11th IADIS International Conference Information Systems 2018

Lisbon, Portugal
14 – 16 April 2018

Editors:

Miguel Baptista Nunes
Pedro Isaias
Philip Powell
Luis Rodrigues

ISBN: 978-1-5108-6769-7

Printed from e-media with permission by:

Curran Associates, Inc.
57 Morehouse Lane
Red Hook, NY 12571

Some format issues inherent in the e-media version may also appear in this print version.

Printed by Curran Associates, Inc. (2018)

For permission requests, please contact International Association for Development of the Information Society (IADIS) at the address below.

International Association for Development of the Information Society (IADIS)
Rua Sao Sebastiao Da Pedreira
No. 100, 30, 1050-209
Lisbon, Portugal

Phone: 351 21 3151373
Fax: 351 21 3151244

secretariat@iadis.org

Additional copies of this publication are available from:

Curran Associates, Inc.
57 Morehouse Lane
Red Hook, NY 12571 USA
Phone: 845-758-0400
Fax: 845-758-2633
Email: curran@proceedings.com
Web: www.proceedings.com

11th IADIS INTERNATIONAL CONFERENCE

INFORMATION SYSTEMS 2018

PROCEEDINGS OF THE
11th IADIS INTERNATIONAL CONFERENCE

INFORMATION SYSTEMS 2018

LISBON, PORTUGAL

14 - 16 APRIL, 2018

Organised by

iadis

international association for development of the information society

Edited by Miguel Baptista Nunes, Pedro Isaias and Philip Powell

Associate Editor: Luís Rodrigues

TABLE OF CONTENTS

FULL PAPERS

SHORT PAPERS

REFLECTION PAPERS

POSTERS

FOREWORD

These proceedings contain the papers of the 11th IADIS International Conference Information Systems 2018, which was organised by the International Association for Development of the Information Society in Lisbon, Portugal during 14-16 April 2018.

The IADIS Information Systems Conference 2018 aims to provide a forum for the discussion of IS taking a socio-technological perspective. It aims to address the issues related to design, development and use of IS in organisations from a socio-technological perspective, as well as to discuss IS professional practice, research and teaching. A set of key areas has been identified. However, these do not aim at being prescriptive, or set in stone, and any innovative contributions that do not fit into these areas have also been considered.

The following main tracks have been object of paper submissions:

- IS in Practice, Technology Infrastructures and Organisational Processes
- IS Design, Development and Management Issues and Methodologies
- IS Professional Issues
- IS Research
- IS Learning and Teaching

The IADIS Information Systems Conference 2018 had 145 submissions from more than 28 countries. Each submission has been anonymously reviewed by an average of 4 independent reviewers, to ensure the final high standard of the accepted submissions. Out of the papers submitted, 25 got blind referee ratings that published them as full papers, which means that the acceptance rate was 17%. Some other submissions were published as short and reflection papers, posters and one tutorial. Extended versions of the best papers will be selected to be published in a special issue of the Journal of Electronic Commerce in Organizations (JECO) journal (ISSN: 1539-2937) and also in the IADIS Journal on Computer Science and Information Systems (ISSN: 1646-3692) indexed by Emerging Sources Citation Index by Thomson Reuters.

The conference, besides the papers' and posters' presentations, also includes a keynote presentation from an internationally distinguished researcher. We wish to thank Professor Bob O'Keefe (Vice-Principal for Student Experience and Dean of the Faculty of Management, Economics & Law, Royal Holloway, University of London, UK), for accepting our invitation as keynote speaker and a Tutorial presented by Dr. Ilia Bider.

As we all know, a conference requires the effort of many individuals. We would like to thank all members of the Program Committee for their hard work in reviewing and selecting the papers that appear in the book of the proceedings. We would also like to thank all the authors who have submitted their papers to this conference. We wish to thank all members of our organizing committee.

Last but not the least, we hope that everybody will have a good time in Lisbon, and we invite all participants for the next year edition of the IADIS International Conference of Information Systems 2019.

Professor Philip Powell, Executive Dean, University of London, UK
Conference Chair

Miguel Baptista Nunes, School of Information Management, Sun Yat-sen University, Guangzhou, China
Pedro Isaias, The University of Queensland, Australia
Program Co-Chairs

Lisbon, Portugal
April 2018

PROGRAM COMMITTEE

CONFERENCE CHAIR

Professor Philip Powell, Executive Dean, University of London, UK

PROGRAM CO-CHAIRS

Miguel Baptista Nunes, School of Information Management, Sun Yat-sen University, Guangzhou, China
Pedro Isaias, The University of Queensland, Australia

COMMITTEE MEMBERS

Adam Wojtowicz, Poznan University of Economics and Business, Poland
Alexis Tejedor De Leon, Technological University of Panama, Panama
Amelia Badica, University of Craiova, Romania
Anastas Mishev, University of SS Cyril and Methodius, Macedonia
Anastasia Constantelou, University of the Aegean, Greece
Andrea Kienle, University of Applied Sciences Dortmund, Germany
Andreas Oberweis, Karlsruhe Institute of Technology (KIT), Germany
Anza Akram, The DaVinci Group, USA
Betim Cico, Epoka University, Albania
Christos Kalloniatis, University of the Aegean, Greece
Claudia Pons, Universidad Nacional de la Plata, Argentina
Demetrios Sarantis, United Nations University, Portugal
Dimitar Trajanov, SS Cyril and Methodius University, Macedonia
Dimitris Karagiannis, University of Vienna, Austria
Dimitris Kardaras, Athens University of Economics and Business, Greece
Dimitris Panopoulos, National Technical University of Athens, Greece
Eddie Soulier, Université de Technologie de Troyes, France
Edward Bernroider, Vienna University of Economics and Business, Austria
Efthimios Tambouris, University of Macedonia, Greece
Eleutherios Papathanassiou, IST College, Greece
Elli Georgiadou, Middlesex University, UK
Euripides Loukis, University of the Aegean, Greece
Francisco Jose Silva Mata, Cenatav, Cuba
François Bergeron, TELUQ, Canada
Goran Velinov, University SS. Cyril and Methodius Skopje, Macedonia
Hans-Peter Steinbacher, University of Applied Sciences, Austria

KEYNOTE LECTURE

HOW USER BEHAVIOUR AND INFORMATION MANAGEMENT ARE NOW CRITICAL FOR IT MANAGEMENT

by Professor Bob O'Keefe, Vice-Principal for Student Experience and Dean of the Faculty of Management, Economics & Law, Royal Holloway, University of London, UK

Abstract

Large scale Information Systems are more difficult and more expensive to develop than at any time in the history of computing. This is in part due to the considerable requirements now placed upon systems, for example, 24/7 working or near immediate processing of transactions, but also due to emerging issues around information architectures, data protection, cyber-security and human-computer interaction. The talk attempts to demonstrate how *user behaviour* and *information management* have grown as critical topics for those managing technology, perhaps as identified by researchers for some years. But both have emerged in rather unpredicted ways, well beyond the boundaries of IT systems.

TUTORIAL

FRACTAL ENTERPRISE MODEL AND ITS USAGE FOR BUSINESS MODEL INNOVATION

by Dr. Ilia Bider
DSV, Stockholm University, Sweden

Abstract

This tutorial introduces a new type of enterprise models called Fractal Enterprise Model (FEM), and its usage for industry level Business Model Innovation. The latter means starting a business that is different from the one already run by the enterprise. A FEM model connects enterprise's business processes with its assets revealing existing assets that can be used in a new business model. The assets can be human-related or infrastructure related, including various IT systems that support the business. A new business model is built by finding another usage for already existing assets; it can be a technologically based transformation, or a human capital based transformation, or both.

KEYWORDS

Business Model, Innovation, Enterprise Modeling, Business Process, Asset

1. BUSINESS MODEL INNOVATION

The pace of changes in the business environment in which a modern enterprise operates requires the enterprise to constantly review its business models in order to survive and prosper in the dynamic world. According to the classification suggested in (Giesen et al., 2007), there are three ways of innovating a Business Model (BM):

1. *Industry model innovation* - which amounts to change the position in value change, entering new markets, and/or other type of radical changes.
2. *Revenue model innovation* - which results in changes in how a company generates revenues, e.g. reconfiguring offerings and/or introducing new pricing models.
3. *Enterprise model innovation* – which involves innovating the structure of an enterprise, such as enterprise goals, business processes, products and/or services

The first type of Business Model Innovation (BMI), which is in the focus of this tutorial, means starting a business that is different from the one already run by the enterprise. The goal of the tutorial is to introduce a systematic approach to this type of BMI.

2. FRACTAL ENTERPRISE MODEL

The enterprise model we use for transformational purpose is called a Fractal Enterprise Model (FEM). It was first introduced in (Bider et al., 2012), and then extended and improved in (Bider et al., 2017). FEM has a form of a directed graph with two types of nodes Processes and Assets, where the arrows (edges) from assets to processes show which assets are utilized by which processes and arrows from processes to assets show which processes help to have specific assets in healthy and working order. The arrows are labeled with meta-tags that show in what way a given asset is utilized, e.g. as *workforce*, *reputation*, *infrastructure*, etc., see an example in Fig. 1, or in what way a given process helps to have the given assets "in order", i.e. *acquire*, *maintain* or *retire* the assets.
A FEM model is built recursively by using a so-called unfolding procedure and two types of archetypes: process-assets archetypes that show which kind of assets might be needed for running a process, and an asset-processes archetype that shows which processes are needed to maintain an asset in order. Unfolding starts with a primary process, a process that delivers value to a customer/beneficiary, by applying process-assets archetypes and alternating them with the asset-processes archetype.

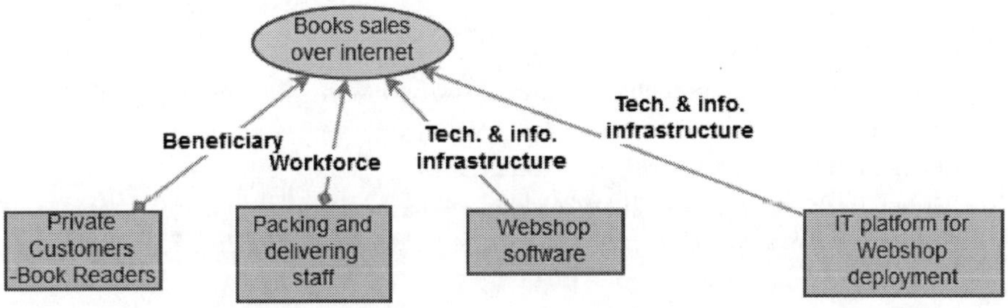

Figure 1. An upper level of a FEM used as an example in the tutorial, adapted from (Bider & Perjons, 2017)

3. USING FEM FOR BMI

Both assets and processes represent capabilities that already exist in the enterprise and can be used as a basis for a transformation. A major organizational change would result in changing FEM. A change that corresponds to an industry model innovation would result in appearing nodes for new primary processes that substitute or complement the old ones. A part of a FEM graph that corresponds to a new primary process would use assets and processes that already exist in the old FEM, though some modification can be made in them. This reuse of nodes from the old FEM in a new one represents employment of the existing capabilities during industrial business model innovation.

The idea of using FEM for business model transformation was first presented in (Henkel et al., 2014), but without any technical details on the transformational procedure. A more recent publication (Bider & Perjons, 2017) presents such a procedure that consists of two steps (1) generating hypotheses, and (2) assessing promising hypotheses. The first step is based on analyzing which asset(s) should be used in a new business activity (new primary process). The second step consists of comparing a FEM for a new business activity with the FEM for already existing one(s), and assessing the differences, in order to understand which assets and processes can be reused and which new ones need to be acquired/developed.

FEM-based BMI is introduced in the tutorial with the help of an example, inspired by Amazon, which while continue its primary business of selling books over the internet, see Fig. 1, added a completely new business of providing a general purpose IT platform. The introduction follows an exercise where the tutorial participants try to innovate a business model of their own organization, or any organization that they worked for or collaborated with. The tutorial is concluded by presenting the results of the exercise by participants and general discussion on FEM-based BMI.

REFERENCES

Bider, I. & Perjons, E., 2017. Using a Fractal Enterprise Model for Business Model Innovation. In *BPMDS 2017 RADAR, CEUR Vol 1859*., pp.20-29.

Bider, I., Perjons, E. & Elias, M., 2012. Untangling the Dynamic Structure of an Enterprise by Applying a Fractal Approach to Business Processes. In *Proceedings of PoEM 2012, Springer, LNBIP 134*. Springer, pp.61-76.

Bider, I., Perjons, E., Elias, M. & Johannesson, P., 2017. A fractal enterprise model and its application for business development. *Software & Systems Modeling*, 16(3), pp.663–89.

Giesen, E., Berman, S.J., Bell, R. & Blitz, A., 2007. Three ways to successfully innovate your business model. *Strategy & Leadership, Vol. 35 Issue: 6, pp.*, 35(6), pp.27-33.

Henkel, M., Bider, I. & Perjons, E., 2014. Capability-based Business Model Transformation. In *Advanced Information Systems Engineering Workshops, Sprnger, LNBIP 178*. Springer, pp.88-99.

Full Papers

AMERICAN APPAREL'S JOURNEY TOWARDS ACCURATE INVENTORY MANAGEMENT: PRELUDE TO OMNICHANNEL RETAILING

Rebecca Angeles
University of New Brunswick Fredericton, Tilley Hall 308B, 7 Macauley Lane, Fredericton, New Brunswick E3B 5A3, Canada

ABSTRACT

This research study features the experience of American (AA), a leading casual fashion apparel manufacturer, distributor, wholesaler, and retailer in deploying the firm's radio frequency identification (RFID) initiative as a way of laying the foundation for attaining omnichannel retailing capabilities. AA is now owned by Montreal-based Canadian firm, Gildan. The prize to be obtained is inventory accuracy; this study focuses on attempts to reach inventory management improvements in the retail stores and other parts of the firm's supply chain. The RFID exploration of AA is successful. This research study also uses the qualitative research method of content analysis of conference transcripts of talks given by a key AA executive who deployed their RFID initiative in the 2012 and 2013 RFID Journal Live! Conferences. AA plans to improve both its brick-and-mortar stores and online ecommerce site to enhance its omnichannel retailing strategy.

KEYWORDS

Radio Frequency Identification (RFID), Supply Chain Management (SCM) for Retailing, Omnichannel Retailing, Inventory Management, Structurational Model of Technology

1. INTRODUCTION

A current noticeable and disturbing development in North America is the closure of brick-and-mortar stores of well-known retail chains. A number of factors related to the economy, the marketplace, and the evolution of e-commerce and mobile commerce-related technologies account for this development. In the meantime, it behooves retailers to plan ahead to assure their survival amidst these adverse forces. One possible way of coping with this challenge is launching an omnichannel retailing strategy. The concept of "omnichannel retailing" emerged dissolving the boundaries separating the physical, virtual, and mobile storefronts. "...The omnichannel concept is perceived as an evolution of the multichannel. While the multichannel implies a division between the physical and online store, in the omnichannel customers move freely between the online (PC), mobile devices, and physical store, all within a single transaction process....the journey should be smooth and should provide a seamless, unified customer experience, regardless of the channels used...." (Pioytrowicz & Cuthbertson, 2014). This research study features the radio frequency identification (RFID) initiative of American Apparel (AA), a Canadian-owned apparel retailer, in its bid to become a top omnichannel retailer in the global marketplace. AA is laying the foundation for full omnichannel retailing capability by establishing a tight inventory management system that will produce inventory count accuracy and reliability.

2. LITERATURE REVIEW

2.1 RFID and Omnichannel Retailing

Today, retailers need to offer customers mobile representations of their brand (Mittal, 2014, p. 4), and seamless cross-channel conveniences such as: order online/pickup in store, direct-to-customer fulfillment (i.e., delivery to homes), and cross-channel returns processing, etc. (Datalogic, 2013, p. 1). The critical role of item-level RFID tagging has been articulated by Bill Hardgrave, founder and former director of the RFID Research Center of the University of Arkansas (Hardgrave, 2015b; Hardgrave, 2012). ".... omnichannel retailing starts with operations --- in particular, those that deliver real-time, accurate inventory data efficiently and cost-effectively. If you don't know what you have, where you have it and when you have it, the great mobile or online app you created for your customers is worthless." (Hardgrave, 2012).

2.2 American Apparel (AA): Firm Background

Founded by CEO Dov Charney and recently acquired by The Gildan Group, a Canadian firm, AA is considered a major manufacturer/wholesaler/distributor/retailer of basic sports apparel for men, women, and children (Read, 2009). AA's retail chain worldwide spans U.S., Canada, Mexico, Europe, and Asia. In 2007-2008, AA pursued rapid retail store expansion, adding about 78 stores to its existing chain. This trend was abruptly interrupted by an 11 percent retail store chain sales decline in 2009 (Xterprise, 2014). Charney addressed inventory-related issues burdening the company by pushing the exploration of RFID first by sanctioning a one-retail store pilot and then, supporting an incremental rollout after that to an increasing number of stores as positive results were posted.

2.3 Structurational Model of Technology

This study applies Orlikowski's "Structurational Model of Technology," (Orlikowski, 1992; Orlikowski & Robey, 1991) to understand how information technology (IT) interacts with organizations. This model draws on Giddens' (Giddens, 1984; Giddens, 1979; Giddens, 1976) theory of structuration, which proposed the concept of the "duality of structure," "...which refers to the notion that the structure or institutional properties of social systems are created by human action, and then serve to shape future human action...." (Orlikowski & Robey, 1991, p. 47).

The structurational model of technology discusses four critical issues (Orlikowski & Robey, 1991). First, IT is the product of human action, which is responsible for the creation, use, and maintenance of different forms of IT. Second, technology is the medium of human action. Third, organizational contexts shape human action within organizations. Fourth, human agents either reinforce or transform the institutional properties of an organization when using IT.

"Structure of signification" refers to the way the concepts and procedures intrinsic to the knowledge embedded in IT directs the manner in which problems are interpreted and work is conducted in the organization (Orlikowski, 1992). "Structure of domination" refers to IT's ability to control the work of organizational members once it is deployed. "Structure of legitimation" refers to the ability of IT to sanction a particular mode of conducting the work and thus, propagate a set of norms about what is considered legitimate business practice. Orlikowski also incorporates the three modalities of structuration --- interpretive schemes, resources, and norms --- in her application of the structures of signification, domination, and legitimation in the deployment of IT in an organization.

3. RESEARCH METHOD

This study uses the case study approach in aligning the concepts prescribed by Orlikowski's framework (Orlikowski, 1992; Orlikowski & Robey, 1991) to the RFID system of AA. The case study is an appropriate methodology in testing the application of a conceptual framework to a real firm. Primary data based on the transcription of the conference presentation of AA Vice President of Technology, Stacey Shulman, during the RFID Journal Live! 2013 and 2012 Conferences. In addition, secondary data sources from academic and trade articles were content analyzed using key concepts in the model.

4. FINDINGS

4.1 Structure of Signification

"The structure of signification" will show how the RFID initiative at AA embedded the way the technology works in the form of concepts and procedures that directed the manner in which inventory management and tracking issues have been interpreted at AA and how business processes have been redesigned to make full use of RFID.

4.1.1 RFID Infrastructure of AA

AA has only one manufacturing site located in Los Angeles, California, where workers attach RFID hangtags with the embedded Avery Dennison AD-220 EPC Gen 2 passive inlay to product items in the packaging process (O'Connor, 2008). The encoded EPC on the tag contains information on the garment's style, size, and color. From this one manufacturing facility, the products are moved to AA's distribution center (DC), also in Los Angeles, where DC workers scan the EPC Gen 2 passive UHF RFID tag embedded in each product's hangtag (Swedberg, 2010). As boxes of products leave the DC, Motorola XR440 fixed interrogators mounted on the DC's dock doors also read tags embedded in cases. EPC data at both the case and product item levels showing reader locations and timestamps are, then, transferred to Vue's TrueVue software platform (O'Connor, 2008).

The key focus of AA's RFID initiative are the retail stores. As of April 26, 2011, AA has installed the Xterprise ARS software in 27 of a total of 250 retail stores in the US, Europe, and Asia (O'Connor, 2011; Swedberg, 2010). The software product at the heart of AA's retail store operations is Xterprise's Clarity ARS, consisting of roughly five modules, which updates the store's inventory databases (O'Connor, 2011).

AA retail stores also use the RetailPro software that simultaneously serves as an enterprise resource planning (ERP), inventory management, and point-of-sale (POS) system. With the software, AA can compare the physical product items with the advanced shipment notices that accompany the goods provided by the factory. At the same time, AA can update its retail store inventory database by recording transactions such as receiving orders and selling product items as reflected by the POS data (O'Connor, 2011). The Clarity ARS software also enables store workers to generate a serial number and encode it into an RFID inlay that could be attached to untagged product items transferred from a non-RFID AA store.

On the hardware side, the following devices are part of the AA RFID system infrastructure in the retail stores (Swedberg, 2010). Fixed Motorola FX-7400 RFID interrogators are used in the store's receiving area to scan the information on the RFID tags of incoming product items. This data is, then, forwarded to the ARS software which records the unique ID numbers associated with the product item's SKU number. Next, items are transferred to the "fill station" where store staffers use an RFID interrogator to scan the RFID tags and separate items that should go to the sales floor from those that will be stored in the backroom. At the sales floor itself, a fixed interrogator scans the RFID tags once again, verifies that the right product items are in the sales floor, and generates alerts when product items are missing or when the wrong items are in the sales floor. As of March 2016 (Swedberg, 2016b; Xterprise, 2014), AA has also been using Alien Technology ALR-9900 fixed readers and in the sales floor, workers have been using handheld Motorola FX3190-Z or Nordic ID Merlin RFID readers.

A later addition to AA's RFID system is an important piece of the firm's omnichannel retailing initiative. As of 2016, AA customers could use Postmate's on-demand delivery service by using a Postmate app on their smartphones to have their AA purchased items delivered to them for a fee of US$1.99 (Swedberg, 2016b). The Postmate app system works with the AA RFID system this way. When a customer inquires about a product item, the Postmate system searches the inventory systems of stores in the area and displays inventory levels for the specific item in those stores. When the customer places an order for that item, the Postmate system sends an alert to the AA retail store that has the item and is geographically closest to the customer. The system also advises the AA store that the Postmate courier is scheduled to pick up the product item for delivery. A store worker in that store, then, uses a handheld RFID reader to quickly locate the ordered product item and check them out as "sold" using the Postmate's software system.

AA has a number of future enhancements to their retail store system in the planning stage (Shulman, 2012). Eventually store workers will work with tablets that will serve as mobile point-of-sale (POS) systems to hasten the process of processing customer orders on the sales floor. This POS system will also automatically update the inventory file to account for products sold. Another feature in the works is the online inventory replenishment system which would automatically generate orders based on inventory counts supported by RFID tag reads.

4.1.2 Impact of RFID System on the Inventory System of AA

The following is the most significant observed impact of RFID item-level tagging on the inventory system of AA. The firm has reached 99.98 percent inventory accuracy level (Shulman, 2012).

4.2 Structure of Domination

A key motivating factor in the adoption of RFID was the 11 percent decline in comparable store sales reported in 2009. Prior to deploying RFID, AA was burdened with inaccurate inventory, out-of-stocks, under-optimized store real estate space, and finally, falling sales (Xterprise, 2014). RFID exploration and ultimately, adoption was triggered by a top-down initiative of its founder and then CEO Dov Charney (Shulman 2012).

Eventually, in 2009, AA signed up Xterprise, an RFID solutions vendor, to take charge of what would turn out to be a succession of pilot projects rolled out through AA's retail chain worldwide. The positive results obtained through the incremental retail store rollout through the years were further reinforced by the support and persistent efforts of AA's Stacey Shulman, who enforced the deployment of an organized and standardized set of business processes that covered receiving, encodings, transfers, replenishment, cycle counting, point-of-sale transaction processing, Geiger counter search/find, and a complete management dashboard reporting (Xterprise, 2014).

4.3 Structure of Legitimation

The RFID initiative at AA has attained a "structure of legitimation" due to a number of developments recently in the retailing industry. Having "structure of legitimation," RFID item-level tagging has been the technological means by which retailers have sanctioned a specific way of developing information systems to address certain business operations needs and propagate a set of norms about what is and what is not "professional" social practice.

What is happening now is that by item-level tagging with RFID for all categories of general merchandise, AA is laying the foundation for omnichannel retailing. This concept is complex, bridges the linkages among the multiple channels of selling to customers, and will require the integration of the IT infrastructure pieces used for capturing, storing, and processing order transactions and creating integrated customer profiles via these different channels. This case study focuses solely on the efforts of AA to achieve a robust inventory management system as its groundwork for taking on the challenge of linking transaction data from the various channels that would have to sit on top of an inventory system serving all these channels.

The other pillar supporting the "structure of legitimation" underlining RFID item-level tagging are the initiatives of the organization called GS1, a nonprofit international organization that develops and maintains standards for supply and demand chains across industries. Firms in the retailing industry use GS 1 electronic product code or EPC global standards that govern the workings of RFID technology. For instance, RFID Gen 2 was released by GS 1 as a worldwide standard for ultra-high frequency (UHF) RFID to simplify visibility, boost read rates, and improve RFID tag performance (Swedberg, 2013b).

4.4 Social Consequences of RFID System

4.4.1 Social Structure and Social Consequences of IT

In looking at the "social structure and social consequences of IT," the structurational model of technology investigates how the IT, in this case, the RFID system for inventory control, is implemented, assimilated, and adopted by the end users, and the consequences of usage (Orlikowski,1991). IT, once again, acts as a medium of human action, and human action is also shaped by the use of IT. The end users' behavior at AA in the process of using the RFID system is mediated by interpretive schemes, resources, and norms perceived to be embedded in the technology. Since the RFID system is a medium of human action at AA, it will shape the end users' behavior in the firm, resulting in facilitating certain outcomes and constraining others.

The most significant change in structure at AA was the ability of the RFID system to put in place standard business processes that governed the movement of product items from the factories to the distribution centers, and finally, to the retail stores (Shulman, 2012). Through the use of Clarity ARS software, AA standardized its business processes around receiving, encoding, transfers, product replenishment, cycle counting, and point-of-sale activities (Xterprise, 2014). Prior to the use of RFID, the different AA retail stores all over the world operated as independent "fiefdoms" (Shulman, 2012).

The second important structural change was the creation of tighter interorganizational linkages and collaboration between AA and the various RFID-related vendors. AA worked closely with Xterprise starting in 2009 when AA piloted the vendor's Clarity item-level RFID software, which was eventually selected for the full chainwide rollout in the following years (Xterprise, 2014). Xterprise provided the software, hardware (in conjunction with other vendor partnerships), and consulting and support services. As of 2014, AA has been relying on Xterprise to support the Clarity ARS software in over 250 AA retail stores covering 20 countries; the most recent deployments have been operational since 2011.

Xterprise eventually developed an installation and kitting method that expedited the rollout of Clarity ARS software in affected AA retail stores (Xterprise, 2014). Providing consulting and training expertise, Xterprise oversaw the brick-and-mortar retail store prep and ARS software installation using Xterprise installers and reader configuration templates. Xterprise maintained and restored AA's databases, and provided ongoing support and maintenance remotely. Eventually, Xterprise was installing the ARS software at the rate of 10-30 stores a week with relative speed and ease.

AA also collaborated with Senitron in testing an RFID solution that would locate product items within designated "zones" in the storefloor and backroom. This solution was initially deployed in the Little Tokyo and Melrose AA stores (Swedberg, 2013a).

Another structural change was the elimination of the use of third party auditors AA used to hire in order to count garments by hand (Xterprise, 2014). Since becoming RFID enabled, AA has been using RFID inventory counts as a source of inputted data into their balance sheet calculations.

AA's relationships with banks have also improved ever since the firm use RFID-based inventory counts (Xterprise, 2014). The banks have more confidence in the accuracy of RFID tracking that they have been able to grant AA better financial packages and thus, increase the firm's liquidity.

4.4.2 Action and Social Consequences of IT

The "action and social consequences of IT" discussion refers to the current and future changes needed in terms of "action initiatives" to optimize changes needed to meet the objectives AA set for its RFID initiative. RFID technology has organized and standardized the business processes around receiving, encoding, store-to-store transfers, replenishment, cycle counting, point-of-sale processing, Geiger counter search/find of product items, and a management dashboard of KPIs (Xterprise, 2014). RFID technology enabled "transparency" in the handling and movement of product items through key points in AA's supply chain --- from the factory to the distribution center and finally, to the retail stores.

The Clarity ARS software system records RFID tag readings as soon as tagged product items are received in AA retail stores. An important feature of the software is a monitor screen report that has color coded horizontal bands indicating the length of time certain product items have been absent from the sales floor (Shulman, 2013; Shulman, 2012). The color shades assigned are such that items that are missing beyond a certain time threshold are flagged and the system sends alerts when these thresholds are exceeded (Shulman, 2012). This monitoring tool is a visual alert to that gives store workers transparent information on the status of product items that should be in the sales floor but are not (Xterprise, 2014). Items missing for more than 90 minutes are placed in the "Absent List." Items in this list are in the store but are missing from the sales floor.

There are also items is what is called an "Unknown List" --- these are items that cannot be located and whose status is unknown. They could be stolen, improperly sold to customers, moved to the stockroom without following proper procedures, etc. Store workers use handheld RFID readers to find these missing items and if found, they are removed from the "Unknown List." Items that remain in the "Unknown List" are given a seven-day grace period beyond which they are declared stolen and are removed from the POS inventory file.

AA also manages and maintains what it calls "bifurcated inventory," which consists of both RFID inventory counts and the POS inventory counts of product items (Shulman, 2013; Shulman, 2012). Store workers need to resolve "discrepancies" between these two inventory system counts everyday; the goal is always to have a discrepancy equal to zero. Each and every store that is RFID enabled is fully informed of its discrepancy level for the day. Discrepancies that are not resolved are written off as "shrink." (Shulman, 2013, 2012).

AA has credited RFID as an enabling technology that has helped instill discipline in its employees so that they are now motivated to reduce discrepancies or better yet, maintain this at the zero level. RFID has made them realize that every product item in the store matters and the RFID technology now forces all employees to be accountable for the disposition of that product item. AA makes it clear that the technology alone has not been responsible for reducing theft. It is the business process that was enabled that depends on RFID transparency enabling features that created the appropriate mindset among their workers (Shulman, 2013).

Store worker morale has been observed to improve on account of the RFID system. Time and labor savings gained from managing the RFID-enabled inventory system has afforded store workers more time to devote to work that has a direct effect on revenue generation like faster processing of receiving and transferring goods, rapid organization of stockrooms, and providing customer service (Read, 2009). AA management plans to use digital "scorecard" signage on the store computer monitors to motivate their different retail stores to improve their performance as they benchmark their store's performance against those of other retail stores (Shulman, 2012).

The introduction of the RFID system in the AA retail stores necessitated what are called "tag-up parties" needed to attach RFID tags to product items already in the retail store shelves after the official RFID system deployment (Xterprise, 2014).

4.5 Measures of Success

AA measured success of its RFID deployment according to certain key performance indicators (KPIs). Clearly, to this day, top management recognizes that its RFID initiative is still a work in progress. But use of periodic milestones is encouraging and keeps the firm on track and firm in its commitment. The most important KPI is inventory accuracy and to date, AA has reached 99.98 percent inventory accuracy.

Another key KPI is inventory replenishment to avoid out of stock situations. Right now, AA has an out-of-stock rate of only under 1 percent on the average across retail stores (Shulman, 2012).

Before the RFID deployment, AA absorbed nearly 60 percent inventory loss due to shrink and had no effective way of dealing with this (Shulman, 2012). Publicly, AA disclosed having attained at least a 50 percent reduction in the incidence of shrink within its retail chain (Xterprise, 2014).

Finally, after the RFID initiative, AA stores have reduced inventory volumes in the stores by about 20 percent and released more brick-and-mortar real estate space for product items that customers are really looking for (Xterprise, 2014).

4.6 RFID and Omnichannel Retailing at AA

Now that AA has attained accurate inventory control, it is poised to pursue omnichannel retailing more effectively. AA relies on the Clarity ARS software system to deliver the most current and accurate view of the inventory levels needed by AA's ecommerce system, to enable this virtual online retailing asset to work with its network of about 250 brick-and-mortar retail stores worldwide in the fulfillment process (Xterprise, 2014). AA uses the ARS software to take and process online orders and identify where the packages should be dropped off --- to other retail stores or distribution centers --- from where they could, again, be picked up and shipped. The Postmate app in customer smartphones piggyback on the ARS software by deploying the final outbound logistical service of delivering the packages to the end customer.

Directly related to AA's omnichannel retailing enhancement initiative, a number of future changes are designed to upgrade customers' brick-and-mortar experience. AA will equip its sales floor workers with tablets that will be able to perform expedited mobile checkouts for customers on the floor. AA also plans to install kiosks that will enable customers to self checkout. AA might pilot digital signage within the brick-and-mortar store using interactions with RFID tagged items.

5. CONCLUSIONS

The obvious limitation of this qualitative study is that the data is based on the RFID deployment experiences of only one firm. But that is in the nature of a case study: the purpose of the methodology is to focus on the minute details of the experience to contribute to the qualitative understanding of the phenomena under study. This limitation is overshadowed by the contribution of this study to the body of literature that uses the structurational model of technology as a theoretical lens for understanding one firm's deployment of different forms of information technologies. Orlikowski's structurational model of technology is only one in a series of theoretical frameworks developed based on Gidden's theory of structuration. The following is a summary of conclusions drawn from the application of this theoretical framework.

"Omnichannel retailing" requires a major transformation in the way retailers operate their business processes in order to meet consumers' needs promptly, fulfilling orders from the position of having a "global view" of the firm's inventories across channels. A key idea in Orlikowski's framework is the centrality of the role of human end users in defining or "structuring" end users' actions with a specific social context that leads to the creation of their distinctive "structure of technology" or "technology in practice." Her theory can be used as a practice lens to enable researchers to appreciate the power of human agency and its transformational potential when the end users apply different forms of technologies to address challenges and problems contextually. RFID, by itself, cannot deliver the benefits targeted by the omnichannel retailing strategy. It is critical that end users of the technology alter business processes of the multiple retailing channels involved and make them work under an overaching framework in order to provide a "global view" of a retailer's inventory levels across channels. The information systems of each channel should also be linked with each other to support a cohesive backend fulfillment system operating as the firm's "retailing central nervous system."

REFERENCES

CMI, 2017, *American Apparel Case Study: American Apparel introduce RFID into their stores*. Available from: http://www.cmilabsplc.com/case_studies/american-apparel-case-study/ . [13 June 2017].

Datalogic, 2013, *Logistics Technology: The Backbone of Omni-Channel Retail.* Available from:http://www.bluestarinc.com/fileadmin/bluestar-typo3/images/Microsites_Misc_Images/Warehouse_Solutions_EU/White_Papers/Datalogic_WP_-_Logistics_Technonolgy - The Backbone_of_Omni-Channel_Retail.pdf. [10 June 2017].

Giddens, A., 1984. *The Constitution of Society: Outline of the Theory of Structure*. University of California Press, Berkeley, California, USA.

Giddens, A., 1979. *Central Problems in Social Theory: Action, Structure and Contradiction in Social Analysis*. University of California Press, Berkeley, California, USA.

Giddens, A., 1976. *New Rules of Sociological Methods*. Basic Books, New York, New York, USA.

Hardgrave, B 2015a, 'Shopping the Planet', *RFID Journal.* Available from: http://www.rfidjournal.com/articles/view?13174. [10 April 2017].

Hardgrave, B 2015b, 'Get Hip to BOPIS', *RFID Journal.* Available from: http://www.rfidjournal.com/articles/view?12911. [10 June 2017].

Hardgrave, B 2012, 'Omnichannel Retailing: You can't do it without RFID', *RFID Journal*. Available from: http://www.rfidjournal.com/articles/view?10247 . [10 June 2017].

Kambil, A & Brooks, JD 2002, *Auto-ID Across the Value Chain: From Dramatic Potential to Greater Efficiency and Profit*. Available from: https://www.rfidjournal.com/whitepapers/download?15. [13 March 2017].

Krippendorff, K., 2000. *Content Analysis: An Introduction to Its Methodology*. Sage Publications, Thousand Oaks, California, USA.

Krippendorff, K., 1980. *Content Analysis: An Introduction to Its Methodology*. Sage Publications, Beverley Hills, California, USA.

McBeath, B 2016, *The Intelligent Integrated Store: MIT Panel Discussion*. Available from: https://www.clresearch.com/research/detail.cfm?guid=F44CB13F-3048-78A9-2F70-6CC256ADD070. [13 June 2017].

Mittal, GS 2014, *Right Integration Strategy: A Cornerstone for Omni-Channel Retail.* Available from: http://www.wipro.com/documents/right-integration-strategy-a-cornerstone-for-omni-channel-retail.pdf. [10 June 2017].

O'Connor, MC 2011, 'American Apparel Adding 50 More Stores in Aggressive RFID Rollout', *RFID Journal.* Available from: www.rfidjournal.com/articles/view?8374/2. [10 May 2017].

O'Connor, MC 2008, 'American Apparel Makes a Bold Fashion Statement With RFID', *RFID Journal.* Available from: www.rfidjournal.com/articles/view?4018. [18 June 2017].

Orlikowski W.J., 1991. Using Technology and Constituting Structures: A Practice Lens for Studying Technology in Organizations. *In Organization Science*, Vol. 11, No. 4, July-August, pp 404-428.

Orlikowski, W.J., 1991. The Duality of Technology: Rethinking The Concept of Technology in Organizations. *In Organization Science*, Vol. 3, No. 3, August, pp 398-427.

Orlikowski, W.J. and Robey, D. 1991. Information Technology and the Structuring of Organizations. *In Information Systems Research*, Vol. 2, No. 2,pp 143-169.

Pioytrowicz, W. and Cuthbertson, R., 2014. Introduction to the Special Issue Information Technology in Retail: Toward Omnichannel Retailing. *In MIS Quarterly*, Vol. 18, No. 4, Summer, pp 5-15.

Read, R 2008, 'American Apparel Case Study Write-Up Robert W. Baird & Co.', *RFID Journal.* Available from: www.rfidjournal.net/PDF_download/American_Apparel_Case_Study.pdf. [3 June 2017].

Roberti, M 2011, 'RFID Delivers Unexpected Benefits at American Apparel', *RFID Journal.* Available from: www.rfidjournal.com/articles/view?8843. [5 April 2017].

Shulman, S. (2013). "Core Store Operations Panel Discussion: American Apparel." Transcription of talk Given at the RFID Journal Live! 2013 Conference, April 30-May 2, Orlando, Florida.

Shulman, S. (2012). "American Apparel." Transcription of Talk Given at the RFID Journal Live! Europe Conference, October 24-25, Oslo, Scandanavia.

Stone, P.J. et al, 1966. *The General Inquirer: A Computer Approach to Content Analysis.* MIT Press, Cambridge, Massachussetts, USA.

Swedberg, C 2016b, 'American Apparel, Postmates Use RFID Visibility for On-Demand Delivery', *RFID Journal.* Available from: www.rfidjournal.com/articles/view?14248. [2 June 2017].

Swedberg, C 2013a, 'American Apparel Displays Real-Time Storewide RFID Inventory Management', *RFID Journal.* Available from: www.rfidjournal.com/articles/view?10906. [16 April 2017].

Swedberg, C 2013b, 'GS1 Ratifies EPC Gen2v2, Adds Security Features, More Memory', *RFID Journal.* Available from: www.rfidjournal.com/articles/view?11168. [4 June 2017].

Swedberg, C 2012, 'American Apparel Adopting RFID at Every Store', *RFID Journal.* Available from: www.rfidjournal.com/articles/view?9202. [1 June 2017].

Swedberg, C 2010, 'American Apparel Adds RFID to Two More Stores, Switches RFID Software', *RFID Journal.* Available from: www.rfidjournal.com/articles/view?7313. [3 May 2017].

Swedberg, C 2008, 'American Apparel Makes a Bold Fashion Statement with RFID. *RFID Journal.* Available from: www.rfidjournal.com/articles/view?4018. [1 May 2017].

The Aberdeen Group 2012, *The 2012 omni-channel retail experience.* Available from: www.stores.org/assets/whitepapers/EpicorThe2012OmniChannelRetailExperience.pdf. [13 July 2017].

Vanheems, R., 2009. Multichannel retailing: Why do multichannel customers deserve special attention. *In Decision Marketing*, Vol. 55,pp 41-52.

Weber, R.P., 1990. *Basic Content Analysis, 2nd edition.* Sage Publications, Newbury Park, California, USA.

Weick, K., 1979. *The Social Psychology of Organizing.* Addison-Wesley, Reading, Massachussetts, USA.

Xterprise, 2014, *American Apparel: Case Study Update: The 10 Crucial Lessons Learned From The First Ever Global RFID Retail Deployment.* Available from: https://www.ramprfid.com/wp-content/uploads/2014/07/American-Apparel-Case-Study.pdf. [13 May 2017].

A SYSTEMATIC MAPPING STUDY ON MOBILE INFORMATION SYSTEMS AND SECURITY

Gizem Öğütçü, Esma Ergüner Özkoç and Murat Paşa Uysal
Department of Management Information Systems, Baskent University, Ankara, Turkey

ABSTRACT

Recent developments in Information Technologies (IT) have brought important and increasingly remarkable changes not only to our daily lives, but also to the way of communication. Combined with various applications, mobile devices, today, also present great opportunities to the business. However, as the widespread use of mobile systems increases, so does the risk to information security, privacy and vulnerability. Contrary to expectations, the intersected research areas of mobile systems and security are relatively scarce, let alone the secondary studies systematically exploring and analyzing the state-of-the-art. In this paper, therefore, we present the preliminary results of a study on mobile information systems and security, which is conducted according to the guidelines of Systematic Mapping Research. The primary purpose is to review the literature on mobile systems and security and provide an overview of this research area. Consequently, the main contributions and outcomes of this study can be identification and synthesizing of possible evidences, finding the trends, gaps and opportunities as well as make them available for future research efforts.

KEYWORDS

Mobile Information Security, Systematic Mapping

1. INTRODUCTION

Along with the development and widespread use of broadband wireless communications technology, downsizing of portable computers and prolongation of battery life, mobility have brought many advantages to our daily life. The tremendous increase in the demand for mobile computing includes mobile communication, mobile hardware and mobile software. Mobile computing devices are capable of various functions, such as, storing, processing, displaying, and communicating data. This can be safety or mission-critical information, such as credentials, personal health records and financial information of customers as well. Especially, the electronic transformation processes in public and private sectors have greatly increased the need for mobility all over the world, such as, e-government, smart city applications, health-care applications, IOT (internet of things) etc. Thus, mobility allows people to manage their business and work anytime and anywhere.

While mobile technologies can bring substantial changes both to the organizations and information systems, they may also be sources of new threats to various data that is stored and processed in mobile systems as well. On the other hand, the global use of mobile systems continues to grow, and as a consequence, most of public and private organizations feel the need of accessing to private and crucial information through mobile applications. In 2020, 6.1 billion worldwide smartphone users are expected to exist (Radicati, 2016), and also the 80% of internet users would have mobile devices and spend their 90% of time by using these devices and applications. (Chaffey, 2016).

In addition to these, personal mobile devices (smartphones, notebooks, PDA's, etc.) continuously gather and process vast amount of personal data, to which access must also be managed and the user privacy must be protected. In the information age, the protection of personal information and ensuring the information security are as vital as ever. For this reason, it is necessary to understand the contents and core concepts of knowledge domain of mobile systems security. If information security cannot be ensured, then, many disasters may occur without compensation; if health information system is corrupted, then, patients' health records can be manipulated; if banking information system is corrupted, then, this can lead to financial crises etc.Mobile information systems can be defined as "the systems that rely on wireless communications and support mobile applications that typically run on wireless devices such as smartphones and mobile phones"

(Borgory et al, 2010). It is crucial to securely access to the data in mobile devices, and thus, the main focus of mobile information security is on the information, which is used, processed or stored in mobile devices and services. Mobile systems usually need different security approaches from the traditional ones, on account of their computing capability, small storage capacity, battery life constraints and small user interfaces. Therefore, traditional security approaches, such as authentication, cryptography, intrusion detection, firewalls and virus protection may not be enough to be able to handle various security issues in mobile environment (Mavridis and Pangalos, 2016).

Mobile security is the protection of portable computing devices, and the networks which they connect to. Portable computing device can have potential security risks ranging from a stolen mobile device to a forced authentication (Ladan, 2016). As mobile communication channels use radio signals instead of wires, mobile security must also tackle with the wireless security threats, such as denial of service, traffic analysis, eavesdropping, session interception, message modification, spoofing and information leakage etc. (Ladan, 2016). Disconnection, bandwidth-interface variability, and heterogeneous networks are the other possible issues that have to be dealt with (Ladan, 2016).

During recent decade, we witnessed various developments in the technical and human aspects of mobile systems, applications as well as their spectacular impacts on both social and business life. A shallow review of literature on mobile systems security also indicates that the proposed solutions are usually platform-depended or domain-specific. Moreover, the intersected research areas of mobile systems and their security are relatively scarce, let alone the secondary studies systematically exploring and analysing the state-of-the-art. In this paper, therefore, we present the results of a systematic mapping study on mobile information systems and security. To the best of our knowledge, the main contribution brought by this research can be described as being the first systematic mapping study on this topic. A generic classification scheme and an online repository for the categorized papers can be regarded as the secondary contributions. Thus, the next parts of this paper include research method, results, and discussion sections.

2. METHOD

The primary purpose of our study was to search the studies on mobile systems and security and provide an overview of this research area. We identified and synthesized evidences, found research trends, gaps and opportunities in order to make them available for future research. The research was conducted according to the guidelines and principles of Systematic Mapping Research Method (Petersen et al., 2008) as depicted by Figure1:

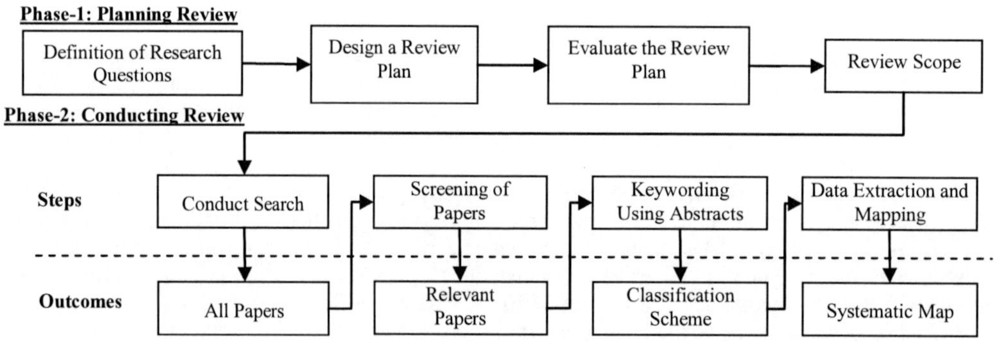

Figure 1. Research Method

2.1 Planning Review

The study began with establishing a research team with the authors. The team formulated research questions, designed and evaluated a review plan (Kitchenham, 2004), and finally, conducted the search. The research questions were as follows:

RQ 1. What are the technical aspects of security in mobile systems?

RQ 2. What are the human aspects of security in mobile systems?

The research limitations led us to use automated search technics in electronic resources, and thus, the digital databases were determined as the main search strategy (Table 1). Additionally, conferences and workshops on security in mobile systems were other possible resources. Asking experienced developers, checking reference lists of primary and secondary studies, and accessing to other web sites were the ancillary procedures addressed by the review plan.

Table 1. Digital Resources

Nu.	Database	URL
1	Science Direct	http://www.sciencedirect.com
2	IEEE Xplore	http://citeseer.ist.psu.edu
3	ACM Dig. Library	http://dl.acm.org
4	Google Scholar	http://scholar.google.com

2.2 Conducting Review

The review process was a means of finding and interpreting available studies relevant to the research questions. The primary and secondary studies were identified by using the search strings on digital databases or browsing through relevant conferences and publications. The structure of search strings were driven by the questions in terms of security and mobile systems context, their features and the problems addressed in the research domains of security and mobile systems (Table 2).

Table 2. Search Strings

Nu.	String
1	mobile AND information AND security AND (problem OR issue)
2	mobile AND information AND security AND "technical aspect"
3	mobile AND information AND security AND "human aspect"

The Google Drive Service was used for both paper storage and information exchange between the researchers. The downloaded studies formed the initial pool of papers in this repository. Initially, the secondary studies and publications similar to the previous reviews were identified. Then, each team member iteratively downloaded potential primary studies until no further relevant papers could be put into the pool. An online spreadsheet in Google Service was updated by the researchers, and thus, it stored the key attributes of all papers, i.e. keywords, abstract, contributions, and the answers to each research question if exist. Although this process is usually during the screening or classification of the reviewed studies, we intentionally executed these recording and sorting procedures at this phase to decrease the risk of missing relevant resources.

2.2.1 Screening of Papers

The research questions, selection criteria and types of papers were main determinants to exclude or screen the papers that were not relevant. The studies that could not answer the research questions were excluded using the exclusion criteria. The application of selection criteria were as: (1) Is the paper relevant and able to answer any of the research questions? (2) Does the paper present any contribution to the research area of security and mobile systems? Therefore, at first, the abstracts explicitly mentioning the phrases, such as, "security and mobile systems", "technical aspects of security in mobile systems", "human aspects of security in mobile systems", were directly included. Next, the papers in the initial pool were reviewed iteratively to look for a theoretical or practical correspondence in the knowledge domain of security and mobile systems. The papers lying outside the intersected knowledge domain of security in mobile systems were excluded. The studies written in English were only the papers included. Finally, the papers published between 2006 and 2016 were included (Appendix).

2.2.2 Keywording and Classification

Initially, the researchers read the abstracts and looked for similar concepts and keywords, which were expected to reflect the context and contributions of the reviewed papers. The set of keywords from different papers were also combined to develop a high level understanding of papers' contribution. The research team also studied the introduction, conclusion or related sections of the papers when abstracts could not allow relevant or meaningful keywords to be chosen. The final set of keywords were clustered to form the categories for the map. Therefore, these categories were also useful to interpret and classify without evaluating each study in detail.

2.2.3 Data Extraction

As aforementioned, the integral part of data extraction occurred when forming the initial pool of papers. At this phase, however, the data extraction took place having completing and sorting the relevant papers into the final classification scheme. When the reviewers were entering the extracted data of a paper into the scheme, they provided a concrete rationale why the paper should be in a certain category. The analysis of data was also focused on presenting the frequencies of publications for each category. After that, it would be possible to see which research categories had been emphasized in the past and also how to identify the gaps and possibilities for future research efforts.

2.3 Reliability and Validity

The study could be affected by various factors, and therefore, several measures were taken to minimize the effects of possible threats to the reliability and validity (internal, external and construct) of this research. For example: (1st) the team members applied a systematic voting procedure for paper selection to decide whether to include or exclude a paper in the paper pool; (2nd) each team member evaluated the papers independently; (3rd) a paper was included in the pool when the majority of members approved, otherwise, it was excluded. (4th) Conflicts on the selection or classification of papers were resolved through online communications and discussions. Consequently, these measures, along with the systematic data extraction and recording methods, and team-based voting procedures, were all to ensure reliability and validity of the research.

3. RESULTS AND DISCUSSION

RQ 1. What are the technical aspects of security in mobile information systems?
As shown in Table 3, there are different issues about the technical aspects of mobile information systems and security. Some of them are about traditional security issues, which are demonstrated by the rows ranging from row 1 to row 9. The other issues are retrieved keywords from reviewed papers. As can be seen, mobile security is a trend topic, especially when considering the technical aspects.

Table 3. Technical Aspects of Security in Mobile Information Systems

Nu.	Technical Aspect	Papers
1	Confidentiality /privacy	5, 12,13, 25, 34, 45, 50
2	Integrity	27
3	Authentication/Identification	1, 2,3, 7, 11, 16,29 33, 38, 56, 57,60
4	Authorization	19, 24
5	Non-Repudation	16
6	Availability (DOS)	18
7	IDS	1, 22, 43, 46
8	Traffic Analysis	9, 26,28, 32, 36, 43, 44,51,58
9	Malware	1, 9, 14, 23, 25, 30, 32, 43,48 49,51, 52
10	Mobile OS (Android/ IOS)	4, 12, 14, 15, 18, 19, 23, 29, 30,32, 34, 42, 47,48, 49,52,54, 55
11	Application	6, 8, 12, 14, 17, 39, 52, 53, 56
12	Device /Architecture	2, 6, 28, 34, 41, 43, 44, 45, 53, 55, 59,60, 61,
13	Network Security / Scheme	3, 7, 9, 21, 23, 26, 33, 35, 46, 51, 57, 61
14	Cloud	2, 8, 22, 24, 27, 32, 33, 38, 40, 41, 58

As seen in the results of the research, technical aspects of the study seem to focus mainly on the search for solutions to the problems arising from new mobile technologies. When all the articles are examined, it is noticed that the most studied topic is the mobile operating system. (Figure 2). Another noteworthy issue is that the vast majority of studies on mobile operating systems are related to the Android OS.

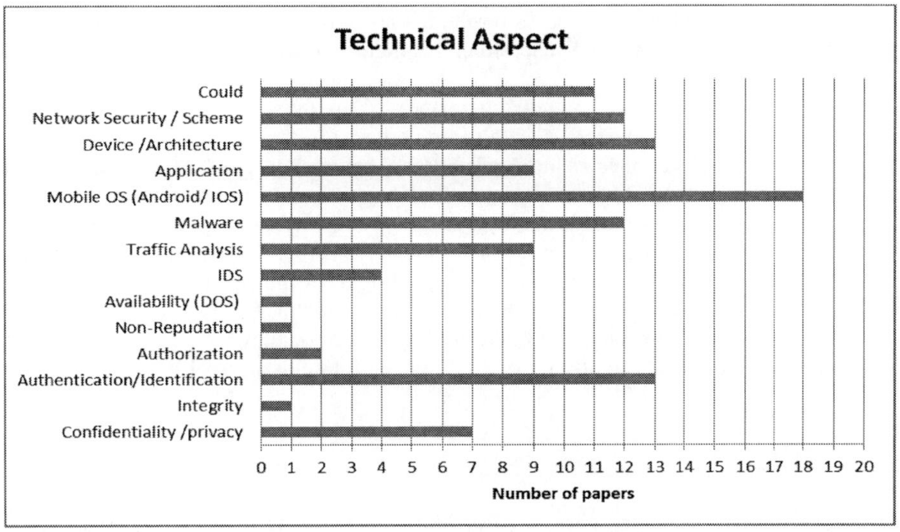

Figure 2. Trend of Studies in Technical Aspect

RQ 2. What are the human aspects of security in mobile systems?

It has been seen that the number of work done in human aspects of mobile information security field is considerably lower than the number of works done in technical aspects. The vast majority of studies in the field of human aspects consist of usability studies in the area of human computer interaction. Another indicator of the study is that other research carried out in the relevant area is related to the information security awareness. However, as it is known, there is a need to improve awareness of information security as well as any technical measures. Studies have shown that studies on mobile information security awareness are not enough. Despite all of these, the policy and model development studies seem to be very few.

Table 4. Human Aspects of Security in Mobile Systems

Nu.	Human Aspects	Papers
1	Model /Hypotise Test	39
2	Awareness	31,37, 61
3	Usability	10, 14, 29, 44
4	Policy	20

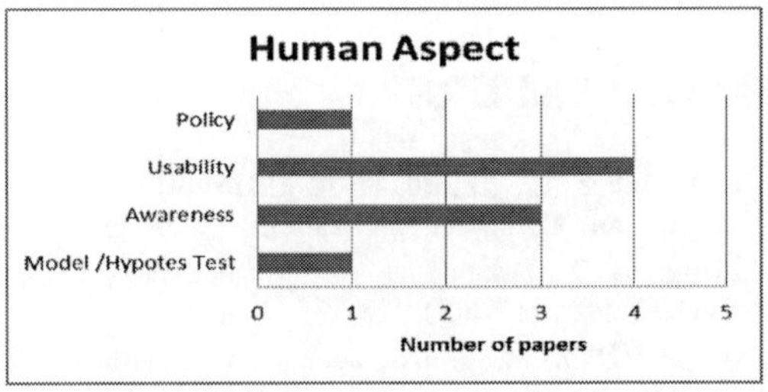

Figure 3. Trend of Studies in Human Aspect

4. CONCLUSION AND FUTURE DIRECTIONS

Today, there is no need to underline or emphasize the importance of mobility, and how the recent decade has brought spectacular developments and revolutionary advances, especially in mobile technologies. Mobile devices, together with their applications, have not only changed the way of our communication means, but also changed our social and business life. As for the research area, we see the proliferation of various papers on mobile systems and security as well. Therefore, this motivated us to conduct the first systematic mapping study on mobile systems and security.

Using a selection strategy, we included 61 papers from the retrieved papers. While planning and conducting the search systematically, it is also important to state the research and space limitations. Therefore, these constraints confined us to report only the preliminary results on technical and human aspects of mobile systems and security. As an emerging technology, it is not surprising to see the studies on mobile systems are in an increasing fashion. However, it is seen that the solutions proposed for mobile systems and their security are usually context-depended and domain-specific. Moreover, they are still away from producing comprehensive and holistic frameworks regarding the technical and human aspects. Consequently, the results and research limitations suggest us to conduct a systematic literature review as a future work, which would be typically of broader and deeper. We hope that this study would help researchers to obtain an overview of the related domain, and also it can shed light on future research efforts.

REFERENCES

Borgy Waluyo, A., Taniar, D., & Srinivasan, B. (2010). Mobile Information Systems in a Hopsital Organization Setting. In K. Khoumbati, Y. Dwivedi, A. Srivastava, & B. Lal (Eds.), Handbook of Research on Advances in Health Informatics and Electronic Healthcare Applications: Global Adoption and Impact of Information Communication Technologies (pp. 493-523). Hershey, PA: IGI Global. doi:10.4018/978-1-60566-030-1.ch030.

Chaffey,D., (2016), URL: (http://www.smartinsights.com/mobile-marketing/mobile-marketing-analytics/mobile-marketing-statistics/), (visited on 25/11/2016)

Kitchenham, B. (2004). "Procedures for performing systematic reviews." Technical Report TR/SE0401, ISSN:1353-7776, Keele University.

Ladan, I., M., Mobile Computing: Security Issues, 11th International Conference on Cyberwarfare and Security, ICCWS 2016, pp: 218-222

Mavridis, I., and Pangalos, G., (2016), Security Issues in a Mobile Computing Paradigm, in Proc. of CMS'97, Communications and Multimedia Security, Vol.3, pp.60-76, 1997.

Petersen, K., Feldt, R., Mujtaba, S. & Mattsso M. 2008. Systematic Mapping Studies in Software Engineering. In: *Proceedings of the 12th international Conference on Evaluation and Assessment in Software Engineering*, Italy, June 26-27 2008, pp. 68-77.

The Radicati Group, Inc,, (2016), URL:http://www.radicati.com/wp/wpcontent/uploads/2016/01/ Mobile-Growth-Forecast-2016-2020-Executive-Summary.pdf, (visited on 25/11/2016)

Wieringa, R., Maiden, N. Mead N. Rolland, C. (2006). "Requirements engineering paper classification and evaluation criteria: a proposal and a discussion." *Requirements Engineering*, 11, 102-107.

APPENDIX: REVIEWED PAPERS

[1]Ab Razak, M. F., Anuar, N. B., Salleh, R., & Firdaus, A. (2016). The rise of "malware": Bibliometric analysis of malware study. Journal of Network and Computer Applications, 75, 58-76.

[2]Ahmad, Z., Mayes, K. E., Dong, S., & Markantonakis, K. (2011). Considerations for mobile authentication in the Cloud. information security technical report, 16(3), 123-130.

[3]Babu, B. S., & Venkataram, P. (2008). Cognitive agents based authentication & privacy scheme for mobile transactions (CABAPS). Computer Communications, 31(17), 4060-4071.

[4]Balachandran, V., Tan, D. J., & Thing, V. L. (2016). Control flow obfuscation for android applications. Computers & Security.

[5]Bayuk, J. L. (2013). Security as a theoretical attribute construct. Computers & Security, 37, 155-175.

[6]Bønes, E., Hasvold, P., Henriksen, E., & Strandenæs, T. (2007). Risk analysis of information security in a mobile instant messaging and presence system for healthcare. International journal of medical informatics, 76(9), 677-687.

[7]Boukerche, A., & Ren, Y. (2008). A trust-based security system for ubiquitous and pervasive computing environments. Computer Communications, 31(18), 4343-4351.

[8]Chen, C. L., Lin, Y. F., Castiglione, A., & Palmieri, F. (2016). A secure payment system for multimedia on demand on mobile VANET clouds. Security and Communication Networks, 9(17), 4378-4390.

[9]Chen, P. S., Lin, S. C., & Sun, C. H. (2015). Simple and effective method for detecting abnormal internet behaviors of mobile devices. Information Sciences, 321, 193-204.

[10]de las Cuevas, P., Mora, A. M., Merelo, J. J., Castillo, P. A., García-Sánchez, P., & Fernández-Ares, A. (2015). Corporate security solutions for BYOD: A novel user-centric and self-adaptive system. Computer Communications, 68, 83-95.

[11]De Marsico, M., Nappi, M., Riccio, D., & Wechsler, H. (2015). Mobile Iris Challenge Evaluation (MICHE)-I, biometric iris dataset and protocols. Pattern Recognition Letters, 57, 17-23.

[12]Dehling, T., Gao, F., Schneider, S., & Sunyaev, A. (2015). Exploring the far side of mobile health: information security and privacy of mobile health apps on iOS and Android. JMIR mHealth and uHealth, 3(1), e8.

[13]Dewri, R., & Thurimella, R. (2016). Mobile local search with noisy locations. Pervasive and Mobile Computing.

[14]Dini, G., Martinelli, F., Matteucci, I., Petrocchi, M., Saracino, A., & Sgandurra, D. (2016). Risk analysis of Android applications: A user-centric solution. Future Generation Computer Systems.

[15]D'Orazio, C. J., Lu, R., Choo, K. K. R., & Vasilakos, A. V. (2017). A Markov adversary model to detect vulnerable iOS devices and vulnerabilities in iOS apps. Applied Mathematics and Computation, 293, 523-544.

[16]Dragoni, N., Massacci, F., Walter, T., & Schaefer, C. (2009). What the heck is this application doing?–A security-by-contract architecture for pervasive services. Computers & security, 28(7), 566-577.

[17]Dye, S. M., & Scarfone, K. (2014). A standard for developing secure mobile applications. Computer Standards & Interfaces, 36(3), 524-530.

[18]Farina, P., Cambiaso, E., Papaleo, G., & Aiello, M. (2016). Are mobile botnets a possible threat? The case of SlowBot Net. Computers & Security, 58, 268-283.

[19]Geneiatakis, D., Fovino, I. N., Kounelis, I., & Stirparo, P. (2015). A Permission verification approach for android mobile applications. Computers & Security, 49, 192-205.

[20]Hovav, A., & Putri, F. F. (2016). This is my device! Why should I follow your rules? Employees' compliance with BYOD security policy. Pervasive and Mobile Computing, 32, 35-49.

[21]Hussain, M., Al-Haiqi, A., Zaidan, A. A., Zaidan, B. B., Kiah, M. M., Anuar, N. B., & Abdulnabi, M. (2016). The rise of keyloggers on smartphones: A survey and insight into motion-based tap inference attacks. Pervasive and Mobile Computing, 25, 1-25.

[22]Iqbal, S., Kiah, M. L. M., Dhaghighi, B., Hussain, M., Khan, S., Khan, M. K., & Choo, K. K. R. (2016). On cloud security attacks: A taxonomy and intrusion detection and prevention as a service. Journal of Network and Computer Applications, 74, 98-120.

[23]Jang, J. W., Kang, H., Woo, J., Mohaisen, A., & Kim, H. K. (2016). Andro-dumpsys: anti-malware system based on the similarity of malware creator and malware centric information. Computers & security, 58, 125-138.

[24]Khalil, I., Khreishah, A., & Azeem, M. (2014). Consolidated Identity Management System for secure mobile cloud computing. Computer Networks, 65, 99-110.

[25]Khan, J., Abbas, H., & Al-Muhtadi, J. (2015). Survey on Mobile User's Data Privacy Threats and Defense Mechanisms. Procedia Computer Science, 56, 376-383.

[26]Kulesza, K., Kotulski, Z., & Kulesza, K. (2006). On mobile agents resistance to traffic analysis. Electronic Notes in Theoretical Computer Science, 142, 181-193.

[27]Lin, C., Shen, Z., Chen, Q., & Sheldon, F. T. (2017). A data integrity verification scheme in mobile cloud computing. Journal of Network and Computer Applications, 77, 146-151.

[28]Liu, Q., Lui, J. C., He, C., Pan, L., Fan, W., & Shi, Y. (2015). SAND: A fault-tolerant streaming architecture for network traffic analytics. Journal of Systems and Software.

[29]Mahfouz, A., Muslukhov, I., & Beznosov, K. (2016). Android users in the wild: Their authentication and usage behavior. Pervasive and Mobile Computing, 32, 50-61.

[30]Maier, D., Protsenko, M., & Müller, T. (2015). A game of Droid and Mouse: The threat of split-personality malware on Android. Computers & Security, 54, 2-15.

[31]Markelj, B., & Zgaga, S. (2016). Comprehension of cyber threats and their consequences in Slovenia. Computer Law & Security Review, 32(3), 513 525.

[32]McNeil, P., Shetty, S., Guntu, D., & Barve, G. (2016). SCREDENT: Scalable Real-time Anomalies Detection and Notification of Targeted Malware in Mobile Devices. Procedia Computer Science, 83, 1219-1225.

[33]Mehrnezhad, M., Toreini, E., Shahandashti, S. F., & Hao, F. (2016). TouchSignatures: Identification of user touch actions and PINs based on mobile sensor data via JavaScript. Journal of Information Security and Applications, 26, 23-38.

[34]Meng, W., Lee, W. H., Murali, S. R., & Krishnan, S. P. T. (2016). JuiceCaster: Towards automatic juice filming attacks on smartphones. Journal of Network and Computer Applications, 68, 201-212.

[35]Merlo, A., Migliardi, M., & Caviglione, L. (2015). A survey on energy-aware security mechanisms. Pervasive and Mobile Computing, 24, 77-90.

[36]Mirsky, Y., Shabtai, A., Shapira, B., Elovici, Y., & Rokach, L. (2016). Anomaly detection for smartphone data streams. Pervasive and Mobile Computing.

[37]Ngoqo, B., & Flowerday, S. V. (2015). Information Security Behaviour Profiling Framework (ISBPF) for student mobile phone users. Computers & Security, 53, 132-142.

[38]Odelu, V., Das, A. K., Kumari, S., Huang, X., & Wazid, M. (2017). Provably secure authenticated key agreement scheme for distributed mobile cloud computing services. Future Generation Computer Systems, 68, 74-88.

[39]Ohk, K., Park, S., & Min, K. S. (2016). The Effect of Personal Information Security Attitude and Perceived Company Information Security Policy on Mobile Banking Acceptance.

[40]Pokharel, S., Choo, K. K. R., & Liu, J. (2017). Mobile cloud security: An adversary model for lightweight browser security. Computer Standards & Interfaces, 49, 71-78.

[41]Saab, S. A., Saab, F., Kayssi, A., Chehab, A., & Elhajj, I. H. (2015). Partial mobile application offloading to the cloud for energy-efficiency with security measures. Sustainable Computing: Informatics and Systems, 8, 38-46.

[42]Safavi, S., Shukur, Z., & Razali, R. (2013). Reviews on Cybercrime Affecting Portable Devices. Procedia Technology, 11, 650-657.

[43]Shabtai, A., Kanonov, U., & Elovici, Y. (2010). Intrusion detection for mobile devices using the knowledge-based, temporal abstraction method. Journal of Systems and Software, 83(8), 1524-1537.

[44]Shen, C., Pei, S., Yang, Z., & Guan, X. (2015). Input extraction via motion-sensor behavior analysis on smartphones. Computers & Security, 53, 143-155.

[45]Sicari, S., Rizzardi, A., Grieco, L. A., & Coen-Porisini, A. (2015). Security, privacy and trust in Internet of Things: The road ahead. Computer Networks, 76, 146-164.

[46]Sobh, T. S. (2006). Wired and wireless intrusion detection system: Classifications, good characteristics and state-of-the-art. Computer Standards & Interfaces, 28(6), 670-694.

[47]Sokolova, K., Perez, C., & Lemercier, M. (2016). Android application classification and anomaly detection with graph-based permission patterns. Decision Support Systems.

[48]Song, J., Han, C., Wang, K., Zhao, J., Ranjan, R., & Wang, L. (2016). An integrated static detection and analysis framework for android. Pervasive and Mobile Computing.

[49]Talha, K. A., Alper, D. I., & Aydin, C. (2015). APK Auditor: Permission-based Android malware detection system. Digital Investigation, 13, 1-14.

[50]Vergara-Laurens, Idalides J., et al. "A-PIE: An algorithm for preserving privacy, quality of information, and energy consumption in Participatory Sensing Systems." Pervasive and Mobile Computing 32 (2016): 93-112.

[51]Wang, P., & Wang, Y. S. (2015). Malware behavioural detection and vaccine development by using a support vector model classifier. Journal of Computer and System Sciences, 81(6), 1012-1026.

[52]Wang, Z., Li, C., Yuan, Z., Guan, Y., & Xue, Y. (2016). DroidChain: A novel Android malware detection method based on behavior chains. Pervasive and Mobile Computing, 32, 3-14.

[53]Weerasinghe, D., Rahulamathavan, Y., & Rajarajan, M. (2013). Secure trust delegation for sharing patient medical records in a mobile environment. Health Policy and Technology, 2(1), 36-44.

[54]Wei, X., & Wolf, M. (2016). A survey on HTTPS implementation by Android apps: Issues and countermeasures. Applied Computing and Informatics.

[55]Wessel, S., Huber, M., Stumpf, F., & Eckert, C. (2015). Improving mobile device security with operating system-level virtualization. Computers & Security.

[56]Wong, K. S., & Kim, M. H. (2016). An enhanced user authentication solution for mobile payment systems using wearables. Security and Communication Networks, 9(17), 4639-4649.

[57]Yan, Q., Han, J., Li, Y., Zhou, J., & Deng, R. H. (2015). Leakage-resilient password entry: challenges, design, and evaluation. Computers & Security, 48, 196-211.

[58]Zhang, Y., Chen, X., Li, J., Wong, D. S., Li, H., & You, I. (2016). Ensuring attribute privacy protection and fast decryption for outsourced data security in mobile cloud computing. Information Sciences.

[59]Zhao, H., & Wang, S. (2011). Data Management Trust System in Pervasive Environments. Procedia Environmental Sciences, 11, 334-338.

[60]Zhou, L., Kang, Y., Zhang, D., & Lai, J. (2016). Harmonized authentication based on ThumbStroke dynamics on touch screen mobile phones. Decision Support Systems.

[61]Zhu, Y., Yan, L., & Li, J. (2016). Mobile Internet Information Security Analysis and Countermeasures. TELKOMNIKA (Telecommunication Computing Electronics and Control), 14(3A), 333-337.

USING THE STRUCTURE OF TACIT KNOWING FOR ACQUIRING A HOLISTIC VIEW ON IS FIELD

Ilia Bider and Martin Henkel
DSV, Stockholm University, Sweden

ABSTRACT

The paper considers the problem of students acquiring a holistic view on the IS discipline via a set of not explicitly connected subjects taught in disparate courses. The main idea is based on M. Polanyi's works on a structure of tacit knowing that can produce "a stereoscopic image from two separate pictures". The images that are used for creating a stereoscopic picture give different perspectives on the same reality, but they do not explicitly refer to each other, the 3-d picture is being created unconsciously by the human mind. This paper demonstrates that a connection between subjects can be created by using the same or tightly connected business cases in different courses that use case based learning combined with computer-based apprenticeship simulation. The paper discusses the main idea, the trial settings, and preliminary results.

KEYWORDS

Digital Learning, Apprenticeship Simulation, Case Based Learning, Knowledge Management, Tacit Knowledge

1. INTRODUCTION

A project for which this paper is a progress report deals with the problem of the fragmented knowledge the students get when studying an Information System (IS) program at a university. The problem is a consequence of that the programs, usually, are structured in terms of subjects, each subject being taught separately and, often, independently from other subjects. The problem is known in all disciplines (Miller, 1988), not only in IS and the most common solution to it is having a special course (Kift et al., 2008) which helps the students to integrate the knowledge from different subjects. In most cases, such a course is a capstone project (Durel, 1993) given in the final year of undergraduate or post-graduate education.

The biggest shortcoming of having a separate course aimed at integration of the fragmented knowledge is the students having their knowledge fragmented in a number of years, which can diminish their desire to stay at the university until the end of their studies. Coupled with the subjects being taught in an academic fashion, this can lead to the students with lesser academic preparedness drop out, or need to extend their stay at the university. The question arises whether there is a solution to the fragmented knowledge problem that would allow making connection between the subjects when they are taught, without waiting to the last year capstone project.

A solution that is under testing in our project is based on the M. Polanyi's ideas on the structure of tacit knowing (Polanyi, 1965). More exactly, his ideas on the ability of human mind of creating a holistic picture from a set of fragmented signals coming from the outside of the human body. This, for example, allows a human being to create a stereoscopic (3-d) image based one two separate flat pictures that does not explicitly refer to each other, but they represent the same reality taken at different viewpoints. Given this ability, interconnection of the courses could be obtained of using learning objects related to the same reality in difference courses, relying on the ability of the human mind to create a "stereoscopic" (holistic picture) from the two, seemingly disjoint subject matters taught in two different courses.

The implementation of the idea of using the structure of tacit knowing for connecting the courses is done in the frame of Case Based Learning (CBL) accepted in our department. The CBL is used in many of our courses in the form of the students completing a practical project during the course where they apply the theoretical knowledge they acquire from teaching/learning activities. Some courses employ projects where students work in groups, others (especially on-line courses) use individually based projects. Each project has a business case, and requires the students to complete some assignments related to this case. The assignments can include building a model, e.g. a process model, or a conceptual model, designing a database or a building a prototype of the system.

To facilitate the students creating tacit connection between the subject matters of different courses, we suggest using the same, or tightly connected business cases in the projects completed in the frame of these courses. For example, in one course the students could be asked to draw a business process model based on the information from the case, and in another - to build a proto-type of an IT-system that would support activities in the process. The connection between the cases can also be less strong, e.g. they concern the same company, for example, a consulting company completing various projects for their customers. This will tie the business cases through the individuals participating in them.

A usual way of presenting a business case to the students is giving them a text description of the case. For testing our idea, however, we use a different way of case presentation, the one that comes from our previous projects (Bider et al., 2015a; Bider et al., 2015b), which is called apprenticeship simulation. The apprenticeship simulation is based on using multi-media capability to present a case to the students, such as recorded inter-views with the stakeholders, web-sites of the companies included in the business case, examples of internal documents, email correspondence, etc. The presentation fragments can be real, e.g. real interviews with people, real companies websites, etc., or totally simulated, e.g. an interview where teachers play the roles of stakeholders, faked websites, etc. Using a mixture of both creates a rich immersive environment similar to what the students will find in their working life after their graduation.

The idea of using CBL projects based on the same or tightly connected simulated business cases was tested in our teaching practice. First, two courses that belong to the same program have been chosen for the test and the results were assessed through a student survey and interviews; then a third course has been added to the trial. In the first hand, the survey and interviews were aimed at finding out whether such courses design helps to connect subject matters taught in different courses. In the second hand, we wanted to find out whether such design has other positive and negative side effects. The preliminary results are positive: (1) the design helps the students to connect the subject matters on the tacit level, (2) the design has some positive side effects, and (3) it does not have substantial negative side effects. Currently, we are extending usage of the same or tightly connected simulated cases to other courses, and continuing investigation of the effects on students learning.

The rest of the paper is structured in the following manner. In Section 2, we give an overview of the knowledge based related to our project. In Section 3, we present the design of business case(s) used in the courses, as well as give a short overview of the courses themselves. In section 4, we give an overview of our investigation of the effects of using the same or interconnected business cases in CBL projects on the students learning. Section 5 presents the conclusions and draws plans for the future.

2. KNOWLEDGE BASE

2.1 Related Works

Our work crosses a number of areas in pedagogical research. To these belong research related to the problem of fragment knowledge, Case Based Learning (CBL), using simulation in education, apprenticeship, apprenticeship simulation, and reuse of learning objects. Due to the space limitations, we cannot give an extensive overview of the works in all these areas, but limit ourselves to some examples.

The problem of fragmented knowledge has been known for a long time (Miller, 1988), but it is still present in all educational disciplines. The most typical solution used for solving this problem is having a special course aimed at integrating the knowledge from the previous courses, such course being usually scheduled at then of the educational cycle (Kift et al., 2008). Often, such course is formed as a capstone project, see for example, (Durel, 1993) that defines a capstone project as "a crowning course or experience coming at the end of a sequence of courses with the specific objective of integrating a body of relatively fragmented knowledge into a unified whole". As has already been mentioned in the introduction, the main drawback of such a solution that we want to avoid is that the knowledge remains fragmented almost to the end of the program.

Case Based Learning (CBL) is a teaching method, where students, through working with a realistic case, are getting an opportunity to apply concepts and theories in complex situations and develop their analytical skills (Herreid, 2005). In its simplest form, a case can be given to the students as a textual description of the organization (Fenstermacher, 2004), but it is possible to refer the students to a real-life organization (Recker & Rosemann, 2009). Cases can be used as a larger part of a course, in the form of project assignments, but can also be used for lectures, seminars, exams, etc.

A case can also be given in the form of a simulated situation. One field where the simulation has been successfully used in teaching is in the medical field where a patient is simulated; see for example (Ellaway et al., 2008). However, such simulations may be complex to create, especially, if the case should cover a multitude of perspectives needed for IS analysis and design. As an alternative, apprenticeship simulation (Bider et al., 2015a; Bider et al., 2015b) has been developed. Rather than simulating a complete business, apprenticeship simulation aims at simulating the situation of an apprentice being guided by a master analyst. The master presents the apprentice (student) with collected documents to analyze and delimited tasks to perform. This approach approximates real apprenticeship that is usually used in professional education (Gowlland, 2014).

Research on reusing course material has so far pointed out positive effects of reuse in terms of increased quality and productivity (Parrish, 2004). The goal of productivity, naturally, puts the focus on creating easy to reuse modules of learning objects (IEEE, 2002) - digital or non-digital assets that may be used for education. Development of learning objects and associated tools has focused on the technical side in terms of platforms and exchange formats (Jesukiewicz, 2009), as well as on metadata standards for describing the pedagogic content (Rodríguez-Artacho, 2004). Research in the reuse of learnings objects has so far pointed towards that limiting dependency between modules simplifies reuse (Boyle, 2003). The approach we present in this paper, have a different goal with reusing cases for teaching – instead of aiming at productivity gains, we primarily aim at letting the students get a holistic view of a discipline. This said, it does not mean that the teachers will not get productivity gains as a side effect of using the same business case in different courses.

2.2 The Structure of Tacit Knowing

In a number of his philosophical works, including (Polanyi, 1965), M. Polanyi presented his view on the structure of tacit knowing that "brings out the joint meaning" from different signals coming from the outside world. A typical example he uses is a stereoscopic (3D) image created from two "flat" pictures "due to slight differences between the two pictures, taken from two points a few inches apart". As Polanyi calls it, "we are *focally aware* of the stereo-image, by being *subsidiarily aware* of the two separate pictures". Our work on creating a holistic view on IS-discipline in the students' heads is based on the capability of human mind to create a holistic picture from two images that are not related to each other besides that they represent the same reality taken from different angles. The problem to solve here is relating the subjects of different courses to the same reality taken from different viewpoints, but without any explicit references between them. In our approach, this is achieved by having the same basic business case for the project assignments in the courses, where the assignments creates different viewpoints, while not explicitly referring to each other.

3. BUSINESS CASE AND COURSES DESIGN

3.1 The Business Case

A business case chosen for the field trial of our approach features two fictional characters, both of them being companies. The first character is a consulting company called ST Transformer that completes projects on behalf of their customers. ST Transformer is meant as being present in all interconnected business cases to be used in various courses in the future. ST transformer is a purely fictional character that does not have any prototype in real life. The roles of consultants working at ST Transformer, e.g. when conducting interviews or facilitating workshops, are played by the teachers in our department.

The second character in the business case is one of the ST Transformer's customers, called Harmony inside. The company helps their clients to deal with the IBS syndrome (where IBS stays for Irritable Bawls Syndrome). The company was started by two dietitians for several years ago, and recently, it came into the phase of growth. This is also a fictional character, but in difference from ST transformer, it has a prototype as a real company. The ladies who started this real company play the roles of the staff working at the fictional company.

The basic information that is reused in all courses that employ the case consist of two websites of the companies (faked), see Figure 1., and two recorded interviews/discussions between the consultants from ST Transformer and the staff from Harmony inside. The interviews are divided in 6 fragments, approximately 5 min each, each fragment being devoted to a specific topic, see Figure 2.

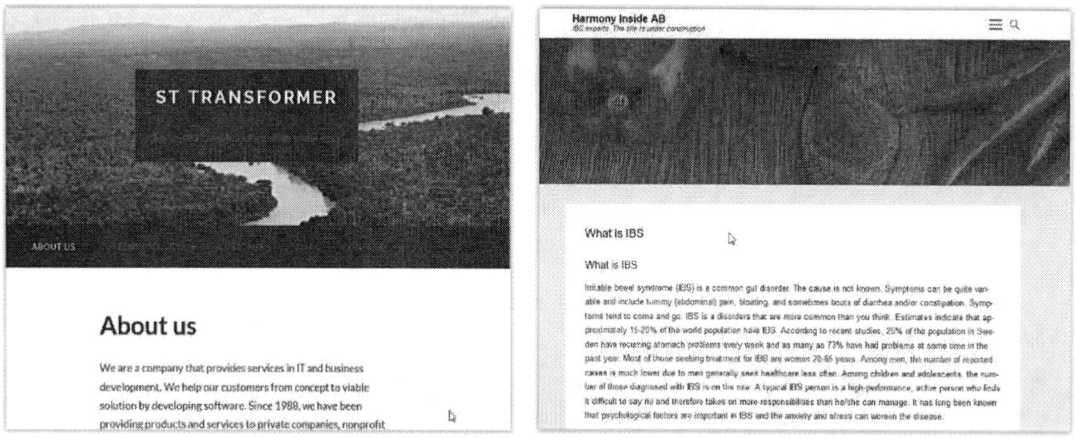

Figure 1. The Fake Website of the Fictional Characters in the Business Case

Figure 2. An Interview Fragment

A course that chooses to use this business case creates a project site where the links to the basic presentation fragments are introduced. An example of a project site used for one of the courses is presented in Figure 3. Besides these links, the project site can include tasks to be completed in the frame of the project and any additional information that might be required for the project. The course teachers are free to choose which interview fragments include in the project, and in which order, for example, irrelevant for a specific project interview fragments can be excluded from a particular project. In addition, the course teachers decide which fragments are the main ones for the project, and which ones only constitute a business context. Here, again, a fragment that is main in one course project can be viewed as just a context in another course project.

3.2 The Courses

Currently, three courses at the department are included in the field trial: Business Process and Case Management (BPCM), Citizen centric service design (SERDES) and Systems Theory, Organization and IT (SYSTOIT). All three courses include elements of enterprise modelling, and use projects related the "Harmony Inside" case for teaching these elements, see Table 1 and text below it. The courses are not explicitly referring to each other, and there is no requirement that a student should take all of them, or should take them in any particular order. In fact, a student can decide to take only one of these courses. The first two courses are mandatory for one MS program (Open eGovernment) and are given online. The third course is a campus course and it is not included in the program. Normally, a student takes BPCM first and SERDES after it. However, some students choose to do it in the reverse order.

Figure 3. An Example of a Course Project Site (BPCM)

Table 1. Overview of the Three Courses

Course	Case contents	Case use
1. BPCM	Video interviews, Companies websites	Business process modelling, Agile business process development
2. SYSTOIT	Video interviews, Companies websites	Variety engineering, Viable System Model (VSM)
3. SERDES	Video interviews, Companies websites, Mails, Screen mockups, see Fig. 4.	Service value network modelling, Information modelling, Domain driven design, API design

The objective of the BPCM course is to give the students broad view on Business Processes (BP), including that there are different approaches to BP modeling, and development, and that the choice of which to adopt depends on the context and task at hand. The course presents to the students two modeling methods in details, workflow modeling with BPMN and State-oriented Business Process Modeling (Khomyakov & Bider, 2000), while giving a short overview of other modeling techniques, alongside with how to choose the one that fits the context and task at hand. The course takes such issues as agile vs. traditional business process development, process architecture and adaptive case management. The Harmony Case is used for a project assignment related to building an executable process model for online consultations given by dietitians, see Figure 3.

SERDES aims at teaching the students software service design in the public sector. It contains elements of theories on service oriented organisations, such as service-dominant logic (SDL). Moreover the course covers the use and design of egovernment service platforms, and the design of service API:s. In the SERDES course, the Harmony Inside case is used for creating enterprise models, including service value networks and information models. Furthermore, the students design a service API based based on the case description. For adjusting the Harmony case to the course, the case has been complemented with additional material. For example, three fictitious mails have been added outlining requirements for the service design that was not a part of the basic case description. Another addition is that a screen mockup has been added (see Figure 1c), that gives the students an idea about what data the future service needs to handle.

SYSTOIT is an introductory course in system theory applied to the organizational context, including usage of IT in the organizations. The course introduces central notions of systems theory, such as system, context, goals, variety, etc. A particular focus is made on teaching Viable System Model of Stafford Beer (Beer, 1979) and its usage for organizational systems diagnostics. The Harmony case is used to support all teaching activities in the course.

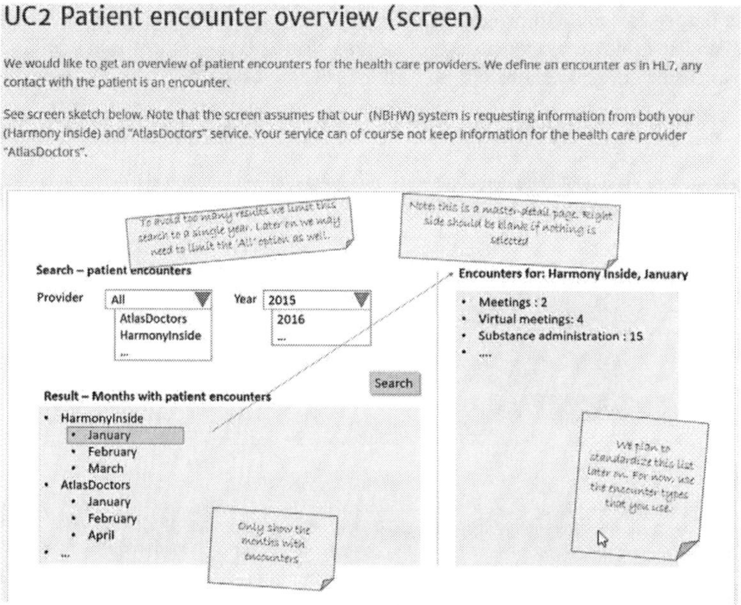

Figure 4. A Mockup Screen Used in the SERDES Course

4. ASSESSMENT OF EFFECTS ON STUDENTS LEARNING

The first round of the three courses included in the field trial was completed during the fall term of 2016 (BPCM and CEDRIS) and spring term of 2017 (SYSTOIT). The second round is now underway. Overall, 11 students finished two of these courses: eight Students attended BPCM + CERDIS, two students attended SYSTOIT + BPCM and one student attended CERDIS + BPCM. To investigate the effects on students learning of having the same case in the projects assignments, we conducted a survey among these students. The participation in the survey was voluntary. Nine students have chosen to answer the questions. In addition, we have interviewed three of these students to get a better understanding of their answers.

Besides the formal questions on the students' background, the survey included questions aimed at clarifying the following issues:

- Whether the students get connection between the subjects from different courses taught in separation
- Possible negative side effects
- Possible positive side effects
- General impression

The questions and answers related to these issues are presented in Table 2. As we can see from the table, there is a consensus among the students that using the same case helped to create a connection between the subjects of the courses that were not explicitly linked to each other. A near consensus has also been reached in the question whether it helped to understand how a company could be viewed from different angles. In comments, the students expressed that it helped to get connection between the subjects as well, e.g. "Seeing different perspectives on the same organization makes it easier to understand new courses and theories".

To better understand in what ways the connection between the subjects has been created, we conducted online interviews with three of the students who participated in the survey. The general conclusion from these interviews was that the students could not explain in which ways the connection had been created, they just felt that it did exist. This fully supports our initial assumption that the connection is created on the tacit level due to the structure of tacit knowing professed by M. Polanyi.

The only possible negative effect we investigated was whether the same course can create a confusion (Question 3). Though one student was undecided on the issue, the rest did not experience any confusion.

The positive effect of gains in learning productivity was reported by almost all students (question 4). This was confirmed with the following type of comments: "The student needs to spend less time familiarizing with the case and can spend more time on the subject matter". However, only about half of the students agreed that reuse made it more interesting to complete assignments (Question 5).

Table 2. Survey Results

<table>
<tr><th colspan="2">Connection between the Courses</th></tr>
<tr><td>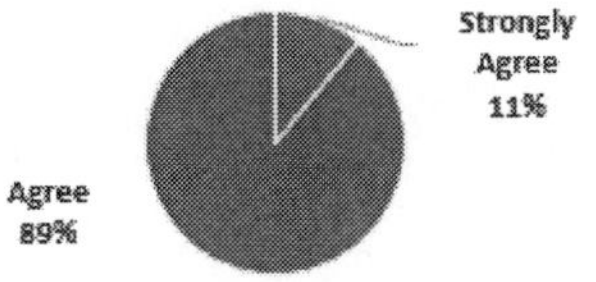

1. Using the same case in two subjects gave me understanding of how the subjects are related</td><td>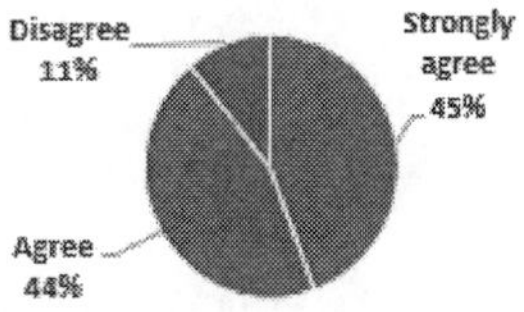

2. Using the same case gave me an understanding of how an organization can be viewed from different perspectives.</td></tr>
<tr><th colspan="2">Possible negative effects</th></tr>
<tr><td colspan="2">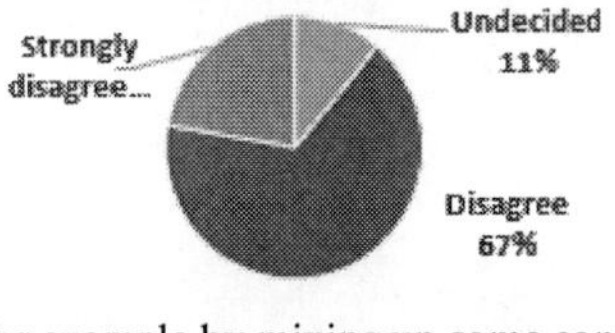

3. Using the same case was confusing, for example by mixing up some concepts from different courses.</td></tr>
<tr><th colspan="2">Possible positive effects</th></tr>
<tr><td>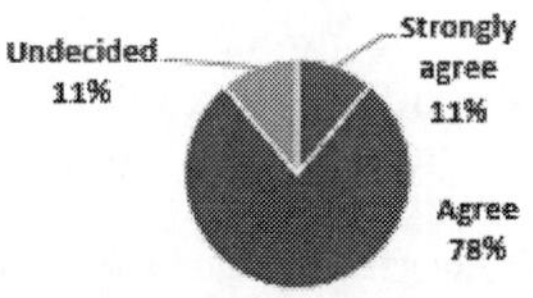

4. Using the same case made it quicker to complete the assignments in the 2nd course.</td><td>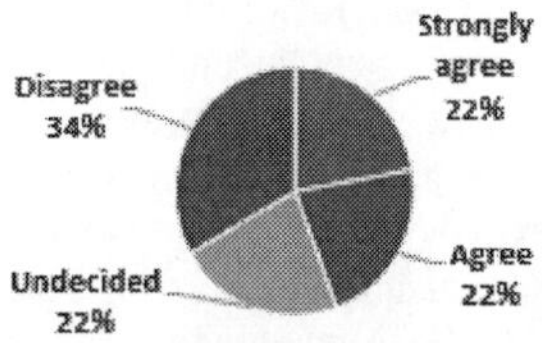

5. Using the same case made it more interesting to do the assignments.</td></tr>
<tr><th colspan="2">General impression</th></tr>
<tr><td>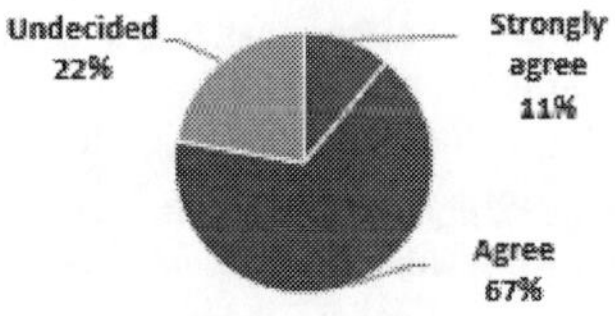

6. If there were a third course using the same case it would be considered as an advantage</td><td>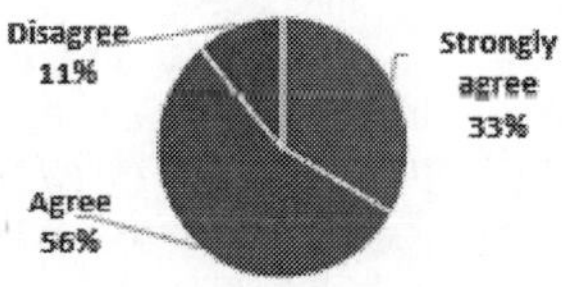

7. Overall, using the same case in several courses is a good idea.</td></tr>
</table>

As far as general impression on the reuse of a cases in different courses is concerned (Questions 6&7), most of the students agreed that it is rather a good approach, though there are potential drawbacks in it, e.g. "The only possible drawback of this approach is that case diversity can enhance student learning, and re-using a case reduces the case diversity a student meets while studying", or " Somewhat decreased motivation; assuming full familiarity with the case without it necessarily being so". Note, that in our preliminary investigation (Henkel et al., 2017) on reusing the case in several courses, the expected results were much more uncertain.

5. CONCLUSION

This paper suggests an innovative approach to dealing with the problem of "fragmented knowledge" the students get in IS related programs that consist of a set of not very tightly connected courses. The approach is based on the structure of tacit knowing uncovered by M. Polanyi that allows a human being to create a holistic picture from a set of disjoint signals coming from outside but representing the same reality taken at different angles. The main idea of the approach is using the same basic business case in different courses. The idea has been tested in a CBL environment using apprenticeship simulation. The trial includes three courses. The results obtained so far, though limited, confirm the initial assumption that using the same, or tightly related business cases in combination with CBL and apprenticeship simulation could facilitate the students to create connection between the subject matters of different courses on the tacit level.

Currently, we are trying to expand the usage of the same case to more courses, and are planning to conduct a broader empirical study. The latter will include a study of the severity of the "fragmented knowledge" problem in the departments programs, and how well our approach deals with it. A kind of connectivity index could be developed for this end.

ACKNOWLEDGEMENT

This work was supported by a grant from Stockholm University. We are grateful to our colleagues Erik Perjons, Stewart Kowalski and Åsa Smedberg who participated in the project and in teaching the trial courses.

REFERENCES

Beer, S., 1979. *The Heart of Enterprise*. Wiley.

Bider, I., Henkel, M., Kowalski, S. & Perjons, E., 2015a. Simulating apprenticeship using multimedia in Higher Education: a case from the information systems field. *Interactive Technology and Smart Education*, 12(2), pp.137-54.

Bider, I., Henkel, M., Kowalski, S. & Perjons, E., 2015b. Teaching enterprise modeling based on multi-media simulation: a pragmatic approach. In Benyoucef, M., Weiss, M. & Mili, H., eds. *Proceedings of 6th International MCETECH Conference, LNBIP Vol. 209*. Montreal, Canada. Springer, pp.239-54.

Boyle, T., 2003. Design principles for authoring dynamic, reusable learning objects. *Australian Journal of Educational Technology*, , 19(1), pp.46-58.

Durel, R., 1993. The capstone course: A rite of passage. *Teaching Sociology*, 21(3), pp.223–25.

Ellaway, R. et al., 2008. Building a virtual patient commons. *Med Teach*, 30, pp.170-74.

Fenstermacher, K.D., 2004. If I had a Model, I'd Model in the Morning. In *Proceeding of OOPSLA'04*. ACM, pp.88-89.

Gowlland, G., 2014. Apprenticeship as a Model for Learning in and Through Professional Practice. In *International Handbook of Research in Professional and Practice-based Learning*. Springer. pp.759-99.

Henkel, M. et al., 2017. Reusing Cases for Teaching Enterprise Modelling — Feasibility Study and Reality Check. In *SCME-iStarT 2017. CEUR Workshop Proceedings Vol. 1954*. CEUR-WS.org, pp.4-14.

Herreid, F.C., 2005. Because wisdom can't be told: Using case studies to teach science. *PeerReview, 7 (2)*, 7(2).

IEEE, 2002. IEEE Std 1484.12.1-2002 *IEEE Standard for Learning Object Metadata*. New York: The Institute of Electrical and Electronics Engineers.

Jesukiewicz, P., 2009. *Sharable Content Object Reference Model (SCORM), 4th Edition Content Aggregation Model*. Advanced Distributed Learning.

Khomyakov, M. & Bider, I., 2000. Achieving Workflow Flexibility through Taming the Chaos. In *OOIS 2000 - 6th international conference on object oriented information systems*. Springer, pp.85-92.

Kift, S.M., Field, R.M. & Wells, I.B., 2008. Promoting sustainable professional futures for law graduates through curriculum renewal in legal education: a final year experience (FYE2). *eLaw Journal*, 15(2), pp.145-58.

Miller, G., 1988. *The meaning of general education: The history of an educational paradigm*. New York: Teachers College Press.

Parrish, P.E., 2004. The trouble with learning objects. *Journal of Educational Technology Research and Development*, 52(1), pp.49-67.

Polanyi, M., 1965. The Structure of Consciousness. *Brain*, LXXXVIII, pp.799-810.

Recker, J. & Rosemann, M., 2009. Teaching Business Process Modelling: Experiences and Recommendations. *Communications of the AIS*, 25, pp.379-94.

Rodríguez-Artacho, M..V.M.M.F., 2004. Modeling Educational Content: The Cognitive Approach of the PALO Language. 7(3), pp.124-37.

COMPUTER INFORMATION SYSTEM CURRICULUM NEEDS REVAMPING A DIGITAL INFORMATION TECHNOLOGY PROGRAM

Bijan Mashaw, Ph.D.
California State University - East Bay, USA

ABSTRACT

We propose an interdisciplinary IT program that integrates general education, critical thinking, business, computer science, and information systems program to create a robust curriculum in Digital Information Technology. The program also allows computing education to cross over to other fields in order to provide a wider market for the computer science and information systems. With the proper planning, the proposed model does not need any new or additional resources.

KEYWORDS

Digital Technology Curriculum, Information Technology Program

1. INTRODUCTION

Traditionally, the Information Systems programs have emphasized business education, and the computer science concentrates on software-technology. Many reports indicate that while there is a shortage for information system professionals, there is a gap between what employers would like to see in technical workers, and what universities provides in the field of information technology. Per Bloomberg Recruiter Report, the most desirable Job Skills that companies need, other than technical competencies, is Strategic thinking, Creative problem-solving, Leadership Skills, and Communication skills (Bloomberg Recruiter Report, 2016). The gap is not limited to the information technology education, or Computer Science. Per McKinsey report, there is a gap between the whole educational system and the job skills that employers need. The report goes further to indicates that even worldwide educational institutions are out of synch with business need particularly in the information technology field. Furthermore, students are also frustrated in matching their interest with a degrees which would help them to find employment. Accordingly, there is a great need for a modified Digital Information Technology education which can accommodate the requirement of employers from stand point of technical, interpersonal and business education. This paper proposes a framework for a multidisciplinary approach for a program to accommodate the employers' hiring requirements. This multidisciplinary program allows incorporating general education, critical thinking, business, computer science, information systems programs, and specialty in a desired field such as system software engineering, web-technology, Database Management Systems, or even other IT field such as Biological Science, Statistical, or Bioengineering.

1.1 The Evolving Areas of Digital Technology

The term "computer" which has been used since 40's, indicates a device that stores and processes data in digital form. The advantage of this device is that it can be programmed to do anything which is desired. Nowadays, a digital system is used to control any device. Therefore, it is appropriate to use digital technology, rather than computer technology. The new areas of digital technology that has received much attention and already developers are tapping applications include the following:

1.1.1 Data-Intelligent Driven Economy

The exponential expansion of the gathering, analyzing, and use of Big Data has tremendous impact on business. Not only has Big Data phenomena have created an opportunity for businesses, but also for developers and providers. However, there are not many educational institutions which offer a program for professional education in this filed.

1.1.2 Mobile Systems

In 2017, approximately 2.5 billion smartphones were used in the world. It is predicted that there would be more than 3 billion smartphone users in 2020. All digital growth are now coming from mobile usage (comScore). Even, majority of e-commerce transactions are done with mobiles. The mobile payment transaction value in US is predicted to be more than $866 billion by 2021 [per Statista, 2017, and Digital Market Outlook, Statista Digital Market Outlook 2016)

1.1.3 Artificial Intelligence

Many of the new technology devices are much more cognitively demanding than the previous technology. The application of Artificial Intelligence is in every object or device. The technique is used in machine learning, digital modelling, business decision making, neuroscience, and diagnostics systems. The universities need to develop programs to prepare work force for the work in this special field.

2. A DIGITAL INFORMATION TECHNOLOGY APPROACH

An ideal program for an undergraduate degree in Digital Information Technology (DIT) would provide the opportunity to obtain the necessary general education, the fundamental knowledge of digital technology, and a focus on the emerging applications of digital technology, yet it would be flexible enough to accommodate the trends and future evolution of the digital technology field. The program should also provide opportunity for specialized work not only in the technical fields, but also in areas such as Big-Data intelligence gathering, Artificial Intelligence, mobile systems, medical, biology, statistics, engineering, etc. The specialization in a specific area should be based on the student's needs or interests, which of course would be demand driven. Opening the door for incorporating the computing education to other fields also has the advantage of expanding the market for computer science programs.

The following sections describes a detailed framework for an interdisciplinary IT program that an integrates general education, critical thinking, business, computer science, and information systems program to create a robust curriculum in Digital Information Technology System for IT Careers. The program also allows computing education to cross over to other fields in order to provide a wider market for the computer science and information systems.

It should be noted that during the past few years, a working group has been established for a new curriculum for Master's programs, and recently has been approved by ACM and AIS. (https://msis2016review.wordpress.com/). The proposed program is different than ACM/AIS MSIS 2016 Global Competency Model. The major difference is that this proposal emphasizes an interdisciplinary and STEM approach for an undergraduate comprehensive autonomous BS degree.

3. PROPOSED CURRICULUM FRAMEWORK

The specific objectives of the B.S. in the Digital Information Technology program are to educate students so that the graduate will have an understanding in areas of communication, problem solving, reasoned decision making and ethics. A graduate in Digital Information Technology will be able to understand the technical aspects of IT, play a key role in the development of leading-edge computer applications in a modern enterprise, and be able to use or manage Digital Information Technology resources effectively. A graduate with this degree would be able to examine information needs critically, find solutions, communicate effectively, perform quantitative functions and apply technology in an area of specialization so that he or she can function effectively in a modern enterprise.

3.1 The Composition of the Program

The proposal is for a Baccalaureate of Science Degree in Digital Technology. Students should complete the units of course requirements in five categories (Figure 1) :

I. General and Global Education
II. General computer science and software engineering
III. Business and Information System Fundamentals
IV. Advance Information Technology skills
V. Specialization in any science field

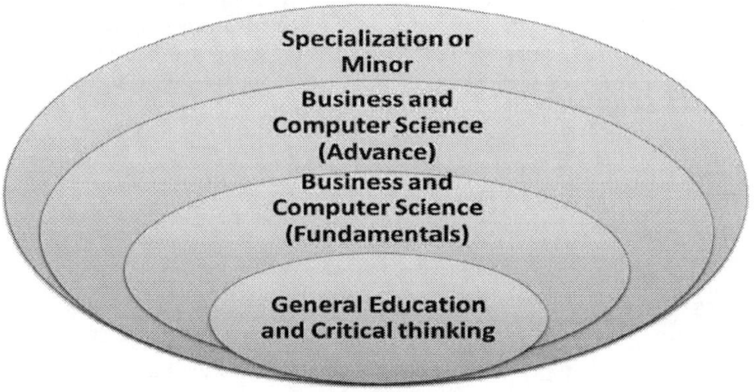

Figure 1. The Categories of Coverage for the Digital Technology Degree

The detailed and the proportions of coverage of the requirements is shown in Table 1.

Table 1. The proportions of Coverage of the Requirements

	% Aprx	No of units (130 units)
General, Science, Critical Thinking & Global Education	35%	45
Business and Information System Fundamentals	15%	20
General Computer Science and Software Engineering	15%	20
Advance Information Technology Skills	15%	20
Specialization in any Science Field	20%	25

This recommended model allows students to have two kinds of concentrations or options: 1) An area in Digital Systems, such as concentration on Web Technology, Security, etc., and 2) An area of concentration in a specialized area of interest and career objectives, such as Computer Science, Biology, Statistics, etc. Each concentration or option in consists of the recommended courses in Digital Technology curriculum. Examples of the concentration areas or option areas are Business Information Systems Development, Database Management Systems and Data Warehousing, System Integration, Big-Data Technology, Artificial Intelligence science, Web-Application Development and Design, E-Business, Telecommunication and Network Systems, Network Security Systems, Computer Science, Software Development and Engineering, and Supply Chain Management Systems/ERP. The composition of the program allows students to obtain a minor in any area such as Computer Science or Software Engineering, Biology, Chemistry, or other area of interest, without additional course requirements, with proper planning (Figure 2.).

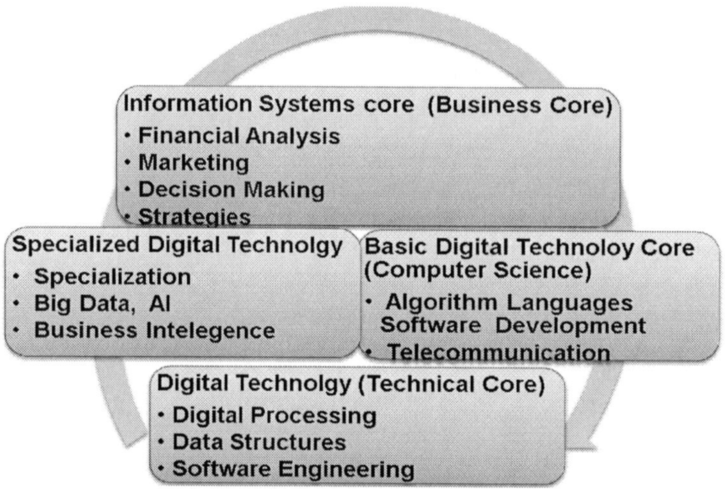

Figure 2. Course Composition of the Requirements

3.2 Implementation

With the proper planning, the proposed model does not need any new or additional resources. Particularly, no new course will be needed to start the program. Implementing such a program is feasible with existing resources by pooling the courses from different disciplines and designing a package to fit the specific needs of the local employers and the interests of the students. The typical courses in the program consist of existing university courses (for GE), business, information systems and computer information systems, and computer science courses. A major portion of the program can come from the existing university GE requirements; but they should be fortified to accommodate the requirements for this major--a strong math and statistical background, written, and oral communication skills, and computer literacy skills. Other recommended areas or courses to be included in GE can be economics, philosophy and/or logic. The business courses can include quantitative analysis, financial analysis, management, marketing, and project management. To implement the Digital Information Technology portion, the courses from Information Systems and Computer Science can be pooled together to create a planned program. The Digital Information Technology courses consist of 4 tiers as follows (Figure 3):

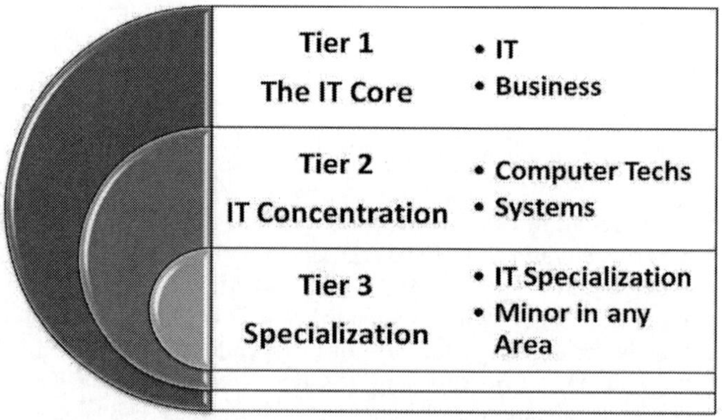

Figure 3. The Tiers and the Course Composition of the Program

3.2.1 Tier 1 -- The IT Cores

The IT cores cover two important fundamentals for an IT education

> **a. The IT Core**--The IT Core should be designed to include fundamentals of problems, data, computer, test, algorithm, process, system, information, language, telecommunication, and software. In practice, the typical courses to cover these topics are already in place in the Computer Science Department or the Information Systems department.

> **b. The Business Core--**The core courses for business contain the tool kit for the essentials and the context of modern business functions such as Financial Analysis, Management, Marketing, Quantitative-Decision Making, Business policies and Strategies, and Project management.

3.2.2 Tier 2 -- The IT Concentration

This tier of IT courses contains a pool of intermediate courses allowing a student to concentrate on an area of interest. Of course, the tier 1 –IT-Core should be the prerequisite for this tier of courses. With the advisor's assistance, a student can take, say 5 or 6 of these "intermediate" courses, per his/her career objectives. For example, if a student desires to major in Computer Science, then the student can take Digital Processing, Data Structures and Algorithms, and Software Engineering.

3.2.3 Tier 3 -- The Possible Specialization

The proposed framework allows a student to specialize in an area of his/her choice for the chosen career. This flexibility allows two kinds of concentration or specialization: 1) within the IT/CS, or 2) in another field such as science, medicine, etc. For example, a specialized area in IT/CS can be Security, Web Technology, etc. In this case, a student can choose say 5 or 6 courses from the pool of advanced IT courses. Examples of an area for specialization based on interest and career objectives can be Computer Science, Information Services, Biology, Statistics, Supply Chain Management, and ERP, etc. In this case, a student can take 5 to 7 courses from outside of the IT/CS, as a "minor", "Track", or "option."

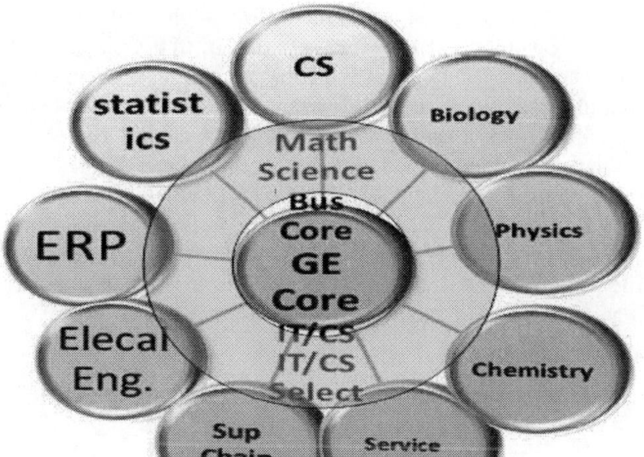

Figure 4. The Possible Specialization

3.3 Setting the Program Objectives

With the proper planning, the implementation of this program can easily meet the ABET's accreditation requirements. ABET's major concern is to make sure that the program's requirements are consistent with its educational objectives. For IT accreditation, the objective of this program should be set as a program that integrates the computing and professional education requirement for careers in Digital Technology. Further, the program's objective should indicate an up-to-date coverage of the basic topics in the computing discipline as well as the advanced/ specialized topics in a professional area (Tier 1 and Tier 2).

The program also should make sure that it covers the mathematics appropriate to the discipline, and indicate that the graduates have the technical ability in the core information technologies; have the ability to integrate IT-based solutions into the solution for a user system; have the ability to identify requirements of a system, and are able to incorporate the requirements into design or development of computer-based systems. Furthermore, as part of the ABET's criteria for IT accreditation, the program should have enough educational experience and course work that covers 1) the necessary technologies and the coursework to cover human computer interaction, programming, networking, and web technologies, 2) the necessary content to include information assurance and security, 3) the maintenance and system administration, and 4) system integration and architecture (ABAT Criteria 5) [1].

The program also needs to have documented measurable educational objectives and a mechanism for continual evaluation and updating. Actually, per ABAT assessment criteria, the program should devise a mechanism that can collect, analyze, and evaluate the achievement of the program outcomes and educational objectives. The result of the evaluation and feedback can be used to improve the program and fine tune it, based on the needs of the program's constituencies.

4. SUMMARY

Computer use, applications, society's view of computers, as well as the divergence of technology and the increase of global economy and infrastructure on computer technology, have all demonstrated the need for drastic redesign and fundamental restructuring of how higher education offers computer science education. It is crucial for today's workforce and tomorrow's technological advances that students receive appropriate and innovative curriculum in computer technology.

This paper proposes a framework for a Digital Information Technology program that can be easily implemented through the Computer Science Department, or the College of Business . The framework suggests an interdisciplinary composition that incorporates courses from the General Education-breadth of the university, fortified to include logic, oral and written communication, economics, and computer literacy, as well as courses from the School of Business and Computer Science. The program suggests courses so that a student will have an understanding in areas of communication, problem solving, reasoned decision making and ethics. A graduate in Digital Information Technology will be able to understand the technical aspects of IT, play a key role in the development of leading-edge computer applications in a modern enterprise, and be able to use or manage IT resources effectively. To implement the program, there is no need for new resources or a new course. The model can be implemented with the existing courses in the university and in the Computer Science Department.

REFERENCES

ABET (2017), Criteria for Accrediting Computing Programs, 2017-2018 Available at http://www.abet.org/accreditation/accreditation-criteria/criteria-for-accrediting-computing-programs-2017-2018/

ACM/IEEE IT Curriculum Guidelines for Undergraduate Degree Programs, 2008. http://www.acm.org/education/curricula-recommendations. As of March 2016.

Barry Lunt , J. Ekstrom , Han Reichgelt , Michael Bailey , Richard Leblanc, IT 2008: the history of a new computing discipline, Communications of the ACM, v.53 n.12, December 2010 [doi>10.1145/1859204.1859236]

Computer and Information Technology Occupations, Publish March 29, 2012, United States Department of Labor, Occupational Outlook Handbook; http://www.bls.gov/ooh/computer-and-information-technology/home.htm

Deagon, Brian, 2013 , Big Data Explosion Is Big Business For Many Investor's Business Daily http://news.investors.com/business/040312-606586-big-data-explosion-fuels-analytics-field.htm?p=full

Education for Sustainable Development (ESD UNESCO) at http://www.unesco.org/new/en/education/themes/leading-the-international-agenda/education-for-sustainable-development/ As of March 2016.

IDC Digital Universe Study, sponsored by EMC, 2012

Impagliazzo, J. 2015. Curriculum Design for Computer Engineering and Information Technology. Global Engineering Education Conference (EDUCON), 2015 IEEE, 18--20 March 2015.

Kuczera, M., Field, S. & Windisch, H. C. (2016). Building skills for all: A review of england. Paris: OECD.

Mashaw, Bijan (2009) Information technology approach in computer science, Journal of Computing Sciences in Colleges, Volume 24 Issue 5, May 2009 Pages 191-197, by Consortium for Computing Sciences in Colleges , USA

Mashaw, Bijan (2009). A Practical Information Technology Program, Journal of International Technology and Information Management, Volume 18, Numbers ¾, 321-336

Mihaela Sabin , Svetlana Peltsverger , Cara Tang, Updating the ACM/IEEE 2008 Curriculum in Information Technology (Abstract Only), Proceedings of the 46th ACM Technical Symposium on Computer Science Education, March 04-07, 2015, Kansas City, Missouri, USA [doi>10.1145/2676723.2691857]

News Feed Item, Third-quarter survey confirms continued growth of cloud computing in industry activity, By PR Newswire, http://cloudcomputing.sys-con.com/node/2466084, November 30, 2012

Paterson, Bill , Mary Granger , John Impagliazzo , Edward Sobiesk , Mark Stockman , Ming Zhang, Should IT2008 be revised?, Proceedings of the 14th annual ACM SIGITE conference on Information technology education, October 10-12, 2013, Orlando, Florida, USA [doi>10.1145/2512276.2512308]

Patterson, David A., Restoring the popularity of computer science, *Communication of the ACM*, vol. 48, No 9, September 2005, 25–28.

Pham, Thu, 2011, Cloud Computing Prompts 2012 Data Center Expansion Plans, Posted October 10, 2011 at http://smartdatacollective.com/onlinetech/41580/cloud-computing-prompts-2012-data-center-expansion-plans

Sabin, M., Alrumaih, H., Impagliazzo, J., Lunt, B., Zhang, M. 2015. Designing an Information Technology Curriculum Framework to Prepare Successful Graduates in 2025. In Proceedings of the 2015 conference on Innovation & technology in computer science education (ITiCSE'15). ACM, New York, NY, USA.

Statista https://www.statista.com/study/41347/mobile-payments-growth-country-comparison-and-usage/)

UNESCO (2015). Sustainable development goal for education cannot advance without more teachers. UIS Fact Sheet No.33. Retrieved from http://www.uis.unesco.org/Education/Documents/fs33-2015-teachers.pdf

Woo, Dan Vesset Benjamin, Henry D. Morris Richard L. Villars, Gard Little Jean S. Bozman, Lucinda Borovick Carl W. Olofson, Susan Feldman Steve Conway, Matthew Eastwood Natalya Yezhkova, 2012, Market Analysis, IDC Worldwide Big Data Technology and Services 2012 – 2015 Forecast. Also Worldwide Storage in Big Data 2013–2017 Forecast, May 2013

THE DEVELOPMENT OF CAPACITY TO SUPPORT HMIS STRENGTHENING IN MOZAMBIQUE

Emilio Mosse and Zeferino Saugene
Eduardo Mondlane University
Maputo, Mozambique

ABSTRACT

Many low-income countries face enormous challenges in implementing their health programs. While implementation of programs has been a possible due to the support of several donors, sustainability of the implemented programs and tools is strongly dependent on several aspects. One of the reasons for the failure of implemented information systems is related to the lack of training strategy at all level and for all users. In this article we provide a case analysis of the implementation of District Health Information System (DHIS2), a Health Management Information System (HMIS) within the health sector of Mozambique that is being used to help the management of health programs. Looking at the strategic training perspective we highlight the role of community around DHIS2 training, trust and use. We examine the function of the various actors in the training processes at the various levels of the health sector in Mozambique, which involved designing strategy, training, human resources and others. The theoretical lens for the analysis is around strategies for the development of capacity to support health information systems. This case helps us to understand the empirical analysis of an ongoing project (the Health Information Systems Programme or HISP), and to analyze some fundamental strategies for implementation and strengthening of the HMIS. The study is based on long participation as co-organizers in the various processes of organization of training and participation of national training courses for managers of several levels of the health system of Mozambique.

KEYWORDS

Health Management Information System, Capacity Building, District Health Information System

1. INTRODUCTION

Health Management Information Systems (HMIS) are one of the six building blocks essential for health system strengthening. HMIS is a data collection system specifically designed to support planning, management, and decision making in health facilities and organizations. We been witnessing that implementation of Health Information System (HIS) in developing countries has been challenging. Through the years, there have been concerns about the amount of investments in resources, i.e., the funding allocated to health sector of developing countries to build or implement their information systems has barely produced the desired result. These concerns require a reflection on the role and the functions of all stakeholders involved taking into account the objective to be achieved.

The University of Oslo (UoO) has been supporting Mozambique's Ministry of Health (MoH) for years specifically in the area of HMIS strengthening. In order to design targeted and relevant strategies for strengthening HMIS, after attempts to introduce computerized HIS, UoO conducted an HMIS assessment during the project start-up phase in 2014 and identified gaps guided systems-strengthening initiatives.

This paper adds to an interpretative understanding of contextual approach adopted in human resource development which aimed at strengthening an MoH capacity, so it can achieve its goals and fulfil its mission through management. Management is concerned with the optimum attainment of organizational goals and objectives with and through other people (Waldron at al., 1987). This process incorporates more than increasing the capacities of staff, among other it includes strategy and policy development, organizational learning capacity, culture of staff, technical competency. At the individual level, human resource development involves gaining insights, changing perceptions, values, and practical skills, as well as attitude and style.

A company needs to engage in systematic human resource development irrespective of how far learning culture has progressed in the organization. Development actions targeting employee competencies must be planned, implemented and assessed (Ritva Laakso-Manninen, 2017)

The aim of this paper is to understand the dynamics of ongoing implementation of HMIS toward the development of capacity and competence. The case study used in this paper is the recently adopted electronic HMIS which has been accepted as standard for management of health data in Mozambique. Maintaining and supporting capacity building routines including encouraging district health workers appears to be straightforward, however, it required the development of a joint strategy by all stakeholders. By understanding the context in which training occur and for whom is addressed to, we provide inputs into the challenges of fulling this task.

This study is part of an on-going research that focuses on understanding the practices employed when customizing generic software systems for healthcare management in developing countries. The approach is also framed in the broader context of implementation and use of DHIS2 to support HMIS in Mozambique, initiated two decades back. The strategy embedded into this study seeks to strengthen processes around the design, implementation and sustainability of HMIS with a focus on the local level of the district and building the capacity of health workers to use information more effectively and be supported by ICTs.

2. RESEARCH METHODOLOGY

This study was carried out in the three regions of Mozambique, over a period of 10 months, from March to December of 2016. The research takes the form of in-depth case study and the epistemological stance is interpretive (Walsham, 2006). Using combined methods as a research strategy, the study design brought together data from observations, interviews, conversations, reflections, and documents. An iterative and reflexive analytic process was used (Stake, 1995), weaving together findings from the several sets of data to confirm, augment, and challenge the understanding of the nature of capacity-building actions, practices and approaches. The following subsections describe the combined-methods approach, including the research context and data collection and analysis activities.

Figure 1. Group of participants of training workshop in the center region of Mozambique

Figure 2. Training session in the North region of Mozambique

The data collection for this study is divided into three phases:

- **For phase i**: the study was carried out in three regions, namely North (Nampula), Center (Sofala) and South (Maputo). These settings where chosen as the center for this particular training. For example, in the Nampula there were participants of the three provinces from northern region namely Niassa, Cabo Delgado and Niassa. In Sofala, participants from four provinces of center region namely Tete, Zambezia, Manica and Sofala and finally the southern region for the four provinces, Inhambane, Gaza, Maputo and Maputo City.

The data was collected through questionnaires to participants and through formal interviews to the provincial directorate staff participating on the referred training. The participants were the responsible for HIS both at the provincial and district levels. During interviews both authors were deeply engaged in building the relationship which afterward helped to interpretatively understand the roles and functions of the participants within the context of implementation of DHIS2.

- **For phase ii**: The second phase of the data collection process was conducted during the second training, specifically in the province of Manica where data managers and decision makers at the level of the central region were present. The data collection consisted of the distribution of questionnaires that after responded were delivered to the researchers during the training.

- **For phase iii**: Finally, the third phase of the data collection was carried out in the city of Maputo, the Ministry of Health. This training was attended by data managers from Maputo City, Maputo province, Gaza and Inhambane provinces. In this phase interviews were carried out and questionnaires were distributed to participants who responded and gave back to researchers.

3. CASE DESCRIPTION

3.1 Mozambique HIS

Mozambique is located in the Southern Region of Africa, and has borders with Tanzania (North), Malawi, Zambia and Zimbabwe (West), and South Africa and Swaziland (South). The country has an area of 799,380 km2, with a total estimated population for 2017 of 29.5 million (INE, 2018), spread over 11 provinces, including Maputo City, which has provincial status. The epidemiological situation of Mozambique is largely pre-transitional, i.e. dominated by communicable diseases, namely malaria, HIV/AIDS, diarrhea, acute respiratory infections and tuberculosis, but with a pronounced rise of non-communicable diseases (cardiovascular diseases, injuries, cancers, etc.), particularly in urban areas (Dos Anjos, 2016).

Strengthening health systems and ensuring increasing equitable access to health services and building management capacity in the public health sector as well as expanding its coverage are top strategic priorities for the country and aim to support the HIS of Mozambique which is organized in four levels, namely: a) the primary level, comprising urban and rural HC; b) the secondary level, comprising general, rural, and district hospitals; c) the tertiary level, comprising the hospitals of the provincial capitals; and d) the quaternary level, represented by the central hospitals of Beira, Nampula, and Maputo and the Specialized Hospitals.

The primary level of the system encompasses a set of basic actions to solve the most common problems in the community where health facilities as health centers are located. Between 70 and 80% of the problems that drive the demand for healthcare can be solved at this level (dos Anjos, 2016).

The secondary level is more differentiated and developed, supporting the primary level technical and organizational problems. This level solves more complex situations than the primary level, referring to other levels of care (tertiary and even quaternary) the solution of situations that go beyond the scope of its competence. The secondary level hospitals have as secondary function to dispense healthcare and constitutes the first level of referral for patients who cannot find solution to their health problems in health centers of their areas of influence. Provincial hospitals provide tertiary healthcare and are the reference level for patients who cannot find solutions for their health problems in district, rural, and general hospitals, as well as for patients from HC located in the vicinity of the provincial hospital, which has neither a rural hospital nor general hospital to which they can be referred. The quaternary level has a regional and national basis and is in charge of the three existing central hospitals in the cities of Maputo, Beira, and Nampula. Each of these central hospitals is responsible for one national territory and for the psychiatric hospitals of Infulene and Nampula (dos Anjos, 2016).

3.2 Community Driven Capacity Building Activities

DHIS2 is a product of the Health Information System Program (HISP) research and development movement initiated in 1994 by researchers from the UoO and the University of Western Cape, South Africa. DHIS2 has become the dominant de facto global health information system of record. It is a platform upon which governments and MOHs across continents are relying upon for analysis, decision-making and investment in the tracking, managing and prevention of disease and pandemics, and for monitoring and evaluation support.

Over the years, the HISP movement thrived and evolved into a diverse and heterogeneous group of entities committed to strengthening public health information systems, including Universities, MOHs, NGOs, social entrepreneurs, individual consultants, and others. The network is built largely on principles of reciprocity, where individual members draw upon the collective good of DHIS2 and associated resources and, in turn, contribute with their individual experiences and technical enhancements (Braa, 2012).

DHIS2 is built on a distributed development approach that involves regional and country health authorities, HISP country teams, open-source communities, and educational institutions. It is the most viable and cost-effective platform on which to build specific and unique data collection systems. DHIS2 is the platform that new donors are examining to pilot their specific health information system-based projects; taking full advantage of its widespread application across the globe and leveraging and contributing to the University environment (Braa, 2012).

To strengthen the regional and local base in developing countries, UoO has established, coordinates, enables and mentors the broader HISP network. Strong communities of practice exist throughout Africa and Asia and the HISP movement is emulated and growing. HISP UoO supports this active and evolving network through the implementation of its PhD and International Master's Programs, and by supporting the series of Regional DHIS2 Academies that yearly attract hundreds of health professionals and contributes to further strengthen regional and national capacity (Braa, 2012).

The Academies provide an intensive training program where participants learn by doing; their also learn about the DHIS2 tools, best practices, new functionality, customization, and advanced use. DHIS2 experts from UoO and the regional groups facilitate these academies. In addition, HISP UoO prepares and disseminates various resource materials, such as DHIS2 technical documentation and user manuals, and supports country teams to conduct end user training. The various DHIS2 mailing lists for developers, implementers and trainers, coupled with strong community based online technical support, provides another rich source of capacity strengthening activities. The content for Online DHIS2 Academies, currently under development, will help to further scale the capacity strengthening activities.

3.3 Country-based Capacity Building Activities

UoO has been, since 2000, collaborating with Mozambique Health Management Institutions such as Universities and MOH. Staff from Eduardo Mondlane University (UEM) were sent to pursue Master and PhD degree on Health Informatics in Norway and subsequently involved in teaching masters students from UEM and support to the Ministry of Health.

From 2014, UoO has taken a number of steps to address the MOH gaps with the aim of strengthening the HMIS in collaboration with MOH. Among other activities, UoO helped MOH to customize and introduce a DHIS2 based data warehouse called SISMA which aimed to replace its old software called 'Modulo Básico'; training sessions have been organized where members of technical team (UoO team together with MOH and health programs) facilitated regional training (for the district and provincial supervisors).

Table 1.

Region		Number of participants per training session
Round 1	North	Seventhly two (72) participants: National Level (4), Province Level (3), District Level (65).
	Center	Sixty-six (66) participants: National Level (3), Province Level (4), District Level (59)
	South	Sixty-three (63) participants: National Level (5), Province Level (4), District Level (54)
Round 2	North	Thirty-five (35) participants: National Level (3), Province Level (3), District Level (29). The result was satisfactory - 65% of the participants were able to generate reports, discuss the results, and in general take advantage of the workshop
	Center	Forth-one (41) participants: National Level (3), Province Level (4), District Level (34). The result was very good - 95% of the participants were able to generate reports, discuss the results, and in general take advantage of the workshop.
	South	Twenty-six (26) participants: National Level (2), Province Level (3), District Level (20). The result was very good - 75% of the participants were able to generate reports, discuss the results, and in general take advantage of the workshop.

Overall, activities performed as part of this collaboration included:

- Development/customization of the system: several meetings with hospital system stakeholders that culminated with the successful development and piloting and posterior roll-out of the system. A user guide was also developed and used during the user training activities.
- Knowledge transfer in data entry and analytics to the MoH team through a number of regional training workshops in 3 cities. Provincial and district supervisors were trained in the use of system for data entry, analytic tools for producing reports, as well as the dashboard app. The purpose of the training was to enhance the district and province supervisors on the fundamentals and use of the system. While the main focus was to build the capacity of district and provincial supervisors in using the systems the team have also developed a preliminary user manual as well as practical exercises for data analysis and reporting.
- Scale-up the system in order to be able to track patients as well has manage inpatient, outpatient and register death certificates: The need to increase the quality of data and the coverage of its usage within the health system, made MoH and the programs to request its expansion by adding modules for patient tracking as well as registration of inpatient and outpatient data.

The active role of its graduates, both at master's and doctoral level, was crucial as they formed the basis of support for the implementation, roll-out and capacity development on DHIS2 in the country. MoH have also allocated its staff to fully participate in the activities listed above. Supportive supervision has been offered to the provinces, districts and facilities regularly and focuses on availability and proper utilization of the system and has been championed by MoH staff. Districts, health facilities staff were coached on data entry, reporting, data utilization, quality of data, and functioning of IT equipment used for data management and communication. Provinces and health programs have been coached on quality improvement with emphasis on utilizing data for making decisions. To further promote data use, health personnel have been supported and encouraged to conduct performance reviews that inform implementation of more improvement activities.

4. DISCUSSION

The study focused on understanding the process through which capacity is developed during the HMIS implementation. The roles and functions of the stakeholders of the HMIS and their relation to the DHIS2 implementation was also evaluated.

Capacity development process has it was presented in the current study was unfold in the following 4 phases: (1) engage stakeholders, (2) assess capacity, (3) formulate a capacity development response, and (4) implement a capacity development response. The study illustrated that several approaches were adopted in implementing software systems, including in-country as well as regional trainings. The two were adopted as both a training approach as well as strategy to enhance knowledge of the personnel responsible for the management of information systems at different levels. Through these trainings the transfer of knowledge from trainers and colleagues to make better use of the system occurred naturally. During the trainings the team of trainers was able to better understand and address capacity building needs

Based on the study outcome, we found that regional training has enabled the personnel responsible for the management of information systems at different levels to gain knowledge in the various processes including data entry and information analysis. Through these training processes, the transfer of knowledge from trainers, supervisors to make better use of the system occurred naturally. During the training, the team of trainers was able to better understand the needs from the user perspective to be integrated in the next development of the new versions of DHIS2.

The qualified and the long experience in information systems, in the management of health information systems, in health informatics of the team of trainers was the key factor for building capacity in the health sector. Following this model of regional training that involved virtually all information system managers at the various levels of the health management system, MOH in collaboration and help from UoO provided a foundation for national implementation, expansion, and use of the Information System. In this way it was possible to measure success by verifying the database that was soon populated with data from practically all health units from all corners of the country.

If on the one hand, there was very high UoO support and the commitment from the top management of information systems management at MOH level. This commitment and efforts meant that in 2016, DHIS2 was declared the country's Health Information System, which revoked the use of the so-called “Módulo Básico”.

After this adoption of DHIS2 as the main system, the various health programs using other data collection information systems requested to be integrated into DHIS2, which doubled the commitment in such a way that at present these Health Programs are developed and enter data directly into DHIS2. A reasonable number of senior managers from various health programs have already attended and continue to request for further training in the use of new system features and functionalities.

Finally, emphasize the key role of training in developing the capacity for HMIS support. An underlying assumption in our arguments is that for the HMIS industry to achieve its declared goals, training can play an effective role. We also advocate the key role of development of capacity through effective training and ongoing support strategies for the success of HMIS in Mozambique. Training, address capacity issues, on how to use the most readily available technology best suited to the organization’s goals embedded in a personnel development plan; with build-in incentives to apply the new skills; empowering/enabling trainees to train others in using the technology; clearly articulating the benefits to personnel development and the linkage of personal performance to team performance and overall organizational efficiency and ability to fulfill its mandate.

5. CONCLUSION

To benefits from the implemented software systems, developing countries need strong institutional capacity. Capacity development is a long-term process, and it can be promoted through a combination of processes and strategies. For instance, shorter-term activities that are driven from the outside and more sustainable need to be combined with longer-term ones that are driven from the inside.

The capacity development approach highlighted in this paper makes the concept of software system ownership tangible and it links the environment, organization and individuals, and promote a comprehensive approach across all three. The principle of development capacity through trainings provided at the academies and at the in-place allows the creation of a strong alliance between the workers who are mainly decision-makers at the local level of the district and province, as well as the trainers who establish a contact line to address the concerns that arise in day-to-day.

We also advocate the key role of development of capacity through effective training and ongoing support strategies for the success of HMIS in Mozambique. An important aspect of this training was to develop the capacities on data and information use within the health staff and on how to use the available technology to best suit the organization's goals embedded in a personnel development plan; with build-in incentives to apply the new skills; empowering/enabling trainees to train others in using the technology; clearly articulating the benefits to personnel development and the linkage of personal performance to team performance and overall organizational efficiency and ability to fulfill its mandate.

REFERENCES

Bansler, J. P., & Havn, E. (1994). Information Systems Development with Generic Systems. Paper presented at the Proceedings of the 1994 ACM conference on Computer supported cooperative work, Chapel Hill, North Carolina, United States.

Birks, M., Chapman, Y., & Francis, K. (2008). Memoing in qualitative research. Journal of Research in Nursing, 13(1), 68-75. doi: 10.1177/1744987107081254

Bossert, T. J. (1990). Can they get along without us? Sustainability of donor-supported health projects in Central America and Africa. Social Science Medicine, 30(9), 1015-1023.

Braa, J., & Sahay, S. (2012). Integrated Health Information Architecture Power To The Users: Design, Development And Use. New Delhi: Matrix Publishers.

Braa, J., Monteiro, E., & Sahay, S. (2004). Networks of Action: Sustainable Health Information Systems Across Developing Countries. MIS Quarterly, 28(3), 337-369.

DEVELOPMENT: A theoretical framework for understanding the practices of modern Finnish organizations. In Haaga-Helia Research, University of Applied Sciences.

dos Anjos Luis, A., & Cabral, P. (2016). Geographic accessibility to primary healthcare centers in Mozambique. International journal for equity in health, 15(1), 173.

INE (2018) ine.gov.mz accessed on March 25th, 2018.

Laakso-Manninen, R. and Viitala, R. (2007) Competence Management and Human Resource

Manya, A., Braa, J., Øverland, L. H., Titlestad, O. H., Mumo, J., & Nzioka, C. (2012). National roll out of District Health Information Software (DHIS 2) in Kenya, 2011–Central server and Cloud based infrastructure. In IST-Africa 2012 Conference Proceedings (Vol. 5).

Rolland, K. H., & Monteiro, E. (2002). Balancing the Local and the Global in Infrastructural Information Systems. The Information Society: An International Journal, 18(2), 87 - 100.

Sahay, S., & Walsham, G. (2006). Scaling of health information systems in India: Challenges and approaches. Information Technology for Development, 12(3), 185-200.

Walsham, G. (2006). Doing interpretive research. European Journal of Information Systems, 15, 320-330.

Waldron, M., Vsanthakumar, J. and Arulraj, S. (1997). Improving the organization and management of extension in Swanson, B., Bentz, R. and Sofranko, A. Improving agricultural extension: a reference manual, Food and Agriculture Organization of the United Nations, Chapter 13.

MOBILE AND WEARABLE TECHNOLOGIES IN HEALTHCARE: A SYSTEMATIC REVIEW AND THE STATE-OF-THE-ART

Tansu Pancar and Sevgi Özkan Yildirim
Middle East Technical University, School of Informatics, Ankara, Turkey

ABSTRACT

Mobile and Wearable Technologies in Healthcare is a rapidly emerging topic in consequence of the technological advances, especially in mobile computing and communication technologies. Mobile phone penetration exceeded over 70% world population with more than 4.7 billion unique mobile subscriptions (GSMA, The Mobile Economy Report 2016). Increased capabilities of mobile devices including smart phones, smart bands and other wearables; provides vast opportunities to easily collect health data. Such data can be used by health professionals to support medical diagnosis and treatment and also by consumers to assist self-motivation to adopt and track healthier daily life practices. Researches on wearable devices collecting health data have various focuses, ranging from sensors, batteries, user acceptance or clinical studies. This review aims to understand and organize the current trends in mobile and wearable technologies in healthcare by proposing a classification of the literature after conducting a systematic review. The review covers 112 publications published between years 2005 and 2016.

KEYWORDS

Wearable Technology in Healthcare, Technology Acceptance in Healthcare, Mobile Devices in Healthcare

1. INTRODUCTION

Mobile Health (mHealth) is defined as the use of portable electronic devices with software applications to provide health services and manage patient information (Källander et al., 2013). Developments in sensors, communication technologies and advances in computing power enabled collecting and processing data from users. E-health is positioned as an emerging field in the intersection of medical informatics, public health and business which utilizes information and communication technology to collect and transmit data (Eysenbach, 2001). One of the most important characteristics of mobile health is its availability anywhere, at any time and to anyone (de Moraes et al., 2016). In parallel with improvements in sensor technology, power consumption and manufacturing, the variety of available wearable devices is also increasing, some of which directly targets consumers, where as some is tailored for specific audiences' such as elder population, users with postural disorders, or pregnant women.

Capabilities and penetration of mobile devices are increasing constantly, and collecting mobile health data is one of the most important subjects regarding these mobile devices, especially smart bands. Use of wireless mobile devices can support continuous health monitoring and encourage healthy behaviors to prevent and reduce health problems (Kumar et al. 2016). Wearable devices combine the benefits of self-monitoring with features increasing motivation (Patel et al., 2015). In a 2012 study of PWC and GSMA, Mobile Health market is expected to grow to 23 Billion USD by 2017 which is nearly 6 times of 2012 market size (PWC 2012) and wearable devices are expected to grow %18 according to Gartner report in 2016 and 2017 (Gartner 2016). With the advances in technology (sensors, energy efficiency, communication technologies), it is expected that health application of wearable devices will also increase.

These devices use multiple sensors to collect vital information via Body Area Network (BAN), whose importance in healthcare increases by providing home healthcare, remote patient monitoring and real-time tele-consultation. (Varga et al., 2014). Wearable devices are used by different audiences with different motivations, health professionals use these devices to track their patients or by consumers for activity or health status tracking.

This study, aims to present current status and trend in wearable devices and tries to classify existing literature into two main areas, namely technology based researches and user related researches. The purpose of this systematic review is to understand, organize and classify the existing literature on mobile health wearables and show the trends in research studies since 2005. This review contains 112 articles published between 2005 and 2016.

2. RESEARCH METHODOLOGY

Initial step of this research was to check the existing literature on use of wearable devices for mobile health applications. A systematic literature review is conducted using Science Direct databased for the articles published after 2005.

Using Science Direct database with "Title, Abstract and Keyword" search for the articles published after 2005 provided below results. 3 sets of keywords are used, first set aimed to reach all articles having any one of these terms which are used interchangeably by using Boolean operator "OR". Second and third set had 1 single word. During the searches these sets are combined with operator "AND" as shown below.

Keyword Set 1: "Mobile Health, M-Health, E-Health, eHealth, mHealth"
Keyword Set 2: "Wearable"
Keyword Set 3: "Acceptance
Search 1: Keyword Set 1
Search 2: Keyword Set 1 AND Keyword Set 2
Search 3: Keyword Set 2 AND Keyword Set 3
Search 4: Keyword Set 1 AND Keyword Set 2 AND Keyword Set 3
Search 5: Keyword Set 1 AND Keyword Set 3

This study, is part of a Technology Acceptance study on wearable devices in mobile health area and Search 3 – 4 – 5 is conducted in order to understand the intersection of acceptance studies for wearable devices and mobile health domain separately.

Table 1. Search Results

	Search 1: Keyword Set 1	Search 2: Keyword Set 1 + Keyword Set 2	Search 3: Keyword Set 2 + Keyword Set 3	Search 4: Keyword Set 1 + Keyword Set 2 + Keyword Set 3	Search 5: Keyword Set 1 + Keyword Set 3
2006	34	0	0	0	1
2007	33	1	1	0	0
2008	32	1	0	0	1
2009	36	1	1	0	1
2010	36	1	0	0	0
2011	71	0	1	0	4
2012	77	1	4	0	1
2013	139	1	1	0	10
2014	182	5	3	1	14
2015	251	11	3	1	8
2016	341	16	12	0	19
2017	39	1	1	0	2
Total	1271	39	27	2	61
		123 unique articles			

123 unique articles reached by Search 2, Search 3, Search 4 and Search 5 were checked manually for relevance to the research subject and how they are related to the topic.

Each article is checked by one of the authors (same author for all articles for consistency) for relevance to the mobile health domain and two focus areas are listed for each article. For example, if an article is focusing on how low power consumption sensors can increase the battery life but not dealing with user side, application areas, system design, user acceptance, it is classified in the technology domain and marked to be located in "Power Consumption" branch of the technology domain. After removing 10 articles without full text, after removing 1 article in French, remaining 112 articles are checked manually and below classification is reached:

Year-based distribution of 112 publications is as shown below:

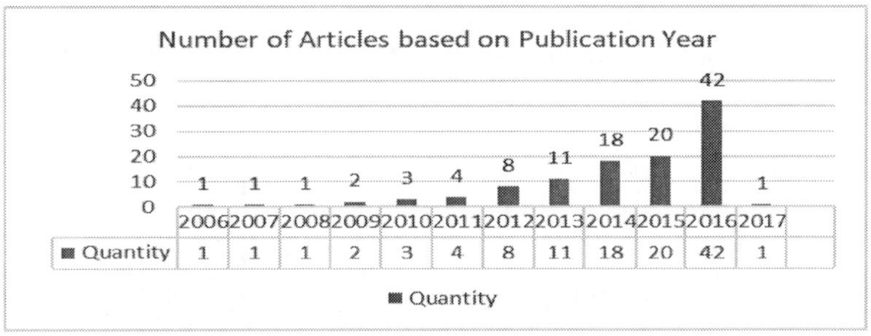

Figure 1. Year Based Distribution of 112 Publication

These 112 articles are published in 68 journals and below table shows journals having more than 2 publications. In addition to these journal articles, there are 4 book chapters related with the topic. The following part discusses the areas depicted in the framework Figure 2.

Table 2. Journals with more than 2 Publication Since 2005

Journal	Quantity
International Journal of Medical Informatics	17
Procedia Computer Science	8
Computers in Human Behavior	7
Procedia Technology	4

3. FRAMEWORK

As explained in methodology section, 112 unique articles are checked manually and classified based on their main focus. Below figure (Figure 2) shows this classification, which is followed by a table (Table 2), showing yearly distribution of these articles based on main focus areas.

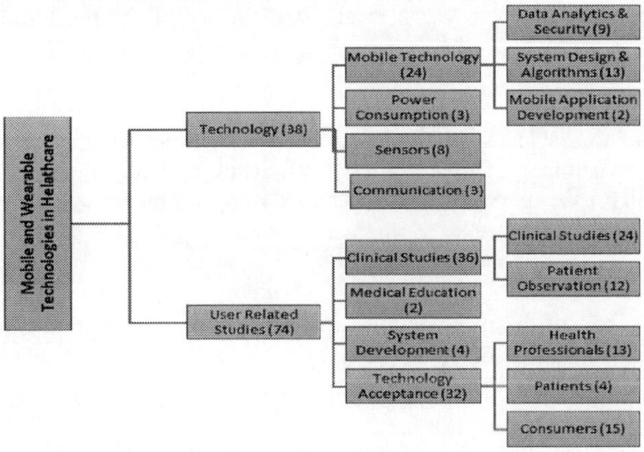

Figure 2. Classification of Mobile Health Research Areas (the number of articles are shown in parenthesis)

Above figure (Figure 2) classifies existing researches on mobile health domain for wearable devices into two main groups with sub-groups. Below table (Table 3) shows the yearly distribution of these studies. This table also gives an idea for the future trends. It is not hard to state that, studies on mobile technology will continue to increase since the capabilities of mobile devices are increasing constantly and increasing capabilities of wearable devices will trigger the researches on mobile technology. Another important topic is the increase in user related studies, especially for Clinical and Technology Adoption studies. Wearable devices are getting mature and started to be used by large communities, not only by early adopters and the need for technology adoption studies emerged, as the usage and interaction with these devices increases.

Table 3. Distribution of Publications by Focus and Year

		Technology				User Related Studies			
Year	Number of Publication	Communication	Mobile Technology	Power Consumption	Sensors	Clinical Study	Medical Education	System Development	Technology Adoption
2006	1					1			
2007	1					1			
2008	1	1							
2009	2		1		1				
2010	3					2		1	
2011	4		1			1			2
2012	8		1		2	3			2
2013	11		2		2	3			4
2014	18	1	4	1		4		1	7
2015	20	1	4		2	6	2		5
2016	42		11	2	1	14		2	12
2017	1					1			
	112	3	24	3	8	36	2	4	32

3.1 Technology

One of the major research area related with wearable devices for mobile health applications is technology used in these devices. It is possible to classify these devices based on the communication technologies and protocols, power consumption and energy efficiency, sensor technologies and collected data and as a final group mobile health technology can be listed including data analytics, security and mobile application development. Below 4 section will briefly mention current status in these areas.

3.1.1 Communication

Wearable devices generally use Wi-Fi technology to collect data from remote sensors. Choosing best access point is an important issue (Norbert Varga et al., 2015) to select the most suitable network environment (Wi-Fi, 3G, 4G, etc.).

3.1.2 Power Consumption

Power consumption of wearable sensors and devices is very important for the seamless operation of these devices, high power consumption and low energy efficiency will require recharging very often. A review study (Rault et al., 2016.) lists previous researches on decreasing power consumption and increasing energy efficiency.

3.1.3 Sensors

Sensors technology is one of the most popular topic in technology area and there are previous literature reviews (Chan et al. 2012, Appelboom et al.2014).

3.1.4 Mobile Technology

Studies in mobile health technology section contains data analytics (Wu et al., 2016, Leff & Yang, 2015, Hossain et al., 2014), with the help of big data analytics, huge amount of data collected via sensors can be analyzed in order to obtain meaningful results, another important issue is data security (Mohan et al., 2016, Moosavi et al., 2015), since health data contains personal information, security and authorization are of great importance and researches focus on information security during collection of data from remote sensors and storage and processing of this data in smart phones or application servers.

3.2 User Related Studies

Second major area is user related studies which includes "Clinical Studies using wearable technologies in order to monitor and improve patient status", "Medical Education using wearable technologies" and "Technology Adoption by different audiences (healthcare professionals, patients, consumers).

3.2.1 Clinical Studies

Advances in mobile technologies for rehabilitation purposes can be used to increase the availability and accessibility for treatments in order to increase effectiveness of treatments (Papi et al., 2015) and observation of patients outside of clinical environment as part clinical studies. There are various usages of mobile technologies for clinical studies in order to monitor and improve patient status.

Wearable technologies also have critical importance for Parkinson patients especially for Freezing of Gait (FOG) disorder, which is hard to study in clinical settings since it is not possible to detect when gait will occur (Factor et al., 2014). Wearable sensors are used to collect data from patients in real-time with a smartphone-based architecture which enabled continuous data collection and analysis (Capecci et al., 2016, Atallah et al., 2012). As a consequence of aging population, fall detection and prevention also gains importance, for the older population falls are still leading causes for injury and death (Ferrari et al., 2012).

3.2.2 Medical Education

As the usage and application of wearable mobile devices in health domain increases, training and education of health professionals also worth studying. As stated before, wearable technology is gaining importance and expected to have a disruptive effect in healthcare provision and education (Sultan, 2015.) The changes in personalized health and collection of data will cause a transformation in providing health service and will effect health professionals as well as patients, which will also effect nursing education by modification of learning environments and teaching methods (Hopia et al. 2015).

3.2.3 System Development

Articles in this category, approaches the topic from a broader perspective and focuses on development and deployment of these systems. Recently developed systems for community health care utilizes wearable devices to monitor user activity and collect data which can be used for various purposes, wearable devices can help predicting seasonal diseases by the data they collect over extended periods of time (Abhimanyu Roy et al. 2016). Due to the changes in industry, most of the current business tasks are knowledge-intensive and ageing of global workforce and preventive healthcare systems using wearable technologies are gaining importance in order to collect health data from employees and predict illnesses (Nikayin et al., 2014).

3.2.4 Technology Adoption

Acceptance and adoption of technology by organizations and individuals is a well-studied area and there are many research studies applying previous models or proposing extensions to existing models. Some examples from selected studies using Technology Acceptance Model (TAM) are listed in below table. (Table 4).

Table 4. Articles using Technology Acceptance Model

Article Name	Author/Year	Audience	Journal	Location
A study on Singaporean women's acceptance of using mobile phones to seek health information	Lim et al., 2011.	Consumer	International Journal of Medical Informatics	Singapore
Learning with mobile technologies – Students' behavior	Ponce et al. 2016.	Consumer, Patient	Computers in Human Behavior	Portugal
Tablet computers in support of rural and frontier clinical practice	Anderson et al, 2013.	Health Professional	International Journal of Medical Informatics	United States
The underlying factors of the perceived usefulness of using smart wearable devices for disaster applications	Cheng & Mitomo, 2016	Consumer	Telematics and Informatics	Japan
Wearable technologies: The role of usefulness and visibility in smartwatch adoption	Chuah et al. , 2016	Consumer	Computers in Human Behavior	Malaysia

Below listed articles (Table 5) use an extension of Technology Acceptance Model (TAM) by proposing new constructs such as Perceived Importance (Dünnebeil et al., 2012), Vanity and Need for Uniqueness (Choi & Kim, 2016) and Perceived Behavioral Control (Alaşehir et al. 2013.), or using constructs from other models like Unified Theory of Acceptance and Use of Technology (UTAUT) or Theory of Planned Behavior (TPB).

Another point that worth noting is the audience of acceptance articles, as discussed in previous sections, researches related with technology do not have an audience and mainly targeted for system developers, and clinical studies mainly focus on patients and physicians together. However, articles about technology acceptance generally have a target audience like consumers, health professionals or patients. Table 3 and Table 4 also shows these intended audiences, and where these audiences are located.

Table 5. Articles using extensions of Technology Acceptance Model

Article Name	Author/Year	Audience	Journal	Location
A cross-sectional investigation of acceptance of health information technology: A nationwide survey of community pharmacists in Turkey	Sezgin & Özkan Yıldırım, 2016.	Health Professional	Research in Social and Administrative Pharmacy	Turkey
Consumers' and Physicians' Perceptions about High Tech Wearable Health Products	Nasir & Yurder, 2015	Consumer + Health Professional	Procedia - Social and Behavioral Sciences	Turkey
Determinants of physicians' technology acceptance for e-health in ambulatory care	Dünnebeil et al., 2012	Health Professional	International Journal of Medical Informatics	Germany
Is the smartwatch an IT product or a fashion product? A study on factors affecting the intention to use smartwatches	Choi & Kim, 2016	Patient	Computers in Human Behavior	Korea
The impact of post-adoption beliefs on the continued use of health apps	Cho 2016.	Consumer + Patient	International Journal of Medical Informatics	Korea
The Role of Gender in Pharmacists Attitudes Towards E-pharmacy Application	Alaşehir et al. 2013.	Health Professional	Procedia - Social and Behavioral Sciences	Turkey
User acceptance of wearable devices: An extended perspective of perceived value	Yang et al., 2016	Consumer	Telematics and Informatics	Korea
Wearable fitness technology: A structural investigation into acceptance and perceived fitness outcomes	Lunney et al., 2016	Consumer	Computers in Human Behavior	United States
Women's use of online resources and acceptance of e-mental health tools during the perinatal period	Fonseca et al. 2016.	Patient	International Journal of Medical Informatics	Portugal
Work in Progress toward Adoption of an e-health Application by Healthcare Personnel: A Model Validation	Sezgin et al. 2014.	Health Professional	Procedia Technology	Turkey

Besides TAM and TAM extension models, other models are also used by researches in order to examine the acceptance of wearable devices for health purposes. UTAUT model is used for a cross-country comparison from consumer perspective (Dwivedi et al., 2016), and in order to evaluate an e-Health system in Australian context (Gajanayake et al., 2016). Among the selected articles, there are 3 literature reviews working on previous studies from health professional perspective (Sezgin & Yıldırım, 2014), ageing population (Peek et al., 2014), and patients for home telemonitoring (Cruz et al., 2014).

4. CONCLUSION

Mobile health is an area gaining importance with the advances in technologies and wearable devices have vast usage in mobile health domain which is expected to increase in the near future. This present review of the literature showed that researches focusing on usage of wearable devices in mobile health can be classified into 2 main areas, technology and user related studies. Research in "technology" area mainly focuses on communication technologies, power consumption, sensors and mobile technology.

"User related" studies are classified as clinical studies, medical education, system development and technology acceptance. It is also possible to divide technology acceptance based on target audience; health professionals, patients and consumers. With the advances in mobile technology, the capabilities of wearable devices are increasing and this led to the increase in clinical studies and technology adoption as more users will start to use and benefit from these devices.

This review aims to provide a state-of-the-art in wearable devices in mobile health domain by classifying previous studies and showing the trend in research focus. Together with the advances in technology and market growth, researches in this area will continue and will remain as a hot topic in the coming years.

REFERENCES

Alaşehir O., Sezgin E., & Özkan S. (2013). The role of Gender in Pharmacists Attitudes towards E-pharmacy Application. Procedia - Social and Behavioral Sciences 83 (1111 – 1115).

Anderson C., Henner T., Burkey J. (2013). Tablet computers in support of rural and frontier clinical practice. International Journal of Medical Informatics, 82 (1046-1058.

Appelboom O., Bruce S. S., Zacharia B. E., Reginster J-Y., & Connolly Jr. E. S. (2014). The promise of wearable activity sensors to define patient recovery. Journal of Clinical Neuroscience 21 (1089–1093).

Atallah L., Wiik A., Jones G. G., Lo B., Cobb J. P., Amis A., & Yang G. Z. (2012). Validation of an ear-worn sensor for gait monitoring using a force-plate instrumented treadmill. Gait & Posture 35 (674–676).

Capecci M., Pepa L., Verdini F., & Ceravolo M. G. (2016). A smartphone-based architecture to detect and quantify freezing of gait in Parkinson's disease. Gait & Posture 50 (28–33).

Chan M., Estève D., Fourniols J-Y., Escriba C., & Campo E., (2012). Smart wearable systems: Current status and future challenges. Artificial Intelligence in Medicine, 56 (137-156).

Cheng J. W. & Mitomo H., (2017). The underlying factors of the perceived usefulness of using smart wearable devices for disaster applications. Telematics and Informatics, 34 (528–539).

Cho J. (2016). The impact of post-adoption beliefs on the continued use of health apps. International Journal of Medical Informatics 87 (75-83).

Choi J., & Kim S. (2016). Is the smartwatch an IT product or a fashion product? A study on factors affecting the intention to use smartwatches. Computers in Human Behavior 63 (777-786).

Chuah S. H-W., Rauschnabel P. A., Krey N., Nguyen B., Ramayah T., & Lade S. (2016). Wearable technologies: The role of usefulness and visibility in smartwatch adoption. Computers in Human Behavior 65 (276-284).

Cruz J., Brooks D., & Marques A. (2014). Home telemonitoring in COPD: A systematic review of methodologies and patients' adherence. International Journal of Medical Informatics 83 (249-263).

de Moraes J. L. C., Souza W. L., Pires L. F., & Prado A. F. (2016). A methodology based on openEHR archetypes and software agents for developing e-health applications reusing legacy systems. Computer Methods and Programs in Biomedicine 134 (267-287).

Dünnebeil S., Sunyaev A., Blohm I., Leimester J. M., & Krcmar H. (2012). Determinants of physicians' technology acceptance for e-health in ambulatory care. International Journal of Medical Informatics, 81 (746-760).

Dwivedi Y. K., Shareef M. A., Simintiras A. C., Lal B., & Weerakkody V. (2016). A generalised adoption model for services: A cross-country comparison of mobile health (m-health).Government Information Quarterly 33 (174–187).

Eysenbach G., (2001). What is e-health? Journal of Medical Internet Research 3(2): e20

Factor S. A, Scullin M. K, Sollinger A. B, Land J. O, Wood-Siverio C., Zanders L., Freeman A., Bliwise D. L, & Goldstein F. C. (2014). Freezing of gait subtypes have different cognitive correlates in Parkinson's disease. Parkinsonism & Related Disorders 20 (1359–1364).

Ferrari M., Harrison B., Rawashdeh O., Hammond R., Avery Y, Rawashdeh M., Sa'deh W., & Maddens M. (2012). Clinical Feasibility Trial of a Motion Detection System for Fall Prevention in Hospitalized Older Adult Patients. Geriatric Nursing 33 (177-183).

Fonseca A., Gorayeb R., & Canavarroa M. C. 2016. Women's use of online resources and acceptance of e-mental healthtools during the perinatal period. International Journal of Medical Informatics, 94 (228–236).

Gajanayake R., Iannella R., & Sahama T., (2016). An Insight into the Adoption of Accountable-eHealth Systems – An Empirical Research Model Based on the Australian Context. IRBM 37(219–231).

Gartner Report, Forecast: Wearable Electronic Devices, Worldwide, 2016.

Hopia H., Punna M., Laitinen T., & Latvala E. (2015).A patient as a self-manager of their personal data on health and disease with new technology – challenges for nursing education. Nurse Education Today 35 (1-3).

Hossain M. S., Masud M., Muhammad G., Rawashded M., & Hassan M. M. (2014). Automated and user involved data synchronization in collaborative e-health environments. Computers in Human Behavior, 30 (485–490).

Källander K, Tibenderana JK, Akpogheneta OJ, Strachan DL, Hill Z, ten Asbroek AHA, Conteh L, Kirkwood BR, Meek SR. (2013). Mobile Health (mHealth) Approaches and Lessons for Increased Performance and Retention of Community Health Workers in Low- and Middle-Income Countries: A Review. Journal of Medical Internet Research,15(1), e17.

Leff D. R., & Yang G-Z. (2015). Big Data for Precision Medicine. Engineering, 1 (277-279).

Lim S., Xue L., Yen C. C., Chang L., Chan H. C., Tai B. C., Duh H. B. L., & Choolani M. (2011). A study on Singaporean women's acceptance of using mobile phones to seek health information. International Journal of Medical Informatics, 80 (189-202).

Lunney A., Cunningham N. R., & Eastin M. S. (2016). Wearable fitness technology: A structural investigation into acceptance and perceived fitness outcomes. Computers in Human Behavior, 65, 114-120.

Mohan M., Kavithadevi M. K., & Prakash J. (2016). Improved Classical Cipher for Healthcare Applications. Procedia Computer Science, 93 (742 – 750).

Moosavi S. R., Gia T. N., Rahmani A-M., Nigussie E., Virtanen S., Isoaho J., & Tenhuen H. (2015). SEA: A Secure and Efficient Authentication and Authorization Architecture for IoT-Based Healthcare Using Smart Gateways. Procedia Computer Science, 52 (452 – 459).

Nasir S., & Yurder Y. (2015). Consumers' and Physicians' Perceptions about High Tech Wearable Health Products. Procedia - Social and Behavioral Sciences, 195 (1261 – 1267).

Nikayin F., Heikkila M., de Reuver M., & Solaimani S. (2014). Workplace primary prevention programmes enabled by information and communication technology. Technological Forecasting & Social Change 89 (326–332).

Papi E., Osei-Kuffour D., Chen Y-M. A., McGregor A. H. (2015). Use of wearable technology for performance assessment: A validation study. Medical Engineering and Physics, 37 (698-704).

Patel, M. S., Asch, D. A., & Volpp, K. G. (2015). Wearable devices as facilitators, not drivers, of health behavior change. Jama, 313(5), 459e460.

Peek S. T. M, Wouters E. J. M., van Hoof J., Luijkx K. G., Boeije H. R., & Vrijhoef H. J. M. (2014). Factors influencing acceptance of technology for aging in place: A systematic review. International Journal of Medical Informatics 83 (235-248).

Ponce B. L., Pereira A., Carvalho L., Mendez J. A J., & Penalvo G. F. J. (2016). Learning with mobile technologies -Students' behavior. Computers in Human Behavior 2016 (1-9

PwC and GSMA, Touching lives through mobile health: Assessment of the global market opportunity, February 2012.

Roy Abhimanyu, Zalzala A. M. S., & Kumar A. (2016). Disruption of things: a model to facilitate adoption of IoT-based innovations by the urban poor. Procedia Engineering 159 (199 – 209).

Santosh Kumar, Wendy J. Nilsen, Amy Abernethy, Audie Atienza, Kevin Patrick, Misha Pavel, William T. Riley, Albert Shar, Bonnie Spring, Donna Spruijt-Metz, Donald Hedeker, Vasant Honavar, Richard Kravitz, R. Craig Lefebvre, David C. Mohr, Susan A. Murphy, Charlene Quinn, Vladimir Shusterman, Dallas Swendeman. (2013). Mobile Health Technology Evaluation. American Journal of Preventive Medicine, 45(2), 228–236.

Sezgin E., & Özkan Yıldırım S. (2016).A cross-sectional investigation of acceptance of health information technology: A nationwide survey of community pharmacists in Turkey. Research in Social and Administrative Pharmacy 12 (949–965).

Sezgin E., & Yıldırım S. Ö. (2014). A Literature Review on Attitudes of Health Professionals towards Health Information Systems: From e-Health to m-Health. Procedia Technology 16 (1317 – 1326).

Sezgin E., Alaşehir O., & Özkan Yıldırım S. (2014). Work in Progress toward Adoption of an e-Health Application by Healthcare Personnel: A Model Validation. Procedia Technology 16 (1327 – 1333).

Sultan N. (2015). Reflective thoughts on the potential and challenges of wearable technology for healthcare provision and medical education. International Journal of Information Management 35 (521-526).

Varga N., Bokor L., & Takács A. (2014). Context-aware IPv6 Flow Mobility for Multi-Sensor based Mobile Patient Monitoring and Tele-consultation. Procedia Computer Science, 40 (222-229).

Varga N., Piri E., & Bokor L. (2015). Network-assisted Smart Access Point Selection for Pervasive Real-time mHealth Applications. Procedia Computer Science 63 (317 – 324).

Wu J., Li H., Cheng S., & Lin Z. (2016). The promising future of healthcare services: When big data analytics meets wearable technology. Information & Management 53 (1020–1033).

Yang H., Yu J., Zo H., & Choi M. (2016). User acceptance of wearable devices: An extended perspective of perceived value. Telematics and Informatics 33 (256–269).

CONCEPTUALIZING BLOCKCHAINS: CHARACTERISTICS & APPLICATIONS

Karim Sultan[1], Umar Ruhi[1] and Rubina Lakhani[2]
[1]*Telfer School of Management,*
[2]*Faculty of Engineering,*
University of Ottawa, Canada

ABSTRACT

Blockchain technology has recently gained widespread attention by media, businesses, public sector agencies, and various international organizations, and it is being regarded as potentially even more disruptive than the Internet. Despite significant interest, there is a dearth of academic literature that describes key components of blockchains and discusses potential applications. This paper aims to address this gap. This paper presents an overview of blockchain technology, identifies the blockchain's key functional characteristics, builds a formal definition, and offers a discussion and classification of current and emerging blockchain applications.

KEYWORDS

Blockchain, Cryptocurrency, Bitcoin, Cryptoeconomics, Definition, Business Applications

1. INTRODUCTION

The concept of blockchain has become so prevalent in the mainstream, that many are heralding it as the next major disruptive technology. There have been comparisons of its importance to that of the Web and even the Internet (Hernandez, 2017; Mougayar, 2016). While at its core, blockchain is just a method of securely storing and distributing information, it is the potential uses of blockchain technology that make it so empowering: sharing asset transactions between disparate agents with unquestionable transparency – all the while without a controlling central authority. Blockchain creates trust through cryptographic operation by, allowing parties to securely exchange value without the use of an intermediary. Many market sectors are poised for disruption and new startup ventures are vying for dominance in these spaces with a fervor not witnessed since the dot.com boom (Nofer et al., 2017). Despite significant interest, there is a dearth of academic literature that discusses the functional technology underpinning blockchains as well as the potential business applications of this technology. This paper aims to address this gap. This paper is intended to serve as a bridge to blockchain: it provides a technological primer to establish the key concepts and then explores industry applications and trends. We will peek underneath the hood, identify key characteristics of the blockchain technology, and build a formal definition. Next, we will offer a discussion and classification of emerging blockchain applications.

2. CONCEPTUAL FOUNDATIONS

2.1 Origins & Underpinnings

The innovation of blockchain technology originated from combining the multi-disciplinary fields of software engineering, distributive computing, cryptographic science, and economic game theory. As depicted in Figure 1, blockchains operate at the intersection of these fields that provide the footing for a stable and scalable software infrastructure, a basis for security of digital assets, support for a global decentralized network of peers along with economic incentives for these peers to be good actors in the network. Real-world blockchain applications comprising these multidisciplinary fields are often discussed under the umbrella term of *Cryptoeconomics* – defined as "*a discipline concerned with the production, consumption and transfer of wealth using computer networks, cryptography, and game theory to enhance prosperity of groups in current and future digital market economies*" (Lielacher, 2017).

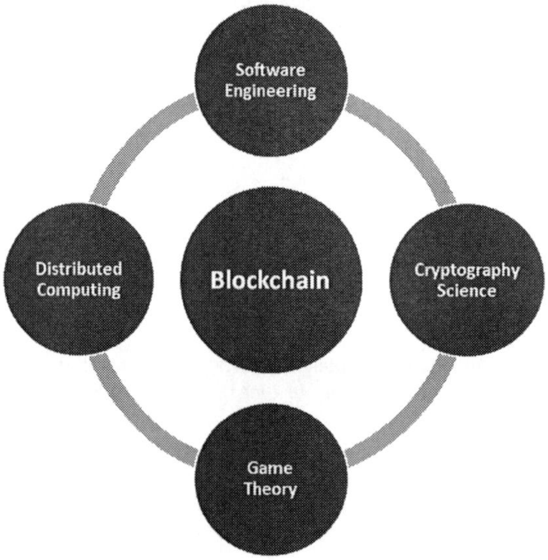

Figure 1. Multidisciplinary Foundations of Blockchain Technology

Blockchain is an underlying construct of Bitcoin, so no discussion of blockchain today is practical without also touching on the Bitcoin cryptocurrency. On October 31, 2008, Satoshi Nakamoto[1] published a brief but groundbreaking paper to a cryptography forum. In it he outlined a way to overcome the double-spend scenario – a problem which plagued previous cryptocurrencies. Despite not mentioning blockchain explicitly, he described its structure as a chain of hashed timestamps: "*Each timestamp includes the previous timestamp in its hash, forming a chain, with each additional timestamp reinforcing the ones behind it*" (Nakamoto, 2008). Although this approach was later refined for Bitcoin, the concept was laid out: a chain of blocks, each cryptographically linked to the previous, using a hash digest. From this we denote that a blockchain is little more than a sequence of records, each hashed and linked to the previous block (Figure 2).

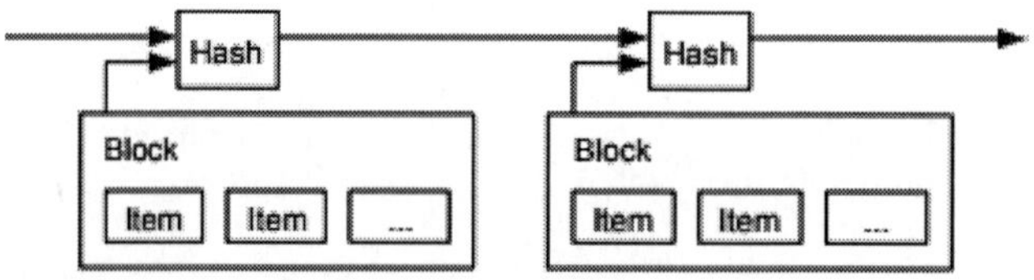

Figure 2. Nakamoto's Blockchain Proposal (Nakamoto, 2008)

However, this approach alone wasn't sufficient to eliminate the double spend issue. In a double spend scenario, the attacker attempts to create a race condition in which they spend the same virtual assets twice before either is validated. For a blockchain to guard against this, Bitcoin needed a method for its network to form consensus. Nakamoto introduced a *Proof-of-Work* model, in which agents would repeatedly hash the block with a random number (nonce) until they achieved a value less than a specified target. Once found, the block would then extend the existing chain. As the blockchain is decentralized over peer-to-peer, any agent

[1] Satoshi Nakamoto was a pseudonym and has spawned numerous conspiracy theories as to the author's, or authors', actual identity, gender and origin.

can participate in the proof-of-work consensus model to validate transactions (Bitcoin incentives agency with potential economic gains).

The Bitcoin cryptocurrency required a construct into which it could record the order of transactions, verify them, and then secure the entry. Blockchain technology provided this mechanism through a collection of ever extending blocks, where each block represents a pool of transactions, and are cryptographically linked to a parent block via a hash digest. Since the blockchain is represented in a freely distributable file, there is no master copy; it is distributed among all parties. The Bitcoin network relies on this decentralized distribution along with the proof-of-work consensus model to coordinate which blocks are added to the chain and to update all other copies.

The blockchain in Bitcoin functions as a database to store transactions, using a series of inputs and output resembling double entry accounting. Interestingly, bitcoin balances are not maintained, just inputs and outputs. There are no "coins" minted and serialized for consumption, as one may think. By traversing the blockchain, the available balance for a user can be quickly calculated. Any attempt to "corrupt" the blockchain and award more coins in a transaction will fail as the blockchain hashes would have to be recalculated – a computationally hard problem – and the blockchain's decentralized nature ensures other nodes will have legitimate copies.

The first usage of Bitcoin dates to January 3, 2009 at which point Nakamoto created the blockchain genesis block (the first block in the chain and the only one not to have a parent block to link to), and issued himself the first 50 bitcoins (Blockchain Luxembourg S.A., 2017; Zohar, 2015). All blocks in the Bitcoin blockchain trace back to this original transaction. This leads to one more observation: blockchains form an immutable historic record of every transaction from the date of origin in a transparent, decentralized data store.

A blockchain gains its secure, immutable nature by combining two innovations: a cryptographic link between records that makes changes progressively more difficult the longer the chain is, and the distribution of the data to all participating nodes on the decentralized network in which it is expected honest nodes outnumber potential attackers.

2.2 Functional Characteristics

Despite being initially linked to Bitcoin, blockchain technology can be used independently in a variety of different use-cases and markets, ranging from insurance to the health industry. A blockchain can be applied in virtually any industry in which assets are managed and transactions occur. It can provide a secure chain of custody for both digital and physical assets through its functional characteristics that facilitate transactions through trust, consensus, security, and smart contracts. These aspects of blockchains are explored in the following sections.

2.2.1 Transactions & Smart Contracts

A transaction is an exchange of assets that is managed under the entity service's rules. Such rules are usually operationalized through scripting languages (e.g. Bitcoin's Forth) and are used for advanced transactions (such as escrow and multi-party signatures) to be performed. These rules also form the basis for smart contracts.

A smart contract is a set of logic rules in the form of a coded script which can be embedded into the blockchain to govern a transaction. The contract is executed autonomously and is used to govern the transaction (Buterin, 2016). In this way, contracts act as smart software agents (Stark, 2016). Once a smart contract is embedded in the blockchain, it becomes an autonomous agent that is permanently tamperproof. An application then reads the code when performing a transaction, executes and processes the results.

The contract nature of a smart contract isn't just restricted to application specific code. It can also be used to codify the terms and condition of an agreement into the transaction workflow. Ethereum (the second largest cryptocurrency after Bitcoin) is an alt-coin technology that has been designed to support smart contracts.

2.2.2 Consensus & Trust

In events surrounding nuclear disarmament near end of the cold war, President Regan made a Russian proverb famous: "trust, but verify." The same could be claimed for blockchain. It is trusted by consensus as all parties must have identical copies of the blockchain; but each participant is responsible for verifying it.

Blockchain's decentralization is a core strength, as a copy of the database file is owned by all actors. In order to ensure the integrity of each copy, a consensus algorithm is required. The consensus algorithm allows the community to ensure that each added block is legitimate. It also prevents attackers from compromising and forking the chain (Coindesk, 2017). Nakamoto suggested using a proof-of-work approach, in which a hard cryptographic puzzle must be solved by miners (Nakamoto, 2008). Miners expend computing resources and are rewarded for their efforts using various incentives. Other consensus models such as proof-of-stake, proof-of-burn, proof-of-elapsed-time, and proof-of-capacity have been proposed in the literature to overcome some of the weaknesses of the original proof-of-work model by attempting to balance fairness and resource expenditure (Kiayias et al., 2017; Zamfir, 2015).

The nature of blockchain is trustless. Blockchain is designed to eliminate the need for any one entity to gate transactions. It establishes a trust model based on a group consensus, where the network validates transactions and authorizes their addition to the chain. There are no middlemen; the notion of trust becomes implicit as each record in the blockchain is verified by the community which holds multiple copies of the blockchain. By removing trust agents from transactions, blockchain has the ability to disrupt many major industries.

Traditional transaction models rely on central authority to act in the clearinghouse role. Trust is granted to the central authority with an expectation that it will remain honest while verifying and clearing transactions. The instances of records reside with the authority. If the central authority is compromised, either intentionally (manipulation) or unintentionally (hacked), the interlocutor can wreak extensive havoc on the system. The blockchain model eliminates the central authority (Figure 3) by instead disseminating copies of the records to all parties. Each participant maintains their own instance of the blockchain. They broadcast changes by forming new blocks and requesting validation based on the rules of the consensus model. Once validated, the block is added to everyone's chain. The process is potentially safer than the traditional model, and the middleman agent isn't required, invoking a disruption to the status quo.

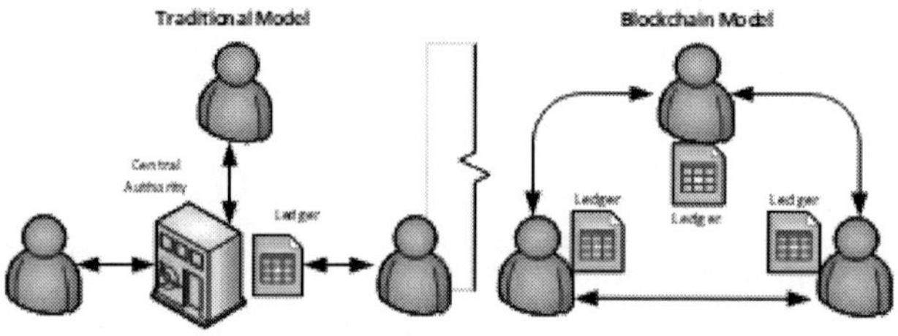

Figure 3. Traditional vs Blockchain Transaction Model

A blockchain relies on mathematics via cryptography to establish independent trust for each transaction, and on computationally expensive consensus models to replace central authorities. Pools of recent transactions are ordered into a block. The block is then cryptographically linked to a chain of blocks (the blockchain) and is verified through a consensus model that involves significant computing resources (mining). As the blockchain is an open-access file replicated on multiple full-nodes of the network, no one entity controls the transaction list. Since each block is hashed and inserted into the chain, it is immutable and serves as a final record of past transactions. An entity cannot change the chain without changing all blocks that follow it, an effort which is computationally hard and expensive. This secures the blockchain and establishes trust independent of a central authority.

2.2.3 Public and Private Blockchains

Blockchains can be classified as public, private or hybrid variants, depending on their application (Buterin, 2015; Mougayar, 2016):

- **Public** – Public blockchains have no single owner; are visible by anyone; their consensus process is open to all to participate in; and they are full decentralized. Bitcoin is an example of a public blockchain.
- **Private** – (also called *permissioned)* Private blockchains use privileges to control who can read from and write to the blockchain. Consensus algorithms and mining usually aren't required as a single entity has ownership and controls block creation.
- **Hybrid** – Also known as consortium, these blockchains are public only to a privileged group. The consensus process is controlled by known, privileged servers using a set of rules agreed to by all parties. Copies of the blockchain are only distributed among entitled participants; the network is therefore only partly decentralized.

Although a public blockchain distributes itself in a decentralized peer-to-peer fashion, this isn't necessarily true for a private blockchain. Private blockchains are those used by enterprises to record asset transactions within a limited user base (restricted scope). Hybrid blockchains can be visualized as very small scale public blockchains; they are decentralized only across a limited participant base.

As a summary, we can formalize the afore-noted features of the blockchain into a list of four core characteristics:

- **Immutable** – (permanent and tamper-proof) a blockchain is a permanent record of transactions. Once a block is added, it cannot be altered. This creates trust in the transaction record.
- **Decentralized** – (networked copies) a blockchain is stored in a file that can be accessed and copied by any node on the network. This creates decentralization.
- **Consensus Driven** – (trust verification) each block on the blockchain is verified independently via a Consensus models which provide rules for validating a block, and often use a scarce resource (such as computing power) to show proof that adequate effort was made. In Bitcoin, this is referred to as the mining process. This mechanism works without the use of a central authority or an explicit trust-granting agent.
- **Transparent** – (full transaction history) since the blockchain is an open file, any party can access it and audit transactions[2]. This creates provenance under which asset lifetimes can be tracked.

3. TOWARDS A DEFINITION

There are many different blockchain definitions offered, ranging from application-specific to the excessively technical. For example, Coinbase, the world's largest cryptocurrency exchange, defines blockchain as "*a distributed, public ledger that contains the history of every bitcoin transaction*" (Coinbase, 2017). As an application-specific definition, this characterization does not account for the fact that blockchains can be reused for other cryptocurrencies and industry applications independently. The Oxford English Dictionary broadens the definition somewhat, defining blockchain as "*a digital ledger in which transactions made in bitcoin or another cryptocurrency are recorded chronologically and publicly*" (Oxford Dictionaries, 2018). This definition also falls short as blockchain technology can be used independently of Bitcoin and other cryptocurrencies. Both these definitions also highlight the role of a blockchain as a digital ledger, and much of the literature would agree with this. However, this domain is evolving rapidly, and ledger usage is simply a feature of the blockchain but not its essence. This feature only pertains to blockchain applications that focus on managing the exchange of value in the case of virtual assets.

A somewhat broader definition is offered by Webopedia where a blockchain is defined as "*a type of data structure that enables identifying and tracking transactions digitally and sharing this information across a distributed network of computers, creating in a sense a distributed trust network. The distributed ledger technology offered by blockchain provides a transparent and secure means for tracking the ownership and transfer of assets*" (Stroud, 2015). While this definition succeeds in capturing more of the characteristics of blockchain, it highlights distribution as a key feature of blockchain computing without acknowledging that blockchains are not just a distributed technology, but also a decentralized one (Swan, 2015b; Wright and De

[2] Websites such as www.blockchain.info provide this service online.

Filippi, 2015). The key distinction here is that while a distributed system partitions work among participants in an optimal fashion, a blockchain requires that each and every participant maintain a full node of the system and enforce its rules independently. In a system where nodes operate on local information (decision locality) to accomplish goals rather than the result of a central ordering influence, this decentralization ensures that pulling the plug is near impossible – only one node needs to remain operational for the network to function.

Evidently, there is a need for a clear and concise definition of blockchain. Based on the theoretical underpinnings of blockchain technology outlined in the previous sections, we provide the following definition of a blockchain:

"a decentralized database containing sequential, cryptographically linked blocks of digitally signed asset transactions, governed by a consensus model."

Through this connotative definition, we aim to highlight the core constituents for blockchain technology in that it is a peer-to-peer networked database governed by a set of rules. Furthermore, blockchains represent a shift away from traditional trust agents and a move towards transparency. As a technological building block, it permits applications from a broad swath of industries to take advantage of sharing, tracking, and auditing digital assets. The next section identifies potential opportunities and use-cases for blockchain technology in different industries.

4. BLOCKCHAIN BUSINESS APPLICATIONS

4.1 Value Proposition of Blockchain Technology

Since the fundamental use-case for blockchain technology is to drive greater transparency and substantiate accuracy of transaction data across the digital information ecosystem, potential applications of such technology are practically endless. In addition to virtual currencies such as Bitcoin, a multitude of other potential blockchain applications and services have been envisioned and discussed by industry pundits and technology research firms (CBInsights, 2018; Mougayar, 2016). To make sense of the blockchain application ecosystem, Mougayar (2016) identifies the value proposition of blockchains as pertaining to the enablement of one or more of six elements denoted by the mnemonic *ATOMIC (Assets, Trust, Ownership, Money, Identity, and Contracts)*. These elements constitute the crux of blockchain business applications by facilitating the creation, management and transfer of digital assets through automated validation rules, cryptographically verified rights and ownerships, and the validation of transactions without requiring intermediaries. Using a blockchain platform implies that each of these six elements is programmable, and by disintermediating these facets, blockchains can enable new services to come to market with cheaper transaction fees and faster execution. In this way, blockchain technology is poised to disrupt many business models which rely on (often costly) intermediaries.

Mougayar (2016) also classifies the role of blockchains as spanning four aspects: blockchain as a development platform; blockchain as a smart contract utility; blockchain as a marketplace, and finally, blockchain as a trusted service application (Rosic, 2017). These potential roles are discussed herewith.

4.2 Blockchain as a Development Platform

At present, the development of blockchain applications and services requires a highly specialized skillset, and the state of the blockchain developer toolkits is immature (Aru, 2017). The introduction of *Blockchain as a Service* (BaaS) platforms such as those by Microsoft (Azure) and IBM (Cloud) provide an inexpensive environment for developers to rapidly prototype on test blockchains before deploying to live ones (Sofia, 2016). Other examples in this space include technology platforms that enable secure sharing of data across industrial networks through blockchain's tamperproof ledgers (e.g. Xage[3]); and technologies that offer blockchain enabled verification of data transactions (e.g. Guardtime[4]). These BaaS solutions form the basis for programmable trust, ownership and identity, and also facilitate the operation and governance of enterprise blockchain applications and services.

---

[3] https://xage.com/

[4] https://guardtime.com/

4.3 Blockchain as a Smart Contract Utility

Smart contracts provide a programmatic interface to blockchains. Smart contract utility is defined as "*being able to perform useful functions to create, maintain or augment the value of digital assets*" (Sorin et al., 2016). The smart contract, when triggered, transacts value based on digital assets. Utility is captured in code and stored on the blockchain. This code is executed when a predetermined condition occurs. Activities often managed by third party central authorities are mitigated to the blockchain instead, disintermediating transactions (Mougayar, 2015). Examples include escrow, multi-party transactions, digital notarization, and time stamping. Blockchain startups such as R3[5] are collaborating with banks and regulators to operationalize blockchains as a new operating system for financial markets (Irrera, 2017). A specific instance of this functionality can be observed in the example of Visa and DocuSign who have partnered to operate a proof-of-concept blockchain project to streamline vehicle leasing experience for customers by simplifying transaction management between multiple parties including sellers, buyers and insurance companies (Hirson, 2015).

4.4 Blockchain as a Marketplace

Any robust ecosystem requires a market for generating value. In the cryptoeconomics marketplace, blockchain provides a payment infrastructure (via cryptocurrencies) and a proof-of-ownership structure (via digital asset tracking). This has enabled peer-to-peer marketplaces with no governing authority, such as OpenBazaar[6] and Soma[7] providing accessible, disintermediated trade (CBInsights, 2018). In these marketplaces, blockchain platforms can be used to directly match buyers and sellers allowing them to transact through smart contracts. Blockchain technology is also being touted as an enabler for next generation online workforce marketplaces in the context of the gig economy that relies on independent contract workers and freelancers for short-term engagements, and the shared economy where consumers increasingly become prosumers. In such instances, blockchain platforms can ensure that service providers are not constrained by any central authority – hence, allowing them to extend flexible offerings, and payment interactions and service transactions can function in a transparent environment (Aitken, 2017).

Overall, as a marketplace enabler, blockchains can be used to operationalize programmable assets, ownership and money.

4.5 Trusted-Service Application

Finally, in its role as a trusted service application, blockchain technology comprises end-to-end functionality by facilitating highly specialized applications for any purpose imaginable. This more generalized use of blockchains to enable all types of applications through a combination of programmable assets, trust, ownership, money, identity, and contracts is sometimes referred to as blockchain 2.0 (Bheemaiah, 2016; Swan, 2015a). On the front-end, trusted service applications built on the blockchain using smart contracts can provide disintermediated, secure services to end users. On the backend, many of these applications reside on public blockchains (e.g. Bitcoin and Ethereum) which cannot be shut down or restricted. Furthermore, many companies now provide APIs (application programming interface) allowing developers to build applications using blockchain protocols and mechanisms (Bheemaiah, 2016).

Based on our discussion of potential blockchain business applications, we propose the following 2x2 matrix (

Figure 4) for mapping industry sectors against blockchain scope (public vs private vs hybrid), and blockchain access (as a service or as application). In this context, an application refers to "*a program designed to perform a function or a suite of related functions of benefit to an end user*" (Horak, 2008), while a service is "*a transport of data and/or applications*" (Horak, 2008).

[5] https://www.r3.com
[6] https://www.openbazaar.org/
[7] https://soma.co/

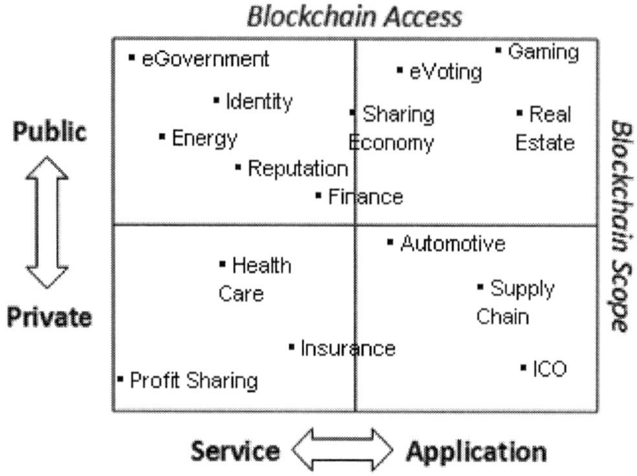

Figure 4. Blockchain Access-vs-Scope Matrix

In order to map horizontal markets on to the above matrix, each offering can be assessed against the following criteria:

- **Access** - Is the primary function to transform data (an application) or to present data (service)?
- **Scope** - Is blockchain usage globally unrestricted (public) or enterprise permissioned (private)?

For contrast, consider the examples of health care and real estate. The health care industry is seeking to facilitate secure transit of patient records via the blockchain. Access is therefore service oriented while the scope remains private to health care partners. In comparison, the real estate industry has shown interest in investigating blockchain for land registration records. This application is meant to be open and transparent to the public.

Overall, these current and envisioned use-cases for blockchain technology are poised to create a global decentralized yet trusted value ecosystem that can lead to exciting new economic opportunities in the public and private sectors alike.

5. CONCLUSION

This paper offers a conceptual overview of blockchains through a description of its underlying technological functions and a discussion of its potential business applications. As outlined, contemporary and future blockchain-based innovations span a myriad of use-cases and industries beyond digital currency and the financial sector. Taking this into consideration, we offer a connotative definition that specifies the core elements of blockchain technology independent of Bitcoin. Furthermore, we describe various functional characteristics of blockchain mechanisms, and offer examples of business applications where these mechanisms can potentially be useful.

REFERENCES

Aitken R (2017) What's The Future Of Online Marketplaces & Blockchain's Technology Impact? Available at: https://www.forbes.com/sites/rogeraitken/2017/10/24/whats-the-future-of-online-marketplaces-blockchains-technology-impact/#6b3a6a0863a0 (accessed 6 January 2018).

Aru I (2017) Full Stack Development Tools Lowering Blockchain Entry... | News | Cointelegraph. Available at: https://cointelegraph.com/news/full-stack-development-tools-lowering-blockchain-entry-barriers (accessed 4 February 2018).

Bheemaiah K (2016) Block Chain 2.0: The Renaissance of Money. Available at: http://www.wired.com/2015/01/block-chain-2-0/.

Blockchain Luxembourg S.A. (2017) Bitcoin Block #0.

Buterin V (2015) On Public and Private Blockchains.

Buterin V (2016) What Are Smart Contracts? A Beginner's Guide to Smart Contracts. *Blockgeeks.*

CBInsights (2018) Banking Is Only The Start: 36 Big Industries Blockchain Tech Could Disrupt. Available at: https://www.cbinsights.com/research/industries-disrupted-blockchain/ (accessed 3 February 2018).

Coinbase (2017) What is the bitcoin blockchain?

Coindesk (2017) A (Short) Guide to Blockchain Consensus Protocols - CoinDesk.

Hernandez K (2017) Blockchain for Development – Hope or Hype? *Institute for Developement (IDS)* April(17): 4.

Hirson R (2015) The Future Of Car Leasing Is As Easy As Click, Sign, Drive | DocuSign Blog. Available at: https://www.docusign.com/blog/the-future-of-car-leasing-is-as-easy-as-click-sign-drive/ (accessed 4 February 2018).

Horak R (2008) *Webster's New World telecom dictionary: [a comprehensive reference for telecommunications terminology]*. Wiley Technology Pub.

Irrera A (2017) Bank-backed R3 launches new version of its blockchain. Available at: https://www.reuters.com/article/us-r3-blockchain/bank-backed-r3-launches-new-version-of-its-blockchain-idUSKCN1C80MS (accessed 3 February 2018).

Kiayias A, Russell A, David B, et al. (2017) PPCoin: Peer-to-Peer Crypto-Currency with Proof-of-Stake. *Proceedings of the 2016 ACM SIGSAC Conference on Computer and Communications Security - CCS'16* 1919(January): 1–27. DOI: 10.1017/CBO9781107415324.004.

Lielacher A (2017) An Introduction to Cryptoeconomics | BTCMANAGER.

Mougayar W (2015) Understanding the Blockchain. *O'Reilly* (May).

Mougayar W (2016) *The business blockchain : promise, practice, and application of the next Internet technology*. Wiley.

Nakamoto S (2008) Bitcoin: A Peer-to-Peer Electronic Cash System. *Bitcoin.org*: 9. DOI: 10.1007/s10838-008-9062-0.

Nofer M, Gomber P, Hinz O, et al. (2017) Blockchain - A Disruptive Technology. *Business & Information Systems Engineering* 59(3): 183–187. DOI: 10.1007/s12599-017-0467-3.

Oxford Dictionaries (2018) blockchain | Definition of blockchain in English by Oxford Dictionaries.

Rosic A (2017) William Mougayar: The Future Of Blockchain? | HuffPost.

Sofia (2016) 3 Companies Leading the Blockchain as a Service (BaaS) Revolution | Lets Talk Payments.

Sorin M, Senyuk S, Ben-Yosef Gelernter D, et al. (2016) Israel : A Hotspot for Blockchain Innovation. *Deloitte*: 1–33.

Stark J (2016) Making Sense of Blockchain Smart Contracts. *Coindesk.com*.

Stroud F (2015) Blockchain: Webopedia Definition. Available at: https://www.webopedia.com/TERM/B/blockchain.html (accessed 12 January 2018).

Swan M (2015a) *Blockchain. O'Reilly Media, Inc.* DOI: 10.1017/CBO9781107415324.004.

Swan M (2015b) Blockchain Thinking : the Brain as a Decentralized Autonomous Corporation [Commentary]. *IEEE Technology and Society Magazine*. DOI: 10.1109/MTS.2015.2494358.

Wright A and De Filippi P (2015) Decentralized Blockchain Technology and the Rise of Lex Cryptographia. *SSRN Electronic Journal*. DOI: 10.2139/ssrn.2580664.

Zamfir V (2015) Introducing Casper "the Friendly Ghost" - Ethereum Blog.

Zohar A (2015) Bitcoin: Under the Hood. *Communications of the ACM* 58(9): 104–113. DOI: 10.1145/2701411.

FORECASTING TOURISM DEMAND FOR LISBON'S REGION THROUGH A DATA MINING APPROACH

Hugo Ricardo[1], Ivo Gonçalves[2] and Ana Cristina Costa[1]
[1]*NOVA IMS, Universidade Nova de Lisboa, Campus de Campolide, 1070-312 Lisboa, Portugal*
[2]*INESC Coimbra, DEEC, University of Coimbra Pólo II, 3030-290 Coimbra, Portugal*

ABSTRACT

Tourism stakeholders such as the government, passenger transport companies, accommodation establishments, restaurants, recreational businesses, among others, rely on tourism demand indicators' forecasts to make decisions. Most of tourism demand forecasting models are time-series and econometric based. Machine learning methods are emerging and have been proved to be quite suitable for non-linear modelling. These methods are part of an interdisciplinary field named "Data Mining" which is known by the process of knowledge discovery in databases (KDD). The core drive of this work is to enhance the available public sources of tourism forecast information and to contribute to the tourism stakeholders' strategy in Portugal. More specifically, a multivariate model to forecast international tourism demand was developed through a Data Mining approach, which assessed models derived by Regression Trees (Random Forests), Artificial Neural Networks and, Support Vector Machines (SVM). The model development was constrained to machine learning methods, publicly available data, and minimum data assumptions. The forecasted demand variable was the nights spent at tourist accommodation establishments in Lisbon's region, one of the country's main foreign tourist destinations. The objectives were achieved, as the selected model (SMOReg, support vector regression) was successful in generalization capability. The accuracy of the produced forecasts provides some evidence of the reliability of the proposed model. If institutions and decision makers have information regarding the evolution of the explanatory variables used in this model, the impact on Lisbon's tourism demand can be assessed, even in case of an emerging recession, as shown using three future plausible scenarios.

KEYWORDS

Forecast, Tourism, Machine learning, Knowledge Discovery, Lisbon

1. INTRODUCTION

International tourism has a significant weight on Portugal's main tourism destinations, namely Algarve, Madeira and Lisbon. According to OECD (2016), 70% of Portugal's tourist demand has its source in international markets. In 2014, the major tourist sources for Portugal were, by order of importance, the United Kingdom, Germany, Spain, France and the Netherlands. The nation's trade balance is positive mainly due to the export of tourism services. It represents almost half of the total service exports (Pordata, 2016). In Lisbon's region, the share of nights spent by non-residents in July'2016 was of 76.4%, according to the Regional Analysis of Turismo de Portugal. It is then clear that Lisbon's region tourism activity heavily depends of international tourist sources. Hence, tourism has a significant role in Portugal's economy, especially in the region of Lisbon which is the one that most contributed to GDP in 2014 (INE, 2016) and ranks second on top 3 national tourism destinations (Turismo de Portugal, 2016).

Tourism industry's players must deal with perishable products such as rooms, airline seats and car rentals, etc. From a macroeconomic point of view, tourism demand forecast is part of the decision-making process that aims at a positive return of the investment on infrastructures and promotion. A country such as Portugal, which depends heavily on tourism income, such forecasting estimates are a starting point for Government policy decisions. From a microeconomic perspective, those forecasts are required to plan, for instance, transportation routes, tours and hotel beds. Hence, it is crucial to forecast tourist arrivals and nights spent at tourist accommodation establishments for long, medium and short-term horizons (Frechtling, 2011).

As stated by most of econometricians, demand can be defined in general terms as the quantity of a good or service that consumers, clients, etc. are willing to pay given a specific price and time span. Hence, tourism demand is the measured desire for tourism products or services regarding a geo-location, as for instance a country, region or city. According to Witt and Witt (1995), there are several metrics that can be used to attain tourism demand, from which the tourist arrivals is the most popular one, followed by expenditure. An alternative measure is nights spent in the destination's tourist establishments. The main advantage of nights spent at tourist accommodation establishments' variable is the capacity to differentiate domestic from foreign tourism and by type of establishment (Cunha and Abrantes, 2013). It is also visible the economic relation of the total duration that tourists stay in a destination and the expenditure in the local commerce and tourism establishments. In relatively recent studies, such as those undertaken by Constantino et al. (2016), and Teixeira and Fernandes (2012) the nights spent at tourist accommodation establishments has been used as a proxy for Mozambique and Portugal's tourism demand, respectively.

An extensive literature is available regarding tourism, and the academic interest in tourism demand forecast has grown (Athanasopoulos et al., 2011; Song and Li, 2008). Most studies are focused in finding the explanatory variables of tourism demand or constructing an accurate forecasting model (Li et al., 2005). Both research streams are related, and to forecast with causal or data-based methods it is advisable to previously identify the determinants of tourism demand. The need for knowledge regarding tourism demand determinants was fulfilled in scientific manner by many economists who modeled tourism demand through econometric methods (Sheldon, 1985). Systematic reviews have shown that the mostly used explanatory variables are the income, price indexes, exchange rates, travel's cost, and demographic variables (Kim et al., 2013).

Recent research reviews on tourism demand modelling and forecasting accuracy by Athanasopoulos et al. (2011) and Kim et al. (2013), show that most of the tourism demand forecasts are time-series and econometric model based. Those authors verified that Artificial Intelligence (a.k.a. machine learning) techniques are emerging. Hence, a shortage of this approach among academic literature is revealed. Traditional methods like time-series or econometric are quite suitable for data characterized by specific behavior such as trend, seasonality and cyclicality (Armstrong, 2001). On the contrary, artificial intelligence methods like the Artificial Neural Networks (ANNs) discard statistic assumptions about the data (Han et al., 2011). These techniques can deal with imperfect and irregular data or nonlinear behavior, and recent studies are demonstrating that their accuracy is satisfactory (Claveria et al., 2014; Constantino et al., 2016; Teixeira and Fernandes, 2012). Although some academic findings point out that there is not a one-fit-all forecast technique for all source markets and forecast horizons, the advantage of using machine learning algorithms is clear under the premise that the system may become chaotic, as stated by Baggio and Sainaghi, (2016).

Given that the economic decisions taken by tourism stakeholders are based on forecasts and likewise on public sources of information, considering a relative worldwide shortage of academic articles regarding Data Mining approaches (data-driven) to estimate tourism demand indicators and, an absence of a public machine learning based multivariate forecasting model in Portugal, this work sought to develop the most accurate multivariate model to forecast international tourism demand through a data-driven approach. The model development was constrained to publicly available data and machine learning methods. The forecasted demand variable was the nights spent by UK residents at tourist accommodation establishments in Lisbon's region.

2. METHODOLOGICAL FRAMEWORK

Data mining refers to the process of extracting meaningful knowledge from databases or information systems by identifying hidden but significant patterns in data. Data Mining (DM) methodologies can be KDD, SEMMA and CRISP-DM, the most complete of the last two (Azevedo and Santos, 2008). This study will follow the CRISP-DM approach (IBM, 2011). It consists in understanding the business or problem, using all the available data in repositories, prepare the data by cleaning, partitioning and modifying, modeling by applying machine learning algorithms, evaluating (assess best models) and deploying by applying the best model to new data. This will be the guideline methodology for the proposed work. The methods used for the modeling step were machine learning based, namely: Regression Trees (Random Forests), Artificial Neural

Networks and, Support Vector Machines (SVM). The multiple linear regression method was used as baseline for the comparison of above non-linear models with a linear one.

This study framework was inspired in light of previous forecasting exercises, such as those by (Cankurt and Subaşi, 2016; Constantino et al., 2016), which attempted to forecast the monthly nights spent at tourist accommodation establishments using machine learning algorithms. Here, due to practical reasons, the chosen tourism source market was the UK, which is one of the top five main tourist's source markets for the region of Lisbon and, thus considered meaningful to the region's economy.

2.1 Data

The target variable has a seasonal component (Figure 1), therefore lagged target variables were added to the original dataset. A preliminary search of explanatory variables for tourism demand in the literature revealed that macroeconomic variables, such as GDP, income and consumer price index are related (Daniel and Ramos, 2002). Most of those variables are available in databases of Eurostat, Instituto Nacional de Estatística (INE, Statistics Portugal) and the UK Office for National Statistics (ONS). Only variables with a monthly frequency were included in the dataset. Rarely used variables, such as google trends, currency exchange rates and stock market index were also included. To guarantee the reliability of data and, that any person can replicate the model, the data sources for the time-series variables used in this study were from official entities and strictly the ones available to everyone in the internet (Table 1).

Table 1. Variables and Data Sources

Source	Variables	Internet address
Instituto Nacional de Estatística (INE)	Nights spent at tourist accommodation establishments in Lisbon's region Number of tourists at accommodation establishments in Lisbon's region	www.ine.pt
UK Office for National Statistics (ONS)	Consumer Price Index (CPI) Retail Price Index (RPI) for Travel and Air Passangers	www.ons.gov.uk/
Eurostat (European Commission)	Financial account - monthly data Consumers - monthly data Harmonised indices - monthly data Harmonised unemployment rates (%) - monthly data Interest rates - monthly data Nights spent at tourist accommodation establishments - monthly data	ec.europa.eu/eurostat
Investing.com	GBP/EUR Exchange Rate Historical Data	www.investing.com
Google Trends	Search words (ex. "Lisbon")	trends.google.pt

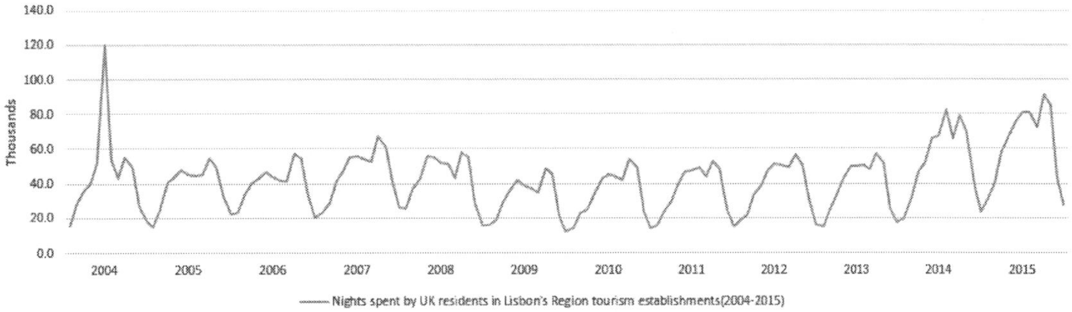

Figure 1. Nights Spent by UK Residents at Tourism Establishments in Lisbon's Region (2004 – 2015)

2.2 Experiments

Three experiments were executed with a data partition of 91% for training (120 instances) and 9% for testing (12 instances) to capture data behavior of most recent years and, with the same set of algorithms applied to 3 different datasets. Between the experiments, a progressive attribute selection was performed to reduce non-relevant variables and to augment the models accuracy, which is further explained.

To compare the models generated by the machine learning algorithms the baseline model was a multiple linear regression (MLR) with no prior testing of assumptions, no attribute selection, no prior check of capabilities (data type, missing values). The set of machine learning algorithms was restricted to a few parameter variation to avoid time consumption and minimize the insertion of multiple heuristics: 2 random forests (first with default parameters, second with attribute importance feature); 3 artificial neural networks (Multi Layer Percepetron – MPL) with default parameter differing in the number of hidden layers (H 2, H 3 and H 4); 4 support vector regression (SMOReg) with default parameters but distinct in the complexity parameter (C 0.5; C 1.0; C 1.5; C 2.0).

For experiment number 1 (Exp.1) the dataset used was the full attribute dataset "TourismDataset.arff" and with the already described data partition and group of ML algorithms. The results are displayed in Table 2. In this experiment, the number of heuristics is the minimum has possible, it is a start point to compare further experiments with selected attributes to improve model's accuracy.

After Exp.1 and, before a new learning process, to eliminate irrelevant variables and at the same time find the attribute interrelationships and bypass linear relationship selection (Arauzo-Azofra et al., 2004), the algorithm used for attribute selection was the Relief algorithm. In Weka software it is named as "ReliefFAttributeEval" (evaluator algorithm) and, in this work it was combined with a search algorithm called "Ranker". Both algorithms were used with the Weka's default parameter configuration. Before applying the Relief attribute selector, to find out the number of attributes to use has threshold in the Ranker's algorithm, the correlation based evaluator algorithm "CfsSubsetEval" combined with the search algorithm "BestFirst" was used. The output informed 19 relevant variables, which were not considered in the next experiment due to the linear constraints. The attribute selection with Relief restricted to 19 variables was performed using the TourismDataset.

For experiment number 2 (Exp.2) the dataset used was the full attribute dataset "TourismDataset.arff" and the dataset "dataset_19_Relief.arff" (19 selected variables) with the previously described data partition and group of ML algorithms (see results in Table 3).

After Exp.2, another attribute selection was done with the best model but, this time, with manual selection of variables to verify the impact on the model's accuracy. It was found that without the variable number of guests at tourist accommodation establishments, the model's accuracy was improved. Results of the Spearman correlation test applied to the selected variables showed strong (linear or non-linear) association between them. Hence, the next dataset was created with 18 variables and named has "dataset_18_Relief_no_hospedes.arff".

For the last experiment (Exp.3), the dataset used was the full attribute dataset "TourismDataset.arff", the "dataset_19_Relief.arff" (19 selected variables) and the "dataset_18_Relief_no_hospedes.arff" (18 selected variables). The results are displayed in Table 4.

2.3 Models Evaluation

In each single experiment the model's evaluation metrics analyzed were the mean absolute error (MAE) and the root mean squared error (RMSE):

$$\text{Mean absolute error: MAE} = \text{mean}(|e_i|),$$
$$\text{Root mean squared error: RMSE} = \sqrt{\text{mean}(e_i^2)}.$$

Additionally, the correlation coefficient (R^2) was used to know how well the predicted values change with the actual values.

3. RESULTS AND DISCUSSION

Analyzing the test results of Exp.1, the Linear Regression outstand the rest of the algorithms in RMSE (and R^2), followed very closely by the MLP H2 which had the best MAE of all (Table 2). Outlier values seem to have similar impact in MLR and MLP, since RMSE is almost equal on both models. The MLR correlation coefficient is quite high, which indicate a relative good fit of the model's test predictions but, the bias measure (MAE) is much lower on MLP, which points toward a better accuracy. MLP showed to have the best performance in modeling an ordered dataset of a high dimension, which may indicate a "presence" of non-linearity relationship. Additionally, has explained before, MLR model cannot be considered reliable for estimation since its assumption were not tested. Nevertheless, MLR works as a benchmark for the experiments.

Table 2. Exp.1 (Top 3 Models)

Dataset	Algorithm	Parameter's options	MAE	RMSE	R^2
TurismDataset	MLR	- default	9.522	11.060	0.964
TurismDataset	MLP	- default with H 2	8.704	11.325	0.939
TurismDataset	SMOreg	- default with C 1.0	10.724	12.106	0.965

After the first attribute selection, Exp.2 was conducted to assess the best trade-off between full and attribute selected datasets and algorithms. In Exp.2, it is evident the superior performance with the attribute selected dataset ("dataset_19_Relief.arff") and the support vector regression algorithm (SMOReg C 2.0) in all evaluation metrics (Table 3). SMOReg C2.0 was then used for the second attribute selection evaluation, where it was achieved a reduction of 3.169 on MAE and of 3.114 on RMSE.

Table 3. Exp. 2 (Top 3 Models)

Dataset	Algorithm	Parameter's options	MAE	RMSE	R^2
dataset_19_Relief	SMOreg	- default with C 2.0	9.255	10.387	0.954
dataset_19_Relief	SMOreg	- default with C 1.5	9.597	10.700	0.953
dataset_19_Relief	SMOreg	- default with C 0.5	9.635	10.858	0.950

The last experiment (Exp. 3) was run to assess the best model with the last dataset "dataset_18_Relief_no_hospedes.arff" (18 selected variables). The SMOReg was still the best model achieved after the attribute selection (Table 4), especially in the RMSE metric, followed by the MLR and MLP (H2). However, the version SMOReg with a C of 1.0 outperformed the version with a C 2.0 by a difference of less 0.06 on MAE. Therefore, it is the selected model for the forecasting exercise. Table 5 displays the model's summary results, and Figure 2 shows the test prediction outputs.

Table 4. Exp. 3 (Top 3 Models)

Dataset	Algorithm	Parameter's options	MAE	RMSE	R^2
dataset_18_Relief_no_hospedes	SMOreg	- default C 1.0	6.024	7.234	0.943
dataset_18_Relief_no_hospedes	SMOreg	- default C 1.5	6.041	7.259	0.942
dataset_18_Relief_no_hospedes	SMOreg	- default C 2.0	6.086	7.274	0.942

Table 5. Summary of the SMOReg C 1.0 Modelling Results

=== Summary ===	
Correlation coefficient	0.9425
Mean absolute error	6.0237
Root mean squared error	7.2338
Relative absolute error	0.2283
Root relative squared error	0.2329
Total Number of Instances	12

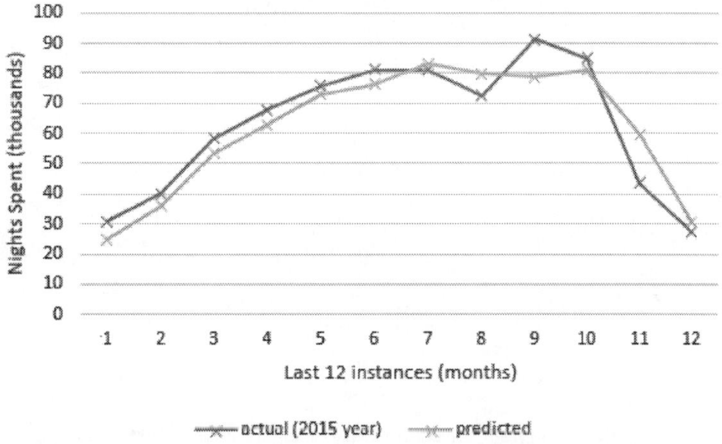

Figure 2. Test Predictions with SMOReg C1.0 (Exp. 3)

Test results for SMOReg C1.0 in Table 5 show a relative absolute error (MAE in percentage) of 22.83% and a Root Relative Absolute Error (RMSE in percentage) of 23.28%. Such results are not so promising of a high forecasting accuracy. However, since the model's generalization capability was roughly tested, due to small number of dataset instances, the forecast exercise was proceeded with the best achieved model.

3.1 Scenario Forecasting

Since the data mining model predicts through interpolation, it is necessary to have accurate observations of explanatory variables in a future period and, in the absence of official data, it would be necessary to undertake several studies for all the input variables to find reasonable estimates for them, which is not viable. In order to forecast the target variable for a 12 month horizon (2016 year) using real data, three future plausible scenarios defined as unfavorable (Scenario 1), moderated (Scenario 2), and favorable (Scenario 3) were established. To obtain the input variables, the averages of the attribute values were calculated in the following way for each scenario.

Scenario 1 (unfavorable) – for each independent variable, it was computed the average of each month of the 2005-2009 period (5 years prior to the financial crises);

Scenario 2 (moderate) – for each independent variable, it was computed the average of each month of the 2011-2015 period (5 years after financial crises), the year 2010 was excluded has it is the inflexion point of the dependent variable;

Scenario 3 (favorable) – for each independent variable, the average of each month of the 2014-2015 (2 years of great growth of the dependent variable);

For the 12 months lagged target variable, the real values of the year 2015 were used and, for the 1 month lagged variable the value of the last instance of the target variable (December's 2015) was used to begin the model's predictions. Every time an estimate was computed for each month, it was used as input value for the 1 month lagged variable attribute. The results are shown in the graphical representation (Figure 3). Due to data availability, the predicted total value was compared to the total actual value (Table 6). The scenario's estimates with highest forecasting accuracy were achieved in scenario 3, which is not surprising because this scenario used the most recent data.

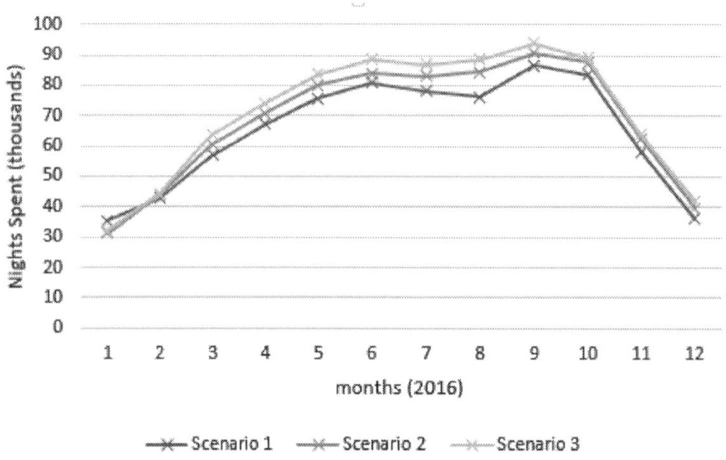

Figure 3. Scenario Forecast h = 12m (year 2016)

Table 6. Forecast Error Evaluation (*Total in Thousands)

Scenarios	Predicted Values (2016)*	Actual Values (2016)*	Absolute Error (%)**
Scenario 1	778.6	845.6	7.92
Scenario 2	818.6	845.6	3.19
Scenario 3	851.1	845.6	0.65

**Absolute Percentage Error formula: $\frac{|\text{Approximate Value} - \text{Exact Value}|}{|\text{Exact Value}|} \times 100\%$

4. CONCLUSION

The objectives of the current study were to enhance the available public sources of tourism forecast information and contribute to the tourism stakeholder's strategy in Portugal. More specifically, to develop a multivariate model to forecast international tourism demand through a Data Mining approach. The forecasted variable was the nights spent at tourist accommodation establishments in Lisbon's region, one of the country's main foreign tourist destinations. The model development was constrained to publicly available data, machine learning methods, and minimum data assumptions.

The selected model (SMOReg) was successful in generalization capability, in resemblance to a similar case study in Turkey by Cankurt and Subasi (2016). Despite of having a high relative absolute error and a high Root Relative Absolute Error in the test phase, the model produced quite accurate forecasts, especially in scenario 3.

As previously discussed, both the European economy and the interest of UK residents in Lisbon's region kept growing slightly in 2016. The "matching" of the total forecasted values of the favorable scenario with the total actual values of nights spent at tourist accommodation establishments in Lisbon's region in 2016, provides evidence of the reliability of the proposed forecasting model.

The integration of this forecasting system with public information systems, such as the recent platform of tourism knowledge management (TravelBI) from the Instituto do Turismo de Portugal, INE databases, Eurostat and other European organizations, would provide up-to-date forecast information to tourism stakeholders.

In summary, if institutions and decision makers have information regarding the evolution of the explanatory variables used in this model, the impact on Lisbon's tourism demand can be assessed, even in case of an emerging recession.

ACKNOWLEDGEMENT

The authors gratefully acknowledge the financial support of "Fundação para a Ciência e Tecnologia" (FCT), Portugal, through the MagIC research center (Centro de Investigação em Gestão de Informação).

This work was also financed through the Regional Operational Programme CENTRO2020 within the scope of the project CENTRO-01-0145-FEDER-000006.

REFERENCES

Arauzo-Azofra, A., Benitez, J. M., & Castro, J. L. (2004). A feature set measure based on relief. In *Proceedings of the fifth international conference on Recent Advances in Soft Computing*(pp. 104-109).

Armstrong, J. Scott (2001). *Principles of Forecasting: A Handbook for Researchers and Practitioners*. Norwell, MA

Athanasopoulos, G., Hyndman, R. J., Song, H., & Wu, D. C. (2011). The tourism forecasting competition. *International Journal of Forecasting*, 27(3), 822–844.

Azevedo, A., & Santos, M. F. (2008). KDD, SEMMA and CRISP-DM: a parallel overview. *IADIS European Conference Data Mining*, (January), 182–185.

Baggio, R., & Sainaghi, R. (2016). Mapping time series into networks as a tool to assess the complex dynamics of tourism systems. *Tourism Management*, 54, 23–33.

Cankurt, S., & Subasi, A. (2016). Tourism demand modelling and forecasting using data mining techniques in multivariate time series: a case study in Turkey. *Turkish Journal of Electrical Engineering & Computer Sciences*, 24(5), 3388-3404.

Claveria, O., Monte, E., & Torra, S. (2014). A multivariate neural network approach to tourism demand forecasting.

Constantino, H. A., Fernandes, P. O., & Teixeira, J. P. (2016). Tourism demand modelling and forecasting with artificial neural network models: The Mozambique case study. *Tékhne*.

Cunha, L. & Abrantes, A. (2013). *Introdução ao turismo* (5ª ed.). Lidel, Lisboa, Portugal

Daniel, A. C. M., & Ramos, F. F. R. (2002). Modelling inbound international tourism demand to Portugal. *The International Journal of Tourism Research*, 4(3), 193.

Frechtling, D. C. (2011). *Forecasting Tourism Demand: Methods and Strategies*. Routledge, New York, USA

Han, J., Pei, J., & Kamber, M. (2011). *Data mining: concepts and techniques*. Elsevier.

IBM. *(2011). IBM SPSS Modeler CRISP-DM Guide, 53.* Retrived from: https://www.ibm.com/support/knowledgecenter/en/SS3RA7_17.1.0/modeler_crispdm_ddita/modeler_crispdm_ddita-gentopic1.html

Kim, N., & Schwartz, Z. (2013). The accuracy of tourism forecasting and data characteristics: a meta-analytical approach. *Journal of Hospitality Marketing & Management*, 22(4), 349-374.

Li, G., Song, H., & Witt, S. F. (2005). Recent Developments in Econometric Modeling and Forecasting. *Journal of Travel Research*, 44(1), 82–99.

Song, H., & Li, G. (2008). Progress in Tourism Management Tourism demand modelling and forecasting—A review of recent research. *Tourism Management*, 29, 203–220.

Teixeira, J. P., & Fernandes, P. O. (2012). Tourism Time Series Forecast -Different ANN Architectures with Time Index Input. *Procedia Technology*, 5, 445–454.

Witt, S. F., & Witt, C. A. (1995). Forecasting tourism demand: A review of empirical research. *International Journal of Forecasting*, 11, 447–475.

OECD (2016). *OECD Tourism Trends and Policies 2016*. Retrieved from: http://www.oecd.org/cfe/tourism/oecd-tourism-trends-and-policies-20767773.htm

Pordata (2016). Table: Exportações de serviços: total e por tipo – Portugal. Retrieved from: http://www.pordata.pt/Portugal/Exporta%C3%A7%C3%B5es+de+servi%C3%A7os+total+e+por+tipo-2352

INE (2016). Table: Produto interno bruto (B.1*g) a preços correntes (Base 2011 - €) por Localização geográfica (NUTS - 2013); Anual. Retrieved from: https://www.ine.pt/xportal/xmain?xpid=INE&xpgid=ine_indicadores&indOcorrCod=0008836

Sheldon, P. J., & Var, T. (1985). Tourism forecasting: a review of empirical research. Journal of Forecasting, 4(2), 183-195.

ENGAGEMENT, CONTEXT AND INFORMATION SYSTEM TRAJECTORY: MODELING CUSTOMER EXPERIENCE IN INSURANCE

Gilles Beaudon[1] and Eddie Soulier[2]
[1]Pôle R&D, La Mutuelle Générale, 1-11 Rue Brillat-Savarin, 75013, Paris, France
[2]Université de Technologie de Troyes, Institut Charles Delaunay, Tech-CICO , 12 rue Marie Curie, 10004, Troyes, France

ABSTRACT

Transformation affecting the insurance market and particularly French health insurance requires traditional actors to transform their customer experience management. Our paper, which relies on the third French mutual health-insurer, tries to settle unified theoretical framework, analysis method and computational framework to address the customer experience complexity in digital environment and avoid strategic misalignment. Outlining the new customer experience information system we examine its dynamic structuration. We approach the fact that this information system must apply the concept of trajectory as primary focus for user engagement. In order to articulate information system and human activity trajectories, we develop the "contextualizing artifact" concept. These findings allow us to elaborate the CST (Context/System/Trajectory) theory and to answer the organization strategic goals. To fulfill its requirements we design the computational framework of the CST theory based on NISPARO service system model.

KEYWORDS

Customer Experience Management, Information system trajectory, Context theory, Customer Engagement, Sociomaterial entanglements, Service interactions modeling, Context Awareness computing systems

1. INTRODUCTION: FROM CUSTOMER EXPERIENCE MANAGEMENT TO CONTEXTUALIZING ARTIFACT

French health-insurance market is completely transforming. From 1156 in 2006 to 560 in 2014 (Juilliard, 2016), mutual health-insurers dropped to 446 in 2016 (Perrin, 2017). Regulatory constraints (tax for mutual health-insurance, Solvency 2, ANI...) upset market's rules. More and more aggressive non-mutual health-insurance actors enter this market. At last, the need for customer personalization grows up. Offering relevant and omni-channel customer experiences is becoming a necessity. Nevertheless, in order to offer omni-channel personalized services, insurers must transform their organizational structure as well as their business models. Additionally they have to improve their digital systems and take advantage of real time data via connected objects.

1.1 Hypothesis and Definitions

Our main hypothesis is the misalignment of organization, business model, service relation, data and information system in many insurance companies. Handling customer experience in the digital environment is complex and needs new theoretical framework, analysis methodology and applications. Our preliminary intuition is that within customer experience domain, a new information system trajectory is organically linked to the dynamic structuration of customer's trajectories. In other words, relationship between information system and actor's activity is an "entanglement" matter (Orlikowski & Scott, 2008). (Orlikowski, 2007) claimed: "the constitutive entanglement of the social and the material in everyday organizational life".. This entanglement presumes that there are no independently existing entities with inherent characteristics. The central argument insists on dealing with the social and the material in the same register. Not reverting to a limited dualism that treats them as separate phenomena.

1.2 Context and Propositions

Our paper relies on the case of a mutual health-insurer, the third one in France. It proposes an artifact to grasp Customer Experience complexity based on Design Science Methodology (Hevner and al., 2004) – the "contextualizing artifact" – which is grounded on commitment/engagement (Becker, 1960; Thevenot, 2001) and trajectory (Strauss, 1992) concepts, together entangled through a consistent "context" apparatus. In order to conceive an application for customer experience management we will study learning decision tree technique applied to a service system model

The second section explores trajectory concept applied to customer experience management system. The third section will hypothesize the crucial role played by customer engagement in information system trajectory. The fourth section will explain how engagement (people activity) and trajectory (system) could be intertwined through a "contextualizing artifact". Finally the last section specifies an application using the NISPARO service system model.

2. CUSTOMER EXPERIENCE INFORMATION SYSTEM TRAJECTORY

To establish a trajectory model is a prerequisite. Trajectories represent states of a "system" or object that we have to observe. What is observed is the customer experience system entangled with customer engagement journeys. And the contextualizing artifact is the experimental apparatus used to characterize the state of the system. To distinguish the states that characterized system and context from classical states's notions (which depend only on the system), we call them "trajectories".

According to (Oiry and al., 2010) analyzing trajectory implies characterizing ingredients. Ingredients are "context elements which act on project's trajectory" (Oiry and al, 2010, p. 85). Thus trajectory and context are conceptually linked: trajectory concept stands at the intersection of interactionism (Strauss, 1992), contextualism (Pettrigrew, 1997) and processualism (Van de Ven et Poole, 1995; Abbott, 2001).

Notions have been defined as follow by (Oiry and al, 2010):

- context : set of elements present in a situation ;
- ingredient : context's element identified by the researcher or the analyst as acting on specific project or system trajectory ;
- engine : ingredients movement and assembling generative mechanism during a trajectory ;
- sequence : trajectory temporal segment which articulates an ingredient set following a significant disposition ;
- turning point : trajectory temporal segment characterized by an intense ingredients disposition reconfiguration leading to a change of trajectory orientation.

In addition, (Strauss, 1993) considers that his concept of trajectory "refers to a course of action but also embraces the interaction of multiple actors and contingencies that may be unanticipated and not entirely manageable (…) To be more exact now, he said, I shall use *trajectory* in two ways (1) the course of any experienced phenomenon as it evolves over time (an engineering project, a chronic illness, dying, a social revolution, or national problems attending mass or 'uncontrollable' immigration) and 2) the actions and interactions contributing to its evolution. That is, phenomena do not just automatically unfold nor are they straightforwardly determined by social, economic, political, cultural, or other circumstances; rather, they are in part *shaped by the interactions* of concerned actors." (p.53-54). These first elements allow analyzing regular movements within a trajectory as well as its brutal reorientation or turning point. If each component could be theorized according to various different perspectives, it is the same for analysis methods of project trajectory within organization (Oiry et al., 2010).

We consider these definitions as a starting point but they do not fulfill the entanglement hypothesis. Thus, we are going to present in the next section the second element of our contextualized artifact, namely, the engagement.

3. USER ENGAGMENT

Today, new insurance approaches around customer experience – InsurTechs, blockchains, smart contracts, peer-to-peer collaborative insurance, behavioral insurance ("pay how you drive", "pay as you live"...), platform strategy, micro-insuring or connected insurance – aim at the core function of "make sure". This function is not challenged by these approaches. But the consequence is a progressing shift from make sure current risks to make sure prevention, prediction or wellness. They will become the core services of the flower of service (Lovelock and Gummesson, 2004) whereas handling risk could be more and more peripheral.

These new insurance approaches underly a problematization (within the meaning of Callon, 1986) around a general movement towards "deinstitutionalization" (health, school, work, friendship, etc.) which comes with the imperative for individuals to "make their experience" (Dubet, 2002). The transition from role to experience is correlative to new processes of subjectivation. With the weakening of institutions, individuals face new difficulties. The meaning of their actions and their experience is not "given" to them by institutions, individuals must construct it themselves. This description is congruent with interactionist's and pragmatics approaches. The « engagement » notion is thus very relevant and the commitment concept formulated by (Becker, 1960) remains a reference. The engagement mechanism reports: "that people engage in consistent lines of activity" (Becker, 1970).

In accordance to it, engagement is an explanatory variable behavior for which some characteristics are identified. First, engagement takes place within a period of time. Second, facing different possible journey, actors choose the one which better serves its goals. Third, the notion of a consistent line of activity implies "consistent behavior". So, the mechanism at the origin of behavior consistency is what Becker named "side bets". In fact, commitments come into being when a person, by making a side bet, links extraneous interests with a consistent line of activity. Side bets are often a consequence of the person's participation in social organizations. As Becker observes, a decision is rarely isolated and goes hand in hand with other decision linked to it: "A person finds that his involvement in social organization has, in effect, made side bets for him and thus constrained his future activity" (p. 36). Thus, this notion is useful to explain the behavior consistency by a kind of "logics of situation".

In more recent sociological research (Thévenot, 2001) has put action and its coordination at the center of his concern through the concept of "regimes of engagement". Thévenot rejects both rationality theory and the different forms of holism. "Sociologists, he said, have heavily relied on practices viewed as habits, dispositions, routines, customs and traditions to account for static perpetuation and reproduction of social order" (p. 66). Besides, inheritors of pragmatism emphasize the dynamics of practice and creativity. Indeed, situations in which actors act are characterized by uncertainty. So actors have to coordinate their situations under uncertain conditions in order to pursue a common intention or goal. Regimes of engagement are mode of coordination between human and environment and with other human beings. Thus, material and social circumstances of any coordinated action implies actually a plurality of modes of engaging the world. How actors deal with the plurality engagement modes is an issue. A central feature of the dynamics of engagement consists in the clues which the agent uses to take hold of the environment and to evaluate the success of his or her engagement. In other words, the dynamics of engagement require making a very complex calculation from the situation to be coordinated. We claim that pragmatics and situated view on action as engagement with the world (situated modes of coordination), and interactionist view of commitment as side bets between extraneous interests with a consistent actual line of activity (linked decisions' temporal ordering) offer a strong ground to explain consistency in behavior. To summarize, any social engagement has a spatial (situated coordinated action) and a temporal (linked decisions from the past) dimensions.

In the first two sections we discussed customer experience management system entangled with user engagements and their trajectories. In the next section we are going to discuss the articulation of the CST theory with contextualizing artifact.

4. ARTICULATION OF INFORMATION SYSTEM AND ENGAGEMENT TRAJECTORIES BY CONTEXT

During two months (October-November 2017) we conducted fifteen exploratory interviews. Interviewees came from various insurer business units – Product Development, Marketing & Sales, Policy Administration, Customer Management and IT – and different hierarchical level – strategic, management, executive and experts. Each interview lasted one and half hour. All have been transcripted. The result showed three main topics: innovation process, strategic context and disruptive insurance approaches. We analyzed them with interpretative methodology leading to more than twenty disruptive approaches. This process has confirmed and highlighted some of our hypothesis:

- Customer experience is a strategic aspect of business transformation and have relevant digital dimension;
- However one of the major issue is to consider this phenomenon beyond its marketing dimension, especially when it concerns linking customer segments and journeys, grasped outside of dynamics and situated engagement or interaction notions;
- Finally, it is difficult to conceive relationship between information system and human activity according to a Sociomaterial Entanglement design pattern, rather than distinguish two elements interacting, and thus ontologically divided.

Then, we follow (Moschetti-Jacob, 2016) for whom the creation of an artifact answering the complexity of customer experience handling in digital environment is a relevant approach. Creation of an artifact to design cross-channel customer journey develop managers' capabilities and can help them reduce the complexity of customer experience management. As a well-known artifact we could mention the service's blueprinting, proposed by (Shostack 1982).

We restrict this artifact to the customer experience management domain, and in particular to the capture of context. The context limits the number of possible states a system could occupy. Thus, we focus on the representation of contextual data that describes the state of a system within a given trajectory. Henceforth this represents what we call "contextualized artifact", which is a computing management tool that professionals can use to reduce the complexity of customer experience management.

In computer sciences, and especially in the context-aware computing field, a context is, according to (Dey, 2001), "any information that can be used to characterize the situation of an entity. An entity is a person, place or object that is considered relevant to the interaction between a user and an application, including the user and applications themselves, and by extension, the environment the user and applications are embedded in". A system is context-aware if it uses context to provide relevant information and/or services to the user, where relevancy depends on the user's task. The context includes all what could be told about an entity or what could describe it. A user, as an entity, may have as context attributes: a location, an emotional state, a cognitive state, an intention, a social setting, and cultural characteristics and so on. (Göker & Myrhaug, 2002) present a context taxonomy in which context elements are divided into five main categories. The task category is about what the user is doing, his goals, tasks, activities. The social one refers to the social aspects of the user, such as information about friends and family or his role. Personal context aggregates mental and physical information about the user such as mood, expertise, disabilities. In the spatio-temporal category are included attributes like time and location, and the environmental context is about user surroundings like things, light, people and information accessed by the user. (Bazire & Brézillon, 2005) consider that "the context acts like a set of constraints that influence the behavior of a system (a user or a computer) embedded in a given task". To sum up, there is no consensual definition because they don't focus on the same topics. As every model of context represents the components of a situation, each feature depends on available sensors, usable data, chosen definition, the representation that researcher has of its effect on entities, actors or interactions and the different scale of analysis. However the context is defined, (Chaari & al., 2005) consider that Dey' definition does not separate enough the data belonging to the context of those belonging to the application (the system), and recommend to distinguish between data of context and data of application and keep them separate. In contrast, because of sociomateriality hypothesis, we believe in the necessity to conceptualize the interplay between (material) technology and (human) use, and to consider that context states and use/technology are entangled.

In any case context presents a structural dimension which could feed a trajectory. What matters are acting contexts' elements (the ingredients) more than just acted contexts' elements (the elements). So, our goal should be to define context' ingredients whose configuration allows a sequence modification within a trajectory, like turning point.

Therefore our contextualized artifact rests on a double hypothesis:

- customer experience information system and consistency activity journeys constitute one single process, according to imbrication perspective (Leonardi et al., 2012), the "intra-action" theory (Barad, 2007), and the entanglement and information system sociomateriality (Orlilowski, 2007 ; 2010 ; Orlikowski and Scott 2008);
- the System/Trajectory pattern makes Context the joining element between System and Trajectory. So, our contextualized artifact could be positioned within the triplet Context/System/Trajectory concept (Figure 1) also call CST theory. Context could be understood through elements which act directly on the experiential trajectory' building.

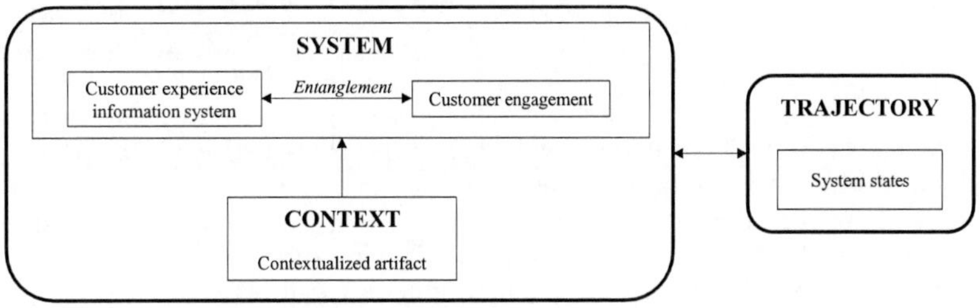

Figure 1. Context-System-Trajectory (CST) Theory

According to the first three sections, CST theory is made explicit. We are now going to discuss how to design an application based on Context-System-Trajectory model in order to cope with insurance issues. This application is based on NISPARO model, adapted from ISPAR service system model and learning decision tree technique.

5. COMPUTATIONAL FRAMEWORK FOR CONTEXT-SYSTEM-TRAJECTORY THEORY

First, we focus on the "System" component. This component is composed of two main sub-components that have to be considered as entangled, customer experience information system and customer engagement. These components' main function is to define customer journeys aligned on health-insurers company strategy. This provides us with the capacity to consider it on a scale from completely predefined journey to open customer journey with a middle step corresponding to a customized journey. Each state could be associated with the strategic nature of engagement negotiated between the insurer and the insured. These states are:

- Risks-insured engagement: insured individual has only "cold contacts" with insurer at anxiety-provoking moment such as claim, ill or death (regarding to health-insurer point of view);
- Risk-prevention engagement: insured individual consider having actions for prevention (self-good health) thanks to new insurance services offer;
- Well-being engagement: insured individual uses voluntarily and instinctively insurer's service to get wellness.

Crossing various elements - customer experience information system, strategic and uncertain nature of customer engagement, and entanglement constraints - lead us to the following System categorization (Table 1).

Table 1. System Categorization of CSP Theory

	No-entanglement system	Half-entangled system	Entangled system
Completely predefined journey and risks-insured engagement	Separate systems (CRM System, Phone calls, Insured-Persons portal, Contract care App)		
Customized journey and risk-prevention engagement		Customer Engagement Hub (CEH), Interaction retention	
Open Customer journey and well-being engagement			Strategic target including smart contracts, collaborative insurance and micro insurance within omni-channel context-awareness information system

Regarding to the CSP theory system categorization we have chosen to focus on relevant intersection between our three dimensions. Nevertheless, this first analysis proves that separate systems are a major issue clearly identified. It provides predefined journey within one channel but no vision of the whole customer journey. Secondly Customer Engagement Hub and interaction retention systems are new concepts for health-insurers but are still not functional. According to Gartner 2017 definition, customer engagement hub (CEH) "is an architectural framework that ties multiple systems together to optimally engage the customer. A CEH allows personalized, contextual customer engagement, whether through a human, artificial agent, or sensors, across all interaction channels. It reaches and connects all departments, allowing, for example, the synchronization of marketing, sales and customer service processes" (https://www.gartner.com/it-glossary/customer-engagement-hub). They represent the first step and most valuable vector for customized and risk-prevention engagement but CEH remains an half-entangled system: it doesn't really take into account the real-world customer' situations nor the ubiquitous and pervasive computing systems they now daily use inside these situations. And it does not take into account service interaction, where the customer and the employee have to work together in order to achieve a mutual understanding to get the task or service done. As (Schneider, 2016) notes: "interactive service work is inherently characterized by uncertainty concerning the outcome or result of the interaction" (p. 6). So almost five elements are implied to serve clients, and constitute the "service system abstraction" (Maglio and al., 2009). We get inspired by (Mili and al, 2016) ontological work on Context Aware Customer Experience Management (CEM), adding service interactions and customer journey analysis to their model of customer experience, as the set of interactions between a company and a customer around the fulfillment of customer's needs:

- "client processes" element, often wrongly mixed up with customer journeys, are every operational procedures and aim at delivering services which are already set out. They are highly supported by current information management systems.

- The "real-world customer' situations" is defined by (Mili and al., 2016) as internal processes, in a sense that a customer has a 'life of his/her own' pursuing his/her objectives of survival and happiness. In the process of pursuing those objectives they have needs that can or need to be fulfilled by a company. Ubiquitous computing develops context-aware CEM applications (CA-CEM) and scenarios that exploit a rich combination of sensor data, customer profile data, and historical data about the customer's interactions with his environment.

- "service interactions" are vivid and performative human interactions which take place between prospects or clients and front-line or back-office service workers (Schneider, 2016).

- "customer journey" analysis results from marketing department and teams modeling in order to bring almost pre-defined customer segments to services offers. This element ordinary belongs also to innovation and/or design firms processes.- some new practices, processes and tools denoted as Customer experience management (CEM) help marketing and sale departments to analyze and exploit their "client's data capital" (i.e. data science) in order to manage customer experience at decision level (behavior studies, recommendations, behavioral targeting, etc.). The tools also help multi-channel customer journey analysis and visualization in order to improve real-time optimization of client outcomes.

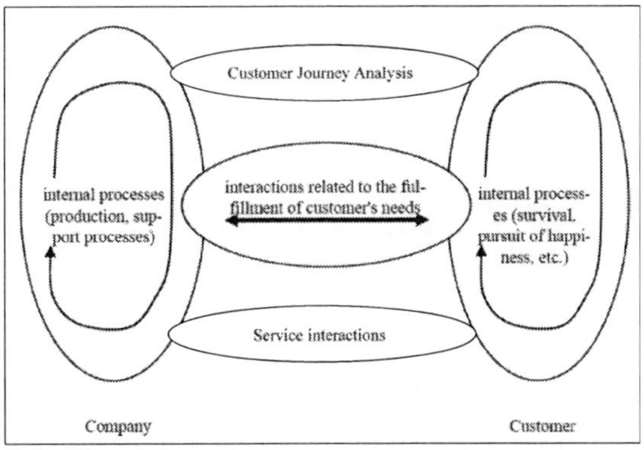

Figure 2. Customer Experience Management Model (inspired from Mili and al., 2016)

Context is the information used in a model for representing real-world situations whereas situations are represented as a meta-level concept over context (Akman and Surav, 1997). Thus, the "context" of the contextualizing artifact surrounds these elements, and it is distributed information from them and their interactions, at service systems level of abstraction. It is why we propose to catch the context of contextualizing artifact from an expanded version of Interact-Serve-Propose-Agree-Realize (ISPAR) model of service systems episodes where a series of activities are jointly undertaken by at least two service systems and produce ten possible outcomes (Spohrer and al., 2008). For example in ISPAR model, realization of the proposed and agreed to service is the desired outcome of a service system (outcome R).

But a proposal may not be successfully communicated or understood by other service systems (-P), and so the interaction may be aborted. Secondly, a proposal may be communicated, but activities between the service systems may not lead to an agreement (-A), and so the service interaction may be aborted, and so on. A case of particular interest is when an interaction between service systems is not service interaction, but nevertheless the interaction may be welcome (W) by both service systems. Here, welcomed (W) non-service interactions should not be minimized, they often lay the foundation for future service interactions that may co-create great value. Despite its relevance ISPAR model is not computerized; service system interaction episodes are not "locked" through any customers real-world situations characterization, service interactions, customer experience visualization and even company's client processes.

We propose to adapt ISPAR model to our insurance business case, and above all for computational purpose. Our generic business case start from the insurer CRM (Salesforce), where the situation of potential or already customer is represented as an *event*. Analyzing such events by data scientists, sales and marketing teams categorized them. We propose our own five event types: Subscription, Certificate, Reimbursement, Claim and Information (asked). The company responds through *tasks* concepts. We propose three types: Action, Service interaction and Information (given). Events and Tasks altogether are represented in Salesforce implementation as an *activity*. Activity object could be fed by any channels, from social network, to phone call, email or IoT sensors. A request comes necessarily from a client as such, thus any request is linked to a contract belonging to back office domain. Thus "activity" here is no longer an interaction nor a situation or an outcome, and it is not possible to link data coming from activity object to customer journey visualization functionality, even if a Proof of Concept is being tested with DataKili tool from AID software publisher (http://www.aid.fr/). To help manager fill this gap we propose the NISPARO model as an extansion of ISPAR model and a main contextualizing artifact application.

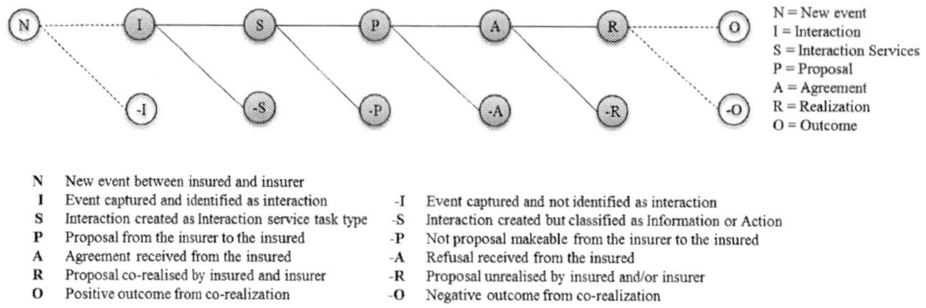

Figure 3. NISPARO Model of a Contextualizing Artifact (Beaudon & Soulier, 2018)

NISPARO could now be completed by two others components of the contextualizing artifact. The first one implements precisely several contexts (plural is here essential) that are now being workable by NISPARO model (fig. 4). We make the hypothesis that in order to turn NISPARO in a more contextual and above all dynamic model, we need to distinguish some "phases" –trajectories - in the overall service interaction phenomenon. As Strauss suggests "*trajectory phasing* represents the researcher's conceptualization of phases, in accordance with changes in the interaction occurring over time 'around' the phenomenon as it evolves. Analytically, these phases are properties of the sequence of interactions" (p.54).

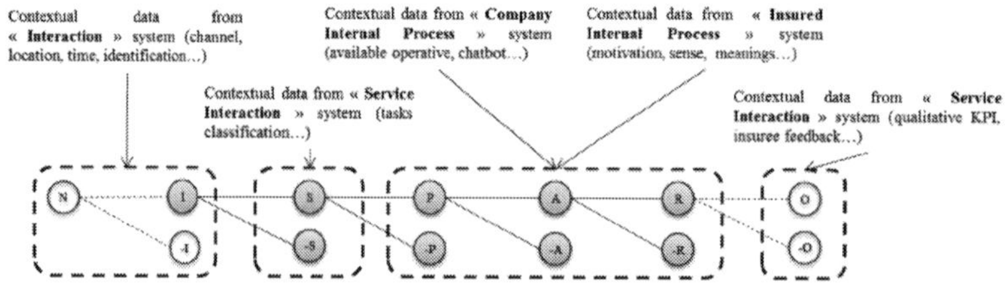

Figure 4. Contexts Aware Customer Experience as Distributed Information along NISPARO Model of Service System Interactions

Thus, even if insurance companies are able to collect a lot of contextual data from the field, interaction in NISPARO model remains a "backcloth" (or static structure) from which a traffic (or dynamic trajectory) must be extricated. Simply speaking, a final trajectory results from a set of choices shaped by interactions in NISPARO abstract model. Predominantly, three questions could be asked: Is there a real-world customer' situation which leads to a welcome non-service interaction? Is there a good Customer Experience induced by a proper client process, a relevant service interaction and a customer journey visualization warning? And finally is there a good outcome from the insured experience perspective? It is then possible to distinguish three main phases in trajectory phasing: initial situation, service interaction situation and outcome situation. Here after, figure 5 shows the second component of the contextualizing artifact. We may use learning decision tree techniques to explore phases and develop an interaction services mining application. The last step will consist in specifying a system able to collect multi-contexts data, and also a method to aggregate NISPARO graphs (i.e. various customer service interactions episodes) within an identified customer journey.

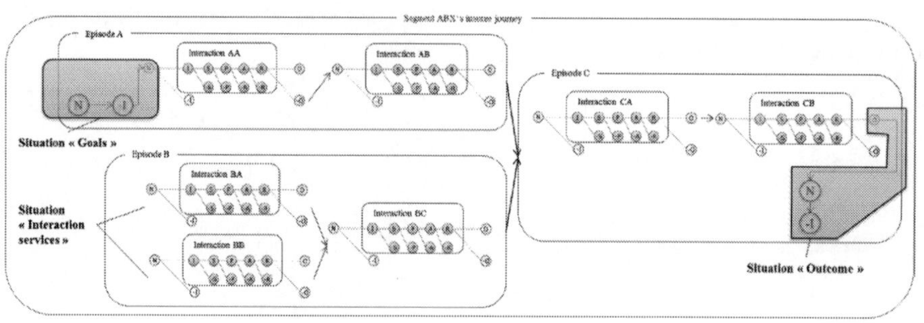

Figure 5. NISPARO and Customer Journeys

6. CONCLUSION

Analyzing new insurers' problematics has emphasized the customer experience relevancy and complexity. To entirely grasp this issue we claim that we need to develop a Context-System-Trajectory theory. To achieve such a theory it is necessary to conceive a new computational framework for customer experience information system and an application to collect, interpret and analyze interactions services. These conclusions rely on multiple arguments. First, the trajectory (states) concept is relevant to analyze customer experience management system entangled with customer engagement journey. Secondly we defined that user engagement has spatial (a situated coordinated action) and temporal (linked decisions from the past) dimensions. It is a challenge to understand customer experience information system's trajectories. Thirdly we develop the CST theory to articulate information system and engagement trajectory related to a contextualizing artifact. This artifact reduces the complexity of customer experience management by outlining state's system with contextual data. Finally we focus on the System dimension to appreciate different computational ways to answer customer experience in insurance. Due to limited entanglement existing approaches, we chose to rely on Customer Engagement Management and Interaction Services previous work. It allowed us to define the NISPARO model and interaction service mining application.

Our work may change insurers' manager views on customer experience. It reveals customer experience complexity beyond its marketing dimension. With CST theory we have a tool to analyze initial situation of customer experience information system versus the targeted one. It exposes a disruptive framework for sensing, interpreting and analyzing interaction services contextual data. Our future works will focus on refining CST theory by articulating it with interaction services concept and develop a proof of concept demonstrating that NISPARO could be used for customer journey analysis.

REFERENCES

Abbott, A.D., 2001. *Time matters: on theory and method.* University of Chicago Press, Chicago.

Akman, V., Surav, M., 1997. The Use of Situation Theory in Context Modeling. *Computational Intelligence* 13, 427–438.

Barad, K.M., 2007. *Meeting the universe halfway: quantum physics and the entanglement of matter and meaning*. Duke University Press, Durham.

Bazire, M., Brézillon, P., 2005. Understanding Context Before Using It, in: Dey, A., Kokinov, B., Leake, D., Turner, R. (Eds.), *Modeling and Using Context*. Springer Berlin Heidelberg, Berlin, Heidelberg, pp. 29–40.

Beckett, R., 2017. Service Ecosystems Supporting High Reliability Assets. *Systems 5*, 32.

Becker, H.S., 1960. Notes on the Concept of Commitment. American Journal of Sociology 66, 32–40.

Becker, H.S., 1970. *Sociological work : Method and substance.* Aldine.

Callon, M., 1986. Éléments pour une sociologie de la traduction. La domestication des coquilles Saint-Jacques dans la Baie de Saint-Brieuc. *L'Année sociologique* n°36.

Chaari, T., Laforest, F., Flory, A., 2005. Adaptation des applications au contexte en utilisant les services web. *In Proceedings of 2th French Spearking Conference on Mobility and Ubiquity Computing*, ACM Press, pp. 111–118.

Chaiklin, S., Lave, J. (Eds.), 1997. *Understanding practice: perspectives on activity and context*, Repr. ed, Learning in Doing: Social, Cognitive and Computational Perspectives. Cambridge Univ. Press, Cambridge.

Dey, A.K., 2001. Understanding and Using Context. *Personal and Ubiquitous Computing 5*, 4–7.

Dubet, F., 2002. *Le déclin de l'institution, L'épreuve des faits*. Seuil, Paris.

Göker, A., Myrhaug, H.I., 2002. User Context and Personalisation. *In Proceedings of the Workshop on Case Based Reasoning and Personalization*, Mehmet H. Göker, Barry Smyth (ed.), Aberdeen, Scotland, pp. 4–11.

Hevner, A.R., March, S.T., Park, J., Ram, S., 2004. Design Science in Information Systems Research. *MIS Quarterly 28*, 75–105.

Juilliard, M.-P., 2016. Une concentration des mutuelles inéluctable... ou presque. *L'Argus de l'assurance*.

Karchoud, R., 2017. Long Life Application dedicated to smart-* usage, thesis, Universidad del País Vasco (UPV) and Université de Pau et des Pays de l'Adour (UPPA)

Leonardi, P.M., Nardi, B.A., Kallinikos, J. (Eds.), 2012. *Materiality and organizing: social interaction in a technological world*, 1st ed. ed. Oxford University Press, Oxford.

Lovelock, C., Gummesson, E., 2004. Whither Services Marketing?: In Search of a New Paradigm and Fresh Perspectives. *Journal of Service Research 7*, 20–41.

Maglio, P.P., Vargo, S.L., Caswell, N., Spohrer, J., 2009. The service system is the basic abstraction of service science. *Information Systems and e-Business Management 7*, 395–406.

Mili, H., Benzarti, I., Meurs, M.-J., Obaid, A., Gonzalez-Huerta, J., Haj-Salem, N., Boubaker, A., 2016. *Context Aware Customer Experience Management: A Development Framework Based on Ontologies and Computational Intelligence*, in: Pedrycz, W., Chen, S.-M. (Eds.), Sentiment Analysis and Ontology Engineering. Springer International Publishing, Cham, pp. 273–311.

Moschetti-Jacob, F., 2016. *Création d'un artefact modulaire d'aide à la conception de parcours client cross-canal visant à développer les capacités des managers des entreprises du secteur du commerce* (Thesis). Paris-Dauphine.

Oiry, E., Bidart, C., Brochier, D., Garnier, J., Gilson, A., Longo, M.-E., Mendez, A., Mercier, D., Pascal, A., Perocheau, G., Tchobanian, R., 2010. Propositions pour un cadre théorique unifié et une méthodologie d'analyse des trajectoires des projets dans les organisations. *Management & Avenir 36*, 84.

Orlikowski, W.J., 2007. Sociomaterial Practices: Exploring Technology at Work. *Organization Studies 28*, 1435–1448.

Orlikowski, W., Scott, S., 2008. *The entangling of technology and work in organizations.* Working paper series, Dept of management information systems and innovation group, London School of Economics London School of Economics.

Orlikowski, W.J., 2010. The sociomateriality of organisational life: considering technology in management research. *Cambridge Journal of Economics 34*, 125–141.

Perera, C., Zaslavsky, A., Christen, P., Georgakopoulos, D. 2014, Context Aware Computing for The Internet of Things: A Survey, IEEE Communications Surveys & Tutorials, Volume: 16, Issue: 1, First Quarter 2014.

Perrin, G., 2017. Santé : la baisse du nombre de mutuelles se poursuit. *L'Argus de l'assurance*.

Pettigrew, A.M., 1997. What is a processual analysis*? Scandinavian Journal of Management 13*, 337–348.

Schneider, A., 2016. Handling the clash between production & consumption. A situated view on front-line service workers'competencies in interactive service, Rainer Hampp Verlag.

Shostack, G.L., 1982. How to Design a Service. *European Journal of Marketing 16*, 49–63.

Spohrer, J., Vargo, S.L., Caswell, N., Maglio, P.P., 2008. The Service System Is the Basic Abstraction of Service Science. *In Proceedings of the 41st Annual International Conference on System Sciences*, IEEE, Hawaii, pp. 104–104.

Strauss, A.L., 1992. *La trame de la négociation: sociologie qualitative et interactionnisme*. Éditions L'Harmattan, Paris.

Strauss, A.L., 1993. *Continual Permutations of Action (Communication and Social Order)*. Aldine Transaction (1634).

Thévenot, L., 2001. Pragmatic regimes governing the engagement with the world, *in: Knorr-Cetina, K., Schatzki, T. Savigny Eike v. (Eds.) The Practice Turn in Contemporary Theory*.

Van de Ven, A.H., Poole, M.S., 1995. Explaining Development and Change in Organizations. *The Academy of Management Review 20*, pp.510-540.

BUSINESS INTELLIGENCE APPLICATION IN ADAPTATION OF SERVQUAL SCALE AT BRAZILIAN HEALTH SYSTEM

Galba Freire Moita[1], Claudio Gonçalves Bernardo[2], Juliana Caetana da Costa[3] and Danilo Afonso de Azevedo[3]
[1]Ministério da Saúde / Universidade de Coimbra (MS/UC), Brasília – Brazil
[2]Universidade de Brasília / Faculdade de Ciências da Informação (UNB/FCI), Brasília - Brazil
[3]Universidade Paulista (UNIP), Brasília – Brazil

ABSTRACT

In a world where data is what most matter, which generate information and knowledge and can be a basis for new strategies, methodologies for its collection, manipulation, transformation and visualization enable diagnoses, solutions to help users perceptions of a system in relation of quality of provided services. This research presents a way of extracting knowledge of specialists and users through the cross-cultural adaptation of Servqual Scale, which resulted in the instrument Quality Saúde (Health quality in portuguese) of measuring expectation and perception from users of Brazilian health system (SUS), measuring their satisfaction. Data were extracted from a relational database in order to be consulted in an organized way, quickly and mainly without unnecessary use of repeated data, bringing integrity. Data were manipulated and transformed using a BI tool, which allowed visualization in an analytical and synthetic way, being able to be analyzed in a micro (small samples of data) and macro (large samples of data), facilitating decision making process, proposing improvements, making diagnoses, proposing solutions.

KEYWORDS

Business Intelligence, Servqual Scale, User Satisfaction, Health Quality, Brazilian Health System

1. INTRODUCTION

Evaluating quality of services is an essential factor when you want to measure customer satisfaction, retain customers and having a broad vision from the consumer perspective of a service. There is a need to evaluate services provided in public health sector as a measure to assist resources management. In an integrative bibliographical research on quality measurement and health user satisfaction in Brazil, the results obtained are timid and there are no records of standardization of quality and satisfaction measurement systems in Brazilian Health System whose acronym in Portuguese is SUS (Sistema Único de Saúde).

A short analysis of the scale proposed in the GESPÚBLICA initiative (Brazil, 2014) reveals much similarity with five dimensions and with 22 questions of original Seervqual scale (Parasuraman *et al.*, 1991a; Berry *et al.*, 1994), but there is no evidence of a process of adequacy through cross-cultural translation and reliability and validity analyzes in construction of satisfaction scale that makes up the IPPS.

In Brazilian health context, two surveys of satisfaction are highlighted: the National Health Service Evaluation Program whose original acronym is PNASS (2015) and the Federal Medical Council (CFM, 2015), both with the goal of evaluating services offered via user-provided notes. According to the Ministry of Health (2015), the PNASS's objective is to evaluate the totality of specialized healthcare centers, outpatient and hospital, with financial resources derived from programs, policies and incentives of the Ministry of Health, regarding the following dimensions: structure, process, outcome, production of care, risk management and user satisfaction in relation to care received. This survey originally was made just for been applied in selected hospitals.

In 2015 the Datafolha Institute (2017), at the request of Brazilian Federal Council of Medicine (CFM), presented a quality survey on the services offered by SUS, where 93% of respondents evaluated services as bad, or regular (0 to 7). According to the survey, for the majority of the population (77%) the government has failed to manage public health resources. In the opinion of 53% of interviewees, SUS does not have enough resources to serve everyone well, in an equitable way. Among the investment dimensions to consider are: i. accessibility - whether the possibility of consumption of the service is accessible to all people everywhere; ii. reliability - whether the service provided is the same as previously promised; iii. effectiveness - verify that the service produced the expected (diagnostic) outcome; iv. efficiency - if the service was done as quickly as possible without losing effectiveness.

The new PNASS was re-launched by SUS (Brazil, 2015), however, this evaluation system only allows institution to be evaluated with binary parameters, "YES" or "NO" in the items that were objects of analysis, not taking into account variations between these parameters. In this research was developed data analysis of data collected by research prototype suggesting a cross-cultural adaptation of Servqual scale for SUS.

These mentioned surveys help to understand that they does not serve its purposes well, because scientific methods with methodological rigor were not applied to structure models that really approximate reality. In this purpose an international scale named Servqual was selected as a proposal for translation and adaptation of Servqual scale in a new instrument named Quality Saúde (Health Quality in portuguese), which is based on the translation field of knowledge in which consolidated theories are targets of transliteration in social actors involved experiences (Barbosa and Pereira Neto, 2017 *apud* Clavier *et al*, 2011; Hartz *et al*, 2008).

In present study, it was based on a collaborative process aimed at establishing the constructs (ideals-forces) to synthesize and apply knowledge aimed at improving services in order to fill knowledge gaps and instruments to transform policies and practices (Barbosa and Pereira Neto , 2017 *apud* CIHR, 2004, p.2; WHO, 2006, p.1) for SUS services management. The applied process can be expanded to other public services, aiming at structuring and validating specific quality scales. Thus was created the following problem question: Is it possible to use BI techniques to analyze the adaptation of the ServQual scale in the Brazilian health system?

Servqual questionnaire model is a selection of quality concepts in the service with a broader understanding, with the objective of basing customer's expectation against the perception of the same client about a service. However, there are no records of standardization of quality and satisfaction measurement systems in SUS. The aim of this article was to treat data obtained through a research that proposes the cross-cultural adaptation of Servqual scale for health quality evaluation, to evaluate services rendered in Brazilian public health, presenting information to assist in decision-making. The following specific objectives have been proposed: i. Define a data model that makes it possible to store collected data in an organized way; ii. Apply processes of extraction, transformation and loading of collected data; iii. Keep the data in a relational database; iv. Produce solutions to visualize collected data presenting them in a way that can accurately evidence obtained results.

Exploratory research was used and for formulation of necessary information for analysis of this work we searched for references in service evaluation area, mainly on Servqual model. This was used in research prototype applied under a PhD thesis developed by Moita *et al.* (2017) with initial results, which resulted in the proposal of Quality Saúde Scale, a measurement instrument of perceived quality (satisfaction and suitability for use) by users, duly adapted to the context of SUS.

The data model was developed based on adaptation made of Servqual scale. Extract, Transform and Load (ETL) processes were applied, which deals with data cleaning coming from several sources to be inserted in Data Warehouse (DW). This process was carried out in three stages: Data extraction; Transformation of data to correct, standardize and eliminate inconsistencies; Loading data into a database. With data available in DW, visualization was prepared in QlikView tool, enabling creation of reports and interactive dashboards.

According Corrêa and Gianesi (1994) "quality in services can be defined as the degree to which customer expectations are met". There is a need to evaluate services provided in public health area as a measure to assist resources management. To that end, Moita (2013) states that it is necessary to evaluate quantity of health services or products (care, examinations, surgeries, hospitalizations) produced by health system or health units, but that requires efficient resource management, that is, it is intended to measure and monitor decisive impact on patients health, society and health system, since it is often perceived that mobilized resources are not monitored from an operative point of view.

2. SERVQUAL QUESTIONNAIRE MODEL

Servqual questionnaire model is a selection of quality concepts in deepening service, with the objective of basing client's expectation in counterpoint with the perception of same about a service. American researchers Parasuraman, Zeithaml and Berry (1988) developed it. Its research method evaluates five aspects defined as dimensions, which are: Reliability; Safety; Empathy; Tangibles; Responsiveness. The questions can be adapted according to service, but the questionnaire applied must meet basic premises to reach its objective of collecting information. They are: i. engaging the participant; ii. communicating appropriately with participant; iii. make participant develop their responses; iv. avoid creating biases or trends of any kind; v. promote interviewer's task easily; vi. seek automated processing of responses.

Figure 1 is a screen of Servqual questionnaire proposed in this research where the interviewee is allowed to inform his basic data. Such personal identification is not mandatory. Data in screen are written in Portuguese.

Figure 1. Basic Data Record Screen

Figure 2 presents screen with one of the questions. In it are presented 5 figures representing grades attributed to interviewee expectation in relation to service performed, the grade 1 for lowest expectation and 5 grade for highest expectation. The same happens for grades attributed to interviewee satisfaction in relation to performed service. Data in screen are written in Portuguese.

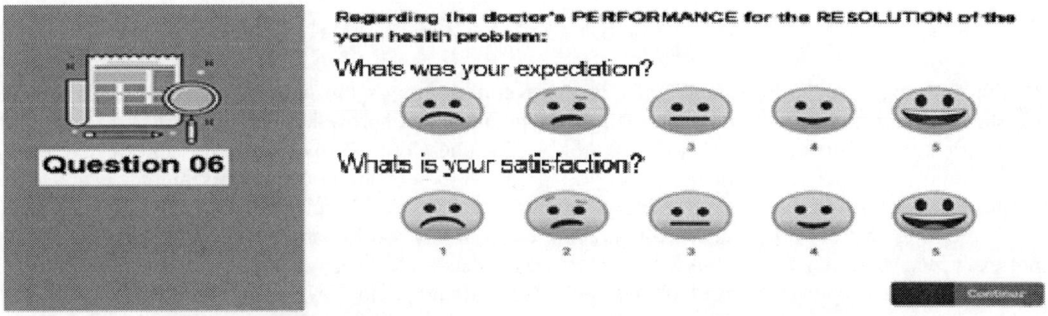

Figure 2. Response Screen In Relation To Interviewee's Expectation And Satisfaction

Business Intelligence (BI) can be defined as a set of methodologies, techniques and tools to perform, collect, analyze and integrate information with main objective of supporting decision-making (Rud, 2009). According to Oliveira *et al.* (2008) BI helps organizations access information synthesized in an easy way for decision-making. In this process, the act of transforming data into useful and meaningful information was destined to distribute this information to those who really need it and who can make right decisions at the right time. Among advantages of using BI can be highlighted discovery of new opportunities, definition of effective strategies based on data and promotion of businesses with competitive advantage in market and long-term stability.

A large amount of data is generated daily and data usage is minimal. Due to this factor, many opportunities to leverage health services in Brazil are lost. In order to control and manage care provided by SUS, information systems developed by Brazilian health ministry are used in most cases, which has one of its goals to define standards for collection and transfer of health information, aiming at databases operational integration and systems developed and implemented within the scope of SUS. One of the most popular information systems is Popular Pharmacy system, which aims to increase access to medicines at more affordable prices for population. This same system served as a model for similar program initiative in Peru. According to Datasus (2017b) it is essential for health management to know about health situation with quality and speed. This information, if it is easy to access and available with quality, becomes a great help for decision making in any area of activity, such as strategic planning, sectoral, control and evaluation, audit, epidemiological investigation. It is in this context that Business Intelligence can be applied in public health, making it possible to obtain excellence in data stored using in various information systems for knowledge production. In this research data were stored in a relational database, and for this research PostgreSQL (2018) was chosen.

On analysis of obtained results, 9,063 responses to each of the items of Quality Saúde scale were obtained in groups of 195 specialists and initial pilot groups aside 506 SUS users via application of software R, version 3.3.2, language which can be used for data manipulation, visualization and statistical analysis, and has more than 5000 additional packages available in repositories, as well as the great data resources of Revolution R Enterprise. For R Project (2017) it is a programming language with a focus on statistics and graphics; is a General Public License (GNU) project and is under open source license, and performs a wide variety of functions.

For the treatment of analyzed results two tools were used: 1. PowerDesigner (Sybase, 2017) has support for several activities such as business process modeling, data modeling, multidimensional data modeling, which stores and controls developed models. PowerDesigner brings impact analysis, design time change management, and metadata management techniques to your user. 2. QlikView (QlikTech, 2017), which covers BI techniques, enables an interactive visualization of information and can be defined as a tool for decision-making. QlikView compresses data and keeps it in its memory, where it is available for use by multiple users. In the case of data sets too large to be stored in memory, this tool connects directly to data source and provides an associative experience for all data used for analysis, regardless of where they are stored.

3. PROBLEMS INVOLVING SATISFACTION SURVEYS

Health in Brazil is in critical condition due to several factors as the lack of investment. Consequently satisfaction surveys emerge in order to highlight the points to be improved, helping managers to apply public funds effectively. Satisfaction surveys in PNASS (2015) and CFM (2015) did not use an effective research method to assess quality of public health services provided to population. Current research does not serve its purpose well, because a rigorous methodology is not applied to sketch results that really approximate reality.

There is no control of participants who are chosen randomly and as consequence people's grade who did not even receive service at that time, the research questions are considered superficial because they do not approach a topic deeply. As a result, the research results are unsatisfactory, since it does not assist managers in decision-making. Based on this, a satisfaction survey was carried out in order to evaluate public health services quality provided to Brazilian population, adapted from parameters of Servqual scale, which resulted in a new instrument adapted to SUS context, named in Portuguese Escala Quality Saúde (Quality Health Scale).

About 5,547 respondents were interviewed, where 701 answered 40 constructs, 2609 answered 20 questions and 2689 answered 14 questions, with answers from 10 Brazilian states: Bahia, Ceará, Federal District, Goiás, Maranhão, Mato Grosso, Pará, Piauí, Rio Grande do Norte and Rondônia. These patients were approached after receiving care at health institution, causing them to answer questionnaire with perceptions acquired when they received services offered by these institutions.

Data obtained in first moment were not able to pass accurate information to interested parties, since they are often inconsistent, mainly due to lack of standardization. In order to avoid these inconsistencies, it was necessary standardize collected data so that this information could be crossed and sketched obtained results. Quality Saúde scale proved to be efficient because significant data were collected and with great potential for analysis. However, it is necessary to maintain a quality standard in information so that there is also quality in information interpretation, providing correct strategies for decision-making. Gross information is not considered useful, data must always be intact, in order to have quality in information.

4. BI IN SERVQUAL SCALE ADAPTATION

In SUS there are no records of quality and satisfaction measurement systems standardization. In an integrative research, only three small jobs of Servqual application in specific contexts were highlighted (Hercos & Berezovsky, 2004; Borges *et al.*, 2006; Cruz & Melleiro, 2007). We also identified two studies with Servqual systematization, but with a sample application summarized in Brazilian hospitals (Albuquerque, 2012; Rosalem, 2013). These surveys apply only the original version of the scale, and it is difficult to measure results by the absence of cross-cultural validation. Thus, this research was applied in the scope of PhD research in development at University of Coimbra by Galba Freire Moita, with initial results verified (Moita *et al.*, 2017) and approved at the research project platform named Brazil Platform (CAAE: 54972816.9.0000.5051). Were selected a group of managers and professionals to form a panel of pilot specialists with 128 professionals and managers after data validation.

Original 22 questions of Servqual scale were adapted for health services (Babakus and Mangold, 2002) and asked the group to suggest and ponder in what dimensions each original question was appropriate and which personal constructs could be better adapted to SUS patients' reality. Afterwards, a questionnaire of 20 questions and a questionnaire of 14 questions were adapted and pondered in the panel of experts and pilot groups, where in these cases the last question represents the patient general satisfaction.

In this way, the application resulted in valuation of original, validated and adapted constructs. Treatment and analysis of collected data, proposed in our study, was used as technological support for application of proposed models and later results systematization. In this case, innovation was using BI tools and techniques as support in cross-cultural adaptation of Servqual scale. Thus, in this research was decided to present aspects of characterization, BI application in initial results obtained in groups of experts and initial pilot groups in order to demonstrate the applicability of techniques developed.

Data treatment was performed based on data standardization. For this purpose, an ER model (entity-relationship model) describing interrelated things of interest in this specific domain of knowledge was created aiming at standardizing tables, in order to maintain data consistency. Initial analysis demonstrated need for data abstraction, placing Institution table as the main entity of the model, because it ends up being related to all other entities. Based on adaptation of Servqual model to public health service, it was necessary to divide issues into three entities, being these; original constructs (TF_CONSTRUCTOS), validated constructs (TF_CV_QUESTOES) and adapted constructs (TF_CA_QUESTOES) whose mission is to store grades assigned by participants.

Afterwards, ETL - Extraction, Transformation and Load processes were applied in data, being applied using programming language R, where they were kept in PostgreSQL database. Data extraction is presented in figure 3, transformation of imported data with R is presented in Figure 4 and data load imported with R is shown in Figure 5.

```
notas.14Q.CEOREG <- `NOTAS-14Q-CEOReg`[5:44, ]
names(notas.14Q.CEOREG) <- `NOTAS-14Q-CEOReg`[4, ]
temp <- `NOTAS-14Q-CEOReg`[57:93, ]
names(temp) <- `NOTAS-14Q-CEOReg`[4, ]
notas.14Q.CEOREG <- bind_rows(notas.14Q.CEOREG, temp)
temp <- `NOTAS-14Q-CEOReg`[106:145, ]
names(temp) <- `NOTAS-14Q-CEOReg`[4, ]
notas.14Q.CEOREG <- bind_rows(notas.14Q.CEOREG, temp)
temp <- `NOTAS-14Q-CEOReg`[158:198, ]
names(temp) <- `NOTAS-14Q-CEOReg`[4, ]
notas.14Q.CEOREG <- bind_rows(notas.14Q.CEOREG, temp)
temp <- `NOTAS-14Q-CEOReg`[211:250, ]
names(temp) <- `NOTAS-14Q-CEOReg`[4, ]
notas.14Q.CEOREG <- bind_rows(notas.14Q.CEOREG, temp)
temp <- `NOTAS-14Q-CEOReg`[263:302, ]
names(temp) <- `NOTAS-14Q-CEOReg`[4, ]
notas.14Q.CEOREG <- bind_rows(notas.14Q.CEOREG, temp)
```

Figure 3. Data Extraction using R language

```
TD_INSTITUICAO <- sqldf(
  "select
  CO_CNES||grupo||subgrupo as ID_INSTITUICAO,
  case when `No. CNPJ` = 999 then NU_CNPJ_MANTENEDORA else `No. CNPJ` end as CNPJ,
  NO_RAZAO_SOCIAL, CASE WHEN `RazÃ£o Social InstituiÃ§Ã£o` IS NULL OR
  `RazÃ£o Social InstituiÃ§Ã£o` = 999 THEN  NO_FANTASIA ELSE `RazÃ£o Social InstituiÃ§Ã£o` END
  AS NO_FANTASIA ,
  `SIGLA Instit.`,
  NO_LOGRADOURO || ' ' || ' ' || NU_ENDERECO || ' ' || ' ' || NO_BAIRRO ||' '
  || NO_COMPLEMENTO || ' ' || Cidade || '-' || UF AS ENDERECO,
  `Cod. Mun.`,CO_CEP,
  case when `CNPJ_Gestor Unid. Agrup.` = 999
  or `CNPJ_Gestor Unid. Agrup.` is null then 'Não Informado'
  else `CNPJ_Gestor Unid. Agrup.` end as `CNPJ_Gestor Unid. Agrup.`,
  case when `RazÃ£o Social Gestor Unid. Agrup.` = 999
  or `RazÃ£o Social Gestor Unid. Agrup.` is null then 'Não Informado'
  else `RazÃ£o Social Gestor Unid. Agrup.` end `RazÃ£o Social Gestor Unid. Agrup.`,
  case when `SIGLA Gestor Unid. Agrup.` = 999
  or `SIGLA Gestor Unid. Agrup.` is null then 'Não Informado'
  else `SIGLA Gestor Unid. Agrup.` end
  `SIGLA Gestor Unid. Agrup.`,
  Grupo,SubGrupo,`Tipo_Agrup.`,Fase_Pesqs,CO_CNES,`Nivel AtenÃ§Ã£o`,`Nivel Complex.`,
  Etapa_Pesqs,`Tipo Instit.`,`Classif. Unid.`,CASE WHEN `Classif. Serv. Atend.` IS NULL THEN 0 ELSE `Classif.
  FROM x
  where CO_CNES is not null"
)
TD_INSTITUICAO <- distinct(TD_INSTITUICAO)
```

Figure 4. Data transformation imported by R

```
################instituicao############################
TD_INSTITUICAO[TD_INSTITUICAO$id_class_servico_atendido == 0, "id_class_servico_atendido"] <- -1
TD_INSTITUICAO[TD_INSTITUICAO$id_municipio == '530040', "id_municipio"] <- 530010
TD_INSTITUICAO <- TD_INSTITUICAO[,-19]

dbWriteTable(con, c("dfdwp", "td_instituicao"), value = TD_INSTITUICAO,append = T,row.names = F)
rm(TD_INSTITUICAO)

################TELEFONE############################

TELEFONE <- select(TD_TELEFONE,id_participante = ID_PARTICIPANTE,
                                nu_telefone = TELEFONE)

dbWriteTable(con, c("dfdwp", "td_telefone"), value = TELEFONE,append = T,row.names = F)
rm(TELEFONE,TD_TELEFONE)
```

Figure 5. Data load imported by R

To data visualization, QlikView BI tool was used, the information was crossed and interactive dashboards were created. According to Gartner (2017), Figures 6 to 9 present some results obtained in this research. In Figure 6, initial dashboard analysis reveals that, when Servqual model was applied in a total of responses obtained in an expert groups, an average of 25 responses per question was obtained in selected phases, and from that average, about 2.30% of answers were scores equal to 1, the mean number of grades 2 was 10.10%, the mean for grades 3 was 19.10%, the mean for grades 4 was 26.88% and the mean score for 5 was 41.70%. Thus, in the stage and phases selected (steps 4, phases 1 and 2), the most received grade was 5, in addition to being able to understand that on average the mean number of grades 1 (lowest grade) is lower than the mean of grade 5 (highest grade).

On the central chart and on the smaller chart, you can see the number of responses received grouped by grade, to give a more detailed view of data being analyzed. Initial dashboard is the starting point for other views, working just like an application, where user can navigate from one screen to another using buttons.

After initial data analysis, where general data are observed without a large level of detail, it is possible to observe more specific data, using filters to reach final objective. Several items can be selected in filters, allowing the manager to view information about all institutions that concern him.

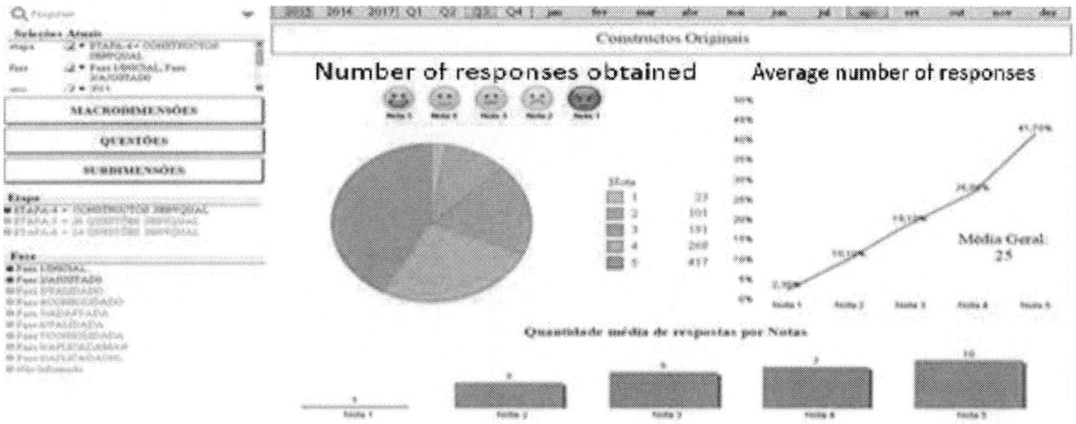

Figure 6. Dashboad QlikView

On the larger bar graph it is possible to compare the average of grade received by institution or set of filtered institutions (General average) in relation to the group that it belongs to, managing entity, microregion and macroregion, grouped by macro dimensions (Tangibility, Reliability, Empathy, Security, Readiness, Access / Accessibility).

The graph at the bottom right is common to all screens because it allows you to see how many responses are being analyzed. The bar chart on the lower left shows the difference between perceived grades and expectations, the red line indicates this difference, and represents a very important analysis within Servqual.

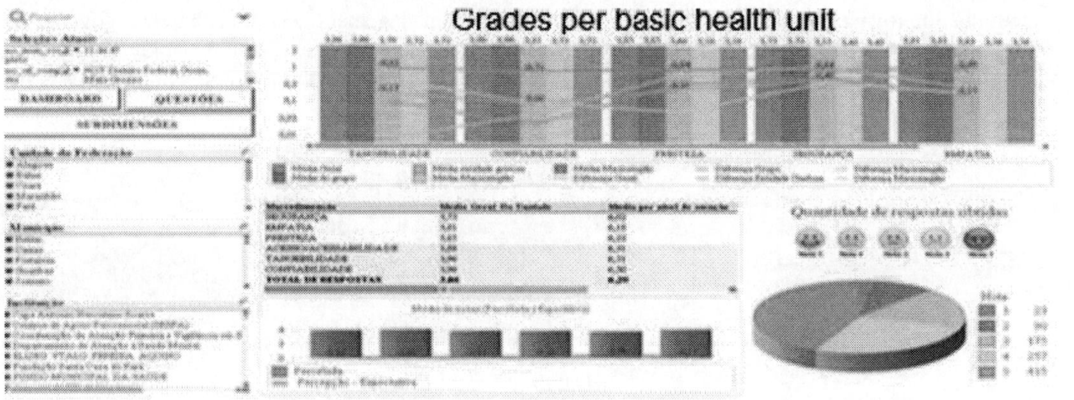

Figure 7. Grade by Macro Dimension QlikView

Figure 8 shows visualization with a higher level of detail, in this screen averages of grades are grouped by questions / constructs, where it is possible to see, for example, quantity of grades 1 that the institution received, or if a filter is not made by data refer to the number of responses for all units that belong to the step and phase selected in dashboard (Figure 6), this table becomes useful when there are a greater number of answers being the object of analysis, in this work we are only showing a sample of data as you can see in pie chart in the upper right corner of the view.

In the above view, it is possible to observe a further level of detail of grades' mean, and in this case mean notes that were obtained by one or more institutions are grouped by sub-dimensions. The central chart and the table present the mean of grades in each sub-dimension, always comparing the institution with the group, managing entity, microregion and macro-region in which that institution belongs.

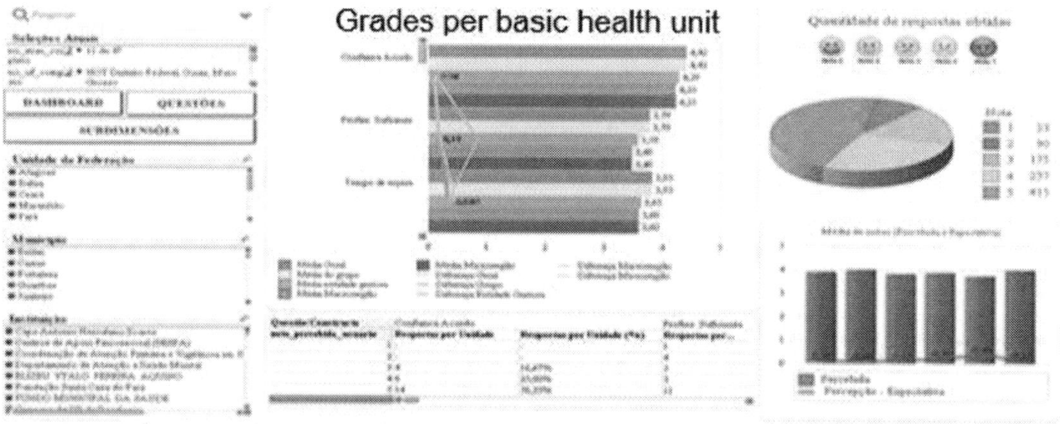

Figure 8. Note by Question QlikView

5. CONCLUSION

Based on what was presented in this research, it can be seen that evaluating quality of services provided to public is of utmost importance. Evaluation of services provided in Brazilian public health with using a scientific method is practically non-existent, which makes it difficult to define strategies to improve services.

Applying BI techniques to a data set such as those generated by satisfaction surveys is of the utmost importance to ensure that collected data can generate quality information. Its application is a focus of this research, in order to allow public managers a powerful visualization of points in which they really need attention, improving strategic decision making and factor management, instrumentalizing governance of quality factors of health units, positively impacting all public health services. From the analysis of these data it is possible, for example, to invest financial resources in areas where the average evaluation was below user's expectation.

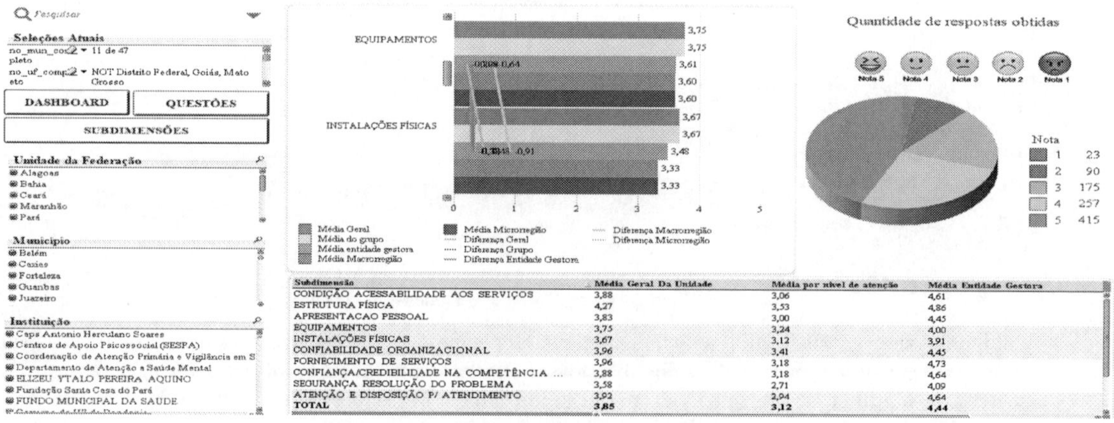

Figure 9. Grades by Subdimension QlikView

Solutions presented in this paper demonstrate a small possibility of analysis for data initially collected; however, in addition to looking at the data in a general and grouped way, comparisons between institutions, municipalities, management entities, macro-regions, microregions, among other possibilities may be useful to assist in the decision-making. Among the possibilities of future works on this research is the creation of articles that can further detail the obtained results with the analysis of dashboards presented here, as well as others that may be created. Foremost, we notice a need to create a software to serve as input of data that are objects of analysis of this work, with main characteristic of being able to be implemented in any platform. Adapting Servqual scale with the objective of evaluating services provided in Brazilian public health allows user perception to be viewed in counterpoint to their expectation, presenting results that really approximate reality, besides highlighting which points should be reviewed by public managers, and can add value in the satisfaction surveys offered by Brazilian Ministry of Health for presenting real results and interpretations.

REFERENCES

Albuquerque, J.D. 2012. *Hospital quality: Analysis of reality in Campina Grande City - Paraíba – Brazil (in Portuguese).* (Doctoral Thesis), Badajoz, Universidade de Extramadura, Espanha.

Babakus, E.; Mangold, G. 1992. *Adapting SERVQUAL Scale Hospital Service: an empirical Investigation.* Health Services Research, 22, Chicago, USA.

Barbosa, L.; Neto, A.P. 2017. *Ludwik Fleck (1896-1961) and knowledge translation: considerations about a concept genealogy (in Portuguese).* Saúde Debate. Rio de Janeiro, Brazil.

Berry, L.L. *et al.* 1994. *Improving service quality in America: Lessons learned; Executive commentary.* The Academy of Management Executive, v. 8, n. 2, p. 21.

Borges, J.B.C, Carvalho, S.M.R., Silva, M.A.M. 2006. *Service quality of hart surgery care of Brazilian health system – SUS (in Portuguese).* Revista Brasileira de Cirurgia Cardiovascular, 25, São José do Rio Preto, SP, Brazil.

Brazil. Ministério da Saúde. 2008. *Nation regulation polices Portaria MS/GM Nº 1.559, de 1º de agosto de 2008 (in Portuguese).* Available in: <http://bvsms.saude.gov.br/bvs/saudelegis/gm/2008/prt1559_01_08_2008.html>. Acessed in: 13 oct. 2017.

Brazil. Ministério da Saúde. 2014. *Good practices for Urgency and Emergency Service Organization and Functioning (in Portuguese): Portaria Nº 354, de 10 de março de 2014.* Available in: <http://bvsms.saude.gov.br/bvs/saudelegis/gm/2014/prt0354_10_03_2014.html> Acessed in 13 oct. 2017.

Brazil. Ministério da Saúde. 2015. *Brazilian health services evaluation program (in Portuguese): Portaria GM/MS Nº 28, de 8 janeiro de 2015.* Available in: <http://bvsms.saude.gov.br/bvs/saudelegis/gm/2015/prt0028_08_01_2015.html> Acessed in 13 oct. 2017.

CFM. *Research reveals that 92% of Brazilian population is insatisfied with Brazilian health system (in Portuguese)*: Conselho Federal de Medicina Brasileiro 2014, Brasília, Brazil.

______. *For 93% of population, Brazilian health system is worst, bad or regular*: Conselho Federal de Medicina 2015, Brasília, Brazil.

CIHR, C.I.O.H.R. 2004.*Knowledge Translation Strategy 2004-2009: Innovation in Action.* CIHR. Ottawa. 2004

Clavier, C.; Sénéchal, Y.; Potvin, L. *A theory - based model of translation practices in public health participatory research. Sociology of Health and Illness.* Henley-on-Thames: Sociology of Health and Illness. 34: 16 p. 2011.

Corrêa, L.; Gianesi, I.G.M. 1994. *Quality and improvement in services systems (in Portuguese).* Administração Estratégica de Serviço. Atlas, São Paulo, Brazil.

Cruz, W.B.S.; Melleiro, M.M. 2007. *Analysis of privaty hospital users satisfaction (in Portuguese).* Revista Escola de Enfermagem da USP. São Paulo, Brazil.

Datafolha. 2017. *Research institute (in Portuguese).* Available in: http://datafolha.folha.uol.com.br/ Acessed in 21 oct.2017.

Datasus. 2017a. *Health informations notebook (in Portuguese).* Available in: <http://www.datasus.gov.br>. Acessed in 21 oct. 2017.

Datasus. 2017b. *System developed by Datasus serves as model for initiative in Peru Program (in Portuguese).* Available in: <http://datasus.saude.gov.br/noticias/atualizacoes/406-sistema-desenvolvido-pelo-datasus-serve-de-modelo-para-iniciativa-de-programa-no-peru>. Acessed in 15 oct. 2017.

De Oliveira, E, Marcondes, K.S; Malere, E.P; Galvão, H.M. 2017. *Services marketing: relationship with customer and strategies for fidelization (in Portuguese).* Revista de Administração da Fatea, v.2, n.2, jan./dez. Available in: <http://www.fatea.br/seer/index.php/raf/article/viewFile/219/176>. Acessed in 14 oct. 2017.

Gartner. 2017. *Gartner Recognizes Qlik® as a Leader in BI and Analytics - Magic Quadrant for Business Intelligence and Analytics Platforms*. Available in: < https://community.qlik.com/docs/DOC-18134>. Acessed in: 04 dec. 2017.

Hercos, B.V.S.; Berezovsky, A. 2004. *Ophthalmologist service quality made to ambulatorial patients of brasilizan health system (in Portuguese) – SUS*. Proceedings of XV Congresso Norte-Nordeste de Oftalmologia, Belo Horizonte, Minas Gerais, Brazil.

Moita, *et al.* 2017. *Tradution, adaptation and cultural validation of Servqual scale in SUS users satisfaction measurement (in Portuguese)*. Proceedings of 3º Congresso Brasileiro de Política, Planejamento e Gestão em Saúde da Abrasco. Natal, Brazil.

Moita, G.F. 2013. *SIG-MASS: management integrated system, monitoring and health services and system evaluation: conceptual introduction* (in Portuguese). In: Congresso CONSAD de Gestão Pública, Brasília, Brazil, 2013.

Parasuraman, A.; Berry, L. L.; Zeithaml, V. A. *Understanding costumer expectation of service*. Sloan Management Review, v. 31, p. 10, 1991.

PNASS. 2015. *Brazilian program to health system evaluation (in Portuguese)*. Available in: http://bvsms.saude.gov.br/bvs/publicacoes/pnass_programa_nacional_avaliacao_servicos.pdf Acessed in 18 jan. 2018.

PostgreSQL. 2018. *The PostgreSQL global development group*. Available in: https://www.postgresql.org/ Acessed in 18 jan. 2018.

R Project, 2017. *R language introdution*. Available in: <https://www.r-project.org/> Acessed in 23 oct. 2017.

Rosalem, V. 2013. *Analysis of actors perception of productivity chain about hospitals services quality in Goiás State (in Portuguese) - Brazil.* Escola de Administração de Empresas de São Paulo, São Paulo, Brazil.

Rud, O.P. 2009. *Business intelligence success factors: tools for aligning your business in the global economy.* John Wiley & Sons, Inc. New Jersey, USA.

Sybase. *SAP PowerDesigner: Enterprise Architecture tools for digital transformation success.* Available in: <https://www.sap.com/products/powerdesigner-data-modeling-tools.html>. Acessed in 01 nov. 2017.

QlikTech, 2017. *Introdution to QlikView*. Available in <https://www.qlik.com/pt-br/products/qlikview> Acessed in 01 nov. 2017

WHO, W. H. O. *Bridging the "Know-Do" Gap: Meeting on Knowledge Translation in Global Health*. WHO. Gen.

KNOWLEDGE ORCHESTRATION AND ACTIVITY OBJECTS IN CROWDSOURCED DIGITAL INNOVATION

Jiayuan Liu
University of Warwick, United Kingdom

ABSTRACT

In this study, I explore how activity objects orchestrate knowledge for crowdsourced digital innovation. Adopting a mixed-methods research approach, my quantitative results from 355 questionnaires corroborate the three hypotheses, and my qualitative evidence collected from 48 interviews enriches my explanations. As a result, I found that by acting as a trigger for expansive learning, and a director and motivator of crowdsourcing communities, activity objects serve to facilitate the sharing, acquisition, and integration of knowledge, coordinating the knowledge heterogeneity and fragmentation for crowdsourced digital innovation.

KEYWORDS

Activity Object, Knowledge Orchestration, Digital Innovation

1. INTRODUCTION

Crowdsourcing communities have increasingly got involved in the process of digital innovation, attracting significant attention to their innovation networks. Such networks are defined as doubly distributed innovation networks, where the organizational and technological control over product components is distributed across firms of different kinds, and knowledge is distributed across heterogeneous specialties (Yoo et al. 2010). However, such innovation networks also create their own challenge: the knowledge heterogeneity and fragmentation (Lyytinen et al. 2015). To address this challenge, a certain amount of orchestration is needed for the network actors to appropriately transfer, accept, and leverage knowledge without sacrificing flexibility and independence. Drawing on a network orchestration model (Dhanaraj & Parkhe 2006), I identify three activities as knowledge orchestration: knowledge sharing, knowledge acquisition, and knowledge integration. As human activity is always mediated by cultural artefacts (Engeström 1999), scholars suggested that activity objects could be a useful starting point in addressing the knowledge orchestration. According to Miettinen (2005), activity objects are partially emergent, partially fragmented and partially contradictory, as well as under-defined, unfolding objects in collaboration; simultaneously, they maintain the activities around the pursuit of themselves. Although many scholars recognized the importance of cultural artefacts (Kaptelinin & Nardi 2006), our understanding of how activity objects serve to orchestrate knowledge for crowdsourced digital innovation is still very limited. Thus, I aim to explore how activity objects influence the sharing, acquisition and integration of knowledge, thereby coordinating its heterogeneity and counter its fragmentation for crowdsourced digital innovation?

2. THEORETICAL BACKGROUND & HYPOTHESIS DEVELOPMENT

According to cultural historical activity theory (Engeström 1999; Kaptelinin & Nardi 2006), an activity's object is emergent, fragmented, and contradictory, and collective human activity is always maintained around the pursuit of a partially emergent, partially fragmented, and partially contradictory object. Hence, an activity object can be viewed as a conflict trigger and a director and motivator of the community that evolves and revolves around itself (Nicolini et al. 2012). Specifically, an activity object can act as a representation for crowdsourced digital innovation from three perspectives. First, because an activity object is inherently multi-faceted, fragmented, and disputed, it can create a socio-material community around itself, into which "a naturally occurring and evolving collection of people" with contradictory interests, orientations and interpretations "engage in particular kinds of activity", and "develop and share ways of doing things as a result of their joint involvement in that activity" (Galagan 1993: 33). As an activity object attracts heterogeneous actors with diverse knowledge boundaries to engage in the process of digital innovation, a crowdsourcing community emerges that absorbs the wisdom of each actor, and triggers reflective learning (Patil & Lee 2016). Second, an activity object is partly predetermined and partly emergent, reflecting the originally embedded, and constantly evolving interests of the actors involved (Nicolini et al. 2012). Because a cultural artefact serves as an object of a crowdsourced digital innovation activity, it enables the collective action to emerge around it according to a shared goal; simultaneously, it is also the result of the practices and expectations of the crowdsourced communities that gather around it (Miettinen 2005). As widely distributed, heterogeneous actors engage in the process of digital innovation, an activity object can help them "find the signal in the noise" while avoiding irrelevant content (Paul et al. 2012). Third, as Leont'ev (1978: 66) emphasized, "the object of an activity is its true motive". An activity object is able to motivate its crowdsourcing communities to continually engage in the process of digital innovation, fuelling the collective activity. Based on the social exchange theory (Lanham 2006), the motives for actors devoting themselves to crowdsourced activities can either be extrinsic or intrinsic (Choudhury et al. 2014). Actors who contribute high-quality knowledge to crowdsourced digital innovation, expect to improve their reputation as a form of extrinsic reward (Jin et al. 2015). Besides reputation, attention, which has become a scarce resource in the information age, is another significant extrinsic motivator (Lanham 2006). In this way, network actors are extrinsically motivated to exchange their knowledge for reputation and attention, which can also be explained in terms of the concept of desire, drive or struggle for recognition (Hegel 1977, 1983). Specifically, social recognition is perceived as a primary source of personal identity, which is especially significant in crowdsourced activities where division of labour is a source of individuality (Miettinen 2005). This kind of social recognition can be achieved by objectified actions and objects (Kojève 1969). This is because, as actors become increasingly recognized by participating in a collective activity, such participation can be objectified in the products of their actions, with their achievements constituting the objectified demonstration of their capability to contribute to their communities and the target activity (Knorr-Cetina 1997). With extrinsic benefits providing the main motivations to initiate the behaviour of knowledge contribution, intrinsic rewards involved in social exchanges that emphasize unspecified obligations, such as social affiliation and feelings of belonging, trust and self-actualization, carry more weight in their motivation of continuous engagement in the community (Sigala & Chalkiti 2015). Nicolini et al. (2012) pointed out that activity objects can trigger intimate emotional attachment that is not restricted to individuals but is performed as an engine of solidarity, a collective obligation and an emotional affiliation, constituting a morally binding force among community members.

As digital innovation is seen as inherently layered, it increasingly pushes heterogeneous actors to connect across multiple boundaries to create new value-in-use, forming a crowdsourced innovation network (Huang et al. 2017). However, such a network brings its own challenges. Specifically, the radical reduction of communication and coordination costs makes affordable the participation in the innovation process of otherwise disconnected actors, distributing the coordination of innovation activities more widely (Yoo et al. 2010). In addition, the loosely coupled layers embedded in the innovation networks enable high levels of flexibility but result in greater fragmentation of the knowledge base common to the network actors (Nätti et al. 2006). Furthermore, the convergence of digital technology combines resources and components in unforeseeable ways, which cumulatively expands the cognitive heterogeneity along the 'rolling edge' of the network actors' capabilities (Yoo et al. 2010). All of this can lead to the knowledge becoming too fragmented and heterogeneous to control. Confronted with this problem, Yoo et al. (2010) suggested that knowledge orchestration could be a solution. Drawing on a network orchestration model (Dhanaraj & Parkhe 2006), I define knowledge orchestration as the combination of knowledge sharing, knowledge acquisition and knowledge integration. First, *knowledge sharing* concerns the ease with which knowledge is transferred within a network (Dhanaraj & Parkhe 2006). Knowledge transfer is predominantly referred to in the network literature as an 'asset' that carries value for a network (Nahapiet & Ghoshal 1998). Particular emphasis is placed on standardizing or establishing compatible methods of communication to facilitate the sharing of this form of intellectual capital across the 'syntactic' boundaries (Carlile 2002), from one actor to the next. Second, when the transferred knowledge is complex and there is not clarity of purpose, then the challenge shifts to the *acquisition of the knowledge*, where a 'semantic' approach (Carlile 2002) is needed to recognize the different ways in which each actor interprets and accepts the disseminated message. Third and last, *knowledge integration* occurs - and the full potential of the innovation network is only realized - if and when the heterogeneous knowledge resources are combined together and transformed into an innovation (Crossan

& Inkpen 1995). Carlile (2002) proposed a 'pragmatic' view of knowledge, and in crowdsourced digital innovation, this poses a challenge for the network actors, namely, fully exploring their unique local context, without losing their ability to interrelate and transform different types of 'hard-won' knowledge into an innovation that transcends its customary pragmatic boundaries.

Drawing on the literature, I develop three hypotheses to examine the impact of activity objects on knowledge sharing, knowledge acquisition and knowledge integration. According to Nicolini et al. (2012), activity objects can create a crowdsourcing community, that is not an integrated whole where parts move in harmony, but is rather a community without unity, in which conflicts abound. Because a wide collection of contradictory assumptions and interpretations regarding problems enables community members to search for optimal solutions, evaluate diverse methods, and question invalid answers, a reflective learning takes place (Scarbrough et al. 2004). Such expansive learning, which involves overcoming heterogeneous boundaries in the transfer and flow of knowledge arising from pre-established cognitive divisions of the community actors involved (Scarbrough et al. 2004), increases their opportunity to share dispersed pieces of knowledge for crowdsourced innovation (Sigalaa & Chalkiti 2015). In addition, when crowdsourcing community boundaries overlap or cross during the process of mutually communicating, discussing, negotiating, and innovating (Boland & Tenkasi 1995), a trading zone may emerge in which a high level of learning flows in multiple directions, and knowledge can travel from one community into another freely, facilitating the mobilization of knowledge (Boland et al. 2007). Furthermore, as a socially interactive cultural artefact, an activity object can drive socio-emotional forces such as trust, commitment and loyalty, and trigger an ethical community culture, conducive to information diffusion and knowledge mobilization (Tsai 2001). Hence, I hypothesize that:

H1: Activity objects serve to foster knowledge sharing for crowdsourced digital innovation.

Because an activity object creates a community around itself with the passage of time, knowledge acquisition is facilitated, because the best way to access knowledge is to interact with the community (Mandl et al. 1996). Specifically, from the perspective of communities of practices, knowledge assimilation is not about absorbing information, but rather is about becoming a part of a community, which is a social process built around informed participation (Engeström 1991). In crowdsourcing communities where learning is identified to be nothing more than accepting socially shared beliefs and practices, activity objects foster the social process of enculturation, promoting the acquisition of knowledge that includes not only procedural and declarative expertise but also social beliefs and values (Lave & Wenger 1991). From the perspective of boundaries of different communities of practice, one platform by which expansive learning occurs is through addressing these boundaries of different communities (Lave 1992). When members of different communities learn from one another, and have to incorporate distributed pieces of knowledge from each member for problem-solving, this process involves the change of their identity, through which expansive learning as well as knowledge acquisition can occur (Merry 1995). At the same time, friction is likely to happen between heterogeneous actors at the boundaries of different communities of practices, as members as a whole iteratively affect each other by building and modifying the changes in each other's identities (Stamps 1997). Such inter-community boundaries are the places where knowledge creation and acquisition occur, where diverse actors engage in an expansive learning to compare and contrast their viewpoints with each community, thereby fostering the assimilation of 'knowledge-in-context' in terms of their various requirements (Paul et al. 2012). Furthermore, activity objects can attach the social desire for recognition and approval to themselves (Miettinen 2005), perceived as a primary source of motives for the members to make contributions to their communities. As the number of actors motivated to contribute their knowledge to crowdsourced digital innovation increases, activity objects broaden the knowledge that improves the conditions essential for the acquisition of knowledge (Davenport & Perusak 1998). Hence, I hypothesize that:

H2: Activity objects serve to foster knowledge acquisition for crowdsourced digital innovation.

Drawing on the potentially contradictory nature of collective activity (Miettinen & Virkkunen 2005), activity objects trigger contradictions and conflicts that can spur expansive learning (Engeström 1987), essential for the coordination and integration of knowledge. Specifically, the cognitive conflicts induced by the object of an activity enable the community members to realize their incomplete ideas, appreciate dissenting views, resolve issues of controversy and create optimal solutions, resulting in a high level of expansive learning (Sockalingam 2000). Such learning plays a critical role in overcoming pragmatic boundaries to the transfer of knowledge resulting from the divisions in practice associated with differing in political interests (Carlile 2002). Furthermore, activity objects can provide the members who pursue reputation improvement with extrinsic motivators for continually contributing to the community. By inducing the desire for recognition among the actors, the object of an activity creates an affective relationship with its actors, with which they are engaging in a collective activity (Miettinen 2005). As more members are motivated to participate in high-order reflective learning, activity artefacts facilitate the exchange of information and the mobilization of cognitive resources that foster the assembly, combination and recombination of heterogeneous pieces of knowledge for crowdsourced innovation. Hence, I hypothesize that:

H3: Activity objects serve to foster knowledge integration for crowdsourced digital innovation.

3. RESEARCH DESIGN: ZHIHU AS AN ACTIVITY OBJECT

In this study, I selected "*Zhihu*"- a Chinese question-and-answer (Q&A) website, where widely distributed actors across heterogeneous communities create questions, crowd-source the search, and vote for high-quality answers- as a representative object of crowdsourced digital innovation activity for three reasons. First, as a community platform, *Zhihu* is able to attract a number of actors with heterogeneous expertise and potentially contradictory interests to engage in the target activity of asking and answering questions, thus creating a crowdsourcing community around it for digital innovation. Because, as a social network website, *Zhihu* is inherently disputatious, it can also act as a trigger of conflict for its crowdsourcing communities, a place where they can engage in an expansive learning by posting challenging Q&As, searching for topics of interest, voting answers up or down and commenting on controversial content. Second, as highly distributed, heterogeneous online actors engage in the process of asking and answering questions, *Zhihu* is able to help them "find the signal in the noise", while avoiding irrelevant content (Paul et al. 2012). Specifically, *Zhihu* supports a voting service such that more authoritative answers can get up-voted to the top of the answer list, while less helpful answers can get down-voted and eventually filtered out (Patil & Lee 2016). In this way, *Zhihu* directs the process of separating high-quality answers from ill-formed alternatives on the basis of the numbers of votes received. The 'invite' function of *Zhihu* also allows users to tag specific individuals in relation to particular questions to try and ensure that these questions are answered by the most authoritative experts. Hence, *Zhihu* directs the crowdsourced digital innovation activity by leveraging appropriate social connections to help users acquire high-quality answers. Third, *Zhihu* serves to motivate its crowdsourcing communities to continually contribute to the collective activity of asking and answering questions, by providing them with extrinsic and intrinsic incentives. In terms of extrinsic incentives, because online users are motivated to exchange their high-quality knowledge for reputation and attention, *Zhihu* is able to recognize, acknowledge and reward the user contributions via its voting mechanism (Jin et al. 2015). In terms of intrinsic incentives, *Zhihu* provides a place where feelings of belonging, loyalty and trust can be engendered among a 'family' of (invisible) friends.

3.1 Quantitative Research and Results

In this study, I used web-based surveys to test the hypotheses. The study population consisted of 500 *Zhihu* users in the groups of digital product innovation, software design and apps use. I distributed 500 questionnaires and deemed 355 usable for the quantitative analysis. To collect reliable data, I asked key informants to respond to the surveys, typically well-known *Zhihu* users with a good reputation and large numbers of up-votes. Of the response population of 355, 301 had been registered on *Zhihu* for more than three years; those with a PhD numbered 105, while those with industrial experience in digital innovation accounted for 65%. In terms of measurement, I first measured *Zhihu* as an activity object (ZH) with four items by asking respondents whether in their crowdsourced digital innovation activity *Zhihu*: (1) created a community around the activity where they engaged in expansive learning and crowdsourced to absorb the wisdom of each other; (2) directed them to find useful answers, while avoiding irrelevant content; (3) motivated them to ask and answer questions by recognizing and rewarding their unique contributions; (4) encouraged them to commit to the activity and their community by triggering feelings of belonging and trust. Second, I used four items to measure knowledge sharing (KS) by asking respondents if they: (1) developed a compatible communication method to promote the transfer of intellectual capital such as experiences, expertise and creative ideas from one actor to the next (Dhanaraj & Parkhe 2006); (2) discussed particular technologies with one another, and accessed the knowledge held by the other members; (3) created and maintained a certain common ground for communication and interaction; (4) promoted mutual transparency, and avoided hiding information from each other during the process of innovation. Third, I used three items to measure knowledge acquisition (KA) by asking respondents if they: (1) recognized and developed the different ways in which each actor interprets and accepts the disseminated message; (2) adequately received and assimilated the shared knowledge resources, increasing their knowledge base (Yang 2005); (3) organized live technology training for the purpose of idea diffusion and solution acquisition (Lynn et al. 2000). Last, I measured knowledge integration (KI) with four items by asking respondents if they: (1) created a full understanding of each other's expertise and developed an ability to scan, filter and engage relevant network actors for problem-solving (Benkler 2006); (2) fully explored each member's unique local context, while carefully interrelating their expertise with that of others (Carlile 2002); (3) maximized the dispersed contributions stemming from a diverse knowledge base while creating a coherent culture; (4) understood how individuals leverage their diverse domains of expertise for innovation.

In terms of a measurement model (Table 1), I first conducted an exploratory factor analysis of the four measures (ZH, KS, KA, KI), by using a principal axis factoring analysis with *Oblimin* oblique rotation with Kaiser normalization rotation. Specifically, KMO was 0.786, indicating that the data was suitable for factor analysis. In addition, the data showed support for the four factors, which had eigenvalues greater than 1 and explained 96.129% of the variance. Furthermore, the measures suitably represented the four factors whereby all the primary loadings exceeded 0.709. Finally, the Cronbach's alpha was 0.906, implying a high reliability of internal consistency. I also conducted a confirmatory factor analysis to estimate the model using SPSS Amos, consistent with Anderson and Gerbing's (1988) two-step approach. First, all indexes displayed a good fit with the model: the observed CMIN was 421.15 with 399 DF, the NFI was 0.990, CFI was 0.980, and RMSEA was 0.021, suggesting a good model fit. Second, I examined the convergent validity by testing the significance of the factor loadings and their gap to the S.E. (Koufteros 1999). All item loadings were above the suggested cut-off of 0.6 (Hair et al., 1998), with a strong significance level. Additionally, all the S.E. values were around 0.1, indicating that all the items had a clear relationship with their own latent variables. Furthermore, all the CR values of the latent variables were above the criterion of 0.7 (Hair et al. 1998), showing a good convergent validity. Finally, all the square roots of the AVE shown on the diagonal of the correlation matrix were greater than the off-diagonal construct correlations, implying a good discriminant validity (Koufteros 1999). With regard to the structural model (Figure 1), I used Amos to test the hypotheses. All the paths were significant, supporting the three hypothesized relationships. The coefficients of *Zhihu* were positive and significant for knowledge sharing (β =.23, $p<.01$), knowledge acquisition (β= .53, $p<.001$), and knowledge integration (β= .19, $p<.01$). This support H1, H2 and H3, indicating that, as an activity object, *Zhihu* fosters the sharing, acquisition, and integration of knowledge for crowdsourced digital innovation.

Table 1. The Result of the Measurement Model

Constructs	Items	Loading	S.D.	C.R.	KMO	Cronbach's α	ZH	KS	KA	KI
Zhihu as an Activity Object	ZH1	.709	.116	.792	.811	.893	.756*			
	ZH2	.823	.100							
	ZH3	.765	.114							
	ZH4	.754	.115							
Knowledge Sharing	KS1	.767	.111	.801	.891	.918	.431	.827		
	KS2	.712	.124							
	KS3	.803	.095							
	KS4	.907	.101							
Knowledge Acquisition	KA1	.801	.129	.751	.767	.907	.311	.225	.763	
	KA2	.822	.135							
	KA3	.711	.092							
Knowledge Integration	KI1	.798	.091	.719	.765	.906	.315	.301	.232	.731
	KI2	.711	.099							
	KI3	.766	.118							
	KI4	.812	.109							

*Square root of average variance extracted

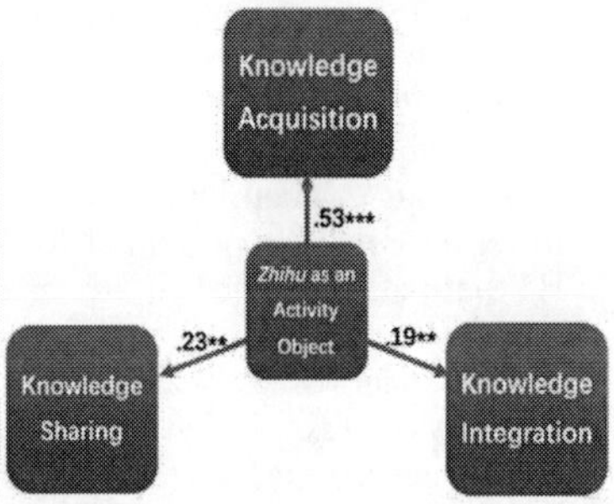

Figure 1. The result of the structural model

3.2 Qualitative Research and Results

In this part, I used interviews to explore how *Zhihu* affects the sharing, acquisition and integration of knowledge, enriching the quantitative results with supplementary evidence. Specifically, I conducted 48 semi-structured interviews. To collect reliable data, I selected those *Zhihu* users who frequently use their expertise to provide high-quality answers. Moving to data analysis, I coded the interview transcripts to identify key themes and categories pertaining to each of the questions. I used some initial codes based on the known theoretical concepts in the literature as a guide to categorize the transcripts. During the process of recursively moving back and forth between original recordings and transcripts, my appreciation of the link between *Zhihu*, knowledge sharing, knowledge acquisition and knowledge integration emerged progressively.

The quantitative result for hypothesis H1 was corroborated by my interview data. Specifically, I found that *Zhihu* created a crowdsourcing community, whose trajectory was shaped by different knowledge relationships, and where contradictions abounded to trigger expansive learning. As one user said: "*Usually one question brings us together. We see the question first, then we come to use our expertise to answer the question. We also look at others' answers, compare and contrast their answers with ourselves. It is normal that we have different views. It is these different interpretations that make us evaluate multiple methods, seek optimal solutions, and abandon invalid answers.*" In addition, some interviewees believed that *Zhihu* triggered socio-emotional forces among them, which promoted the information flow and fostered the knowledge diffusion. Specifically, one user highlighted how *Zhihu* created an ethical and cohesive culture within his community: "*Because we are all interested in iOS 10.1.1, it is easy for us to discuss the function of this system, its potential and its bugs. So, it is not weird that during the process of asking and answering questions together, we can generate a high trust in each other's willingness and competence to solve problems.*" My qualitative data similarly made further sense of hypothesis H2. Most interviewees highlighted the role of *Zhihu* in separating valuable answers from alternatives in directing them in the acquisition of high-quality knowledge. Specifically, *Zhihu* provides a space where valuable answers generally get up-voted to the top of the answer list, while irrelevant content gets down-voted and eventually filtered out. The 'invite' mechanism of *Zhihu* also leveraged proper social connections to help its users gain authoritative answers from primary information sources, by allowing them to tag persons who have direct evidence on specific questions. As one interviewee highlighted: "*Zhihu is an amazing place. For example, when you ask a question about comparing Huawei Mate 9 with iPhone 7, it is possible that it will be a designer working within Huawei who provides you with a (very authoritative) answer.*" Nevertheless, some interviewees argued that an answer from such primary knowledge sources does not necessarily represent a higher quality response. In order to find the "real" signal in the noise, *Zhihu* engages its users in a reflective dialogue, where they are empowered to access a pool of diverse answers, compare and contrast their answers with others, and negotiate their perspectives mutually, fostering the assimilation of 'knowledge-in-context' in terms of their various requirements (Paul et al., 2012). As one user reported: "*Many people up-vote the answers from primary information sources, but I only respect logic. If the logic of an answer convinces me, I will give it an up-vote. If not, I tend to argue with the answer provider, in order to create a better answer.*" In addition, some interviewees believed that *Zhihu* propelled them to continually engage in the process of creating questions and formulating answers, by providing them with reputation and attention. Specifically, I found that *Zhihu*'s function of assessing the helpfulness of responses attracted answers from many users pursuing reputation improvement. This was reflected in one interview: "*When I receive up-votes from others, I can really feel their approval of my answer. This gives me more confidence to answer other questions, in order to achieve more up-votes. I want to use my expertise to help others solve problems, but I also want social recognition for my contribution. These two requirements don't conflict with each other.*" As increasing knowledge is contributed via the answer posting, *Zhihu* broadens the knowledge available to its users, fostering conditions essential for the acquisition of knowledge. Last, the quantitative results for hypothesis H3 were also enriched by my interviews. Most users highlighted that *Zhihu* brought them into contact with cognitive conflicts that encouraged them to realize their incomplete ideas, embrace dissenting views, resolve controversial issues, and seek optimal solutions. Thus, one interviewee reported: "*Although we share a common interest, we have different experiences. It is normal that we have various ways of thinking*". Hence, these interviewees were empowered to engage in a significant learning critical to overcoming pragmatic barriers to the transfer of knowledge resulting from the divisions in practice, and conducive to the transformation of knowledge for innovation. This was seen in one interview: "*When we group together around one specific question that we all are interested in, we can have a full picture of each other's expertise, thereby recognizing the knowledge needed for answering this question, tinkering with various pieces of knowledge in parallel, and developing a shared understanding for problem-solving.*"

4. DISCUSSION, IMPLICATIONS AND CONCLUSION

In combination, my quantitative and qualitative results demonstrate how activity objects serve to orchestrate knowledge for crowdsourced digital innovation. Therefore, I make two contributions. My first contribution is to recognize *Zhihu* as a trigger for expansive learning, and a director and motivator of crowdsourcing communities in facilitating the sharing, acquisition and integration of knowledge, thereby presenting a novel private-collective model for crowdsourced digital innovation with an integration of personal investment and collective action (Trompette et al. 2008). Specifically, this private-collective model for crowdsourced digital innovation involves an effective coordination between mutually dependent collective action and personal investment (Trompette et al., 2008). With regard to collective action, I identified the ability of *Zhihu* to direct the qualifying process to ensure the attainment of high-quality answers, and even support the shift from highly credible ideas to potential innovation opportunities. This co-evaluation process combines quantitative and qualitative means. For the quantitative measures, the crowd can evaluate an answer's usefulness via voting, with more authoritative answers getting up-voted, and less popular ones getting down-voted and filtered out. By attributing a "like" to an answer to indicate how many users favour it, *Zhihu* directs the process of separating high-quality content from alternatives, which saves significant time and allows crowdsourcing communities to make more accurate decisions. For the qualitative means, the crowd may offer their various opinions on certain questions, comment on answers given or convert novel ideas into feasible plans. For example, *Zhihu*'s 'invite' mechanism enables the crowd to tag users in relation to certain questions to obtain more useful answers. Thus, I highlighted the capacity of *Zhihu* to shape the collective activity and "find the signal in the noise" for crowdsourced digital innovation (Paul et al. 2012). In terms of personal investment, I recognized the ability of *Zhihu* to encourage the investment of the diverse knowledge resources of intrinsically and extrinsically motivated users in the creation of Q&As, promoting the aggregation of added-value contributions to crowdsourced digital innovation (Trompette et al. 2008). For the extrinsic incentives, I emphasized *Zhihu*'s ability to provide its users with a space to compete for each other's attention and promote their future engagement, by recognizing and rewarding their differing contributions, based on the fact that online communities tend to exchange their knowledge for attention. As Lanham (2006) indicated, social recognition indeed dominates free-riding incentives, and a member with a larger audience size may contribute more to the community. I also highlighted the capacity of *Zhihu* to give its users intrinsic incentives. Whereas crowdsourcing communities are seen as densely interconnected networks of actors, *Zhihu* not only offers a space for knowledge orchestration, but it also encourages reciprocal behaviours by identifying, detailing and highlighting user contributions. Thus, *Zhihu* creates a sense of community, builds a tone of collaboration, and concentrates shared norms of trust, gratitude and respect that members have toward each other to motivate them to contribute without an a priori specified reward in sight. For my second contribution, the focus on the independent role of an activity object as a trigger for expansive learning and a director and motivator of knowledge orchestration contributes a novel understanding of the roles of material artefacts and humans in crowdsourced digital innovation. Orlikowski (2007) perceived material artefacts as technical objects or managerial instruments, which are generally utilized to sustain and support the daily work in the hands of managers who speak on their behalf. Vázquez (2006) emphasized the active role of managers as the agents of control through supervision or normative means. Drawing on this work, I have highlighted the active role of these material artefacts in enabling networks of actors to freely share, acquire and integrate knowledge, and in mediating dialogue between differing perspectives, maximizing the wisdom of the crowd for digital innovation. In this way, my research provides a new insight into how material artefacts can coexist with other types of formal managerial control in a beneficial manner, geared toward coordinating the fragmented and heterogeneous knowledge for crowdsourced digital innovation. Specifically, I gave prominence to activity objects that have been applied to collaborative development within virtual communities of practice (Hemetsberger & Reinhardt 2009), and linked crowdsourcing communities to digital innovation. 'Crowdsourcing', combining 'crowd' in terms of 'the wisdom of crowds' and '(out)sourcing' in the sense of opening up the R&D process to a distributed network of heterogeneous actors via an open call, is a key trend that has been studied by many scholars (Bayus 2013; Howe 2006). Communities, seen as the basic organic force, are essential for achieving network effects (Surowiecki 2004). By viewing crowdsourced digital innovation as an object-oriented, culturally mediated and collective human activity (Engeström 1999), I presented the ability of activity objects to orchestrate knowledge by providing expansive learning, direction, and motivation for the crowdsourced digital innovation activity.

In terms of theoretical implications, by treating *Zhihu* as an activity object that creates crowdsourcing communities around it for digital innovation, I add to the work of Mladenow et al. (2014) and Trompette et al. (2008), who linked crowdsourcing to open innovation and recognized a community platform as an "interesting" subject for scholars. My focus on *Zhihu*'s role as a director and motivator presents a novel private-collective model for crowdsourced digital innovation, with the integration of collective action in distinguishing high-quality content from alternatives, and the personal investment of fragmented and heterogeneous knowledge resources. Thus, my study has a theoretical implication for the development of new collaboration rules among virtual crowdsourcing communities, for managing tensions to trigger expansive learning, for identifying extrinsic and intrinsic incentives to enhance individual involvement, and for establishing the collective brain to direct the innovation activity. I also furnish two practical suggestions. First, my focus on *Zhihu*'s director role has a practical implication for the design of such a Q&A website. By emphasizing *Zhihu*'s capacity to select the best answers, generally from primary information sources, I suggest that such community platforms should promote the creation of social networks based on a real-name registration policy, which provides users with improved credibility when judging others' authoritativeness. Second, for those firms aiming to cooperate with crowdsourcing communities to leverage differentiated cognitive resources into something that creates novel meaning, my study provides a practical implication for the identification of motivation to encourage involved actors to contribute to crowdsourced activities.

REFERENCES

Boland, R. J., Lyytinen, K. and Yoo, Y. (2007), "Wakes of Innovation in Project Networks."

Carlile, P. R. (2002), "A pragmatic view of knowledge and boundaries: Boundary objects in new product development," *Organization Science*, 13 (4), 442–455.

Davenport, T. H. and Perusak, L. (1998), *Working knowledge*, Boston, MA: Harvard Business School.

Dhanaraj, C and Parkhe (2006), "Orchestrating innovation networks," *Academy of Management Review.*

Engeström, Y. (1999), "Activity theory and individual social transformation."

Galagan, P. A. (1993), "The search for the poetry of work," *Training and Development* 47 (10), 33-37.

Granovetter, M. S. (1973), "The Strength of Weak Ties," *American Journal Of Sociology* (78).

Hegel, J. (1977), *Phenomenology of spirit* (A.V. Miller, Trans.). Oxford, UK: Oxford University Press.

Jin, J., Li, Y., Zhong, X. and Zhai, L. (2015), "Why users contribute knowledge to online communities: An empirical study of an online Q&A community," *Information & Management,* (52), 840–849.

Kaptelinin, V. and Nardi, B. A. (2006), *Acting with Technology: Activity Theory and Interaction Design*.

Knorr Cetina, K. (1997), "Sociality with objects: social relations in post-social knowledge societies".

Lanham, R. A. (2006), *The Economics of Attention: Style and Substance in the Age of Information*.

Lave, J. and Wenger, E. (1991), *Situated learning: Legitimate peripheral participation*.

Leont'ev, A. N. 1978. *Activity, Consciousness, and Personality*, Englewood Cliffs, NJ: Prentice Hall.

Lyytinen, K., Yoo, Y., Richard, J. and Boland, J. (2015), 'Digital product innovation within four classes of innovation networks', *Information Systems Journal*, 1-28.

Miettinen, R. (2005), "Object of activity and individual motivation," *Mind, Culture, Activity* 12(1).

Miettinen, R. and Virkkunen, J. (2005), 'Epistemic objects, artefacts, and organizational change'.

Mladenow, A., Bauer, C. and Strauss, C. (2014), "Social Crowd Integration in New Product Development: Crowdsourcing Communities Nourish the Open Innovation Paradigm."

Nätti, S. and Halinen, A. and Hanttu, N. (2006), "Customer Knowledge Transfer and Key Account Management in Professional Service Organisations."

Nicolini, D., Mengis, J. and Swan, J. (2012), "Understanding the Role of Objects in Cross-Disciplinary Collaboration," *Organization Science* 23 (3), 612–629.

Patil, S. and Lee, K. (2016), "Detecting experts on Quora: by their activity, quality of answers, linguistic characteristics and temporal behaviors," *Social Network Analysis and Mining* 6 (5), 1-11.

Rennstam, J. (2012), "Object-Control: A Study of Technologically Dense Knowledge Work".

Rheinberger, H. (1997), *Toward a History of Epistemic Things: Synthesizing Proteins in the Test Tube*.

Scarbrough, H., Swan, J., Laurent, S., Bresnen, M., Edelman, L. and Newell, S. (2004), "Project-Based Learning and the Role of Learning Boundaries," *Organization Studies,* 25 (9), 1579–1600.

Sigala, M. and Chalkiti, K. (2015), "Knowledge management, social media and employee creativity," *International Journal of Hospitality Management* (45), 44–58.

Trompette, P., Chanal, V. and Pelissier, C. (2008), "Crowdsourcing as a way to access external knowledge for innovation: Control, incentive and coordination in hybrid forms of innovation."

Yoo, Y., Henfridsson, O. and Lyytinen, K. (2010), "Research Commentary The New Organizing Logic of Digital Innovation: An Agenda for Information Systems Research," *Information Systems Research.*

STREAMLINING PROCESSES FOR DIGITALIZATION

Azeem Lodhi, Veit Köppen, Gunter Saake and Klaus Turowski
Institute for Technical and Business Information Systems
University of Magdeburg, Magdeburg, Germany

ABSTRACT

New trends and technological developments bring opportunities and threats for enterprises at the same time. Organizations which do not adapt their strategies have to fight for their survival. Information Technology plays vital role in this evolution. Enterprises still need a seamless process from idea initiation till its implementation and improvement. The gap exists between the research and its application in an enterprise. Organization need to streamline their processes for Digitalization. In this paper, we provide an analytical framework for analysis and improvement of business processes. We also propose an analytical process modelling language to support the framework and to identify the deficiencies in processes. We also provide constructs and patterns of our proposed modeling language which are independent of a specific modeling language. The analytical business process modeling language is further explained with the help of a case study and demonstrated by extending an existing modeling language.

KEYWORDS

Business Process Modeling, Performance Representation, Business Process Analysis, Analytical Framework, Improvement

1. INTRODUCTION

The business world is competitive and fierce competition exists between companies due to globalization, emerging technologies, and digitalization. Even small companies with niche characteristics give competition to well-established companies and have a reach to wider international markets. A research in 2014 indicated that in the span of 14 years (since 2000), 52% of companies in the Fortune 500 have disappeared from the list (either gone bankrupt, been acquired or ceased to exists) (Wang, 2014). Only 12% companies (60 in total) still in Fortune 500 list since 1955 as analyzed in (The American Enterprise Institute, 2017). Old products are replaced by new products and services (e.g. camera films with digital cameras).

In the past three decades, significant technological development has been made and reached to wider society. This has not only increased the competition between companies, but also raised the expectation of customers. Therefore, enterprises seek new ways to provide innovative and quality services to satisfy customer's needs. Different enterprises attract and involve customers with digital experiences. These new ways also paved the way for new business models to generate more revenue and serve different customer segments.

There are different levels of developments and their implementations in organizations with respect to time as discussed in (Khan & Turowski, 2016b). At universities and research institutes, significant developments have been made in research. These developments are industrialized or applied in organizations after a certain period of time (3-6 years approximately) on enterprise level. For example, the term "Internet of Things" coined in 1999 by (Ashton, 1999) and "Cyber-Phyiscal System" in 2006 in (Lee, 2008). At manufacturing level, these developments come after a long time, as technology remain at the time of machine purchase and lasts as long as it works. This relation is shown in the Figure 1. A company which uses the latest technology at all levels coupled with business model is guarantee for its success (Khan & Turowski, 2016a).

In order to respond to the changes in the business world with existing infrastructure, enterprises continuously try to streamline their organizational structure and operations. This is carried out through effective design and analysis of operations. It requires understanding of operations and its performance evaluation. Evaluation is considered as first step for improvement.

It is quite challenging for analysts to understand the existing infrastructure, performance, and deficiencies of an enterprise. In this paper, we provide an analytical framework which help to understand the processes and their performance. After such analysis, organizations can be able to find out the possible deficiencies in processes and will be able to take steps for its improvement. We also propose the constructs of analytical modelling language which can be used to extend the existing modeling languages for performance analysis purpose.

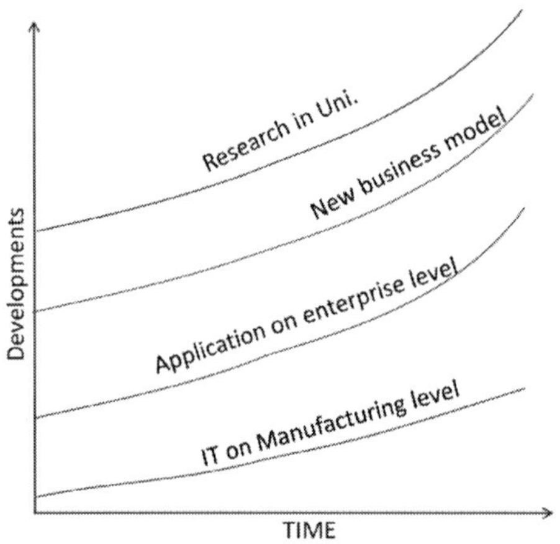

Figure 1. Research & its Implementation (adopted from (Khan & Turowski, 2016b))

The structure of this paper is as follows: In Section II, we discuss the business context and challenges for organizations. This helps the reader to understand the challenges in this domain. In Section III, we provide an analytical framework for analysis of business processes followed by Section IV where we propose the Analytical Business Process Modeling Language to support our framework by discussing our proposed modeling language with its patterns. In Section V, we explain the proposed modeling language with the help of a case study using business process modeling notations (BPMN). In Section VI, we summarize our paper and provides an outlook.

2. BUSINESS CONTEXT, DRIVERS AND CHALLENGES FOR ORGANIZATION

Customers' demands are fulfilled by enterprises which do business for several reasons like satisfying stakeholders (executives, employees, and customers), monetary gain, or increase in reputation (Lodhi et al., 2011b). To maintain the competitive position in the market, enterprises provide new products and services. This trend of competitiveness triggers other enterprises to provide better services in order to keep or strengthen their position in the market.

Vision is developed by its stakeholders followed by the strategy to fulfill it, whereas business model plays a vital role for the implementation of the strategy. Business processes (BP) are defined to carry out the operations of an enterprise. We refer this as a business perspective and represented in the Figure 2(on left side). Different aspects have to be investigated on the business level due to digitalization such as business models (and business patterns), business process management practices and their impact on supporting information technology.

Business processes are executed by organizational resources. During the execution of business processes data is generated and used for its processing. The execution of processes is supported by different applications and managed by technological entities. This is referred as an enterprise architecture perspective and represented in the middle of the Figure 2. Enterprise Architecture is renowned field of the research. The information and communication technology (ICT) is a critical enabler in digitalization. Often a holistic view of relevant processes, data, applications, and technological infrastructure is missing in the organizations. This is due to the fact that sometimes processes are complex and long which includes automated and manual process steps.

On the right side of the Figure 2, automation perspective is shown. This shows how different technological systems interact with each other during the industrial operations. On Enterprise level, orders are received and planned for manufacturing. Manufacturing Execution System (MES) monitors and controls the execution of orders supported by Supervisory control and data acquisition (SCADA) and programmable logic controller (PLC) components. On the lowest level, actuators perform actions on the raw material and turn it into the products. Different sensors are used to collect the data during this process like quality attributes, machines and environmental conditions. Business perspective is disciplined by an enterprise architecture and operated by industrial automation on wider scale. The relationship between these perspectives is shown in Figure 2.

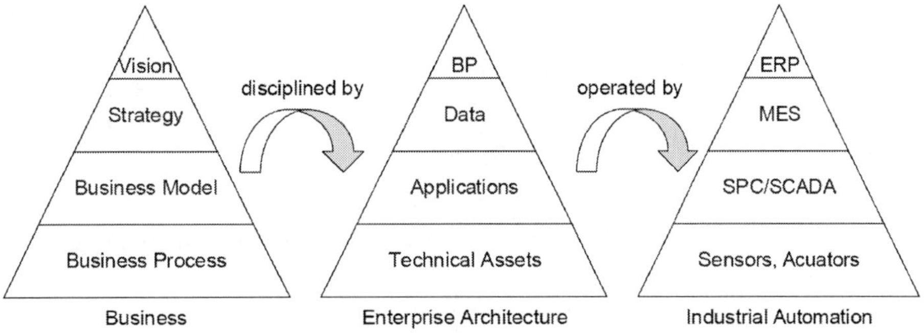

Figure 2. Relationship between Management Perspectives of an Enterprise

3. AN ANALYTICAL FRAMEWORK

In enterprises, different silo systems exist which can be applications and their databases. In reality, the communication between silos is not seamless. Different other applications, interfaces and macros are used to fulfill this task. The situation is more challenging in bigger organizations at manufacturing level where process chains are lengthy and majority of the processes are executed manually supported by different customized applications on old systems. Enterprises find it difficult to decide from where to start and what changes should be carried out for improvement. Complexity in business process is due to various factors like inter-dependencies between activities, stakeholders, involved elements, their attributes, and applications. Research in business process improvement needs to address these complexity issues and provide support to decide which action should be taken for business process improvement.

In order to provide the required support for business process improvement, a complete framework for analysis is required to be specified. This framework should address issues like data collection from silos, its integration, computation with business rules, and representation in business process models. We also need clear directions like defining steps for improvement, and mechanism to carry out the changes. An abstract picture of the overall framework is shown in the Fig. 3.

Enterprise data warehouse systems, extract the data from different legacy systems and applications and then integrate with each other. This data is also combined with Manufacturing Execution System logs which registers different events (like business object ”received”, ”processed”, ”successfully completed”) during the process execution. Different application log files are also collected from the systems.

Different techniques related with process mining (van der Aalst & Weijters, 2004) attempt to solve the issues related with data collection (Khan et al., 2010, Ingvaldsen and Gulla, 2008) and its conversion (van Dongen & van der Aalst, 2005, Günther & van der Aalst, 2006). Similarly in (zur Muehlen, 2008), author proposes a data format for recording business events. This BPAF (Business Process Analytics Format) helps in correlating and aggregating business events from different systems to one location. In (Grigori et al., 2004), authors store data from logs into a data warehouse for different analysis. Therefore, data is collected from log files of information system and converted into a suitable format for analysis (this data is sometimes referred as process trace data).

Afterwards, several techniques (like process mining algorithms (Rozinat & van der Aalst, 2006, van der Aalst, 2005, van der Aalst et al., 2005) and business process intelligence (Grigori et al., 2004)) are applied on process trace data to extract knowledge. Application usage mining (Kassem & Rautenstrauch, 2005) techniques analyze user's behavior with applications and attempt to improve the interaction between applications, humans and their working. Similarly, other techniques can also be applied like balance scorecards and other process metrics.

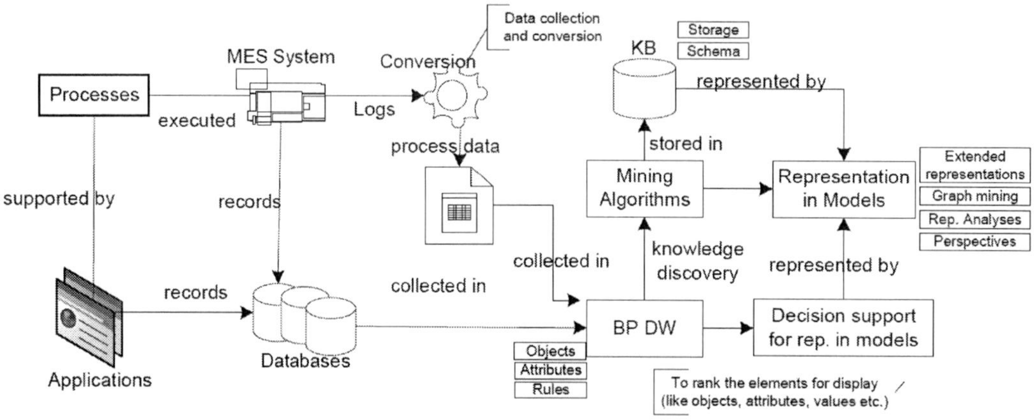

Figure 3. Framework for Business Process Improvement and Analysis

A knowledge base is also required to store the gathered information and knowledge from analysis techniques. Several issues are needed to be further investigated like what would be the schema design or format for storage? How the knowledge will be reflected as a company's best practices or used in enterprise operations?

The extracted knowledge and information are represented in a graphical form for intuitive understanding. For this purpose, depending on the stakeholders, certain information is filtered or provided with more details (context). Therefore, a decision support system is required which will rank the knowledge for representation with context to stakeholders. This is also very important to reduce the cognitive load of users in graphical business process models while representing performance details and other knowledge.

Graphical representation of extracted knowledge and process trace data also provide an opportunity to apply different methods like graph mining (Lodhi et al., 2010). Similarly, extended business process models help analysts to understand processes and identify deficiencies in business processes. We discuss the extended representation and benefits in the following section.

4. ANALYTICAL BUSINESS PROCESS MODELING LANGUAGE

Different stakeholders are involved in enterprises at different levels. In (Lodhi et al., 2011a), we discuss different stakeholders and their participation in business process elements. The performance is usually evaluated in form of quantitative measurements which help to indicate about quality. Business processes and its elements are evaluated in different dimensions like time, cost, and quality. In order to achieve the real benefits of evaluation of all important dimensions, their attributes should be part of the evaluation for a particular product, process, or employee.

We design analytical business process modeling language (ABPML) by performing a thorough analysis of business process performance analysis requirements (Lodhi et al., 2014, Lodhi et al., 2010), existing modeling language (Lodhi et al., 2011b), and different analytical tools (like ProM (van der Aalst et al., 2009, Ingvaldsen et al., 2005)). We do not only include the best of breed features, but also include some innovative features which provide help in analyzing business processes and identifying deficiencies. Therefore, the problem/solution search space is well investigated and considered in designing the new modeling language.

Here, we take the assumption that the analytical data is already available from the analytical framework discussed in previous section and just needs to be represented. The analytical data can be extracted from executional data (process trace data) or database tables.

In design science, a language specification includes constructs, models, method, and instantiation components. Therefore, we address these components for specification of our proposed analytical modeling language. These are correspondingly discussed in the following.

Constructs provide the vocabulary and symbols which are used to represent a problem or a solution (Hevner et al., 2014) or just representing a situation. Constructs are used to represent the tangible or intangible elements of a process. They are used to represent activities, process participants (resources, places), events (communication between elements), gateways (decisions), and other involved objects (materials, orders). Therefore, they are basic building blocks of a graphical model. Semantic defines the meaning of symbols and relationship with each other.

4.1 BPMN as an Example Case Study

We use the basic constructs of Business Process modeling Notations (BPMN) as described in the BPMN [1] standard (BPMI and OMG, 2006). We have select BPMN as it is rigorously defined and has widely accepted as a standard (defined by OMG) for modeling and communicating business processes. It is implemented in different modeling tools and rich in representation. Similarly, various extensions are also proposed in order to suit different business needs. Therefore, adoption of our proposed modeling language will not be a challenge in industry.

For our analytical modeling language, we propose some other constructs as an extension and also define the context in which some of the basic constructs have different semantics (meanings and relations) as compared to BPMN standard. Those constructs are used only in a defined context for performance analysis.

BPMN graphical notations are divided into four basic categories (BPMI and OMG, 2006). These categories are discussed briefly as follow.

Flow objects consist of activities, involved decision nodes for their order (sequential, parallel, iterations), and events of processes.

Connecting objects, as the name implies are used to connect activities and other elements with each other using different arrows which represent messages and associations between them. This core set of elements defines the control flow perspective of processes.

Different modeling elements are grouped through **Swimlanes** which use pools and lanes (BPMI and OMG, 2006). A pool is used to represent process participants while lanes are used to partition these participants and their activities from one to another. A process participant can either be an organizational entity within an organization or different organizations for collaboration in a process. Mostly, organizational perspective is provided by using Swimlanes constructs.

In BPMN, additional information about the process such as involved data object and guidelines for operations are provided by **artifacts**. These elements consist of data objects, annotations and group constructs.

To accommodate different requirements, we combine constructs to build models for analysis in different perspectives, and call them patterns. Different allowed combinations are explained here which also define the method of constructing the models in the analytical process modeling language. Depending on the user's requirements, models are built at different level of granularity to facilitate the understanding of processes. We further explain these constructs and their semantics with the help of our proposed patterns.

4.2 Modeling Patterns

Patterns are used to share knowledge and solve problems (Khan et al., 2011). Therefore, in our context, we define patterns as a combination of constructs to analyze the process and its elements in a particular perspective for improvement.

[1] http://www.bpmn.org

Each pattern intends to analyze performance with a particular focus involving certain dimensions and their attributes. Here, we provide four patterns for visualization of business process performance (with respect to business process modeling language). We consider these four patterns as the most important and frequent in business process analysis.

The analytical data can be used to identify which activities, organizational resources, and involved elements add more value to the enterprise. Based on this information, activities, organizational resources, and involved elements are classified in a particular dimension. The classification of process elements based on performance depends on the metrics used in the enterprise. Overall average values can be used for this classification and threshold values can be set. We recommend that only few classes should be defined for less cognitive loads of models. Enterprises can define their own metrics.

Based on the organizational metrics and values, different colors can be used to indicate the effect of the business objects, like green for optimal cost, yellow for high cost, and red for very high cost. Similarly, these classes can be represented in other dimensions as well like quality and time. Although the relation of cost and time, is not as simple as discussed in (Vullers et al., 2007). Once such metrics are defined, then they can be represented using our proposed patterns in our modeling language.

Table 1. Pattern and Characteristics

Patterns	Purpose	Constructs
Time	Analyze the performance of resources and activities with respect to time	Swimlanes, activities
Cost	Analyze the performance from the cost perspective like material and resources	Swimlanes, activities, colors
Path	To understand the activities which will be fruitful	Edges, activities, colors
History	To understand which activities are frequently executed in process	Edges, thickness, activities

4.2.1 Time Pattern

Time pattern focus on representation of process element's performance from time aspect. A few classes and characteristics in this dimension are classified in Table 1 and represented in Section V with BPMN. Some examples are idle time and working time.

4.2.2 Cost Pattern

Cost is an important factor in business processes. This pattern observes the performance of process elements from cost and other related aspects involving material and other resources. Different colors can be used to distinguish between high cost and low cost elements of process. Similarly, process elements can also be grouped based on the cost incurred by them.

4.2.3 Path Pattern (Time-Cost Pattern)

The time-cost pattern is helpful to decide at which path the execution will be effective (or beneficial for the organization). In case of different available paths, a path with company best practice can be colored to distinguish it from other options. Similarly, problematic paths (incurring cost and problems) can also be distinguished using colors from the others.

4.2.4 History Pattern

History path pattern represents which path is taken in most of the process executions. A thick edge represents that this particular path is taken by most of the cases during execution compared to a thin edge path which represent the opposite.

The proposed patterns, their elements, and meanings are summarized in Table 1. In the following patterns, different other attributes of the dimensions can be added and correspondingly represented using our proposed modeling language and its cognitive aspects (like colour, shape, and size). The above mentioned patterns are further explained with the help of an case study in V.

5. CASE STUDY

Instantiation demonstrates the feasibility of a proposed modeling language to solve the problem and its benefit. For this purpose, we take a small example of a real life scenario. This typical purchasing scenario may have different implementations (order of activities and roles) in organizations depending on the size of organization and requirements. For the sake of simplicity, we take if from a very small company which do not have complex processes like big organization.

Consider a typical purchasing scenario where a customer orders a product. Once the order is received, the product is checked in the stock. If the product is available, then it is shipped to the customer. An invoice is also generated and the payment process also starts. If the product is not in stock, then a production order is created for manufacturing the product. In this way, the customer order scenario is completed. Several processes are involved in successfully completing this order-scenario like fulfilling an order request, transfer of payment, manufacturing the product, quality evaluation, and shipping process.

In production, first, the production order is created by a foreman for the required products. Once the production order is created the assignments of resources are made like scheduling of machines and persons for manufacturing. In parallel to this, the raw material is also collected from the store or suppliers. Afterwards, the product is manufactured by workers. On completion of product manufacturing, quality inspector examines the quality of the manufactured product. If the quality of the product is at the desired level, then the shipping process and financial processes are started. Otherwise, the quality of product is brought to the desired level by sub-process "fix quality". Therefore, the overall order is completed and marked as completed. This production process is shown in Figure 4 using BPMN.

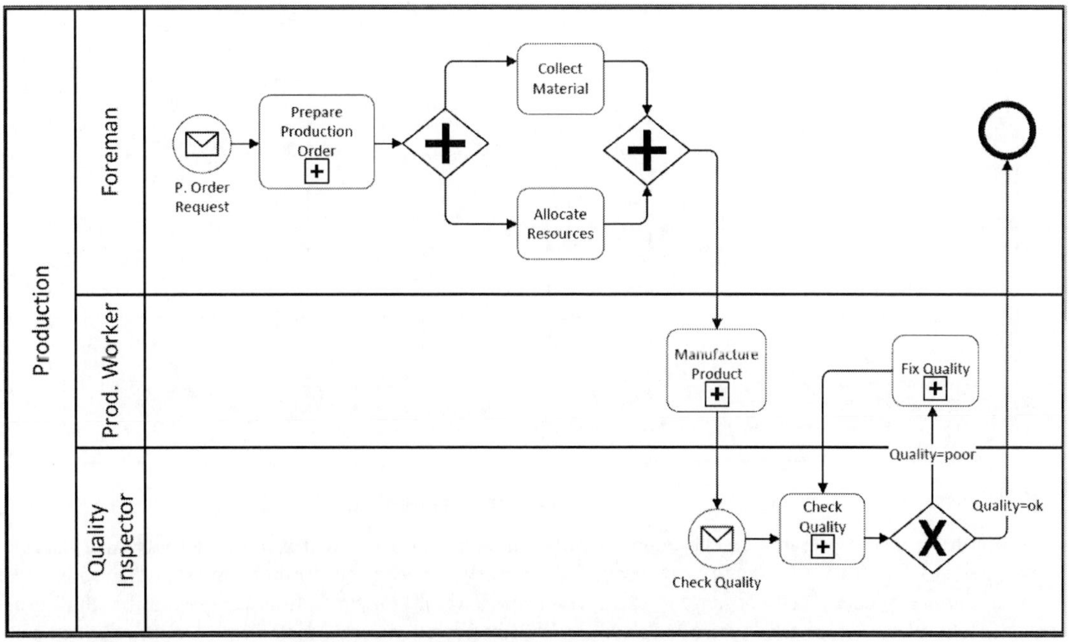

Figure 4. Production process in BPMN

When all these steps are recorded in information systems, we can use this data to analyze the performance of organizational elements and ordering of activities.

The whole process can be analyzed with abstract details like how much time it takes to complete the order. Bar chart like representations are suitable at an abstract level. However, at the managerial level the process can be analyzed with more graphical details that help to identify deficiencies and improve the process. For this detailed representation, we discuss our proposed patterns in the context of this example.

In BPMN, Swimlanes (pool and lane) are used to represent process participants and their interaction during execution. We propose to use Swimlanes not only to see participant interaction, but also the performance of organizational resources and activities. Based on collected data, process participant performance should be computed and their lanes should be colored (like green, yellow, and red). Similarly, activities can also be aligned using Swimlanes based on their computation in a particular dimension and their attributes. Consider Figure 5, where three classes are defined in cost dimension to arrange the process activities and their involved elements.

Similarly, different dimension can also be defined as pools where lanes represent further attributes of these dimensions like in time dimension, Idle time can be defined as an attribute and other classes (like high, medium, and low) align activities for representation. Moreover, different dimensions and their attributes can be combined with one another for further business process analysis.

When we represent performance details using Swimlanes in the BPMN model, we can find out which activities are consuming time and taking high costs. Afterwards, these activities can be further investigated to identify their deficiencies for improvement.

Similarly, successful paths (or best practices) can be determined by evaluating the performance of processes and its involved elements. The successful paths can be represented by coloring the edges. The frequency of execution on a particular path can be represented by changing the thickness of edges (connecting objects). This corresponds to the history pattern of proposed modeling language.

Based on these extended notations, we represent an extended business process model of our production process in Figure 6. The colors red, yellow, and green represent activities with high, medium, and low cost respectively. In order to avoid confusion, in this figure, we only colored the activities to represent the performance aspects whereas Swimlanes are kept with their classical BPMN semantics (BPMI and OMG, 2006), such as process participants.

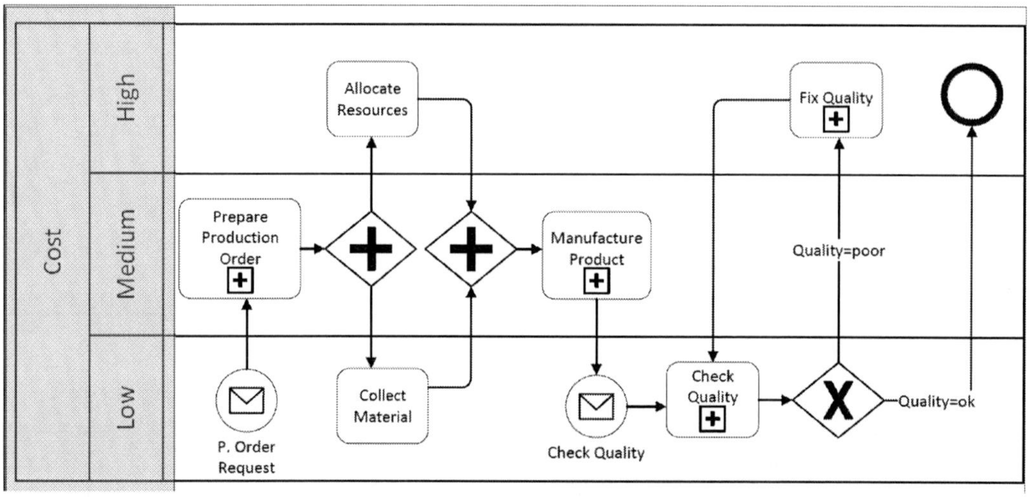

Figure 5. Cost of activities in ABPML

Figure 6, also represents that the quality of production is poor and frequently activity “fix quality” is executed to improve the quality of product. Similarly, it can be further investigated why activity “manufacture product” is consuming extra resources, which may result a representation that product manufactured by certain employee often need quality fixes or often certain paths with loops are executed.

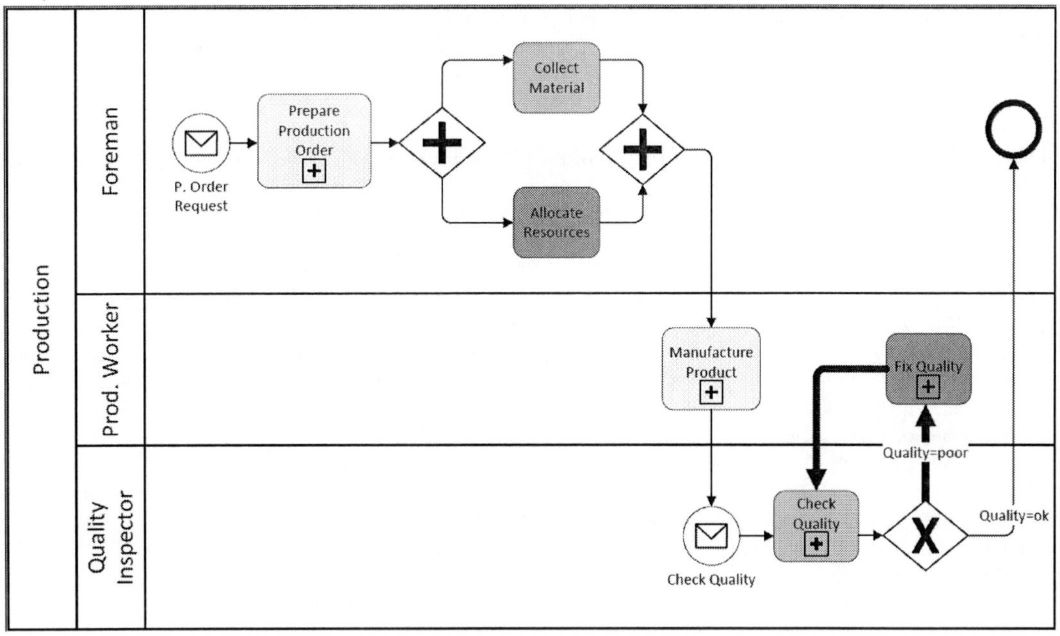

Figure 6. Production process in ABPML

6. SUMMARY AND OUTLOOK

In this paper, we presented a design science artefact (an analytical framework and modeling language) to solve the problem of performance analysis of business processes. We followed the design science guidelines for the specification of the framework. In order to support our analytical framework, we also devise and presented the patterns of proposed modeling language for performance analysis. These patterns are explained with the help of an example using a rigorously defined modeling language (BPMN). The patterns are independent of modeling language and can be used to extend any modeling language.

REFERENCES

Ashton, K., 1999, 'That 'Internet of Things' Thing'. RFiD Journal, http://www.rfidjournal.com/articles/view?4986.

BPMI and OMG, 'Business Process Modeling Notation Specification, Final Adopted Specification'. http://bpmn.org/Documents/OMG\s\do5(F)inal\s\do5(A)dopted\s\do5(B)PMN\s\do5(1)-0\s\do5(S)pec\s\do5(0)6-02-01.pdf

Grigori et al., 2004, 'Business process intelligence', *Computers in Industry* 53(3), 321–343.

Günther C. and van der Aalst W., 2006, A generic import framework for process event logs, in J. Eder S. Dustdar, eds, '*Workshop on Business Process Intelligence*', Vol. 4103, Springer, pp. 81–92.

Hevner et al., 2004, 'Design science in information systems research', *MIS* Q. 28(1), 75–105.

Ingvaldsen et al., 2005, Empirical business models, in '*CAiSE Short Paper Proceedings*', Vol. 161 of CEUR Workshop Proceedings, CEUR-WS.

Ingvaldsen and Gulla 2008, 'Preprocessing support for large scale process mining of SAP transactions', *Business Process Management Workshops* 4928, 30–41.

Kassem, G. and Rautenstrauch, C. 2005, Application usage mining to improve enterprise workflows: ERP systems SAP R/3 as example, in M. Khosrow-Pour, ed., 'Managing Modern Organizations Through Information Technology', *Information Resources Management Association*, chapter 86, pp. 358–362.

Khan et al., 2011, Service variability patterns, in '*Proceedings of the 30th international conference on Advances in conceptual modeling: recent developments and new directions', ER'11,* Springer-Verlag, Berlin, Heidelberg, pp. 130–140.

Khan et al., 2010, Applying process mining in SOA environments, in A. Dan, F. Gittler F. Toumani, eds, *'Service-Oriented Computing ICSOC Service Wave 2009 Workshops'*, Vol. 6275 of Lecture Notes in Computer Science, Springer, pp. 293–302.

Khan, A. Turowski, K. 2016 a, 'A preliminary study on industry 4.0', *Journal of Industrial and Intelligent Information,* 4(3), 230–234.

Khan, A. Turowski, K. 2016 b, A survey of current challenges in manufacturing industry and preparation for industry 4.0, in *'Proceedings of the First International Scientific Conference Intelligent Information Technologies for Industry (IITI 16)'*, Vol. 450 of Advances in Intelligent Systems and Computing, Springer, Cham.

Lee, E. 2008, Cyber physical systems: Design challenges, in *'Object Oriented Real-Time Distributed Computing', 11th IEEE International Symposium*, IEEE Computer Society, pp. 363–369.

Lodhi et al., 2010, Investigation of graph mining for business processes, in '*Proceedings of The International Conference on Intelligence and Information Technology ICIIT*', Vol. 2, IEEE Computer Society, Lahore, Pakistan, pp. 293–297.

Lodhi et al., 2010, Post execution analysis of business processes: Taxonomy and challenges, *Technical Report 9*, University of Magdeburg.

Lodhi et al., 2011 a, Business process improvement framework and representational support, in '*Proceedings of The Third International Conference on Intelligent Human Computer Interaction (IHCI)'*, Advances in Intelligent and Soft Computing, Springer, Prague, Czech Republic.

Lodhi et al., 2011 b, Business process modeling: Active research areas and challenges, *Technical Report 1*, University of Magdeburg.

Lodhi et al., 2014, Business process modeling language for performance evaluation, in '*47th Hawaii International Conference on System Sciences (HICSS'14)'*, Vol. 00, pp. 3768–3777.

Rozinat, A. and van der Aalst, W. 2006, Decision mining in ProM., in *'International Conference on Business Process Management (BPM 2006)'*, Vol. 4102, Springer-Verlag, Berlin, Germany, pp. 420–425.

The American Enterprise Institute, Fortune 500 firms 1955 v. 2017: Only 60 remain, thanks to the creative destruction that fuels economic prosperity accessed on 25.01.2018 at http://goo.gl/BgRxZj.

van der Aalst, W. 2005, 'Business alignment: Using process mining as a tool for delta analysis and conformance testing', *Requirement Engineering* 10(3), 198–211.

van der Aalst et al., 2005, 'Discovering social networks from event logs', *Computer Supported Cooperative Work* 14(6), 549–593.

van der Aalst et al., 2009, ProM: The process mining toolkit, in A. K. A. de Medeiros B. Weber, eds, *'Proceedings of the BPM 2009 Demonstration Track'*, Vol. 489 of CEUR Workshop Proceedings, CEUR-WS.org, pp. 1–4.

van der Aalst and Weijters, A. 2004, 'Process mining: A research agenda', *Computers in Industry* 53, 231–244.

van Dongen and van der Aalst, 2005, A meta model for process mining data, in M. Missikoff A. D. Nicola, eds, *'Proceedings of the Open Interop Workshop on Enterprise Modelling and Ontologies for Interoperability, Co-located with CAiSE'*, Vol. 160 of CEUR Workshop Proceedings, CEUR-WS.org, Porto, Portugal.

Vullers et al., 2007, Performance measures to evaluate the impact of best practices., in *'Proceedings of Workshops and Doctoral Consortium of the 19th International Conference on Advanced Information Systems Engineering (BPMDS)'*, Tapir Academic Press Trondheim, pp. 359–368.

Wang, R. 2014, Constellation's 2014 outlook on dominating digital business disruption, *Technical Report 01/2014,* Constellation Research Inc.

zur Muehlen, M. 2008, 'Business process analytics format (BPAF) Document Number WFMC-TC-1015', Workflow Management Coalition USA.

MOBILE TECHNOLOGIES AND ENTREPRENEURIAL DEVELOPMENT – IDENTIFYING THE MISSING LINK

Atika Ahmad Kemal
Lord Ashcroft International Business School, Anglia Ruskin University, UK

ABSTRACT

The phenomenal diffusion and explosive growth of mobile technologies in developing economies has sparked off an information revolution that has reframed the subject of development for policy makers, practitioners and academics. The use of mobile phones by rural micro-entrepreneurs addresses one of the fundamental challenges in creating relative wealth for poverty alleviation in rural communities. This paper uses meta-analysis, as a methodology, to review the ICT literature on mobile technologies and frames it under Porter's Value Chain and System framework. It analyses how mobile technologies integrates informal actors in the value chain to undertake business activities. However, the framework is confined to an economic lens, and being deterministic, fails to highlight the social processes that underpin economic activities. Alternatively, the paper proposes a socio-technical framework that illuminates how mobile phone usage amplifies 'social networks' for micro-entrepreneurs within the value chain. By intertwining the social and geographical connections, technology enables new communications patterns to evolve for business success. As contribution to the ICT literature, the paper presents new insights on technology's role in transforming market channels through the creation of social wealth for inclusive development. Also, it signifies how mobile technologies may offer financial services- via mobile banking- to boost entrepreneurial development in rural communities.

KEYWORDS

Mobile technologies, Micro-Entrepreneurs, Economic Development, Social Networks, Entrepreneurial Development, Developing Countries

1. INTRODUCTION

Mobile technologies are usually classified as Information Communication Technologies (ICTs) that are mobile, support real time two-way communications that have leapfrogged traditional fixed line telephone infrastructures (Rashid and Elder, 2009). Since these technologies work using the radio spectrum, they do not rely on physical infrastructures, for example, roads and phone wires. Base-stations are powered using their own generators where electrical grids are absent. Thus, the diffusion of mobile technologies, as major forms of communication in rural communities, especially in developing nations is exponentially high (ITU, 2017).

According to Sachs (2005), *'mobile phones are the single most transformative technology for development'* (cited in Etzo and Collender, 2010, p. 661) in reshaping structures and processes for socio-economic development (Bada and Madon, 2006; Heeks, 2008). However, mobile phones, other than smart phones, serve as communication tools for the poor (Aker and Mbiti, 2010; Komunte, Rwashana and Nabukenya, 2012). Since they serve as a platform for multiple applications, many services have now gone mobile, namely, banking, entertainment, health and education (Komunte, Rwashana and Nabukenya, 2012).

Whilst developing countries are still lagging behind in overall ICT usage and applications, mobile technologies are more accessible and cost effective tools for low income populations to bridge the digital divide (Katsina and Abdulkareem, 2012; ITU, 2017). In rural communities, mobile phones are the dominant mode of communication, acting as a mediating tool, to connect them to the information society (Komunte, Rwashana and Nabukenya, 2012). Moreover, studies demonstrate that mobile technologies address the fundamental challenges that many rural micro-entrepreneurs face; in terms of limited access to fixed telecommunication and physical infrastructures, affordability in owning a personal landline phone and lack of digital capabilities for using computers and internet for business requirements (Wolcott, Kamal and Qureshi, 2008; Makoza and Chigona, 2012).

Studies divulge that mobile phones have greater impact on economic growth in developing countries, as opposed to developed countries, which are well covered by landline telephony (Rabayah and Qalalwi, 2011). While the infiltration of mobile networks in rural communities is high, they bypass the expensive infrastructure barriers attributed to fixed landline telecommunications. Beyond connectivity and accessibility, mobile phones offer the ease of mobility, security and convenience to micro-entrepreneurs, without their having to rely on physical infrastructures, such as roads (Donner, 2006; Jenson, 2007). With the increase in affordability of handsets, with the exception of smartphones, mobile phones have penetrated the lower income strata of rural populations and are tools for pro-poor growth (Rashid and Elder, 2009; Heeks, 2009; Aker and Mbiti, 2010).

Whilst many studies have focussed on the adoption and diffusion of mobile phones, there is little research that theorises the economic effects of mobile technology use by micro-entrepreneurs in developing countries. Hence, the aim of the paper is to address this gap and analyse how mobile phones support the livelihood activities of rural micro-entrepreneurs through a systematic review of the literature. In what follows, section 2 reviews the literature on the economic significance of mobile technologies by rural micro-entrepreneurs. Section 3 outlines the methodology- a systemic literature review. In section 4, the literature is framed and analysed under Porter's Value Chain and System Model. Section 5 proposes a socio-technical framework that illuminates how social networks may be integrated into the framework. In the end, section 6 concludes how the creation of social assets leads to inclusive development, including innovative platforms, such as mobile banking, for the sustainable livelihoods of rural micro-entrepreneurs.

2. MOBILE PHONE USAGE BY RURAL MICRO-ENTREPRENEURS

As classified in the literature, micro-enterprises employ between 0-5 employees, and are categorised as 'livelihood micro-enterprises' that constitute the rural, informal economic sector in developing economies (Liedholm and Mead, 1999; Leidholm, 2002; Duncombe and Heeks, 2005). While supporting the social and business needs of micro-entrepreneurs, mobile technologies are strategic tools for wealth creation and poverty reduction (Donner and Escobari, 2010; Aker and Mbiti, 2010). Since mobile phones require basic literacy levels, as compared to other ICT devices, they are popular tools within the less educated class of rural micro-entrepreneurs (Akpan-Obong, 2007). Certain features make them particularly attractive, for example, short messaging servicing, has innovated use for mobile banking applications (Rashid and Elder, 2009; Donner, 2009). Donner (2009) highlights how mobile services offer integrated platforms for information sharing, coordination, marketing and financial transactions for rural micro-entrepreneurs. However, lack of literacy, SMS not in the native language and complex user interfaces, are some challenges faced by micro-entrepreneurs. Other barriers are high costs of service and call charges, poor connectivity and quality of service which limits mobile usage in rural areas for micro-entrpreneurs (Aker and Mbiti, 2010).

While some scholars argue that the role of mobile technologies is 'global', others criticise the 'one size fits all' model in disputing that usage models differ between developed and developing countries (Castells, 2007). In developed nations, mobile phones offer a 'supplement' role, in contrast to developing nations, where they are the first link to the communications network. Under such circumstances, mobile technologies are valued more for their connectivity and convenience, rather than for their mobility and ease of use. Studies show that the common-use asset model, as seen in the case of the Grameen Village Phone in Bangladesh, is now becoming obsolete due to constant evolving information needs under fluctuating economic, social, cultural and institutional factors affecting the businesses of micro-entrepreneurs. The Grameen Phone operators (GPO) also known as 'village ladies' hire out time-based use of their mobile phones for a small fee to rural women micro-entrepreneurs. However, they are gradually disappearing as the personal owbership of mobile phones is rapidly penetrating in communities (Boettiger, Toyama and Abed, 2012). James (2016) nonetheless, looks at the challenges of rapid scaling-up of village phone projects in poor micro-communities in Bangladesh.

Nonetheless, the flexibility of mobile phones, over other ICT's, has made mobile communications a popular tool for social and business communication among micro-entrepreneurs (Donner, 2006, 2007; Donner and Escobari, 2010; Ilahiane and Sherry, 2012). This is because mobile phones are attached to a person rather than a location. Since many micro-entrepreneurs have no fixed place of business, mobile phones offer them the flexibility of working from remote sites (Donner, 2006, 2007; Ilahiane and Sherry, 2012). Scholars argue that the the separation of business from personal functions need to be replaced with more integrated approaches to mobile phone use (Donner 2009; Ilahiane and Sherry, 2012). Other studies suggest that mobile phones have a limited role in supporting the economic activities of micro-entrepreneurs and they significantly do not increase incomes (Chew, Ilavarasan and Levy, 2010; Sife, Kiondo and Lyimo-Macha, 2010). However, the discourse that mobile technologies play a significant role in economic development for micro-entrepreneurs is an area that is still under researched.

3. METHODOLOGY

This study adopts meta-analysis, as a methodology, for analysing the literature on mobile technology usage by micro-entrepreneurs in developing countries. The studies included in this review were located through a comprehensive search of publicly available literature, mostly through manual electronic searches of the following databases: EBSCO, Primo, Google Scholar, SAGE Journal Online, ACM Digital Library, and Elsevier Science. Although search strategies varied depending on the tool used, the search terms included the keywords 'mobile technology usage and micro-entrepreneurs', 'mobile phones and micro-entrepreneurial development' and 'mobile phones and economic development' in developing countries. The literature search produced studies that were initially screened as part of the systemic review process. Initially, around 250 studies were yielded from the search, inclusive of those articles which informed the literature review section in this paper. After applying the inclusion criteria (mobile phone usage for micro-enterprises/ micro-entrepreneurs in developing countries) 30 studies were selected for the purposes of developing codes/categories for thematic analysis of the literature. Specific themes from studies were coded, collated and categorised drawing on Porter's framework. This included themes from the 1) value chain; *operations, marketing, sales, procurement and after sales service*, and 2) value system; *external linkages with suppliers, traders and customers.* This framework constitutes the theoretical lens to analyse the economic activities of micro-entrepreneurs using their mobile phones, and thereby, present new themes that reflect on deficiencies of the framework. While Porter's value chain and system model (Porter and Millar, 1985; Porter, 1998) has been used by some scholars in the past, as an analytical framework (Jagun, Heeks and Whalley, 2008; De Silva, Ratnadiwakara and Soysa, 2009; Donner and Escobari, 2010; Rabayah and Qalalwi, 2011), this paper expands the review and conceptualises emerging themes into this framework. The themes coded drew on the concepts in the value chain and system which are presented in the next section.

Notably, the terms micro and small enterprises (MSE) and small and medium enterprises (SME) were acronyms that combined two distinct sizes of enterprises into a single reference. They were used interchangeably in the literature. However, with no commonly accepted definitions of the thresholds between micro-small and medium, there were often implicit conceptual overlaps between the acronyms in studies. Hence, some researchers conveniently conflated results from studies between micro and small enterprises (Donner, 2004; Donner and Escobari, 2010; Rabayah and Qalalwi, 2011; Donner 2009a; Komunte, Rwashana and Nabukenya, 2012) and for small and medium enterprises (Frempong, 2009). Also, universal standards were absent to distinguish between 'formal' and 'informal' enterprises (Ilahiane and Sherry, 2012; Chew, Ilahiane and Levy, 2011; Donner, 2004, 2007).

4. PORTER'S FRAMEWORK

Porter's value chain (1985) comprises of i) primary activities, or internal core processes of an enterprise (inbound logistics, operations, outbound logistics, marketing, sales and after sales service) and ii) supporting functions (procurement, technology development, human resource and firm infrastructure). The value system highlights the enterprise's relations with customers, suppliers and agents/retailers (see Figure 1).

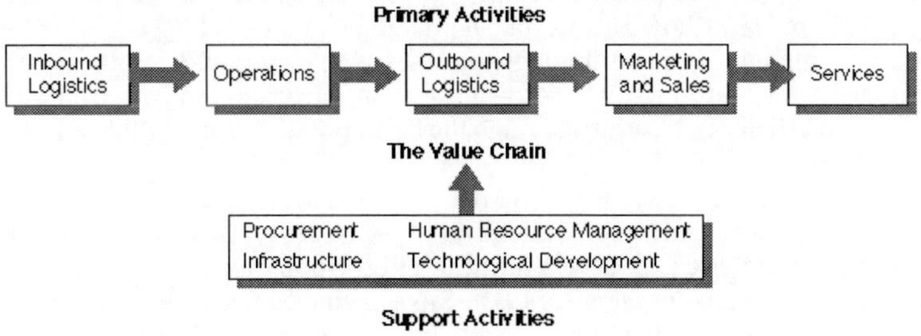

Figure 1. Porter's Value Chain and System Model (1985)

4.1 The Value Chain

Few studies evidenced that mobile phone usage by micro-entrepreneurs elevated the 'operational efficiency' for the production of goods and services. This is because studies primarily focussed on the individual economic activities of micro-entrepreneurs who were not engaged in the manufacturing sector (Donner and Escobari, 2010). Analysis through Porter's value chain revealed that mobile phones supported the 'core operations' and increased efficiencies for cloth weavers in Nigeria. By reducing the travel time for journeys - to and from suppliers and customers – mobile phones considerably reduced the transaction time for micro-entrepreneurs (Jagun, Heeks and Whalley, 2008). Another study showed that owing to issues of trust, mobile phones were unable to completely replace physical travel for 'inbound/outbound logistics'. Other complexities arising from the interactions between customers and suppliers made the physical presence of retailors mandatory in the value chain (Molony, 2006).

Studies illustrated that mobile phones reduced inbound/outbound logistic costs- pertaining to supplier/customer search and travel costs. Due to reduced transaction costs, overall production costs were significantly lowered to boost efficiency, productivity and growth of businesses (Bayes, Braun & Akhter, 1999; De Silva, Ratnadiwakara and Soysa, 2009; Mittal et al., 2010; Sife, Kiondo and Lyimo-Macha, 2010; Aker and Mbiti, 2010). Another study showed that mobile phone usage, sometimes, locked suppliers into forward contracts, which prevented them from taking advantage of higher spot prices (Molony, 2008). While using mobile phones for communications assisted retailers/sellers to integrate the deciding and selling stages together, this reduced market price variations. Previously, disjoint systems within the value chain failed to address market fluctuations (De Silva, Ratnadiwakara and Soysa, 2009). Hence, mobile technologies disseminated useful information which improved 'marketing and sales' activities for micro-entrepreneurs and enhanced their human and financial capabilities (Mittal et al., 2010). Further, Komunte (2015) found that women entrepreneurs in Uganda gained in mainstream operations, especially, marketing and sales, information inflow, customer service delivery, increased business processes and profits, which facilitated increased productivity and enterprise transformation. Hence, mobile phones waere perceived as an economic tool that liberated women entrepreneurs from poverty.

Analysis of primary activities within the value chain insinuated that mobile phones played a critical role to streamline the marketing, sales (downstream) and procurement (upstream) activities for micro-entrepreneurs in enabling them to achieve business goals (Donner, 2004, 2009; Jagun, Heeks and Whalley, 2008; Aker, 2008; Donner and Escobari, 2010; Essegbey and Frempong, 2011). Specifically, Jenson's (2007) research on the fishing industry in Kerala revealed that mobile phones supported the marketing and sales activities of fishermen within the value chain. Fishermen were able to sell their catch at the most competitive prices to achieve uniform prices across all markets. This strategy eliminated waste through perfect adherence to the 'Law of One Price' which increased the welfare of both producers and consumers. Jenson (2007) argued that the 'spill over' gains for small fisherman improved market functioning, thereby, spreading the digital divide more uniformly across the society.

Under Porter's framework, Aker's (2008) study of grain traders in Niger examined the role of mobile phones in supporting the procurement, sales and marketing activities in the value chain. The study reflected that mobiles phones assisted grain traders to access market information to reduce price variances that improved market efficiency. This diminished the intra-annual coefficient for variation which lowered intra-annual price risk for customers to increase their welfare. The net effect of these changes maximised daily profits for traders. Hence, in markets where traders practiced local monopoly in pricing, consumer's increased access to information, through mobile phones, enhanced their overall welfare (Aker and Mbiti, 2010; Carmody, 2012). By contrast, mobile phones also adversely created unequal markets and affected seller's behaviour to sell less quantities, especially in markets where mobile usage was low (Aker, 2008). Boateng et al. (2104) revealed how mobile phones used in micro-trading activities by women traders in Nigeria, enhanced communication and trading processes that improved revenue acquisition and increased decision making and control. Similarly, micro-entrepreneurs from Myanmar, who were early adopters of mobile phones, reaped efficiency benefits although they also posed threats for those who lagged behind in the market (Ling et al., 2017).

Studies from Palestine (Rabayah and Qalalwi, 2011) and Ghana (Essegbey and Frempong, 2011) confirmed that mobile phones underpinned the primary activities of micro-entrepreneurs. Within the value chain, mobile phones were used to access critical information that decreased operational costs whilst maximising revenues for micro-entrepreneurs (De Silva, Zainudeen and Ratnadiwakara, 2008; Frempong, 2009; De Silva, Ratnadiwakara and Soysa, 2009; Rashid and Elder, 2009; Aker and Mbiti, 2010; Sife, Kiondo and Lyimo-Macha, 2010). Similarly, research from the Carribean countries showed how mobile technology motivated and stimulated economic growth, through greater market integration and penetration, increased productivity, reduced price fluctuations and increased price dispersion (Maghionyeodiwe and Annansingh-Jamieson, 2017). Scholars have argued how mobile phone usage by micro-entrepreneurs augmented efficiencies within business operations and increased productivity of goods which boosted sales and profits for micro-entrepreneurs (Rashid and Elder, 2009; Aker and Mbiti, 2010; Rabayah and Qalalwi, 2011). Studies suggest that mobile technologies helped micro-entrepreneurs streamline and manage their supply chains more effectively, as information necessary for decision making, were fast tracked within business cycles (Jagun, Heeks and Whalley, 2008; Aker and Mbiti, 2010). Some micro-entrepreneurs used their phones to provide after sales service to customers which cemented trust and loyalty within the value chain (Molony, 2006; Essegbey and Frempong, 2011). Furthermore, mobile technologies serve in procuring raw materials for the inbound operations to underpin the activities in the value chain (Jagun, Heeks and Whalley, 2008; Aker, 2008).

4.2 Value System

Porter's value system analysed how micro-entrepreneurs used mobile technologies to foster and build their external relationships with key agents. The literature presented that mobile phones increased the flow of information in the upstream and downstream channels that promoted coordination amongst various suppliers and customers in the value system (Donner, 2004, 2006; Molony, 2006; Aker, 2008; Jagun, Heeks and Whalley, 2008; Frempong, 2009; Aker and Mbiti, 2010; Sife, Kiondo and Lyimo-Macha, 2010; Essegbey and Frempong, 2011; Rabayah and Qalalwi, 2011; Smith, Spence and Rashid, 2011). Mobile phones fortified existing business ties and established new linkages with business partners in the value system (Donner, 2006; Donner and Escobari, 2010). However, Molony (2008) argued that mobile communications strengthened existing business ties only.

Within the value system, mobile technologies enabled micro-entrepreneurs to expand or amplify markets through the creation of value networks with new customers (Donner, 2006, 2009, Jenson, 2007; Molony, 2008; Jagun, Heeks and Whalley, 2008; Aker, 2008; Essegbey and Frempong, 2011; Smith, Spence and Rashid, 2011). Jenson (2007) portrayed that mobile technologies helped Kerala fishermen decide where to sell their catch to capture new markets. Similarly, Aker (2008) observed that grain traders in markets with cell phone coverage had greater access to information that enabled them to expand in more extensive markets. Hence, mobile phones created new business opportunities and markets for micro-entrepreneurs. However, the use of mobile technologies by larger, formal enterprises posed risks and dangers for smaller micro-entrepreneurs by subjecting them to greater competitive pressures (Kleine, 2009). Duncombe's (2016) study suggested how mobile phones were used as an information source to provide agricultural data for effective planning and policymaking in the development of the agricultural sector. Fu and Akter's (2016) research in India also illustrated how mobile phones enhanced intervention in agricultural extension service delivery- in significantly improving the amount, quality and speed of service delivery. There were also benefits in terms of greater knowledge and awareness of new agricultural practices, and farmers' aspirations to try new technology in the future.

Porter's value system highlighted that mobile phones assisted middlemen, wholesalers and traders to perform their roles more effectively. This is because technology replaced and mediated existing relationships with more open and transparent market structures (Aker, 2008; Jagun, Heeks and Whalley, 2008; Donner, 2009; Aker and Mbiti, 2010; Donner and Escobari, 2010). In doing so, technology reconfigured traditional market chains within the value system (Jagun, Heeks and Whalley, 2008; Aker, 2008; Aker and Mbiti, 2010). Jagun, Heeks and Whalley (2008), in their study of cloth weavers in Nigeria, accentuated the significance of the *'aso oke'* supply chain - characterised by intermediaries who played an imperative role in the supply chain. By providing critical information to buyers and sellers, intermediaries reduced financial risks for weavers. Within the *'aso oke'* supply chain, both micro-entrepreneurs and buyers were dependent upon intermediaries who created new buyers and sellers and established new relationships to expand business markets. Here it is argued that mobile phones did not reduce the information asymmetry between weavers and the coordinator-weaver. Molony (2006) further highlighted how mobile phones were perceived as a facilitating technology for extending trust-based relationships beyond business networks.

5. INTEGRATING SOCIAL LINKAGES IN THE FRAMEWORK

Porter's framework is a process theory which helps analyse how mobile phones supported the economic activities of micro-entrepreneurs in developing countries. Researchers have criticised Porter's value chain and system (1985, 1998) for being a purely 'deterministic' economic model that measures enterprise growth (Jagun, Heeks and Whalley, 2008). Limited to an economic lens, it failed to address the role of social networks in the value chain that may affect enterprise success and growth. As the framework is confined to the economic processes and activities that support micro-entrepreneurs, it is argued that social chains may complement the economic processes in the value chain and system. Alternatively, based on the literature, the paper proposes how the inherent shortcomings in the model may be overcome by integrating social processes in the chain for increasing economic assets.

Thus, the paper identifies how mobile phones increased the 'social assets' of micro-entrepreneurs by intertwining the social and geographical connections that enabled business communication patterns to evolve (Donner, 2004, 2006; Aker and Mbiti, 2010; Sife, Kiondo and Lyimo-Macha, 2010; Smith, Spence and Rashid, 2011). However, it is argued that mobile technologies failed to substitute face-to-face communications within social networks for micro-entrepreneurs, but were used for consolidating trust amongst parties (Molony, 2006; Donner, 2006, 2007; Frempong, 2009). Donner's (2006) research from Rwanda evidenced that majority of calls made by micro-entrepreneurs were social, but were beneficial to foster trust for business contracts, despite the 'blurring' between the social and business domains (Donner, 2009). In addition, studies articulate that mobile technologies 'amplified' social networks (Donner, 2009; Donner and Escobari, 2010) by strengthening existing social ties (Donner, 2004, 2006, 2007; Rashid and Elder, 2009). Other researchers argued that mobile communications created new social networks amongst micro-entrepreneurs (Molony, 2008). Ilahiane and Sherry (2012) argue that mobile phones transformed social communication networks that were integrated within the *'bricolage'* for the pursuit of economic interests. Hence, mobile phone usage was perceived as an integral article of faith, as technology nurtured economic and symbolic values for micro-entrepreneurs. As the benefits from social networks 'spilled' into other networks from using mobile telephony, social networks were closely knitted into economic and business networks (De Silva, Ratnadiwakara and Zainudeen, 2011). Moreover, there is evidence that mobile technologies promoted stronger kinship bonding and social capital through improved family relationships that enhanced socio-economic opportunities for micro-entrepreneurs (De Silva, Ratnadiwakara and Zainudeen, 2011; Ilahiane and Sherry, 2012).

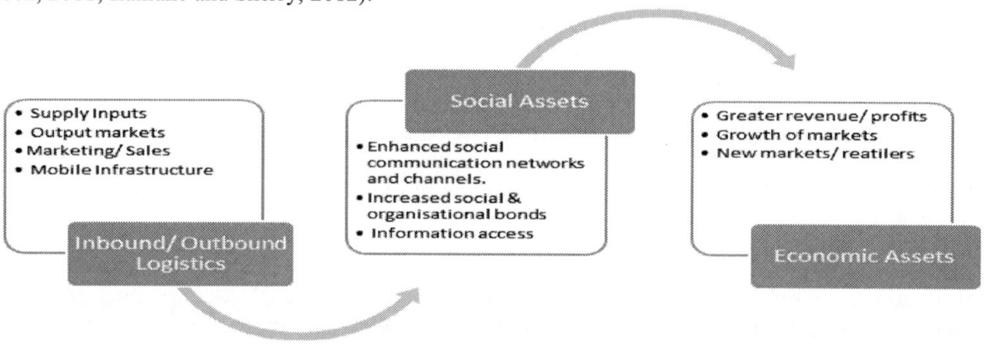

Figure 2. Mobile Technologies Increase Economic Assets through Social Linkages

Figure 2 illustrates an alternative socio-technical perspective by integrating social linkages in the framework. It illustrates that technology usage amplifies social networks which increases social assets which in turn augments economic assets within the value chain. By intertwining the social and geographical connections, technology enables new communications patterns to evolve for business success. This argument extends Porter's deterministic framework and offers valuable insights for micro-entrepreneurs. While Porter's value chain neglected the 'social' role of technology for business development, this paper presents new perspectives on examining technology's contribution. It sheds light on how the usage of mobile technologies by informal actors creates social wealth for expanding into new markets. Additionally, the injection of mobile money into the current value chain and system may transform socio-economic processes for micro-entrepreneurial development. By offering financial resources, such as credit, payments and saving facilities – via mobile banking- this new process may evoke micro-entrepreneurial activities in the value chain and contribute towards financial inclusion.

6. CONCLUSION AND CONTRIBUTIONS

Although mobile technologies play a vital role in economic development, there is little evidence presented that they transform economic markets (Donner and Escobari, 2010). Further, the economic approaches of 'mobile technologies for development' overlooks the social dimensions that contribute towards business success. Hence, policymakers, practitioners and researchers need to create inclusive strategies to integrate social networks within more deterministic practices that currently exist for business development.

Further, it is essential to recognise that a new 'global digital divide' at the BoP is emerging- a population with limited digital capabilities which cannot afford and use sophisticated mobile technologies (Carmody, 2012). Therefore, a holistic approach is required to overcome these challenges with greater support from policymakers and practitioners to ensure that informal actors at the BoP are integrated within inclusive development approaches (Komunte, Rwashana and Nabukenya, 2012; Katsina and Abdulkareem, 2012). In order to underpin the 'mobiles for development' discourse, researchers need to question the feasibility of mobile developmental projects over other low-tech approaches. Mobile technologies may not necessarily be the 'silver bullet' for millions of households without adequate policies and practices focused at the community level (Aker and Mbiti, 2010).

The paper concludes that mobile technologies play a vital role in increasing incomes for micro-entrepreneurs within the value chain. However, as theoretical contribution, the paper looks beyond pure deterministic economic processes within Porters Value Chain and System. First, it extends the framework through integrating social processes that create social assets which are vital for increasing monetary assets. Thus, the creation of social capital underpinned economic activities for micro-entrepreneurs that led to business success. As this missing link in the chain is identified, an alternative socio-technical framework is proposed. Second, the injection of mobile money into the current value chain and system may transform economic processes for micro-entrepreneurial development and financial inclusion. This conceptualisation contributes towards the growing body of literature on mobile banking that is gaining popularity in rural communities in developing countries. Whilst current research provides scarce evidence that mobile technologies help people start new businesses (Donner and Escobari, 2010), this paper conceptualises how mobile technologies may offer alternative channels to deliver financial resources – via mobile banking to micro-entrepreneurs. This may enable micro-entrepreneurs to start their businesses with the availability of credit and conduct financial transactions. As mobile banking, based on branchless banking models, is becoming popular in developing countries, this may lead to financial innovation in rural communities.

Nonetheless, the paper bridges the gap between theory and practice and offers rich insights for practitioners to implement policies that combine social and economic perspectives for developing innovation strategies. This paper contends that economic activities are dependent upon social networks to transform business and market structures. The paper has implications in framing policies for businesses, financial institutions, mobile operators and development practitioners for advancing micro-entrepreneurial development in rural communities.

REFERENCES

Aker, J. and Mbiti, I., 2010. Mobile Phones and Economic Development in Africa. *Journal of Economic Perspectives,* 24 (3), pp.207-232.

Aker, J., 2008. Does Digital Divide or Provide? The Impact of Cell Phones on Grain Markets in Niger. *Center for Global Development Working Paper,* (154).

Amaghionyeodiwe, L. and Annansingh-Jamieson, F., 2017. An Investigation into the Impact of Mobile Technologies on Economic Growth and Employment in the Caribbean. Athens Journal of Business and Economics, 3 (3), pp. 263-278.

Boateng, R., Hinson, R., Galadima, R. and Olumide, L., 2014. Preliminary insights into the influence of mobile phones in micro-trading activities of market women in Nigeria. Information Development, 30(1), pp. 32–50.

Boettiger, S., Toyama, K. and Abed, R., ed., 2012. Natural Obsolescence of Village Phone. *Proceedings of the Fifth International Conference on Information and Communication Technologies and Development*. Atlanta, Georgia USA, March 12-15 2012, ACM.

Carmody, P., 2012. The Informationalisation of Poverty in Africa? Mobile Phones and Economic Structure. *Information Technologies & International Development,* 8 (3), pp. 1-17.

Chew, H. E., Levy, M.R. and Ilavarasan, P.V., 2011. The Limited Impact of ICTs on Microenterprise Growth: A Study of Businesses Owned by Women in Urban India. *Information Technologies & International Development,* 7 (4), pp.1-16.

Chew, H.E., Ilavarasan, P.V. and Levy, M.R., 2010. The Economic Impact of Information and Communication Technologies (ICTs) on Microenterprises in the Context of Development. *The Electronic Journal of Information Systems in Developing Countries,* 44 (4), pp.1-19.

De Silva, H., Ratnadiwakara, D. and Zainudeen, A., 2011. Social Influence in Mobile Phone Adoption: Evidence from the Bottom of Pyramid in Emerging Asia. *Information Technologies & International Development,* 7 (3), pp.1-18.

Donner, J. and Escobari, M.X., 2010. A Review of Evidence on Mobile Use by Micro and Small Enterprises in Developing Countries. *Journal of International Development,* 22 (5), pp.641-658.

Donner, J., 2009a. Mobile-based Livelihood Services in Africa: Pilots and Early Deployments. *Communication Technologies in Latin America and Africa: A Multidisciplinary Perspective,* pp.37-58.

Donner, J., 2009b. Blurring Livelihoods and Lives: The Social Uses of Mobile Phones and Socio-economic Development. *Innovations: Technology, Governance, Globalization,* 4 (1), pp.91-101.

Duncombe, R. and Heeks, R., 2005. Information & Communication Technologies (ICTs), Poverty Reduction and Micro, Small & Medium-scale Enterprises (MSMEs): A Framework for Understanding ICT Applications for MSMEs in Developing Countries. Vienna: *United Nations Industrial Development Organization.*

Duncombe, R., 2016. Mobile Phones for Agricultural and Rural Development: A Literature Review and Suggestions for Future Research. *The European Journey of Development Research*, 28, (2), pp. 213-235.

Duncombe, R., 2006. Using the Livelihoods Framework to Analyze ICT Applications for Poverty Reduction through Microenterprise. *Information Technologies & International Development,* 3 (3), pp.81-100.

Essegbey, G.O. and Frempong, G.K., 2011. Creating Space for Innovation - The Case of Mobile Telephony in MSEs in Ghana. *Technovation,* 31 (12), pp.679-688.

Esselaar, S., Stork, C., Ndiwalana, A. and Deen-Swarray, M., 2007. ICT Usage and Its Impact on Profitability of SMEs in 13 African Countries. *Information Technologies & International Development,* 4 (1), pp.87-100.

Frempong, G., 2009. Mobile Telephone Opportunities: The Case of Micro-and Small Enterprises in Ghana. *Info,* 11(2), pp.79-94.

Fu, X. and Akter, S., 2016. The Impact of Mobile Phone Technology on Agricultural Extension Services Delivery: Evidence from India. *The Journal of Development Studies*, 52 (11), pp. 1561- 1576.

Heeks, R., 2009. Emerging Markets IT and the World's "Bottom Billion. *Communications of the ACM*, 52 (4) pp.22-24.

Ilahiane, H. and Sherry, J.W., 2012. The Problematics of the "Bottom of the Pyramid" Approach to International Development: The Case of Micro-Entrepreneurs' Use of Mobile Phones in Morocco. *Information Technologies & International Development,* 8 (1), pp.13-26.

Jagun, A., Heeks, R. and Whalley, J., 2008. The Impact of Mobile Telephony on Developing Country Micro-enterprise: A Nigerian Case Study. *Information Technologies & International Development,* 4 (4), pp. 47-65.

James J., 2016. Micro, Macro and Scaling-Up Effects. In: *The Impact of Mobile Phones on Poverty and Inequality in Developing Countries.* SpringerBriefs in Economics. Springer, Cham

Jensen, R., 2007. The Digital Provide: Information (technology), Market Performance, and Welfare in the South Indian Fisheries Sector. *The Quarterly Journal of Economics,* 122 (3), pp.879-924.

Komunte, M., 2015. Usage of Mobile Technology in Women Entrepreneurs: A Case Study of Uganda. *The African Journal of Information Systems*, 7 (3), pp.52-74.

Komunte, M. and Rwashana, AS., 2012. Comparative Analysis of Mobile Phone Usage among Women Entrepreneurs in Uganda and Kenya. *African Journal of Computing & ICT,* 5 (5), pp.74-86.

Liedholm, C. and Mead, D. C., 1999. *Small Enterprise and Economic Development. The Dynamics of Micro and Small Enterprises.* London and New York: Routledge.

Ling, R., Parekh, P., Zainudeen, A., & Galpaya, H., 2017. Rationalization of mobile telephony by small-scale entrepreneurs in Myanmar. *Information, Communication & Society*, 1-17.

Makoza, F. and Chigona, W., 2012. The Livelihood Outcomes of ICT Use in Microenterprises: The Case of South Africa. *The Electronic Journal of Information Systems in Developing Countries,* 53 (1), pp.1-16.

Molony, T., 2008. The Role of Mobile Phones in Tanzania's Informal Construction Sector: The Case of Dares Salaam. *Urban Forum,* 19 (2), pp.175-186.

Porter, M.E., 1995. *Competitive Advantage: Creating and Sustaining Superior Performance.* New York: The Free Press.

Rabayah, K. and Qalalwi, K., 2011. The Impact of Mobile Telephony on Developing Countries Enterprises: A Palestinian Case Study. *The Electronic Journal of Information Systems in Developing Countries,* 46 (4), pp.1-20.

Smith, M.L., Spence, R. and Rashid, A.T., 2011. Mobile Phones and Expanding Human Capabilities. *Information Technologies & International Development,* 7 (3), pp.77-88.

THE INFLUENCE OF IS ON KNOWLEDGE SHARING IN MULTINATIONAL MANUFACTURING NETWORKS: EXPERIENCES FROM ALBANIAN AND MACEDONIAN PLANTS

Kreshnik Vukatana[1], Adrian Besimi[2], Kozeta Sevrani[1], Zamir Dika[2], Betim Çiço[2] and Elira Hoxha[1]
[1]*Faculty of Economy, University of Tirana, Tirana, Albania*
[2]*South East European University, Tetovo, Macedonia*

ABSTRACT

This paper addresses the topic of knowledge sharing in multinational manufacturing companies. Its purpose is to examine the role and influence of Information Systems (IS) in knowledge sharing and knowledge transfer, with specific focus in Albanian and Macedonian manufacturing plants. The study covers companies with headquarters (HQ) located in European countries. The paper presents a literature review related to the importance of ISs as knowledge enablers for manufacturing networks and their role in competitive advantage of the companies. Furthermore, a review on Enterprise Systems, Management Information Systems and Knowledge Management Systems is presented. A qualitative research methodology is used and the data are collected through semi-structured interviews from seven manufacturing plants. The data are analyzed to find the role of the subsidiary plants within the network and their position as senders or receivers of knowledge through the means of ISs. The data highlight the tendency of the companies to cover all their business processes using ISs. Even in the cases where they are not implemented, their wish is to have fully functional systems in the near future. Another fact emerged from the data is that knowledge transfer between the plants in the manufacturing networks are heavily supported by ISs, where the tools used and analyzed in this paper are supporting very well the knowledge transfer.

KEYWORDS

Knowledge Sharing, Information Systems, Manufacturing Networks, Multinational Companies

1. INTRODUCTION

The manufacturing plants of multinational companies (MNCs) located in different countries, need to communicate and to share knowledge between each other, in order to improve their processes and maintain their competitive advantage (Abdullah and Liang, 2013). These statements are developed and reinforced by many researchers (Chang et al., 2012; Fang et al., 2010). According to these authors, a significant competitive advantage of MNCs is based in their ability to create and transfer knowledge from head offices to subsidiaries abroad and vice-versa.

The aim of this study is to contribute to the understanding of information and knowledge transfer in multinational organizations through information systems. The framework for the research is provided by the scientific co-operation between Eastern Europe and Switzerland in the SCOPES program, which consists of researchers from different Universities of Switzerland and Eastern Europe countries. The main purpose of the framework research is studying the role of Eastern European manufacturing sites in manufacturing networks, regarding the influence of absorptive capacities, but this paper focuses only in the influence of IS in this typology of multinational companies networks. According to O'Brien and Marakas (2012) in the definition from their book, "an information system can be any organized combination of people, hardware, software, communications networks, data resources, and policies and procedures that stores, retrieves, transforms, and disseminates information in an organization". Our interest is mainly on knowledge and information sharing through ISs amongst different players within the manufacturing network of plants, by categorizing them in

Enterprise Resource Planning (ERP), Customer Relationship Management (CRM), Supply Chain Management (SCM), Knowledge Management Systems (KMS), Management Information Systems (MIS), Transaction Processing Systems (TPS), Decision Support Systems (DSS) and Executive Information Systems (EIS).

The data collected for our study is part of a three-year research conducted within the project "Strengthening the role of Eastern European Manufacturing Sites in Manufacturing Networks: The Influence of Absorptive Capacities". The research teams were from Switzerland, Romania, Albania and Macedonia and the interviewed companies (thirteen in total), matched the criteria of being a manufacturing plant, part of a manufacturing network in Europe. The interviews were taken during the period of August 2016 to January 2017. In order to get a better understanding on knowledge sharing and specifically how does IS support the knowledge flow between manufacturing plants, these thirteen plants were examined and analyzed through 24 examples of knowledge transfer projects. Some findings of the study are published in a joint paper (Szász et al., 2017), published by Springer in October 2017, where it is stated that an important precondition of the central role of IS in transferring knowledge, is the data quality and strategic commitment towards it. In the study, the manufacturing plants were divided in senders and receivers of knowledge. The data analysis showed that knowledge sending plants saw IS less beneficial for transferring knowledge then knowledge receiver plants who in contrast with them, saw IS as a primary enabler of knowledge transfer that may or may not be complemented with personal interaction.

2. LITERATURE REVIEW

A good starting point for our study is described by Iyengar et al. (2015) who concluded through the findings of their research that "Higher internal IT use by the franchisee will lead to higher knowledge transfer effectiveness" and that "Higher internal IT use will lead to greater franchisee absorptive capacity" that we are arguing to be so and tried to verify in our project. Jasimuddin et al. (2012) propose a knowledge transfer framework that extends the knowledge share also to other important components such as knowledge storage and knowledge administration within the knowledge transfer process. Madsen (2014) also states that IT systems along with organizational culture enhance knowledge sharing between HQs and their subsidiaries.

Sook-Ling et al. (2015) in their paper, describe an in-depth research of several aspects of IS and knowledge transfer within organizations by focusing on several major research gaps and thus covering them by providing a framework on examining whether the current information infrastructure in companies is encouraging effective knowledge management to quickly expand new business processes, techniques and decisions.

Roberts (2000) in his paper questions the role of IS in transferring knowledge and argues that technology can not entirely replace the face-to-face interaction between the sender and the receiver, which is one of the reasons that our interview considers the aspect of on-site training, in addition to the IS as a facilitator for knowledge sharing.

Different types of enterprise systems are implemented by most of nowadays organizations in order to gain efficiency in business processes, effectiveness in supply chains, and a better understanding of customer needs and behaviors. These systems help organizations in gaining competitive advantages and improving the company's profitability. As part of these systems ERP is an open-source or commercial software that enables the integration of transaction-oriented data and business processes throughout an organization (Markus et al., 2000). In other words, ERP is acclaimed as an enterprise-wide package that will tightly integrate all necessary business functions into a single system with a shared database (Lee and Lee, 2000; Shanks and Seddon, 2000). Anyway, from a critical point of view there are risk factors in enterprise-wide implementation as shown in Sumner (2000) work, which identifies the major risk factors associated with ERP projects and then compares these with the risk factors associated with implementing traditional management information systems projects. Based on her findings, risk factors associated with ERP projects include the danger of customization, the challenge of using external consultants, and the investment in recruiting and re-skilling technology professionals and business analysts.

In the context of multinational organizations, the adoption of CRM practices and solutions can improve the process of knowledge acquisition in different local markets, allowing multinational corporations to define and develop both local and global strategies according to regional demands, allowing different subsidiaries to develop long-term learning relationships with their local customers. The use of CRMs systems is becoming increasingly important to improve customer lifetime value as stated in Winer (2001) work. However, CRM systems implementation is challenging. In general, the failure rates for CRM projects have to be taken in consideration. Some of the problems with implementing the CRM arise because the local organizational culture was not taken in consideration and assessed properly before the implementation started (Brendler 2001).

SCM is a system for the management of information flows between and among activities in a supply chain, to maximize total supply chain effectiveness and corporate profitability. The challenge for firms today is not just to take up a SCM initiative but to implement it successfully. An informatics perspective is vital since information flow is an integral part of SCM and material flow is closely dependent on information flow. But SCM initiative can be a failure unless one is aware of the issues that may arise during its planning or implementation (Varma et al., 2006). As mentioned by Groznika and Trkman (2015) there are six important issues to be considered when talking about SCM, as strategic insights, business redesign, supply chain risks, frameworks and standards, performance measurement and the problematic related to IS support for SCM. The last issue is the one that interest us most, so from technological perspective SCM relates to internal and external systems for facilitating information transfer between the different sites of a MNC. SCM includes also various functional areas of an organization and is affected by the interaction and communication between employees. One of the main goals of SCM software is to enlarge flows through collaboration and for this making a tool available is not enough. Employees of different sites must be motivated to use the tool for sharing useful information in order to make its use effective. In this direction, a study related to the improvement of information flows compared various information technologies (Ruppel, 2004). The findings showed that choosing the right technology to adopt does not guarantee its effective use. The key factor that affects knowledge sharing is the successful implementation of these information technologies.

The interaction between these systems is also very important because companies run on interdependent applications (SCM, CRM, and ERP). If one application has a poor performance, the entire customer value delivery system is affected. For example, no matter how much effort a company has put in having a great CRM, if its SCM system does not work properly and the customer never receives the finished product, the company will lose that customer.

A KMS generally refers to the technology set in place to capture, disseminate and retrieve knowledge. For example, an Intranet can be referred to as a KMS depending on how it was designed. A KMS is a special class of information system applied to managing organizational knowledge (Alavi, 2001). Many organizations have implemented knowledge management systems, only to find that employees do not use them (Hansen and Von Oetinger, 2001). In some cases, employees avoid the formal KMS and continue to share knowledge person-to-person, but in other cases, employees simply do not share knowledge. Key problems cited include motivating employees to share knowledge (Reinholt et al., 2011), incentivizing knowledge sharing (Bock et al., 2005), instilling trust (He et al., 2009) and creating effective processes for knowledge sharing (Durcikova and Gray, 2009).

The systems and technologies mentioned above are the ones analyzed in our work mainly for the purpose of knowledge share between the plants of MNCs. Meanwhile in our interviews we got information also for other information systems in place that the companies might have. So, for study purpose we asked about the three primary types of MIS, available to support decision making across the company levels that are TPS, DSS and EIS. TPS is used in analyzing everyday data and operations and assists in making structured decisions (Baltzan, 2018). The information or knowledge generated from this system can be transferred to DSSs which uses different internal and external sources of detailed data for enabling high-level managers to examine and manipulate large amounts of information for decision making. One of the main categories of DSSs is communications-driven DSS which through IS and communication technologies supports the sharing of tasks and knowledge between groups (Kautish and Thapliyal, 2012). Whereas the EIS as a specialized DSS is used in the strategic level of decision making, by enabling senior-level executives for unstructured, long-term decisions that requires judgment, evaluation, and insight. Expert Systems are a kind of EIS with the main focus in knowledge transfer.

3. METHODOLOGY

This study is based mainly on a qualitative research methodology, focused on an exploratory approach, in order to examine in detail only a specific type of companies. The companies taken in consideration were all manufacturing multinational networks, where the head office of each of them was located in a European country. More specifically, the headquarters of the companies were located in Austria, Belgium, France, Greece, Italy and Switzerland, while they had plants spread across Europe and beyond. The research included several topics (products, processes, technologies and services) related to the process of creation and distribution of knowledge in an international network of manufacturing plants. We wanted to learn how is the flow between sending and receiving in the network for the above topics, letting the interviewed determine through a Likert scale (none, low, medium, high) the right weight for both directions. The findings are analyzed later in this paper.

The main method of data collection was through a semi-structured interview, conducted uniformly in each manufacturing company. Researchers have participated in multiple interviews in different countries to enable a uniform understanding of data collection. The paper focuses mainly on the qualitative data from the interviews conducted within the Albanian and Macedonian manufacturing plants and for comparative matters we will refer to quantitative data from the project. The qualitative methodology approach used to perform in depth analyses for the identified results is the case study research for a small number of companies (Baxter and Jack, 2008) and the type of case study conducted is the descriptive one (Yin, 2018). Eight interviews were conducted, for a total of seven companies in these two countries. All the eight interviewed employees were listed high in the organizational hierarchy. To ensure anonymity, identification codes were assigned to each company, from A1 to A4 for Albanian plants and M1 to M3 for Macedonian plants. Confidentiality was guaranteed to interviewees and to the companies, as well.

4. DATA ANALYSIS AND DISCUSSION

Table 1 shows data about the type of industry and the country where the interview was conducted. As seen from the table, the manufacturing plants fall in different industries, thus the findings are not related to any particular industry. It is worth noting that there are different types of plants: new ones, where buildings, technology and processes are implemented anew; existing plants with existing buildings and technology adapted to the new production processes; and another type of existing plants where the technology and production process are transferred from the other most experienced plants within company.

Table 1. Interviewed Companies by Industry

Country	Industry	Sub Total
Albania	Aluminum production	1
Albania	Cement and concrete production	2
Albania	Construction materials production	1
Macedonia	Steel industry	1
Macedonia	Automotive industry	1
Macedonia	Construction materials production	1

The targeted companies for this research had to fulfill several conditions, such as: being a manufacturing plant in Albania or Macedonia, having a plant and headquarter in Europe, and the network of manufacturing plants must be more than three units within the company. The location of plants in different countries brings an added value to the research due to the mix of cultures and managerial culture.

Table 2 shows the location of manufacturing plants and the position within the company structure, of the persons interviewed. Most of them were Chief Executive Officers (CEOs), sometimes called plant managers and in one case the Chief Technical Officer (CTO). This managerial level of their position means they have a full frame of production processes and operations in the plant, which brings added value to the quality of the data collected.

Table 2. Position within Company of Interviewees, by Plant Location

Plant location	Position
Albania (A1)	Chief Executive Officer
Albania (A1)	Chief Human Resources Officer
Albania (A2)	Chief Executive Officer
Albania (A3)	Chief Technical Officer
Albania (A4)	Chief Executive Officer
Macedonia (M1)	Chief Executive Officer
Macedonia (M2)	Chief Executive Officer
Macedonia (M3)	Chief Executive Officer

Table 3 shows for each plant, its role on sending and receiving knowledge. On the other hand, table 4 shows the plant age in years. The two tables are strongly related with each-other.

Table 3. The Role of Manufacturing Plants from Albania and Macedonia in the Knowledge Network Flow

Company Abbreviations / Plant roles	A1	A2	A3	A4	M1	M2	M3
Knowledge sending	medium	low	low	none	none	medium	medium
Knowledge receiving	medium	high	high	high	high	high	medium

The role of plants in the network related to "knowledge sending", in both countries is low or none. Only in plant A1, M2 e M3 is medium. This means that the examined plants can be considered mostly as receivers especially in the strategic decision making level. But there is knowledge flow in the other direction also. For the Macedonian plants, as the plant managers said, the plants age was a factor of experience in production processes to share knowledge with newer plants in the network of the same company. Meanwhile, A1 was the plant with the newest technology in its network and its key factor of success was the knowledge on innovation to share with the other plants.

Table 4. Plant Age by Country Location

Company Abbreviations	A1	A2	A3	A4	M1	M2	M3
Plant age in years	6	8	12	9	4	19	13

Concerning the "knowledge receiving", it seems clear that is a lot of knowledge flowing from headquarter or other plants of developed countries to Macedonian and Albanian plants, this due to the limited experience of workforce and to the new technologies and processes brought by the parent company.

All the interviewed companies, both Albanian and Macedonian companies have implemented Information Systems in general, but the type of these systems is different for different companies, due to the profile of the business and the manufacturing network specifics.

From the data collected through the interview, in Table 5 is shown a short summary. What emerges from these data is that most of the companies are mainly focused on Enterprise Applications such as Enterprise Resource Planning (ERP), where the majority are based on SAP software, rather than dedicated ad-hoc systems. This applies both to Albanian and Macedonian companies, showing a high level of usage of IS within the plants, but in most of the cases operated and invested directly by the headquarters.

Another interesting fact is that Decision Support Systems (DSS) is missing in Macedonian and Albanian companies. These DSSs seemed to be included as integrated part of the ERP systems in use, such as MIS reports which are mainly used in daily/weekly routines, in the companies that were part of the study. From this analysis can be perceived that in both, Macedonian and Albanian companies the decision making is made mainly in the HQ, therefore the majority of the IS systems that handle decision making like DSS are not in place.

Table 5. Information Systems in Place by Plant Location

Information Systems in place \ Company Abbreviations	A1	A2	A3	A4	M1	M2	M3
Enterprise Resource Planning (ERP)	Yes	Yes	Yes	Yes	Yes	Yes	Yes
Knowledge Management System (KMS)	No	Yes	No	No	Yes	Yes	No
Customer Relationship Management (CRM)	Yes	No	Yes	Yes	Yes	Yes	No
Supply Chain Management (SCM)	No	No	Yes	No	Yes	Yes	Yes
Transaction Processing System (TPS)	Yes	No	No	No	Yes	Yes	No
Management information system (MIS)	Yes	Yes	No	No	No	Yes	No
Decision Support System (DSS)	No	No	No	No	No	Yes	No
Executive Information Systems (EIS)	No	No	No	No	No	No	No

The analysis of Supply Chain Management (SCM) shows that the majority of manufacturing plants heavily depend on the Supply Chain from the HQ, but in some cases the companies have some autonomy. This is due to the fact that some plants are established in Macedonia or Albania for the raw materials closeness, as it is for the metal and cement industry. In these cases the SCM is in place. What emerged as result of interviews is that most of interviewed managers are in favor of using SCM in their plants.

Knowledge Management Systems (KMS) usage is important for these manufacturing networks and our findings show that half of the companies have KMS in place or partially. In some cases it was mentioned during the interviews that they do use various tools for the information and knowledge sharing but not necessarily in place dedicated KMS systems.

5. CONCLUSION

This paper analyzed the influence of IS in knowledge sharing, through a case study in networks of manufacturing MNCs of Albanian and Macedonian plants.

The tendency of the companies, as seen from the data analysis and the interviews conducted, is to cover all their business processes using IS/ERPs. Even in the cases where they are not implemented, their tendency is to have fully functional systems in the near future and this brings added value to the local manufacturing plants, to synchronize activities and processes within the network of companies plants.

Our findings did conclude that even in the cases of Macedonian or Albanian manufacturing plants, in relation to the capabilities of emerging countries is that the knowledge transfer between the plants in the manufacturing networks are heavily supported by IS, and the tools that we analyzed that were used, are very well supporting this knowledge transfer. There is no particular tool used, but in all cases there is an IS that is being leveraged by the manufacturing plants from Macedonia and Albania as "receivers", where all the knowledge relies on, and this knowledge is further used in many manufacturing processes.

ACKNOWLEDGEMENT

We would like to thank the Swiss National Science Foundation (SCOPES Joint Research Project IZ73Z0_152505) for the financial support provided for the research project discussed in this paper.

REFERENCES

Abdullah N. A. H. N. and Liang L. Y., 2013. Knowledge Sharing between Multinational Corporation's Headquarters and Subsidiaries: the Impact of Manager's Role, Compensation System and Cultural Differences. *Journal of Economics and Behavioral Studies*. Vol. 5, No. 10. pp. 660-668

Alavi, M. and Leidner, D. E., 2001. Review: Knowledge Management and Knowledge Management Systems: Conceptual Foundations and Research Issues. *MIS Quaterly*, 25, pp. 107-136.

Baltzan, P., 2018. *M: Information Systems 4th ed.* McGraw-Hill Education, New York.

Baxter, P. and Jack, S., 2008. Qualitative Case Study Methodology: Study Design and Implementation for Novice Researchers. *The Qualitative Report*, 13(4), pp. 544-559.

Bock, G., Zmud, R.W., Kim, Y. and Lee, J., 2005. Behavioral intention formation in knowledge sharing: Examining the roles of extrinsic motivators, social-psychological forces, and organizational climate. *MIS Quarterly*, 29(1), pp. 87–111.

Brendler, W., 2001. 8 Critical factors that make or break CRM. *Target Marketing*, (24:4), pp. 57-61.

Chang, Y. Y., Gong, Y. and Peng, M. W., 2012. Expatriate Knowledge Transfer, Subsidiary Absorptive Capacity, and Subsidiary Performance. *Academy of Management Journal*. Vol. 55, No. 4, pp. 927-948.

Durcikova, A. and Gray, P., 2009. How knowledge validation processes affect knowledge contribution. *Journal of Management Information Systems*, 25(4), pp. 81–108.

Fang, Y., Jiang, GL. F., Makino, S and Beamish, P. W., 2010. Multinational Firm Knowledge, Use of Expatriates, and Foreign Subsidiary Performance. *Journal of Management Studies*. Vol. 47, pp. 27-54.

Groznika, A. and Trkman, P., 2015. Current Issues and Challenges of Supply Chain Management. *Economic Research-Ekonomska Istraživanja*, 25:4, pp. 1101-1112.

Hansen, M.T. and Von Oetinger, B., 2001. Introducing t-shaped manager: Knowledge management's next generation. *Harvard Business Review*, 79(3), pp. 106–116.

He, W., Fang, Y. and Wei, K. K., 2009. The role of trust in promoting organizational knowledge seeking using knowledge management systems: An empirical investigation. *Journal of the American Society for Information Science and Technology*, 60(3), pp. 526–537.

Iyengar, K., Sweeney, J.R. and Montealegre, R., 2015. Information technology use as a learning mechanism: The impact of IT use on knowledge transfer effectiveness, absorptive capacity, and franchisee performance. *Mis Quarterly 39*: pp. 615-641.

Jasimuddin, S.M., Connell, N. and Klein, J.H., 2012. Knowledge transfer frameworks: an extension incorporating knowledge repositories and knowledge administration. *Information Systems Journal 22*: pp. 195-209.

Kautish, S. and Thapliyal, M. P., 2012. Concept of Decision Support Systems in relation with Knowledge Management – Fundamentals, theories, frameworks and practices. *International Journal of Application or Innovation in Engineering & Management (IJAIEM)* Vol. 1, Issue 2.

Lee, Z., and Lee, J., 2000. An ERP Implementation Case Study from a Knowledge Transfer Perspective. *Journal of Information Technology* (12:2), pp. 281-288.

Madsen, A. S., 2014. Knowledge Sharing in a Multinational Corporation. A case study of knowledge sharing between HQ and subsidiaries and the integration of marketing strategies. *Copenhagen Business School Master Thesis*. July 2014.

Markus, L., Axline, S., Petrie, D. and Tanis, C., 2000 . Learning from Adopters' Experience with ERP Problems Encountered and Success Achieved. *Journal of Information Technology* (15: 2), pp. 245-265.

Reinholt, M., Pedersen, T. and Foss, N., 2011. Why a center network position isn't enough: The role of motivation and ability for knowledge sharing in employee networks. *Academy of Management Journal*, 54(6), pp. 1277–1297.

Roberts, J., 2000. From know-how to show-how? Questioning the role of information and communication technologies in knowledge transfer. *Technology Analysis & Strategic Management 12*: pp. 429-443.

Ruppel, C., 2004. An information systems perspective of supply chain tool compatibility: the roles of technology fit and relationships. *Business Process Management journal* 10 (3): pp. 311-323.

Shanks, G., and Seddon, P., 2000. Editorial: Enterprise Resource Planning (ERP) Systems. *Journal of Information Technology* (15:2), pp. 243-244.

Sook-Ling, L., Ismail, M.A. and Yee-Yen, Y., 2015. Information infrastructure capability and organisational competitive advantage: framework. *International Journal of Operations & Production Management 35*: pp. 1032-1055.

Sumner, M., 2000. Risk Factors in Enterprise-wide/ERP Projects. *Journal of Information Technology* (15), pp.317-327.

Szász, L., Scherrer, M., Deflorin, P., Sevrani, K., Cico, B., Besimi, A., Vukatana, K. and Rácz, B., 2017. The Role of ICT-Based Information Systems in Knowledge Transfer within Multinational Companies. In: Lödding H., Riedel R., Thoben KD., von Cieminski G., Kiritsis D. (eds) Advances in Production Management Systems. The Path to Intelligent, Collaborative and Sustainable Manufacturing. APMS 2017. *IFIP Advances in Information and Communication Technology, Vol. 513*. Springer, Cham.

Varma, S., Wadhwa, S. and Deshmukh, S.G., 2006. Implementing supply chain management in a firm: issues and remedies. *Asia Pacific Journal of Marketing and Logistics* 18 (3): pp. 223-243.

Winer, R. S., 2001. A Framework for Customer Relationship Management. *California Management Review*, 43(4), pp. 89–104.

Yin, R. K., 2018. *Case Study Research Design and Methods* (5th ed.). Sage Publication, Inc., USA.

MANAGING AGILE AND DEV-OPS ACTIVITIES THROUGH A CONSOLIDATED WEB PORTAL: SOUTH AFRICAN CASE STUDY

Abdel Kader Doukoure Gaoussou and Dr. Ernest Mnkandla
College of Science, Engineering & Technology, School of Computing, University of South Africa, Johannesburg, South Africa

ABSTRACT

Modern approaches to software project and operations management have shifted from traditional waterfall models. Nowadays, firms require a novel understanding of the agile philosophy and Dev-Ops. As the number of software suites and services available to facilitate agile related practices increasingly grows, organizations need to manage the large amount of data generated by these tools. In effect, during project lifecycles, extensive usage of such technologies can yield an unmanageable amount of scattered information views for stakeholders. Further problems arise when this information results in seemingly conflicting sources of truth. In such cases, inaccurate information can negatively inform project management and engineering activities. The current paper aims to address this issue by conducting a case study at a South African start-up where a web-based portal is designed for the consolidation of information specifically pertaining to agile and Dev-Ops activities. Underpinned by an activity theory centered framework, the research discusses how the developed tool was designed. The paper concludes by describing how the proposed information system was perceived to positively impact agile teams during our case study.

KEYWORDS

Agile, Dev-Ops, Project Management, Activity Theory

1. INTRODUCTION

Modern firms are moving away from traditional waterfall models (Mwansa, 2016, p. 382). In South Africa, some studies show the adoption of agile practices in more than eighty percent (80%) of companies surveyed (*ibid.* 2016). This has resulted in an increased reliance on agile-compatible software suites and services.

While the number of services available to facilitate agile related practices grows, organizations need to manage the large amount of data generated by these tools. In effect, during project lifecycles, extensive usage of such technologies can yield an unmanageable amount of scatted information views for stakeholders. Further problems can arise when this information results in seemingly conflicting sources of truth. In these cases, inaccurate information can negatively inform project management and engineering activities.

To address this, the current study describes the design and implementation of an IS to facilitate the management of agile and Dev-Ops activities.

2. AGILE AND RELATED PRACTICES

Organizations need to be attentive to the way in which they run their projects. On the South African scene for example, agile approaches have been shown to decrease IT project failure rates (Joseph, Marnewick and Jan Santana, 2016, p. 338). Local academia seems to indicate that the most prolific methodologies in use include Scrum, Extreme Programming and Kanban (*ibid.* 2016):

- *Scrum advocates short unit works which are built in a series of fixed-length iterations called sprints.* (Radigan, 2017, para. 2).

- *Extreme Programming (XP) advocates short development cycles called releases to improve productivity*(Mwansa, 2015, p. 30).
- *In Kanban projects, items are visualized with cards onto a task board* (Beck et al. in Nakazawa and Tanaka, 2016, p. 1). *These boards will include technical details valuable to assignees and allow team members to be updated with task status throughout the project at any time.*

As agile has positively influenced business perception of software teams, operations staff members have not always benefited from the same appreciation. In many organizations, application internals and detailed systems architecture are not always well understood by operations staff. Conversely, software engineers are not always in tune with infrastructure basics and critical environment variables such as platform dependencies, network limitations etc. This situation has led to the emergence of Dev-Ops as an engineering model geared towards an increase of collaboration, communication and integration between software and operations engineers (Di Nitto *et al.*, 2016, p. 12).

Dev-Ops encourages the sharing of responsibilities and accountability between software and operations engineers (Perera, Bandara and Perera, 2016, p. 282). It often encompasses three principal activities which include a build phase with Continuous Integration and testing; a release phase with Continuous Delivery and Deployment; and an Operate phase which contains tasks related to the operations support domain.

The move towards agile methods for teams and the emergence of Dev-Ops as an engineering paradigm to support this philosophy illustrates the need for innovative disruptive technology to support projects. In the next sections, we proceed to present a snapshot of agile and Dev-Ops technologies available.

2.1 Managing an Overwhelming Amount of Technology in Agile Settings

Because agile teams increasingly require reliable software services to conduct their daily activities, these services need to address needs such as reliable code source control, infrastructure a project management capability, as well as enabling Dev-Ops. Organizations can leverage a combination of cloud offerings and software services to address these project needs. The table below provides a snapshot of these services:

Table 1. Technology Options Available to Agile Teams

Agile Team Project Requirement	*Available service*
Infrastructure	• **AWS** • **Microsoft Azure** • **Digital Ocean**
Source Control	• **Bitbucket** • **GitHub**
Project Management	• **JIRA** • **Trello** • **Microsoft PPM** • **Redmine**
Dev-Ops	• **Slack** for ChatOps • **Jenkins** for CI/CD • **TeamCity for** CI/CD

During the current research exercise, we conducted a case study at a South African start-up which runs its daily activities by utilizing many of the tools mentioned above, in the next section we proceed to introduce this local organization: GZ Consulting Services.

2.2 Case Study: Presenting GZ Consulting Services

GZ Consulting services(GZCS) is an agile technology start-up located in Gauteng, South Africa. GZCS projects are essentially managed through scrum, Kanban boards and teams embrace Dev-Ops. Software engineers are expected to be able to perform certain operational tasks such as deploying code, writing scripts etc. and infrastructure operators are expected to be able to contribute code when required. In addition, the firm has a heavy cloud footprint.

GIT is the source control management system used with private GITHUB cloud repositories. Project leaders leverage a private Atlassian JIRA cloud instance to manage software and business projects. Amazon EC2 cloud infrastructure is used to host runtimes such Java enterprise grade products, web applications built in

NodeJS etc. Continuous integration (CI) is performed with a Jenkins instance hooked into the source control system to build, test and deploy.

The list of tools utilized by the firm is not exhaustive and the sheer number of these technologies has led to the generation of an immense amount of data for project teams.

3. BACKGROUND TO THE PROBLEM AND RESEARCH OBJECTIVE

When running agile projects, organizations can experience challenges in keeping workloads integrated among team members (Stillwell and Coutinho, 2015, p. 1). Moreover, agile environments have often yielded poor documentation and a lack of traceability management (Palihawadana *et al.*, 2017, p. 130). In the case of engineers for example, there is an additional need to provide updated and consistent environment information to ensure smooth running of engineering tasks ((*ibid.* 2017). If an organization decides to adopt new methodologies and technology tools, this often initially has implications regarding reduced efficiency while increasing overhead costs (Logigear, 2013, para. 2). Moreover, usage by project teams of the latest technology trends or tools does not guarantee the delivery of quality software.

At GZCS, engineers need to access many different systems to get information sets that are often related when not redundant. Project managers for example would like to have more practical insight into feedback from engineers. This is because task updates from technical staff does not always convince project leaders, and they would like to be able to monitor practical development progress without having to know the intricacies of navigating through the command line of a GIT system for instance.

In effect, at the term initial exchanges with staff members in regards of their perception of effective agile practices at the firm and possible limitations, our central research question emerged:

> *How could an information system be designed to improve the management of agile and Dev-Ops activities?*

The research objective tilted therefore towards the design of an information system (IS) which would consolidate data from a firm's internal tools into a consolidated information to improve the management of agile and Dev-Ops activities. We were hence inclined to sketch a model describing key motivators for the development of such a tool:

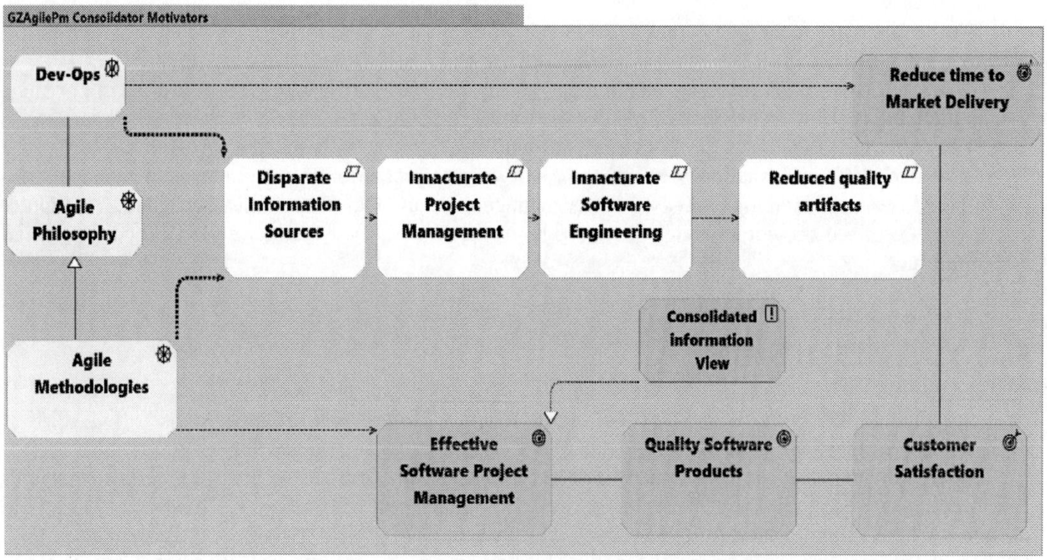

Figure 1. Motivators for an Information Consolidation Tool

We thus proceed to discuss the design of our proposed tool "*GZAgilePM Consolidator*" by first introducing the theoretical foundation and conceptual framework underpinning this study.

4. THEORETICAL FRAMEWORK

The works of Vygotsky and Leontiev in the early 1920s contributed to the emergence of Activity Theory (AT) as a lens to facilitate understanding of human activity (Hasan and Kazlauskas, 2014, p. 9). Initially grounded in the field of human psychology, this theory has also been used in other fields including ethnography, human-computer interaction systems research, communications, education etc. (Karanasios, Riisla and Simeonova, 2017, p. 1).

Research projects underpinned by an Activity Theory(AT) lenses suppose at least three key methodological requirements (Hasan and Kazlauskas, 2014, p. 12):

- The identification of the main activities to be observed in conjunction with each activity's subject, object and outcome.
- The identification of actions which constitute these activities and their mediating tools.
- The description of interactions between and throughout the identified activities

AT is attractive to IS researchers as it facilitates studies which cover a maximum amount of alternative contexts in terms of ubiquitous computing analysis (Achour et al. in Iadis, 2012, p. 66).

4.1 Applying an Activity Theory Lenses in the Current Study

The current study aimed to result in the design of an IS which would facilitate the management of agile and Dev-Ops activities. Activity Theory in the context of IS research can be used to place technology as the central tool which mediates actions of individuals in the community (Hashim and Jones, 2007, p. 6). In this light, underpinned by an AT informed framework, we have identified:

- Agile engineering as Central Activity 1 (We also include Dev-Ops in this).
- Agile project management as Central Activity 2.
- The local African start-up and software engineering industry as Mediator 1.
- GZ Consulting Services (local African software house also described as GZ CS)'s organizational culture as Mediator 2.
- The entire agile technology stack GZ CS uses to build its software for the African market as Internal Mediators.
- An IS named "GZAgilePM consolidator" as the principal technology Tool and Mediator meant to facilitate the continuous delivery of quality software.
- The entire GZ CS team as the Community around which the activity system revolves.
- A consolidated information view of agile software project information for project managers and the entire software engineering team as to better manage agile and Dev-Ops related activities as the Outcome.

Having described the cornerstones of the current study's activity system, we next proceed to detail our system design.

5. SYSTEMS DESIGN

An experimental tool referred to as "***GZ-Agile Project Management Consolidator***" (GZAPMC) was designed to facilitate management of agile and Dev-Ops activities during our case study.

The IS implemented services two central activities in the form of Agile Engineering (this includes activities considered in the Dev-Ops realm) as well as Agile Project Management. The core actors considered during implementation of the Agile PM consolidator system were project managers and engineers at GZCS.

For our system to provide intended functionality to users such as retrieving data from the tools already in use at GZ Consulting Services, a credentials registration module is required. This functionality is used to secure internal users data. It is also used to store essential third-party credentials which enables the system to authenticate users to cloud services and backend systems we require information from. Once this is done, project managers and software engineers have access to a consolidated view of software project information aggregated from various sources used at GZ Consulting services. Additionally, users can initiate a complete project creation workflow which will synchronize and integrate the developed system's artefacts to tools already in use at the organization and hence monitor them as well.

The web portal technical design was essentially informed by the Model-View-Controller pattern. This architectural style preconizes segregation of the presentation layer from business layers as well as backend data (Wu, 2016). In addition to the tool implemented, three main backends which the Agile PM Consolidator would have to integrate to were identified: A Source Control Management System, the current Project Management system in use at GZ Consulting Services, and a Continuous Integration and Deployment service used by engineers at the firm. The designed web application leverages an application programming interface layer (API) which performs some of the integration to third party systems. The front end seamlessly integrates to the source control system via plugins and it leverages similar technologies and an API layer to integrate with the project management system (Atlassian JIRA) currently used as well as the CI/CD tool (Jenkins).

GZ Agile project management consolidator interacts via APIs calls with the current systems in use at the firm to retrieve, post and aggregate data. The next illustration depicts the overall picture of how the system was designed and includes the business, application and technology views considered:

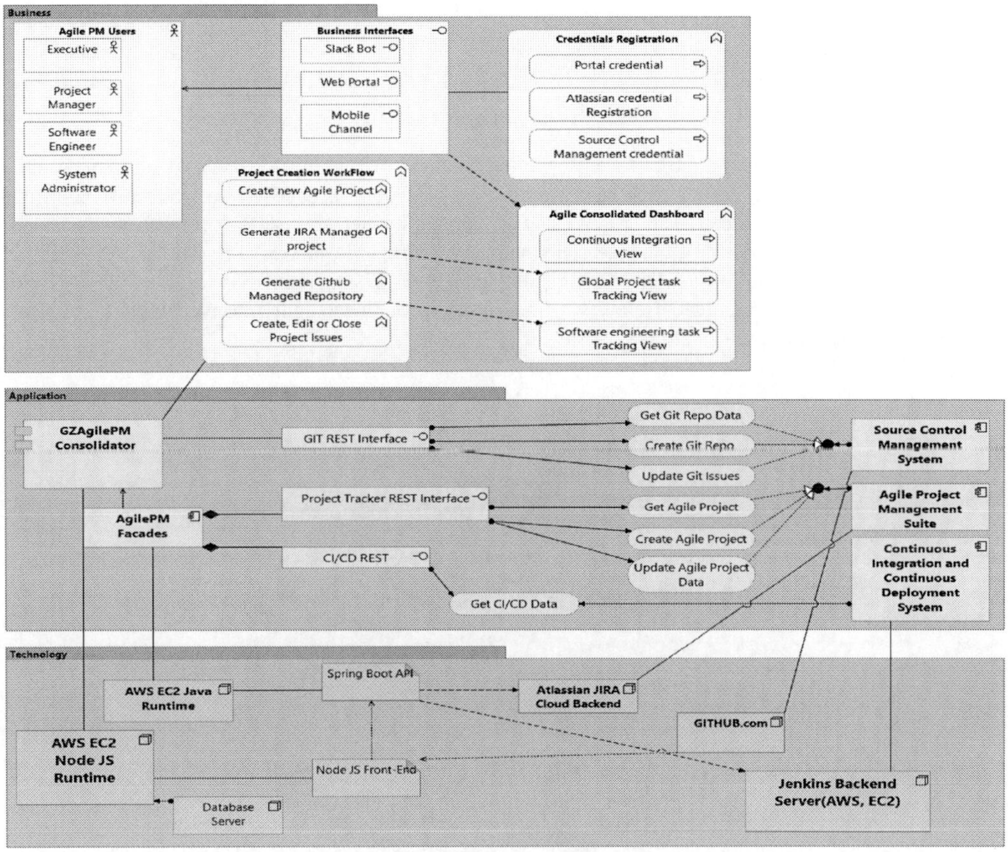

Figure 2. GZAPM Consolidator Full View

Figure 2 above complements the previous two illustrations of the system by adding the technology stack which forms the foundation of our IS. The entire system runs on Amazon Cloud EC2 Linux infrastructure. The front-end built with NodeJS, leverages SpringBoot APIS that expose a collection of façades to call back end services such as Atlassian JIRA, GITHUB and Jenkins.

6. PRELIMINARY EVALUATION

To gage our tool's usability and retrieve user perceptions, after deployment, we provided GZ Consulting Services staff with access the tool's portal. The figures below include sample key integrations the developed tool provides:

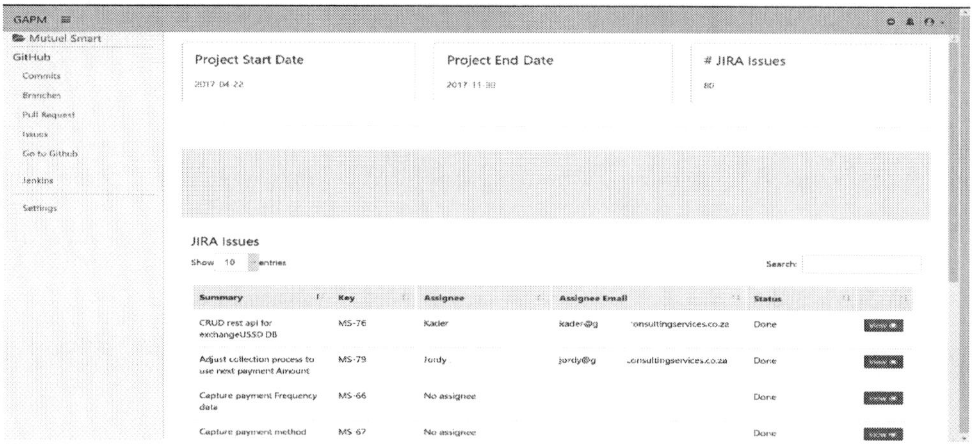

Figure 3. GZAPMC Atlassian Integration

After having introduced the tool to staff, we left the system running for 6 weeks and encouraged users to interact with the portal during their daily activities. We then proceeded to collect data through direct observations and semi-structured interviews of GZ Consulting Services staff during project management and engineering activities. After this, the researcher shared an electronic survey to try and capture staff perceptions and understanding of agile and Dev-Ops related concepts. The survey also enabled us to capture usage information, end user sentiment. Below we present some of the insight retrieved with QDA Miner during analysis of the survey data.

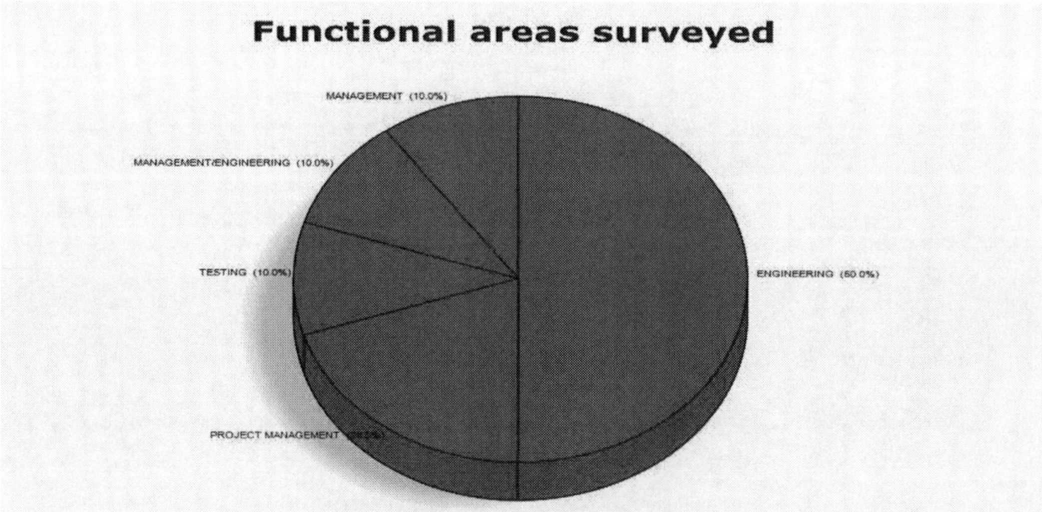

Figure 4. QDA Miner Surveyed Functional Areas

Feedback from engineers indicated usefulness in providing a single point of entry to engineering activities and CI information. The convincing argument was that an engineer well versed in agile and Dev-Ops practices would find the tool useful and insightful because it reduces the number of systems one needs to be knowledgeable about to get things done in an agile team setting.

In regard to project management activities, one administrator seemed overwhelmed by the main portal dashboard and did not believe the system would provide him anything relevant not already accessible. Another project manager's view was that the system could now help him recon engineer feedback during stand-up meetings and JIRA task updates, with actual activity velocity on source control systems and Dev-Ops tooling dashboard. The figure below illustrates GZ AgilePM Consolidator integration to the CI system:

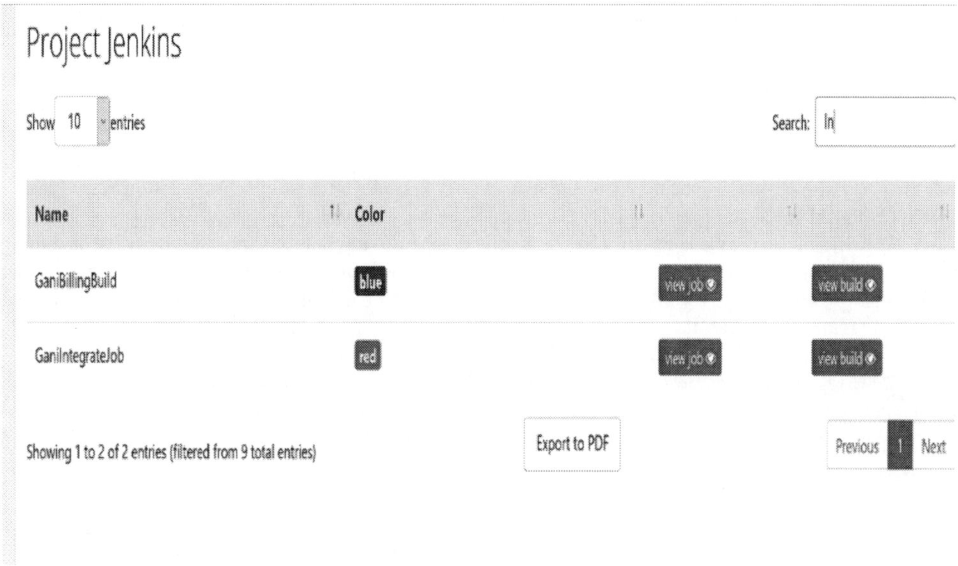

Figure 5. GZAPMC CI/CD Integration

7. CONCLUSION

This paper described the design of GZAPMC, a tool implemented to consolidate information from a firm's internal systems. GZAPMC ambitions to facilitate management of agile and Dev-Ops activities by aggregating project information into a central portal. With this tool, engineers are able to monitor project activities such as code commits, checkouts and artifact deployment from agile 3rd party tools. Feedback retrieved during the case study from participants seems to paint the tool built as useful to both project management and engineering staff in their daily activities. GZAGPMC reduces point of entries to access project information and presents a unified or centralized version of the truth. This is argued to indeed facilitate the management of agile and Dev-Ops activities. Future research informed by this case study will be conducted to determine how the agile consolidator information portal built, could fit in the bigger agenda of improving software quality and thus facilitating the delivery of quality software products to markets.

ACKNOWLEDGEMENT

For their invaluable contribution in the architecture design and engineering of GZAPM, the authors need to acknowledge:
Herve Ntubi, EMPLOG
Jonathan Mayunga, INTEGROVE,
Jordy Mugeni, Standard Bank of South Africa

REFERENCES

Hasan, H. and Kazlauskas, A. (2014) 'Activity Theory: who is doing what, why and how', *Being Practical with Theory: A Window into Business Research*, pp. 9–14. doi: 10.3102/0034654306298273.

Hashim, N. H. and Jones, M. L. (2007) 'Activity Theory : A framework for qualitative analysis', *Qualitative Research*, pp. 3–5. Available at: http://ro.uow.edu.au/cgi/viewcontent.cgi?article=1434&context=commpapers%5Cnhttp://ro.uow.edu.au/cgi/viewcontent.cgi?article=1434&context=commpapers.

Iadis (2012) 'IADIS International Conference Information Systems 2012', in Nunes, M. B., Isaias, P., and Powell, P. (eds) *IADIS International Conference Information Systems*. Berlin: IADIS, International Association for development of the information society, p. 460.

Joseph, N., Marnewick, C. and Jan Santana, M. (2016) 'Agile Software Development and IT Project Performance in South Africa: A positive relationship?', in. Orlando, Florida, USA: International Association for Management of Technology, pp. 338–358.

Karanasios, S., Riisla, K. and Simeonova, B. (2017) 'Exploring the use of contradictions and tensions in activity theory studies: an interdisciplinary review', in *33rd EGOS Colloquium: The Good Organisation*. Copenhagen: Loughborough University Institutional Repository, pp. 0–9. Available at: https://dspace.lboro.ac.uk/2134/26026.

Logigear (2013) *How to Select the Right Tools for Testing in Agile ?*, *http://www.logigear.com*. Available at: http://www.logigear.com/blog/agile/using-tools-for-testing-in-agile/ (Accessed: 20 December 2017).

Mwansa, G. (2015) *Exploring the development of a framework for agile methodologies to promote the adoption and use of cloud computing services in South Africa*. University of South Africa.

Mwansa, G. (2016) 'An investigation into agile development methodologies in use by small , medium and micro enterprises in South Africa', in *2016 International Conference on Advances in Computing and Communication Engineering (ICACCE)*. Durban, pp. 381–386.

Nakazawa, S. and Tanaka, T. (2015) 'Prototype of Kanban Tool and Preliminary Evaluation of Visualizing Method for Task Assignment', *Proceedings - 2015 International Conference on Computer Application Technologies, CCATS 2015*, pp. 48–49. doi: 10.1109/CCATS.2015.21.

Nakazawa, S. and Tanaka, T. (2016) 'Development and application of kanban tool visualizing the work in progress', *Proceedings - 2016 5th IIAI International Congress on Advanced Applied Informatics, IIAI-AAI 2016*, pp. 908–913. doi: 10.1109/IIAI-AAI.2016.156.

Di Nitto, E. *et al.* (2016) 'A software architecture framework for quality-aware DevOps', in *Proceedings of the 2nd International Workshop on Quality-Aware DevOps - QUDOS 2016*, pp. 12–17. doi: 10.1145/2945408.2945411.

Palihawadana, S. *et al.* (2017) 'Tool support for traceability management of software artefacts with DevOps practices', *3rd International Moratuwa Engineering Research Conference, MERCon 2017*, pp. 129–134. doi: 10.1109/MERCon.2017.7980469.

Perera, P., Bandara, M. and Perera, I. (2016) 'Evaluating the Impact of DevOps Practice in Sri Lankan Software Development Organizations', pp. 281–287. doi: 10.1109/ICTER.2016.7829932.

Radigan, D. (2017) *Scrum A brief look into using the scrum framework for software development*, *www.atlassian.com*. Available at: https://www.atlassian.com/agile/scrum (Accessed: 3 May 2017).

Stillwell, M. and Coutinho, J. G. F. (2015) 'A DevOps approach to integration of software components in an EU research project', *1st International Workshop on Quality-Aware DevOps, QUDOS 2015 - Proceedings*, (c), pp. 1–6. doi: 10.1145/2804371.2804372.

Wu, M. (2016) 'Design and implementation of J2EE and MVC model based enterprise information management system', in *Proceedings - 2016 International Conference on Intelligent Transportation, Big Data and Smart City, ICITBS 2016*, pp. 424–427. doi: 10.1109/ICITBS.2016.115.

A CYBERSECURITY MODEL FOR MOBILE DEVICES AIMED AT SMES THAT USE FREELANCERS AND BYOD SCHEMES

Ramon Bruderer[1], Moises Villena[1], Manuel Tupia[1] and Mariuxi Bruzza[2]
[1]*Pontificia Universidad Católica, Avenida Universitaria 1801 San Miguel, Lima, Peru*
[2]*Universidad Laica "Eloy Alfaro" de Manabi, Ciudadela Universitaria S/N, Manta, Manabí, Ecuador*

ABSTRACT

Small and Medium Sized enterprises (SMSs) that provide services related to information and communications technologies (ICT) have developed a human resources scheme with its labor force being mainly made up of freelancers. These companies' lower costs even in infrastructure by allowing this kind of employees to use their own computer equipment (e.g., computers, servers, multiple devices) following the Bring Your Own Device (BYOD) mode. However, this results in more vulnerable devices to cyberattacks. This article intends to put forward a cybersecurity management model applicable to this type of companies, oriented to mobile devices which allow for securing confidentiality, integrity and availability of the information managed by them. This model is composed of three main components: processes, management indicators or metrics and the implementation guide of the model itself. ISO 27032 standards and NIST standards have been mainly used. Meanwhile, to test the model's validity, the expert judgment will be used as a validation tool.

KEYWORDS

Cybersecurity Model, Mobile Devices, BYOD, Information Security, SME

1. INTRODUCTION

At present a wide consensus regards cyberattacks as one of the major threats to the security and privacy of the information managed by the companies. The increasing number of attacks in several countries around the globe are quite evident; among these cases is the Stuxnet case. This was a malicious computer worm designed to destroy uranium enrichment facilities in Iran (Berghel, 2015). Another case involves hackers who infiltrated the network of one of the companies managing the nuclear plants in South Korea and stole material information on the design of reactors and the plants' employees (ISACA, 2010). Likewise, Sony was the victim of a theft of a great amount of company information regarding employees and planning documents, and some of the company's computers got infected as well. Many other similar events took place throughout 2017 in companies such as Deloitte, WannaCry, NotPetya, Equifax, Maersk, Forever 21. Some of them were disclosed to the public with the availability, confidentiality and integrity of the information of people or organizations being affected (Castillo, 2018).

The small and medium sized enterprises face huge economic challenges in their early stages of their life. One of them is the monetary liquidity issue even in the payment of their human resources. This topic is critical for service providers of information and communications technology (ICT) as they allocate a very high percentage of their expenses to the payment of human resources (human intensive character). This is why they advocate for the hiring of staff on a freelance basis, allowing these employees (for example, programmers, designers, architects, analysts, testers) to bring their own technological equipment to the workplace so as to lower costs in the infrastructure area. This company policy is usually called "Bring your own device" (Vaca Herrera, Ron and Rabadao, 2017).

Despite the benefits they may obtain, on many occasions SMEs are not aware of data security and privacy risks they might have introduced with these practices since their information (confidential, private) will now be circulating through non-controlled or monitored devices or unprotected (Flores, Qazi and Jhumka, 2016). Additionally, it is worth highlighting the widespread use of mobile devices which exhibit vulnerabilities that make them sensitive to cyberattacks. They are both used to develop technology within the companies and remotely use systems and applications that can manage confidential information (ISACA, 2015). Hence it is necessary that the companies establish a set of good practices of information security and data privacy so as to protect freelancers' information assets contained in mobile devices under BYOD schemes.

This paper will introduce a cybersecurity model that enables the protection of information managed or stored in mobile devices. The content of the article is organized as follows: Section 2 briefly explains the proposed model, Section 3 introduces the model components, Section 4 lays out each component, Section 5 conducts the validation by expert judgment, and finally Section 6 contains the conclusions arrived with such a contribution.

2. MODEL EXPLANATION

This article introduces a cybersecurity model for mobile devices mainly based on ISO 27032 standard (ISO, 2012) and the cybersecurity framework of NIST in its version 1.0 (NIST, 2017). Additionally, the model is partially based on (Tupia, Bruzza and Rodríguez, 2018). The model uses categories, subcategories, objectives and the results of the structure of the NIST framework. After using the model indicators, the model will be reviewed to determine whether this is helping to improve the security of the organization's mobile devices. Below are the components that make up the proposed model.

2.1 Components

The model of cybersecurity introduced is made up of 3 components displayed below:

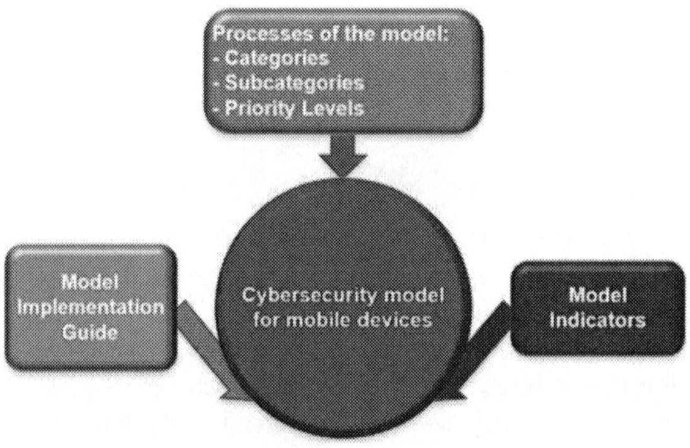

Figure 1. Component of Proposed Model

2.2 Component 1 - Processes Model

The model processes are composed of three parts as follows: model categories, subcategories related to the categories and model's priority levels.

2.2.1 Categories

Sets of outcomes expected or objectives of the controls expected to be achieved. Each of these categories is related to a basic cybersecurity activity, including identification, protection, detection, response and recovery. These categories with their core cybersecurity activity related will be drawn from NIST cybersecurity framework (NIST, 2017).

For the definition of model subcategories both NIST (NIST, 2017; Ross, 2013) and ISO 27032 (ISO, 2012) will be reviewed. With such information, the most appropriate subcategories will be defined to enhance cyber-security of mobile devices. Once subcategories are defined, it will be determined to which category of the NIST cyber-security framework belongs said subcategory. These categories which at least one subcategory belongs to will be included in the model. A example can be seen on table 1:

Table 1. Sample of a Category with only one Subcategory

Category	Subcategory	Priority
Data security and privacy	Data stored and broadcasted by mobile device is protected	None (inside de category, the subcategory is unique)

Figure 2 displays all the model categories and subcategories.

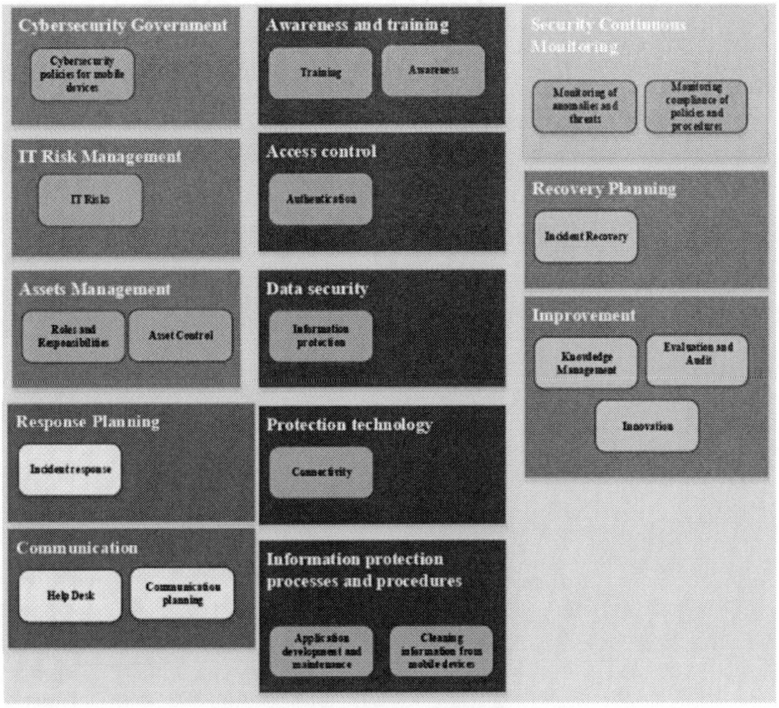

Figure 2. Model Categories and Subcategories

Table 2 shows the relationship between a category, its respective subcategories, the descriptions of these subcategories and the references with the standards on which we have based to define the model (fundamentally the NIST SP-800 series and the family ISO 27000).

Table 2. Detail of Subcategories

Category	Subcategory	Description	Reference
Assets Management	Roles and Responsibilities	Security responsibilities and roles of mobile devices are established and assigned.	NIST SP 800-124 (Souppaya and Scarfone, 2013), ISO 27032 (ISO, 2012)
	Assets Control	Mobile devices, installed applications and their users are all inventoried and classified. In addition to it, in the case of mobile devices these are secured and managed.	NIST SP 800-124 (Souppaya and Scarfone, 2013), ISO 27032 (ISO, 2012), NIST SP 800-53 (Ross, 2013), NIST SP 800-45 (Tracy et al., 2007), NIST SP 800-121 (Padgette et al., 2018), NIST SP 800-164 (Chen, Franklin and Regenscheid, 2018), NIST SP 800-118 (Scarfone and Souppaya, 2009)

Cybersecurity Government	Cybersecurity policies for mobile devices	Mobile devices information security policy approved, formalized, disseminated and implemented	NIST SP 800-124 (Souppaya and Scarfone, 2013), NIST SP 800-164 (Chen, Franklin and Regenscheid, 2018), NIST SP 800-118 (Scarfone and Souppaya, 2009), NIST SP 800-61 (Karen et al., 2012)
IT risk management	IT Risks	Risks of applications and devices are identified, assessed and treated	NIST SP 800-163 (Quirolgico et al., 2018), NIST SP 800-124 (Souppaya and Scarfone, 2013), ISO 27032 (ISO, 2012)
Raising awareness and formation	Training	Users are trained on threats to mobile devices and security procedures for mobile devices	NIST SP 800-118 (Scarfone and Souppaya, 2009), NIST SP 800-124 (Souppaya and Scarfone, 2013), ISO 27032 (ISO, 2012)
	Raising awareness	Users are aware of policies and responsibilities in the management of mobile devices and applications	NIST SP 800-61 (Karen et al., 2012), NIST SP 800-121 (Padgette et al., 2018), NIST SP 800-124 (Souppaya and Scarfone, 2013)
Access Control	Authentication	Mechanisms of authentication and security for mobile devices established	NIST SP 800-124 (Souppaya and Scarfone, 2013)
Data Safety	Information Protection	Data stored and broadcasted by mobile devices are protected	NIST SP 800-124 (Souppaya and Scarfone, 2013), NIST SP 800-118 (Scarfone and Souppaya, 2009) NIST SP 800-45 (Tracy et al., 2007)
Protection Technology	Connectivity	The networks all mobile devices are connected to are managed	NIST SP 800-124 (Souppaya and Scarfone, 2013), ISO 27032 (ISO, 2012)
Information processes and procedures for protection	Development and maintenance of applications	Development and maintenance of applications is managed	NIST SP 800-124 (Souppaya and Scarfone, 2013), NIST SP 800-88 (Kissel et al., 2014), ISO 27032 (ISO, 2012)
	Cleaning information from mobile devices	The cleaning of information from mobile devices is managed	NIST SP 800-124 (Souppaya and Scarfone, 2013), NIST SP 800-88 (Kissel et al., 2014)
Continuous monitoring of security	Monitoring of anomalies and threats	Security of mobile devices is monitored	NIST SP 800-124 (Souppaya and Scarfone, 2013), ISO 27032 (ISO, 2012)
	Monitoring of compliance with policies and procedures	Compliance with security policies and procedures for mobile devices is monitored	NIST SP 800-124 (Souppaya and Scarfone, 2013), ISO 27032 (ISO, 2012)
Response Planning	Response to incidents	Incident response procedure implemented	NIST SP 800-61 (Karen et al., 2012), ISO 27032 (ISO, 2012)
Communication	Help Desk	Help desk for incident report is implemented	NIST SP 800-184 (Bartock et al., 2016), ISO 27032 (ISO, 2012)

	Communication Planning	Communication plan is implemented	NIST SP 800-184 (Bartock et al., 2016), ISO 27032 (ISO, 2012)
Recovery Planning	Recovery of incidents	Recovery procedure of incidents is implemented	NIST SP 800-184 (Bartock et al., 2016), ISO 27032 (ISO, 2012)
	Knowledge Management	Lessons learned are implemented	NIST SP 800-61 (Karen et al., 2012)
Improvement	Evaluation and Audit	Categories are audited periodically	NIST SP 800-163 (Quirolgico et al., 2018)
	Innovation	Last innovations of security for mobile devices are reviewed and implemented	ISO 27032 (ISO, 2012)

2.2.2 Subcategories

Control objectives or outcomes expected of cybersecurity intended to be achieved. Each subcategory is related to one category.

2.2.3 Priority Levels

This is the procedure whereby the implementation order of categories is determined, to then allocate priority levels to subcategories related to said categories so that the recommended order is determined at the time of the model implementation.

As a reference, this section suggests priorities at the time of implementing model categories and subcategories. It will be accomplished in two parts: first, model categories will be prioritized in a descending direction by implementation order. Then for subcategories related to each category a priority level will be assigned to determine the order to follow when implementing subcategories within one category. The table 3 below outlines the aforementioned:

Table 3. Detail of Priority Levels

Category	Subcategory	Priority level
Cybersecurity Government	Cybersecurity policies for mobile devices	None
	Roles and Responsibilities	Priority 1
Assets Management	Assets Control	Priority 2
IT Risk Management	IT Risks	None
Raising Awareness and Training	Training	Priority 2
	Raising awareness	Priority 1
Data Security	Information Protection	None
Access Control	Authentication	None
Protection Technology	Connectivity	None
Processes and procedures for information protection	Development and maintenance of applications	Priority 1
	Cleaning of information from mobile devices	Priority 2
Continuous monitoring of security	Monitoring of anomalies and threats	Priority 1
	Monitoring the compliance of policies and procedures	Priority 2
Response Planning	Reponses to incidents	None
Communication	Help Desk	Priority 1
	Communication Planning	Priority 2
Recovery Planning	Incident Recovery	None
Improvement	Knowledge Management	Priority 2
	Evaluation and Auditing	Priority 3

2.3 Component 2 – Indicators

Model indicators will be used to assess model functioning. Indicators will be defined for model subcategories which will include the indicator's purpose. In terms of the values taken from such indicators the model's effectiveness will be determined. An example is showed on table 4:

Table 4. Sample of an Indicator Description

Attribute	Description
Name	Percentage of lesson learned implemented
Purpose	Test if past incidents have been learned an internalized by the organization.
Measurement method	Number of lessons learned implemented/Total of lessons learned identified
Subcategory	Knowledge management – Lessons learned from incidents are implemented
Reference value allowed	50% (at least 50% of lessons learned must be implemented in a time)
Measurement frequency	Quarterly

The model will rely on indicators that enable verification whether or not the security of mobile devices is improving in the organization. To assess these indicators, the model will have previously implemented the incident management, so at the time of measuring required values of indicators, differentiation can be made among incident types. The table 5 below outlines said indicators:

Table 5. Model Indicators

Category	Subcategory	Priority level
Cybersecurity policies for mobile devices	Policy Status (approved, formalized, disseminated, implemented)	Verify the progress status of implementation of policies
	# of infringement of policies	Verify if policies are being useful or if they are only documents
Roles and Responsibilities	# of roles not assigned to users	Verify if all roles created have been assigned
	# of incidents occurred due to non-compliance of responsibilities assigned to users	Verify if users fulfill their responsibilities or not
Assets Control	# of unknown applications and devices	Verify if inventories were properly conducted
	# of errors in the classification	Verify if all devices and applications are properly classified
IT Risks	# of failures detected in the security of mobile devices	Verify if mobile devices are properly secured
	# of incidents materialized due to risks accepted	Verify if risks have been dealt with properly enough
	# of incidents materialized due to risks which impact was poorly assessed	Verify if risks have been properly assessed
	# of incidents materialized due to risks not identified	Verify if all risks were identified
Raising Awareness and Training	# of incidents occurred not reported or poorly reported	Verify if users are becoming aware
	# of errors of users during response processes or incident recovery	Verify if training was conducted properly
	% of approved from the total of trained	Verify if training is being understood
Authentication	# of unauthorized accesses	Verify if safety measures for access control are enough
Protection of Information	# of filtrations of information stored	Verify if data is properly protected
	# of alterations in the information flow of each mobile device	Verify if data is properly protected
Connectivity	# of unauthorized devices hooked up to the network	Verify if networks where mobile devices are connected to are being monitored and protected properly
Development and Maintenance of Applications	# of applications without enough security measures implemented	Verify if applications have safety measures implemented that guarantee the security of the information managed by them
	# of security updates of developed applications	Verify if applications are properly developed or if they need to be patched on a regular basis
Cleaning of information of mobile devices	# of failures in the cleaning process of information in mobile devices	Verify if the information from devices is properly erased

Monitoring of Anomalies and Threats	# of unauthorized changes in the settings of mobile devices not detected on time	Verify if devices have not gone through any unauthorized changes in their settings
Monitoring of compliance with policies and procedures	# of non-compliance with policies or procedures not detected on time	Verify if monitoring procedures are being conducted in a properly
Incidents Response	# of delays on incident responses	Verify if they are responding with the speed required
	# of incidents not controlled properly	Verify if they are responding properly to incidents
Help Desk	# of times help desk is reported as busy	Verify if help desk works properly
Communication Planning	# of information filtrations during communication of occurrence of an incident	Verify if the communication plan is working properly
Incident Recovery	# of failures in recovery	Verify if incidents are being recovered properly
	# of delayed recoveries	Verify if incidents are being recovered properly
Knowledge Management	% of lessons learned implemented	Verify if past incidents are being learned
Evaluation and Audit	# of audits conducted	Verify if audits are being made to test model operation
Innovation	% of innovations for security of mobile devices implemented	Verify if they are updating security innovations

2.4 Component 3 – Implementation Guide

The model implementation guide will serve for the model implementation which consists of a series of activities recommended for the implementation of each of the model's subcategories. These activities will not only be grouped into subcategories but categories as well. The order to be followed for the implementation of said activities will be established in terms of priority levels of model subcategories and categories. Besides, the guide will lay out a procedure to conduct self-evaluation of the organization status and will also suggest a government structure to put the model into action.

3. EXPERTS JUDGEMENT VALIDATION

To validate the model, expert judgment must be used. This process is made up of several stages, among which the preparation stage stands out as goals are set for what needs to be validated with expert judgment. The expert recruitment stage will appoint the experts that will validate the model; and the elicitation stage will select and execute the experts' information collection method required to validate a model. Finally, the aggregation stage will summarize all information extracted from the previous stage (Benini et al., 2017).

4. CONCLUSION

This paper has introduced the cybersecurity model for mobile devices designed along with its components. Throughout this model design, it was noted that the model implementation guide did require activities to implement the model as well as self-evaluation so as to appraise the current status of the organization cybersecurity. Based on that, this guide determined which activities to accomplish and which should not be conducted. Although this is yet to be tested in an organization, this will significantly reduce cybersecurity risks related to mobile devices since the information used for the model preparation is based on internationally recognized standards such as ISO 27032 and NIST standards, which guarantees the validity of such information.

REFERENCES

Bartock, M., Cichonski, J., Souppaya, M., Smith, M., Witte, G. and Scarfone, K. (2016). *Guide for cybersecurity event recovery*. [online] Available at: http://nvlpubs.nist.gov/nistpubs/SpecialPublications/NIST.SP.800-184.pdf.

Benini, A., Chataigner,, P., Noumri, N., Parham, N., Sweeney, J. and Tax, L. (2017). *Expert Judgement. The use of expert judgment in humanitarian analysis Theory, methods and applications*. [online] Geneva: Assessment Capacities Project - ACAPS. Available at: https://www.acaps.org/sites/acaps/files/resources/files/acaps_expert_judgment_-_full_study_august_2017.pdf.

Berghel, H. (2015). Cyber Chutzpah: The Sony Hack and the Celebration of Hyperbole. Computer, 48(2), pp.77-80.

Castillo, T. (2018). *Los mayores ataques Cibernéticos del 2016-2017*. Economia Digital. Available at: https://www.economiadigital.es/tecnologia-y-tendencias/los-diez-mayores-ataques-informaticos-de-2016_188964_102.html

Chen, L. (2012). Guidelines on Hardware-Rooted Security in Mobile Devices. [online] Nist.gov. Available at: https://csrc.nist.gov/csrc/media/publications/sp/800-164/draft/documents/sp800_164_draft

Flores, D., Qazi, F. and Jhumka, A. (2016). *Bring Your Own Disclosure: Analysing BYOD Threats to Corporate Information*. 2016 IEEE Trustcom/BigDataSE/ISPA, [online] pp.1008-1015. Available at: http://ieeexplore.ieee.org/document/7847052/

ISACA (2015). *Cybersecurity guidance for small and medium-sized enterprises*. 1st ed. Illinois: ISACA Publishing.

ISACA. (2010). *Securing Mobile Devices*. 1st ed. Illinois: ISACA Publishing.

ISO (2012). *ISO/IEC 27032:2012 Information technology - Security techniques - Guidelines for cybersecurity*. ISO International.

Karen, S., Tom, M., Grance, T. and Paul, C. (2012). *Computer Security Incident Handling Guide*. [online] Nvlpubs.nist.gov. Available at: http://nvlpubs.nist.gov/nistpubs/SpecialPublications/NIST.SP.800-61r2.pdf [Accessed 10 Feb. 2018].

Kissel, R., Regenscheid, A., Scholl, M. and Stine, K. (2014). *Guidelines for Media Sanitization*. [online] Available at: http://nvlpubs.nist.gov/nistpubs/SpecialPublications/NIST.SP.800-88r1.pdf

NIST (2017). Framework for Improving Critical Infrastructure Cybersecurity. [online] Nist.gov. Available at: https://www.nist.gov/sites/default/files/documents/draft-cybersecurity-framework-v1.11.pdf

Padgette, J., Bahr, J., Batra, M., Holtmann, M., Smithbey, R., Chen, L. and Scarfone, K. (2018). *Guide to Bluetooth Security*. [online] Nist.gov. Available at: http://csrc.nist.gov/publications/drafts/800-121/sp800_121_r2_draft.pdf

Quirolgico, S., Voas, J., Karygiannis, T., Michael, C. and Scarfone, K. (2018). *Vetting the Security of Mobile Applications*. [online] Nist.gov. Available at: http://nvlpubs.nist.gov/nistpubs/SpecialPublications/NIST.SP.800-163.pdf.

Ross, R. (2013). *Recommended security controls for federal information systems SP 800-53*. 4th ed. Gaithersburg, MD: U.S. Dept. of Commerce, National Institute of Standards and Technology.

Scarfone, K. and Souppaya, M. (2009). *Guide to Enterprise Password Management*. [online] Nist.gov. Available at: http://csrc.nist.gov/publications/drafts/800-118/draft-sp800-118.pdf

Souppaya, M. and Scarfone, K. (2013). *Guidelines for Managing the Security of Mobile Devices in the Enterprise*. [online] Nist.gov. Available at: http://nvlpubs.nist.gov/nistpubs/SpecialPublications/NIST.SP.800-124r1.pdf

Tracy, M., Jansen, W., Scarfone, K. and Butterfield, J. (2007). *SP 800-45 Version 2, Guidelines on Electronic Mail Security | CSRC*. [online] Nist.gov. Available at: http://csrc.nist.gov/publications/nistpubs/800-45-version2/SP800-45v2.pdf

Tupia, M., Bruzza, M. and Rodríguez, F. (2018). *An information security framework for ubiquitous services in e-government structures: a Peruvian local government experience*. 2016 Federated Conference on Computer Science and Information Systems (FedCSIS), [online] pp.1309-1316. Available at: http://ieeexplore.ieee.org/document/7733415/

Vaca Herrera, A., Ron, M. and Rabadao, C. (2017). *National cyber-security policies oriented to BYOD (bring your own device): Systematic review*. 2017 12th Iberian Conference on Information Systems and Technologies (CISTI), [online] pp.1-4. Available at: http://ieeexplore.ieee.org/document/7975953/ [Accessed 10 Feb. 2018].

READINESS FRAMEWORK OF ENTERPRISE RESOURCE PLANNING (ERP) IMPLEMENTATION AT SMALL AND MEDIUM COMPANY (SME)

Ria Puspadewi N. Yosoenarto, Putu Wuri Handayani and Ave Adriana Pinem
Faculty of Computer Science Universitas Indonesia, Depok, Indonesia

ABSTRACT

This study aims to analyze and develop a framework that can be used to assess a SMEs' company's readiness to implement Enterprise Resource Planning (ERP). This study used qualitative approach with empirical study on relevant researches and case studies at three SMEs manufacturing company in Indonesia. Correspondent from the case study companies are top management officers that will be involved in ERP implementation process. Result from this study is an assessment framework that can be used to assess company's readiness to implement ERP system. This model consists of three domains, namely technology (e.g. system change, infrastructure, relative benefits, ease-of-use, innovation result, sources, team assignation, team creation, and knowledge and skill), organizational (e.g. aligned objective, process change, top management support, scope, risk planning, feasibility study, consultant, company's size, and project manager), and environment (e.g. culture, decision making mechanism, communication, competitor, industry type, and partner and target market). The readiness framework then implemented to evaluate the readiness of SME's and the result shows that the readiest domain is technological and followed by organizational and environment domain. Organizations need to improve their system change, risk planning, feasibility study, communication and partner and target market process to increase the readiness because those indicators are the lowest readiness rate in each domain.

KEYWORDS

Readiness, System Implementation, ERP, SMEs

1. INTRODUCTION

Bank of Indonesia aware that increasing number of SMEs have an important and strategic impact on building the national economic (Bank Indonesia, 2015). In 2012, SMEs in Indonesia dominated the market with total up to 56 million enterprises or 99,99% from the total enterprise (Kementerian Koperasi dan Usaha Kecil dan Menengah, 2013). Obviously, the rapid growth of the enterprise needs an empowerment to make those SMEs have competitive advantage to increase the national economic. Seeing how the competitive advantage rely on how those SME innovate, it is safe to say that IT and internet are major components for company's competitive strategic (Bank Indonesia, 2015; Beheshti, 2006). Thus, make Enterprise Resource Planning (ERP) as a tool to increase company's competitive strategic.

Small and Medium Enterprises (SMEs) adopt an ERP as a technology innovation to stay competitive (Ahmadi, et al., 2014; Deshmukh & Thampi, 2014). ERP, especially in manufacture SMEs can be used to solve a lot of challenges and give advantages to company such as cost reduction, effective process, growth control, and competitive advantages (WorkWise Software, 2015). ERP implementation will integrate all business process in the company (e.g. inventory, production, operational and selling, and accounting and finance) into one database as an information hub that provides an accurate, real-time, and critical information for company (WorkWise Software, 2015).

There are several studies which focusses on developing framework to assess SMEs that implemented ERP. First study (Ahmadi, et al., 2014) focused on building a framework to assess SMEs company's readiness to implement ERP system using a TOE framework and fuzzy cognitive maps. Result shows that the proposed framework indeed can be used to assess and map the relationship between dependent activities that increase the company's readiness. Second study (Ahmadi, et al., 2015) is related to the first study, in this study, the purpose is to test the previous framework to assess the company's ERP implementation readiness with budgetary constraints using a manual FCM construction that rely solely on interviewee knowledge. Result shows that although the proposed framework is tailored for SMEs, it also can be used to assess a large sized company's ERP implementation readiness. Third study (Razmi, et al., 2009) also assess the company's readiness to implement ERP system. This study based on critical success factors that used a practical framework with fuzzy analytic network process methodology (F-ANP) to identify weak (low readiness) area for company to implement ERP successfully. Result shows that the proposed model is a robust tool to assess and measure company's readiness to implement ERP system. Fourth study (Ramdani, et al., 2013) explored the technology, organization, and environment (TOE) factors as SMEs influencer to adopt enterprise application (EA). This study used an empirical study with direct interview to the correspondent as a data collecting method. Data then processed using SEM-PLS method. Result shows that TOE factor undoubtedly is an influencer for SMEs to adopt EA. Lastly, fifth study (Awa & Ojiabo, 2016) explored the TOE framework as a determinant model of ERP adoption at SMEs. Proposed TOE framework consists of 12 factors then tested with purposive sampling and snow ball method using a survey questionnaire with executives from 6 SMEs and processed using a logistic regression test. Result shows that among TOE framework, technology is the most influential domain that contribute to company's decision to adopt ERP.

Thus, ERP implementation needs a meticulous and careful readiness assessment to succeed (Kwahk & Lee, 2008; Awa & Ojiabo, 2016; Razmi, et al., 2009; Ahmadi, et al., 2015). Readiness assessment can be used as a benchmark whether the company is ready to implement ERP or not. This study aims to identify influencing factors; and build a readiness assessment model out of those factors to develop the right system tailored to meet company's requirement. Hence, this study could provide guidance for SME to assess SME readiness before implementing ERP.

2. LITERATURE REVIEW

Enterprise Resource Planning (ERP) is a first generation of enterprise system that developed to integrate and support all main function throughout the organization (Motiwalla & Thompson, 2012). ERP implementation is a complex process, requires a lot of time, and intensive resources (Tanyani & Gilaninia, 2015; Motiwalla & Thompson, 2012). ERP implementation is a risky process which often failed (Hidayanto, et al., 2013). Therefore, before an organization implement an ERP system, it is necessary to identify, plan and understand the implementation risk as early as possible (Hidayanto, et al., 2013). Thus, it is very important for company to assess its readiness to implement ERP system (Ahmadi, et al., 2015).

Enterprise Resource Planning Readiness emphasizes on the importance of readiness management before a company run an ERP implementation project (Ahmadi, et al., 2015). Risk that may be occur have to identified and anticipated on the early stage [18] (Hidayanto, et al., 2013). There are three main domains that can be used to assess company's readiness to implement ERP system, i.e. organizational, social, and technical domain [11] (Ahmadi, et al., 2015). Ahmadi et.al. [11] (Ahmadi, et al., 2015) stressed that there are two main issue that affect company readiness to implement ERP system, i.e. how to identify influencer factor and how to build a readiness assessment model considering those influencing factors.

3. METHODOLOGY

This research identifies the problem with interviewing the top management correspondent from case study company to identify relevant and critical issue in the company. Result from the problem identification is an occurring problem in the company. After problem identification, research question is built based on the problem, previous study, interview, also formal and non-formal analysis. Research question then analyzed with relevant journal, books, and study with 5C methodology principle, resulting a theoretical framework and an interview instrument that used for data collecting. Data collecting based on 3 main domains i.e. technology, organization, and environment due to previous study that shows that those are the main factors that influence enterprises adoption of ERP [13,15,6]. Collected interview data from the top management of the case study company then mapped into a framework to assess company's readiness to implement ERP with a statistic descriptive coding method. The software used to model the framework are Ms. Excel, OmniGraffle, and MentalModeler. Second data collecting was held by using a Forum Group Discussion to achieve consensus and deeper validation for the collected data. Validated data then built into one framework that can be used to assess company or organization readiness to implement ERP system. Proposed framework then can be used in case study company or any other company that in the process of implementing ERP system.

4. RESULT AND ANALYSIS

Figure 1 shows the result from this research as a readiness framework assessment to implement ERP system that consists of three main domains which will be explained further on Appendix.

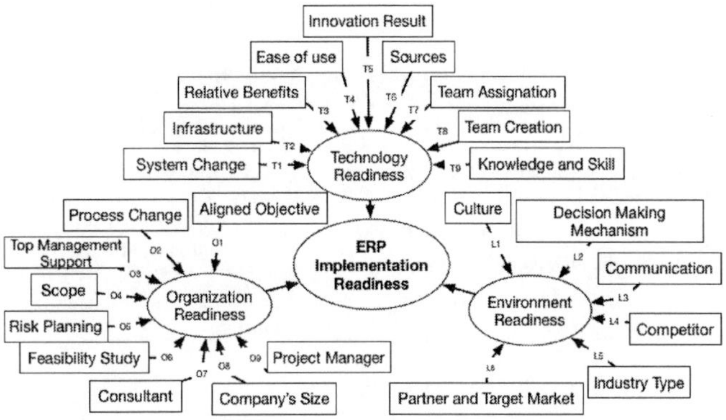

Figure 1. Readiness Framework Assessment Model

4.1 Testing the Framework

The readiness framework assessment then will be tested on several SMEs company that plan to implement ERP system. Testing the framework consists of two phases. First, testing using interview method to correspondent from case study company, and second, testing the interview result with a forum discussion group that attended by main correspondent from the case study company to gain a general readiness of SMEs in implementing ERP system. The readiness assessment on both first and second method will be measured by using the following readiness value in Table 1.

Table 1. Readiness Assessment Value

State Number	*State*	*Crisp Value*
Readiness State 1	Not ready	0
Readiness State 2	Very weakly ready	0.2
Readiness State 3	Weakly ready	0.4
Readiness State 4	Moderately ready	0.6
Readiness State 5	Strongly ready	0.8
Readiness State 6	Very strongly ready	1

This paper adopts the readiness assessment value from Ahmadi, et.al. [13] with a range of readiness state from 1 to 6. For readiness state 1 as not ready with crisp value 0, readiness state 2 as very weakly ready with crisp value 0.2, readiness state 3 as weakly ready and with crisp value 0.4, readiness state 4 as moderately ready with crisp value 0.6, readiness state 5 as strongly ready with crisp value 0.8 and readiness state 6 as very strongly ready with crisp value 1.

Value given on each variable on the domain will be discussed with the correspondent to get an accurate value that represent the real state of the company. Assessment will be proceeded by finding the average value from each correspondent on Table 2. Assessment will be done with a repository terms as follows:

1. For $0 < X \leq 0{,}2$ then company valuation will be on scale "not ready" and / or "very weakly ready".

2. For $0,2 < X \leq 0,4$ then company valuation will be on scale "very weakly ready" and / or "weakly ready".

3. For $0 < X \leq 0,2$ then company valuation will be on scale "weakly ready" and / or "moderately ready".

4. For $0 < X \leq 0,2$ then company valuation will be on scale "moderately ready" and / or "strongly ready".

5. For $0 < X \leq 0,2$ then company valuation will be on scale "strongly ready" and / or "very strongly ready".

Table 2. Correspondent Demographic Profile

	Company 1	*Company 2*	*Company 3*
Position	Vice President	Vice President	Production Manager
Education	Bachelor Degree	Bachelor Degree	Bachelor Degree
Been working for (up until 2017)	11 years	34 years	30 years
Experience (Latest 5 years)	Implemented transaction and stock handling system	Implemented purchase order, stock handling, and production planning system	Implemented EDFP system (production)
Secondary Correspondent	President, and Head of Finance	Head of Administration, and Head of Finance	Head of Production

Table 3 contains assessment result from each company.

Table 3. Assessment Result

Domain	Variable	Code	Readiness state			Value of 3 Company	
			C1	C2	C3	Total	Average
Technology	System change	T1	0.2	0.2	0.6	**1.00**	**0.33**
	Infrastructure	T2	0.6	0.8	1	**2.40**	**0.80**
	Relative benefits	T3	1	1	1	**3.00**	**1.00**
	Ease of use	T4	0.6	0.4	0.2	**1.20**	**0.40**
	Innovation result	T5	1	0.8	0.2	**2.00**	**0.67**
	Sources	T6	0.6	0.8	0.8	**2.20**	**0.73**
	Team assignation	T7	1	0.8	1	**2.80**	**0.93**
	Team creation	T8	0.6	0.6	1	**2.20**	**0.73**
	Knowledge and skill	T9	1	1	0.4	**2.40**	**0.80**
Organization	Aligned objective	O1	1	1	0.2	**2.20**	**0.73**
	Process change	O2	0	0.2	0	**0.20**	**0.07**
	Top management support	O3	1	1	0.6	**2.60**	**0.87**
	Scope	O4	0.8	0.8	1	**2.60**	**0.87**
	Risk planning	O5	0	0	0	**0.00**	**0.00**
	Feasibility study	O6	0	0	0	**0.00**	**0.00**
	Consultant	O7	0.2	1	1	**2.20**	**0.73**
	Company's size	O8	0.8	0.6	1	**2.40**	**0.80**
	Project manager	O9	1	1	1	**3.00**	**1.00**
Environment	Culture	L1	1	1	0.4	**2.40**	**0.80**
	Decision making mechanism	L2	0.2	0.4	0.4	**1.00**	**0.33**
	Communication	L3	0.2	0.2	0	**0.40**	**0.13**
	Competitor	L4	1	0	1	**2.00**	**0.67**
	Industry type	L5	1	1	1	**3.00**	**1.00**
	Partner and target market	L6	0	0.2	0.2	**0.40**	**0.13**

Result from Table 3 is very subjective on each company's readiness. Based on this, forum group discussion was conducted on testing the framework to increase the accuracy and provide validation. Results from second method then mapped into Figure 2 to assess the relationship of each indicators. Based on matric value in Figure 2, each domain of readiness is calculated and the results from the calculation can also be seen on Figure 2. The total ERP implementation readiness can be calculated using average formula. From the result, total ERP implementation readiness is 0.61 which means that readiness state is still on the moderately ready state.

There's no significance different of the readiness from each domain. The largest number of assessment is technologies readiness with value of 0.66 followed by organization readiness with value of 0,65 and environment readiness with value of 0,53. In the technology dimension, system change has the lowest readiness value. Organization need to assess their system and identify every change that would be needed. The change management implementation could help with this issue. In the organization domain there two indicators with readiness value of 0.00 which are risk planning and feasibility study. The planning phase of the ERP implementation must allocate more time in assessing the risk and the feasibility of the initiative. For the environment domain, communication and partner and target market need to be improved. The identification of all stakeholders and communication between them have to be formulated in advance to increase the communication effectiveness.

	Technology readiness	System change	Infrastructure	Relative benefit	Ease of use	Innovation result	Resources	Team assignation	Team creation	Knowledge and skill
Technology readiness										
System change	0									
Infrastructure	1									
Relative benefit	1									
Ease of use	0									
Innovation result	1									
Resources	1		1							
Team assignation	1									
Team creation	1							1		
Knowledge and skill	1				1			0		
Organization readiness										
Aligned objective										
Process change										
Top management support										
Scope										
Risk planning										
Feasibility study										
Consultant										
Company's size										
Project manager										
Environment readiness										
Culture										
Decision making mechanism										
Communication										
Competitor										
Industry type										
Partner and target market										
Total ERP implementation readiness										

	Organization readiness	Aligned objective	Process change	Top management support	Scope	Risk planning	Feasibility study	Consultant	Company's size	Project manager
Technology readiness										
System change										
Infrastructure										
Relative benefit										
Ease of use										
Innovation result										
Resources										
Team assignation										
Team creation										
Knowledge and skill										
Organization readiness										
Aligned objective	1									
Process change	0									
Top management support	1		1							0
Scope	1									
Risk planning	1									
Feasibility study	1									
Consultant	1					1	0			
Company's size	1					1		1		
Project manager	1									
Environment readiness										
Culture										
Decision making mechanism										
Communication										
Competitor										
Industry type										
Partner and target market										
Total ERP implementation readiness										

	Environment readiness	Culture	Decision making mechanism	Communication	Competitor	Industry type	Partner and target market	Total ERP implementation readiness
Technology readiness								0.66
System change								
Infrastructure								
Relative benefit								
Ease of use								
Innovation result								
Resources								
Team assignation								
Team creation								
Knowledge and skill								
Organization readiness								0.65
Aligned objective								
Process change								
Top management support								
Scope								
Risk planning								
Feasibility study								
Consultant								
Company's size								
Project manager								
Environment readiness								0.53
Culture	1							
Decision making mechanism	0							
Communication	0		1					
Competitor	1							
Industry type	1					1		
Partner and target market	0							
Total ERP implementation readiness								0.61

Figure 2. Readiness Value Matrix

5. DISSCUSION AND CONCLUSION

In this research, we have addressed a framework that can be used to assess company's readiness to implement ERP system. The framework has three main domains i.e. technology, organization, and environment. Each domain has several variables. Technology domain has nine variables, organization domain also has nine variables and lastly, environment domain has six variables. The proposed framework then used to assess company's readiness to implement ERP system in Indonesia. Results shows that SMEs readiness in general is still on the moderately ready state (total readiness score is 0.61 out of 1.00), which can be improved to increase chance of successful implementation. There's no significance different of the readiness from each domain. The largest number of assessment is technologies readiness followed by organization readiness and environment readiness. Organization need to improve the system change, risk planning, feasibility study, communication and partner and target market to improve the readiness of ERP implementation.

REFERENCES

Ahmadi, S., Papageorgiou, E., Yeh, C. & Martin, R., 2014. Managing readiness-relevant activities for the organizational dimension of ERP implementation. *Computers in Industry,* 23 December, 68(68), pp. 89-104.

Ahmadi, S., Yeh, C., Martin, R. & Papageorgiou, E., 2015. Optimizing ERP readiness improvements under budgetary constraints. *Int. J. Production Economics*, Volume 161, pp. 105-115.

Awa, H. & Ojiabo, O., 2016. A model of adoption determinants of ERP within T-O-E framework. *Information Technology & People,* 29(4), pp. 901-930.

Bank Indonesia, 2015. *Bank Indonesia Informasi UMKM.* [Online] Available at: http://www.bi.go.id/id/umkm/penelitian/nasional/kajian/Documents/Profil%20Bisnis%20UMKM.pdf [Accessed 27 Desember 2017].

Beheshti, H., 2006. What managers should know about ERP/ERP II. pp. 184-193.

Deshmukh, P. & Thampi, G., 2014. *Empirical analysis of factors influencing ERP implementation in indian SMEs.* s.l., IEEE, pp. 2058-2062.

Hidayanto, A. N., Hasibuan, M. A., Handayani, P. W. & Sucahyo, Y. G., 2013. Framework for measuring ERP implementation readiness in small and medium enterprise (SME): A case study in software developer company. *Journal of Computers,* July.8(7).

Kementerian Koperasi dan Usaha Kecil dan Menengah, 2013. *Sandingan Data UMKM 2012-2013.* [Online] Available at: http://www.depkop.go.id/pdf-viewer/?p=uploads/tx_rtgfiles/sandingan_data_umkm_2012-2013.pdf [Accessed 27 Desember 2017].

Kwahk, K. Y. & Lee, J. N., 2008. The role of readiness for change in ERP implementation: Theoretical bases and empirical validation. *Information and Management,* 45(7), pp. 474-481.

Liu, C. & Ruan, H., 2012. *A comparative study on the competitiveness of china key IT enterprises clusters.* s.l., IEEE, pp. 380-383.

Motiwalla, L. & Thompson, J., 2012. *Enterprise systems for management.* New Jersey: Pearson Education Inc..

Ramdani, B., Chevers, D. & Williams, D., 2013. SMEs' adoption of enterprise applications A technology-organisation-environment model. *Journal of Small Business and Enterprise Development,* 20(4), pp. 735-753.

Razmi, J., Sangari, M. & Ghodsi, R., 2009. *Developing a practical framework for ERP readiness assessment using fuzzy analytic network process.* Iran, ScienceDirect, pp. 1168-1178.

Tanyani, H. & Gilaninia, S., 2015. Enterprise resource planning readiness assessment. *Arabian Journal of Business and Management Review (OMAN Chapter),* September, 5(2), pp. 8-13.

WorkWise Software, 2015. *Why today's manudacturers need a modern ERP system.* [Online] Available at: https://www.workwisellc.com/erp-software/the-need-for-a-modern-erp-system/ [Accessed 15 September 2017].

APPENDIX

Variable	Indicator	Sources
System change	Before ERP implementation stage, it is important to identify and implement the necessary changes in the existing systems of the organization.	(Razmi, et al., 2009) (Ahmadi, et al., 2014)
Infra-structure	The availability of ICT infrastructures significantly determines SMEs' adoption of ERP.	(Ahmadi, et al., 2014; Ramdani, et al., 2013; Awa & Ojiabo, 2016)
	Technology infrastructure positively affects readiness.	
	Technology infrastructure refers to a shared technology platform (e.g., computer hardware, software, and networking technologies) that are necessary to implement new technology solutions throughout an organization	
Relative benefits	The degree to which an innovation is perceived as consistent with the existing values, past experiences, and needs of potential adopters.	(Ramdani, et al., 2013; Miles, et al., 2014)
	The system goals, deliverables and expected benefits are considered along with the project risks, costs and needed resources to justify the investments in the ERP system.	
Ease of use	The degree to which an innovation is perceived as relatively difficult to understand and use.	(Ramdani, et al., 2013)

Innovation result	The degree to which the results of an innovation are visible to others. ICT that have been seen to make impacts in the industry, in which an SME operates, are more likely to be viewed in a favourable light.	(Ramdani, et al., 2013)
Sources	The availability of the needed organizational resources for adoption ERP implementation demands valuable resources from the organization such as time, money and personnel. Resource requirements are critical to realize the benefits associated with an ERP package and should be determined early in the project. The resources must be provided and allocated according to a resource plan which is an important part of the project management program.	(Ramdani, et al., 2013; Ahmadi, et al., 2014)
Team assignation	In an ERP project, several parties must cooperate with each other but each accomplishes different tasks based on their given responsibility. It is important to assign the responsibilities for the ERP project. Assigning the responsibilities is one of the main parts of the project management program which is critical to the success of ERP implementation.	(Razmi, et al., 2009)
Team creation	The demographic composition of the decision making team significantly determines SMEs' adoption of ERP facilities. Best organization's employees must be assigned to the project team The project team should be balanced, cooperative and cross functional. People in the project team work on a full time basis. The areas where team members lack knowledge must be identified and resolved using qualified consultants	(Razmi, et al., 2009; Ahmadi, et al., 2014)
Knowledge and skill	Involving people with both business and technical knowledge into the project team is critical to achieve success. Not only the higher level, but also the lower level management must support the changes required by the ERP system, the successful implementation of the system requires commitment and cooperation of personnel from all segments of the business. ERP implementation is about people, not process or technology. Therefore, the role of personnel in the ERP implementation success or failure is inevitable. The personnel must be convinced and recognize the need for change and be properly prepared for changes to prevent resistance and chaos at the implementation stage. The personnel involvement in the project is also important; because they will actually be the users of the system so they must have enough IT skills and knowledge on ERP concept.	(Razmi, et al., 2009)
Aligned objective	The organization must carefully define why the ERP system will be implemented and what critical business needs the system will address What business values the ERP system is intended to deliver. Aligning the ERP implementation goals and the organizational goal.	(Ramdani, et al., 2013) (Razmi, et al., 2009) [6]
Process change	The processes needing improvement should be identified and necessary adjustments should be made prior to ERP implementation stage. This is important in designing the system architecture and will ensure that the selected ERP system will reflect the complete business processes.	(Ahmadi, et al., 2014; Awa & Ojiabo, 2016)
Top management support	Getting top management support about the project Top management can stimulate change by communicating and reinforcing values through an articulated vision for the organisation	(Ramdani, et al., 2013; Razmi, et al., 2009)
Scope	The scope of the ERP project must be clearly defined. It should be determined whether only a few functional units are involved in the project or the system implementation takes place over the entire organization. For organizations with multiple sites, it should be determined whether the system is implemented globally or restricted to certain sites. The affected business processes are also determined in the project scope. The project scope directly affects the implementation time and cost of the project. A project scope that is too broad can cause severe problems. It is also important to establish realistic milestones and delivery dates for the ERP project	(Ramdani, et al., 2013; Razmi, et al., 2009)
Risk planning	Planning project risks Project risks need to be defined to make sure that the project runs smoothly and problem-free. In case a problem occurred, a defined project risks will make it easier to solve them.	(Ahmadi, et al., 2014)
Feasibility study	Conducting an ERP system implementation feasibility study for the organization. Feasibility study will make sure that the project is feasible.	(Ramdani, et al., 2013; Ahmadi, et

		al., 2014)
Consultant	Using ERP consultant before making decision about ERP system.	(Ramdani, et al., 2013; Ahmadi, et al., 2014)
	External ICT support refers to the availability of support for implementing and using ICT.	
	Firms are more willing to adopt new ICT if they feel there is adequate third-party's support.	
Company's size	The size of SMEs significantly determines the possibility of adopting ERP facilities.	(Ramdani, et al., 2013)
	Firm size positively affects readiness.	
	Larger firms have a greater need, resources, skills and experience and the ability to survive failures than smaller firms. Thus, it can be argued that larger SMEs are more likely to adopt EA.	
	The positive impact of firm size may be derived from the fact that larger firms have more resources and competencies.	
Project manager	Selecting well-qualified and knowledgeable project champion because the importance of project championship in an ERP implementation is greater than other information systems implementations.	(Razmi, et al., 2009; Ahmadi, et al., 2014)
	The commitment of the project champion is critical to drive consensus and oversee the entire project.	
	The project champion must be a high level official in the organization. He/she should be a real advocate of the project and must continually manage resistance and change during the implementation.	
Culture	Organizational culture plays an important role in the implementation stage. It can be a facilitator or a major impediment to change.	(Razmi, et al., 2009; Ahmadi, et al., 2015)
	ERP system brings a new way of working and communicating, the success and acceptance of the system is heavily dependent on the organizational culture.	
	The successful implementation of ERP systems requires a corporate culture that emphasizes the value of sharing common goals over individual pursuits and the value of trust between partners, employees, managers and corporations	
Decision making mechanism	The collection of information, the effectiveness and accuracy of data, and the retrieval process are the elements of decision mechanism that play an important role in the ERP project.	(Razmi, et al., 2009)
	It is always necessary to possess accurate and effective information to make the right decisions. The speed of information retrieval is another important factor in making decisions at the right time.	
Commu-nication	Expectations and goals of the ERP project must be communicated effectively among stakeholders and throughout all levels of the organization.	(Razmi, et al., 2009)
	It is necessary to have a communication plan in place for all stages of the implementation, which should include the rationale for the ERP implementation, change management strategies, the project scope.	
	Communication should be open, clear and complete to be effective and poor communication creates many problems for the ERP project	
Compe-titor	Competitive pressure significantly determines SMEs' adoption of ERP solution.	(Ramdani, et al., 2013)
	Competitive pressure has been identified as one of the best predictors of organisational adoption of ICT.	
	Competition in the adopter's industry is generally perceived to positively influence the adoption of ICT. This is argued to be even more evident if the innovation directly affect the competition	
	It can become a strategic necessity to adopt the new technologies to compete in the marketplace.	
Industry type	Industry in which the firm operates has been argued to influence the adoption of ICT.	(Ramdani, et al., 2013; Awa & Ojiabo, 2016)
	Service industries, which rely on the processing of information, depend on ICT.	
	Manufacturing industry rely more on ERP systems.	
Partner and target market	Trading partners' readiness significantly determines SMEs' adoption of ERP solution.	(Ramdani, et al., 2013; Awa & Ojiabo, 2016)
	Market scope refers to the market area that a firm chooses to operate in from local to international markets. Working on a wider market area introduces a high level of complexity in dealing with legal and cultural issues.	
	Firms tend to expand their ICT infrastructure beyond their organisational boundaries through the development of inter-organisational business systems.	
	Competitive market means collaboration with partners, but also copes with the competition on the market.	

PREDICTING OPINION LEADERS IN LARGE SCALE ENTERPRISE ONLINE SOCIAL NETWORKS

Maryam Shahbazi[1], Nazim Choudhury[1], Majid Shahbazi[2] and Prof. Deborah Bunker[3]
[1]*Faculty of Engineering & IT, the University of Sydney, Sydney, Australia*
[2]*Faculty of Computer Engineering, Najafabad branch, Azad University, Iran*
[3]*Discipline of Business Information Systems, the University of Sydney, Sydney, Australia*

ABSTRACT

Increased application of Enterprise Online Social Network (EOSN) platforms at workplace extended the origin of influence on corporate social communities from management to unofficial opinion leaders who influence individual's decision-making through EOSN platforms. This study attempted to examine the relation between network structural positions and behaviors of EOSN users and their ability to influence others via EOSN platforms. By analyzing the pattern of user interactions via EOSN platform (Yammer), this study revealed that over ($N \cong 33\%$) of users' who voluntary participated at online communities were triggered by less than ($n \cong 3\%$) of opinion-makers in EOSN platforms. Correspondingly, the results of this study showed that memberships in various online workgroups, structural position of actors in social networks, and degree of actors and groups' online activities largely impact on user's ability to become an opinion leader or an influential feature within corporate social environments. Considering these facts, this study proposed a model to compute influence score which represents the ability of an EOSN's user in influencing others in decision making. Subsequently, a set of predictor features were extracted to successfully predict this score.

KEYWORDS

Enterprise Online Social Network (EOSN), Information System (IS), Yammer platform, Influence measure, Online Communication

1. INTRODUCTION

Social Media platforms connected people and moved most of their social and professional activities to online environments. Due to the privacy issues and sensitivity of the confined information, publicly available social media services are incapable of conforming towards organizational requirements. Further, these services do not support sufficient functionalities for secure document storage and proprietary knowledge management (Wiesneth, 2017). Consequently, a new class of social media services, known as Enterprise Online Social Network (EOSN), has emerged with a view to improve communicate, collaborate and sharing knowledge among enterprise social members. EOSN platforms reduced the cost of interactions, facilitated collaboration in entities and enabled users to preserve their social and work-related relations at the same time (Mantymaki and Riemer, 2016). They provided employees with the visibility on others interaction and activities which increase the opportunity for social learning at workplace (Leonardi et al., 2013). Studies showed employees use enterprise social network platform (Yammer) for various purpose such as; problem solving, idea and work discussion, task management, events and updates as well as informal talk. Other studies also explored various aspects of EOSN including; understanding the impact of informal communication at work, educational usage through informal learning, knowledge management and sharing (Ebner et al., 2010, Zhang et al., 2010). However, one aspect of EOSNs is yet to be explored that has received considerably lower attention from the scholars, although, arguably it is widely explored regarding public social media, is to derive a model to identify influential users, alternatively known as opinion leader, within the context of EOSN. Recognition of existence of opinion leaders is an interesting topic in various areas of public online social networks researches, for instance; the use of opinion leaders in influencing public at political or economic decision making events, such as; daily purchasing and voting has been well studied (Aleahmad et al., 2016). However, the focus of this study is identifying the opinion leaders in corporate societies and the possibility of guiding enterprise social opinion through internal online platforms. For this purpose, this study follows both statistical and network approaches to define an ensemble of features that will not only help predict influential users in EOSN but also can further be extended to identify the similar in public social media.

Social influence which is part of the broad content area of social sciences is when one person or group's opinions, attitudes, emotions, or behaviors are affected by influence of others (Goldsmith and SpringerLink, 2015). The concept of influence from social network perspective depicts the power and proficiency of a social actor to influence the decision, attitudes and activities of others informally and it plays a vital role in defining the function of a society, such as voting. Influencers used by researchers to control the process of information transmission or diffusion of rumors (Yang et al., 2017). These critical users are also important to managers as they play key roles in voluntarily share and transfer knowledge within corporate social networks, viral marketing (Zhu, 2013), etc. The definition of influence is broad and influence measures reveal different results with respect to the concept of study and network's property. Lazarsfeld et al. envisaged the idea of 'opinion leaders' in their seminal work (Lazarsfeld et al., 1944) as a metaphor of influential users by mining the diffusion process where the opinion leaders are positioned between the mass media and the rest of the community in regards to the flow of innovative ideas. Although influential individuals have been often known as super spreaders (Sheikhahmadi and Nematbakhsh, 2017), they also can be central actors in preventing, manipulating or reforming the spread process. Influential users exercise the power of maneuvering the decision of others either positively or negatively (Guldbrandsson et al., 2012) or disproportionately impact the diffusion of information (Bakshy et al., 2011).

Identifying these influencers within organizational context is crucial to comprehend and improve the corporate social culture and policy. For instance; identifying the social opinion leaders within the organization will help in understanding current trends and key concerns of the staffs and members to bridge the gap between executives and employees. Moreover, influential employees or opinion leaders within an organization can help build positive opinions towards events and rapidly diffuse the positive attitude to promote company-wide social harmony and stability (Chen et al., 2014). Likewise, as identified by Wu, Morstatter, Hu, & Liu, recognizing influential users in both large and small communities may help managing disseminating misinformation and immunizing communities from the adverse effects of misinformation (Wu et al., 2016) which is essential for having a healthier workplace. Furthermore, with the help of EOSN, organizations are now allowing workers to have their own voice on organizational decisions. The influential users not only may help swaying their voices accordingly but also help in recognizing others within the organization. Since recognition is a social act, it will consequently generate motivated employees towards company's success.

Considering abovementioned studies, in this paper, we attempted to develop a novel framework to develop a subset of discriminative features for a given EOSN to identify its influential opinion leaders. In the subsequent sections, we will define an influence score for each actor within EOSN regarding the degree of consideration they received from their peers following their activities in online forums. By mining the network and sub-networks structures, and dynamics of the online social activities, we extracted a set of features which directly associated with the degree of influence in EOSN. These features are then fed into a regression model to successfully predict the influence scores, and finally, the model is applied to real-world EOSN data sets to measure its viability.

2. DATASET AND RESEARCH METHODOLOGY

Yammer, an EOSN service found in September 2008 and used by more than 100,000 companies with a user base of more than four million (Riemer and Scifleet, 2012), is a service organized using the concept of networks where each network typically represents one company. Anyone is capable of creating a network for a company by registering with his/her email address and corporate colleagues' on the platform and depending on the setup, new users can easily join the network with the help of corporate email addresses serving as their identifier. Resembling the web front-end features of public social networks, like Twitter or Facebook, Yammer platform provides shared workspaces, private messaging, document sharing and paid advanced administration and security features. Like Twitter, it is built upon the rationale of 'follower' principle, however, unlike Twitter; it provides a group feature can be used for work or non-work groups' collaboration and discussions. A set of members within a network can form a group discussion board according to the topical interests or types of project within the company. In this respect, two types of groups can be formed, firstly, public groups those are open to join and where messages can be viewed by any network user and secondly, private groups those are only visible to the group members and these require invitations for the new members to join in. Like Twitter and Facebook, members can like, reply to a post or mention other members in their posts or reply to a posts to draw others' attention into the respective topics. Every post has a Unique Identifier (UID) and is automatically assigned to a thread which also has its unique UID. Moreover, every member of a group receives notification of a new post and will be able to react to the post voluntarily. All responses to a post will be grouped under the same thread UID of the original post. Each thread UID denotes a unique context or topic where interested users deliberately follow or participate in the respective discussion.

Two datasets used in this study are drawn from Yammer platform collected from two companies over 123 and 608 days. For privacy reason, the companies name and information here is unspecified. Data sets respectively contain 6195 and 25053 posts, 15042 and 28327 replies, 5937 and 11932 mentions, 12359 and 15547 likes, and 716 and 2429 notifications. They also contain 12242 and 25127 unique thread UIDs to denote the number of discussion contexts/topics.

Interaction of 5787 users in 51 work groups created the first data set and 19098 users and 771 public and private work groups were included in the second set.

In the following sections, we describe the methodology followed in this study to define a users influence score and a set of feature subsets those will be used to successfully predict the influence score.

2.1 Influence Score

Organizations leverage their knowledge resources by consolidating them into shared sources such as intranet and EOSNs and such repositories became integral to overall organizational functioning. Pursuant to 'Public Goods Theory' (Samuelson, 1954) and 'Expectancy Theory'(Vroom, 1964), the consumption and demand for information commodity derived from the information it contains and its benefits to users. Hence, the level of contribution at collective activities such as online communities are directly correlated with the perceived value of information shared within the platform and its benefits to users in a group (Rafaeli and LaRose, 1993). Drawing on this, we also assumed that the perceived value of the public information produced by a given post, posted by an individual user for all other EOSN users, is correlated to the degree of participations at the discussion and response the post receives. Alternatively, EOSN users will only participate in an online conversation, created by an individual user, if it creates value him/her or it is beneficial to his/her own sake.

Considering the aforementioned facts in conjunction with tracing users' tendency to participate at online discussions, created by opinion leaders, this study quantified users' influence scores and ranked users in regards to their ability of activating other user via EOSN. For instance; if a user 'X' created a new discussion forum (i.e., topic thread) by posting to the public, X's influence score was computed by the number of users who reacted to the post or showed interests by either replying, liking or mentioning others to the post under the same thread. Analogues to different Twitter information diffusion topologies, this study observed three different online social activities (i.e., like, reply, mention) in Yammer EOSN. However, instead of building three different layers of social networks depending on three different types of interactions, this study considered one aggregated network where the actors are EOSN users and links denote any types of interactions between them.

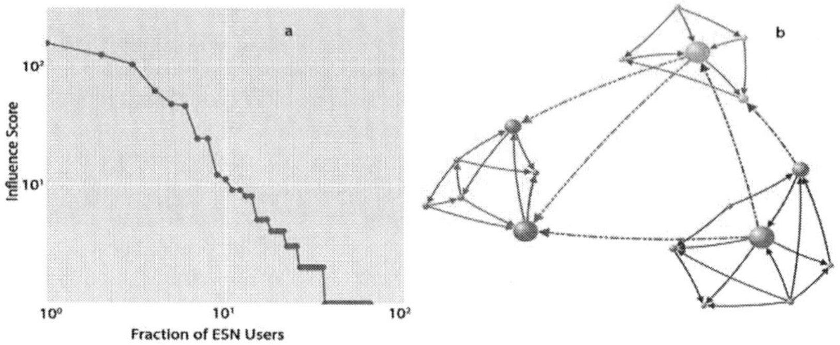

Figure1. (a) Distribution of influence score (b) The abstract network representation of an EOSN demonstrates three discussion forums (Threads with unique thread IDs)

In Figure 1(a), we present the distribution of influence scores computed for the EOSN analyzed in this study. At both companies over one third of those who participated at group discussions were triggered by less than 3% of discussion creators and the distribution follow Pareto principle. In figure 1(b), we present an abstract network representation of directed network considering four different types of asymmetric social interactions (Post, Like, Notification, Mention) that were used to calculate the influence score for a user. When a user creates a new discussion thread by posting a topic to the public, all members of the work group receive a notification and can observe not only the context of the post but also every related activities and responses. However, not all group members react to all threads; so, the dotted links in the network 'b' denote only inter-discussion board interactions. All interactions are asymmetrical and therefore the corresponding network is directional. The number of in-degree denotes the number of users reacted to a post and considered as the degree of the influence for the origin of the discussion. This score also denotes the number of people activated by the post creator.

2.2 Predictor Feature Extraction

Social network refers to a relational system consist of actors and links those represent ties or relationships among actors. Actors can range from individuals, communities, groups, scholars or any entities able to form different types of relationships with their peers. In social networks, in one hand, each actor can influence others or be influenced by others and on the other hand, it is widely perceived that information, rumor or piece of messages can be passed through the links of underlying social networks. Due to these characteristics, social network has predominantly emerged as an indispensable medium of information diffusion. Further, according to C. Zhang, Sun, & Wang, two different terminologies, namely, 'influence maximization' and 'social contagion' leverage the link structure of social networks instead of the actual message content exchanged and widely impact the information propagation mechanism (Zhang et al., 2013). Among these two, the former represents the problem of identifying some seed users being most influential and can motivate others in the network. Therefore, this study attempted to mining the link and community structure to find out the influential staffs within the structure of EOSN. Since this study exploit the community structure of EOSN users and the multiple group membership of EOSN users, we assume that the possibility of any types of interactions within a group can be reciprocated and hence the interactions are bidirectional. Therefore, in this study, the network of group membership is an undirected network. In addition, multiple interactions between two users are considered as one interaction. Therefore, the resultant network is also unweighted network.

In Figure (2), this study presents an abstract representation of an EOSN considering three communities colored as red (A), green (B) and blue (C). Each community is a work group within the enterprise where users may experience single or multiple group memberships. Links in this network are bidirectional since it is believed that users' interactions via online social networks can be reciprocated. User 'u' is member of three work groups and is able to observe and react to other members' activities.

Group membership is considered as important feature of EOSN users in this study since any interaction performed by any user in EOSN is visible to his/her group members. For example, a post in EOSN either liked or replied by one user, will also be visible to his/her group members. Activities of members with multiple group memberships are visible to all the corresponding group members. For example, in Figure 2 actor u is a member of multiple groups and has high visibility to others. This allows actor u to exert more bridging power in this corporate social network. In following section, we describe the set of features constructed in this study to predict the influence score of users in EOSN. The first two variables created based on the structural position of nodes within Yammer network and the last two variables has been defined using the network of interaction of users via the EOSN platform.

2.2.1 Group Affiliation Score

This feature denotes the total number of users in different groups for those a user has membership. If n_i denotes the number of members in a work group g_i then group affiliation score f_g for a user u is computed as:

$$f_g^u = \sum_{i=0}^{G} |n_i| \text{ where } u \in g_i$$

Where G denotes the total number of work groups in an EOSN. In figure 1(b), sizes of the actors are proportionate to their group affiliation score.

2.2.2 Betweenness Centrality

The betweenness centrality of an EOSN user u is computed considering the network in Figure 2 as:

$$f_b^u = \sum_{v \neq u \neq t}^{n} \frac{p_{vt}(u)}{p_{vt}} / n$$

Where, p_{vt}denotes the geodesic distance/shortest path between user v and t and $p_{vt}(u)$ denotes the number of shortest paths that include user u and n denotes the total number of groups in the network.

2.2.3 Community-aware Score

Considering each work group as a community within an EOSN, this study scored each group in regards to the total number of different social activities occurred within group. For example, in Figure 1(b), within the blue community, there are 13 different links denoting any type(s) of interactions (i.e., like, reply, mention) within the group. Likewise, in green group there are eight links and in red group there are 10 links or total number of interactions. Depending on the number of links we scored different work groups in regards to the frequency of activities taking place within the group. Considering these community scoring, this study assigned each user a community aware score in regards to their group memberships relative to the maximum membership possibilities (n=50 groups). For example, if user 'x' is a member of two groups (i.e., Red and Green), its community-aware score can be computed as ($6 = \frac{8+10}{3}$) since red is scored as 10 and green as eight and there are only three groups in this network (n=3). For the sake of brevity, in this study, we denote this score using f_c^u.

2.2.4 Social Interaction Score

This score is defined by the total number of activities (like, reply, mention) exhibited by a user excluded the number of replies, 'likes' and mentions of a user that he/she performed on his/her own post. This feature is denoted by f_s^u and reflects on the effect of users' attitude and behaviour towards others on stability of interactions in dynamic communication.

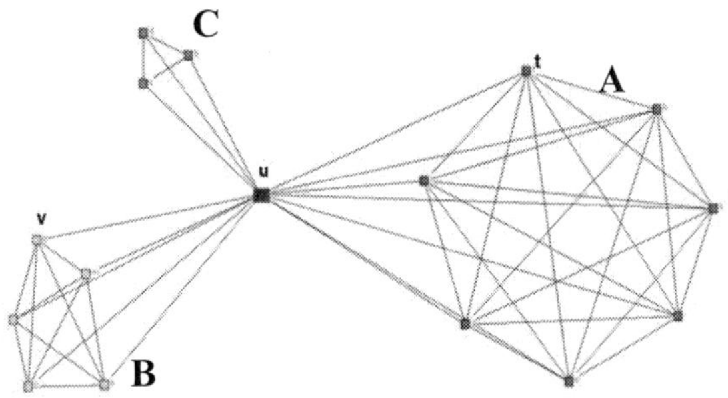

Figure 2. An abstract representation of undirected network developed from user group membership within an EOSN

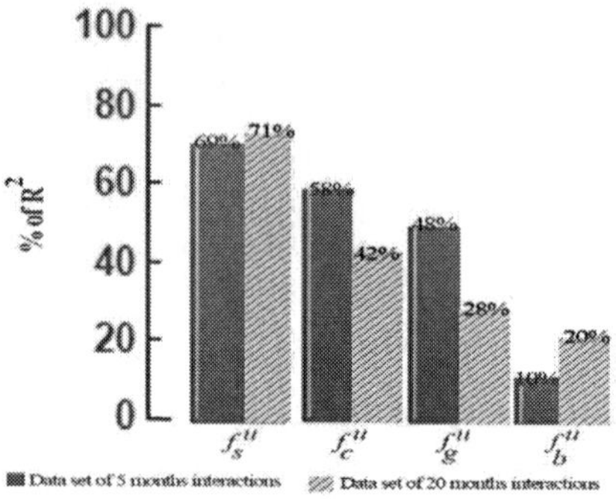

Figure 3. Feature importance in predicting the influence score

2.3 Prediction Model

To develop a prediction model, this study used both linear and support vector regression (SVR) to predict the influence score with the help of the aforementioned extracted features. In SVR, linear regression is performed in a high dimensional feature space using ε-intensive loss function proposed by the study in (Chapelle and Vapnik, 2000). It simultaneously attempts to reduce model complexity $||w||^2$ where w denotes the weight vector of the model $f(x_i, w)$ and x is the input features. This is performed by introducing non-nengative slack variables ξ_i , $i = 1,2, \ldots, n$ to measure the deviationof training samples outhside the ε-intensive zone. Therefore, SVR can be formulated as an optimization problem as follows:

$$\boldsymbol{min}\left\{\frac{1}{2}||w||^2 + C\sum_{i=0}^{n}(\xi_i)\right\} \qquad \textit{Subject to } \boldsymbol{y_i - f(x_i, w) \leq \varepsilon + \xi_i \text{ and } \xi_i \geq 0}$$

A detail description of the optimization problem considering both primal and dual problem can be found in the study by Smola & Schölkopf in (Smola and Schölkopf, 2004). To solve non-linearity in regression problem, support vector regression also uses kernel function to efficiently handle the optimization problem. This includes computing one Lagrange multiplier per training sample instead of one weight per feature. The well-known machine learning library WEKA (Hall et al., 2009) was used for the purpose of support vector regression.

3. RESULTS

In table 1, we present the results from linear regressions. We observed that both linear and non-linear regression have similar performances in regards to predicting the influence scores in this study. Considering the correlation measures we can conclude that features constructed in this study are strongly correlated with the degree of influence a few users in EOSN experience over others in decision making.

In Figure (3), this study presents the feature importance in regards to their ability to successfully predict the percentage of variability present in the computed influence scores. It is evident that the last feature which denotes the social interaction score concedes the highest performance followed by betweenness centrality and community-aware ranking. However, group affiliation denotes the lowest performance. It is noteworthy that, all together, the predictor variables represented by the extracted features in this study can successfully predict over 70% of the total variability present in the influence score.

Table 1. Model Summary

$f_g^u + f_b^u + f_c^u + f_s^u$			
Linear Regression	*RMSE*	*Std Error of the Estimate*	*P-Value*
5 months online interactions	0.777	140.85	0.000
20 months online interactions	0.705	50.35	0.000

4. DISCUSSION AND CONCLUSION

Enterprise Social Online platforms, such as; Yammer, connected employees via online communities to share their ideas and communicate and collaborate efficiently. Users voluntarily participate in online communities to gain the value of the information available on the platform. The unsupervised virtual connection via Enterprise Online Social Network (EOSN) platforms raises the phenomenon of influence propagation via online platforms, and, given that some opinion makers can also be sources of influence within online social networks. Considering the importance of influencers in areas of organizational management such as; communication and knowledge management, this study examined the association of structural and interactive attributes of enterprise social networks with user's ability to influence others in EOSNs. Drawing on structure of inter-organizational communication via Yammer social platform, we defined an influence score for each user and developed a novel model to predict influential users within ESON with respect to their ability to activate others by spreading information via enterprise social networks. We extracted four important features reflect on the structure and dynamic of the networks by exploiting the users and communities' interactions and positions within the structure of the EOSN. Communities defined by work groups in the corporate environment and the interactions records drawn out the network of discussion boards. The results of this study indicated the individuals' influence ability significantly correlated with both their network structural position and activities via online social platform. Digging into the results revealed that the degree of influence is considerably subjective to the users and communities' interactions and the dynamic of the network. The dynamics of interaction within communities and users' attitude towards others' online activities significantly promote the users' ability of influence, however, the number of direct neighbors and groups were less effective on the degree of influence. This means users who are member of active online groups are more likely to influence others within the whole network compare with those who are member of sluggish communities and this is regardless of the number of social communities' members. In an organization obviously not many employees could be influential and our research showed only less than 3% of opinion creators are the real opinion leaders. Using our model we can identify and predict those opinion leaders within organizations aims to promote or control the influence of these members to support the organizational goals and performance.

In this study, due to privacy reason we did not have access to the content of the posts, however, information transmission is commonly topic sensitive. Hence, in our future study we will apply our model on public social online platform Tweeter to examine the role of the context of the posts (Tweets) in being an opinion leader within social networks. We will also trace the patterns in opinion leaders' activity using time-series analysis methods to reveal footprints of organizational events in enterprise social online activities and predict users' behaviors in the future events. We will also examine the practice of our new model on other types of human networks, for instance: cellular /mobile network, etc.

REFERENCES

2014. *Social Data Analytics: Collaboration for the Enterprise,* San Diego, Morgan Kaufmann [Imprint].

Aleahmad, A., Karisani, P., Rahgozar, M. & Oroumchian, F. 2016. OLFinder: Finding opinion leaders in online social networks. *Journal of Information Science,* 42, 659-674.

Bakshy, E., Hofman, J. M., Mason, W. A. & Watts, D. J. Everyone's an influencer: quantifying influence on twitter. Proceedings of the fourth ACM international conference on Web search and data mining, 2011. ACM, 65-74.

Chapelle, O. & Vapnik, V. Model selection for support vector machines. Advances in neural information processing systems, 2000. 230-236.

Chen, D., Lü, L., Shang, M.-S., Zhang, Y.-C. & Zhou, T. 2012. Identifying influential nodes in complex networks. *Physica A: Statistical Mechanics and its Applications,* 391, 1777-1787.

Chen, Y., Wang, X., Tang, B., Xu, R., Yuan, B., Xiang, X. & Bu, J. Identifying Opinion Leaders from Online Comments. Chinese National Conference on Social Media Processing, 2014. Springer, 231-239.

Ebner, M., Lienhardt, C., Rohs, M. & Meyer, I. 2010. Microblogs in Higher Education–A chance to facilitate informal and process-oriented learning? *Computers & Education,* 55, 92-100.

Goldsmith, E. B. & Springerlink 2015. *Social Influence and Sustainable Consumption,* Cham, Springer International Publishing.

Guldbrandsson, K., Nordvik, M. K. & Bremberg, S. 2012. Identification of potential opinion leaders in child health promotion in Sweden using network analysis. *BMC research notes,* 5, 424.

Hall, M., Frank, E., Holmes, G., Pfahringer, B., Reutemann, P. & Witten, I. H. 2009. The WEKA data mining software: an update. *ACM SIGKDD explorations newsletter,* 11, 10-18.

Lazarsfeld, P. F., Berelson, B. & Gaudet, H. 1944. *The people's choice: How the voter makes up his mind in a presidential election,* New York, Duell, Sloan and Pearce.

Leonardi, P. M., Huysman, M. & Steinfield, C. 2013. Enterprise Social Media: Definition, History, and Prospects for the Study of Social Technologies in Organizations. *Journal of Computer-Mediated Communication,* 19, 1-19.

Mantymaki, M. & Riemer, K. 2016. Enterprise social networking: A knowledge management perspective. *International Journal Of Information Management,* 36, 1042-1052.

Rafaeli, S. & Larose, R. J. 1993. Electronic Bulletin Boards and "Public Goods" Explanations of Collaborative Mass Media. *Communication Research,* 20, 277-297.

Reinhardt, W. Communication is the Key-Support Durable Knowledge Sharing in Software Engineering by Microblogging. Software Engineering (Workshops), 2009. 329-340.

Riemer, K. & Scifleet, P. Enterprise social networking in knowledge-intensive work practices: A case study in a professional service firm. ACIS 2012: Location, location, location: Proceedings of the 23rd Australasian Conference on Information Systems 2012, 2012. ACIS, 1-12.

Samuelson, P. A. 1954. The Pure Theory of Public Expenditure. *The Review of Economics and Statistics,* 36, 387-389.

Sheikhahmadi, A. & Nematbakhsh, M. A. 2017. Identification of multi-spreader users in social networks for viral marketing. *Journal of Information Science,* 43, 412-423.

Smola, A. J. & Schölkopf, B. 2004. A tutorial on support vector regression. *Statistics and computing,* 14, 199-222.

Vroom, V. H. 1964. *Work and motivation,* New York, Wiley.

Wiesneth, K. 2017. *Enterprise Social Networks–Contributions to Research with respect to Actor Roles in Knowledge Management, the Role of Formal Hierarchies, and Network Evolution.*

Wu, L., Morstatter, F., Hu, X. & Liu, H. 2016. Mining misinformation in social media. *Big Data in Complex and Social Networks*, 123-152.

Yang, L., Tian, Y., Li, J., Ma, J. & Zhang, J. 2017. Identifying opinion leaders in social networks with topic limitation. *Cluster Computing,* 20, 2403-2413.

Zhang, C., Sun, J. & Wang, K. Information propagation in microblog networks. Proceedings of the 2013 IEEE/ACM international conference on advances in social networks analysis and mining, 2013. ACM, 190-196.

Zhang, J., Qu, Y., Cody, J. & Wu, Y. A case study of micro-blogging in the enterprise: use, value, and related issues. Proceedings of the SIGCHI Conference on Human Factors in Computing Systems, 2010. ACM, 123-132.

Zhao, D. & Rosson, M. B. How and why people Twitter: the role that micro-blogging plays in informal communication at work. Proceedings of the ACM 2009 international conference on Supporting group work, 2009. ACM, 243-252.

Zhu, Z. 2013. Discovering the influential users oriented to viral marketing based on online social networks. *Physica A: Statistical Mechanics and its Applications,* 392, 3459-3469.

REFLECTIONS ON THE IMPEDIMENTS TO INFORMATION SYSTEMS STRATEGIC ALIGNMENT IN PUBLIC SECTOR ORGANISATIONS IDENTIFIED THROUGH A PROCESSUAL LENS

Anne Burke[1] and Joseph McDonagh[2]
[1]*School of Business, Letterkenny Institute of Technology, Letterkenny, Donegal, Ireland*
[2]*Trinity Business School, Trinity College Dublin, Dublin, Ireland*

ABSTRACT

Why are there still issues in aligning information systems (IS) and business strategies despite the fact there has been over three decades of research? In this paper we reflect on the impediments to strategic alignment identified through a processual lens. Failure to align business and IS strategies may result in misused resources and failed IS projects. IS in Public Service Organisations (PSOs) has been discussed in the literature as an aid to delivering new and better services to citizens, increasing efficiency and transparency, and improving accountability in public sector procedures and management. Although challenges with alignment in the public sector are identified as a recurring theme by government audit functions, a review of the literature indicated that most studies were concentrated in the private sector, using a variance approach with few focused on strategic alignment within PSOs. A review of the literature identified an insufficient understanding of the impediments to IS alignment as an emerging strategic process in PSOs, from both a theory and practitioner perspective. This paper presents an interpretive processual longitudinal case study with alignment being viewed as an unfolding sequence of events necessitating a longitudinal approach to data collection. A process model of strategic alignment emerged from this case study illustrating the conditions, using process theories, under which certain impediments could be expected to occur therefore adding to existing knowledge on strategic alignment impediment. While the findings are from a single PSO, the results shed light on a globally-persistent management concern for the past thirty years.

KEYWORDS

Strategic Alignment, Processual Approach, Impediments

1. INTRODUCTION

Given the complexity of government structures, managing public sector Information Systems (IS) is considered to be increasingly important (Van Grembergen, 2004) as is public sector IS strategic alignment. Alignment between business and IS strategies is not easy to accomplish or maintain (Ciborra, 1997) in public or private organisations, however, there is a paucity of empirical research into strategic alignment in Public Service Organisations (PSOs). Since the 1980s, researchers have been interested in establishing what enablers and impediments emerge in the strategic alignment process. The focus of this paper is a reflection on the impediments to the process of aligning business and IS strategies in PSOs using a processual lens. Section 2 outlines the background to the research. In section 3, the theoretical concepts underpinning the research are introduced and briefly discussed. Section 4 gives an overview of the research methodology, with the analysis and findings being presented in section 5. Reflections on the impediments identified through a processual lens are outlined in section 6. The following section, 7, brings the paper to a close.

2. BACKGROUND TO THE RESEARCH

With the rise of e-business, organisations have become increasingly reliant on IS (Huang et al., 2013). However, there are often challenges with IS in PSOs and in our review of Value For Money studies emerging from government audit functions across the United States of America, United Kingdom, and Ireland over three decades, the alignment of IS and business strategies is depicted as an ongoing challenge for PSOs (Burke & McDonagh, 2010). However, these studies did not explore in-depth the underlying causes or circumstances resulting in misalignment. The studies were carried out at a particular point in time and did not have the scope longitudinally to delve further into the underlying conditions giving rise to the identified challenges. A more research paper by Dwivedi et al., (2015) call for IS challenges to be studied from multiple perspectives, to move beyond narrow considerations of the IS artefact, and to venture into underexplored organizational contexts, such as in PSOs. Therefore there is a need for ongoing empirical research to understand how the process of strategic alignment in PSOs can be better managed to increase the degree of alignment and reduce the impact of impediments.

3. LITERATURE OVERVIEW

The research presented in this paper is built on the following sets of scholarly literature: the nature of strategy process, process theory and processual research, and IS strategic alignment. These are now briefly introduced.

Processual research in strategic management focuses on the formation of strategies, which conventionally have been conceptualised as the consequence of decision and/or planning processes. This necessitated an understanding of the nature of the strategy process, but alongside that, a general understanding of the literature on the approaches to strategy-making – particularly in relation to principal schools of thought. There are several schools of thought with respect to strategy. Three of the most influential are: 'Rational', 'Emergent', and 'Processual'. There have been many debates on the relative advantages of the rational (comprehensive, formal, rational planning) versus emergent-processual (adaptive, participative). Both the rational and emergent schools are the forerunners to the 'processual' school approach. Rational and emergent approaches to the strategy process are near opposites while the third perspective, the 'processual' approach, is shown to integrate both (Chakravarthy and White, 2002).

Processual research is founded on the examination of actual organisational decision-making thus leading to more representative concepts of process, highlighting the fact that strategies are often arrived at circuitously and, to a degree, inadvertently. Scholars (the first being Mohr in 1982) have drawn a contrast between variance approaches, which conceive explanations as relationships among dependent and independent variables, and processual ones which build explanations from observed "patterns in events, activities, and choices over time" (Langley, 2009, p. 409). The variance approach is oriented towards large sample sizes, structural explanations, and generalizable results, whilst processual approaches are qualitative in nature and oriented towards the dynamic study of behaviour within organisations, focusing on the core themes of organisational context through the temporal order and sequence of events that unfold over time (Van de Ven and Poole, 1995).

The suitable temporal periods for process research may fluctuate from a few days, weeks, or months to very long periods of time and offers explanations in terms of patterns in events, activities, and decisions over time (Langley et al., 2009). However, as Van de Ven (1992) suggests, it is not just the processes that are critical but also the underlying logic that gives meaning and significance to these processes. So the contributions from process studies can also be regarded as meanings which sometimes reflect the interpretations of participants, or instead recognise the researcher's own interpretive processes. Van de Ven and Poole (1995) recognised a set of four basic process theories which they propose cover the variety of theories used to describe change both individually and collectively. The four theories are categorised as: life cycle theories (grounded in the notion of genetic predetermination), teleological theories (grounded in goal-driven behaviours and learning), dialectical theories (grounded in cycles of confrontation and resolution among opposing forces), and evolutionary theories (grounded in the processes of variation, selection and retention). We found little research on strategy process in the public sector with the majority of studies taking a variance approach focusing solely on strategy content ignoring the temporal dimension (Andrews et al., 2011).

Reich and Benbasat (1996, p. 56) describe strategic alignment as: "the degree to which the mission, objectives and plans contained in the business strategy are shared and supported by the IT strategy." The literature clearly shows that strategic alignment "continues to be elusive, and in all of the geographies it ranks in the top ten management concerns; ranking 1st in both the world and Europe" (Luftman and Derksen, 2014, p. 6), and has been a top management concern for both IS management and business executives for over three decades (Chan and Reich, 2007, Derksen and Luftman, 2014). Scholars have tried to ascertain factors that contribute as either enablers or impediments to this process of strategic alignment (Hussin, King, & Cragg, 2002). An impediment is referred to as a key area that if mismanaged is a barrier to strategic alignment (Luftman et al., 1999b). Based on the review of the strategic alignment research, a number of influential factors were synthesised: strong leadership and senior management support for IS, business/IS communication and shared domain knowledge, partnership in planning, prior IS success, planning sophistication and governance. However, Chan and Reich (2007b, p. 309) suggest: "It is not enough to simply understand the factors involved in alignment, one must understand the interrelationships among the factors." Opinions in the literature differ as to whether strategic alignment is a process (King & Teo, 1997; Campbell, 2005), or an end-state (Avison et al., 2004). The latter view is dominant (Earl, 1989) and therefore, the necessity to continuously maintain and sustain strategic alignment dynamically is seldom recognised. Hirschheim and Sabherwal (2001, p. 87) contend that strategic alignment is not an end-state but, rather, a "process of continuous adaptation and change".

Strategic alignment is also viewed as having intellectual and social dimensions which underpin the ongoing alignment of business and IS strategies (Reich and Benbasat, 2000). Most strategic alignment studies focus on the technical deliverables in relation to planning content and methodologies, that is, focusing on the intellectual dimension alone. They do not include the social dimension which would encompass communication, interpretation and integration, and how collective and departmental levels within the organisation create mutual understanding in the strategic alignment process (Balhareth et al., 2012). Research on strategic alignment clearly indicates that attaining and sustaining alignment is highly dependent on social dimensions rather than intellectual dimensions alone. The social dimension of the dynamic process of strategy-making has been well described by Pettigrew (1992) in the strategic management literature, but less well explored in the strategic alignment literature.

Although challenges with the alignment of IS and business strategies in PSOs are identified as a recurring theme by government audit functions, the IS strategic alignment literature indicates that most studies were concentrated in the private sector, with very few focused on strategic alignment in PSOs (Bourn, 2007). Indeed, we found perspectives on the process of strategic alignment in PSOs largely underrepresented. Rocheleau (2006) also argues that IS in the public sector presents different challenges than those faced within the private sector due a number of dissimilarities. The three main dissimilarities between public and private organisations are: firstly, their ownership; secondly, unlike their private counterparts, PSOs are funded largely by taxation rather than fees paid directly by customers; and thirdly, PSOs are controlled predominantly by political forces, not market ones (Boyne, 2002).

Therefore, this paper in the following sections addresses the shortcomings of the strategic alignment literature, focusing on the impediments to the process of aligning business and IS strategies in PSOs.

4. RESEARCH METHODOLOGY

This research involved a longitudinal in-depth case study to obtain rich data (both real-time and retrospective) from which a detailed process narrative was produced. We chose a single PSO that was involved in the IS strategy-making process at the time of the research and had instigated previous IS strategies. The PSO is responsible for the delivery of core public sector services to 1.7 million people and employs 25,000 administrative staff spread across 12 departments. Regarding the efforts to produce IS strategy-making and strategically align them to business strategies, two distinct periods were explored: 2004–2010 (retrospectively) and 2010–2014 (retrospectively and real-time) each with a sequence of events. The aim was to collect processual, historical, and contextual data. The data was not only gathered longitudinally but was also primary and secondary in nature, reflecting the need to gain both an understanding of the strategy-making process context and the views of participants at multiple levels of the organisation representing the PSO collectively and in individual departments. Therefore, it was collected through observation, interview, and archival and secondary documentation, permitting both the combination and cross-validation of contextual and temporal data to provide useful insights into organisational events and processes.

The data for the first time period (2004-2010) was gathered from archival data and retrospective accounts given by participants via interview. It is not as detailed in comparison to the next time period (2010-2014) in which it was possible to observe first-hand many of the events that took place (Langley, 1999) and follow the strategy-making process in real-time via attendance at workshops and real-time accounts given in participant interviews. Twenty-four interviews (11 unstructured and 13 semi-structured) were conducted that produced a vast quantity of data. Additionally, extensive access was given to IS strategy-making documents. As part of the data collection, four internal IS strategy workshops were attended during 2010. In a processual study, having retrospective data is vital (Bizzi and Langley, 2012). A range of over thirty organisational documents was reviewed for the study. A complete case study database for this research was maintained using NVivo 10 qualitative data analysis software.

The final stage in this case study research was the development of a phased model of strategic alignment from the detailed analysis of the case data.

5. ANALYSIS AND FINDINGS

The case narrative provided the initial analysis of the case data. Narrative has been described as being particularly useful for analysing data where an interpretive approach to theory building has been chosen (Langley, 1999). The data analysis began by placing the data onto the two timelines (temporal bracketing) and developing a narrative around that timeline in order to arrive at a processual view (Langley, 1999) and identify the phases of strategic alignment. From the two timelines four preliminary phases emerged. That allowed the demarcation of themes and aggregate dimensions by comparing key events (Nag et al., 2007). After providing a description of what happened in the two time periods over the four phases, preliminary analysis was carried out to explore why events unfolded as they did and identify some impediments to the process of aligning business strategy and IS strategy. The baseline for the coding was the identification of sixty-four codes into which blocks of text (from the interview transcripts, notes from workshops, the case narrative, and secondary documentation) were aggregated in NVivo10 for second level analysis. The codes were based on the research question, literature, and collected data. The initial focus was on identifying critical events; later renamed as core social work. They encapsulated those social events identified as being necessary to the achievement of a technical deliverable in relation to the process of strategic alignment, i.e. the development of business principles. Next, the core social work and technical deliverables were grouped under one of four phases with a predominant focus. This in turn led to the identification of distinctive characteristics of the various phases over time. In examining the dominant focus of each phase, the external and internal contexts were analysed to see how they influenced the strategic alignment process. Additionally, the main participants engaging in each of the phases were identified as to whether they were acting at a collective or departmental level.

The impediments in each phase were then identified. Firstly, the emerging process model was related to earlier work on impediments (Chan et al., 2006, Hussin et al., 2002, Luftman et al., 1999a, Reich and Benbasat, 1996) and process theorising (Langley, 1999). Next, participant interviews and the critical events coded from the data sources were reviewed. The most prominent impediments were cross-referenced again with the literature before settling on eight that seemed to be clearly linked to a particular phase.

Impediments were classified as being either intellectual or social. Social impediments have a direct link with people involved in the creation of alignment, whilst intellectual barriers have a direct link to the content and structure of strategy and strategy-making methodologies (Reich & Benbasat, 1996). Impediments were grouped under one of the four phases if, they appeared in a phase in both time periods. If an impediment appeared in more than one phase, it was linked to the earliest one and, where an intervention was made by management within that phase, it should not then reappear in a later phase. A number of impediments were either discarded due to the fact that they only appeared in one time period or could be subsumed as part of another impediment. All these findings, together with the case study narrative, coded text blocks, and process theory, were used to draw a full phased model of strategic alignment in a PSO (Pentland, 1999; Langley, 1999).

Not only was it observed that there was a multiplicity of levels involved in the process of strategic alignment, but that different types of events were taking place at a collective level and departmental level, which motivated social interactions among levels and between departments. The case analysed IS strategies for two periods that initially showed a high degree of alignment with the PSO's strategy, but were difficult to embed across departments. In summary, the emergence of two distinct but yet intersecting levels were observed that influenced the process of strategic alignment: the collective level and the departmental level. Findings from the case show that misalignment was not automatically the result of just one impediment in a particular phase. The first temporal phase of the strategic process to emerge referred to the efforts made to **establish** business principles that would underpin the business strategy which, in essence, should have driven all IS projects. Work then tended to focus on getting business executives at a collective level to **endorse** the newly-formed IS strategy. In the next phase that emerged from both time periods, efforts were focused on **embedding** the IS strategy into the organisation as a whole via individual departments. The last phase to emerge referred to the process of **evaluating** whether value was realised from the IS strategy. Eight impediments were identified. Four of these were intellectual: *planning, governance, IS structure,* and *value realisation.* The social ones were: *leadership, partnership, commitment,* and *culture.*

The findings led to the development of a phased model of strategic alignment in PSOs composed of seven characteristics and four phases, as shown in Table 1. The holistic processual model is intended to identify the impediments to strategic alignment in terms of patterns in events and choices that emerge over time (Mohr, 1982), and explain how and why these impediments overlap and are interdependent (Chan and Reich, 2007). The ***dominant focus*** characteristic describes the principle driver of action in each phase. The ***level of engagement*** describes the level of the organisation that is most engaged in driving the process of strategic alignment. The ***degree of alignment*** can range from high to medium for each phase. The ***core technical deliverables*** identify and formally document what technical products are important in each phase. The ***core social work*** relates to socially organized human work engaged in by more than one actor in the socially constructed environment of business and IS domains. The two final characteristics refer to ***intellectual*** and ***social impediments***. The strategic alignment process has high levels of intellectual and social interactivity. Therefore, individuals engaged in work of a social nature and complex technical deliverables become crucially interdependent. This tight coupling means that error in any particular process can quickly cascade into more significant events and potentially lead to strategic misalignment.

Table 1. Phased Model of Strategic Alignment in PSOs

Phased Model of Strategic Alignment				
CHARACTERISTICS	**PHASES**			
	Establishing	**Endorsing**	**Embedding**	**Evaluating**
Dominant Focus	Principles	Strategy	Projects	Value
Level of Engagement	Collective	Collective	Departmental	Departmental
Degree of Alignment	High	High	High/ Medium	Medium
Core Technical Deliverables	Developing Business Principles	Defining Enterprise Architecture	Delivering Projects	Reviewing Projects
Core Social Work	Collaborating	Sharing	Coordinating	Assessing
Intellectual Impediments	Planning	Governance	IS Structure	Value Realisation
Social Impediments	Leadership	Partnership	Commitment	Culture

6. REFLECTIONS ON THE IMPEDIMENTS IDENTIFIED THROUGH A PROCESSUAL LENS

A key strength of the developed model is depicting the dynamic, evolving nature of strategic alignment. This model reflects the perspective that it is not to be understood as a set of deterministic causal relationships, but rather as a continuous process of interactions between people, IS, and contexts. An important source of learning about strategic alignment is from identifying impediments. As long as organisations attempt to align business and IS strategies, impediments will likely transpire. Impediments, although nearly unavoidable and frequently expensive, can offer insight from which to learn. Learning from impediments includes acknowledging that unforeseen, impeding events have transpired and taking time to reflect on these impediments diminish the likelihood of these happening again (Lyytinen and Robey, 1999). Reflecting on impediments and why they occur may enable awareness that reduces misinterpretations of particular situations and recognition of failings that hinder strategic alignment. This research revealed insights into impediments using a processual lens. It also stressed the importance of on-going learning and review (Galliers, 2006) and, given its processual lens, the unintended consequences arising not only from the dynamic nature of alignment (Sabherwal and Chan, 2001), but also the emergent nature of strategy-making (Mintzberg and Waters, 1985).

The use of a processual lens provided an opportunity for deeper analysis of the case data than would have been possible if a variance research lens had been used. The additional analysis, which consisted of examining the data associated with each of the four phases to identify the unique characteristics of each phase and discern how these unfolded in the process of strategic alignment, led to distinct intellectual and social impediments in each phase. The findings suggest it is phase two which experiences the highest impact of impediments to strategic alignment - unclear governance and the lack of close business-IS partnership. For practitioners both in PSOs and the private sector, this means organisations should develop business and IS strategies together to ensure that they support each other to consequently overcome impediments and achieve a high degree of strategic alignment.

Another practical implication of this research is the need to create an IS governance structure aimed at cohesively managing all aspects of the process of aligning business and IS strategies across the organisation and at an individual department level. The importance of IS governance cannot be underestimated. This case study highlighted the influence of governance and its impact on communication and partnership. The data further suggests that strong engaged IS executives and a culture that encourages sharing increases the level of trust in IS and promotes knowledge-sharing and integration. This research thus proposes that business-IS partnership enables communication between the business executives and IS executives and that communication between the business executives and IS executives enhances business-IS partnership. Therefore, IS executives and the business executives must find a way to communicate, in a language that both parties understand and with which they are comfortable. Hence, organisations should recognise the importance of inviting IS executives to the strategy-making table.

Another key impediment affecting alignment is the lack of credibility-building, in terms of underpinning the business principles, meeting user requirements, delivering good quality work, and managing timelines and budgets. Low levels of business executive engagement with IS, as a result of their difficulties with IS projects in the past, can lead to lack of senior management commitment. This finding is consistent with past studies; however, the data suggests that it is not only the past record of IS success that increases the strategic alignment, but also the present outcomes. In practice, organisations should ensure that IS consistently delivers results that satisfy the business needs, and that requires value realisation processes to be monitored before, during, and after project implementation. This research found that there was almost no incidence of systematic post-implementation reviews.

As discussed above, the theory underlying the model is a process one. The model describes the dynamic process of strategic alignment over four phases in which it may be impacted by various impediments. As described previously, there were 12 departments within the PSO with an overarching IS strategy being developed over two temporal periods; leading to events which were the product of the interplay between two opposing forces: the sense making of the PSO identity as a system of public service organisations at a collective level and individual departmental identities at a departmental level with collaborative engagement necessary between these two levels during the strategic alignment process. The proposed model shows two levels of engagement: the level of the PSO as a collective system of public service organisations which develop and implement an overall IS strategy and that of the departments which struggle to defend their IS needs based on the sense making processes of an organisational identity.

The subsequent analysis of strategic alignment in the organisational context exhibited as predominant, teleological and dialectical behaviours explained by teleological and dialectical theories. Teleological behaviour was found when a group of participants decided on and moved toward a shared organisational goal, such as underlying business principles. Impediments to strategic alignment occurred at various phases when participants could not reach consensus on a goal or when the conclusions reached were subject to individual and group biases – silo mind-set. In contrast, dialectical behaviour was found to apply when different departments conflicted and confronted one another on an issue – e.g. prioritisation of projects, allocation of resources.

At a departmental level, each department made sense of the IS that would enable the organisation as a collective system of public service organisations achieve its business principles. The departmental decisional events further influenced how decisions were taken at the overall organisational level at a collective level, like a specific implementation approach that would be reflected by the functionality of an organisation wide IS. Moreover, the overall events of the PSO shaped departmental IS strategies given the reciprocal influence between individuals' perceptions and the social and historical context in which they have developed over time (Orlikowski, 2002). Thus, it can be inferred that the underlying processual theory for driving strategic alignment across multiple departments was dialectical and subjected to colliding forces and contradictory values that competed with each other. Therefore, some of the impediments identified in the model directly relate to the dialectical theory or departments struggling to defend their IS needs based on the processes of making sense of its overall organisational identity.

Each impediment was designated as being explained by either teleological or dialectical theory. The analysis suggested that these two theories provided a cohesive viewpoint that linked the impediments to strategic alignment at two levels – collective and departmental. The case study clearly shows that strategic alignment is driven by the behaviours of individuals, especially those in leadership positions, trying to create a new IS strategy and aligning it to the business principles. However, it was also evident that organisations are complex entities, comprised of many goal-directed individuals whose purposes may be incompatible. As opposing individuals interact in an effort to achieve their respective goals, organisations may change in response to negotiations or resolutions of conflicting interests. This mechanism for achieving strategic alignment is dialectical because it conceives the IS strategy as a product of the interplay between opposing forces. A teleological force occurs through an individual actor exhibiting goal-seeking behaviour. Dialectical forces result from clashes between individual teleological forces. This confirms the need for ongoing studies and examinations of processes whereby such goals are attained and to what degree process events, and those who partake in those events (Lyytinen and Newman, 2008), impact the process of strategic alignment. A comprehensive understanding of the developed model will provide valuable insights into the impediments that influence the process of strategic alignment and offers opportunities for future research in understanding the process of strategic alignment.

7. CONCLUSION

The advantage and contribution of the model is that it considers both the traditional technical deliverables of strategic alignment along with the social dimension, incorporating actors involved in producing the technical deliverables, following a novel processual analysis of the case data that is useful and relevant for practitioners and researchers. While the extant literature has described the factors that impede the process of strategic alignment, there is almost no systematic research that considers these impediments over a phased period of strategic alignment or uses processual theory to explain them.

When reviewing these findings a number of limitations should be taken into account. As this is an interpretive processual case study, the conclusions do not claim to be generalizable and do not assert to be verifiable facts (Walsham, 1995). The choice to limit the data to a single case was made by choosing depth over the generalisability of the findings. Selecting a single case does not mean that the findings cannot be used by other researchers or that they are invalid, but does mean that academics and practitioners should interpret the findings with the circumstances of the original case in mind.

The model offers a planning and diagnostic tool for public sector managers intending to engage in the process of strategic alignment. The research findings offer fresh insight into the strategic alignment process, and also facilitate the amalgamation of a number of assertions about the social and intellectual dimensions of strategic alignment by comparing prior research with individual characteristics of the model.

REFERENCES

Andrews, R., Boyne, G. A., Law, J. and Walker, R. M. (2011) 'Strategy Implementation and Public Service Performance', *Administration & Society,* 43(6), pp. 643-671.

Avison, D., Jones, J., Powell, P. and Wilson, D. (2004) 'Using and validating the strategic alignment model', *Journal of Strategic Information Systems,* 13, pp. 223-246.

Balhareth, H. H., Liu, K. and Manwani, S. 'Achieving Business and IT Alignment from Organisational Learning Perspectives'. *Proceedings of World Academy of Science, Engineering and Technology*: World Academy of Science, Engineering and Technology.

Bizzi, L. and Langley, A. (2012) 'Studying processes in and around networks', *Industrial Marketing Management,* 41(2), pp. 224-234.

Bourn, J. (2007) *Public Sector auditing: is it value for money?* . Chichester, West Sussex, England: John Wiley & Sons Ltd.

Boyne, G. A. (2002) 'Public and Private Management: What's the Difference?', *Journal of Management Studies,* 39(1), pp. 97-122.

Chakravarthy, B. and White, R. E. (2002) *Strategy process: Forming, implementing and changing strategies. Handbook of strategy and management* London: Sage Publications.

Chan, Y. E. and Reich, B. H. (2007) 'State of the Art IT alignment: what have we learned?', *Journal of Information Technology,* 22, pp. 297-315.

Chan, Y. E., Sabherwal, R. and Thatcher, J. B. (2006) 'Antecedents and Outcomes of Strategic IS Alignment: An empirical investigation', *IEEE Transactions on Engineering Management,* 51(3), pp. 27-47.

Derksen, B. and Luftman, J. (2014) *European key IT and Management Issues & Trends for 2014. Results of an International Study.* Available at: http://blog.cionet.com/wpcontent/uploads/2014/02/ITTrends_2014print.pdf.

Earl, M. J. (1989) *Management Strategies for Information Technology.* Europe: Prentice Hall.

Galliers, R. D. 'On confronting some of the common myths of Information Systems strategy discourse: towards a revised framework'. *OLKC Conference proceedings*: Citeseer.

Hirschheim, R. and Sabherwal, R. (2001) 'Detours in the Path Towards Strategic IS Alignment', *California Management Review,* 44(1), pp. 87-108.

Huang, S.-J., Wu, M.-S. and Chen, L.-W. (2013) 'Critical success factors in aligning IT and business objectives: A Delphi study', *Total Quality Management & Business Excellence,* 24(9-10), pp. 1219-1240.

Hussin, H., King, M. and Cragg, P. (2002) 'IT Alignment in Small Firms', *European Journal of Information Systems* 11(2), pp. 108-127.

Langley, A. (1999) 'Strategies for Theorizing from Process Data', *The Academy of Management Review,* 24(4), pp. 691-710.

Langley, A., Smallman, C., Tsoukas, H. and Van de Ven, A. (2009) 'Academy of Management Journal special research forum call for papers: Process studies of change in organization and management', *Academy of Management News,* 56(1), pp. 1-13.

Luftman, J. and Derksen, B. (2014) 'European key IT and management issues & trends for 2014', *CIONET Europe and Business & IT Trend Institute.*

Luftman, J., Papp, R. and Brier, T. (1999a) 'Enablers and inhibitors of business-IT alignment', *Communications of the AIS,* 1(3), pp. 1-33.

Luftman, J. N., Papp, R. and Brier, T. (1999b) 'Enablers and inhibitors of business-IT alignment', *Communications of the Association for Information Systems,* 1, pp. 1-32.

Lyytinen, K. and Newman, M. (2008) 'Explaining information systems change: a punctuated socio-technical change model', *European Journal of Information Systems,* 17(6), pp. 589-613.

Lyytinen, K. and Robey, D. (1999) 'Learning failure in information systems development', *Information Systems Journal* 9, pp. 85-101.

Mintzberg, H. and Waters, J. A. (1985) 'Of Strategies, Deliberate and Emergent', *Strategic Management Journal,* 6(3), pp. 257-272.

Nag, R., Corley, K. G. and Gioia, D. A. (2007) 'The intersection of organizational identity, knowledge, and practice: Attempting strategic change via knowledge grafting', *Academy of Management Journal,* 50(4), pp. 821-847.

Reich, B. and Benbasat, I. (1996) 'Measuring the Linkage between Business and IT Objectives', *MIS Quarterly,* 20(1), pp. 55-81.

Reich, B. and Benbasat, I. (2000) 'Factors that Influence the Social Dimension of Alignment between Business and IT Objectives', *MIS Quarterly,* 24(1), pp. 81-113.

Rocheleau, B. 2006. Public and Private Information Systems: How Are They Similar? Hershey, PA: Idea Group Publishing.

Sabherwal, R. and Chan, Y. E. (2001) 'Alignment between business and IS strategies: a study of prospectors, analyzers, and defenders', *Information systems research,* 12(1), pp. 11-33.

Van de Ven, A. H. and Poole, M. S. (1995) 'Explaining development and change in organizations', *Academy of Management Review,* 20(3), pp. 510-540.

DON'T STOP ME NOW: EMERGENT ORGANISATIONAL PRACTICES ON SOCIAL MEDIA

Maxim Viktor Wolf[1], Julian Sims[1] and Huadong Yang[2]
[1]*Birkbeck, University of London, UK*
[2]*University of Liverpool, UK*

ABSTRACT

This study investigates communication practices within three UK corporates. This paper presents findings from a comparative qualitative case study with data collection in a series of semi-structured interviews. Each organisation has a different strategic approach to social media use internally and externally. However, many of the practices are similar across all cases. The findings suggest that organisations are failing to control social media use top-down and instead should re-align their strategies to support and guide bottom-up social media use to reap benefits of new connections and relationships. The results have theoretical and practical implications. The study uncovers how new technologies are introduced into organisational praxis, how social media use is motivated and how interest conflicts between the management and employees regarding technology use can be resolved. Practically, the study highlights successful strategies to encourage and align social media use with organisational goals.

KEYWORDS

Social Media, Qualitative Case Study, Technology Adoption, IT Strategic Value

1. INTRODUCTION

This paper presents the results of a multiple-case study on social media use in organisations. The focus of the study are the actual practices of social media use in organisations and the juxtaposition of the "on the ground" practices with organisation's strategy. The context for the study is the HR communication process: strategies and practices aimed at establishing a consensus between the management and the employees, and alignment of individual and organisational goals. The question is whether social media use can (and does) support the communication process or disrupt it?

The study adopts a qualitative interpretative multiple case study design (Yin, 2009) and applies within-case and cross-case analysis to build theory from the data collected through semi-structured interviews. The cases represent different manifestations of social media use strategies in terms of control, neutrality and encouragement, and different emergent practices (Eisenhardt, 1989; Rouse & Daellenbach, 1999).

The study employs a socio-material view, investigating the effects of practices of IT use on organisations' strategy, performance, business processes. Placing the IT into a specific business setting, the study answers the calls for research in two distinct areas: social media use from Information Systems perspective (Diga & Kelleher, 2009; Griffith & McLean, 2014; Leonardi, Huysman, & Steinfeld, 2013 2013; Oestreicher-Singer & Zalmanson, 2013), and social media use from HR perspective (Brown & Vaughn, 2011; Haar & White, 2013). The findings are applicable to both academic communities: IS research is inherently multidisciplinary and benefits from studies which look at technology adoption in different business areas (Huang, Baptista, & Galliers, 2013; Whittington, 2006). Business and HR research is complemented by considering the role of technology in the shaping of organisational life (Billington & Billington, 2012; Boudreau & Lawler III, 2014; Orlikowski & Scott, 2008).

Traditionally, intra-organisational communications are top-down controlled content creation and sharing processes (Bowen & Ostroff, 2004; Huang et al., 2013 2013). Specifically, the HR Management communication process: communications between management and employees, requires top-down strategic approach and alignment of content creation and delivery (Bowen & Ostroff, 2004). A strong HR communication system has the properties of distinctiveness, consistency and consensus. *Distinctiveness* requires the communication to originate from a legitimate source, be visible (i.e. reach the intended recipient), and to be relevant to the recipient. *Consistency* is achieved when communications carry the same content over time and space. I.e. similar content is delivered from management at different levels (space) and to employees at different stages (time). *Consensus* is the agreement among employees and management about what the message content is. It requires alignment of messages and practices, and provision of feed-back mechanisms to ensure that management's messages have been received and interpreted by the employees.

Inherently democratic, social media use is bottom-up, uncontrolled and uncontrollable user content creation and distribution (Boyd & Ellison, 2008; DesAutels, 2011). Access to (many) social media is free. Many platforms provide tools for content creation and sharing (Kietzmann, Hermkens, McCarthy, & Silvestre, 2011; Leonardi et al., 2013). It is difficult for organisations to block access to social media for their employees and to prevent social media use in general. The collision of the two worlds: top-down control of inter- and intra-organisational communication and bottom-up "free for all" content creation on social media, deserves further investigation (Kane, Alavi, Labianca, & Borgatti, 2014 & Borgatti, 2014).

2. SOCIAL MEDIA USE – STRATEGY AND PRACTICE

This study in three large UK corporations follows the principles of comparative case studies (Eisenhardt, 1989; Yin, 2009). The data for each study was collected in a series of interviews and first analysed "within case". The findings from each case were then compared with each other to highlight differences and similarities in strategic approaches and actual practices. This section starts with a brief introduction of the case selection process followed by an introduction of each case study organisation. The strategy and practices in each organisation are described and compared across the cases in the main body of the paper. Finally, select theoretical lenses are discussed which support the explanation of value-creation for organisations through social media use. Specifically, the effects of social media use on the strength of HR communication system (its consistency, distinctiveness and consensus) are discussed in the final sub-section.

2.1 Case Study Findings

All organisations are UK-Based multinational corporations operating globally. As the employees report their (sometimes deviant) use of information technology, to ensure anonymity, all organisation's names, internal software systems, and all employee names are coded. Any identifying information has been sanitised and removed. The organisations are given code-names representing their country (UK) and broad area of business (Banking, Outsourcing and Consultancy). Each participant was assigned a code in the format UKxNN, whereby "x" represented the company (Bank: B, Consulting: C, Outsourcing: O), and "NN" is the ordinal number of the interview. It bears no relationship to the participants position in the company. During the interview transcription all names were replaced with either interviewee-code or "colleague" whenever a participant referred to one of their colleagues by name. The quotes provided in this paper are near-verbatim, with some minor grammar corrections and filler words (e.g. "like, you know, well") removed for readability.

The studies were selected following the logic of theoretical relevancy (Rouse & Daellenbach, 1999). The aim of the selection process was to identify cases with different approaches to social media use. The guiding idea is that by comparing the differences in settings and outcomes patterns of "conditions" or "configurations" may emerge which lead to or prevent expected outcomes (Rihoux & Ragin, 2009). Activities on social media by over thirty organisations were assessed from the viewpoint of how active the "organisation" was on social media (official accounts on Twitter, Corporate Pages on Facebook, YouTube and LinkedIn), and how engaged were the employees (comments and replies on Twitter, YouTube and Facebook, memberships in official Employee Groups on LinkedIn, existence of alternative Employee and Alumni Groups on LinkedIn). The organisations were ranked against each other (organisation A was more active than organisation B etc) and "high and low" performers were selected (Figure 1).

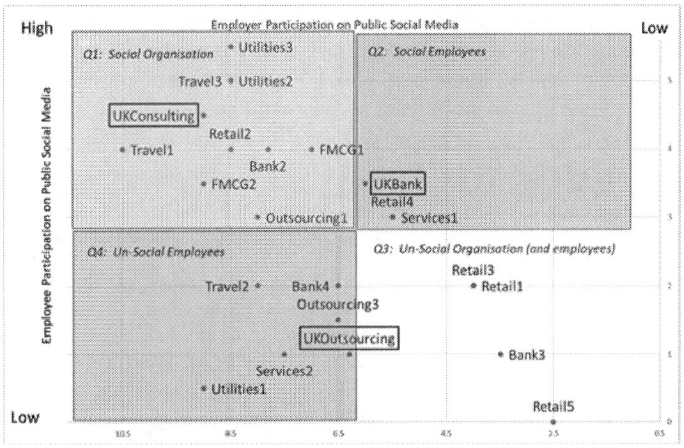

Figure 1. Participation on Social Media selection Matrix

Ten of the "most interesting" firms have been selected. These included five firms from the square 1 (above average firm and employee engagement), three from the square 4 (above average firm, below average employee engagement) and two from the square 2 (below average firm, above average employee engagement). Organisations which do not use social media at all (square 3) have been excluded from the study: the aim is to understand how organisations use social media, and why some firms are successful in building engagement (square 1), whereas others try to build engagement and are less successful (square 4) or do not try to create engagement when they could (square 2). The selection and assessment process has been presented and discussed at IS conferences to ensure its viability (Wolf, Sims, & Yang, 2015).

The interpretative case studies were coded using NVivo software and the vignettes from three organisations, highlighting different representations of social media use, are presented in the following sections.

The organisations are presented in the order of social media strategy: UKBank actively controls and limits social media use, UKOutsourcing is neutral and does not have a strategy, UKConsulting actively encourages and supports social media use as part of their business processes.

2.1.1 UKBank Case Study

UKBank is a financial services organisation with headquarters in London which has operations in multiple countries worldwide. Many employees are employed in retail and outside the central office, however, most of the interviews were conducted in and with employees from the head office. The relationships within the company's headquarters are segmented and team-centric. Even teams sharing the same floor tend not to know the other teams well.

Top-down approach to social media in UKBank is one characterised by the ideas of "control" and "information". Several explanations are provided to justify the need for controlled social media use and for restrictions placed on employee's use of these platforms (Table 1).

Table 1. UKBank's Top-Down Approach to Social Media Use

Participant	Statement	Summary
UKB1	… you expect any feedback? I don't think that's the intention, because these comms by their nature are to inform people	Broadcast without feedback
UKB2	[internal communication on social media] must be targeted, relevant and timely	Controlled broadcast
UKB4	[using twitter in HR function is not permitted as it sits] within the marketing function. This is still an area which is heavily guarded we would not use this within resourcing	Limiting access to social media to defined functions
UKB4	[access to LinkedIn] is blocked from corporate computers	Physical barriers to access
UKB4	have a way to control of what people have as part of their [LinkedIn] profiles	Expectation of controlling information
UKB5	[limitations are driven] definitely from external forces, whether it's UK TRA, whether it is US laws	Policy and legislative barriers to access
UKB6	we are a bit hampered by technology and security, because we are quite tight	Policy and legislative barriers to access

Several social media are blocked within UKBank and access to some platforms is limited to certain functions e.g. Marketing has access to Twitter, and some recruiters have access to LinkedIn. UKBank is currently implementing an internal social media tool, however (rather ironically) the main purpose of the tool is to deliver targeted information to employees, rather than to seek engagement.

At the practice level, however, employees and, specifically, recruiters deviate from prescribed procedures and use social media platforms despite erected physical, policy and procedural barriers (Table 2).

Table 2. UKBank's Bottom-Up Social Media Use

Participant	Statement	Summary
UKB1	… different [LinkedIn] groups that have been created by other alumni or different people but not managed by our business	Employee/Alumni engagement outside UKBank
UKB2	[I am] using LinkedIn ... to know how things are going in each other's careers…You never know when we may need each other; It is a good way	Employee/Alumni engagement outside UKBank
UKB3	[posting jobs on personal LinkedIn profile] will increase the job's publicity"	recruiters' personal accounts for job adverts
UKB4	on the Blackberry we do not have WhatsApp, [but I am] using LinkedIn, WhatsApp and emails to contact potential candidates	personal devices/accounts to connect to candidates
UKB5	[I would] use personal LinkedIn account to post a link to our roles, so that my contacts know about it […] to get more people [to apply]	recruiters' personal accounts for job adverts
UKB6	[I] go on there [LinkedIn Groups] on my own personal mobile […] Depending of what their skillset is, there is always a need for keeping in touch with people	personal devices/accounts to connect to candidates

The (deviant) use of social media is motivated by variety of factors. Significantly, recruiters see it as part of their job to connect with candidates using whatever means necessary – e.g. via personal devices and accounts on LinkedIn and WhatsApp. Another motivation for social media use despite regulations, is the maintenance of relationships with current and former employees.

2.1.2 UKOutsourcing Case Study

UKOutsourcing is a UK-Based services company providing a variety of outsourcing solutions to government and private businesses across the globe. While each of the service lines (e.g. "Security", "IT-Services") is operated as its own business, there is a drive to unify the UKOutsourcing-Brand and to enforce a firm-wide approach to HR and employer brand. Despite a strong top-down initiative to engage employees on internal social media, the expected levels of participation are not being achieved.

Top-down approach to social media in UKOutsourcing is characterised by the "lack of interest" from the top-tier management and a push from middle-management to use social media as a "shrinker" and "glue" within the organisation (Table 3).

Table 3. UKOutsourcing's Top-Down Approach to Social Media Use

Participant	Statement	Summary
UKO1	we don't have a social media strategy, we've got people strategy and we have got an approach to engagement which complements people strategy which complements business strategy	Lack of social media strategy
UKO2	we have the challenge with not having the senior leadership of the social media strategy	Lack of social media strategy
UKO3	[LinkedIn is] all about sharing content, sharing the right content, to be more engaging, be thought leaders	Desire to engage on public social media
UKO3	[we need to have a] strategy around content creation, align that with market strategy, business development, engagement, employee engagement, all tied up together	Desire for a top-down support
UKO4	comms team passively watch the twitter feed about UKOutsourcing, but we don't proactively post	Policy is to "watch" but not engage
UKO4	all along we are looking for this senior stakeholder ownership	Lack of top-tier management involvement
UKO6	[internal social media is] more personal, and possibly I would not communicate with half of people if I was using outlook	Desire for closer collaboration

UKOutsourcing is using LinkedIn for pro-active candidate search and recruitment, which is supported by the group's HR Director. An internal social media platform has been introduced without top-down ownership by efforts of middle-management (UKO2) who decided to "take the forgiveness role rather than asking for permission". However, some managers actively prohibit their employees from accessing the internal platform, because "of perception that you are playing rather than working. It has got social in the title" (UKO3).

At the practice level, employees use the internal platform to connect, recruiters use LinkedIn "as prescribed" for candidate searches, and extend their use beyond what is expected (Table 4).

Table 4. UKOutsourcing's Bottom-Up Social Media Use

Participant	Statement	Summary
UKO1	from a linkedin prospective we have saved the business 2 million pounds	Changes in direct sourcing
UKO2	You are trying to get to know each other and we had some quite fun things posted on our resourcing sort of page	Building relationships
UKO3	on LinkedIn, if someone responds to one of our post, we are trying that they get a response back	Active engagement on LinkedIn
UKO4	from the internal engagement side, we have got a CEO who is absolutely brilliant on Yammer	Top-managers using social media
UKO5	I don't really use it [LinkedIn]. It's just something we were all asked to do	Compliance with social media policy
UKO6	[for posting jobs on LinkedIn there are] standard templates approved by management [but] I try and make it a little different	Deviation from prescribed format to be engaging

The use of social media deviates from prescribed policy. E.g. UKO3 attempts to reply to post in LinkedIn groups contrary to the policy to "watch but not engage". Despite active involvement in strategy, some top-managers are reported to use internal and external social media. The motivations for social media use include collaboration with (remote) colleagues, financial savings through direct sourcing, and creation of "affiliation".

2.1.3 UKConsulting Case Study

UKConsulting is an IT consultancy organisation operating worldwide. There is a variety of internal and external social media used by the management and employees. The utilisation does not (always) happen in a consistent or transparent manner, however, social media tools are being used at different levels and for a variety of purposes.

UKOutsourcing declared itself a "social media company" and actively encourages social media use. Public and in-house social media are accessible and there is no limitation on what platforms can be used (Table 5).

Table 5. UKConsulting's Top-Down Approach to Social Media Use

Participant	Statement	Summary
UKC1	UKConsulting has its own products that they want companies to use, they have "Networking": an internal social media portal	social media use built around consultancy offering
UKC2	CEO of UKConsulting has a personal blog	Visible top-management engagement
UKC3	It is good to use it [social media], and the management uses that too in a positive way	Visible top-management engagement
UKC3	have a number of [own] social media products ... , so we have to use the products we are offering	Policy to use social media
UKC4	I don't think the organisation is trying to promote it.... The drive is not necessarily from the organisation but rather from the individual	Employees encouraging social media use
UKC5	... this social score actually affects people's pay raises	Monetary incentives for social media use

Several internal social media platforms are available including internal blogs and communication tools. Some of the platforms are semi-public, allowing partners and customers to be involved in conversations. In addition, the employees are getting involved in product-related groups on public social media. As there are no reported physical or policy limits to social media use, it is difficult to observe any deviation from policy or regulations (Table 6).

Table 6. UKConsulting's Bottom-Up Social Media Use

Participant	Statement	Summary
UKC1	[LinkedIn is] quite useful to understand where your old colleagues are working and what's going on and where people are now	Maintaining Relationships
UKC2	I use [LinkedIn] for information about the industry I am in. It affects my clients and I need to have the technical knowledge	Self-training on social media
UKC3	"Networking" is knowledge sharing platform, … where we can communicate with colleagues and sometimes with clients	Collaboration on social media
UKC4	there is another internal tool which is similar to LinkedIn and twitter: you can follow someone on their page … [it is] a way to improve that side of the relationship	Building Relationships
UKC5	I want to share as much information to everyone. I want to give my connections up and get my social score higher so that's in line with company's goal	Compliance with policy

Employees explain their social media use through personal motivations such as establishing and maintaining relationships with colleagues, self-improvement through learning about the industry and related products, as well as top-down motivation through compliance and incentives.

2.2 Cross-Case Analysis

The three organisations under investigation have different approaches to social media use. The motivations for control and encouragement are different. However, on the shop-floor-level, practices of, and motivations for social media use are similar across the organisations (Table 7).

Table 7. Cross-Case Comparison of Social Media Strategies and Practices

	UKBank	UKOutsourcing	UKConsulting
Top-Down approach	Control and limit access Broadcast Information	Monitor social media activity Broadcast information Direct hires on LinkedIn	Engage employees, partners and customers on social media Encourage content creation
Top-down motivations	Regulatory compliance, information control	Brand building, savings in recruitment	Knowledge sharing, information, relationships
Bottom-up practices	Direct employee/alumni engagement Recruiter/candidate conversations	Employee/management engagement Recruiter/candidate conversations	Employee/management engagement Knowledge transfer and sharing Relationship building
Bottom-up motivations	Maintain relationships Perform better at job	Maintain relationships Perform better at job	Maintain Relationships Perform better at job Share and acquire knowledge

Regardless of the top-down approach to social media use, all organisations report similar uses of social media. These include "relationships", "doing the job", and "improving oneself". Maintaining relationships includes current colleagues (for example, to be able to ask for help, to share knowledge), as well as former colleagues (for example, to keep in touch on a personal level, or to find the next job). Using social media to perform the job includes examples of UKBank's recruiters deviating from policy and using personal LinkedIn accounts to find and attract better candidates, UKOutsourcing's recruiters deviating from approved job-templates to make them more appealing, and UKConsulting's employees engaging in product-forums to learn and teach about the firm's offerings. Self-improvement has been reported in all organisations by employees e.g. using LinkedIn to learn about their industry, company or competitors.

Social media use, whether sanctioned or not, appears to contribute to strengthening of interpersonal relationships. Stronger emotional ties are contributing to distinctiveness of messages (Gilbert & Karahalios, 2009). Organisations which are involved in creation of such ties can benefit from this and use social media to complement their overall HR strategy.

Organisations cannot prevent social media use. Those organisations which do not engage with bottom-up use, jeopardise the consistency of communications. For example, UKBank has lost legitimacy and control over social media use policy, its employees deviating from rules and circumventing barriers. Some employees in UKOutsourcing report departmental silos being replicated on internal social media. Whereas UKConsulting encourages cross-departmental, an even extra-organisational content creation and sharing, adding to transparency

Consensus based on shared understanding, agreement of rhetors, and perceived fairness of practices (Bowen & Ostroff, 2004) can also be impacted by social media use. In organisation with management participating on social media, the understanding of messages can be verified and validated, resulting in a two-way dialogue (Kent & Taylor, 1998). Employees in UKConsulting comment on manager's posts and blogs, and receive feedback. In UKOutsourcing managers try to actively engage with the employees in open discussions on (internal) social media to validate messages and to establish a shared understanding. In UKBank different departments have different approaches to social media use, the management is not participating on any public social media which, in turn, leads to a lack of a shared understanding among employees on company's policy and strategy.

Social media use in organisations appears to be emerging independently of organisational strategy. It is up to the organisations to adapt their approach to social media use to reap the potential benefits of tighter relationships and improved communication capabilities with wider reach, instantaneous feedback and democratic access.

3. CONCLUSION

This study uncovers how organisations practice social media use in the domain of HR management. The findings suggest that organisations are failing to control and limit social media use by their employees. The deviations from prescribed behaviours, however, are not motivated by "bad will" on the side of the employees. The employees use social media for (in their opinion) the company's benefit. Whether allowed or not, recruiters and non-HR employees share job posting to their friends and colleagues to help their organisations attract more (and better) candidates. Employees spend time on social media to share their professional knowledge with their peers inside and outside of the organisation and in return to benefit from their peers' experiences.

The research contributes to current IS literature by describing and analysing social media adoption practices in organisational context. One of the aspects uncovered here is the fluidity of knowledge going in- and out of organisations. The porous boundaries where information is "leaking" outside the organisation and "trickles" in from the outside through the involvement of customers, suppliers and partners have been recognised in other research (Hanna, Rohm, & Crittenden, 2011; Jussila, Kärkkäinen, & Leino, 2011; Saldanha, Mithas, & Krishnan, 2017) and deserve a dedicated attention beyond the scope of this research.

The study further contributes to HR literature by showing how bottom-up social media use can complement the top-down strategic approach to HR communications (Ostroff & Bowen, 2016). A further contribution to HR literature is the introduction of a "technology"-focus into this field (Hauptmann & Steger, 2013; Heffernan & Dundon, 2016).

Practitioners can use the findings to develop their current social media strategies and policies, and to seek alignment of these strategies with emergent practices.

Further studies in this emergent and developing area are necessary to validate the findings. First, additional practices and motivations can be discovered. Second, the cases represent different industries, and validations studies within an industry would further strengthen the arguments. Third, quantitative studies measuring the impact of "stronger relationships" and "knowledge sharing" would provide additional data to challenge or support the claims. Finally, studies investigating possible malicious social media use practices would enhance our understanding of this emergent phenomenon. There is still much to discover: Don's stop me now!

REFERENCES

Billington, M. G., & Billington, P. J. (2012). Social Media Tools for Leaders and Managers. *Journal of Leadership, Accountability and Ethics, 9*(6), 11-19.

Boudreau, J., & Lawler III, E. E. (2014). Stubborn traditionalism in HRM: Causes and consequences. *Human Resource Management Review, 24*(3), 232-244.

Bowen, D. E., & Ostroff, C. (2004). Understanding HRM–Firm Performance Linkages: The Role of the "Strength" of the HRM System. *Academy of Management Review, 29*(2), 203-221.

Boyd, D. M., & Ellison, N. B. (2008). Social Network Sites: Definition, History, and Scholarship. *Journal of Computer-Mediated Communication, 13*, 210-230.

Brown, V. R., & Vaughn, E. D. (2011). The Writing on the (Facebook) Wall: The Use of Social Networking Sites in Hiring Decisions. *Journal of Business and Psychology, 26*, 219–225.

DesAutels, P. (2011). UGIS: Understanding the nature of user-generated information systems. *Business Horizons, 54*(3), 185-192.

Diga, M., & Kelleher, T. (2009). Social media use, perceptions of decision-making power, and public relations roles. *Public Relations Review, 35*, 440–442.

Eisenhardt, K. M. (1989). Building Theories from Case Study Research. *Academy of Management, 14*(4), 532-550.

Gilbert, E., & Karahalios, K. (2009). *Predicting tie strength with social media.* Paper presented at the Proceedings of the SIGCHI conference on human factors in computing systems.

Griffith, M., & McLean, R. (2014). *Unleashing Corporate Communications: Social Media and Conversations With Customers.* Paper presented at the Annual Conference of the UK Academy of Information Systems, Oxford, 2014.

Haar, J. M., & White, B. J. (2013). Corporate entrepreneurship and information technology towards employee retention: a study of New Zealand firms. *Human Resource Management Journal, 23*(1), 109-125.

Hanna, R., Rohm, A., & Crittenden, V. L. (2011). We're all connected: The power of the social media ecosystem. *Business Horizons, 54*, 265—273.

Hauptmann, S., & Steger, T. (2013). "A brave new (digital) world"? Effects of In-house Social Media on HRM. *Zeitschrift für Personalforschung, 27*(1), 26-46.

Heffernan, M., & Dundon, T. (2016). Cross-level effects of high-performance work systems (HPWS) and employee well-being: the mediating effect of organisational justice. *Human Resource Management Journal, 26*(2), 211-231.

Huang, J., Baptista, J., & Galliers, R. D. (2013). Reconceptualizing rhetorical practices in organizations: The impact of social media on internal communications. *Information and Management, 50*(2), 112-124.

Jussila, J. J., Kärkkäinen, H., & Leino, M. (2011). *Benefits of social media in business-to-business customer interface in innovation.* Paper presented at the Proceedings of the 15th International Academic MindTrek Conference: Envisioning Future Media Environments.

Kane, G. C., Alavi, M., Labianca, G., & Borgatti, S. P. (2014). What's different about social media networks? A framework and research agenda. *MIS Quarterly, 38*(1), 275-304.

Kent, M. L., & Taylor, M. (1998). Building Dialogic Relationships Through the World Wide Web. *Public Relations Review, 24*(3), 321-334.

Kietzmann, J. H., Hermkens, K., McCarthy, I. P., & Silvestre, B. S. (2011). Social media? Get serious! Understanding the functional building blocks of social media. *Business Horizons, 54*(3), 241-251.

Leonardi, P. M., Huysman, M., & Steinfeld, C. (2013). Enterprise Social Media: Definition, History, and Prospects for the Study of Social Technologies in Organizations. *Journal of Computer-Mediated Communication, 19*, 1-19.

Oestreicher-Singer, G., & Zalmanson, L. (2013). Content or community? A digital business strategy for content providers in the social age. *MIS Quarterly, 37*(2), 591-616.

Orlikowski, W. J., & Scott, S. V. (2008). Sociomateriality:Challenging the Separation of Technology, Work and Organization. *The Academy of Management Annals, 2*(1), 433-474.

Ostroff, C., & Bowen, D. E. (2016). Reflections on the 2014 decade award: Is there strength in the construct of HR system strength? *Academy of Management Review, 41*(2), 196-214.

Rihoux, B. t., & Ragin, C. C. (2009). *Configurational comparative methods : qualitative comparative analysis (QCA) and related techniques*. Thousand Oaks: Sage.

Rouse, M. J., & Daellenbach, U. S. (1999). Rethinking research methods for the resource-based perspective: isolating sources of sustainable competitive advantage. *Strategic Management Journal, 20*(5), 487-494.

Saldanha, T. J., Mithas, S., & Krishnan, M. S. (2017). Leveraging Customer Involvement for Fueling Innovation: The Role of Relational and Analytical Information Processing Capabilities. *MIS Quarterly, 41*(1).

Whittington, R. (2006). Completing the practice turn in strategy research. *Organization studies, 27*(5), 613-634.

Wolf, M., Sims, J., & Yang, H. (2015). *Theoretical Sampling – ALIAS: a Case selection framework for research on social media engagement.* Paper presented at the Annual Conference of the UK Academy of Information Systems, Oxford, 2015.

Yin, R. K. (2009). *Case Study Research: design and methods*. Thousand Oaks, CA: Sage.

MULTIDIMENCIAL FRAMEWORK FOR CROSSCORPORATE BUSINESS SOCIAL NETWORK (BSN)

Nikolay Sterev, Valentin Kisimov, Tsvetana Stoyanova and Venko Andonov
University of National and World Economy, Sofia Bulgaria

ABSTRACT

The new millennia economy is defined as "sharing economy" and covers variety of economic sectors where the re-circulation of goods and exchange of services is done. The sharing economy uses digital platforms in order the re-circulation to be organized. Nevertheless, the focus of the sharing economy is placed on the individuals. But they are also playing different roles in variety of business organizations. So, there is an uncovered field when individuals participate in sharing economy as business' role players.

The paper focuses on identifying and analysis of elements of the framework that explain the social interaction between two corporations. The preliminary hypothesis is that any corporation has established its own business social network (BSN) and has organized data transfer among the corporate participants of the BSN, but different staff members of this BSN interact with other corporation members as a part of the industrial and business chains of the economy.

Thus, the paper uses to define three layers of the corporate BSNs as: BSN, economic impacts of BSN; social impacts of BSN. **1.) Business Social Network (BSN)** is similar to Traditional Social Network (TSN), but works only inside a single corporation and, where the focus of BSN is on the corporate needs and especially on functioning on specific corporate entities like HR division, Big solution crafting, etc. Core of the BSN is the cooperation, project specific teaming, and business and solution generation discussions inside in a corporate division from one side or between particular divisions from the other. **2.) Economic and social impacts** express these elements of quantitative and qualitative indices of the business goals that are based on the function of the BSN. These indices are very important for the functioning of the contemporary sharing corporation and they could be neglected in the traditional corporations as: time saving; information partaking; social group participation and etc.

The structure of the paper covers the next 5 elements: **Introduction**: the definitions of the sharing economy and digital platform's solutions are given. Specific technical solutions are also proposed making technology differentiation between BSN and TSN. **1. Framework of BSN**: the explanation of the 3 core layers of BSN is proposed. A set of the economic and social impacts of BSN is also presented. **2. B2B BSN logical protocol**: this protocol works with business objects, which are elements of partners' BSN, supporting the social data exchanges between BSN and helping in better cross-business cooperation. Security policy are used as constraints for the protocol communications, which policy can be dynamically implemented into appropriate Firewalls and routers inside each of the corporate-partner infrastructure. Technical solution for those business objects and their integration in BSN are proposed. **3. B2B Economic and Social BSN protocols**: these protocols are elements of the interaction of the partners BSNs and they are specific in digital era. Although these protocols are part of the traditional cross-business cooperation, they need to be redefined according to enlarged cross- corporate data exchange and the restrictions of the corporate security policy. Business and social solutions for these business objects and their integration in BSN are proposed. **Conclusions**: the main results of the research are summarized. Some limitations of the practical implication of the cross- corporate BSNs are also discussed.

KEYWORDS

Sharing corporation, Business Social Network (BSN), B2B, Cross- Corporate BSN, Economic and Social Business Impacts

1. INTRODUCTION

The environment that surround contemporary business has been changing very fast as a result of development of new technologies as internet: starting with development of the internet technology in 1990s (web 0.0) and enlargement to the Emotional web in 2010s (web 5.0). So did the business information systems: starting with group of components (computers) that carry on different information, and enlarging to group of components generally organizing electronically data interexchange (Hardcastle, 2008)

Nevertheless, the business information has to be kept inside of the single corporation opposite to the wide open communication channels used of the individual users through Web 5.0 technologies. Thus, the business information kept is one of the most important tasks while the business information system is established.

So, the contemporary challenge to the business information system's developers is to organize and interexchange the information securely in the web 5.0 informational ocean. This means that the best business information system has to be more social and emotional oriented one, but not less secure than the traditional one.

Finally, as the different information components operate in open source mode to different users, they could be defined as a network of computer components as different users cooperating in sharing information while doing their employment/business activities. But this network is open and the sharing information through networks (basically B2B or B2C) possesses as positive as well as negative impacts over the business activities (Ricciardi, 2014).

The main benefits of networking are: establishment opportunities to ask questions and receive feedback, and learning from other's "best practices", and saves time, energy and resources. Respectively, the relationship between different users in the Business networks are set as a point of development of the business information system (Håkansson & Snehota, 1995; Bouzdine & Bourakova-Lorgnier, 2004).

Furthermore, AT&T (2008) predicts that the social networks could change the way of doing business as well as the organization of business networks. The main point of view is that collective (social) intelligence will lead better innovations, business and personnel excellence.

So the next step is to develop not just Intelligent Business Network, but Business Social Networks (BSN).

2. FRAMEWORK OF BSN

The recent expansion of the social networking is based on the opportunities that SNs provide to people for establishing connections with colleague or friends by person-to-person communications (Barczyk and Duncan, 2011). In this content, the social networks, means of Traditional Social Network (TSN), are based on establishment of social media as a set of Internet-based applications that allow free exchange of User Generated Content through them. (Kaplan and Haenlein, 2010; Benkler 2006). The advantages of traditional social medias and TSN is based on the given flor to people to share ideas, to cooperate and collaborate more easily and more quickly than ever before.

Business networks (BN), basically represent the main elements of TSN, but as Jones, Hesterly and Borgatti (1997) define: they are "persistent and structured set of autonomous firms (as well as nonprofit agencies) engaged in creating goods or services based on implicit and open-ended contracts". The given definition explains the Traditional Business Network (TBN) as a set of inter-firm relationships (e.g. those that exist between suppliers and a producers) (Blundel and Smith, 2001).

As the Talarowska C. and D. Tuzinovic (2008) stated the social characteristics (as demographic ones) influence the benefits of TBN, the phenomenon of Business Social Networking (BSN) explains the combination of: 1. Information system, 2. Business network (TBN), 3 Social network (TSN). So, the main requirement is that the Corporate networks is organized in three-layers in order that conceptual architecture of it consists of:

- **Business Social Network** Layer – it defines the objects (users, groups, documents, data points, etc.) and the relationships between them (for example, a user sharing a document; a group discussing statistical data) and how they are stored and processed, including the rules and constraints defined by the business requirements.
- **Economic Impacts** (EI) Layer – it defines economic indicators of the business entity and the bi-directional relationships between each one of them and the properties of the Business Social Network Layer.
- **Social Impacts** (SI) Layer – it defines social indicators of the business entity, the relationships between each one of them, the Economic Impacts Layer and the Business Social Network Layer.

A relationship through the layers might flow in both directions – an event or a series of events in the BSN might influence the indicator values on the upper layers as well as a change of the indicators on the SI and EI layers might lead to a specific change inside the Social Network layer.

As shown on Figure 1, the relationships might be dynamic – on each iteration of the self-updating process, the interactions might include a different set of indicators and social network properties.

In the case of B2B communication, assuming both sides have implemented the three-layer architecture described above, the interaction between the companies is implemented on the **Business Social Network** layer as a set of web services exposing data and actions on both sides of the relationship, according to predefined rules and constraints.

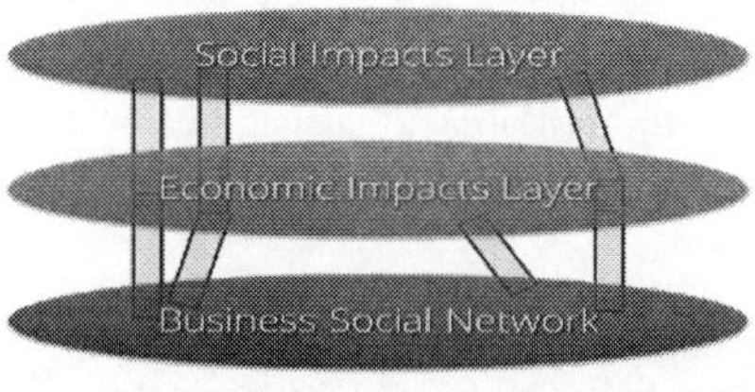

Figure 1. The Conceptual Three-Layer Architecture

The interaction between different entities (e.g. divisions, subdivisions, project-based teams) across the two enterprises should start by creating a group on the side of the initiator. The role of the initiator, as defined by the internal policies, is a constraint to what kind of group can be created and which features can be enabled.

As a part of the business discussion group instantiation, the initiator should specify one or more data structures (Figure 2), which can serve as a basic for discussion and inter-business collaboration. Each data structure has the following properties:

- one or more **data fields** – the field has a name, data type and source (if available), as well as permission settings (which participants in the group can read them, modify existing values or create new ones);
- **data** structure **permissions** (for the whole structure)
- **data** structure **source**(s) – can be internal information systems (like ERP's, CRM's, HR systems) or external open data (e.g. statistics, currency rates).

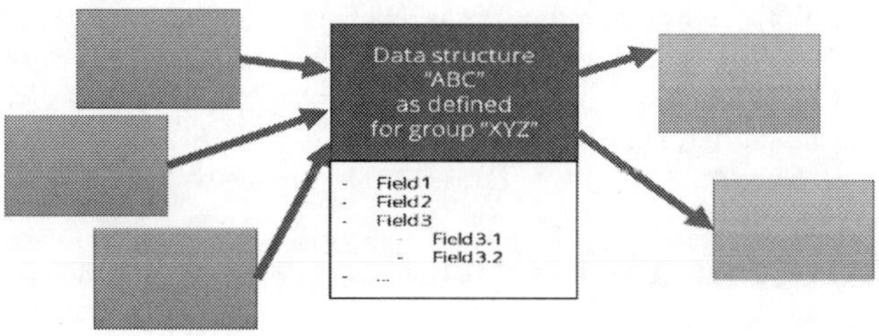

Figure 2. A Specific Data Structure Defined for a Specific Group, Including the Data Sources (Information Systems) and Potential Targets (for Machine Learning)

Additionally, the users of the Business Social Network with predefined high level access (e.g. CEO, division managers, designated business analysts) have access to the generated data (in the groups) and can feed the data (manually or continuously) to machine learning algorithms, capable of classification (for example, sentiment analysis (Pak and Paroubek, 2010.), which might classify a given discussion as positive, negative, neutral or other categories as necessary for the Economic and Social Impact layers) and prediction (for example, predicting the value of a Social layer indicator in the next month based on a recurrent neural network (RNN) model (Mandic and Chambers, 2001).

The Economic impact (EI) as well as Social impact (SI) layers is organized in order to cover the business networks in the single corporation as well as to manage the relationship between different staff members (users) of the business network.

According to this approach the EI layer is organized following the main business processes (Figure 3) (Dulak, 2014).

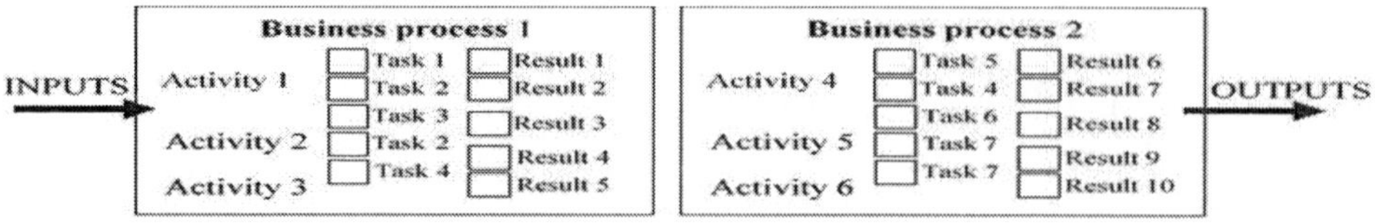

Figure 3. The Conceptual EI Layer

The explanation of the EI layer is that it consists all business processes as a collection of activities that takes one or more inputs and creates an outputs that is valuable to the customers (Brady et al. (2001) in Damij and Damij, 2014; Burattin, 2015). The inputs and outputs explain the Business networking in order the single business process to operates.

The SI layer explains the inter-relations between different persons (users) of the social network. According to Ellison and Boyd (2013) social networks are web-based services that allows different individuals to build their own personal profile and to participate in different social groups through sharing connections (connection list) to each other's. The driving forces for social networking are explained as: maintaining offline friendship; psychology motivation to share daily expressions; personal data broadcasting; satisfying the personality and cultural expectations (Figure 4) (Popkins, 1998; Boag, 2011).

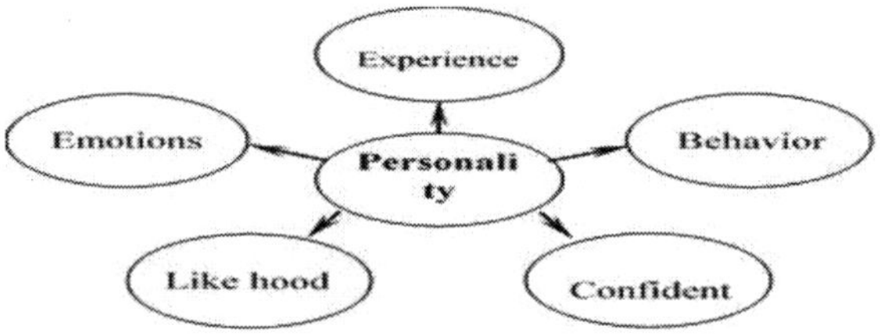

Figure 4. The Conceptual SI Layer

One of the problems of interconnection between EI and SI layers is that the contemporary corporations are too slowly and not so effective in participation of social networking. The social networking is just intra-company relations that cover just employees as a network member/users. Effects of social networking is percept as a part of B2B or B2C marketing process where they use just blogging or viral advertising.

But to define how the corporations has to be effective at social networking we need to see in depth the logical (data) protocols that different layers use.

3. B2B BSN LOGICAL PROTOCOL

The connection between two corporations according B2B approach needs to establish separate teams in any of the business entities. The created business discussion or teaming group is replicated on the **paired Business Social Network** layer and the communication is implemented through standards-based web services. This technological solution allows for a secure and policy-based information exchange and allows the development of third-party applications and extensions on top of the protocol.

The protocol for data exchange defines: the type of the requested operation; the user or automatic process, who initiated it; one or more complex parameters. Additionally, the operation might subscribe with a callback address for a delayed response (when the operation is asynchronous).

The data communication channel is secured by using the Diffie-Hellman algorithm for asymmetric key exchange (Boyko, MacKenzie and Patel, 2000 in: Preneel B. (eds), 2000), where the exchanged key is used for symmetric encryption of the data itself. This approach allows for fast encryption and decryption without relying on a manual (and possibly interceptable) exchange of encryption keys.

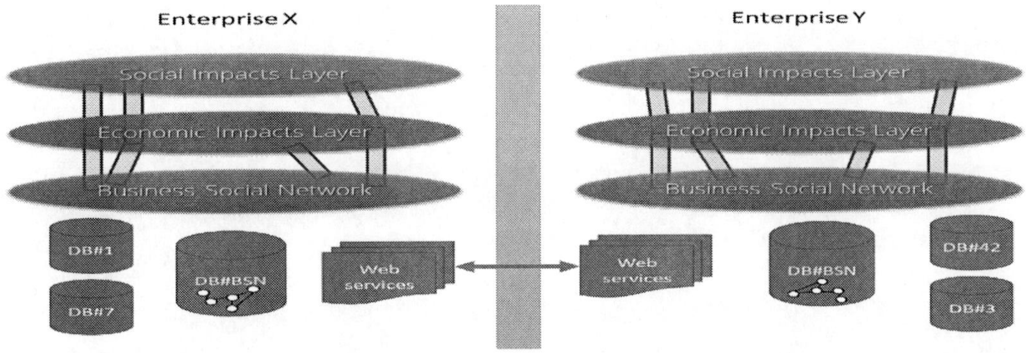

Figure 5. The Data Exchange for the B2BBSN Communication is performed through Standards-Based Web Services on the Business Social Network Layer. These Web Services serve as a façade for the Data Stored in the Databases of the Social Network itself, including Additional Internal Business Information Systems (typically ERP Systems)

Since business collaboration can be performed on multiple dimensions – with multiple other companies and divisions, all of them in different roles and relationship types, it is necessary for each communication channel to be able to filter the data exchange according to a very specific ruleset (Figure 6).

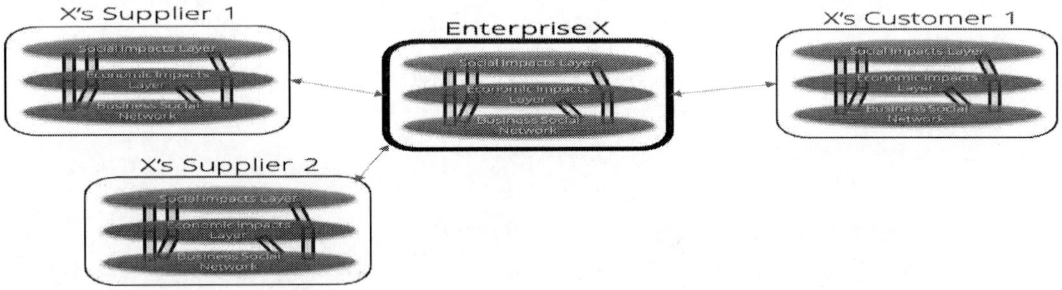

Figure 6. Each Enterprise Might Have Different Types (and Scopes) of Communication going through their Business Social Network Instances

For example, the communication with the suppliers might follow a different set of rules than the communication with the B2B customers. Even further, the communication with each supplier can be quite specific and therefore defined separately.

The definition of the rules of the B2B BSN communication protocol consists of: allowed (whitelisted) sources of communication; allowed (whitelisted) targets of communication; allowed operation (action) types; allowed data structures (or just specific fields of a given data structure).

In order to define a mapping between two indicators in different layers, the BSN administrator needs to specify: the **source indicator** (the name, the type of the value – typically a number, percentage, or a relative value); the **target indicator** or a target object in the social network layer (the name and the type); a **function** that is executed on a change in the source indicator in order to modify the value or a given property of the target object. Currently, the function is expressed with the JavaScript programming language, however it might be beneficial to develop higher-level methods to create these expressions in order to allow for non-technical people to control the behavior of the system.

4. B2B ECONOMIC AND SOCIAL BSN PROTOCOLS

The B2B EI protocol explains the rules of data transfer between the given two corporations. Basically, the rules cover: the position of responsible staff; the rights and obligations of the responsible staff; information data access and etc.

The B2B EI protocol also define the possible cross-corporation process matches (Figure 7) (Stoyanova, 2015).

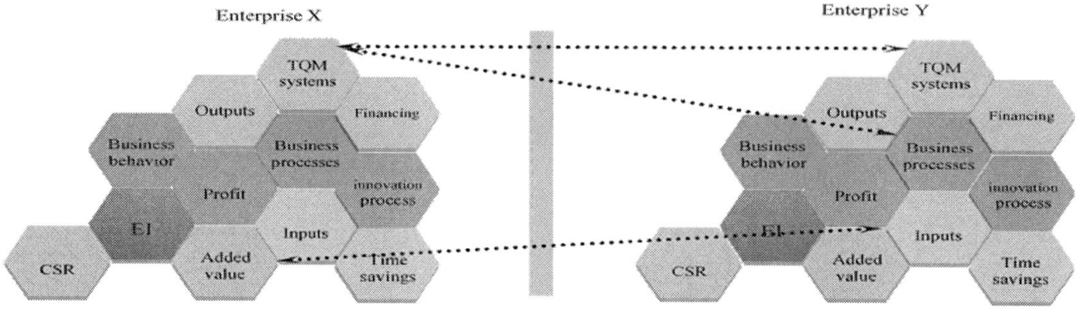

Figure 7. The Data Exchange for the B2B EI Communication is Performed through Indirect Standards-Based Web Services

The B2B SI protocol explains the rules of data transfer between any two persons that are employees of the given two corporations. Basically, the contemporary corporations do not give the exact rules but prohibited items or activities in the social networks. Thus, the B2B SI protocol has not to keep an eye on the employees, but to organize and to manage the data shared between any two persons: the position of staff; the emotions, awareness, confident of the employees and other psychological elements of their personality expression.

The B2B EI protocol also define the possible social matches (Figure 8).

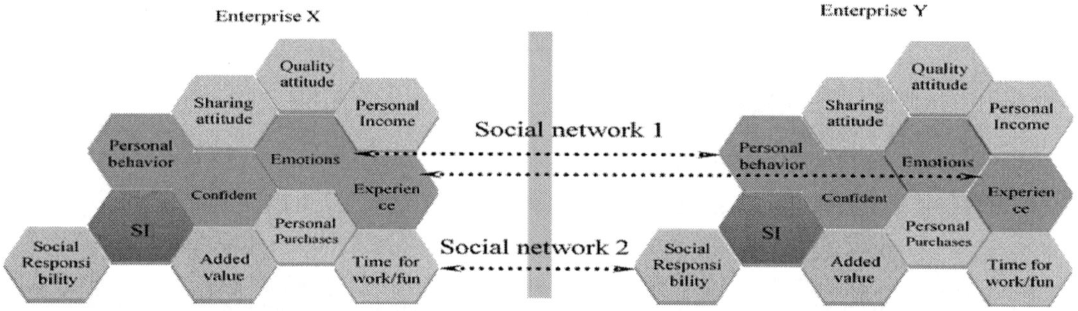

Figure 8. The Data Exchange for the B2B SI Communication is Performed through Direct Web Network Services

Finally, there is inter-connection between B2B EI and B2B SI protocols. The vertical connection between EI and SI protocols depends on the existing Traditional Business Network. The elements of the information data exchange are defined by the Business process' management software or is stated in the internal management documents.

Nevertheless, the elements of TBN are **data fields**, **data permissions,** and **data source**(s).

The results of this inter-connection depends on the organization of the intra-business network and could include (Figure 9):

- Improvement of the business processes (for example: new product development);
- Improvement of the management processes (for example: business strategy excellence);
- Improvement of the business outputs (for example: goods' quality improvement);
- Improvement of the business inputs (for example: cost and time savings);
- Improvement of the social benefits (for example: new added value for the society).

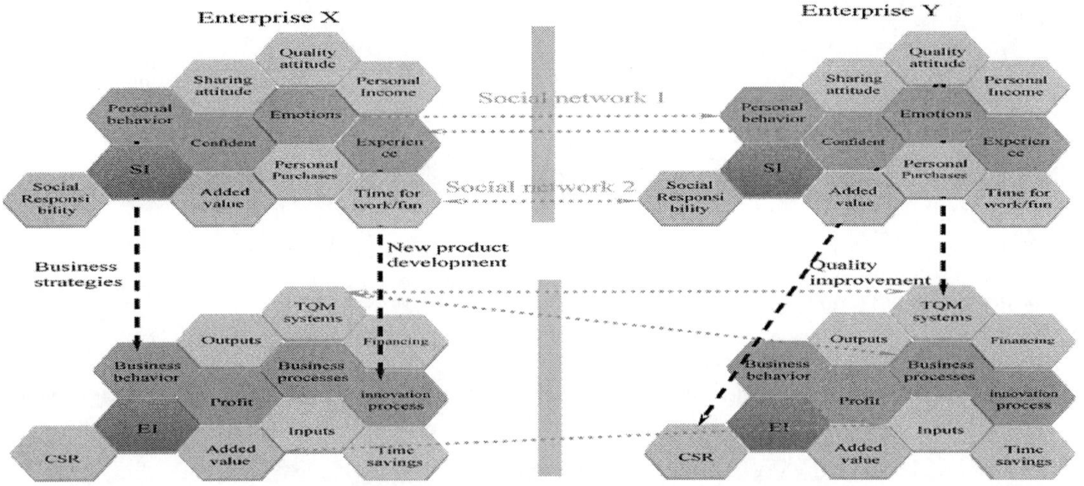

Figure 9. The Data Exchange between the B2B EI and B2B SI Protocols

The efficiency of the B2B BSN model might be evaluated in two separate directions: **business efficiency** and **technological efficiency**. The business efficiency can be measured by metrics like: the usage of the social network, the trend of the values economic and social indicators. The technological efficiency can be measured by metrics like: system performance, latency, cross-corporate communication performance.

5. CONCLUSIONS

Development of technical tools of cross-corporate business social networks (BSN) continues. But a number of authors point out that it was expanding volume of information about the business behavior (Economic impacts: EI) and individual social behavior (Social impact: SI) disseminated through these modern tools are the basis of "knowledge based economy".

The problem area could be divided in some separate problems that could deeply investigated:

1. **technical parameters** of BSN and B2B BSN protocols: current research covering the formulation of lean behaviors tied to logical data models of information technology as follows:

- Logical separation and independence of the data: surveys show the existence of three types (or layers) data models - conceptual, logical and physical (Simsion, 2005), incl.: terms and nature of the information and its relationships, structural constraints and rules.
- Modeling data process with standard solution for any type of modern information systems as they implement the relational data model defined by Codd (1970). The data management process is too complicate bases on too many approaches depending on the model data, specific requirements and behavioral patterns of end users of the system, generating queries and commands to the database (Poolet, 2005).

2. **logical parameters** of EI, SI and resp. B2B SI and B2B EI protocols. In this connection, a critical problem for missing established and generally accepted database solutions is scalability. According to EI and Si layers and their B2B protocols, there is growing amount of information content and B2B relations. In this case we can refine - maintain the normal operation of business social network in a growing number of users, content, links between them (Hoff, 2009).

ACKNOWLEDGEMENT

The paper is prepared as a part of the research activities under the project "Knowledge Economy based on business platforms and enterprises' networks" (DN 05/17/2016), financed by the Bulgarian National Science Fund.

REFERENCES

AT&T, 2008, *The Business Impacts of Social Networking*: A White Paper in Cooperation with Early Strategies Consulting, https://www.business.att.com/content/whitepaper/WP-soc_17172_v3_11-10-08.pdf

Barczyk C., D. Duncan (2011), Social Networking Media as a Tool for Teaching Business Administration Courses, *International Journal of Humanities and Social Science*, Vol. 1 No. 17 / 2001

Benkler Y. (2006), *The wealth of networks: how social production transforms markets and freedom*, New Haven, Conn: Yale University Press, pp.528

Blundel, R. and D. Smith (2001), *Business Network Report*, Research Report to the Small Business Service, Glasgow

Boag S., 2011, Explanation in personality psychology: "Verbal magic" and the five-factor model, *Journal Philosophical Psychology*, 2011 Apr 1; 24(2): 223–243, doi: 10.1080/09515089.2010.548319

Bortoli S., P. Bouquet, and T. Palpanas, Social Networking: Power to the People, http://www.w3.org/2008/09/msnws/papers/Bortoli-FSNW2009.pdf

Bouzdine T., M. Bourakova-Lorgnier, 2004, The Role of Social Capital within Business Networks: Analysis of Structural and Relational Arguments, *Proceedings of The Fifth European Conference on Organisational Knowledge, Learning and Capabilities*, 5-6 April 2004, Innsbruck, Austria, https://warwick.ac.uk/fac/soc/wbs/conf/olkc/archive/oklc5/papers/e-3_bouzdine.pdf

Boyko V., MacKenzie P., Patel S., 2000, Provably Secure Password-Authenticated Key Exchange Using Diffie-Hellman. in: Preneel B. (eds) *Advances in Cryptology* — EUROCRYPT 2000, Lecture Notes in Computer Science, vol 1807. Springer, Berlin, Heidelberg

Brady, A. J., Monk, F. E., & Wagner, J. B., 2001, Concepts in enterprise resource planning. Boston: Course Technology Thomson Learning.

Codd, E.F., 1970, A relational model of data for large shared data banks. Communications of the ACM. 13, 6, 377–387

Damij N. and T. Damij, 2014, *Process Management*, Progress in IS, DOI 10.1007/978-3-642-36639-0_2, # Springer-Verlag Berlin Heidelberg, 2014

Dulak J., Jozkowicz A., Loboda A. (edd.), 2014, *Angiogenesis and Vascularization*, Chapter 2: Business process.

Ellison, N.B. & Boyd, D., 2013, Sociality through Social Network Sites. in Dutton, W. H. (Ed.), *The Oxford Handbook of Internet Studies,* Oxford: Oxford University Press, pp.151-172.

European Union, 2010, *Social Networks Overview: Current Trends and Research Challenges*, doi:10.2759/1559

Håkansson H. and I.Snehota, 1995, *Developing Relationships in Business Networks*, T.J. Press (Padstow) Ltd, Padstow, Cornwall

Hardcastle E., 2008, *Business Information System*, BookBooN.com, http://www.promeng.eu/downloads/training-materials/ebooks/business-information-systems.pdf

Hoff, T., 2009, Why are Facebook, Digg, and Twitter so hard to scale, http://highscalability.com/blog/2009/10/13/why-are-facebook-digg-and-twitter-so-hard-to-scale.html

Jones, Hesterly and Borgatti (1997), A General Theory of Network Governance: Exchange Conditions and Social Mechanisms, *he Academy of Management Review* Vol. 22, No. 4 (Oct., 1997), pp. 911-945

Kaplan, A. and Haenlein, M. (2010), Users of the world, unite! The challenges and opportunities of social media, *Business Horizons*, 53(1), pp. 59-68.

Kent J., 2008, Social Networking Sites: will they survive@ http://www.nobleworld.biz/images/Kent2.pdf

Mandic, D. P. and J. A. Chambers, 2001, *Recurrent neural networks for prediction: learning algorithms, architectures and stability*. New York: John Wiley, 2001

Pak, A. and P.Paroubek. 2010, Twitter as a corpus for sentiment analysis and opinion mining, *LREc*. Vol. 10. No. 2010

Poolet M. A., 2005, Performance-Tuning the Data Model: Configuring the Database, http://sqlmag.com/t-sql/performance-tuning-data-model-configuring-database

Popkins N. C., 1998, The Five-Factor Model: Emergence of a Taxonomic Model for Personality Psychology http://www.personalityresearch.org/papers/popkins.html

Ricciardi F., 2014, *Innovation process in Business networks*, ch. 2. Business Networking: Possible Positive and Negative Impacts on Innovation and Excellence, http://www.springer.com/978-3-658-03438-2

Simsion, G.C., 2005q *Data modeling essentials*. Morgan Kaufmann Publishers, Amsterdam; Boston

Stoyanova T., 2015, *Strategic Management,* Sofia, Avangard Prima, pp.98-100

Talarowska C. and D. Tuzinovic (2008), Business networks: A study of managers in small companies and their perceived benefits of formal business network participation, Kristianstad University

Vaisman A., 2012, An Introduction to Business Process Modeling, http://cs.ulb.ac.be/conferences/ebiss2012/files/vaisman_ebiss2012.pdf

DETERMINANTS OF A SUSTAINABLE USE OF THE HEALTH INFORMATION SYSTEM IN THE SUB-SAHARAN AFRICA CONTEXT

Edison Wazoel Lubua[1, 2] and Philip D. Pretorius[1]
[1]*School of Information and Computing Science, North-West University, South Africa*
[2]*Institute of Accountancy Arusha, Tanzania*

ABSTRACT

This study was done in Tanzania, a close representation of the Africa Sub-Sahara. The intention of the study was to evaluate user factors determining the sustainable use of the Health Information System in the Sub-Saharan context. A sustainable use supports the achievement of corporate objectives. Our review of the literature identified four (4) variables cited to decide the use of the information system: Self-efficacy, the degree of system resistance, the approach used to deploy a Health Information System, and the extent which the use of the Health Information System is perceived to support corporate objectives. These were used in hypotheses formulation. This study followed the quantitative procedures. The survey design was adopted, where data were collected through a closed survey questionnaire. Both systematic and random sampling methods were used in obtaining a scientifically acceptable sample. Analytical models engaged in the analysis included: One Way ANOVA and Ordinal regression. They tested the categorical and causal relationship between variables. The following results were observed: Self-efficacy determined the degree of resistance and the extent which the use of the Health Information System supports corporate objectives, user resistance determined the extent which the use of the Health Information System supports corporate objectives, and the relevance of the approach used to implement the Health Information System determines the extent which the use supports corporate objectives. Moreover, the implementation of the Health Information System is not in a good shape. This is the reason why the majority of respondents want to drop it. It is more striking to learn that the category of respondents who are more conversant with the system are more eager to drop it than their counterpart.

KEYWORDS

Determinants of the Use, Sustainable Use, Health (Hospital) Information System, Africa

1. INTRODUCTION

Health is a vital investment at the centre of government services (Prinja, et al., 2016). Unfortunately, health services remain a challenge to many countries, including the African continent (Buntin, Burke, Hoaglin, & Blumenthal, 2011). The sector is embattled by inadequate human resources and infrastructure, necessary to meet the population size (Prinja, et al., 2016; Buntin, Burke, Hoaglin, & Blumenthal, 2011). Therefore, innovative technologies are essential to ease the tension (Grut, Mji, Braathen, & Ingstad, 2012). For example, the Health Information Systems (HIS) provide tools for managing patients' information, necessary in decision making across different actors (Mehdi, Hassan, Soheila, & Jamileh, 2013; Mimbi & Bankole, 2015). Moreover, they assist in strengthening evidence basis, which are necessary for policy formulation, effort evaluation, innovation, governance assessment, and other issues related to mobilisation of resources and accountability in the medical sector (Mimbi & Bankole, 2015; Cillers & Flowerday, 2013).

Regardless of the importance of ICTs in healthcare services, often times, the implementation is reported to lack sustainability (Mimbi & Bankole, 2015). A sustainable project supports the vision and mission of the organisation of its deployment. First, sustainability requires the technology (in use) to be accepted by its users (Schoen, et al., 2012). Studies by Venkatesh, Thong, and Xu (2016) and Farzandipur, Jeddi and Azimi (2016) suggested that user acceptance of a new information system is influenced by technological, human, and organisation factors. Basically, human factors include things such as user's knowledge of the technology, and emotional preparedness – all these contribute to self-efficacy (Farzandipur, Jeddi, & Azimi, 2016). In the current study, we consider self-efficacy as the ability of the technology user, to comfortably apply the technology in his activities.

Studies highlight that in the case where human factors are ignored, users are likely to resist the use (Lee & Mendlinger , 2011; Venkatesh, Thong, & Xu, 2016). In this regard, it is invaluable to address factors for user resistance of the new system, for the project to be a success (Mehdi, Hassan, Soheila, & Jamileh, 2013). Furthermore, organisational factors can also cause resistance to the system use, provided that post-implementation environment is poor (Khalifa, 2014; Farzandipur, Jeddi, & Azimi, 2016). Therefore, the system implementation approach must be designed in a careful manner to enhance the sense of project ownership, and lower the chance for resistance implementation (Mimbi & Bankole, 2015). Moreover, the approach must take to consideration the change management process in its design. The ultimate goal (of introduced changes and the involved process) is to have a Health Information System, which supports corporate goals, through its implementation (Sharifian, Askarian, Nematolahi, & Farhadi, 2014). In our study, we are interested in the sustainability of the Health Information Systems, and its determinants. In ouru definition, a sustainable Health Information System adequately supports users' operations in making their contribution to the corporate goal.

2. STATEMENT OF THE RESEARCH PROBLEM

The population index of many developing countries (in the African content) shows a rapid growth (United Nations Economic Commission of Africa, 2016). With this growth, it is necessary for social services to match the needs (Sharifian, Askarian, Nematolahi, & Farhadi, 2014). Nevertheless, many countries are often failing to meet this objective, because of factors such as funding, manpower, and even political will (Moucheraud, et al., 2017). Health services are at the centre of other social services, and core for human survival (Khalifa, 2014). Unfortunately, the health sector is overly stretched due to the outweighing population (United Nations Economic Commission of Africa, 2016). Arguably, the increase in the population affects the management of operations; this is the reason for introducing Health Information Systems (HIS). The system is used to enhance efficiency in operations. Unfortunately, indicators suggest that this purpose is not adequately met (Mwiruka, 2018). With these revelations, this study was established to evaluate the impact of user factors toward a sustainable use of a Health Information System, at the Tanzania National Hospital.

2.1 Objective

This paper evaluated user factors determining the sustainable use of the Health Information System. Our study was based on the national hospital of Tanzania Information System. The following factors are considered by the study: self-efficacy, the relevance of the approach used in introducing the system, and the degree of user resistance.

2.2 Literature

The importance of Health Information Systems is indisputable in the issuance of proper health services to citizens (Cillers & Flowerday, 2013). With the increase of human population across the world, many health centres are subjected to the increase of health incidents than the intended capacity (Mehdi, Hassan, Soheila, & Jamileh, 2013). It is necessary to extend current hospital facilities, and increase the efficiency of service providers (English, Masilela, Barron, & Schonfeldt, 2011). The Health Information Systems is useful in improving the efficiency. Unfortunately, the sustainability of these information systems facilities (in the African context) is questionable due to complaints accompanying the service issuance (Moucheraud, et al., 2017). According to Lee and Zakaria (2012), a sustainable use of the Health Information System is the use of the system, which supports corporate objectives. With this knowledge, the current study decided to evaluate the impact of self-efficacy, the approach used to introduce the system, and user resistance in defining the sustainability of the use of the Health Information System.

The study by Venkatesh and Bala (2008) identified computer self-efficacy among key variables for the use of information related technologies. Self-efficacy is the belief and ability of an individual to demonstrate certain behaviours and it involves the quality of judgements and possessed skills (Venkatesh, Thong, & Xu, 2016). In the case where technology users believe that their efficacy is low, their choices, aspirations and effort mobilisation will be affected negatively (Lubua & Semlambo, 2017; Gagnon, et al., 2012). This is the reason why the study by Lee and Mendlinger (2011) suggested that people with high efficacy are capable to use their effort to have positive results. In this study, we test the influence of self-efficacy to the sustainable use of the Health Information system in the Tanzania national hospital. Furthermore, the study evaluates the impact of the level of resistance to the system. Resistance is simply the rejection of the system use, and it is the opposite of user acceptance suggested through studies by Venkatesh and Bala (2008), and Venkatesh, Thong, and Xu (2016). The study by Moucheraud et al (2017) and Venkatesh, Thong and Xu (2016) cites the cost of switching between technologies and self-efficacy as determinants of the level of resistance by technology users. A more competent user finds the use to be easy and enjoyable, which are good factors for the adoption (Buntin, Burke, Hoaglin, & Blumenthal, 2011). Moreover, other users are concerned with the loss of control and the dissatisfaction with the technology use among the causes of resistance (Ngafeeson & Midha, 2014). Nevertheless, the study by Mwiruka (2018) conducted in Tanzania suggested that users were not worried of their control or dissatisfied with the implementation of the Health Information System. This is the reason for adopting self-efficacy, user resistance and a sustainable use of the Health Information System in our analysis.

Moreover, the literature suggests that extent which the method for introducing a new system is accepted by users determines the success of the technology implementation (Venkatesh & Bala, 2008). One method of introducing a new system requires a complete and direct replacement of the old system (Hendriks, 2012; Lee & Zakaria, 2012). If the new system becomes a success, the organisation is likely to benefit within a short time of implementation, and vice versa (Mehdi, Hassan, Soheila, & Jamileh, 2013). Alternatively, the implementation may allow parallel running, where the old and new systems are operating at a given time (Hendriks, 2012; Khalifa, 2014). The old system provides backup in the event of failure, however, it is unfortunate that running two systems is more expensive (Khalifa, 2014). Another method of implementation allows the new system to be implemented in phases replacing the old system in stages (Lee & Zakaria, 2012). To some extent, the method favours staff because they get used to the system gradually. The other alternative is to install a pilot system, where the new system is tried in an environment similar to the business (Hendriks, 2012). In the current study, the implementation of the Health Information System was through a complete replacement of the old manual system. It is possible that the implementation procedure was not fully accepted by end users, and the rest of the National Hospital Community.

Generally, the original concept about this study was developed as a result of the conversation between the principal researcher and a system administrator of the Tanzania National Hospital. Knowing feedbacks they receive from clients and employees, in their general operation, we decided to evaluate the impact of self-efficacy, user resistance, the relevance of the approach used to introduce the system to the perceived extent which the system supports corporate objectives. The following hypotheses summarises studied relationships.

Hypotheses One: The perceived self-efficacy determines the extent which the Health Information System supports the implementation of corporate objectives

Hypothesis two: The perceived self-efficacy determines the degree of resistance

Hypothesis three: The perceived degree of resistance determines the extent which the Health Information System supports corporate objectives

Hypothesis four: The perceived relevance of the approach of implementation determines the degree of resistance toward the use of the Health Information System

Hypothesis five: The perceived relevance of the method of implementation determines the perceived extent which the Health Information System supports corporate objectives

2.3 Methodology

This is a quantitative survey study, objective in its operationalisation (Coviello, 2013). The results are generalisable to a population, with an environment similar to that of the study (Babones, 2015). The choice of the quantitative approach was necessary to test hypothetical relationships stated in the previous section. Table 2 summarises key variables of the study with their measurements.

Table 1. Variables of the Study with Their Measurement

Variable	Description	Measurement
Age group	This is the age group which the respondent belongs	Ordinal
Level of education	This is the highest level of education attained by the respondent	Ordinal
Work experience	Number of years in the current position	
Specialisation	The speciality of the respondent	Nominal
Self-efficacy	The ability of using the HIS in office operations	Ordinal
The degree of resistance	The perceived unwillingness to use the HIS	Ordinal
The perceived relevance of the approach for HIS implementation	The relevance of the method used to implement the Health Information System	Ordinal
The perceived extent which the current use of HIS supports corporate objectives	The current status of using the system.	Ordinal

This study was conducted at the National Hospital of Tanzania, based in Dar Es Salaam. The introduction of the Health Information System aimed to enhance efficiency. The study used employees of the National Hospital of Tanzania as its population, where the total number of medical practitioners was 1200 (Muhimbili National Hospital, 2017). This is the category of employees who frequently contact clients. In this population, we formed a sampling frame of 300 people, through systematic sampling; this ratio is supported by Bartlett, Kotrlik, & Higgins (2001), given that data are non-continuous. This was followed by a sample of 146 respondents, through random sampling. Moreover, data collection was through close-end questionnaire, where the purpose was to capture data relevant for quantitative analysis (Friborg & Rosenvinge, 2013). Before analysis, we ensured that data were correct and complete, through the inspection of collected questionnaires. Moreover, data were coded and captured to the SPSS, where techniques for analysis, such as descriptive statistics, One Way ANOVA, Ordinal regression model were applied.

Furthermore, the study conducted the validity testing to ascertain what it measures (Mohamed, Sulaiman, Sern, & Salleh, 2015). We attained the content validity through ensuring that members of the sample are those who meet the criteria of the sample. Moreover, we ensured the validity of the construct in different ways. First, the literature highlighted on theories related to the main theme of the study, with their propositions. The knowledge was used as the basis for conceptualisation and hypotheses formulation. Furthermore, we engaged two senior researchers, of the same field, to verify the validity of our assumption. Moreover, we conducted a pilot study with 15 respondents, with the purpose of understanding whether the research tool extracted the right data, and was clear to respondents. On the other hand, we tested the reliability of the study to verify the consistency of the measurements. The observed Cronbach Alpha value was 0.866, which is above the minimum acceptable ratio (Williams, 2007; Mohamed, Sulaiman, Sern, & Salleh, 2015). Generally, the study observed ethical principles for research approved by the National Research Foundation of South Africa.

2.4 Results

The intention of this study was to evaluate determinants of the sustainable use of the Health Information System. The sustainable use is defined through the extent which the use of the Health Information System supports corporate objectives. Our main discussion revolves around four key variables: Self efficacy, the desire for resistance, the comfortability with the approach used to introduce the system, and the extent which the current use supports corporate objectives. Moreover, the study engages demographic variables (table 3) in its discussion. The discussion relates these variables with the extent which the current use support corporate objectives. Demographic variables are included because numerous studies acknowledge that they impact the use (Lubua, Semlambo, & Pretorius, 2017; English, Masilela, Barron, & Schonfeldt, 2011).

Table 2. Demographic Information

Demographic variable	Descriptive statistics			The extent which the use of the HIS supports corporate objectives
	Measurements	Freq.	Percent	
Age group	Less than 30 Years	25	17.1	ANOVA, P-Value = 0.022
	30-39 Years	44	30.1	
	40-49 Years	51	34.9	
	Above 50 yeas	26	17.8	
	Total	**146**	**100**	

The gender of respondents, level of education, the specialisation and work experience did not show a significant categorical relationship with the extent which the use of the Health Information System (HIS) supports its corporate objectives. The One Way ANOVA test shows that the p-value is greater than the threshold that is 0.05. Therefore, the study disregards these variables in its discussion. On the contrary, the age of respondents showed a significant categorical relationship with the One Way ANOVA (P=0.022). Furthermore, the descriptive information shows that respondents with the age below 30 years, and those with the age above 50 years showed the strongest perception toward the extent which the current use of the Health Information System supports corporate objectives. The average mean was 3.8, and that of the respective age groups recorded their mean as 4.0 and 4.3; the scale used was 1 = strongly disagree and 5 = strongly agree. Our next discussion focuses on key variables of the study, refer table 4.

Table 3. Determinants of the Extent which the use of the HIS Supports Corporate Objectives

	Input variable	Output variable	Parameter estimates for input variable (p-value)		Nagelkerke r-square
1	Self-efficacy (Model fitting Information – p=0.041)	Extent which the use of the HIS supports corporate objective	Very low	0.005	0.071
			Low	0.020	
			Moderate	0.027	
			High	0.018	
			Very High	RV*	
2	Self-efficacy P=0.003	Degree of resistance	Very low	0.008	0.113
			Low	0.010	
			Moderate	0.000	
			High	0.660	
			Very high	RV*	
3	Degree of resistance (0.000)	Extent which the use of the HIS supports corporate objective	Very high	0.000	0.366
			High	0.001	
			Moderate	0.000	
			Low	0.138	
			Very low	RV*	
4	The perceived relevance of the method of implementation (0.000)	The degree of resistance	Highly irrelevant	0.000	0.264
			Irrelevant	0.000	
			Moderate	0.000	
			Relevant	0.001	
			Highly relevant	RV*	
5	The perceived relevance of the method of implementation (0.000)	Extent which the use of the HIS supports corporate objective	Highly irrelevant	0.003	1.0
			Irrelevant	0.001	
			Moderate	0.006	
			Relevant	0.075	
			Highly relevant	RV*	

RV* - Reference value

Self-efficacy. This sub-section intended to show the extent which respondents can comfortably use the Health Information System (HIS) in their operations. The analysis suggested that 59.6 percent of respondents are comfortable/highly comfortable with the use of the Health Information System. Moreover, it was necessary to know whether the perceived comfortability with the use, determines the perceived extent which the use of the HIS supports corporate objectives. The observed Ordinal regression p-value for the model fitting information is 0.041, confirming that the model is relevant for testing this relationship. Furthermore, the p-values for parameter estimates, of the input variable, suggest p-values which are less than the threshold (all parameter p-values < 0.05). Therefore, the study confirms that self-efficacy significantly determine the perceived extent which the use of the HIS supports corporate objectives. The higher the efficacy, the more the idea is supported, and vice versa. The literature identifies the following things to contribute to a low efficacy: the perceived ease of use and the extent which the system integrates user's activities (Venkatesh, Thong, & Xu, 2016; Grut, Mji, Braathen, & Ingstad, 2012). The study by Farzandipur, Jeddi and Azimi (2016), recommends trainings, and the review of the system to accommodate key make all activities.

Moreover, the study conducted an additional analysis to show whether the level of efficacy determines the degree of resistance toward system use. User resistance is the degree which the user is not willing to use the HIS in its current state. Statistics show that 78.8 percent of respondents are willing/highly willing to drop the Health Information System, should they be given the choice. More users are resisting the system use.

Moreover, the ordinal regression results suggest a significant difference across parameters of the input variable except for respondents with a high efficacy. In this case, the parameter called "very high efficacy" was set as a reference value. The parameter with the insignificant difference had a p-value greater than 0.05, which is 0.066. Overall, descriptive information are surprising. For example, 68.4 percent of respondents with a low efficacy want to drop the HIS, while 87 percent of those with a high efficacy share this position. Nevertheless, in both categories, above half of the sample disregards the system. This is not a good sign. It is possible that those with high efficacy have a better understanding that the system does not adequately address operational issues. This could be the reason for denouncing the system. One of the reasons for resisting the use of the system includes poorly communicated changes (English, Masilela, Barron, & Schonfeldt, 2011; Grut, Mji, Braathen, & Ingstad, 2012). The technical team needs to engage users for effectiveness.

The degree of resistance. In previous paragraphs, the study engaged the degree of resistance as a dependent variable. This part uses the degree of resistance as the input variable, in a relationship with the perceived extent which the use of the Health Information System (HIS) supports corporate objectives. In summary, 71.92 percent of all respondents do not accept the proposal that the HIS should be dropped. This is a good percent, however, the remaining portion needs the attention of hospital administrators. Additional analysis showed whether the perceived degree of resistance determined the perceived extent which the HIS support corporate objectives, in its current status of operations. The p-value for the model fitting information was 0.000, showing that the model fits for testing this relationship. Furthermore, we examined the regression results against each parameter of the perceived degree of resistance, provided that a parameter "very low" was set as a reference value. The five levels Likert scale was used. All parameters of the input variable showed a significant difference from the reference value, except those with a low resistance. The p-value for those with a low resistance (0.138) was above the threshold (0.05). Respondents who perceive a low resistance and those who perceives a very low resistance are very close to each other; this is the reason for the insignificant difference in their perception on the extent which the HIS supports corporate objectives. Overall the Nagelkerke r-square value was 0.366, suggesting a 36.6 percent of the impact. Therefore, those who perceive a low and high resistance toward the use of HIS, significantly differ on their perception toward the support of HIS to corporate objectives.

The perceived relevance of the approach of implementation. The approach adopted in the implementation of a new system impacts user acceptance (Hendriks, 2012; Ngafeeson & Midha, 2014). In our analysis, we found that 71.9 percent of respondents are uncomfortable/highly uncomfortable with the approach used in introducing the Health Information System (HIS). This percent is high. The ordinal regression tested whether the observed variation on the level of comfortability with the approach determined the degree of resistance toward the use of the HIS. The results revealed the following: the model fitting information p-value was 0.000, and the Nagelkerke r-square value was 0.264. Moreover, all the parameter estimates showed the p-value less than the threshold ($p<0.05$). Therefore, different parameters of the perceived relevance of the approach used resulted in a significant difference to the perceived degree of resistance. Therefore, users who are uncomfortable with the approach used to introduce the HIS, are likely to resist its use, and vice versa. The influence is by 23.4 percent.

Moreover, the study tested the impact of the implementation approach to the degree which the HIS is perceived to support corporate objectives. The following results were observed: The *model fitting information* p-value was 0.000, and the *Nagelkerke r-square* value was 1.0. Moreover, except for respondents who suggested that the approach used in introducing the system was relevant, the rest of the variable parameters showed a significant difference to the extent which the HIS is perceived to support corporate objectives. The reference value was the parameter suggesting that the approach was highly relevant. The descriptive information shows that all respondents who are uncomfortable with the approach used in introducing the HIS, do not consider HIS to adequately support corporate objectives, and vice versa. Since only 59.6 percent are comfortable with the use of HIS, there is a need to review the model for introduction. Issues such as the comprehensiveness of the system, skills and competence need to be addressed (Mehdi, Hassan, Soheila, & Jamileh, 2013; Sharifian, Askarian, Nematolahi, & Farhadi, 2014).

2.5 A Recast to Propositions

Four (4) key variables were used in formulating hypotheses for testing. The variables were: Self-efficacy, the degree of resistance, the perceived relevance of the approach for introducing the Health Information System (HIS), and the extent which the HIS is perceived to support corporate objectives. It was observed that self-efficacy determined the degree which the HIS supports corporate objectives. Self-efficacy is high, when users have the required technical skills, and the system use becomes easy (Lee & Zakaria, 2012). Moreover, self-efficacy was approved to determine the level of resistance toward to system. Furthermore, the perceived resistance determines the degree which the system favours the execution of the organisation's objectives. Even if the system is good, resistance affects its use (Farzandipur, Jeddi, & Azimi, 2016). In another relationship, the study confirmed that the perceived relevance of the approach for the system implementation determines both the degree of resistance and whether the system use favours execution of corporate objectives. In general, a system that fails to support corporate objectives lacks a key element of its sustainability (Friborg & Rosenvinge, 2013). In the current study, only 14.4 percent of respondents agree that the system adequately supports the achievement of corporate objectives. Therefore, the system faces the prospect of being rejected and dropped. With these results, the study proposes figure 1 to represent its findings.

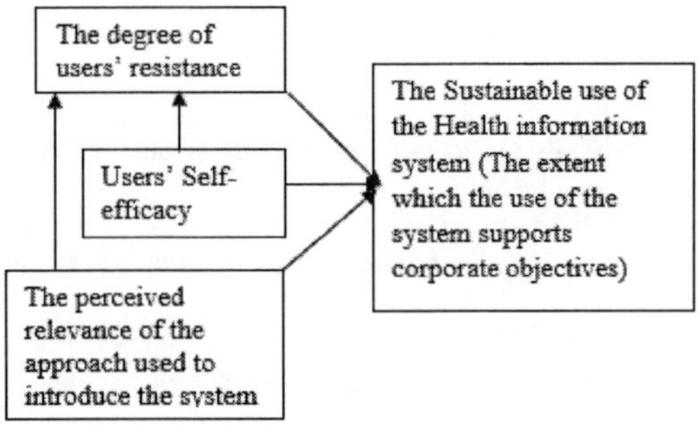

Figure 1. Determinants of the sustainable use of the Health Information System

3. CONCLUSION

This study evaluated determinants for a sustainable use of the Health Information Systems (HIS). Four variables were key in framing and operationalising this study: Self-efficacy, the degree of resistance, the approach adopted in introducing the system and the degree which the HIS is perceived to support corporate objectives. The analysis concluded the following: Self-efficacy determines the degree of resistance and the degree which the HIS is perceived to support corporate objectives, the perceived relevance of the approach used to introduce the HIS determines the degree of resistance and the degree which the HIS is perceived to support corporate objectives, and the degree of resistance determines the degree which the HIS is perceived to support corporate objectives. Moreover, the following recommendations are important:-

- It is surprising that respondents with higher efficacy have a higher desire to drop the system, than those with low efficacy. This is not a good sign. People who have a better understanding of the system should be in the position to support it, the fact that this is the opposite, suggests that the post-implementation status is not good. The organisation needs to investigate this.
- The organisation needs to evaluate the approach used to implement the system. It work less in current setting. Unfortunately, it affects the degree of resistance and the support of corporate objectives.
- The group with low efficacy need to be addressed. Low efficacy has a negative impact to the acceptance of the system, and its use in supporting corporate objectives.

ACKNOWLEDGEMENT

We acknowledge the support by Ms. Faith Mwiruka in data collection process.

REFERENCES

Lee, J.-W., & Mendlinger , S. (2011). Perceived Self-Efficacy and Its Effect on Online Learning Acceptance and Student Satisfaction. *Journal of Service Science and Management, 4*(1), 243-252.

Babones, S. (2015). Interpretive Quantitative Methods for the Social Sciences. *Socialogy, 50*(3), 453-469.

Bartlett, J., Kotrlik, J., & Higgins, C. (2001). Determining appropriate sample size in survey research. 19(1), . *Information Technology, Learning, and Performance Journal, 19*(1), 43-50.

Buntin, M. B., Burke, F. M., Hoaglin, C. M., & Blumenthal, D. (2011). The Benefits Of Health Information Technology: A Review Of The Recent Literature Shows Predominantly Positive Results. *Health Affairs, 30*(3), 464-471.

Cillers, L., & Flowerday, S. (2013). Health Information Systems to Improve Health Care: A telemedicine Case Study. *SA Journal of Information Management, 15*(1), 1-5.

Coviello, N. E. (2013). Integrating Qualitative and Quantitative Techniques in Network Analysis. *An International Journal, 8*(1), 39-90.

English, R., Masilela, T., Barron, P., & Schonfeldt, A. (2011). Health Information Systems in South Africa. *10*(1), 1-7.

Farzandipur, M., Jeddi, F. R., & Azimi, E. (2016). Systematic review of factors influencing the adoption of information and communication technologies by healthcare professionals. *Acta Informed Medicine, 24*(1), 51-55.

Friborg, O., & Rosenvinge, J. H. (2013). A comparison of open-ended and closed questions in the prediction of mental health. *Quality and Quantity, 47*(3), 1397-1411.

Fullerton, A. S. (2009). A conceptual framewok for ordered logistic regression model. *Socialogical methods and research, 38*(2), 306-347.

Gagnon, M., Desmartis, M., Labrecque, M., Car, J., Pagliari, C., Pluye, P., . . . Légaré, F. (2012). Systematic review of factors influencing the Adoption of Information and Communication Technologies by Healthcare Professionals. *Journal of Medical Systems, 36*(1), 241-277.

Grut, L., Mji, G., Braathen, S. H., & Ingstad, B. (2012). Accessing community health services: challenges faced by poor people with disabilities in a rural community in South Africa. *African Journal of Disability, 59*(2), 1-7.

Hendriks, C. J. (2012). Integrated Financial Management Information Systems: Guidelines for Effectives Implementation in the Public Sector of South Africa. *South African Journal of Information Management, 14*(1), 1-9.

Khalifa, M. (2014). Technical and Human Challenges of Implementing Hospital Information Systems in Saudi Arabia. *Journal of Health Informatics in Developing Countries, 8*(1), 12-25.

Lee, H. W., & Zakaria, N. (2012). External Factors in Hospital Information System (HIS) Adoption Model: A Case on Malaysia. *Journal of Medical Systems, 36*(4), 2129–2140.

Lubua, E. W., & Semlambo, A. (2017). The Influence of the Ease of Use and Perceived Usefulness t o the Adoption of Mobile Money Services in SMEs in Tanzania. *The Information Technologist, 14*(2), 131-141.

Lubua, E. W., Semlambo, A., & Pretorius, P. (2017). Factors influencing the use of social media in the learning process. *South African Journal of Information Systems, 19*(1), 1-7.

McCullagh, P. (1980). Journal of the royal statistical society. *42*(2), 109-142.

Mehdi, K., Hassan, B., Soheila, S. G., & Jamileh, M. Z. (2013). The impact of IT infrastructures on Iranian nurses' and students' health information-seeking strategies. *Program, 47*(4), 369-383.

Mimbi, L., & Bankole, F. (2015). ICT and Health System Performance in Africa. *26 Australian Conference on Information Systems* (pp. 1-15). Adelaide: ACIS.

Mohamed, M. M., Sulaiman, N. L., Sern, L. C., & Salleh, K. M. (2015). Measuring the Validity and Reliability of Research Instruments. *Procedia, 204*(24), 164-171.

Moucheraud, C., Schwitters, A., Boudreaux, C., Giles, D., Kilmarx, P. H., Ntolo, N., . . . Bossert, T. J. (2017). Sustainability of health information systems: a three-country qualitative study in southern Africa. *BMC Health Services Research*, 1-11. doi:10.1186/s12913-016-1971-8

Muhimbili National Hospital. (2017). *About Muhimbili National Hospital.* Retrieved February 25, 2018, from www.mnh.or.tz/index.php/about-us

Mwiruka, F. (2018). *Factors influencing the sustainable use of Hospital Information Systems in Tanzania.* Arusha: Institute of Accountancy Arusha.

Ngafeeson, M., & Midha, V. (2014). An Exploratory Study of User Resistance in Healthcare IT. *International Journal of Electronic Finance , 8*(1), 74–94.

Prinja, S., Gupta, A., Verma, R., Bahuguna, P., Kumar, D., Kaur, M., & Kumar, R. (2016). Cost of Delivering Health Care Services in Public Sector Primary and Community Health Centres in North India. *PLOS, 11*(8), 1-15.

Schoen, C., Osborn, R., Squires, D., Doty, M., Rasmussen, P., Pierson, R., & Applebaum, S. (2012). A survey of primary care doctors in ten countries shows progress in use of health information technology, less in other areas. *Health affair, 31*(12), 2805–2816.

Sharifian, R., Askarian, F., Nematolahi, M., & Farhadi, P. (2014). Factors Influencing Nurses' Acceptance of Hospital Information Systems in Iran: Application of the Unified Theory of Acceptance and Use of Technology. *Health Information Management Journal, 43*(3), 23-28.

United Nations Economic Commission of Africa. (2016). *The Demographic Profile of African Countries.* Addis Ababa: Economic Commission for Africa.

Venkatesh, V., & Bala, H. (2008). Technology Acceptance Model 3 and a Research Agenda on Interventions. *Decision Sciences, 39*(2), 273-315.

Venkatesh, V., Thong, J. Y., & Xu, X. (2016). Unified Theory of Acceptance and Use of Technology: A Synthesis and the Road Ahead. *17*(5), 328-376.

Williams, C. (2007). Research methods. *Journal of Business & Economic Research, 5*(3), 65-72.

BEING CONTROLLED: EXPLORING CONTROLLEES' VIEW ON CONTROL IN IS PROJECTS

Roman Walser and Peter Virag
Vienna University of Economics and Business
Welthandelsplatz 1, 1020 Vienna, Austria

ABSTRACT

Control is often implemented in IS projects to increase project success. A typical control relationship involves two parties: A controller, who is executing control and a controllee, who is being controlled. While there is no doubt that effective and efficient control can positively influence project success, previous research has mainly focused on the controller perspective. This primarily includes the managerial aspect of control choice, i.e. creating a set of control mechanisms for a project. However, it is arguable that also the controllees' perception of control has a considerable impact on their behavior and the resulting control effectiveness and efficiency. To close the current gap in research and get a better understanding of the controllee perspective on IS project control, explorative interviews with experienced IS project team members in Austria were held. Our summarizing content analysis yields three main findings. First, the familiarity of the project team members with each other is a crucial factor determining the perceived appropriate amount of control. Second, controllees prefer control that focuses more on the outcome rather than on their way of working. Finally, control might have a better connotation than expected and could be even seen as an opportunity to make achievements visible to supervisors.

KEYWORDS

IS Project Control, Control Congruence, Control Experience, Perceived Appropriateness

1. INTRODUCTION

One of the most important activities to promote value creation from information technology resources is the control of information systems (IS) projects. Existing literature has shown that both in case of internal and outsourced projects using different software development methodologies, control mechanisms can have positive effects on project outcomes (Gopal and Gosain, 2010; Kirsch, 1996, 1997; Tiwana and Keil, 2009).

Experience has shown that IS projects, which are often lengthy and expensive, are more prone to failure compared to projects in other fields (Irani, 2010). Possible reasons for this could be the uncertain and changing business requirements (Whyte and Bytheway, 1996), complexity of information systems that often lead to unforeseen escalations (Mahring and Keil, 2008), intangibility of deliverables (Snow et al., 2007) and significantly different educational and professional experiences of participants (Tiwana and Keil, 2009). This high risk of project failure makes control in IS projects essentially important as it can help projects speed up and stay within budget (Heumann et al., 2015).

In this paper we define control as "any attempt to motivate individuals to behave in a manner consistent with organizational objectives" (Kirsch, 2004) and IS project control as "the attempt to intentionally affect the behavior of another person or group as a means to achieve objectives related to designing, developing, operating, using and managing information systems" (Cram et al., 2016).

There are various control modes, mechanisms and styles available to controllers; the amount and intentions behind control are also variables to consider. Over the past two decades, a number of studies have been carried out to advise controllers on how to control IS projects. Nevertheless, data in those studies were mainly based on controllers' experiences (Wiener et al., 2016). This focus on the controller's view on control is surprising because control is usually seen as a dyadic relationship consisting of both controllers and controllees (Kirsch, 2004). However, the controllees' view on control has rarely been examined so far, which is problematic because a common understanding between controller and controllee can minimize control loss

(Narayanaswamy et al., 2013). We assume that a number of factors influence the controllees' perceptions and experiences of control. For example, company culture and size could affect the optimal amount of control, and, since control in IS projects is generally seen as a tool to fight agency problems such as appropriation and moral hazard (Eisenhardt, 1989), we presume that control mechanisms are necessarily undesirable for controllees. Therefore, this research paper is aimed at providing insights into the controllees' perception of control. More precisely, we try to find answers to the following research questions:

"How do controllees experience control in IS projects and which factors influence controllees' perception of control?"

We believe that our study can shape the way of thinking about how controls should be applied in IS projects. It is relevant for research because it provides novel insights for gaining a better understanding of the perception of control. In addition, our research can guide practitioners (such as IT project managers) to fine-tune their control portfolio that may have a positive impact on project performance. The remainder of this paper is structured as follows. First, we provide an overview of the research on IS project control and describe the main concepts relevant for this paper. After introducing the chosen research methodology, the results of our explorative interviews are presented. Subsequently, we elaborate on theoretical and practical implications. Finally, we reflect on contributions and limitations of the study.

2. THEORETICAL BACKGROUND

Controllers in IS projects play a crucial role in selecting and implementing control. Most previous research see control as a dyadic relationship between a controller and a controllee. Controllers are typically middle managers, an IS project manager for example, and controllees are members of his team. Controllers are individuals who exercise control in order to regulate the behavior of controllees. Although the analysis of this paper is at project level, it is important to note that other controller groups might also exist in an organization, for example senior IT executives exercise control over IS projects. (Wiener et al., 2017).

Controllers can choose specific actions called control mechanisms that help to achieve organizational goals. Control mechanisms specify who will do what and when. (Cram et al., 2016). For instance, a control mechanism is when business representatives are asked to provide user stories at the beginning of a software development project in order to validate requirements.

Control mechanisms can be categorized into different control modes. These control modes represent a unique collection of actors and techniques to achieve control. Table 1 shows an adapted version from literature (Cram et al., 2016; Kirsch, 1996; Wiener et al., 2016) to give an overview of the different control modes and to outline some corresponding control mechanisms. Control modes can be formal and informal. Formal controls are input, behavioral and outcome controls and they focus on enforcing previously defined plans and emphasize accountability. Informal controls are clan and self-control and they are used to create shared values and norms (Gregory and Keil, 2014). A controller can choose from a wide variety of control mechanisms when creating a project control portfolio.

Table 1. Control Modes and Exemplary Mechanisms

Control modes	**Control mechanism example**	
Input control: Specifying and monitoring resource allocation (human, financial, material)	- Recruitment - Training programs - Changes in allocation of funding	*Formal*
Behavioral control: specifying and monitoring and rewarding actions of subordinates	- Mandated software development methodology - Regular status meetings - Weekly progress reports	
Outcome/Output control: specifying and monitoring employees level of output	- Defining project milestones - Functional specifications - Number of code lines to be submitted each week	
Clan Control: social mechanisms (norms, values) that motivate goal-oriented behavior	- Ceremonies and rituals - Working overtime - Socialization (e.g. Team dinner)	*Informal*
Self-control: self-monitoring behavior based on intrinsic motivation, individual standards and objectives	- Developing elegant code - Work autonomy - Self rewarding	

A diverse portfolio is important for example because input and behavioral control play a significant role in successfully enacting clan control (Eng et al., 2012). Another important characteristic of control is how much it is exercised. In other words, control amount refers to the extent the controller uses control mechanisms to exercise control over controllees. It reflects the collective influence of controller on controllee to affect what the latter does. In outsourced settings, Rustagi and his colleagues (2008) found that outsourced tasks, which are of higher uncertainty call for a larger amount of control. However, technical knowledge on the client side (controller) or when the client trusts the vendor (controllee) mitigates the necessary amount of control (Rustagi et al., 2008).

While the configuration of the control portfolio is an important control activity, control consequences are also determined by control enactment. It describes the interaction between the controller and the controllee through which the controller implements formal control and promotes informal control. (Wiener et al., 2016). Control enactment can be conceptualized through control style and control congruence. Control style describes the interaction between the controller and the controllee. An authoritative control style can be used to ensure and enforce compliant controllee behavior. It is a top-down control style that emphasizes bureaucratic norms. Using this control style, the controllee typically has minimal influence over how the control is configured. In contrast, an enabling control style promotes collaboration and frequent interaction. It is important to mention that these two styles are conceptualized as end points on a scale and usually one of them is a dominant but not an absolute choice of style (Gregory et al., 2013). Control congruence is the degree of similarity between the controller and controllee perceptions of enacted controls. There are two types of congruence. First, communicational congruence refers to the shared understanding between the controllee and the controller about the enacted controls. Second, evaluational congruence is defined as the level of agreement between the controllee and the controller about the appropriateness of the enacted controls (Wiener et al., 2016).

Finally, the concept of control purpose focuses on why controllers enact control. It is defined as intentions underlying the controller's choice and implementation of specific control mechanisms. While the primary focus of control is the supervision and monitoring of controllees (i.e. appropriation oriented control), coordination is also an important aspect of control. Such aspect is present because of the complexity of IS projects and the difficulties associated with managing resource and task interdependencies. Thus, the goal of coordination oriented control is to maximize the value of project resources unlike in appropriation oriented control where the purpose is to minimize agency problems such as moral hazards (Remus et al., 2015). Understanding the differences between control purposes is important because if e.g. the selected control mechanisms are primarily targeted towards managing appropriation concerns, they can become ineffective as they ignore the need to coordinate with and among stakeholders. Furthermore, appropriation oriented controls can become counterproductive as they may diminish the feelings of autonomy and responsibility and can negatively affect satisfaction and performance of controllees (Donaldson, 2008).

In summary, prior IS control literature conceptualizes control activities from a controller perspective and focuses on performance effects on a project level. To the best of our knowledge, only one study investigates control effects on controllees: a study from Remus and his colleagues (2016) focuses on how control modes and control styles relate to controllee task performance and job satisfaction. The authors found that both formal and informal controls increase job performance but only informal control has a positive effect on job satisfaction. While the controllee perspective is present in the control congruence concept, it does not investigate controllee behavior in case of low level of congruence (Remus et al., 2016). For example, possible detrimental behavior of controllees (e.g. keeping project information private or distorting information) is a largely neglected area even though it is arguable that it leads to decreased control efficiency and effectiveness. Therefore, our study concentrates on controllees' perception of control and factors influencing their perception. We expect that control is generally undesirable and that controllees have preferred control modes.

3. METHODOLOGY

Due to the lack of previous research in the field, explorative interviews were held to better understand the controllees' perspective on IS project control. In particular, semi-structured personal interviews were conducted with a judgment sample of three IS project team members. We chose interview partners who have been repeatedly working in projects with a clear connection to IS, such as programming or IS consulting projects. As we wanted to gain a better understanding of the common situation where a (potentially unexperienced) project team member is controlled by a supervisor, it was important that the interview partners have never held a leading role within a company or within a project team. This is because people who have already taken a leading role within the dyadic control relationship might have another view on control. Our judgment sample included interviewees both with and without a university degree. Each interview was conducted individually and lasted between 50 minutes and one hour. Two of the interviewees worked for large and internationally operating organizations (employing more than 25,000 people). The two organizations covered IT consulting as well as programming activities. The third interviewee worked for a small- to medium sized programming organization employing approximately 50 people.

To provide our interviewees with some orientation, we started our interviews with a brief introduction. This included a simplified description of the term 'control'. For our interviewees, we defined control as any attempts by supervisors to ensure that employees act in a way that is beneficiary for the project. We chose this definition because it is easier to understand for practitioners without academic background but still close enough to the more precise definition given in the introduction of this paper. To keep the direction of the interview open for as long as possible and to avoid biases, we did not give any concrete examples of control mechanisms during the first half of the interview. Furthermore, we briefly explained the dyadic control relationship and the two parties (i.e. controller and controllee) involved. Afterwards, we wanted to investigate whether control awareness contributes to control congruence. This is arguable because low awareness would impede the acquirement of a shared understanding of control. The third thematic block was about personal perception and addressed the controllees' perceived appropriateness of control. Towards the end of the interview, we wanted to check the relationship between congruence and the controllees' attitude towards control, arguing that either low congruence leads to a negative attitude or vice versa. An overview of the contents is given in table 2. All interviews were recorded and notes were taken to capture observations like facial expressions or gestures, which might support the subsequent analysis.

Table 2. Structure of the Explorative Interviews

Thematic block	Contents
1: Introduction to and information about the interviewee	- Clarification of roles and responsibilities within a project - Assessment of experience and competence - Getting an idea of the person and his/her character
2: Control awareness and assessment of own concernment	- How does the team ensure project success - Assessment of extent and importance of control in own environment - Assessment of own control involvement compared to colleagues
3: General personal perception of control (regarding appropriateness)	- Impairment due to control mechanisms - Impact of control on work (what makes control intrusive, disturbing) - Factors justifying more control
4: Attitude towards control	- How do employees generally see control - Preferred control characteristics - Observed impact of control on previous project success

Qualitative research offers a wide range of methods for acquiring knowledge from data. Apart from hermeneutic approaches, qualitative and content analyzing approaches can be even further subdivided depending upon the applied techniques and procedures (Mayring, 1991). Considering the purpose of our research and the length restrictions for this paper, we decided to perform a summarizing content analysis. It aims to compactly outline the main findings of data (such as interviews) and gives a high level of flexibility. To avoid individual biases, three researchers were involved in the analysis. We also see it as the appropriate approach because we made small adaptions to the interview guideline based on learnings from the first run. We present the results of our interviews in the subsequent chapter, followed by a separate downstream discussion to clearly separate one from another.

4. RESULTS

Overall, the interview partners fulfilled the requirements of having project experience without ever having any leading role within the company. The answers to our introductory questions (e.g. work experience, education, operating role within company) let us believe that our interviewees represent a considerable part of typical IS project team members.

Control awareness: When asked about control in their environment, all of our interviewees stated that they are well aware of being surrounded by control within their project setting. However, they had difficulties to name some exemplary control mechanisms. In general, the importance of control for successful project completion was acknowledged. The controllees stated that control is particularly important in their industry because IS projects are typically conducted at fixed prices. This means that their employer has to bear the costs for any delays or quality issues.

Regarding own concernment, one interviewee observed that employees lower in the hierarchy are less affected by control mechanisms. He assumed that this is due to the lower hourly rates of younger professionals resulting in a lower financial impact in case of inefficiencies. Moreover, the interviewee observed greater acceptance of errors and room for deviations in case of unexperienced employees. For employees on the same hierarchical level within an IS project team, our interview partners did not experience any differences regarding control amount.

Perception (regarding appropriateness): Overall, the interviewed controllees found that the control amount in their project environment is appropriate. Control mechanisms mainly consisted of regular status meetings or project milestone evaluation. When asked for an estimation, two interviewees stated that they spend approximately ten percent of their work time for activities that are related to control and coordination. Both of them observed that this workload related to control is two or three times higher for employees holding a leading role.

When we asked them about circumstances which would justify the implementation of a larger control set within a project, they consistently determined the familiarity of the project team members with each other as the crucial factor. This is because employees who are familiar with each other know what they can expect from their colleagues and therefore less control and coordinating tasks are necessary. The project size per se was not seen as a decisive factor because they already experienced situations where "more control than necessary" was implemented in lager projects although the project team members knew each other very well. One of the interview partners criticized that some project managers assume that a larger project automatically requires more control.

Attitude towards control: We found a rather neutral attitude towards control among the interviewed controllees. One of them even mentioned some positive aspects: according to him, control mechanisms can help to make own efforts and achievements visible to controllers, who are usually also supervisors. Moreover, he stated that control mechanisms can also give valuable feedback for personal development and further (intrinsically motivated) improvement.

All interviewees stated that they prefer control mechanisms which focus on the outcome of their efforts because they appreciate a high degree of freedom and flexibility during work. For our interviewees, it was only important that the milestones are clear from the beginning. Automated control throughout the project (e.g. automated recording of working times) was seen very critically and manual but more time-consuming control mechanisms were preferred instead. Moreover, the interviewees indicated that they wish for control mechanisms that don't make them feel small, even if the controller is superior within the project team.

5. DISCUSSION

Overall, we recognized a considerable level of awareness regarding control. To give an example, all interviewees acknowledged the importance of regular status meetings and other coordination tasks. However, already at the beginning of the interviews we saw how hard it was for our interview partners to think of other concrete control mechanisms. This indicates that existing control mechanisms are not very intrusive for the interviewed controllees. Another explanation could be that implemented control mechanisms are not too time-consuming for the controllees. As the employees are usually not directly affected by the negative consequences of failed projects, we were surprised by the controllees' empathy for the controllers. One interviewee remarkably outlined the importance of control in his environment although he has never held a leading role. In case of employment contracts where overtime is compensated with a flat fee, the situation might be different and project issues could also have a direct negative impact on the controllees if they have to do more unpaid overtime. However, we had the impression that the controllers in that case have clearly justified the implementation of control mechanisms so that the employees understand the situation and behave as required.

The first main finding we want to highlight is that from the viewpoint of the interviewed controllees, a higher budgeted project does not automatically justify a greater control amount. Intuitively, for a controller it might seem reasonable to determine the required control amount based on the size (i.e. budget) of a project. This is because in many cases, the budget of a project will correlate with the number of employees involved and also with the overall complexity of a project. Based on the insights we could gain from the interviews, it might be a good idea to focus more on the familiarity of the project team members instead of the mere headcount. When our interviewees talked about larger projects they recently participated in, they clearly indicated a level of annoyance whenever they did not agree with the implemented amount of control. To increase controllees' willingness to behave in a way that promotes control efficiency and effectiveness, we thus suggest reducing the control amount in accordance with the familiarity of the project team members. Finally, whenever employees have to carry out fewer activities that are only related to control (without generating project value), additional cost savings might be achieved. This does not mean that there should never be an extensive control set implemented in an IS project. Instead, the project team members' level of familiarity with each other should be considered as one of many factors potentially influencing the appropriate amount of control in a project.

Second, our interviews have shown that controllees have a quite pronounced understanding regarding the necessity of control in IS projects. In general, they are willing to cooperate and conduct additional work steps that are necessary for the control mechanisms to be efficient and effective. Our results indicate that controllees only behave detrimentally if they find a control mechanism unnecessary or inappropriate. However, they prefer control mechanisms which focus on their results rather than on their way of working and this would suggest the implementation of outcome control. IT project management points out the importance of recognizing deviations as early as possible so that countermeasures can be taken at lower costs. We are aware that outcome control is usually located later in a project that might make the correction of deviations more costly. Also, in line with other research pointing out the importance of trust within a project setting (e.g. Sauer and Reich (2009)), it might be beneficial for project success to focus more on informal control. This is because control that gives the controllees more freedom and flexibility has the potential to increase intrinsic motivation and willingness to comply with control mechanisms.

Third, we were surprised by the rather positive attitude towards control that our interviewees have shown. There might be a prevailing negative connotation of 'control' in practice. This is not surprising because implementation of control is often justified with the almost compelling existence of goal incompatibilities (Ouchi, 1979), information asymmetries (Dalton et al., 2007) or controllees' moral hazard (Fama and Jensen, 1983). Moreover, control is said to potentially have negative impacts on aspects such as trust (Mohr and Spekman, 1994). Contrary to those negative connotations, one of our interviewees even stated that he sees a big opportunity in control. He said that control is a good means for him to make his personal achievement visible to his supervisors. Because personal achievements serve as a crucial input for decisions on promotion within his organization, he rather saw control more as an opportunity than as a burden or harassment.

Seeing control also as an opportunity for controllees comes up with two conflicting implications: on the one hand, by emphasizing this aspect a controller could increase the controllees' motivation to behave in a way that is supporting control effectiveness and efficiency. To give an example, employees might be more willing to submit desired information regarding working hours or work package progress. On the other hand, the controller has to keep in mind that the information communicated by the controllee might be glossed over to gain a better impression of the own work. This could be counterproductive for the purpose of the implemented control, where objective information is crucial. For controllers to further increase control effectiveness and efficiency, it therefore might be valuable to consider this two-sided aspect.

6. CONCLUSION

The goal of this study was to get a better understanding of how controllees experience control in IS projects and which factors influence their perception of control. For this, we conducted three explorative interviews with IS project team members and performed a summarizing content analysis. First, we found that controllees are highly aware of control mechanisms. Second, we could observe the prevailing assumption that controllers tend to automatically implement a larger control set in higher budgeted projects. Furthermore, a key finding of our study is that there is a strong correlation between the level of familiarity amongst the project team members and the amount of control they find appropriate: our findings suggest that an informal relationship among controllees makes control more inappropriate. Finally, rather surprisingly our study has shown that controllees' attitude towards control can be positive if it makes their efforts more visible. This finding implies that the agency view of control might be too narrow.

This paper contributes to research by presenting individual level control experiences of controllees. Our results suggest that the hierarchical position in the organization and familiarity of the project team are key variables in shaping control experiences, control congruence and thus control performance. For practitioners these findings are important because they may explain ineffective control modes, mechanisms and reasons behind employee dissatisfaction and underperformance.

As with any research, our work is subject to limitations. First, we only had one interviewee from each organization, which could result in a level of subjectivity and personal bias in our data. Second, it was difficult to investigate causality between some of our research phenomena. For example, it is not obvious that it is the hierarchical position that determines how much a controllee is affected by control mechanisms. Not all employees seek leadership opportunities and a specialist role can be attractive to a large set of experienced employees as well. Therefore, an alternative explanation could be that it is the amount of job experience that influences how much control mechanisms affect controllees, whereas young professionals may be more permissive with control mechanisms. Future studies that investigate control from controllees' perspective should hence also include individual characteristics, which might influence control perception. For example, it would be interesting to examine how national culture, educational background or the amount of job experience shape the sense of control. For this, a longitudinal case study or action research would allow researchers to have in depth discussions with controllees and explore the dynamics of changes in control perception.

We hope that our work contributes to the academic discourse and inspires further theoretical progress in the field of IS project control.

REFERENCES

Cram, W.A., Brohman, K. and Gallupe, R.B. (2016), "Information Systems Control: A Review and Framework for Emerging Information Systems Processes", *Journal of the Association for Information Systems*, Vol. 17 No. 4, pp. 216–266.

Dalton, D.R., Hitt, M.A., Certo, S.T. and Dalton, C.M. (2007), "The Fundamental Agency Problem and Its Mitigation", *The Academy of Management Annals*, Vol. 1 No. 1, pp. 1–64.

Donaldson, L. (2008), "Ethics Problems and Problems with Ethics: Toward a Pro-Management Theory", *Journal of Business Ethics*, Vol. 78 No. 3, pp. 299–311.

Eisenhardt, K.M. (1989), "Agency Theory: An Assessment and Review.", *Academy of Management Review*, Vol. 14 No. 1, pp. 57–74.

Eng, C., Chua, H., Lim, W.-K., Soh, C. and Sia, S.K. (2012), "Enacting Clan Control in Complex IT Projects: A Social Capital Perspective", *MIS Quarterly*, Vol. 36 No. 2, pp. 577–600.

Fama, E.F. and Jensen, M.C. (1983), "Separation of Ownership and Control", *The Journal of Law & Economics*, Vol. 26 No. 2, pp. 301–325.

Gopal, A. and Gosain, S. (2010), "Research Note —The Role of Organizational Controls and Boundary Spanning in Software Development Outsourcing: Implications for Project Performance", *Information Systems Research*, Vol. 21 No. 4, pp. 960–982.

Gregory, R.W., Beck, R. and Keil, M. (2013), "Control Balancing in Information Systems Development Offshoring Projects", *MIS Quarterly*, Vol. 37 No. 4, pp. 1211–1232.

Gregory, R.W. and Keil, M. (2014), "Blending bureaucratic and collaborative management styles to achieve control ambidexterity in IS projects", *European Journal of Information Systems*, Nature Publishing Group, Vol. 23 No. 3, pp. 343–356.

Heumann, J., Wiener, M., Remus, U. and Mähring, M. (2015), "To coerce or to enable? Exercising formal control in a large information systems project", *Journal of Information Technology*, Vol. 30 No. 4, pp. 337–351.

Irani, Z. (2010), "Investment evaluation within project management: an information systems perspective", *The Journal of the Operational Research Society* , Vol. 61 No. 6, pp. 917–928.

Kirsch, L.J. (1996), "The Management of Complex Tasks in Organizations: Controlling the Systems Development Process", *Organization Science*, Vol. 7 No. 1, pp. 1–21.

Kirsch, L.J. (2004), "Deploying Common Systems Globally: The Dynamics of Control", *Information Systems Research*, Vol. 15 No. 4, pp. 374–395.

Kirsch, L.S. (1997), "Portfolios of Control Modes and IS Project Management", *Information Systems Research*, Vol. 8 No. 3, pp. 215–239.

Mahring, M. and Keil, M. (2008), "Information technology project escalation: A process model", *Decision Sciences*, Vol. 39 No. 2, pp. 239–272.

Mayring, P. (1991), "Qualitative Inhaltsanalyse", *Handbuch Qualitative Forschung: Grundlagen, Konzepte, Methoden Und Anwendungen*, Psychologie Verl. Union, pp. 209–213.

Mohr, J. and Spekman, R. (1994), "Characteristics of partnership success: Partnership attributes, communication behavior, and conflict resolution techniques", *Strategic Management Journal*, Vol. 15 No. 2, pp. 135–152.

Narayanaswamy, R., Grover, V. and Henry, R.M. (2013), "The Impact of Influence Tactics in Information System Development Projects: A Control-Loss Perspective", *Journal of Management Information Systems*, Vol. 30 No. 1, pp. 191–226.

Ouchi, W.G. (1979), "A Conceptual Framework for the Design of Organizational Control Mechanisms", *Management Science*, Vol. 25 No. 9, pp. 833–848.

Remus, U., Saunders, C., Wiener, M., Mähring, M. and Kofler, M. (2016), "Control Modes Versus Control Styles : Investigating ISD Project Control Effects at the Individual Level", *Thirty Seventh International Conference on Information Systems*, pp. 1–21.

Remus, U., Wiener, M., Mähring, M., Saunders, C. and Cram, A. (2015), "Why do you control? The concept of control purpose and its implications for is project control research", *International Conference on Information Systems: Exploring the Information Frontier, ICIS 2015*, pp. 1–19.

Rustagi, S., King, W.R. and Kirsch, L.J. (2008), "Predictors of Formal Control Usage in IT Outsourcing Partnerships", *Information Systems Research*, Vol. 19 No. 2, pp. 126–143.

Sauer, C. and Reich, B.H. (2009), "Rethinking IT project management: Evidence of a new mindset and its implications", *International Journal of Project Management*, Elsevier Ltd and IPMA, Vol. 27 No. 2, pp. 182–193.

Snow, A.P., Keil, M. and Wallace, L. (2007), "The effects of optimistic and pessimistic biasing on software project status reporting", *Information & Management*, Vol. 44 No. 2, pp. 130–141.

Tiwana, A. and Keil, M. (2009), "Control in Internal and Outsourced Software Projects", *Journal of Management Information Systems*, Vol. 26 No. 3, pp. 9–44.

Whyte, G. and Bytheway, A. (1996), "Factors affecting information systems' success", *International Journal of Service Industry Management*, Vol. 7 No. 1, pp. 74–93.

Wiener, M., Cram, A. and Remus, U. (2017), "The View From the Top – How Senior Executives Exercise Control Over Information Systems Projects to Enhance Performance", *Proceedings of the 25th European Conference on Information Systems (ECIS)*, No. July, pp. 1423–1438.

Wiener, M., Mähring, M., Remus, U. and Saunders, C. (2016), "Control Configuration and Control Enactment in Information Systems Projects: Review and Expanded Theoretical Framework", *MIS Quarterly*, Vol. 40 No. 3, pp. 741–774.

RANSOMWARE: RECOMMENDATIONS AGAINST THE EXTORTION

Shubham Goel[1], John Bambenek[2] and Dr. Masooda Bashir[1]
[1]*School of Information Sciences, University of Illinois Urbana Champaign, USA*
[2]*Department of Computer Science, University of Illinois Urbana Champaign, USA*

ABSTRACT

The dramatic rise in ransomware attacks in the last few years has made headlines all over the world. With the invention of new attack techniques, ransomware has become the most prolific and profitable type of cyber-attack of all time. In this paper, we provide the first comprehensive guide for organizations and individuals to protect against ransomware by analysing the differences, commonalities, and best practices among 49 reports that are widely available. Our research reveals that individuals and organizations should take both proactive and reactive approaches that take into account both pre-attack and post-attack strategies. In addition, we present protective measures that are specific to governments, corporations, and researchers/online communities/media while differentiating between technical and operational recommendations.

KEYWORDS

Malware, Ransomware, Malicious activities, Underground Economy, CyberCrime

1. INTRODUCTION

Ransomware attacks are on the rise as the value of digital information as a commodity increases [Cisco, 2016] [InfoSec Institute, 2017]. Ransomware is a form of malicious software that holds personal computers or organizations' information systems hostage until a ransom is paid. The first known ransomware attack dates to 1989 [Ladan et al., 2016]; however, the term was not coined until 2005, the same year in which organized crime in Russia produced the first modern ransomware, GPCoder Trojan [Ladan et al., 2016]. Since then, more than 300 different families of ransomware have been identified. Ransomware typically encrypts files so they are inaccessible, notifies the victim, and provides decryption instructions. Attackers exfiltrate data and sensitive information and then extort victims with the threat of dumping the information online, misusing the information, or deleting the data. Unlike other cyber-attacks, motives for ransomware attacks are typically monetary, which can lead to enormous damage and hardship for individuals and organizations. However, a few recent attacks have been motivated to cause maximum destruction and disruption to target organizations since the amount collected is minimal [Bill Conner, 2017].

According to an FBI report, ransomware was a billion-dollar industry in 2016 [Ladan et al., 2016], with around 4,000 computers are affected every hour. IBM Security reports that 70 percent of business victims paid the ransom in 2016. Furthermore, to avoid having their information made public, nearly 50 percent of organizations did not report ransomware attacks to law enforcement [IBM, 2016]. Most ransoms are requested in digital currency (e.g., bitcoins) and therefore many organizations are stockpiling cryptocurrencies to ensure faster recovery of their data [Phil Mccausland, 2017].

Although there are numerous reports and recommendations published by governments, corporations, news media, and online communities, there is a lack of scholarly research on best practices to guard against this threat. Therefore, our research is focused on analyzing, summarizing, and identifying the differences and commonalities among various best-practice recommendations given in published reports. We believe this will serve as a first step towards creating a comprehensive guide for individuals and organizations to defend against ransomware. Our long-term aim is to provide an exhaustive report highlighting protections that are focused and specific to an organization, including technical and operational recommendations. In our framework, recommendation which relies on technology are categorized as technical recommendations and recommendations which are more business and administrative-centric are labeled as operational recommendations.

2. BACKGROUND INFORMATION & RELATED WORK

Ransomware are generally transferred via Spam email campaigns, smishing, or web exploit kits. A study by IBM [Acutec, 2017] found that 40 percent of spam emails were infected with ransomware in 2016. After getting onto the machine, ransomware executes its files and connects to the Command and Control (C&C) server. C&C servers are used to remotely send malicious commands to the compromised network or a computer. The information received by the C&C server includes IP addresses and access permissions for the account that executed the ransomware. This C&C server sends instructions to encrypt the files and, once the ransomware receives the encryption key, it starts propagating and encrypting files from folders to removable media.

Although each ransomware has a different mechanism, there are quite a few similarities, one of which is encryption. Encryption of ransomware is so strong that decryption is infeasible, with a few exceptions. Earlier ransomware such as Cerberv1, Jigsaw and TeslaCryptV1 are among those that can be decrypted with the help of a decryption tool [No more ransom, 2016]. One of the encryption methods used by attackers is Advance Encryption Standard (AES) (128/256) symmetric cryptography [Ladan et al., 2016] to encrypt a victim's files, along with an RSA-2048 key to encrypt the AES key. It is not possible to break this encryption method as of this writing. Ransomware leverages spam messages to trick users to open it. If a user opens the attachment to the spam email, the user's file will become encrypted and a message with payment details will be displayed. Figurel shows a typical propagation of ransomware adapted from a blog on Algosec [Erik, 2016].

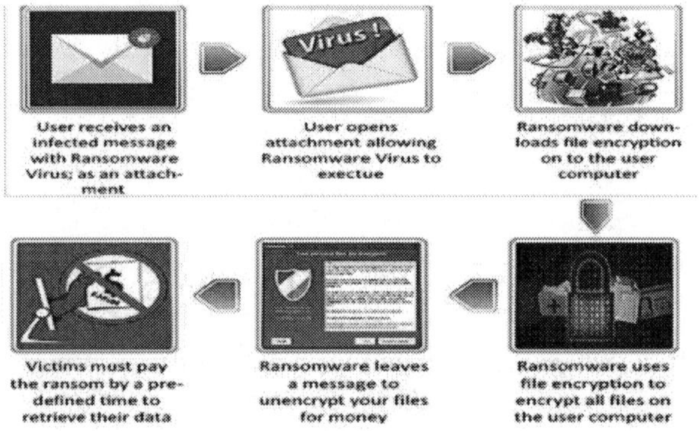

Figure 1. Ransomware Propagation

To the best of our knowledge, there are no publications that analyse and report on the assessment of best practices against ransomware. However, a few recent publications focused on technical protections and mechanisms against ransomware are related to this research and thus will serve as our literature review in this section.

One such study provides a brief overview of mitigation strategies [Samir, 2014]. The research provides a list of preventive measures such as creating backups, installing antivirus software, and updating software. The author discussed the various infection mechanisms like cryptowall, cryptolocker, police ransomware, SMS ransomware and MBR ransomware. Additionally, the author concluded the paper with a brief study about the monetization of the ransom and the popularity of cryptocurrency.

In recent years, a prominent author Kharraz and his colleagues have been actively researching and publishing on ransomware and their contributions provide real-time and other technical solutions against ransomware. For example, in a recent study Kharraz et al. provide insight into the evolution of ransomware, different ransomware families, and evolution techniques [Kharraz et al., 2015]. The authors collected the samples from Anubis, public malware repositories, and other security forums, and ran each for 45 minutes to confirm whether it was a ransomware attack. According to their paper, current ransomware samples started attacking the user's files right after the malicious program was executed by the user. Their paper also discusses the deletion mechanism and found that 35.6% of samples do not perform any encryption mechanisms, and they delete the users' files if they do not pay. This research discusses the mitigation strategies with the help of API Call monitoring. A study about the mode of payment is also presented, in which all the ransomware families are categorized in different payment modes. Most families take an untraceable payment, but it shows that the recent trend is changing to bitcoin since it is a better method of transfer and the attackers feel that it is hard to trace.

In another study Kharraz et al. reported on a real-time solution against ransomware called Redemption. It is an endpoint solution that differentiates between benign and malicious ransomware requests [Kharraz et. al., 2016]. The first part of Redemption is a lightweight kernel module that intercepts process interactions, stores the event, and manages the changes in a protected area. The second is a user-mode daemon, called a behavioural monitor and notification module that assigns a malice score to a process, and is used to notify the user about the potential malicious behaviour of a process. The authors proposed a behaviour-based and content-based detection. Their paper provided a usability experiment for 28 participants to test the usability of Redemption and concluded that all the participants found the system to perform normally when it was running.

Another group of researchers proposed a solution with few similarities to Redemption. They proposed Paybreak, which defends against Cryptographic Ransomware. Paybreak observes the use of symmetric keys and decrypts the files for some ransomware families including the famous locky and crypto locker [kolodenker et. al., 2017]. Paybreak stores the encrypted key in the key vault and the user can decrypt the key vault and the files using the private key. The paper also includes the benchmarking and the performance impact on the system and the results showed no significant slowdown. The main drawback of Paybreak is if the attackers know about the vault, they can input the vault with garbage values before encrypting the files, and thus delay or prevent recovery.

As seen in this literature review, most of the published research studies are based on technical solutions against ransomware. While these are important and valuable papers, it may be difficult for individuals without a strong technical background to implement these solutions. More importantly, there are no research studies focused on best practices and protections against ransomware that are specifically aimed at individuals and organizations that can provide guidelines for how to proactively and reactively prepare for this type of an attack. Hence our goal was to provide this much-needed list of recommendations that an individual or organization can use to develop their defense against ransomware.

3. METHODOLOGY

The rising threat of ransomware has caused organizations to publish frequent reports to make sure their employees and clients are safe. In this study, we identified and collected 49 reports that were generated by governments, corporations, media, and online communities. Inclusion criteria for these reports were that reports should be published between January 1, 2016 and June 1, 2017. We selected these dates because there was a dramatic rise of ransomware threats in 2016 and there was an increase in ransomware advisories and guides in the same year [Herb, 2017]. We included all the reports that were publicly available and published in English. We excluded reports that aimed to publicize a product or sell a product, were password protected, or which mainly referenced other reports.

We used Google search to find these reports with keywords “Ransomware Best practices”, “Ransomware defenses”, “Ransomware tips”, “Ransomware strategies”, “Post-attack ransomware strategies”, “Pre-attack ransomware strategies”, “Ransomware detection”, and “Ransomware advisory”. If there were multiple reports from the same organization, we compiled the reports into one report before doing the analysis. Our initial assessment of these 49 unique reports showed that all the reports included similar recommendations in a variety of ways that were not specific or organized. For example, although most reports included strategies for individuals and organizations to take, they were not presented in such categories as “pre-attack” or “post-attack”. In addition, similar recommendations about how to protect an information system were scattered throughout the reports and difficult to follow. Therefore, our initial data collection task was to organize and categorize the recommendations in a manner that can be used systematically for further analyses. Thus, the remainder of this section will show the steps we took to review and organize the details of the reports so that our readers can follow our research methodology.

The first step in our data organization was to categorize the recommendations as either “pre-attack” or “post-attack” strategies. Pre-attack means all the practices which should be considered before any attack to prevent or restrict the harm caused by the attack. Post-attack implies all the practices which should be adopted after the attack has occurred to minimize the damage or to restart business operations. In addition, we analyzed and distinguished the strategies as either "technical" or "operational" recommendations. Technical recommendations include recommendations that rely primarily on technology, such as backup, antivirus, and software upgrades and patches. Operational recommendations include business-centric recommendations like business continuity planning, risk management, and contacting the authorities, i.e. notifying law enforcement agencies. Furthermore, we classified the recommendations based on the entity or sector that generated the report, namely, governments, corporations, or online communities/researchers/media. We termed this classification a "sector-wise" assessment of the recommendations. This assessment highlighted the most recommended practices across the three sectors: Governments, Corporations, and Online Communities/ Researchers/Media.

3.1 Sector-Wise Analysis

Our dataset includes three sectors, namely Governments, Corporations, and Online Communities/ Researchers/Media. Most of our sources come from information security/cloud companies (63% percent), which were actively reporting about ransomware attacks, followed by Corporations (27%) and Governments (10 %).

We included 5 government organizations: United States-CERT, CERT-In (India); National Cyber Security Center-United Kingdom; Canada Cyber Security Center; and Singapore-CERT. A computer emergency response team (CERT) is a government expert group that handles computer security incidents. There were government organizations apart from these listed in this section which released ransomware advisories, but we didn't include those because either they were not published in English or they were protected by a password.

We included reports from the top 50 Information Security companies as per Cyber Security Ventures [13]. Additionally, some reports in this section are from major cloud providers. The corporations include: Deloitte, PWC, EY, Rapid7, I-Sprit, Carbon Black, SecureWorks, Ziften, BT, ForcePoint, Herjavec Group, Norton, Palo Alto Network, EMC^2, Sophos, Trend Micro, Alien Vault, Druva, Digital Guardian, Ivanti, HighTouch Technologies, Microage, Novicus, Giant Stride, Online Tech, Carbonite, Rackspace, Assurestor, Infiniwiz, Beazley Group and CDWG.

The remainder of the recommendations come from online Communities, researchers, and media sources, including ISACA (Information Systems Audit and Control Association); ENISA (European Union Agency for Network and Information Security); SEI-CMU (Software Engineering Institute – Carnegie Mellon University), Osterman Research, WeLiveSecurity, Dark Reading, Information Security Buzz, VinRansowmare, ToolBox, Quest Systems, Wired, NY Times and The VOIP Report.

4. RESULTS

From these 49 reports, we identified 59 unique factors, common to all reports, that provide protection against ransomware. Table 1 gives the list of all the recommended practices. We believe that it is necessary for organizations to prepare both proactive and reactive strategies against ransomware. Hence, we divided the recommendations as pre-attack and post-attack strategies. In addition, our assessment distinguished between technical and operational practices highlighting all the best practices. Furthermore, our study provides a sector-wise comparison which is comprised of the most recommended practices across these three sectors namely Government, Corporation, and Online Communities /Researchers/ Online Media. Below are the results of our analyses.

Table 1. Overview of Recommended Security Practices

Recommendations			
Backup	Pay Ransom	Endpoint Security	Mitigation Toolkit
Antivirus	Alert all	Robust Policy	BIOS Clock Change
Red Team Testing	Backup Security	Testing	Block N/W access
Hide Network Share	Firewall(IDS/IPS)	Authentic Software	Disabling Remote Desktop
Log Management	Delete Registry	Restrict Tailgating	Encryption Implementation
Web Browser Security	Safe Mode	Cyber Insurance	Shutdown
Pen Testing	External Device	Updates/Patches	Whitelisting
Vulnerability Assessment	Decrytper Check	Backup Frequency	Software Restriction Policy
Threat Intelligence	Restore/Reimage	Social Media Policy	Snapshot of system
Two Factor Authentication	Find Source/ Scope	Training	Network Segmentation
URL and Email	Port Block/Close(Open)	File Extension	Changing Password
Block Malicious IPs	Business Continuity Plan	Scanning Mails	Contact Authority
Data Protection Solution	Block Executable files	Virtualization	Disable JavaScript & Flash
Disable File Sharing	FSRM/File Monitor	Disable Macros	File Access Controls
Account Privileges	Ensure Database Integrity	Disconnect Systems	

4.1 Top 10 Recommended Practices

Our analysis has revealed the top 10 recommended practices across all the sectors. Clearly, Backup is the most recognized practice against ransomware with 42 reports recommending it. The following are the most recommended practices after backup: Updates/patches (39), Training (31), Account Privileges (25), Scanning Mails (24), Antivirus (24), Disable Macros (22), Pay ransom (19), Firewall (18) and Filters (17).

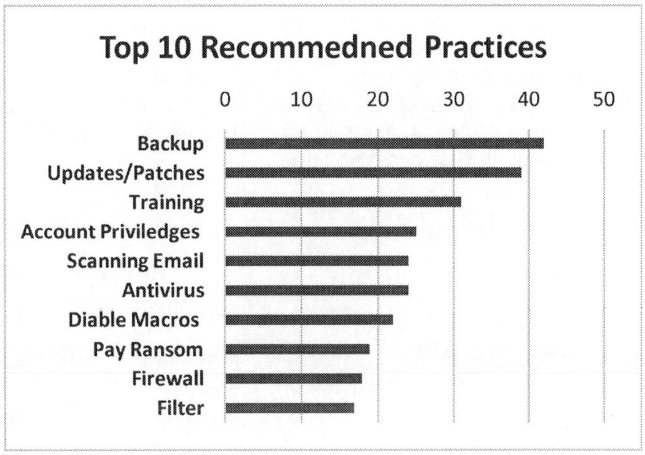

Figure 2. Top 10 Recommendations

4.2 Pre-Attack and Post-Attack Technical

Our analysis revealed that it would be practical to divide the recommendations into pre-attack and post-attack strategies. Therefore, we separated these reports into technical and operational recommendations based on our evaluation. As shown in Figure 3, the top pre-attack technical recommendations are backup (42), updates/patches (39), account privileges (25), scanning emails (24), antivirus (24), disable macros (22), firewalls (18) and filters (17).

In ransomware attacks, time is crucial since most organizations are given between 48-72 hours to pay the ransom. Therefore, it is in the organization's best interest to keep the downtime of their information systems to a minimum while having solid post-attack strategies in place to deal with the ransomware attack. As Figure 4 shows, the top post-attack technical recommendations given by all three sectors are restore/reimage and decrypter check.

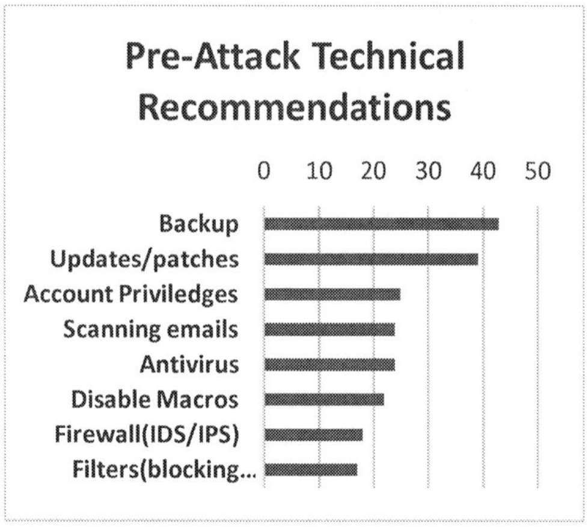

Figure 3. Pre-Attack Technical Recommendations

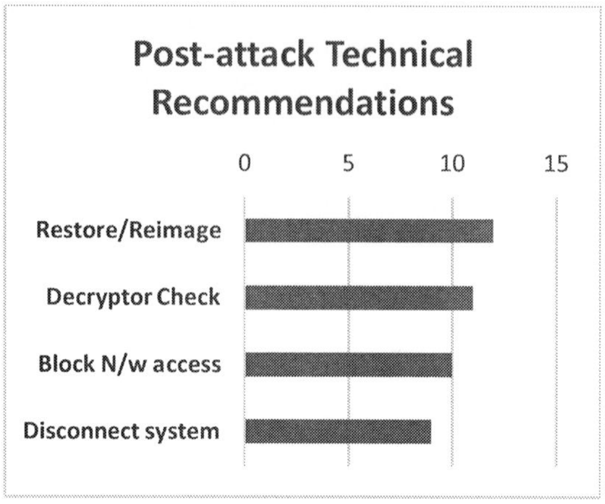

Figure 4. Post-Attack Technical Recommendations

4.3 Pre-Attack and Post-Attack Operational

As stated earlier, operational recommendations include the business-centric recommendations, which are equally as important as the technical ones. Our assessment, shown in Figure 5, indicates that the most followed pre-attack operational practices are training (63%) and business continuity/incident response planning (27%). Training is crucial in preventing against ransomware since the majority of ransomware infects via spam emails and malvertising campaigns, which are often not known to employees. Business continuity planning includes establishing regular back-ups of data, on and offline, so that even if organizations are locked out of their systems, they can continue their operations. For example, in the case of hospitals, it is important to continue operations even after an attack, and a good continuity plan will help to reduce the downtime for restoring the business operations.

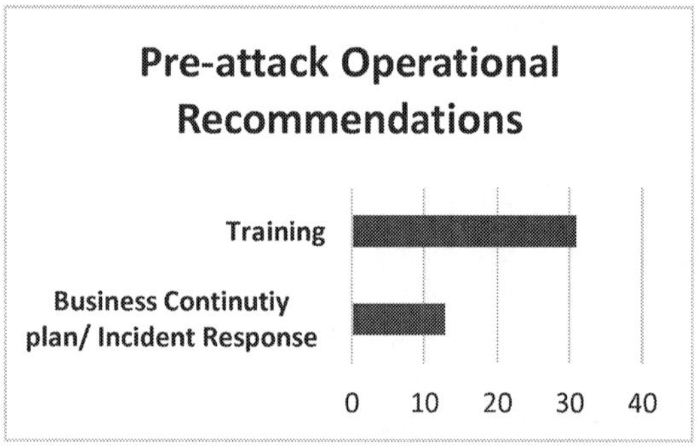

Figure 5. Pre-Attack Operational Recommendations

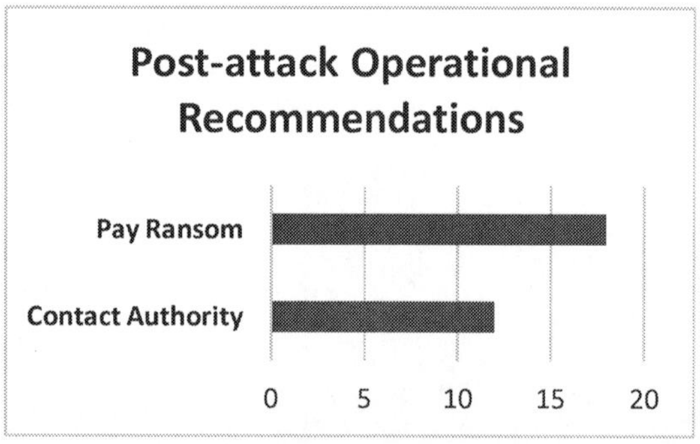

Figure 6. Post-Attack Operational Recommendations

Figure 6 shows the post-attack operational recommendations that include pay ransom (18), contacting authority (12), finding the source/scope (6) and alerting all (1). Not all the reports suggest paying the ransom, but there are few important ones that do (18). One such report was about an incident when people asked an FBI official about the ransom payment, and the FBI official suggested to pay the ransom to get the decrypted files back [Mohit Kumar, 2015]. The encryption techniques used in ransomware make it difficult to get the decrypted files, and many reports (31) do not recommend paying the ransom since it motivates and supports the adversary's intentions. When it comes to lifelong data or sensitive documents, or when the value of attacked data is much greater than the ransom itself, it becomes challenging to decide whether to pay the ransom or not. Organizations and individuals should evaluate all the outcomes, since there have been cases where the victims paid the ransom but did not get the files back [Phil Mccausland, 2017]. Shortage of time makes it difficult for the victim to decide, but if the defense mechanism is followed, one can avoid the dilemma of paying the ransom.

4.4 Sector-Wise Technical Recommendations

The impact of ransomware is on a massive scale; some industries are more frequently affected, such as government, healthcare, IT, energy, and finance. Therefore, it is necessary to highlight and study sector-wise recommendations and look at their approaches against ransomware. This section highlights the technical recommendations by all three sectors. The technical recommendations given by government organizations are backup, filters (blocking URLs, attachments), firewalls, account privileges, access controls, disabling the macros, whitelisting settings and ensuring database integrity.

The top technical recommendations given by online communities/researchers/news media include backup, filters, scanning emails, updates/patches, account privileges, disabling macros, and blocking network access after an attack.

The top technical recommendations by corporations, which include some of the top 50 information security companies, include backup, antivirus, scanning emails, firewalls, updates/patches, account privileges, disabling the macros, backup security, and endpoint security. It is important to note that while government sectors are not focusing on endpoint security devices, corporations are recommending many steps towards securing these devices to reduce the cyber-attacks.

4.5 Sector-Wise Operational Recommendations

Operational recommendations are often neglected because companies do not realize the worth of spending on trainings and risk management frameworks. We identified the major operational recommendations by corporations. The most recommended ones are training, contacting the authorities, paying ransom, and business continuity plans.

There are very few non-technical recommendations suggested by online community/researchers/ media. Training and ransom payment are the only operational recommendations that are suggested by this sector.

Government CERTs did not focus on the operational recommendations and mostly suggested technical practices. The only operational recommendations suggested by the government organizations is contacting the authority. It is important for the government CERTs to talk about the operational practices since these recommendations also contribute in making a secure system. Often, startups and small companies lack a dedicated IT team and hence have few people who can inform them about information security practices, so recommendations from government sources can be put to good use.

5. FUTURE WORK AND LIMITATIONS

Cybercriminals have taken the ransomware game to the next level by introducing services like RaaS and making anyone capable of launching attacks to extort money. There is still a lot of research to be done in order to understand the economics of ransomware. For example, in some recent attacks there was no apparent financial motive and the files were never decrypted even after the ransom was paid [Arjun, 2017]. In addition, research studies that investigates ransomware payments would be essential since it seems dubious that the only motive behind such attacks are financial. The amount that is collected from WannaCry and Petya [Arjun, 2017] is minimal, and it is unclear why some countries are affected more than others. The motive behind the attack is still not clear, and security researchers have different views on this topics. Future work would also involve analysis of ransomware genealogy since every ransomware has a different method of propagation. In addition, an in-depth analysis of ransomware and how it affects sectors like Healthcare, IT, Financial and small businesses is needed. Furthermore, it is important to assess the sensitivity of the data that is corrupted by ransomware across all industries. There has been limited research on propagation and priority mechanism of the files and folders.

One of the main limitations in our current study was the lack of prior scholarly published articles in our focused topic area, which limited us in comparing our results to prior findings. In addition, it is difficult to assess and report on the effectiveness of any of the top recommendations without a feedback loop from the individuals and organizations that have utilized these recommendations. As stated in the methodology section, our current analysis includes only reports that were publicly available and hence we may be missing vital recommendations that are not publicly available. Furthermore, since there are no known scholarly published standards or guidelines for individuals and organizations to date for pre-attack or post-attack best practices against ransomware, which makes the extent of our recommendations limited.

6. CONCLUSION

To summarize, we have collected and analyzed 49 reports from governments, corporations and research/ online media/ online communities that give best practices for defending against ransomware. Our assessment reveals that there is no single way of protecting yourself or your business through a single practice and that organizations should follow a guide and make a layered defense mechanism against ransomware. This research gives in-depth insight into best practices from sectors like Governments, Corporations and Online Communities /Researchers/ Online Media. Sector-wise recommendations can be helpful for specific industries to select a dedicated set of practices that are specific to their needs since it is difficult and financially burdensome to adopt all the recommended practices. For individuals, practices like backup, updates, antivirus and scanning mails are the top recommendations and are somewhat easy to adopt practices. In conclusion, to maintain the sanctity of data, advance preparation and adopting best practices will be the best possible way of avoiding ransomware and therefore organizations and individuals should choose both proactive and reactive approaches.

REFERENCES

A.Kharraz et al. 2015. Cutting the Gordian Knot: A Look Under the Hood of Ransomware Attacks. *International Conference on Detection of Intrusions and Malware, and Vulnerability Assessment (DIMVA), volume 9148 of Lecture Notes in Computer Science, Springer International Publishing. Milan, Italy.*

A. Kharraz et al. 2017. REDEMPTION: Real-time Protection Against Ransomware at End-Hosts. *Research in Attacks, Intrusions and Defenses.*

Arjun Kharpal. 2017. Hackers who infected 200,000 machines have only made $50,000 worth of bitcoin.

Acutec Study. 2017. How Ransomware Can Affect Businesses. Acutec UK.

Bill Conner. 2017. Ransomware as a Service- The next great cyber-threat.

Cisco, 2016. Midyear Cyber Security Report. Pp. 4-8.

Cyber Security 500. 2017. Cybersecurity ventures.

Erik Barnett. 2016. Would you like your Data Back? It will cost only $1000 – Love, Ransomware.

Harshada U. Salvi, Ravindra V. Kerkar. 2016. Ransomware: A Cyber Extortion. *Asian Journal of Convergence in Technology*, India, pp. 1-2.

Herb Weisbaum, 2017. Ransomware: Now a billion dollar a year rime and growing. NBCNews.

InfoSec Institute. 2017. A brief summary of encryption method used in widespread ransomware.

Kolodenker et. Al. 2017. PAYBREAK: De- fense against cryptographic ransomware. *Asia Conference on Computer and Communications Security (New York, NY, USA, 2017), ASIA CCS '17.*

Ladan Nikrayan Hayes. 2016. The History of Ransomware: Where it started and where it's going. SpiderOak.

Mohit Kumar. 2015. FBI suggest ransomware victims – Just pay the ransom.

Phil Mccausland. 2017. Companies are stockpiling bitcoins in anticipation of ransomware attacks. NBCNews.

Samir Thakkar, 2014. Ransomware- Exploring the Electronic form of Extortion. *International Journal for Scientific Research & Development* Vol 2, Issue 10. India.

TOWARDS A NEW REUSE CAPABILITY AND MATURITY MODEL

Siham Younoussi and Ounsa Roudies
Mohammed V University in Rabat, Ecole Mohammadia d'Ingénieurs (EMI), Siweb Research Team, Morocco

ABSTRACT

Current literature argues that adopting software reuse becomes a necessity for organizations to face competition and stand-out from the others, with proposing large range of techniques and methods. However, there is a high upfront risk of reuse adoption, because a significant initial organization investment is required with no guaranteed results. Several reuse maturity models are proposed in the literature to help organizations implementing an efficient reuse program, but they suffer from various issues that limit their adoption by organizations. Therefore, RCMM, the new Reuse Capability and Maturity Model, proposes new reuse practices, inspired by Agile approaches and Devops movement, that aim to assist companies obtain the real benefits of software reuse, and assess their current adoption of reuse best practices. This paper is a continuity of the research that refines and details the RCMM, it defines the Reuse Process Areas, Reuse Goals and Reuse Practices of this model.

KEYWORDS

Software Reuse, Capability and Maturity Model, Maturity Level, Reuse Practice, Reuse Process Area, Agile Approache

1. INTRODUCTION

For any organization, improving the business performance means perfecting their software development (Younoussi and Roudies, 2015). Systematic reuse offers great potential of significant gains for an organization, by reducing costs and efforts, and accelerating the time to market of software products (Younoussi and Roudies, 2015). However, developing and adopting adequate reuse strategies remain challenging, because of factors relating to organization's structure and culture (Garcia, 2010). That's why organizations need to reinforce reuse practices and process, towards an effective software reuse adoption model.

Several studies (Garcia, 2010), (Spoelstra, 2010), (Koltun and Hudson, 1991), (T. Davis, 1993), (Anshul and Sumesh, 2017) were interested on the industrial application of reuse, and especially on reuse maturity models. To benefit from reuse strengths and benefits, a significant initial organization investment is required, with defining strategy for adopting reuse in the correct way. Specific reuse maturity models are proposed in the literature, but most of them are either incomplete, or complex or not validated or not applicable in every context, like the Rise-RM (Garcia, 2010) (only in Brazilian software development companies).

Thus, a new maturity model for reuse (RCMM) was proposed in our last article (Younoussi and Roudies, 2018), in order to overcome limitations of the proposed models in the literature, to support organizations in the definition, evolution, and implementation of successful reuse program. The aim of the RCMM is: 1) To identify maturity model based on Reuse Maturity levels, Reuse Process Area and a set of Reuse Practices; 2) To identify capability model based on capability levels; and 3) To define model to assess the state of reuse practices by determining its score and relevance.

As RCMM model structure was already presented and accepted on our last work (Younoussi and Roudies, 2018), this work will define the 6 maturity levels of the model with providing Reuse Process Areas, Reuse Goals and Reuse practices and focus on the first three maturity levels.

The paper is organized as follow: section 2 presents related works, section 3 presents an overview of the RCMM model with reuse maturity levels covering reuse goals and practices, and finally a brief conclusion and future work are pointed-out in section 4.

2. RELATED WORKS

Several contributions in the field of software reuse research have been done, and some of reuse maturity models have been proposed to face the reuse adoption problem in organization. To identify these approaches, a survey was conducted and presented in our latest paper (Younoussi and Roudies, 2016). The aim of that article (Younoussi and Roudies, 2016), was to present some of the representative and relevant reuse models and framework on the literature and to propose a comparative study of these models based on some relevant criteria.

In the following some excerpts from these studies are presented:

In 1991, Koltun and Hudson (1991), presented the Reuse Maturity Model (RMM), with the aim to assess processes of an organization for achieving high levels of reuse (Younoussi and Roudies, 2016). The model consists of five maturity levels, like the levels defined by the CMMI model.

In 1993, Ted Davis (1993), presented the Reuse Capability Model (RCM), as a basis for understanding and improving an organization's reuse capability. The model has two components: an assessment model and an implementation model. The implementation model contains four stages and defines 21 Critical Success Factors corresponding to issues most critical to improving reuse capability.

Spoelstra in 2010 proposes a management tool for addressing software reuse issues, in the agile development organizations. The model is based on two main components, a reuse maturity model which consists of 5 maturity levels, and an assessment method which defines a way to assess the state of a reuse using score and relevance (Spoelstra, 2010).

The RiSE-RM model (Garcia, 2010), was proposed in 2010, a solution for adoption of software reuse in an incremental and systematic way and defined in accordance with the international standard ISO/IEC12207 (2008), and fulfills the requirements for reference process models as defined in the International Standard 15504-2 (2003). The model also complies with CMMI-DEV version 1.2 (2006) and MPS.BR (SOFTEX, 2007). The model consists of 7 maturity levels, 6 process capability levels that helps the organizations in assessing their maturity to implement reuse and determine the capability level of processes of the organization (Garcia, 2010).

Soora in 2014 presented the idea of domain engineering (Product Line engineering) as one of the key ideas for the implementation of systematic software reuse (Soora, 2014).

Anshul in 2017 proposed a framework called Software Reuse Division or SRD, which is dedicated to reuse of software components (Anshul and Sumesh, 2017). The framework is presented as a hierarchical structure with defining roles & responsibilities of persons, and has been measured using a comparison based approach with the RiSE– Reference Model (Garcia, 2010).

The presented models suffer from several problems that limits their acceptance by organizations that are interest in the Reuse process improvement, and want to stand-out in competitions for software projects. Most of works propose adoption reuse in atomic way rather than a systematic and incremental way. Few models like Rise-RM (Garcia, 2010) and Reuse Management Tool (Spoelstra, 2010) proposed to use systematic and incremental approach for implementing reuse in organizations and presented some reuse factors.

3. OVERVIEW OF THE REUSE CAPABILITY MATURITY MODEL

3.1 Methodology

Some studies were conducted (Younoussi and Roudies, 2015), (Younoussi and Roudies, 2016), to analyze several reuse models in the literature. Based on this analysis and on our proper experience on software organization, a decision was made (in (Younoussi and Roudies, 2018)) to combine, the following models:

1- CMMI-DEV v.1.3 (2010); 2- Rise-RM with some modifications based on expert recommendations (Garcia, 2010); 3- Reuse Management Tool (Spoelstra, 2010).

Rationales for basing our model on Rise-RM (Garcia, 2010) and Reuse Management Tool (Spoelstra, 2010) and more details about the methodology was given in (Younoussi and Roudies, 2018). The proposed model will also benefit from advantages of CMMI-DEV version 1.3 (2010) which is considered as the most international standard used in organization describing incremental steps to mature processes, based on best practices derived from many years of empirical study and contains some of sub-practices for reuse.

Limitations of the chosen models are the following:

- Rise-RM (Garcia, 2010):
  - Is not applicable under all circumstances and in every context (Only Brazilian companies) (Garcia, 2010)
  - Based on CMMI-DEV version 1.2 (old version)
  - No Reuse Assessment Method was proposed to evaluate the company reuse capability.
  - There is no practices in this model.
  - Model should be complement with new process area with different companies and domains (Garcia, 2010)
- Reuse Management Tool (Spoelstra, 2010):
  - Validation process is based on the perception of the researcher and the opinions of experts.
  - Proposed for agile development organizations.
  - Based on CMMI-DEV version 1.2 (old version)
- CMMI-DEV v.1.3 (2010):
  - Has only some sub-practices for software reuse, such as reuse design and reuse code (Garcia, 2010)
  - Not specialized on the reuse activities

In order to overcome the majority of these limitations, a new REUSE CAPABILITY MATURITY MODEL was proposed (Younoussi and Roudies, 2018), completed with recent popular approaches applied in software organization as Lean (Poppendieck, 2007) and Devops (Hüttermann, 2012) to aid organizations to be more competitive.

3.2 RCMM Architecture

The RCMM (Younoussi and Roudies, 2018) defines 6 Reuse Maturity Levels composed by several Reuse Process Areas. Each Reuse Process Area has a Reuse Goal and its related Reuse Practices. For each Reuse Practice, two components are defined: Sub-practices and work product (See Figure A).

In the following, the definitions of these elements are given:

- Reuse Maturity levels: A maturity level in RCMM is defined as the overall degree of reuse process capability that a company possesses (Srivastava and Nair, 2017).
- Reuse Process Area: A reuse process area is a cluster of related reuse practices that must be performed to achieve a maturity level. The improvement in the activities related to a reuse process area is accomplished when all practices of that area and its reuse goal are performed.
- Reuse Goals: A reuse goal describes the unique characteristics that must be performed to satisfy the reuse process area.
- Reuse practices: The reuse practices describe the activities that are expected to result in achievement of the reuse goals of a reuse process area.
- Sub-practices: a sub-practice is a description that provides guidance for interpreting and implementing the reuse practice.
- Work product: a list of the outputs that resulted from a reuse practice. In our model, it's an artifact including files, documents, parts of product, processes, specifications, etc.

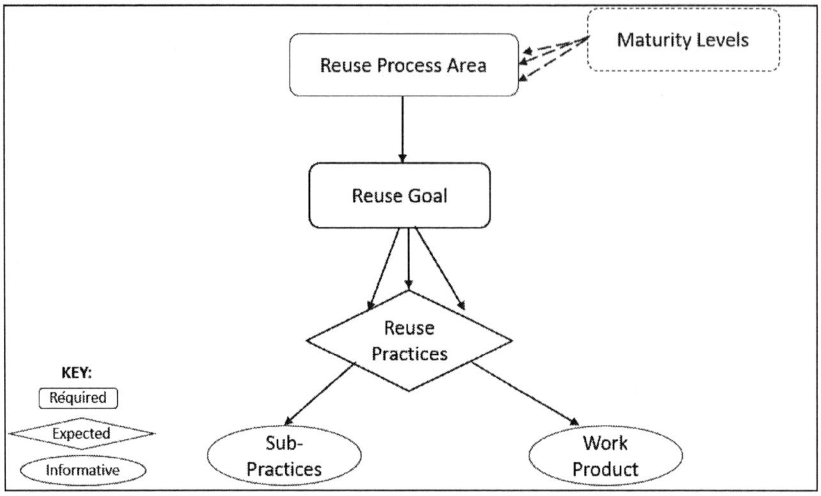

Figure 1. The Proposed RCMM Model Component (Younoussi and Roudies, 2018)

3.3 Reuse Maturity Levels, Goals and Practices

RCMM has 6 Reuse Maturity Levels that describe an evolutionary path for an organization that wants to improve its reuse process. Reuse maturity levels where adapted from the Maturity levels presented by Rise-RM (Garcia, 2010), and Management Tool Model (Srivastava and Nair 2017). Each maturity level consists of a set of reuse process areas. Each reuse Process area has a reuse goal and its related reuse practices. For an organization wants to reach a particular reuse maturity level, it must satisfy all of the set of reuse practices that are targeted for improvement.

In this section, reuse maturity models are presented, and details of 3 levels are provided. This work will be limited on the presentation of reuse Goals and reuse practices of levels 2, 3 and 4. Advanced levels will be detailed on future works.

Defined reuse practices are retrieved from models: CMMI-DEV v.1.3 (2010); Rise-RM (Garcia, 2010); Reuse Management Tool (Spoelstra, 2010), and are adapted and completed by literature (ISO/IEC, 2003) , (ISO/IEC, 2006), (T. Davis, 1993), (Anshul and Sumesh, 2017). So for levels 2,3 and 4 each Reuse process Area has a Reuse Goal and some practices (PR1, PR2, etc.).

3.3.1 Level 1: Informal

In this level, no formal reuse processes are defined and reuse practice depends on individual initiative, based on previous experience (Spoelstra, 2010). The copy past from previous projects is the most used, even if some other reuse practices can be found such as Component based Development, Design Patterns, etc., reuse costs and benefits are unknown at this level (Garcia, 2010). No practices are defined in this level.

3.3.2 Level 2: Initial

This level is defined by a basic usage of reusable assets like documents, design, code… (Garcia, 2010), to aid in the implementation of new components and documentation. Basic reuse techniques and tools are identified and recommended to be used by the organization, and are evaluated by defining policies to ensure their consistent application (Garcia, 2010). Organization builds its first reusable artifacts (code, test, documentation…) which are, packaged and published in a shared area to promote reuse in several projects (Garcia, 2010).

Reuse Process area: Basic Reuse Techniques and Tools (BRTT)

Reuse goal: Basic reuse techniques and tools are identified and recommended to be used by the organization.

RP1: Define and document a set of reuse techniques and tools [Rise-RM-BRT1(Garcia, 2010)]

RP2: Establish tools or environment to support activities towards the reuse activities [Rise-RM-BRT2 (Garcia, 2010)]

RP3: Establish a shared area in the organization for packaging and publishing reusable artifacts produced by the company [Rise-RM-BRT3 (Garcia, 2010) ; ISO/IEC 15504-REU.2 - BP04(ISO/IEC, 2003), (ISO/IEC, 2006)]

RP4: Establish and maintain a configuration management plan for reusable artifacts [Rise-RM-BRT4 (Garcia, 2010); Management Tool – Factor 10 (Spoelstra, 2010)]

Reuse Process Area: Reusable Artifacts Implementation (RAI)
Reuse goal: reusable software artifacts are defined and implemented.

RP1: Identify requirement similarities for developing reusable artifacts in the most generic way [Rise-RM-RAI1 (Garcia, 2010); Management Tool – Factor 7 (Spoelstra, 2010); Davis - Similarity/variation definition (T. Davis, 1993)]

RP2: Define reusable artifact interfaces [Rise-RM-RAI2 (Garcia, 2010); Davis - Asset development factor (T. Davis, 1993)]

RP3: Define unit test for each reusable artifact according to its specification and on different possible reuse context [Rise-RM-RAI3 (Garcia, 2010); Davis - Asset evaluation and verification (T. Davis, 1993)].

RP4: Implement reusable artifacts identified as similar requirements (RP1), and based on defined interfaces (RP3) [Rise-RM-RAI4 (Garcia, 2010)]].

3.3.3 Level 3: Planned

At this level, a standard reuse strategy is defined for the different reuse levels (code, design and documentation) and reusable artifacts are categorized and stored.

Software reusable artifacts previously constructed are reusing for projects independently of the business issues. Organization will plan its reuse efforts based on several reuse practices which are standardized and deployed in the whole organization (Garcia, 2010).

Reuse Process Area: Software Development with Reuse (DWR)
Reuse goal: Reusable artifacts are selecting, adapting, integrating and testing, and their effort for integration into the system is estimated.

RP1: Perform search activity to identify potential reusable artifacts to be reused in the part of application which did not need to be built from scratch [Rise-RM-DWR1 (Garcia, 2010); Davis - Asset identification (T. Davis, 1993); ISO/IEC 15504_REU.1 - BP05 ((ISO/IEC, 2003), (ISO/IEC, 2006))]

RP2: Implement a decision-making process, to decide whether to reuse, build or buy some artifact [Rise-RM- DWR2 (Garcia, 2010)]]

RP3: Perform testing of combined reusable artifacts at whole, to detect integration errors [Rise-RM- DWR3 (Garcia, 2010); Davis - Asset evaluation and verification (T. Davis, 1993)].

RP4: Estimate the reuse effort for the reusable artifacts integration into the System [Rise-RM- DWR4 (Garcia, 2010); Davis - Asset evaluation and verification (T. Davis, 1993); ISO/IEC 15504_REU.2 - BP03 ((ISO/IEC, 2003), (ISO/IEC, 2006)); Devops-Continuous programming (Hüttermann, 2012)]

Reuse Process Area: Define Reuse Standards and Quality Criteria (DRS)
Reuse goal: Reuse standard are and unified rules are defined.

RP1: Establish and maintain a set of reuse standards for the different reuse levels (code, design and documentation) [Rise-RM-DRS1 (Garcia, 2010)]

RP2: Identify development components that will be placed under reuse standards [Rise-RM- DRS2 (Garcia, 2010)]

RP3: Define and maintain tailoring criteria and guidelines for the company's reuse standards [Rise-RM- DRS3 (Garcia, 2010)]

RP4: Track and control the reuse standard changes [Rise-RM- DRS4 (Garcia, 2010)]

Reuse Process Area: Planning for Reuse (PR)

Reuse goal: Reuse strategy and plan are defined and documented, and reuse committee is selected for managing reuse goals.

RP1: Define a reuse plan with a set of goals [Management Tool – Factor 5 (Spoelstra, 2010); Davis - Planning and direction (T. Davis, 1993)].

RP2: Define and share a strategy to reach the reuse goals [Rise-RM- RGD3 (Garcia, 2010); ISO/IEC 15504_REU.3 - BP01 ((ISO/IEC, 2003), (ISO/IEC, 2006))]

RP3: Establish and document the reuse strategy in the project plan [Rise-RM- RGD2]

RP4: Design a reuse committee responsible for managing the reuse goals and reuse strategy [Rise-RM- RGD4 (Garcia, 2010); Management Tool – Factor 3 (Spoelstra, 2010); Davis - Organizational commitment (T. Davis, 1993)].

Reuse Process Area: Reusable Artifacts Management (RAM)

Reuse goal: A process management of reusable artifacts is implemented to manage reusable artifacts threw repository.

RP1: Implement a reusable artifacts management process [Rise-RM-RAM1 (Garcia, 2010); ISO/IEC 15504_REU.2 - BP01((ISO/IEC, 2003), (ISO/IEC, 2006))]; Davis - Process definition and integration (T. Davis, 1993)].

RP2: Establish repository or library system to manage (store, search, retrieval and evolve) the different versions of the reusable artifacts [Rise-RM- RAM2 (Garcia, 2010); Management Tool – Factor 13 (Spoelstra, 2010); ISO/IEC 15504_REU.2 - BP04 ((ISO/IEC, 2003), (ISO/IEC, 2006))], SRD framework – Factor 14 (Anshul and Sumesh, 2017); Devops- Architecture (Hüttermann, 2012)]

RP3: Establish a classification scheme for assets [ISO/IEC 15504_REU.2 - BP02 ((ISO/IEC, 2003), (ISO/IEC, 2006)); Rise-RM- DRS3 (Garcia, 2010); Management Tool – Factor 10 (Spoelstra, 2010)]

RP4: Review and update the classification scheme constantly to reflect the evolution of the registered artifacts [Rise-RM- DRS3 (Garcia, 2010)]

3.3.4 Level 4: Managed

In this level, the reuse program is defined and supported by management by designing a reuse committee with a leader and responsibilities. Reuse processes and activities are standardized and integrated into the software development life cycle (Garcia, 2010), (Spoelstra, 2010). At this level, the company can evolve a systematic way to produce its product (Garcia, 2010). A procedure defining the domain scope is identified and commonalities and variabilities are specified, which is in line with the software product line approach.

Reuse Process Area: Maintain Traceability Among Reusable Artifacts (TRA)

Reuse goal: Traceability between reusable artifacts is defined and documented to maintain the relationships between the different reusable artifacts.

RP1: Define A traceability framework to establish all relationships among the reusable artifacts and the way they relate to each other [Rise-RM-TRA1 (Garcia, 2010); SRD framework – Factor 16 (Anshul and Sumesh, 2017); Davis - Tool support (T. Davis, 1993)].

RP2: Define and document a set of traceability requirements for the development process of the company [Rise-RM- TRA2 (Garcia, 2010); Management Tool – Factor 7 (Spoelstra, 2010); SRD framework – Factor 11 (Anshul and Sumesh, 2017)]

RP3: Integrate the traceability requirements in the development process to maintain the relationships between the different reusable artifacts [Rise-RM- TRA3 (Garcia, 2010); Management Tool – Factor 7 (Spoelstra, 2010); SRD framework – Factor 11 (Anshul and Sumesh, 2017)]

RP4: Manage traceability information and version control in the Software configuration management [Rise-RM- TRA4 (Garcia, 2010); Management Tool – Factor 10 (Spoelstra, 2010); SRD framework – Factor 11(Anshul and Sumesh, 2017)].

Reuse Process Area: Manage Reuse Unit (MRU)

Reuse goal: A reuse unit is created integrating the reuse committee, to monitor and control reuse issues in the company.

RP1: Establish a reuse dedicated team with a leader by the top management of the company [Rise-RM-MRU1 (Garcia, 2010); Management Tool – Factor 2 (Spoelstra, 2010); SRD framework – Factor 2 (Anshul and Sumesh, 2017); Davis – Organizational commitment (T. Davis, 1993)].

RP2: Define a set of rules and responsibilities for the reuse team [Rise-RM- MRU2 (Garcia, 2010); Management Tool – Factor 3 (Spoelstra, 2010) ; SRD framework – Factor 3 (Anshul and Sumesh, 2017)]

RP3: Establish a communication cannel for propagating reuse information within and outside the organization [Rise-RM- MRU4 (Garcia, 2010); Management Tool – Factor 4; SRD framework – Factor 4 (Anshul and Sumesh, 2017)]

RP4: Encourage the reuse team to pursue opportunities and give him the autonomy to make decisions. [Lean – Respect People (Poppendieck, 2007)]; Lean- Create Knowledge (Poppendieck, 2007)]

Reuse Process Area: Reuse Integration into the Software Life Cycle (REI)

Reuse goal: Reuse practices are integrated into the company's software process.

RP1: Integrate reuse activities into the software life cycle [Rise-RM- REI1 (Garcia, 2010); Davis – Process definition and integration (T. Davis, 1993)].

RP2: Establish a communication cannel for propagating reuse information within and outside the organization [Rise-RM- MRU4 (Garcia, 2010); Management Tool – Factor 4 (Spoelstra, 2010); SRD framework – Factor 4 (Anshul and Sumesh, 2017)]

3.3.5 Level 5: Quantitively Managed

At this level the reuse program is quantitatively managed, reuse processes are controlled using quantitative analysis techniques and methods (Garcia, 2010), (Spoelstra, 2010). Software product quality goals are established and documented into the reuse plan (Garcia, 2010). the company is able to evolve in a systematic way to produce its products based on target domain. Functions are identified to measure reuse costs and benefits within reuse program to evaluate if it is valuable to invest or not in one or more reuse scenarios (Garcia, 2010).

In this work only practices are resented, practices details will be given in future works.

Reuse Process Area: Domain Analysis (DA)
Reuse Process Area: Asset Quality Control (AQC)
Reuse Process Area: Reuse Cost Model (RCM)

3.3.6 Level 6: Anticipating/Optimization

In this level company investigate and analyze new business opportunities based on the return on reuse investment analysis (Garcia, 2010). Predictable reusable assets and High payoff assets are identified, to satisfied new business demands and customers' needs, in a much shorter time.

Reuse Process Area: ROI and Market Conditions Analysis
Reuse Process Area: Reusable Assets Predictability

4. CONCLUSION AND FUTURE WORK

Organizations try to adopt software reuse because of its potential effect on competitiveness. The reuse community (Spoelstra, 2010), (M. Davis, 1992), (T. Davis, 1993), (Rine and Nada, 2000), agrees that characterizing reuse with maturity models and adoption reuse processes is a clear sign of progress towards making reuse a natural part of development (T. Davis, 1993).

This paper presented RCMM, a new Reuse Capability and Maturity Model (Younoussi and Roudies, 2018) based on international standards, and completed with literature approaches to help organizations implementing an efficient reuse program. The idea is to propose a common maturity model, covering a wide category of software. As CMMI is indeed very popular in software engineer community, we choose to adopt its way of evaluation and concepts. However, a sixth level of maturity was introduced because reuse processes are indeed not recommended at institutional level. Practices as Agile approaches and Devops movement are also considered.

In this paper, the six Maturity Levels are presented, composed by Reuse Process Area, Reuse Goals and Reuse Practices. For level 1 to 4 associated Reuse goals are described and 34 Reuse practices are defined.

As a future work, advanced levels of the RCMM model will be detailed (Level 5 and 6) with reuse goals and reuse practices, and validation of the model will be performed. The validation of the model is underway by an expert panel gathering both practitioners and academics. Thus, process areas and practices and their relationships to the maturity levels are being evaluated. A second validation will be performed by some software companies to assess the feasibility and completeness of the model.

REFERENCES

Anshul, K. Sumesh, S., 2017. A Comparison Based Framework for Reuse Adoption in an Organization. *Indian Journal of Computer Science and Engineering (IJCSE)*.

CMMI, 2010. *CMMI for Development, Version 1.3*. www.sei.cmu.edu

Davis, M. J., 1992. Stars Reuse Maturity Model: Guidelines for Reuse Strategy Formulation. *Proceedings of the Fifth Annual Workshop on Institutionalizing Software Reuse*. Palo Alto, California, USA, pp. 1-6.

Davis, T., 1993. The reuse capability model: A basis for improving an organization's reuse capability. *Proceedings of the 2nd International Workshop on Software Reuse*. Lucca, Italy.

Garcia, V.C., 2010. RiSE Reference Model for Software Reuse Adoption in Brazilian Companies. From web site http://ivanmachado.com.br/research/rise/thesis/files/2010_ViniciusGarcia_phd.pdf accessed on 25/03/2016.

Hüttermann, M., 2012. Introducing DevOps. *DevOps for Developers*. Apress, Berkeley, CA, p. 15-31.

ISO/IEC, 2008. *ISO/IEC 12207 Systems and Software Engineering - Software Life Cycle Processes*. International standard, ISO (the International Organization for Standardization) and IEC (the International Electrotechnical Commission).

ISO/IEC, 2003. *IS 15504-2: Information technology – Process assessment – Part 2: Performing an assessment*

ISO/IEC, 2006. *IS 15504-5: Information technology – Process Assessment – Part 5: An exemplar Process Assessment Model*.

Koltun P., and Hudson, A., 1991. A reuse maturity model. *4th Annual Workshop on Sofware Reuse, Hemdon,* Virginia.

Poppendieck, M., 2007. Lean software development. *Companion to the proceedings of the 29th International Conference on Software Engineering*. IEEE Computer Society, p. 165-166.

Rine D. C., and Nada, N., 2000. An empirical study of a software reuse reference model. *Information and Software Technology,*Vol. 42, pp. 47-65.

Soora S.K., 2014. A Framework for Software Reuse and Research Challenges. *International Journal of Advanced Research in Computer Science and Software Engineering*, Vol. 4, No. 10, 441-448.

Spoelstra, W., 2010. Reusing Software Assets in Agile Development Organizations-A Management Tool. From web site http://essay.utwente.nl/59917/1/MA_thesis_W_Spoelstra.pdf accessed on 30/03/2015.

Srivastava, D.K. and Nair, P., 2017. An Extensive Conception of Reusability in Software Component Engineering. *Proceedings of International Conference on Communication and Networks, Advances in Intelligent Systems and Computing*. Springer, Singapore, pp. 449-457.

SEI/CMU, 2006. *CMMI for Development, Version 1.2*

SOFTEX, 2007. *MPS.BR - Brazilian Software Process Improvement, General Guide (Version 1.2)*. Technical report, Association for Promoting the Brazilian Software Excellence – SOFTEX.

Younoussi, S., Roudies, O., 2015. All about software reusability: a systematic literature review. *Journal of Theoretical & Applied Information Technology*. vol. 76, no 1.

Younoussi, S., Roudies, O., 2016. Capability and maturity model for Reuse: A comparative study. *Cloud Computing Technologies and Applications (CloudTech),2nd International Conference on IEEE*. Morocco, Marrakech, p. 302-308.

YounoussI, S. and Roudies, O., 2018. A New Reuse Capability and Maturity Model: An Overview. *Proceedings of the 2018 International Conference on Software Engineering and Information Management*. ACM, Casablanca, Morocco, pp. 26-31.

Short Papers

MIGRATING GOOGLE CLOUD SDK TO THE CLOUD CASE STUDY: GAE LAUNCHER

Orges Çiço[1], Zamir Dika[2], Betim Çiço[2] and Kozeta Sevrani[1]
[1]*Faculty of Economy, University of Tirana, Tirana, Albania*
[2]*South East European University, Tetovo, Macedonia*
[3]*Computer Engineering Department, Epoka University, Tirana, Albania*

ABSTRACT

In this paper we propose the implementation and migration of the existing cloud SDK (Software Development Kit) on the cloud platform. Moreover an integrated development environment (IDE) fully supporting Google Cloud Python SDK (Software Development Kit) on the cloud infrastructure has been part of the ongoing development within the scope of this work. Our architecture fulfills the need to have an IDE environment totally independent from personal desktop environments. The working architecture and a business model of the online IDE and SDK are presented. Further discussion is made how this migration could become part of the rest of cloud infrastructures and maybe provided as a core service .

KEYWORDS

Google Cloud SDK, Integrated Development Environment, Cloud Services

1. INTRODUCTION

We propose the migration of the current cloud Software Development Kit (SDK) on the cloud PaaS (Platform as a Service) infrastructure.

Since many global web applications today are commonly implemented on the cloud infrastructure this proves their dependability on the latter.

Development has become a critical issue for cloud designers (developers and project managers) which struggle with a whole set of different programming languages, tools, SDKs and environments. This arises the need of development environments that are fully operational within the cloud infrastructure.

First we describe the current trends in cloud development and then we provide with the current state of the art of other providers offering similar services. Either ad-hoc (Code Run, JAVAWIDE) or third party solutions (Bespin)have been adopted so far. Advantages of utilizing online development environments have been largely understood and discussed (A. van Deursen et al. 2010, A. Zeller 2007, R. Frost 2007).

After we discuss the adopted methodology in migrating the Google Cloud SDK into its own PaaS infrastructure, the case study features and capabilities of a running application called GAE Launcher (Google App Engine Launcher) are described together with a business model so that it can evolve into a self sustainable system.

The case study results not only prove the feasibility of fully supporting cloud development tools within the cloud infrastructure by relying on REST API (representational state transfer application programming interfaces), but it also opens up new challenges for better collaborative project managements, faster deployments and better utilization of the cloud from the application designers, developers and project managers.

2. BACKGROUND

2.1 Cloud SDK and IDE Tools

The cloud SDK commonly represents a set of tools for Cloud Platforms, which allow the end user to fully exploit the cloud infrastructure at different service level (PaaS, IaaS). Such tools are usually part of CLI (Command Line Interface) or GUI (Graphical User Interface) interfaces mostly common in the major cloud providers. The SDK-s also support multiple programming languages and the primary objective is to allow not just development but also management of virtual clusters of computers.Each of which have the similar properties to personal computers and provide primarily virtualization of basic computing components and I/O, thus the systems can provide services starting from Web servers and continuing with CRM, database, computation, etc.

Most of the services for every major cloud provider such as Amazon, Azure and Google operate with on-demand or pay per use strategy (Amazon Web Services, Google Cloud Tools,Microsoft Azure). The platforms are very flexible for every individual, business or governmental sector.

The approach for developing and deploying applications is also similar to using enterprise desktop based tools containing either IDE or SDK and sometimes both. Worth mentioning gcloud/GAE, AWS and Visual Studio for Google, Amazon and Azure Cloud respectively.

Sometimes the third party tools/plugins are also available and offer a flexibility of choices for different Operating Systems or working environments. One good reference is how Google Tools have been adopted for such purpose (Google Cloud Tools).

The set of programming languages and environments supported proves the flexibility of current cloud platforms to support a large scale of technologies, Table 1.

Table 1. Supported Programming Languages of Major Cloud Providers

Cloud Provider	Denomination	PaaS Supported Programming Languages
Google	Google App Engine	Go, PHP, Java, Python, Node, .NET, Ruby
Amazon	AWS Elastic Beanstalk	Java, .NET, PHP, Node.js, Python, Ruby, Go
Microsoft Azure	Azure Cloud Services	Java, .NET, PHP, Node.js, Python, Ruby

The establishment of an integrated Cloud based IDE environment on demand would not just reduce the scale of licensing, but also contribute into optimizing individual, business and enterprise resources when it comes to development of large scale applications. Most developers won't be restricted from proprietary tools of third party entities and shall rely mostly on the cloud infrastructure they prefer to keep their development going. This would not just reduce the operational cost but also help in increasing the productivity and collaborative approaches for distributed working environments.

Moreover within the Google Cloud infrastructure as well as in the others, already exist solutions for debugging in real time, such as Stackdriver Debugger. It offers debugging in production capabilities and synchronizing with different versioning repositories such as Google Cloud Source Repository, GitHub, Bitbucket or GitLab (Stackdriver).

This approach is fully integratable with the idea of collaborative development environment running on the cloud platform.

3. STATE OF THE ART

There have been few but important initiatives related to move development environments on Web Browsers. Some of them were specifically related to particular needs such as embedded computing and software development (J. Hausladen et al. 2014) others more general (L. Wu et al. 2011). One of the first was founded since 2010 by providing basic features for code highlighting and more advanced related to cloud code deployment for major providers such as AWS (Amazon Web Services), Microsoft Azure, Google App Engine. Only recent environments have however tried to fully integrate the IDE with the cloud SDK by facilitating not just the development, testing and debugging but also the deployment process.

3.1 Cloud 9

Founded in 2010 proves the concept of moving IDE oriented services to the Web. Thus code development and accessibility is made easy enough and relies on browser development.

Acquired from the Amazon Cloud Services, it relies on the web EC2 Operating System or other web oriented technology such as Aurora filesystem and the RDBMS for database management. Moreover team collaboration is made easy by full integration of repositories such as Github, Bitbucket with the online shared workspaces (Cloud9).

3.2 Condevy

Condevy was originally launched in 2012 and has become since then a popular cloud based development environment.

Developers can work with shared, scalable and distributed workspaces, which result in better compilation and deployment times. The environments are commonly set up as sandboxes where all the necessary configuration are pre-arranged so that the development process can focus primarily towards the final application. This has become since then the common approach for Dockers exploitation, commonly done behind the scenes also from Condevy (Condevy).

4. METHODOLOGY

In this section we shall describe the possibility of adopting similar concepts for a general purpose IDE environment (encapsulating the different cloud SDK). While in the next section we shall provide with a feasibility sample of the model developed on the PaaS of Google Cloud Platform.

Based on the previous sections we propose that the model should include several entities :

1. Browser based SDK fully integrated with the different service layers (PaaS, IaaS) and their REST API-s or client libraries
2. Browser based IDE encapsulating the SDK functionalities running on the platform
3. Development tool that fully exploits the pay per use or pay as you go model
4. Coding Synchronization through Versioning or Agile Environments (GitHub, Jira etc.). The developers can also use other offline IDE-s with their common environment and synchronization is made from collaborative repositories.

Integrating the development environment platform in the cloud and treating it as a usual service layer shall provide end cloud users not only with an integrated development environment which can scale at demand, but also provide development teams with better upfront cost evaluation, help them focus on fast and efficient coding and meeting project deadlines, rather than setting up collaborative environments.

Community based open source coding will be facilitated even further throughout team collaborations.

Figure 1 shows that most cloud providers can adopt the service as a third party cloud application at software layer.

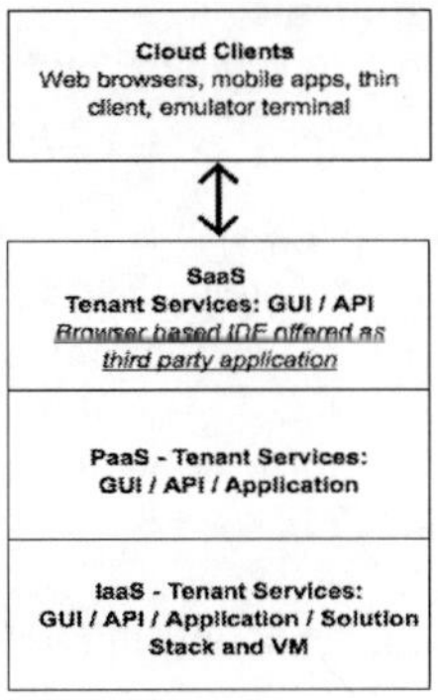

Figure 1. Browser based IDE/SDK running on Cloud Webserver and integrated into the SaaS

Proof of the concept and model adoption is presented in the following section, where actual development and integration of the GAE Launcher service has been performed for one of the major cloud providers (Google Cloud).

5. CASE STUDY - GAE LAUNCHER

The section presents the actual migration of the google cloud python SDK-s libraries from their desktop environment to the Google App Engine. The deployment process which was previously done from the desktop application has been made possible to be completed from a GAE VM.

Moreover, a simple code interpreter has also been developed offering the possibility to implement and link the code getting deployed directly on the cloud. GAE Launcher has also the possibility to synchronize with local code which can be uploaded on GitHub repositories.

More features can be added in the future and the development could become part of the cloud infrastructure by playing a key role and not just act as an application running on Google PaaS which can later be part of the SaaS application pools.

Thus more functionalities from gcloud tool could contribute for creating a more sophisticated development environment fully integrated to the cloud.

5.1 Migrating GAE Desktop SDK to the Cloud

The migration of the Google App Engine Launcher python SDK from desktop to the GAE environment has involved the modification of several SDK libraries and their adoption with client libraries (Django Support). In particular the appcfg.py has been adopted to run on the GAE VM (Virtual Machine) environment. Common modifications relate to limitations to the environment such as lack of file system, spawning of processes etc. Thus other cloud services such as google cloud storage and sql have been used instead of local filesystem. And the application has to run as a single web service process. Thus the major changes to the Google SDK code (Google Cloud Python API, Google Cloud Tools) are related to modifying the appcfg.main(argv) as below:

```
def main(argv):
  logging.basicConfig(format=('%(asctime)s %(levelname)s %(filename)s:' '%(lineno)s %(message)s '))
  try:
    result = AppCfgApp(argv).Run()
    if result:
      sys.exit(result)
  except KeyboardInterrupt:
    StatusUpdate('Interrupted.')
    sys.exit(1)
```

which is then passed a list of arguments representing the functionality to be run. Common tasks are :

1. **Authentication and Deploy Arguments:**
   argv = ["./google/appengine/tools/appcfg.py", 'update', '/gaelauncher/' + 'user @gmail.com' , "--email=" + 'user@gmail.com', "--passin"]
2. **Rollback Arguments:**
   argv = ["./google/appengine/tools/appcfg.py", 'rollback', '/gaelauncher']
3. **Creating/Deleting/Editing project** source code acquired from google cloud storage (or git repositories). Preliminary condition is that the project should already be a registered project on the Google Cloud Console.
4. **Getting logs** For each operation performed the user can visualize current logs. For this purpose the google-cloud-sdk logservice.py module has been exploited. One example displaying error logs is as follows:
   tot_logs=logservice.fetch(end_time=end_time,minimum_log_level=logservice.LOG_LEVEL_ERROR,include_app_logs=True)

The first step in accessing the application as a SaaS solution was to perform the user authentication with the backend. There are two methods adopted for this purpose :

1. Exploiting the username and password for the user and as a list of arguments upon project deployment. Drawback is that end user has to provide the credentials to the application, alongside full permission to other different services. Thus this makes the approach not the best option.
2. OAuth 2 for web server authentication, is a more secure approach (OAuth2 Python API). Moreover there exist full support for integrating it with Django Framework (GAE Launcher as PaaS Application).

Next section discusses further opportunities alongside the features offered so far for the integration. The entire code has been integrated into Django Framework 1.11 based on Python 2.7.

The environment shown in Figure 1, currently allows users to perform common tasks already available from the desktop GUI SDK application (Google App Engine Launcher):

- Create/Delete project
- Edit existing project files
- Cloud deployment on the GAE VM
- Rollback of deployment processes
- Logging retrieval
- Integration with other google cloud services for debugging

Figure 2 a,b,c,d. displays some of the currently developed features.

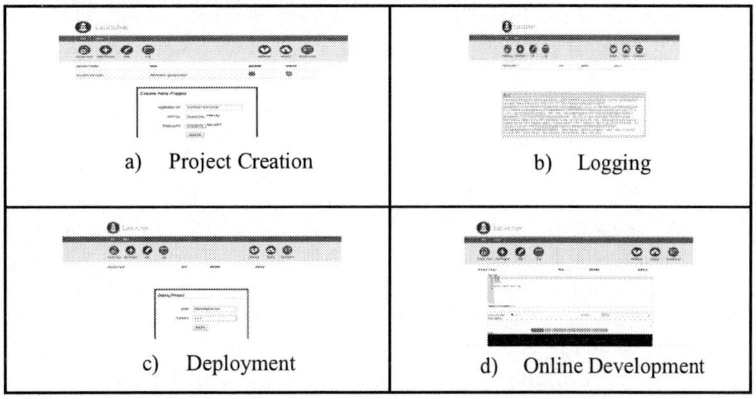

Figure 2. Developed features of the Cloud SDK on the Google Cloud Infrastructure (GAE Launcher as PaaS Application)

Further integration with cloud based PM tools such as Asana and Jira are part of the important features to be considered and developed.

6. CONCLUSION

Major cloud providers are becoming aware of the developer needs and already supporting online development tools, although most of them are still relying on old fashioned downloadable SDK-s. The major benefit of the presented case study, like any other service, it can provide new features based on cloud end user demands as well as generate solid revenues for every provider adopting the business models relying on it.

The present solution proposed in this paper GAE Launcher provides all the features already offered from the Desktop SDK application but integrating further new services which have already been offered online for a long time (Git repositories, PM tools etc.).

Offline provisioning and online synchronization solution as well as integration with other existing tools, by means of plugins or addons, should become part of the core functionalities of the service, so that developers would still feel comfortable continuing their work even when online connection is lost.

Future trends will prove the effectiveness and allow more cloud providers to adopt the proposed platform and models, where machine learning and artificial intelligence will ease the cloud application development process.

REFERENCES

A. van Deursen, A. Mesbah, B. Cornelissen, A. Zaidman, M. Pinzger, and A. Guzzi,2010, *Adinda: a knowledgeable, browser-based IDE*; In ICSE, pp.203-206.

A. Zeller, 2007,*The future of programming environments: Integration, synergy, and assistance*

Amazon Web Services: https://en.wikipedia.org/wiki/Amazon_Web_Services

Bespin: https://mozillalabs.com/skywriter/2010/10/01/bespin-0-9a2-released-skywriter-update/

CodeRun: http://www.coderun.com/ide/

Cloud9: https://aws.amazon.com/cloud9/

Condevy: https://codenvy.com/

Django Support: https://developers.google.com/api-client-library/python/guide/django

GAE Launcher as PaaS Application : http://gaelauncher.appspot.com/

Google Cloud Python API : https://cloud.google.com/resource-manager/reference/rest/v1/projects/create

Google Cloud Tools: https://cloud.google.com/docs/overview/developer-and- admin-tools

JAVAWIDE: http://www.javawide.org

J. Hausladen, B. Pohn and M. Horauer,2014,*A cloud-based integrated development environment for embedded systems*, IEEE/ASME 10th International Conference on Mechatronic and Embedded Systems and Applications (MESA), Senigallia, pp. 1-5.

L. Wu, G. Liang, S. Kui and Q. Wang,2011, CEclipse: *An Online IDE for Programing in the Cloud,*2011 IEEE World Congress on Services, Washington, DC, pp. 45-52.

Microsoft Azure : https://en.wikipedia.org/wiki/Microsoft_Azure

OAuth2 Python API: https://developers.google.com/api-client-library/python/auth/web-app

R. Frost, 2007,*Jazz and the eclipse way of collaboration*, Ieee Software, pp. 114-117

Stackdriver: https://cloud.google.com/debugger/

INVESTIGATING A TECHNIQUE TO ANALYSE SOCIAL MEDIA DATA

Lizani Botha, Estelle Taylor and Magda Huisman
North-West University, South Africa

ABSTRACT

Businesses have adopted social media as a way to enhance customer relationship management, and to meet communications objectives and business goals. Vast quantities of user-generated content are created on a daily basis through social media platforms and the amount of content grows exponentially. Companies can gain advantage by analysing available social media data, but they still face challenges when using social media platforms, especially to manage the vast amounts of user-generated content. The purpose of this study is to investigate techniques that can be used by a company to analyse social media data effectively. A computer-aided analysis technique was used. Twitter data (tweets) were collected and analysed. A basic framework was created which can be used by companies to determine sentiment and opinions from social media data. The framework can serve as a guideline for companies that are struggling with the effective use of social media platforms.

KEYWORDS

Social Media, Social Media Data, Sentiment Analysis, Opinion Mining, Data Mining

1. INTRODUCTION AND PROBLEM STATEMENT

Businesses have adopted social media as a way to enhance customer relationship management, and to meet communications objectives and business goals (He *et al.*, 2013; Jeffrey, 2013; Kaplan & Haenlein, 2010). A company can gain advantage over another company by analysing publicly available social media data (He *et al.*, 2013). It is critical for companies to have effective management of user-generated data and that this data is utilized correctly (Gundecha & Liu, 2012). By analysing the content posted by a user/consumer, a business can gain data and information, which can lead to improving decision making regarding future marketing campaigns, brand awareness and customer relationship management. By using social media data and data-mining techniques, sentiment analysis and opinion mining can be done to determine a customer's/client's response regarding a product, brand or service. The aim of sentiment analysis and opinion mining is to automatically extract opinions that are expressed within the user-generated content (Gundecha & Liu, 2012).

Research regarding the use of social media within and by companies is still in the early stages (Ahmed, 2015; Dickinson & Hu, 2015; Hanna *et al.*, 2011; Kietzmann *et al.*, 2011; Merril *et al.*, 2011; Adedoyin-Olowe *et al.*, 2013; Zhang *et al.*, 2011; Trainor *et al.*, 2014). Kärkkäinen *et al.* (2010) indicate that very few academic studies have been done regarding the adoption of social media in organizations. From the above it can be seen that companies can gain advantage by analysing available social media data, but that they still face challenges when using social media platforms, especially to manage the vast amounts of user-generated content. The purpose of this study is to investigate techniques that can be used by a company to analyse social media data.

2. METHOD OF INVESTIGATION

The research follows a positivistic research paradigm. The positivistic research paradigm is known as the dominant research paradigm used when studying information systems and information technology in an organization (Orlikowski & Baroudi, 1991). Computer-aided analysis techniques are used. Twitter data (tweets) are collected and analysed. This data is used to perform sentiment analysis and opinion mining. Open-source software is used to analyse the Twitter data by using a data- or text mining technique.

3. LITERATURE STUDY

In this section social media is defined, followed by a brief discussion on the mining of social media data.

3.1 Defining Social Media

Kaplan and Haenlein (2010:60) claim that there seem to be confusion among managers of companies and academic researchers about the term social media. Kärkkäinen *et al.* (2010) define the term social media as "applications that are fully based on user-generated content and this user-generated content or user activity plays a significant role in increasing the value of the application or the service." Kaplan and Haenlein (2010:61) define the term social media as "a group of Internet-based applications that build on the ideological and technological foundations of Web 2.0 and that offer the opportunity to create and exchange User-Generated Content (UGC)." A definition of social media can be formed from the above-mentioned definitions; Social media is Internet-based applications, which create the opportunity for users to create and share content and activities, which may include different forms of media, such as text, images, videos, etc.

Different techniques and strategies can be applied when a company decides to use social media, for example using a social media framework, choosing the most suitable social media platforms, ensuring that the content is timeless, using content in such a way that the company becomes the influencer, characterizing customers, using social media tools and templates, etc. After a comparison of techniques has been done, a company can then adjust its current social media strategy or framework and identify new opportunities and current weaknesses (AMEC, 2013). A social media framework or model should reflect how social media is supposed to work with respect to the company and the consumers. After a company has decided on the social media measurement process that will be used, the company should determine which social media platform's data will be used. The techniques that will be used to analyse the data also need to be determined. By using data-mining, text mining and web mining, a company can extract sentiment and opinions.

3.2 Mining Social Media Data

Data-mining is used to extract hidden information from not-structured or semi-structured data. According to Agrawal and Batra (2013:118), "data-mining is an important step of the knowledge discovery process". A clear distinction can be drawn between data-mining, text mining and web mining. In text mining, the analyser of the text applies certain aspects, techniques and methods of data-mining. Hotho *et al.* (2005:1) define text mining as "the process of extracting interesting information and knowledge from unstructured text."

4. DATA-GENERATION METHOD USED FOR TWITTER DATA

Twitter data (tweets) can capture information, and customers' feelings and opinions about any topic, product, brand or service imaginable. This is the main reason why the researchers chose to use tweets to perform sentiment analysis and opinion mining. Today, there is a variety of ways to gather Twitter data; a person can use a programming language, such as Python with a library known as Tweepy, Twitter Firehose, Google Sheets, etc. (Russell, 2014:9). Whichever process a person chooses to gather Twitter data; the process will involve using Twitter's Streaming Application Programming Interface (API). Before gathering Twitter data, a person should have a Twitter account. When using a programming language, such as Python in conjunction with Twitter's API, a person will have to gain access to Twitter's API. The data format will depend on the method used when gathering Twitter data. For example, when using Python and the Twitter Streaming API, the data will be returned in JSON format. For this study, the researchers used Twitter's Streaming API in conjunction with Google Sheets, as this method allows for free, easy and fast gathering of Twitter data.

Google Sheets offers a simple add-on, known as Twitter Archiver. This add-on allows a person to search Twitter for a specific topic, keyword or hashtag and saves the collected data to a spreadsheet. This add-on gathers all the tweets it can from Twitter's history and updates the spreadsheet with new tweets every hour. Twitter Archiver will gather the last 1 000 tweets or tweets that have been posted in the last 5-7 days. Tweets were gathered from three companies: an international company in retail, and two South African companies, one company in banking and the other company in insurance.

4.1 Using Rapidminer Studio

For this study, the researchers chose to make use of Rapidminer Studio to determine sentiment and opinions of customers who tweeted about their experience and their perception of a certain company. Rapidminer Studio is an open-source software platform that enables a user to make use of machine-learning techniques to perform data mining and text mining, as well as business analytics and predictive analytics (Rapidminer, 2014:19). The researcher chose this software platform because of its user-friendliness and the fact that the platform can handle great volumes of data. Rapidminer Studio can be used by companies on a daily basis to determine sentiment and opinion of their clients/customers. Data can be imported into a previously built process and depending on the quantity of data results can be viewed graphically within minutes. The basic principles of how a process works in Rapidminer Studio is depicted in Figure 1.

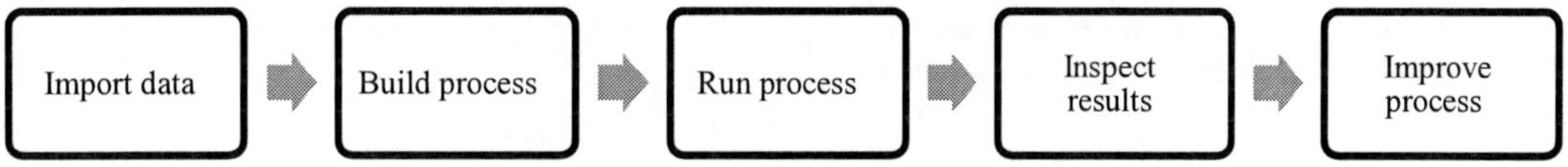

Figure 1. How a process works in Rapidminer Studio

4.2 Results Obtained from Twitter Data

Before data collection commenced, two companies in different business areas were chosen, namely retail and banking. In the past, data mining has been applied successfully in these business areas. The chosen companies' names will be kept anonymous during the discussion of results and will be referred to as Company X and Company Y.

4.2.1 Company X

Company X is a large enterprise with approximately 9 000 employees in South Africa alone. The company has 25 brands that are currently being sold across South Africa. 5 994 tweets concerning Company X were gathered and analysed. All tweets were gathered within a timeframe of a month. All duplicate tweets were removed. The AYLIEN Text Analysis extension returns five attributes of each tweet as results: the polarity, the polarity confidence, the subjectivity, the subjectivity confidence and the tweet text. The polarity indicates the sentiment, while the subjectivity indicates the opinion. The polarity confidence and subjectivity confidence range from 0 – 1, and a value close to 1 indicates a higher confidence level. Table 1 presents the sentiment and the average confidence levels of polarity for Company X. Only 17.60% of the tweets concerning Company X were positive, while 75.48% were neutral and 6.92% were negative.

Table 1. Average Confidence Levels of Polarity for Company X

Sentiment	***Number of tweets classified***	***% of overall tweets***	***Average polarity confidence***	***Overall average of polarity***
Positive	1055	17.60	0.72	
Neutral	4524	75.48	0.80	0.77
Negative	415	6.92	0.67	

42.53% of the tweets were classified as subjective meaning that an opinion was tweeted while 57.47% were objective meaning that a fact was tweeted. The results regarding the average confidence levels of subjectivity levels are presented in Table 2.

Table 2. Average Confidence Levels of Subjectivity for Company X

Opinion	*Number of tweets classified*	*% of overall tweets*	*Average subjectivity confidence*	*Overall average of subjectivity*
Subjective	2549	42.53	0.97	
Objective	3445	5 7.47	0.97	0.97

Only the positive and negative tweets were used when aggregating the sentiment. Only 1 470 tweets concerning Company X were classified as either positive or negative. 441 tweets were used as a sample of the process described in section 6.4.2. Rapidminer Studio and the process built to aggregate sentiment determines the sample size based on the number of tweets gathered, as well as the sample size that will be used for validation and testing. A Support Vector Machine (SVM) was applied within the process. The accuracy of the model was 79.14%, indicating 20.86% error in the model, which can be reduced. 45 tweets that were actually positive were predicted as positive, and six tweets that were actually negative were predicted as positive. 86 tweets that were actually positive were predicted as negative and 304 tweets that were actually negative were predicted to be negative. The results regarding the precision of the sentiment determined for Company X are presented in Table 3.

Table 3. Precision of Sentiment Determined for Company X

	True positive	*True negative*	*Class precision*
Pred. positive:	45	6	88.24%
Pred. negative:	86	304	77.95%
Class recall:	34.35%	98.06%	

4.2.2 Company Y

Company Y is a South-African company specializing in banking and providing financial services to customers/clients. 620 tweets concerning Company Y were gathered within a timeframe of a month. All duplicate tweets were removed. Only 27.42% of the tweets were classified as positive, while 41.77% were classified as neutral and 30.81% were classified as negative. The average confidence levels of polarity for Company Y are presented in Table 4.

Table 4. Average Confidence Levels of Polarity for Company Y

Sentiment	*Number of tweets classified*	*% of overall tweets*	*Average polarity confidence*	*Overall average of polarity*
Positive	170	27.42	0.82	
Neutral	259	41.77	0.71	0.76
Negative	191	30.81	0.76	

53.39% of Company Y's tweets were subjective (an opinion regarding the company), while 46.61% were classified as objective (a fact stated regarding the company). The average confidence levels of subjectivity for Company Y are presented in Table 5.

Table 5. Average Confidence Levels of Subjectivity for Company Y

Opinion	*Number of tweets classified*	*ercentage of overall tweets*	*Average subjectivity confidence*	*Overall average of subjectivity*
Subjective	331	53.39	0.99	0.98
Objective	289	46.61	0.98	

To test the precision of the sentiment analysis, a decision tree was applied and an example of the results for Company Y's tweets is given below. Different words are identified in the tweet. From the results below an interpretation of the word 'great' can be made according to the TF-IDF score. This score is used to rank the importance of words, as well as the frequency of a word. If the TF-IDF score for the word 'great' is greater than 0.081 then a tweet with the word 'great' in was classified as positive and if the TF-IDF score is smaller than 0.081 the tweet was classified as negative.

The accuracy of the model was 85.82%, indicating 14.18% error in the model, which can be reduced. The Validation operator makes use of random sampling when choosing tweets to train and test through the model. From the 361 tweets classified either as positive or negative, a sample size of 261 was used. Rapidminer Studio and the process built to aggregate the sentiment determines the sample size of the data sets for validation and testing. 92 tweets that were actually positive were predicted as positive. Six tweets that were actually negative were predicted as positive. 31 tweets that were actually positive were predicted as negative and 132 tweets that were actually negative were predicted to be negative. The precision of sentiment determined for Company Y is presented in Table 6.

Table 6. Precision of Sentiment Determined for Company Y

	True positive	*True negative*	*Class precision*
Pred. positive	92	6	93.88%
Pred. negative	31	132	80.98%
Class recall	74.80%	95.65%	

5. CONTRIBUTION OF THIS STUDY AND FUTURE WORK

Social media data play a significant role in a company and sentiment analysis and opinion mining can be performed on this data to gain insight into a company's customers or clients. For this study, the researchers chose to make use of Rapidminer Studio to determine sentiment and opinions of customers who tweeted about a company. Results obtained from the analysis of Twitter data were discussed and companies are encouraged to use software platforms, such as Rapidminer Studio, to determine sentiment and opinions. The processes built in this software platform for this study can be adapted for future research.

A basic framework was created which can serve as a guideline or tool for companies that are struggling with the effective use of social media platforms. The framework consists of 11 guidelines that can be followed.

1. Align the company's social media goals with the company's goals/business objectives.
2. Prioritize social media goals.
3. Identify a timeframe.
4. Identify the target audience.
5. Re-examine the social media goals set.
6. Test various types of content on different social media platforms.
7. Identify the platform from which social media data will be collected.
8. Make use of techniques or methods to gather social media data.
9. Analyse the social media data.
10. Analyse the results and determine social return-on investment.
11. Evaluate the process on a regular basis.

The basic framework developed in this study can be elaborated on, tested and adjusted according to the type of company and/or type of customer. A limitation of this study was that the techniques, methods, strategies and developed framework were not tested in practice.

REFERENCES

Adedoyin-Olowe, M., Gaber, M. M. & Stahl, F. 2013. *Survey of Data Mining Techniques for Social Media Analysis* [Online]. Available: http://arxiv.org/vc/arxiv/papers/1312/1312.4617v1.pdf [Accessed 9 November 2015.

Agrawal, R. & Batra, M. 2013. A Detailed Study on Text Mining Techniques. *International Journal of Soft Computing and Engineering,* 2, 118 - 121.

Ahmed, W. 2015. *Using Twitter as a data source: An overview of current social media research tools* [Online]. Available: http://blogs.lse.ac.uk/impactofsocialsciences/2015/07/10/social-media-research-tools-overview/ [Accessed 26 January 2016.

AMEC. 2013. *Unlocking Business Performance* [Online]. Available:http://amecorg.com/wpcontent/uploads/2013/06/Social-Media-Valid-Framework2013.pdf [Accessed 19 January 2016.

AMEC. 2014. *AMEC's Social Media Measurement Framework: User Guide* [Online]. Available: http://www.social-media-measurement-framework.org/wp-content/uploads/2014/06/SocialMedia-Measurement-Framework.pdf [Accessed 19 January 2016.

Dickinson, B. & Hu, W. 2015. Sentiment Analysis of Investor Opinions on Twitter. *Social Networking,* 4, 62-71.

Gundecha, P. & Liu, H. 2012. *Mining Social Media: A Brief Introduction* [Online]. Available: http://www.public.asu.edu/~pgundech/book_chapter/smm.pdf [Accessed 10 July 2015.

Hanna, R., Rohm, A. & Crittenden, V. L. 2011. We're all connected: The power of the social media ecosystem. *Business Horizons,* 54, 265-273.

He, W., Zha, S. & Li, L. 2013. Social media competitive analysis and text mining: A case study in the pizza industry. *International Journal of Information Management,* 33, 464-472.

Hotho, A., Nürnberger, A. & Paaβ, G. 2005. *A Brief Survey of Text Mining* [Online]. Available: http://citeseerx.ist.psu.edu/viewdoc/download?doi=10.1.1.210.158&rep=rep1&type=pdf [Accessed 9 July 2015.

Jeffrey, A. 2013. *Social Media Measurement: A Step-by-Step Approach* [Online]. Available: http://www.instituteforpr.org/wp-content/uploads/Social-Media-Measurement-Paper-Jeffrey-6-4-13.pdf [Accessed 19 January 2016.

Kaplan, A. M. & Haenlein, M. 2010. Users of the world, unite! The challenges and opportunities of Social Media. *Business Horizons,* 53, 59-68.

Kärkkäinen, H., Jussila, J. & Väisänen, J. 2010. *Social media use and potential in business-to-business companies' innovation* [Online]. Available:http://dspace.cc.tut.fi/dpub/bitstream/handle/123456789/22019/karkkainen_social_media_use_and_potential.pdf?sequence=1 [Accessed 29 January 2015.

Kietzmann, J. H., Hermkens, K., Mccarthy, I. P. & Silvestre, B. S. 2011. Social media? Get serious! Understanding the functional building blocks of social media. *Business Horizons,* 54, 241-251.

Merril, T., Latham, K., Santalesa, R. & Navetta, D. 2011. *Social Media: The Business Benefits May Be Enormous, But Can the Risks – Reputational, Legal, Operational – Be Mitigated?* [Online]. Available: http://www.acegroup.com/us-en/assets/ace-progress-reportsocial-media.pdf [Accessed 26 January 2016.

Orlikowski, W. J. & Baroudi, J. J. 1991. Studying Information Technology in Organizations: Research Approaches and Assumptions. *Information Systems Research,* 2, 1-28.

Russell, M. A. 2014. *Mining the Social Web,* Sebastopol, California, O'Reilly Media, Inc.

Trainor, K. J., Andzulis, J., Rapp, A. & Agnihotri, R. 2014. Social media technology usage and customer relationship performance: A capabilities-based examination of social CRM. *Journal of Business Research,* 67, 1201-1208.

Zhang, M., Jansen, B. J. & Chowdhury, A. 2011. Business engagement on Twitter: a path analysis. *Electron Markets,* 21, 161-175.

POLITICAL PARTICIPATION IN TIMES OF BOLOGNA AND SOCIAL WEB – A GROUNDED THEORY FROM A STUDENTS´ POINT OF VIEW

Gerald Wolf
Faculty of Humanities, University of Cologne, Albertus Magnus Platz, 50923 Cologne, Germany

ABSTRACT

Today's students, as adolescents and young adults in general, are publicly perceived to be less engaged in conventional politics than previous student generations. This PhD dissertation deals with the question if the Social Web plays a role as a new medium of political participation and how young adults use it politically. In other words the aim of this thesis is to reveal more about students´ attitudes to and experience with political participation in times of Bologna and Social Web. Employing a qualitative-empirical research design to analyse empirical data gathered in guided interviews, I decided to use and work with the methodology of Grounded Theory by Strauss and Corbin. The concept of mediatization is the theoretical frame of my doctoral thesis.

KEYWORDS

Political Online Participation, Social Web, Mediatization, Life-World Of Students, Grounded Theory

1. INTRODUCTION

In the last decade media underwent a remarkable change which can be described with concepts like digitalisation (transformation of analogue to digital technology) convergence (merging different media for example the convergence of TV and Internet, Internet and Smartphone) pluralisation (multiplication of media forced by the digitalisation, mp3-player, Smartphones, tablets, etc.) and diversification (highly visible web offers) (Hugger, 2014, p.7). This fundamental change affects almost everybody but especially young people.

1.1 Students in Times of Bologna – a Net Generation?

The "Digital Natives" (Prensky, 2001; Palfrey & Gasser, 2008) "Net Generation" (Tapscott, 1997) or "Millenials" (Howe & Strauss, 2000), have grown up with these new technologies. Smartphones, tablets, laptops, the Internet, online resources and instantaneous access are simply a main part of their life-worlds respectively their lives. The way things are done is a digital (Oblinger & Oblinger, 2005).

Having this in mind I ask the following question: The students in times of Bologna – a Net Generation? Since they have grown up with new media they can be characterised with special characteristics: visual orientation, multitasking, active learning, tolerance towards minorities, team orientation, fast change of attention, well informed and so on. Besides these positive descriptions, however, there are also critical voices. Rolf Schulmeister identified the "Net Generation" and the "Digital Natives" as a myth (Schulmeister, 2009), Jones and Shao stated that these terms do not capture the processes of change that are taking place (Jones & Shao, 2011). Furthermore, empirical analyses (Busemann & Gscheidle, 2010) of media usage data disprove the thesis of the "Digital Natives" in general.

1.2 Bologna

It is not only the media change that affects young people´s lives. The area of higher education in Europe is also passing through a far-reaching process of change initiated by the Bologna reform (Schmatz et al., 2015). Different studies (Bargel, 2008; Multrus et al., 2010; Ramm et al., 2014) assert that the mentality of the contemporary student generation has changed compared to the previous generations: They are labour oriented and look for practical experience to increase their employability which plays a central role. Nowadays the university is not the centre of a student´s life.

The multifaceted changes that are taking place in today's student life have an age related component that is most obvious with the newest waves of technology. Prominent amongst these are the uses of e-Learning platforms (e.g. ILIAS) social networking sites (e.g. Facebook (messenger) for communication, discussions and networking) and the use of Smartphones or tablets to access the mobile Internet (e.g. WhatsApp) (Jones & Shao, 2011, p.4).

Basically I am interested in how students of the University of Cologne experience and describe their daily university life. What do they think about the bachelor / master structure, the employability and the concept of workload? In the light of the current economy climate the employability for example is a central aspect of importance.

1.3 Social Web

With the Internet, especially through Social Web new forms and possibilities of political participation emerged. Via social networking sites like Facebook, Instagram, etc. micro blogging platforms like Twitter, etc. open sourced encyclopaedias like Wikipedia, video sharing platforms like YouTube, etc. almost everybody is able to create and spread self-produced contents and even get involved in different (political) discussions or discourses.

In this context Bruns coins the term 'produser' (Bruns, 2009). The infrastructure of Web 2.0 makes it easy to get engaged online for or against a political issue, for example the initiation of an online-petition (with change.org, avaaz.org, campact.de), organisation and mobilisation of demonstrations (e.g. the mobilisation via internet against the demo Hooligans against Salafists 2.0, on the 25th of October 2015 in Cologne), flash mobs or smart mobs via Facebook or Twitter and afterwards watching on YouTube. Social Web or the participatory Web refers to a new spirit of self-confidence among Internet users. But all the mentioned advantages and possibilities are hiding the "dark side" of Social Media. Fake news, social bots, filter bubbles, social propaganda are just a few negative phenomena related for example to the presidential elections in the USA, the presidential elections in Austria and the access of the populists. In other words: Social Media seem to influence voters behaviour and as a consequence the election results. Research indicates that faked-up stories on Facebook or Twitter could appeal opinion-forming and that is alarming. In this context my PhD-project works on recommendations for action with regard to media literacy.

2. THEORETICAL FRAMEWORK

The concept of mediatization is the theoretical frame of my doctoral thesis. Study, work, free time, politics, economy and other parts of society and culture rely more and more on media communication. In order to grasp these media change and the developments that depend to that I refer in particular to the concept developed by Friedrich Krotz.

Krotz understands mediatization as a meta process, as a long term development that includes media change and the respective change in culture and society (Krotz, 2007; Livingstone, 2009). For that reason, Friedrich Krotz defines the term meta process as follows:

"By using the term meta process we want to point out that these are long-term and culture-crossing changes, processes of processes in a certain sense, which influence the social and cultural development of humankind in the long run. More in detail, they are conceptual constructs, by which science as well as persons in their everyday life sum up certain developments, their causes, forms of expression and consequences and therewith make the world manageable". (Krotz, 2007, p.27)

Having this in mind, mediatization is comparable to individualization, globalization and commercialization. Mediatization proceeds on different levels:

- the macro-theoretical level as the transformation of culture and society,
- the meso-theoretical level as the transformation of institutions and finally
- the micro-theoretical level as the change of social and communicative action.

There are two traditions within the mediatization research: the "institutionalist tradition" and the "social constructivist tradition" (Hepp, 2013). It is not possible here to describe and discuss the traditions in detail but for my thesis I set the focus on the "social constructivist tradition". While in the "institutional tradition" media are understood as independent social institutions with their own sets of rules (Hepp & Krotz, 2014), from the social constructivist point of view the role of various media (especially digital media) moves into the foreground as part of the process of the construction of social and cultural reality.

In this sense, mediatization refers to the process of construction of socio-cultural reality by communication (Schütz & Luckmann, [1979] 2003, Krotz, 2001). Within this tradition I move the individual (the students of the University of Cologne) and its social and communicative action in the centre of analysis. In a further step, I want to link the concept of mediatization with the social life world perspective, because the "mediatized worlds" are life-worlds that rely on communication media (Lundby, 2014, p.5).

2.1 Research Question

Strauss & Corbin offer notes, which characteristics a research question should have to work and analyze with the Grounded Theory Methodology:

"The research question in a qualitative study is a statement that identifies the phenomenon to be studied. It tells the readers what the researcher specifically wants to know about this subject" (Strauss & Corbin, 1998, p.41) The main research question reads as follows: **How respectively in which manner young people use the Social Web in order to get involved in political participation processes?**

As can be seen, the main research question contains an orientation for action (confrontation with political topics in the Social Web) as well as an orientation of processes (political media activity). The political media activity of young people is the phenomenon which has to be analyzed in depth.

"Another important aspect of the research question is that it helps to establish the boundaries of what will be studied. It is impossible for any investigator to cover all aspects of a problem" (Corbin & Strauss, 2008, p.25). The target groups of this thesis are students of the University of Cologne.

2.2 Research Design and Methodology

This project employs as I mentioned before a qualitative-empirical research design. I started with explorative expert interviews with students working in student´s union executive committee and student associations to get in the field of higher education participation. Additionally, I talked with social media experts about the relevance and role of political participation of the Internet. The results and awareness of these explorative expert interviews has been integrated into the development of the guided questionnaire. The guided questionnaire contains questions among students′ course of study, attitude to the Bologna-reform, significance of Internet use in everyday life and on the University (e.g. e-learning) usage of (different) Social Web applications, political participation in the internet and University, politics and political interest, effects from online participation to offline participation and vice versa, flash mob as a new form of political participation. Till today I conducted and transliterated 20 guideline oriented interviews (in the sense of theoretical sampling) with engaged and not engaged students of the University of Cologne. The data collection and analysis are interrelated processes. One of the main essentials of the Grounded Theory is that the analysis begin as soon as the first bit of data is collected, it's just work in progress. Coding means to break up data, scrutinizing parts of my interviews very closely. The aim is to produce concepts and categories that seem to fit the data. First open categories: access, interest, opinion – opinion formation, expression of opinion, sensitization, communication, networking, mobilization, organisation.

2.3 First Results

For axial coding I am using the coding paradigm developed by Anselm Strauss and Juliet Corbin (1996) to ensure conceptual development and density. One important part or better said essential of political participation in the Social web is the opinion formation process: For example, this opinion formation process (see Figure 1) could be compared in terms of the coding paradigm – for conditions, strategies/interactions, context, and consequences.

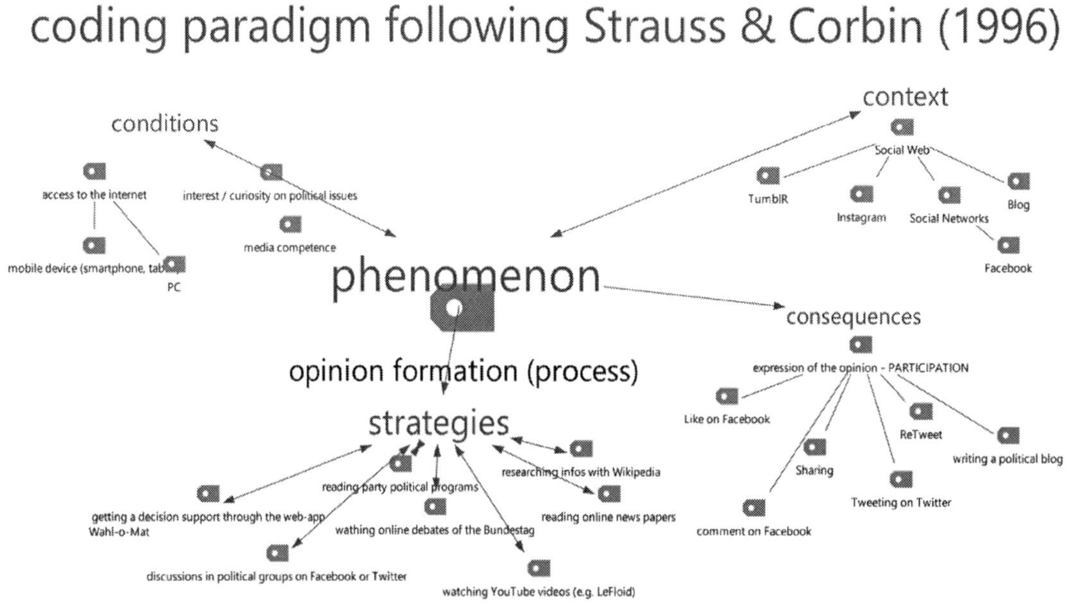

Figure 1. Coding Paradigm: Categorie Opinion Formation (Process)

Access: An often mentioned category in my interviews or let me say an "in-vivo Code"– a precondition getting engaged online is "access". If you haven´t access you are not able to participate (Carpentier, 2011). Further conditions getting involved in political online processes are basically "interest/curiosity on political online issues" and "media competence".
Opinion: Another very important category from the interview-statements of the students is "Opinion". To get engaged politically you have to have an opinion. The category Opinion has some characteristics:
Opinion formation process: YouTube Videos for example could lighten up the "*opinion forming process*". This could lead to an "expression of opinion". In the next step of analysis the expression of the opinion on Facebook for example can be described on a dimensionality scale from low to high:
Low: Pushing the Like Button – just one click. Clicking the Like Button as a form of low-threshold form of participating or just slactivism?
Middle: Comment an article on Facebook, or re-tweet on Twitter, or commenting a photo on Instagram.
High: Writing a blogpost on a political blog, or an article on Facebook or writing a tweet to a political issue.
As you can see these are the first categories which I discovered from my empirical data. Currently I am working on the axial coding. The first axis as you could see in figure 1 is the opinion formation process, just one part of the complex phenomenon of online participation. It´s work in progress.

3. CONCLUSION

The aim of my PhD thesis is a contribution to the current mediatization discourse on the basis of empirical data. With my research I try to reveal and delineate the change of participation especially with the advent of online participation possibilities. My methodological approach offers the possibility to develop a system of categories by comparing various parts of my interview data. The special emphasis is to develop a grounded theory through qualitative analysis.

Furthermore I want to understand the online participation processes, how and why students are participating politically in the Internet especially in the Social Web. For the future the main objective would be the transfer from online participation to the real world – just like from the "like button" to a meaningful vote!

REFERENCES

Bargel, T., 2008. *Wandel politischer Orientierungen und gesellschaftlicher Werte der Studierenden. Studierendensurvey: Entwicklungen zwischen 1983 und 2007.* Bundesministerium für Bildung und Forschung, Bonn, Germany

Bruns, A. 2009. *From Prosumer to Produser: Understanding User-Led Content Creation.* Paper presented at Transforming Audiences, London, 3rd-4th Sep. 2009.

Busemann, K., and Gscheidle, C., 2010. Web 2.0: Nutzung steigt – Interesse an aktiver Teilnahme sinkt. Ergebnisse der ARD/ZDF-Onlinestudie. In: *Media Perspektiven* 7-8, 2010, pp.359-368.

Carpentier, N. 2011. The concept of participation. If they have access and interact, do they really participate? In: *Communication Management Quarterly* (21), 2011, pp. 13-36.

Corbin, J. and Strauss, A., 1998. Grounded Theory Research: Procedures, Canons and Evaluative Criteria. In: *Zeitschrift für Soziologie*, Jg. 19, Heft 6, 1990, pp.418-427.

Hepp, A. 2013. Mediatisierung. In: J. Schröter, *Handbuch Medienwissenschaft*. Metzlar Verlag, Stuttgart & Weimar, Germany.

Hugger, K.-U. 2014. Digitale *Jugendkulturen: Von der Homogenisierungsperspektive zur Anerkennung des Partikularen.* In: K.-U. Hugger, (Eds.). Digitale Jugendkulturen. 2. Auflage, Springer VS; Wiesbaden, Germany, pp.11-31: 2014,.

Jones, C. and Shao, B., 2011. *The Net generation and digital natives: implications for higher education.* Paper presented at the Generation United Conference, Cologne, 3rd-4th March 2011.

Krotz, F. 2001. *Die Mediatisierung des kommunikativen Handelns. Der Wandel von Alltag und sozialen Beziehungen, Kultur und Gesellschaft durch die Medien.* Westdeutscher Verlag, Opladen, Germany.

Krotz, F. and Hepp, A.,2012. Mediatisierte Welten: Forschungsfelder und Beschreibungsansätze – Zur Einleitung. In: Krotz F. and Hepp A., *Mediatisierte Welten* VS Verlag Springer Fachmedien, Wiesbaden, Germany 2012, pp. 7-23.

Krotz, F., 2007. *Mediatisierung. Fallstudien zum Wandel von Kommunikation.* VS Verlag für Sozialwissenschaften, Wiesbaden, Germany.

Livingstone, S., 2009. On the Mediation of Everything. In: *Journal of Communication*, 59 (1), pp. 1-18.

Lundby, K. 2014. Mediatization of Communication. In: Lundby, K. (Ed.) *Mediatization of Communication. Handbooks of Communication Science*. De Gruyter Mouton, pp 3-35.

Multrus, F. et al, 2010. *Studiensituation und studentische Orientierungen. 11. Studierendensurvey an Universitäten und Fachhochschulen.* Bundesministerium für Bildung und Forschung, Bonn, Germany.

Oblinger D. and Oblinger J., 2005. *Educating the Net Generation.* EDUCAUSE - Transforming Education through Information Technologies, Washington DC. USA.

Palfrey, J. & Gasser, U., 2008. *Born Digital. Understanding the First Generation of Digital Natives.* Basic Books New York. USA

Prensky, M., 2001. Digital natives, Digital immigrants. In: *On the Horizon* 9, No. 5. pp 1-6.

Ramm, M., et al, 2014. *Studiensituation und studentische Orientierungen. 12. Studierendensurvey an Universitäten und Fachhochschulen.* Bundesministerium für Bildung und Forschung, Berlin, Germany.

Schmatz, R. et al. 2015. *Students as costumers: The Net Promoter Score as a measure for loyalty and satisfaction in Higher Education.* Paper presented at the EAIR-Conference on the Danube University Krems, Austria, 30th Aug. – 2nd Sep. 2015.

Schulmeister, R., 2009 *Gibt es eine Net Generation? Widerlegung einer Mystifizierung*. Paper presented at the Hamburg-International Conference, Germany, 4th -6th May 2009.

Schütz, A. and Luckmann, T., 2003. *Strukturen der Lebenswelt*. UVK Verlagsgesellschaft mbH, Konstanz, Germany

Strauss, S. and Corbin, J., 1996. *Grounded Theory: Grundlagen Qualitativer Sozialforschung*. Beltz Psychologie, VerlagsUnion. Germany.

Tapscott, D. 1997. *Growing up digital: The rise of the net generation.* Oracle Press Series. New York, USA.

VISUALIZING THE SYNTAX OF GRADUAL TRANSITIONS IN TEACHING DATABASE MODELING

Adi Katz
Sami Shamoon College of Engineering (SCE), Ashdod, Israel

ABSTRACT

Database conceptual modeling is an essential skill for Information Systems (IS) practitioners, but is a complex cognitive activity that is error prone. Finding an appropriate pedagogy to deliver the topic to novice database designers has been a challenge for IS educators. TSSL, a model that is known in the area of human-computer interactions (HCI) is applied in the area of relational database schema modeling as a theoretical framework, to explain a pedagogic approach of visually emphasizing the syntax of the hierarchical nature of schemas, in the aim of reducing the potential cognitive complexity of novice database designers. The approach puts focus on the syntactic level of TSSL, to visually emphasize gradual transitions between hierarchic levels of the schema. While this paper explains the approach, at the next phase an empirical experiment will test the effectiveness of the approach by comparing the performance and attitudes of students that are exposed to the syntax of gradual transitions in hierarchical schema structure, to those who are not.

KEYWORDS

Database Conceptual Modeling, TSSL, Pedagogy, Visualization

1. INTRODUCTION

This paper offers a pedagogical approach for effectively delivering the activity of database schema modeling to novice database designers. Modeling users' requirements is an essential task in information system analysis and design, to correctly capture users' reality and to ensure that the intended system would meet organizational goals (Dahan et al., 2014). Modeling database schemas according to organization scenarios is a complex cognitive process for novice database designers, therefore it is error prone. Students in database courses frequently demonstrate the difficulty to think like data modelers (Watson, 2006). Previous pedagogic works in database modeling show attempts to deal with the challenges of effectively delivering the complex topic using different approaches (Watson, 2006, Al-Dmour, 2010, Katz & Shmallo, 2015). The current approach adopts and exploits the idea known in the area of human computer interactions (HCI), that there are multiple levels of human interaction with an artifact. While in HCI the idea is used in the context of interacting with a system's interface, in database design the context is interacting with an organizational description of requirements and constraints.

The new approach suggested, is to emphasize the syntax of the hierarchical structure of database schemas characterized by two main gradual transitions between different hierarchical levels, which can be useful for IS educators. The approach is especially focused on reducing modeling errors that were previously found and mapped into dichotomous categories of additions and omissions. On the one hand, novice database designers tend to add redundant relations and relationships between relations. On the other hand, they often fail to define crucial relationships between existing relations (Katz and Shmallo, 2015).

When learning, novices' working memory resources can quickly become overwhelmed by task complexity and, as a result, their learning process will suffer (Artino, 2008). Cognitive load theory provides a framework for designing instructional materials, since it is focused on identifying instructional designs that can effectively reduce unnecessary cognitive burden on the learner (van Merriënboer & Sweller, 2005). According to cognitive load theory, among types of cognitive load is an 'extraneous cognitive load', which may result from ineffective instructional techniques (Sweller, 1998). Since extraneous cognitive load is imposed by the ways information is presented, educators can control this type of cognitive load to reduce it. The complexity of course material depends critically upon the way in which it is described. To achieve simplification in database modeling IS educators must find the right representation. Visualization had been found as means for supporting learning by decreasing extraneous cognitive and by enhancing comprehension (Schwamborn et al, 2011). Also, hierarchy is one of the most effective ways of organizing complexity and serves as a major facilitating factor enabling comprehension as it allows representations at different levels of detail, with a manageable complexity at each level (Flood & Carson, 1993; Simon, 1962). In line with these findings, the current approach puts emphasize on visualizing hierarchic levels in database schemas.

TSSL, a four-level model (Foley et al., 1990) known in the area of human computer interactions (HCI) to explain human interaction with systems is applied here as a theoretic lens for analyzing the conceptual activity of database schema modeling and for understanding the usefulness of the new approach. TSSL that is usually used as a theoretical framework to guide interface designers can be utilized as a guide for database instructional designers in the context of modeling organizational requirements in terms of a database schema. TSSL supports the idea that visualizing the syntax of a hierarchical schema structure characterized by gradual transitions, has a high potential to reduce the extraneous cognitive load in database modeling.

2. APPLYING TSSL FOR UNDERSTANDING DATABASE MODELING

TSSL, an abbreviation for: task, semantics, syntax and lexicon, is a multilayer model for user activity, originally developed and used as a conceptual framework for designing user interfaces (Foley et al., 1990). The idea of four levels of interaction can be applied as a lens for understanding the conceptual activity of database schema modeling and for demonstrating the applicability of a new pedagogic approach for delivering the topic to novice database designers. In the area of relational database schema design, while the upper levels of TSSL, task and semantics, are close to the organizations' or users' realities, the lower levels, syntax and lexicon, can be affected by the pedagogical implementation of educational practitioners.

Schema modeling is a process often solved by, top-down and bottom-up techniques, interchangeably. Database educators should integrate both top-down and bottom-up approaches in database design (Kung et al., 2013). Alongside the top-down path, we pursue a bottom-up influence, in which visualization choices deliberately made by educators at the lower TSSL levels (lexical and syntactic), will promote the higher levels of comprehending (semantic) and fulfilling the goal of designing a proper schema for organizational users (task). Since TSSL is applied to the pedagogy of database modeling from an instructional designer (educator) perspective, we dwell on the lower levels and particularly on the syntactic level. An appropriate bottom-up influence can be achieved when the syntactic level integrates the lexical level's building blocks, in a way that creates a deeper understanding of the entities (relations) and relationships between entities at the semantic level, to accomplish an appropriate expression of organizational database requirements at the highest task level. The syntactic level, with a proper instructional design using visualizations aids (such as relative locations, sizes, and colors) can promote the comprehension of entities at the semantic level, leading to a higher performance in the task of schema modeling. We now explain each TSSL level.

Task At the uppermost level, in database modeling, the task level is about organization requirements and constraints that have to be met. The goal of database designers is to define a database schema that properly expresses an organization's description of needs. Each schema includes relations with attributes, keys (primary and foreign), and connections (relationships) between relations.

Semantics At this level, designers are required to understand the meaning of entities and relationships. They decide what attribute of an entity unambiguously identifies its records. Also, given different attributes that are candidates for serving as the primary key (PK) of a relation, they decide which one is most preferable. Different considerations and consequences are taken into account at this level. A crucial aspect at this level is to identify the nature of the relationships among entities, in terms of cardinality ratios (1:1, 1: N, M: N respectively).

Syntax Database modeling educational practitioners can use different syntaxes to display the structure and combination of the building blocks of database schemas. Since extraneous cognitive load is imposed by the way information is presented, this level is extremely important for reducing and coping with the cognitive load that arises from an organizational description of requirements and constraints. A proper syntactic representation organizes the information in a way that eliminates difficulties in understanding of the entities and relationships of a given organizational context at the upper semantic level. Prominent modeling errors made by database students (Katz and Shmallo, 2015) can be reduced by simplifying the relational schema to a hierarchic structure, and by emphasizing two parallel transitions that occur when moving up or down the hierarchy.

The nature of many complex systems, characterized by a hierarchic structure enables their comprehension (Simon, 1962). Hierarchical structuring removes the complexity of large schemes generated by organizational modeling (Gandhi et al., 1994). Hierarchical organization of materials serves as a retrieval cue for recall, with a general–specific structure, that helps locate particular items (Najarian, 1981). According to the current pedagogic approach, visualizing the syntax of gradual transitions across levels of a schema's hierarchy, serves as a guide for database students in the process of modeling organizational descriptions.

The hierarchical structure is characterized by two gradual transitions from parent to child levels of the hierarchy (or vice versa when going bottom-up). One is a semantic gradual transition in terms of changes in the degree of abstraction. Going top-down, the first level starts with entities in the real-world that are clear, tangible and straightforward and gradually going down the hierarchic levels, relations represent entities that are relatively either more abstract (e.g. events), specific, detailed, and usually more complex to comprehend. The other transition is simple to visualize; the relations' PKs gradually expand to include more fields, when moving between levels down the hierarchy. A relation's PK includes the PK of its parent-relation and additional field/s, or a combination of the PKs of mutual parents.

Lexicon In database modeling, lexicon is about the visual appearance of separate components in the schema's diagram - relations, keys, fields, and relationships. For example, it is common to display a relation as a table with columns and rows, specify that an attribute is a PK by underlining its text, and draw lines that connect relations to express relationships between them.

The gradual semantic transition in relations' abstraction levels and the gradual syntactic transition in PKs' expansion occur in parallel. As previously mentioned, schema modeling is a process in which top-down and bottom-up are interchangeably used techniques. On the one hand, the semantic level serves as conceptual guidance for physically positioning relations in the syntactic level and for properly defining the PKs. On the other hand, the syntactic level of relative relation locations and relative PK sizes (key expansion) increases the comprehensibility of the schema structure and the meaning of entities. Painstaking attention to both transitions may encourage database students to go both ways, top-down and bottom-up interchangeably.

Figure 1 demonstrates the two gradual transitions from parent to child levels of the hierarchy, on an online flower shop scenario. The relative location of relations is a choice made by educators at the syntax level: placing the parents above and closest to their direct children helps visualize the hierarchy and prevents the creation of incorrect relationships. For clarity, direct parents and children should be placed at a minimum distance (one hierarchy level) from one another, when possible. Sometimes the parents of a joint child are not at the same hierarchical level; in these cases, the distance between the 'higher' parent and the child is the distance from the 'higher' parent to the 'lower' parent plus one more level. The expanding PK keys can be visually illustrated by drawing rectangles within rectangles, or by using identical colors for identical fields (colors are not demonstrated in Figure 1).

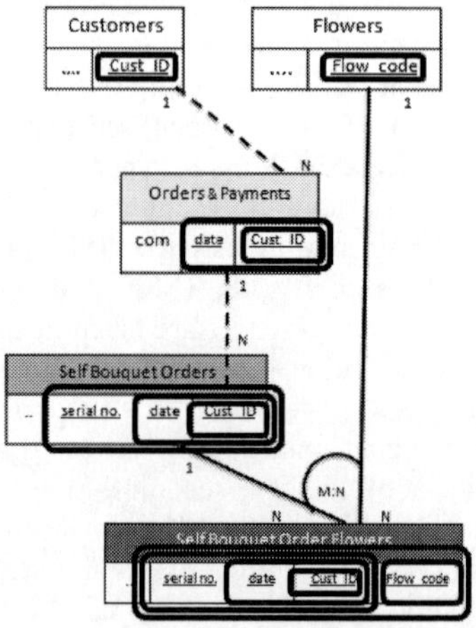

Figure 1. Visualizing the Gradual Transitions in Hierarchical Levels

3. CONCLUSION

The pedagogic approach has been implemented in the last two years in an academic college of engineering in a "Databases" course. Solutions for homework assignments and test questions in schema modeling improved in comparison to the solutions in the previous years, in terms of the types and amount of errors and in grades, but a controlled experiment to investigate whether the approach improves database modeling significantly, was not yet conducted. A planned experimental study will compare a group of students who will learn schema modeling through a traditional teaching approach (control group) to a group of students who will be exposed to a learning process that emphasizes the syntax of gradual transactions between hierarchical levels of a schema (experimental group). The experimental study is designed as a one factor with two treatments. This kind of assignment of participants to treatment groups is often used in experimental evaluation of modeling techniques (Dahan et al., 2014). In order to compare between the traditional approach and the current one, database design educators will analyze the quality of the students' schemas in terms of the number and the types of errors found. The results of the comparison will enable us to reach a conclusion regarding the effectiveness of the current approach in educating database schema modeling.

In the process of evaluating the effectiveness of the current approach, a computerized supporting tool is currently designed to be implemented in database courses. An initial prototype exists, but a detailed description of its features is beyond the scope of this paper. The tool contains an area on the screen that presents a textual scenario (uploaded from a pool of pre-written scenarios) and a working area that is divided horizontally into different hierarchical levels (the user can at any time add or remove levels with dedicated hierarchical icons). The user can select and then 'drag and drop' words that represent entities from the textual scenario to the working area in order to create relations. Once a table is shown in the working area, the user can select and then 'drag and drop' words that represent the table's attributes, from the textual scenario into that table. Throughout the solution process, visualization techniques such as colors and rectangles of different sizes will automatically mark the gradual transitions between hierarchical levels of the schema. For example, mutual PK fields of different relations will appear in identical colors to highlight the gradual expansion of PKs, and serve as a visual aid in the process of creating proper FK-PK connections. Figure 2 shows a print screen of the prototype of the database modeling supporting tool at its current design stage. The prototype serves to evaluate students' attitudes towards the approach, using user testing techniques such as observations and interviews (Shneiderman et al., 2016). If the approach would be found useful, it could guide the development of computer-based environments for learning and exercising database schema modeling.

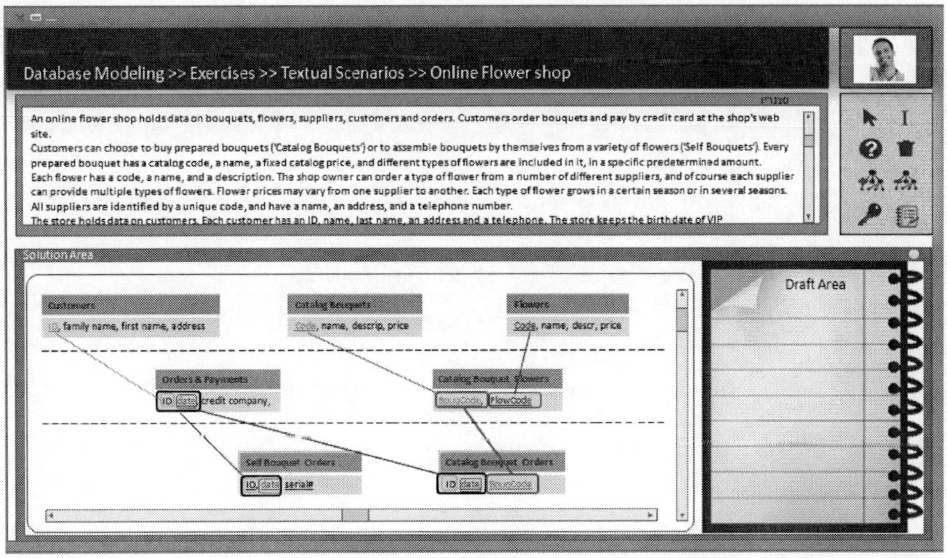

Figure 2. A Computerized Tool for Supporting Database Modeling (reprinted from "Applying TSSL in Database Schema Modeling: Visualizing the Syntax of Gradual Transitions.," by Katz, A., 2018, *Journal of Technology and Science Education, in press*. Creative commons license)

REFERENCES

Al-Dmour, A. 2010. A cognitive apprenticeship based approach to teaching relational database analysis and design, *Journal of Information & Computational Science*. Vol. 7, pp 2495-2502.

Artino Jr, A. R. 2008. Cognitive Load Theory and the Role of Learner Experience: An Abbreviated Review for Educational Practitioners. *AACE Journal*, Vol. 16, No. 4, pp 425-439.

Dahan, M., et al, 2014. Comparing the Impact of the OO-DFD and the Use Case Methods for Modeling Functional Requirements on Comprehension and Quality of Models: A Controlled Experiment. *Requirements Engineering*, Vol. 19, No. 1, pp 27-43.

Flood, R. L., & Carson, E. R. 2013. *Dealing with Complexity: an Introduction to the Theory and Application of Systems Science*. Springer Science & Business Media.

Foley, J. D., et al, 1990. John f. Hughes. *Computer Graphics Principles and Practice*. Addison-Wesley, Reading, Massachusetts.

Gandhi, M., et al, 1994. Leveled Entity Relationship Model. *In International Conference on Conceptual Modeling*, Berlin, Heidelberg, pp 420-436.

Katz, A. 2018. (in press). Applying TSSL in database schema modeling: Visualizing the syntax of gradual transitions. *Journal of Technology and Science Education*.

Katz, A & Shmallo, R 2015. Improving Relational Data Modeling through Learning from Errors, *Proceedings of the IADIS Multi Conference of Computer Science and Information Systems MCCSIS 2015, Theory and Practice in Modern Computing (TPMC 2015)*, Las Palmas de Gran Canaria, Spain, pp 198-202.

Kung, H. J., et al, 2013. Comparing Top-Down with Bottom-Up Approaches: Teaching Data Modeling. *Information Systems Education Journal*, Vol. 11, No. 1, 14.

Najarian, S. E. 1981. Organizational Factors in Human Memory: Implications for Library Organization and Access Systems. *The Library Quarterly*, Vol. 51, No. 3, pp 269-291.

Schwamborn, A., et al, 2011. Cognitive Load and Instructionally Supported Learning with Provided and Learner-Generated Visualizations. *Computers in Human Behavior*, Vol. 27, No. 1, pp 89-93.

Shneiderman, B., et al, 2016. *Designing the User Interface: Strategies for Effective Human-Computer Interaction*. Pearson.

Simon, H. A. 1962. The Architecture of Complexity. *Proceedings of the American Philosophical Society*, Vol. 106, No. 6, pp 467–482.

Sweller, J. 1988. Cognitive Load during Problem Solving: Effects on Learning. *Cognitive Science*, Vol. 12. No. 2, pp 257-285.

Van Merriënboer, J. J., & Sweller, J. 2005. Cognitive Load Theory and Complex Learning: Recent Developments and Future Directions. *Educational Psychology Review*, Vol. 17, No. 2, pp 147-177.

Watson, R. T. 2006. The Essential Skills of Data Modeling. *Journal of Information Systems Education*, Vol. 17, No. 1, pp 39-41.

A FRAMEWORK FOR TRACKING AND ASSESSMENT OF CURRICULA EVOLUTION

Vangel V. Ajanovski
Faculty of Computer Science and Engineering - Ss. Cyril and Methodius University
Rugjer Boshkovikj 16, Skopje 1000, Macedonia

ABSTRACT

A framework for tracking and assessment of the evolution of curricula at a diverse institution is proposed (ranging from a single educational departmental-level organization to the scale of an integrated university) and the evaluation of a prototype system implementation of such a framework is discussed. The effort builds upon the conceptual integration of two approaches to analysis of curriculum structure that have been used in the past – curriculum mapping for investigating possible duplicate topics in the knowledge coverage of a certain discipline, or gaps in the knowledge coverage of that discipline that students might have, against evolutionary curriculum reconstruction where a day-to-day process is introduced to manage revisions and changes during curriculum reconstruction. This proposal extends the existing practices on a long-term time-scale and can be used to analyse and cross-check in more depth the differences and effects of curriculum development efforts in the history of a single institution, or even be used to analyse and compare differences and effects of curriculum development efforts across many partner institutions.

KEYWORDS

Information Systems, Curriculum Development, Curriculum Mapping, Curriculum Assessment

1. INTRODUCTION

Science and technology are in a state of unprecedented development and expansion in the past decades. Interdisciplinary studies are more and more prevalent, even in combinations that have not occurred in the past. To introduce students to the new fields, new curricula are constantly developed and existing ones are reconstructed. This largely influences the teaching processes and general educational management. In this paper, a framework is proposed that enables the assessment of the evolution of curricula and comparison of the curricula differences across a long time-frame. The framework can be operated at the level of a single department, at the institutional level of a complex or diverse institution, or even across institutions.

2. A CASE-STUDY OF LONG-TERM CURRICULA EVOLUTION

This proposal builds upon the author's experience in teaching IS (Information Systems) and related courses over the period of twenty years at two institutions. During the whole period, different curricula structures were implemented at the institutions, making it hard to compare the curricula differences even within a single revision, and nearly impossible to grasp the overall development over a long time frame.

As an example of how curricula structures evolves over time – the partial evolution of the curricula in the field of IS at the author's institution(s) is presented in Table 1. *Note that due to space constraints, the list includes information on only 3 revisions out of the total 8 that occurred in the period of analysis.* It is obvious that in some periods the field was covered by only few elective courses, while it was a larger curricula structure in other periods – a study program in one period, a specialization in another. Over many revisions, the list of courses covering the field fluctuated, and course syllabi and their executions varied significantly over time – semesters in which the courses are offered have changed, workloads in hours and ECTS credits have changed, the list of covered topics has changed, technologies taught have changed, etc.

Table 1. Case-study of the evolution of the Information Systems (IS) field over 3 curricula reconstructions at the author's institution. *Due to space constraints, only the courses related to IS are listed, and only parts of relevant plans*

Curriculum organization structures and sub-structures and courses	Semester	Lectures	Exercises	ECTS
Study Plans Revision 1 (3 study programs, IS is represented in the core and as a specialization in 1 program):				
◦ **The core of both study programs**				
Course: Databases	5	3	4	N/A
◦ **Study Program: Applied Informatics** (includes 2 areas)				
▪ **Elective specialization: Software Engineering**				
• **The core of the specialization**				
Course: Information Systems	7	2	4	N/A
• **Elective sub-specialization: Information Systems**				
Course: Databases 2	8	2	3	N/A
Course: Geographical Information Systems	8	2	3	N/A
Study Plans Revision 2 *(introduces ECTS, the study program from Rev. 2 is split into 6 full new study programs):*				
◦ **The core of all study programs includes 2 courses related to IS**				
Course: Databases	4	3	4	8
Course: Software Project Management	8	2	3	4
◦ **Study Program: Information Systems** *(all listed courses are in the core and are mandatory)*				
Course: Information Systems	5	2	3	6
Course: IS Analysis and Design	6	2	3	6
Course: Data Mining	6	2	3	6
Course: Capstone Group Project	7	2	4	4
Course: IS Implementation	8	2	4	6
Course: Software Project Management	8	2	2	4
Study Plans Revision 3 *(restructuring of the top-level structure of study programs warranted by new legislation)*				
◦ **Study Program: Informatics** *(4 study programs from Rev. 3 were merged into 1, so IS program is merged too)*				
▪ **The core of the study program** *(again includes only one course related to IS)*				
Course: Databases	5	2	5	8
▪ **Specialization in IS** *(an elective one, possible if a student voluntarily enrols and finishes all its courses)*				
Course: Information Systems	6	2	3	6
Course: IS Analysis and Design	7	2	3	6
Course: IS Implementation	8	2	4	6
Course: Software Project Management	8	2	3	6
Course: Data Mining	8	2	3	6

3. EVOLUTION ASSESSMENT MODEL

The case-study discussed in section 2, shows that it is sufficiently hard to understand the many structural changes in curricula over long time-frame even for a smaller set of courses of a single specialization. In the general case, when investigating a large and diverse institution the complexity rises. The proposal is that instead of tracking programs and courses, the core bits of the learning knowledge covered in courses should be tracked. An inventory of all knowledge pieces should be identified and mapped one-by-one to a standard and well-known Body of Knowledge (BoK) structure. In that way, the evolution can be assessed in terms of the coverage of the BoK in each revision, giving stability of the process and a reference for comparisons.

The idea for this method stems from the Curriculum Mapping technique, see (Uchiyama & Radin, 2009). In the paper (Ajanovski, 2017a) an evolutionary process of curriculum reconstruction was introduced, and in (Ajanovski, 2017b) the application of curriculum mapping was discussed for analysis of the coverage of Reference Curriculum Guidelines. This proposal aims to integrate the two approaches. First, it extends the evolutionary curricula reconstruction – originally intended for iterative management of the process of a single reconstruction, to cover multiple revisions of both content and structure over a longer time-frame. Second, it merges the concept of curriculum mapping – instead of using it to control the quality of the process within a single revision, it will be used to map how each piece of knowledge migrates from a curriculum to a curriculum over many historical revisions. Finally, data-driven content analysis of the curricula, as in (Mendez, Ochoa, & Chiluiza, 2014; Sekiya, Matsuda, & Yamaguchi, 2015) can be applied to further explore the trends, or streamline the process of manual mapping.

The domain of the proposed assessment process is defined over three constituent models – the model that defines the study program structure and how it evolves across the many revisions in the history of a diverse institution, the model that elaborates BoK of the investigated field and the model that defines a single curriculum revision and it's curriculum mapping on a topic-by-topic level against the BoK (see Figure 1). This solution enables the curricula assessment over many *Institutions*, each one having multiple study *Plans* (overall revisions of the curricula at a certain moment in time), with multiple study *Programs* leading to one or several *Degrees*. In our model, a *Curriculum* denotes the fact that a certain *Subject* area will be taught within a certain study *Program* and can be tailored to have a specific title, workload, syllabus, activity and exam types. As designed, it enables capturing of the variance in teaching methods across programs. Further, each *Curriculum* can be a complex of many curricula, linked through a graph of *CurriculumLinks* of various *LinkTypes*. To track the evolution over time a graph of *CurriculumRevisions* is separately maintained.

Many things can change over time. The program names and subject-area titles can change as the science and practice in the field evolves, and together with the field - the studies will be revised. Therefore it is necessary to map the contents to a certain stable reference guideline that defines the field and is stable over long periods. The system captures how the planned execution of each curriculum, topic-by-topic, is mapped to certain standardized BoK definitions. A list of *CurriculumTopicsCoverage* elements is created, and lecture by lecture they are linked to *Topics* and *LearningObjectives* from the chosen BoK and respective *KnowledgeArea* and *KnowledgeUnit*.

While each curriculum revision is independently mapped, the fact that it is done topic-by-topic against a fixed set of items from a reference BoK enables analysis of how these standard topics from the BoK are covered in our curricula. Hence, we can easily understand the evolution, by mere searching and filtering per area, unit or topic, or at the level of learning objectives. In our case, an effort was made to map each course of the IS-related structure to the ACM curriculum guidelines and their respective BoK (Joint Task Force on Computing Curricula, Association for Computing Machinery (ACM) and IEEE Computer Society, 2013).

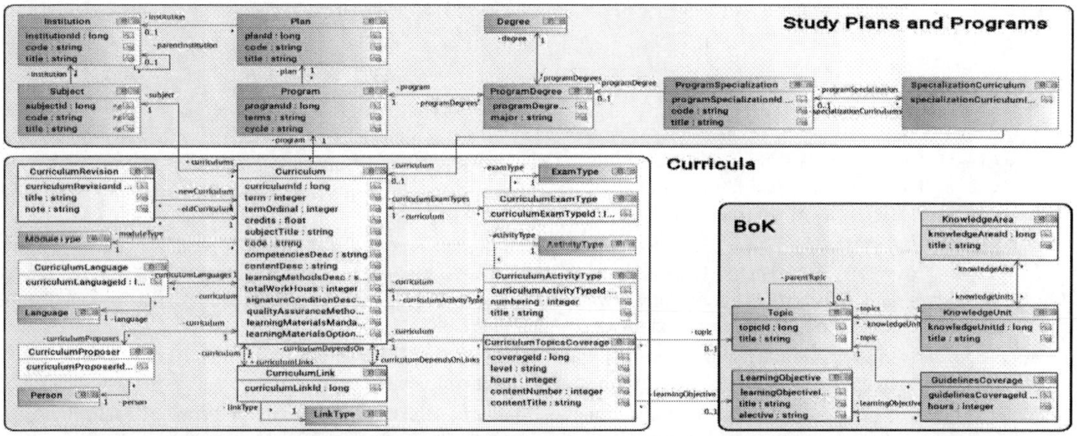

Figure 1. UML class diagram showing the domain model for the proposed assessment process. In the case of the author's institution the mapped Body of Knowledge (BoK) corresponds to the well-known ACM Curricula Guidelines

4. EVALUATION AND FUTURE WORK

A prototype web-based information system was implemented enabling editing of the curriculum definitions and revisions and many types of queries and reports. The system was tested against historical curricula structures at the author's institutions in the period 1990-2017 and curriculum mapping was enabled for all the IS-related courses spanning the whole period. The systems allows querying on curricula that include a certain items from the BoK and displays the results both as heat maps showing how the BoK are implemented and comparison maps on how the queried item is included in courses (Figure 2a), but also in the form of a graph of all revisions in the selected and related courses over time (Figure 2b). When a series of curricula teach the same topic, the graph-based interface can be used to both visualize and manage the respective associations.

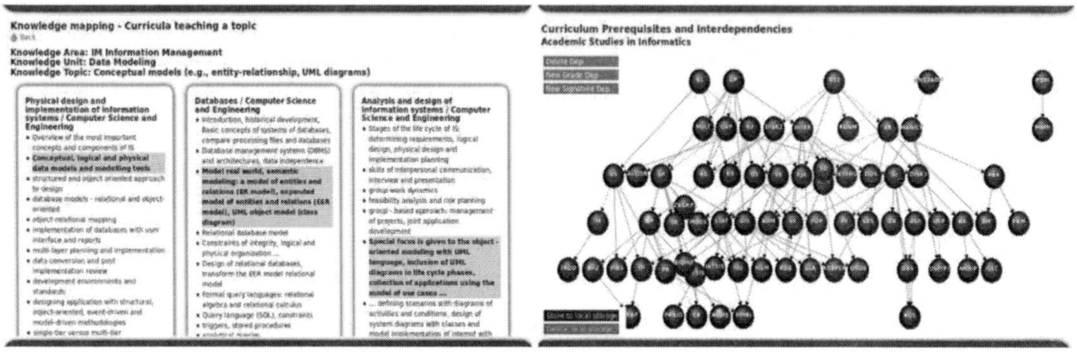

Figure 2. a) Mapping UI for visualizing the coverage of a queried topic from the BoK across several curricula. b) Graph-based UI for visualizing and editing curriculum associations and revisions based on the queried topic

The research will continue towards using learning objectives as units for mapping (Gluga, Kay, & Lever, 2013) and enabling multiple-BoK mapping. This is important in situations where a many BoKs exist (e.g. inter-disciplinary environments). Also, the effect of the curricula structure over student performance will be investigated (Herbert, de Salas, Lewis, Dermoudy, & Ellis, 2014).

ACKNOWLEDGEMENT

The work is result of the project Study Information Systems of the Next Generation, partially financed by the Faculty of Computer Science and Engineering (Ajanovski, 2018). The project results are open-sourced.

REFERENCES

Ajanovski, V. V. (2017a). Evolutionary Curriculum Reconstruction: Process Model and Information System Development. In *Proceedings of the 18th Annual Conference on Information Technology Education* (pp. 89–94). New York, NY, USA: ACM. https://doi.org/10.1145/3125659.3125698

Ajanovski, V. V. (2017b). Information System for Mapping the Coverage of Reference Curriculum Guidelines in the Teaching Curricula of a Higher-Education Institution. In *Proceedings of the 14th International Conference for Informatics and Information Technology (CIIT 2017)* (pp. 10–15). Mavrovo, Macedonia: Faculty of Computer Science and Engineering. Retrieved from http://ciit.finki.ukim.mk

Ajanovski, V. V. (2018, March). Student Information Systems of the Next Generation [Project Development Website]. Retrieved March 25, 2018, from https://develop.finki.ukim.mk/projects/sisng

Gluga, R., Kay, J., & Lever, T. (2013). Foundations for Modeling University Curricula in Terms of Multiple Learning Goal Sets. *IEEE Transactions on Learning Technologies*, *6*(1), 25–37. https://doi.org/10.1109/TLT.2012.17

Herbert, N., de Salas, K., Lewis, I., Dermoudy, J., & Ellis, L. (2014). ICT Curriculum and Course Structure: The Great Balancing Act. In *Proceedings of the Sixteenth Australasian Computing Education Conference - Volume 148* (pp. 21–30). Darlinghurst, Australia, Australia: Australian Computer Society, Inc. Retrieved from http://dl.acm.org/citation.cfm?id=2667490.2667493

Joint Task Force on Computing Curricula, Association for Computing Machinery (ACM) and IEEE Computer Society, I. C. (2013). *Computer Science Curricula 2013: Curriculum Guidelines for Undergraduate Degree Programs in Computer Science*. New York, NY, USA: ACM. Retrieved from https://dx.doi.org/10.1145/2534860

Mendez, G., Ochoa, X., & Chiluiza, K. (2014). Techniques for Data-driven Curriculum Analysis. In *Proceedings of the Fourth International Conference on Learning Analytics And Knowledge* (pp. 148–157). New York, NY, USA: ACM. https://doi.org/10.1145/2567574.2567591

Sekiya, T., Matsuda, Y., & Yamaguchi, K. (2015). Curriculum Analysis of CS Departments Based on CS2013 by Simplified, Supervised LDA. In *Proceedings of the Fifth International Conference on Learning Analytics And Knowledge* (pp. 330–339). New York, NY, USA: ACM. https://doi.org/10.1145/2723576.2723594

Uchiyama, K. P., & Radin, J. L. (2009). Curriculum Mapping in Higher Education: A Vehicle for Collaboration. *Innovative Higher Education*, *33*(4), 271–280. https://doi.org/10.1007/s10755-008-9078-8

IMPROVING DOCUMENT RETRIEVAL WITH A CLUSTERING BASED RELEVANCE FEEDBACK SYSTEM

Johannes Darms and Jens Dörpinghaus
Fraunhofer Institute for Algorithms and Scientific Computing
Schloss Birlinghoven, Sankt Augustin, Germany

ABSTRACT

Relevance feedback for document retrieval systems is a technique where user feedback is used to improve a query response. In this work we propose a system that uses multiple clusterings and a semi-supervised heuristic to improve a query response. The heuristic creates an optimal cluster w.r.t. the relevance feedback based on multiple clusterings. We justify the explicit separation of the optimization process and the clustering process by time and space constrains. The evaluation of the heuristic on a corpus containing 1.660 documents from MEDLINE showed promising results. We were able to obtain better results as a single clustering after a few iterations.

KEYWORDS

Relevance Feedback System, Document Clustering, Search Engine

1. INTRODUCTION

In Information System and especially in document retrieval system the returned data is always a response to a user's request. No matter on how specific a request may be, the user will consider parts of the response more or less correct. This feedback, either explicit or implicit, gathered can be used to improve a request (Salton, 1997). Much work has been performed either on improving ranking functions (Radlinski, 2005), retrieval functions (Joachims, 2002) or on personalizing query responses (Shen, 2005). However best to our knowledge, search engines still return some irrelevant results that do not fulfill the user's query.

Following Cohn's "it is easier to criticize than to construct" metaphor (Cohn, 2003). We imagine a relevance feedback system initially returning a coarse result and after gathering some positive and negative feedback the system returns a finer result. This looping process is either stopped by the user or the system. However the feedback can be interpreted as, if this document is relevant - similar documents are also relevant. Naively a better response can be achieved by returning documents that are similar to documents, considered relevant by the user. Though which similarity measure should be used and at what threshold should be stopped? These questions relates with the cluster hypothesis, "Documents in the same cluster behave similarly with respect to relevance to information needs." (Manning, 2008). Hence we propose a relevance feedback system based on clustering.

In this work we describe a heuristic to generate an optimized cluster based on n different clusterings with respect to the relevance feedback. Therefore we first define clustering based on similarly measures, show rationales for optimizing based on clusterings instead of optimizing a single clustering process and penultimate evaluate the heuristic on a real word MEDLINE based dataset. Last we discuss our findings and give an outlook on further work to be done.

2. CLUSTERING

Document clustering and clustering in general is based on the assumption, that documents within one cluster are more similar to each other than to document outside the cluster (Manning, 2008). Based on this a function to measure the similarity of two documents is needed $sim : D \times D \rightarrow \mathbb{R}_0^+$. Thus two documents x, y are grouped in one cluster if $sim(x, y) \geq e > 0$. Following the higher $sim(x, y)$ the more similar both documents are to each other. If the assignment to only one cluster is allowed it is considered as hard clustering, whereas if multiple assignments are possible it is known as soft clustering. We consider soft clustering to be only allowed if $l > sim(x, y)$, thus if the similarity is above a threshold l $(l \geq e)$ both documents must belong to one cluster. Below that and above the threshold e an assignment to multiple clusters is allowed. Furthermore a document can belong to no cluster at all.

Using these definitions a soft clustering problem can be transferred into a hard Clustering problem by setting $l = e$. In the reminder we use clustering in the meaning of soft clustering. Subsequent clustering can be defined by a function $CL : D \rightarrow \{C \cup \{NULL\}\}$ that assigns each document a cluster label $C \subseteq \mathbb{N}$ or to $NULL$ indicating no assignment.

We use $CL^{of} : C -> S \subseteq D$, to refer to all documents within the same cluster as the argument and use $CL(S), S \subseteq D$ to refer to all cluster labels used to assign elements of the set S. Accordingly $|CL(D)|$ refers to the total number of cluster labels used.

2.1 Similarity Measures

As we talk about clustering based on similarity measures and yet no other constrains than a $D \times D$ mapping to $\mathbb{R}_0^+$ is required. Any similarity measure can be written as a linear combination $sim(x, y) = \sum_i^{m \in \mathbb{N}} a_i f_i(x, y)$. Hence one can define a similarity measure as a weighted combination of m similarity measure, possible one measure per dimension of the document. Following the weights can be adjusted to obtain an optimal clustering, for example a boosting like approach as proposed by Frossyniotis in 2004. To reassess a clustering, if new information becomes available, the process needs to know which measure lead to a decision. Assuming the m components $f_i : D \times D \rightarrow \mathbb{R}_0^+$can be normalized to $D \times D \rightarrow [0,1]$ and further refined to $D \times D \rightarrow \{0,1\}$ to reduce complexity. If $m = 1$ and $a_1 = 1$ and f_1 is a decision function. Then for all documents $x, y \in D, sim(x, y) = f_1(x, y) = 0$ $holds$ $cl(x) \neq cl(y)$. Thus we know which component lead to the decision for or against an assignment. This is not true for $m > 1$, see **Lemma 1** for a proof.

Lemma 1: Given a clustering process with $m > 1$ and $sim(x, y)$ as a sum of decision functions and $|C| > 1$. Then $cl(x) \neq cl(y)$ does not imply $f_i(x, y) = 0, \forall x, y \in D$ and a fixed $i \in \{1, \ldots, m\}$.

Proof 1: Let $x, y, z \in D$ with$cl(x) \neq cl(y), cl(x) = cl(z)$ and$cl(z) \neq cl(y)$. Thus$sim(x, y) = 0$ and $sim(z, y) = 0$ and $f_i(x, y) = 0$ and $f_i(z, y) = 0$ for all x, y, z and a fixed $i \in \{1, \ldots m\}$. We can now apply the triangle inequality and obtain $sim(x, z) \leq sim(x, y) + sim(y, z) = 0$. Thus $sim(x, z) = 0$ and we can follow, that the similarity must always be null. But $sim(x, y) \equiv 0$ implies, that $c(x, y) \equiv 0$ and thus $|C| = 1$. The clustering process can only have one cluster. This is contradictory to the requirement.

Thus for a combination of similarity functions we cannot decide which part introduced an error or lead to the correct decision. Following an optimization cannot be performed on an obtained clustering, with only access to the result of the similarity function without access results and weights of the components within. Subsequent having access to the results m functions and weights is equivalent to having m clusterings each performed by a different f_i $i \leq m$. Considering the lower space consumption by only storing obtained clusterings. We claim that it's more viable to optimize the combination of m individual clusterings than optimizing a single similarity measure of one clustering. Additionally to the rationale above this also makes an optimization independent of the used clustering algorithm and further allows a decoupling of clustering and optimization process.

3. HEURISTIC TO OPTIMIZE A CLUSTERING

To optimize a clustering a function is needed which decides if an assignment with respect to the clustering is correct or not. Such a function $f : -> \{0,1\}$ evaluates to 1 if the assignment is correct and otherwise to 0. This function depends on the document, the overall clustering and may also on additional information and can be arbitrary complex. For a user of an information system this problem is way simpler. Seeing many grouped documents, he/she can easily mark a document as correctly or wrongly grouped based on his opinion. This feedback can be used to optimize a clustering, due the nature of a binary feedback it can only be used to optimize one of many clusters. In the following we assume such a function that encodes user feedback, and n different clusterings $CL_1 \ldots CL_n$, over the same data, to be given and propose a heuristic to optimize one cluster based on n clusterings. We like to emphasize that only one cluster and not the overall clustering is optimized.

With the given function f a set $F = F_P \cup F_N$ can be constructed which groups some documents by the user feedback. $F_P = \{d \in D \mid f(d) = 1\}$ $F_N = \{d \in D \mid f(d) = 0\}$. The heuristic is based on the initial stated idea, that if a user considers one document correct he probably finds similar documents correct as well. Analogously for wrong documents. Therefore the heuristic is built upon iterative union and intersection of clusters.

The function o is called iteratively with a fixed value for x for each $cl_i \in \{cl_1, \ldots, cl_n\}$. In each iteration the result of the previous iteration is passed as cl_m to the next iteration. This is repeated for k values of $x \in F, k \leq |F|$. After the last iteration cl_m is a cluster optimized based on the user feedback. For the first iteration cl_m can be empty or arbitrary initialized.

$$o(x, F_N, F_P, cl_m, cl_i) = \begin{cases} cl_m \setminus cl_i{}^{of}(cl(x)), x \in F_N \\ cl_m \cup cl_i{}^{of}(cl(x)), x \in F_P \end{cases}$$

4. PPLICATION ON A REAL WORLD DATASET

Dörpinghaus (2017) et al. introduced a clustering method using pseudo stable sets. A benefit of this approach is that no information next to the data and a similarity function is needed to obtain a "perfect" clustering w.r.t. the similarity measure. Therefore we used it in our evaluation. The used dataset consists of two sets each 830 documents large. Both sets where obtained using SCAIView (Younesi, 2012) with different queries, "escherichia AND pili" (D_1) and "cerevisiae AND cdc*"(D_2). Both queries have been published in Iliopoulos, 2000, Theodosiou, 2008.

We performed two clustering, using the pseudo stable sets method with different similarity measures. (1) Jaccard Similarity (Jain, 1988) based on the Medical Subject Headings (MeSH) Terms (Lipscomb, 2000) manual annotated to the documents. (2) Term frequency, a inverse document frequency measure based on weighted words (Manning, 2008). These initial clustering have been evaluated with a F1-Measure using D_1 as a reference (Manning, 2008). The performance is far from optimal ($F1\ of\ best\ cluster = [0{,}24.0{,}28]$) but as expected since we planned to use both clusterings as input for the optimization heuristic. To mimic the needed user feedback we randomly sampled with replacement 23 documents from the 1660 documents. If a drawn sample originated in D_1 we consider it as a positive user feedback, otherwise as a negative feedback. We like to note that we sampled from the same set as we used to evaluate. One can argue this is flawed, but for this early evaluation and the small amount (1.3%) of data sampled this can be neglected. The results are displayed in Table 1. As it can be seen the recall increases or stays constant with the number of iterations (samples seen), no matter if an intersection (negative feedback) or union (positive feedback) is performed. Notable is that the precision increase in the first iterations and stays fairly constant even though the cluster size increases. Hence the overall quality (F1) increases. Even after two iteration the heuristic achieved a better result than a single clustering and doubled the performance after 9 iteration starting with an initial empty cluster.

Table 1. Evaluation of the Proposed Heuristic (Due to Space Constrains Some Iteration are Left Out)

Samples	0	1	2	3	4	8	9	10	12	13	14	15	16	17	18	19	23
Cluster Size	0	95	250	290	289	383	536	571	582	575	**697**	747	739	**732**	775	760	862
Precision	0%	33%	62%	70%	70%	80%	78%	81%	82%	83%	**86%**	83%	85%	**86%**	83%	84%	83%
Recall	0%	4%	19%	24%	24%	37%	50%	56%	57%	57%	72%	75%	76%	76%	78%	77%	**86%**
F1	0%	7%	29%	36%	36%	51%	61%	66%	67%	68%	79%	79%	80%	81%	80%	81%	**85%**

5. CONCLUSION AND FURTHER WORK

We defined clustering based on similarity measures. Showed that an optimization of clustering based on a weighted combination of similarity measure isn't as viable as optimizing a clustering based on m different clusterings, with the rational of less space consumption and the decoupling of the clustering and optimization process. We introduced a heuristic doing such an optimization based on relevance feedback. Subsequent we evaluated our heuristic on a real world dataset with a standard F1-Measure. The evaluation reveals that the proposed algorithm does optimize. Notable is the steep increase in performance using the heuristic considering an empty start set and poor performing individual clustering. However the heuristic is only experimental evaluated on one fairly small dataset with only two groups. Further work has to be done to assess the quality on larger and more diverse real word datasets and also on artificial ones in the typical shapes (donuts, banana and half circles). Nevertheless the results are promising, considering that after a few iterations a reasonable result is already obtained.

Taking these findings to the initial introduced use case, as a relevance feedback system for a search engine, we can sketch such a system based on a preprocessing by multiple unsupervised clustering processes using many arbitrary similarity measures. And a simple heuristic to optimize a response to the relevance feedback. We plan to integrate that sketched system into the SCAIView document retrieval system. Additionally the sketched system can also be used as a basis for system which allows dynamic document retrieval similar to the task proposed in the TREC Dynamic Domain Track (Yang, 2016). Participating systems are expected to adjust their systems dynamically to complex and exploratory searches based on provided relevance feedback.

REFERENCES

Cohn, David, Rich Caruana, and Andrew McCallum. "Semi-supervised clustering with user feedback." *Constrained Clustering: Advances in Algorithms, Theory, and Applications* 4.1 (2003): 17-32.

Dörpinghaus, J., Schaaf, S., Fluck, J., Zimmermann, M.: Document clustering using a graph covering with pseudostable sets. In: Proceedings of the 2017 Federated Conference on Computer Science and Information Systems. Annals of Computer Science and Information Systems, pp. 329(338. IEEE, (2017))

Frossyniotis, D., Aristidis Likas, and Andreas Stafylopatis. "A clustering method based on boosting." *Pattern Recognition Letters* 25.6 (2004): 641-654.

Iliopoulos, I., Enright, A., Ouzounis, C.: Textquest: Document clustering of medline. Biocomputing 2001, 384(2000)

Jain, Anil K., and Richard C. Dubes. *Algorithms for clustering data*. Prentice-Hall, Inc., 1988.

Joachims, Thorsten. "Optimizing search engines using clickthrough data." *Proceedings of the eighth ACM SIGKDD international conference on Knowledge discovery and data mining*. ACM, 2002.

Lipscomb, Carolyn E. "Medical subject headings (MeSH)." *Bulletin of the Medical Library Association* 88.3 (2000): 265.

Manning C., Prabhakar Raghavan and Hinrich Schütze, Introduction to Information Retrieval, Cambridge University Press. 2008.

Radlinski, Filip, and Thorsten Joachims. "Query chains: learning to rank from implicit feedback." *Proceedings of the eleventh ACM SIGKDD international conference on Knowledge discovery in data mining*. ACM, 2005.

Salton, Gerard, and Chris Buckley. "Improving retrieval performance by relevance feedback." *Readings in information retrieval* 24.5 (1997): 355-363.

Shen, Xuehua, Bin Tan, and ChengXiang Zhai. "Implicit user modeling for personalized search." *Proceedings of the 14th ACM international conference on Information and knowledge management*. ACM, 2005.

Theodosiou, T., Darzentas, N., Angelis, L., Ouzounis, C.A.: Pured-mcl: a graph-based pubmed document clustering methodology. Bioinformatics 24(17), 1935/1941 (2008).

Yang, Grace Hui, and Ian Soboroff. "TREC 2016 Dynamic Domain Track Overview." *TREC*. 2016.

Younesi, E., Toldo, L., Mueller, B., Friedrich, C.M., Novac, N., Scheer, A., Hofmann-Apitius, M., Fluck, J.: Mining biomarker information in biomedical literature. BMC medical informatics and decision making 12(1),148 (2012).

A HIGH LEVEL SCIENTOMETRIC ANALYSIS OF WEBSITE QUALITY RESEARCH

Adel M. Aladwani
Department of QM & IS, College of Business Administration, Kuwait University, Kuwait

ABSTRACT

This work-in-progress study reports the initial results of a scientometrics assessment of website quality research. The statistical analyses reveal a number of findings including that research in the area is growing and distributed unevenly across many different scientific disciplines.

KEYWORDS

Website Quality, Scientometrics, Research Assessment

1. INTRODUCTION & BACKGROUND

Although website quality research has been in the rise during the past 20 years, little is known about the productivity and impact of the major contributors to the area. Therefore, this study will try to provide an early scientometric assessment of this multidisciplinary stream of research. Scientometrics is a scientific discipline concerned with examining all aspects of information including scholarly research using a number of techniques to provide a valid description of its foundations and contributions (Garfield, 1979, Price, 1963, Pritchard, 1969, Garfield, 1955, Egghe and Rousseau, 1990). Although several information systems have carried out a number of scientometrics analyses related to many information systems issues (Lowry et al., 2013, Zhang et al., 2011, Willcocks et al., 2008), to our knowledge, no study has focused on website quality research specifically.

The literature is rich with articles focusing on "research about research" (Gallivan and Benbunan-Fich, 2007), which depend for the most part on scholarly assessment research in the information science discipline (Pritchard, 1969, Egghe and Rousseau, 1990). According to Truex et al. (2009), similar investigations can be categorized as journal rankings, individual productivity assessment, or metrics/methods improvements. The first category of research is concerned with assessing the quality/influence of research sources in the area using a number of techniques including citations analysis and related measures. Recent example investigations in this area include those by Lowry et al. (2013), Zhang et al. (2011), and Willcocks et al. (2008). The second category is concerned on assessing individual researcher's contributions and/or impact. Example studies in this category include Meho and Rogers (2008) study, which examined the citation counting and ranking as well as the h-index indicators of 22 human-computer interaction scholars across the Scopus and Web of Science databases. Another example study in this category is that of Hu and Chen (2011) who examined the productivity and h-index scores of 232 information systems researchers based on Google Scholar citations. The third category of "research about research" is concerned with developing metrics and methods that facilitate the measurement of scholarly influence. Example research efforts in this area can be found in the information science discipline notably in the works of researchers such as Garfield (1972), Hirsch (2005) and Egghe (2006).

Website quality research is concerned with the evaluation of the salient technical and/or non-technical features of a website (commercial or otherwise) and the evaluation of its various implications (e.g., Aladwani, 2017, Aladwani, 2013, Aladwani and Palvia, 2002, Olsina et al., 1999, Palmer, 2002, Parasuraman et al., 2005, Eysenbach et al., 2002). This stream of research is progressively making its way into mainstream literature in many disciplines including information systems, computer science, marketing, medical informatics, and engineering, to name a few. The interest in the concept of website quality stems from its documented influence on many important individual and organizational outcomes (Wells et al., 2011, Aladwani, 2006, DeLone and McLean, 2003, McKnight et al., 2002). A major sign of this growing attention manifests in the mounting number of documents on the topic. Given the rising attention among researchers in the area, it is important to shed light on this trend.

One way to analyze this important yet under studied knowledge base is by carrying out a scientometrics study. Therefore, this study will try to describe research productivity across scientific disciplines using high-level scientometrics analyses. In doing so, it seeks to provide several insights to researchers and policy makers in the form of answers to a number of basic questions such as: how many website quality articles have been published globally?, what is the country-level research output on the topic?, what is the organizational-level productivity in the area?, how many sources have published articles about the subject?, who are the most productive and influential authors in this field?, and which terms are most frequently appearing in this stream of research?

2. METHODS

We followed a number of steps: (1) collected the required data, (2) ranked the countries, institutions, and authors according to research productivity, (3) identified the top 10 entries along each measure, and (4) interpreted the results. The website quality research dataset was downloaded on November 25th, 2017 from the Web of Science© database after a comprehensive using a Boolean search of two sets of title terms: (website, web, "e-commerce", "e-government", etc.) and (quality, usability, accessibility, etc.). No additional criteria were used to construct the query besides search keywords and the time span (between 1996 and 2017).

3. ANALYSIS & RESULTS

To address the research questions of this study, we used descriptive statistics to analyze overall measures of website quality research data on country, institution, source, and author levels. Overall, the research corpus consisted of 7,237 documents, appeared in 3,900 academic outlets, and written by 16,533 authors from 4,522 institutions and 113 countries. Research productivity in the area is increasing since 1996 ($R^2 = .70$, $p < .01$). The dataset spans numerous scientific disciplines (information systems, computer science, marketing, medical informatics, engineering, education, psychology, etc.) and includes all document types such as journal articles, conference papers, books, book chapters, reviews, book reviews, software reviews, letters, editorials, and many other types of scholarly outputs. For the purpose of this study, the analyses were performed on the first five document types.

The results reveal that the total number of documents produced by the top ten countries (USA, China, England, Spain, Taiwan, Germany, South Korea, Italy, Canada, and Australia) is 4,677 (65% of the total number of documents in our dataset). The minimum number of documents is 183 (Australia) and the maximum is 1,440 (USA), a difference of 1,257, averaging 467.7. Research output in the website quality area is somewhat concentrated with two of the top ten countries (USA and Peoples Republic China) representing close to 57% of the total. The USA alone accounts for approximately 31% of overall research productivity in the area. With 1,440 documents, USA is more than three times bigger than the average across the top ten countries.

The findings also reveal that, together, the ten most productive institutions in our dataset (University of Washington, Purdue University, University of Hong Kong, University of Manchester, Indiana University, Polit. Milan, Hong Kong Polytechnic University, Penn State University, Tsinghua University, and University of Granada) contributed 324 website quality documents that spread from 29 (Hong Kong Polytechnic University and Penn State University, among others) to 44 (University of Washington). Approximately 40% of the institutions produced 29 documents (below the average of 32.4). Research productivity is distributed relatively evenly across all ten institutions. The top two universities in our dataset account for approximately 25% of total number of documents.

A total of 312 website quality articles appeared in the top ten academic outlets in our corpus (Journal of Medical Internet Research, Computers in Human Behavior, Universal Access in the Information Society, Government Information Quarterly, Web Engineering, Proceedings, Computers Helping People with Special Needs, Proceedings, International Journal of Human-Computer Studies, Social Science Computer Review, Expert Systems with Applications, and Journal of Web Engineering). The distribution ranges from 24 (Expert Systems with Applications and the Journal of Web Engineering) to 49 (Journal of Medical Internet Research), a difference of 25, averaging 31.2. The distribution is positively skewed as the average of 31.2 is much greater than the median of 28. The total number of documents is relatively concentrated with 41% of the total represented by three of the ten publications. The top publications list is dominated by computer science and engineering journals.

The top ten most productive researchers (Calero, C; Huang, GQ; Olsina, L; Rossi, G; Cyr, D; Kuo, CFJ; Rocha, A; Chevalier, A; Aladwani, AM; and Loiacono, ET) in our dataset wrote 96 website quality articles. The distribution ranges from six (Aladwani, AM; and Loiacono, ET) to 18 (Calero, C), averaging 9.6. Author level productivity scores are relatively concentrated with 54% of the total represented by four of the authors. The top two researchers represent approximately 31% of the overall number of documents. The list of most productive authors is dominated by computer science researchers. An important note here is that in our initial analysis, we faced some challenges with names' accuracy. Zhang, Y, for example, was listed as the most productive author in the area with 25 articles. After manually double checking the data, it was clear that this name was mistakenly concatenated with those of other authors (e.g., Zhang, Yi; Zhang, Ye; Zhang, Yang; Zhang, Yin; Zhang, Yuejin; and several other variations). A similar problem was found with many other authors' names (e.g., Lee, S; Lee, J; Zhang, L; Wang, J; and Kim, H, etc.). Moreover, some names repeatedly appear together as co-authors (e.g., Caro, A and Piattini, M with Calero, C) so to avoid double counting only the name of the most productive author was included in the list. Therefore, the list was reconstructed by moving backwards from the most frequent names to the most frequent and accurate ones.

Citations analysis of the top authors (Parasuraman, A et al.; Eysenbach, G et al.; Palmer, J et al.; Cyr, D et al.; Venkatesh, V et al.; Flavian, C et al.; Aladwani, AM et al.; Willard, L et al.; You, F et al.; and Jain, E et al.) offers different results, however. The total accrued citations by the top ten authors are 6,742. The values range from 333 (Jain, E et al.) to 1,606 (Parasuraman and his colleagues); the average is 674.2. The distribution is positively skewed and the total number of citations is dominated by two of the ten researchers (47%). Parasuraman and his colleagues' citations (1,606) are more than two times bigger than the average of citations across the top ten authors. The list of most influential authors is dominated by marketing and information science researchers.

The distribution of terms in our corpus (Web Service, Implementation, Accessibility, Student, Platform, Web Application, Architecture, Patient, Solution, and Network) ranges from 542 for the term solution to 1,109 for the term "web service", a difference of 567. The average is 802.5. The distribution is positively skewed and the occurrences are relatively evenly spread. The top two terms account for more than 27% of the occurrences. The list of most recurring terms is consistent with the list of most active researchers; the list is dominated by computer science keywords. This result is somewhat expected because 50% of the entries in our dataset are classified as computer science articles. Moreover, the term "student" gives an indication that most field studies in the area rely on college students as research subjects.

4. CONCLUSIONS

The goal of this work-in-progress study was to carry out a scientometrics analysis of website quality research from 1996 to 2017 as reported in Web of Science©. The paper reports summaries of overall country, institutional, source, author, and term level characteristics and reveals a number of findings including: (1) research on website quality is growing and distributed unevenly across many different scientific disciplines, (2) extant research in the area is dominated by computer science contributions, (3) most of the efforts in the area come from few countries; mainly from USA and China, (4) the list of top universities is dominated by American and Asian institutions, (5) the list of top publications is dominated by computer science and engineering journals, (6) the list of most productive authors is dominated by computer science scholars, whilst the most influential authors list is dominated by information science and marketing researchers, and (7) the list of most recurring terms is dominated by computer science keywords. The findings offer a number of helpful insights for researchers and research policy makers. Future research is, however, needed to shed more light on these findings.

REFERENCES

Aladwani, A. M., 2006. An empirical test of the link between web site quality and forward enterprise integration with web consumers. *Business Process Management Journal,* Vol. 12 No. 2, pp. 178-190.

Aladwani, A. M., 2013. A cross-cultural comparison of Kuwaiti and British citizens' views of e-Government interface quality. *Government Information Quarterly,* Vol. 30 No. 1, pp. 74-86.

Aladwani, A. M., 2017. Compatible quality of social media content: Conceptualization, measurement,and affordances. *International Journal of Information Management,* Vol. 37 No. 6, pp. 576-582.

Aladwani, A. M. and Palvia, P. C., 2002. Developing and validating an instrument for measuring user-perceived web quality. *Information and Management,* Vol. 39 No. 6, pp. 467-476.

DeLone, W. H. and McLean, E. R., 2003. The DeLone and McLean model of information systems success: A ten-year update. *Journal of Management Information Systems,* Vol. 19 No. 4, pp. 9-30.

Egghe, L., 2006. An improvement of the h-index: the g-index. *ISSI Newsletter,* Vol. 2 No. 1, pp. 8-9.

Egghe, L. and Rousseau, R., 1990. *Introduction to informetrics: Quantitative methods in library, documentation and information Science.* Elsevier, Amsterdam, Netherland.

Eysenbach, G., et al., 2002. Empirical studies assessing the quality of health information for consumers on the World Wide Web: A systematic review. *Journal of the American Medical Association,* Vol. 287 No. 20, pp. 2691-2700.

Gallivan, M. J. and Benbunan-Fich, R., 2007. Analyzing IS research productivity: An inclusive approach to global IS scholarship. *European Journal of Information Systems,* Vol. 16 No. 1, pp. 36-53.

Garfield, E., 1955. Citation indexes for science: A new dimension in documentation through association of Ideas. *Science,* Vol. 122 No. 3159, pp. 108-111.

Garfield, E., 1972. Citation analysis as a tool in journal evaluation. *Science,* Vol. 178, pp. 471-479.

Garfield, E., 1979. *Citation Indexing. Its theory and application in science, technology and humanities.* Wiley, New York, NY.

Hirsch, J. E., 2005. An index to quantify an individual's scientific research output. *PNAS,* Vol. 102 No. 46, pp. 16569-16572.

Hu, P. J.-H. and Chen, H., 2011. Analyzing Information Systems Researchers' Productivity and Impacts: A Perspective on the H Index. *ACM Transactions on Management Information Systems,* Vol. 2 No. 2, pp. 1-8.

Lowry, P. B., et al., 2013. Evaluating journal quality and the association for information systems senior scholars' journal basket via bibliometric measures: Do expert journal assessments add value? *MIS Quarterly,* Vol. 37 No. 4, pp. 993-1012.

McKnight, D. H., et al., 2002. Developing and validating trust measures for e-commerce: An integrative typology. *Information Systems Research,* Vol. 13 No. 3, pp. 334-359.

Meho, L. and Rogers, Y., 2008. Citation counting, citation ranking, and h-index of human-computer interaction researchers: A comparison between Scopus and Web of Science. *Journal of the American Society for Information Science and Technology,* Vol. 59 No. 1, pp. 1711-1726.

Olsina, L., et al., 1999. Specifying quality characteristics and attributes for websites. *First ICSE Workshop on Web Engineering (WebE-99),* Los Angeles, CA.

Palmer, J. W., 2002. Web site usability, design, and performance metrics. *Information Systems Research,* Vol. 13 No. 2, pp. 151-167.

Parasuraman, A., et al., 2005. E-S-QUAL: A multiple-Item scale for assessing electronic service quality. *Journal of Service Research,* Vol. 7 No. 3, pp. 213-233.

Price, D. d. S., 1963. *Little Science, Big Science.* Columbia University Press, New York, NY.

Pritchard, A., 1969. Statistical bibliography or bibliometrics? *Journal of Documentation,* Vol. 24, pp. 348-349.

Truex, D., et al., 2009. Assessing scholarly influence: Using the Hirsch Indices to reframe the discourse. *Journal of the Association for Information Systems,* Vol. 10 No. 7, pp. 560-594.

Wells, J. D., et al., 2011. What signal are you sending? How website quality influences perceptions of product quality and purchase intentions. *MIS Quarterly,* Vol. 35 No. 2, pp. 373-396.

Willcocks, L., et al., 2008. The ranking of top IS journals: A perspective from the London School of Economics. *European Journal of Information Systems,* Vol. 17 No. 2, pp. 163-168.

Zhang, C., et al., 2011. Quality-structure index: A new metric to measure scientific journal influence. *Journal of the American Society for Information Science and Technology,* Vol. 62 No. 4, pp. 643-653.

KNOWLEDGE MANAGEMENT FOR THE CONSERVATION OF BIODIVERSITY AND THE SUSTAINABILITY OF ECOSYSTEM SERVICES

Johan Manuel Redondo, PhD
Catholic University of Colombia
Research Institute of Biological Resources Alexander von Humboldt, Colombia

ABSTRACT

The main difficulty in the management of socio-ecological systems is misinformed decision making that leads to wrong interventions of the landscape, which translates into the loss of biodiversity and ecosystem services. The aim of this paper is to develop spaces for the formulation of socio-ecological problems, oriented to the generation, transfer and application of knowledge with which decisions are taken to solve socio-ecological problems. In this way, in this article is presented a proposed knowledge management structure for decision making on socioecological systems oriented to the conservation of biodiversity and the sustainability of ecosystem services. It is concluded that the great efforts being made by organizations of any style within the framework of knowledge management are wasted if this management does not return to the problems that generated them to help them resolve. This depends, to a large extent, on the capacity that the organization possesses to be articulated transdisciplinarity in exercises of joint construction of knowledge.

KEYWORDS

Knowledge Management, Socio-Ecological Systems, Biodiversity Conservation, Ecosystem Services, Socio-Ecological Balance

1. INTRODUCTION

The main difficulty in the management of socio-ecological systems is misinformed decision making that leads to wrong interventions of the landscape, which translates into the loss of biodiversity and ecosystem services (Ray-Vallete, H., 2017).

Figure 1 shows a representation of the socioecological systems in which, starting from the main ecological structure and following the orange trace, it is seen that the main ecological structure performs functions that give rise to the ecosystem services that, in the Social sphere is interpreted as benefits, which are valued according to the mental models and scientific capacities of the moment, generating a set of decisions that affect the main ecological structure in a positive or negative manner, according to the assessment that have received their services. In this way, it is distinguished in this systemic representation that everything is woven together, and that it is precisely this interdependence that can guide decisions towards the conservation of biodiversity and the sustainability of ecosystem services.

In developing countries, the research agendas of specialized centers and the administrative processes of public institutions disrupt decision-making processes, ignoring the fact that these processes are fed from and to the problems related to biodiversity and ecosystem services to give them a solution. This situation demands the definition of knowledge management frameworks that allow the institutional articulation for the conservation of biodiversity and socio-ecological balance (Raum, S. 2018).

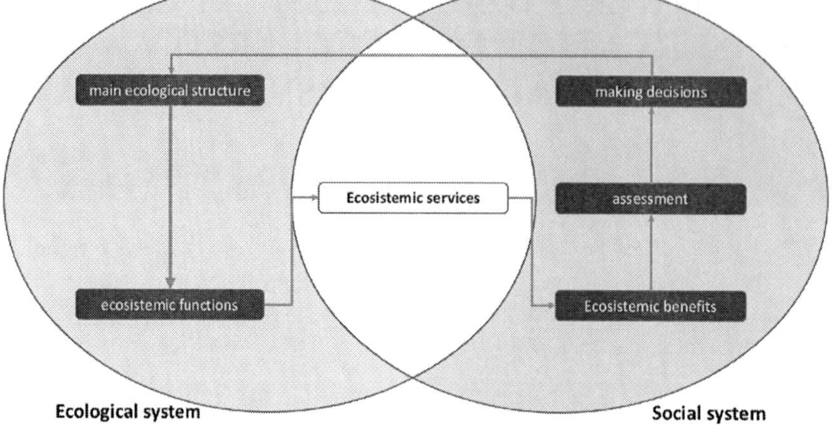

Figure 1. Conceptual scheme for the evaluation and evaluation of Ecosystem Services, leading to the establishment of policy options and management measures by decision makers. Adapted from TEEB (2008)

In this sense, an intergovernmental framework between political and scientific institutions has been developed to strengthen the relationship between them and achieve the sustainable use of biodiversity, long-term human well-being and sustainable development called Intergovernmental Science-Policy Platform on Biodiversity and Ecosystem Services IPBES (IPBES, 2016). To achieve this goal, the Platform has four functions: to catalyze the generation of new knowledge; to produce assessments of existing knowledge; to support policy formulation and implementation; and to build capacities relevant to achieving its goal. These interconnected functions are realized in the Platform work programme. However, the IPBES framework shows more concern for a conceptual framework on biodiversity and ecosystem services than on the management itself of the socio-ecological knowledge that is obtained.

The aim of this paper is to develop spaces for the formulation of socio-ecological problems, oriented to the generation, transfer and application of knowledge with which decisions are taken to solve socio-ecological problems. In this way, in this article is presented a proposed knowledge management structure for decision making on socioecological systems oriented to the conservation of biodiversity and the sustainability of ecosystem services.

2. THE DOUBLE LOOP OF KNOWLEDGE MANAGEMENT TO ADDRESS PROBLEMS IN SOCIO-ECOLOGICAL SYSTEMS

From an abstract perspective, dealing with socio-ecological problems or any other type of problems has the same steps. It begins with a clear formulation of the problem and turns on it after a methodological process through which its solution is proposed (Calvet et.al. 2015). In this sense there seems to be not much to say. However, about the problems in socio-ecological systems, it should be highlighted the difficulty that exists for decision makers in aligning their agendas with the agendas of biodiversity needs and ecosystem services in landscapes, particularly due to the lack of knowledge of the relationships that these have with all human activities (Balvanera, P., 2012). For this reason, even some scientific development institutions end up working for the strengthening of political agendas without a premeditated intention and fall into the game in which one should not fall when working on socio-ecological systems: the game of disciplinarily and ignorance of the importance of connections in socio-ecological systems (Eastwood, et al.2016). In this way, biodiversity and socio-ecological services end up becoming disconnected parts of the system whose value is established in the number of individuals, hectares, tons, cubic meters, etc. which are counted, and which are measured by specialists not interested in establishing the relationships that determine the quantities (Mancini, M, et al. 2018).

The lack of interest and ignorance of educational institutions in the underdeveloped nations to teach the socio-ecological as something in which everything is woven together, ends up determining the dynamics of the social with the ecological, affecting the conservation of biodiversity and the balance between them (La Rosa, et al. 2016). In this context, the decision-maker, oriented towards development, is unable to define a medium and long-term path in which this development guarantees the welfare of the socially, in respect of the ecological, because he only sees sustainability the economic aspect (Hasegawa, Okabe, & Taki. 2018). On the other hand, those interested in ecological issues underestimate the needs of the decision maker in terms of seeking welfare and often stick to their own agendas of a disciplinary type (Fagerholm, et al. 2016).

This panorama of disciplinary disarticulation and its effects on the treatment of the essential problems of socio-ecological systems that cannot be dissolved in disciplines and that are made increasingly critical by the growing power of transformation of the human being, has been treated general form by speeches like the one of the complex thought of Edgar Morin from at least three decades back, nevertheless, continues being a problem for our species.

In this sense, the knowledge management framework proposed in this document supposes the disciplinary break from transdisciplinary work, understood as the work carried out by different disciplines in which besides trying to work together they also try to understand each other. With this context, a proposal for the management of knowledge in the institutions responsible for the conservation of biodiversity and the sustainability of ecosystem services is presented below, which will constitute a double loop of knowledge management to address problems in socio-ecological systems, see figure 2.

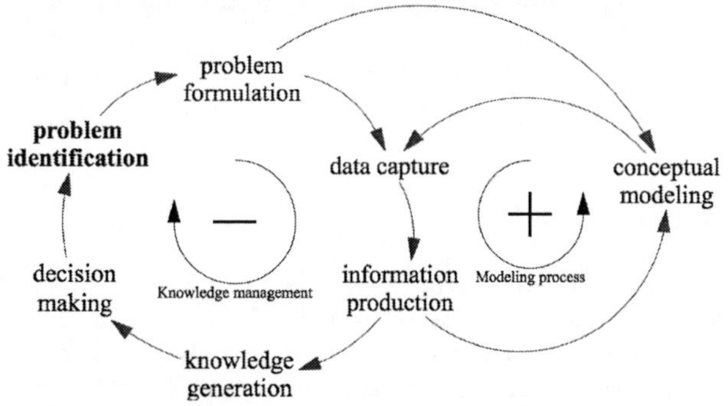

Figure 2. Double Loop of Knowledge Management to Address Problems in Socio-Ecological Systems

2.1 Identification and Formulation of Problems

The main basis of discussion is to initiate management with the identification and formulation of a problem of interest to the decision-maker related to socio-ecological systems. These problems involve the transformation of the landscape by the change of land use or other anthropic activities necessary for the welfare of society. Here management implies the understanding of the landscape as a system in which everything is woven together, precisely because the landscape is a complex system. Therefore, it is expected that the problems are identified from the decision maker with the support of a transdisciplinary team that assists in the formulation of the problem. With the problem formulated, the articulation of different research, consultancy and/or advisory actors that contribute to solving the problem from their capacities is simple.

2.2 Conceptual Modeling

With the problem formulated, the step to follow is the proposal of conceptual models from which the data capture that will be required to solve the problem is determined. The conceptual models demand rigorous exercises of revision of the state of the art, together with the consideration of the inclusion of systems of knowledge different from the western ones, in exercises of disciplinary and cultural inclusion. These conceptual models must consider, mainly, the relationships between the different attributes of the landscape because, as is known, it is the relationships that allow the behavior of the system to be established (Sterman, 2000), which in turn enunciates the interest of considering both the direct relationships as indirect of the system in consideration of the transformations that this exhibit during the time.

2.3 Data Capture

The capture of data is a fundamental activity to recognize the state of the systems, as well as to feed the models that have been established for the generation of information oriented to solve the formulated problems. The data captured may be conditioned by the formulation of the problem or by the conceptual model of the problem. For the first case, the existence of previous methodologies that require the data to be solved is assumed, while in the second case, a previous conceptual modeling is required with which the work methodology is defined and, therefore, the data that is required to meet the new methodology.

2.4 Information Production

The production of information is the exercise by which the conceptual model and the captured data are considered to generate information with which at least one solution to the problem proposed is provided. This process is cyclical in the sense in which its generation does not necessarily have to be effective from the first attempt, reason for which it is necessary to return on the conceptual model and on the data capture to verify the reasons why the methodology is not responding to the needs of the problem. In the generation of information, it must be understood that what is solved is a problem and, therefore, the technique or set of techniques that best solve the problem must be identified, since it has been seen in practice that much is insisted on solving different problems with the same technique, which also establishes a single type of scope of the answer and in the end it ends up losing the sense, because the problems of interest are no longer addressed but the problems for the technique. In the production of information should also be considered the type of outputs that will be obtained for the results, which are conditioned by users, decision makers, who will address the problem in question directly.

2.5 Knowledge Generation

The generation of knowledge is the moment of the management process in which the transfer of knowledge is made to the decision maker, therefore it is mediated by the instruments and dissemination techniques that are available. This moment is very important because it justifies all the effort made, since an empowered decision-maker of the learned information transforms assertively and opportunely the socio-ecological system it manages. For this reason, it must be taken into account that, the interests of the transdisciplinary work team that carried out the generation of information do not necessarily correspond to the interests that the decision maker has on the same results, the frameworks are different. In addition, since the decision maker has a different function and most likely a different disciplinary training, the how's of the elaboration of the results are not as important as the results themselves for later decision-making, making their communication end in undesirable conflicts and, therefore, in the rejection of the results.

2.6 Decision Making

Finally, it is considered for the success of knowledge management that decision making is made from the previous process that has been mentioned. In this regard, the technicalities considered for the achievement of results and the ability to carry out the disclosure, can be dismissed only because of the lack of interpersonal skills on the part of those who carried out knowledge generation activities ranging from the formulation of the problem to the generation of knowledge, basically because the decision maker always considers the relevance of trust on the methodologies and this is expressed in the way they approached him throughout the process.

3. CONCLUSIONS

It is concluded that the great efforts being made by organizations of any style within the framework of knowledge management are wasted if this management does not return to the problems that generated them to help them resolve and that this depends, to a large extent, on the capacity that the organization possesses to be articulated transdisciplinarily in exercises of joint construction of knowledge.

In this context, local and global organizations responsible for the management of biodiversity and ecosystem services should consider the broad framework proposed in this document for knowledge management, so that their activities do not fall outside a framework in which can be implemented to solve essential problems of the complex realities in which they are framed.

REFERENCES

Abiteboul, S. et al, 2000. *Data on the Web: From Relations to Semistructured Data and XML.* Morgan Kaufmann Publishers, San Francisco, USA.

Gretchen, D. 1997. *Nature Services, societal dependence on natural ecosystems.* Island Press, Washington D.C.

Millennium Ecosystem Assessment, 2005. Ecosystems and Human Well-being Millennium Ecosystem Assessment. ISLAND PRESS. Washington.

Business Dynamics:Systems thinking and modeling for a complex world. 2000. Boston.

Bodorik P. et al, 1991. Deciding to Correct Distributed Query Processing. *In IEEE Transactions on Data and Knowledge Engineering*, Vol. 4, No. 3,pp 253-265.

Binder, C. R., J. Hinkel, P. W. G. Bots, and C. Pahl-Wostl. (2013). Comparison of frameworks for analyzing social-ecological systems. *Ecology and Society* 18 (4), 1-26.

Ray-Vallete, H., Mathé, S., Sales, J. (2017). An assessment method of ecosystem services based on stakeholders perceptions: The Rapid Ecosystem Services Participatory Appraisal (RESPA) . *Ecosystem Services, 28,* 311-319.

Costanza. R., D 'arge. R., De Groot. R.,Farberk. S., Grasso. M., et. al.(1997). The value of the world's ecosystem services and natural capital. *Nature.* 387 (15).

IDEAM, 2011. Aportes del IDEAM para la definición y aplicación de la Estructura Ecológica Nacional. Instituto de Hidrología, Meteorología y Estudios Ambientales *–IDEAM-*. Bogotá D.C., Colombia. 43 p.

Raum, S. (2018). A framework for integrating systematic stakeholders análisis in ecosystem services research: stakeholders mapping foto forest ecosystem services in the UK. *Ecosystem services.* 170-184. 29.

Hasegawa, Y., Okabe, K., & Taki, H. (2018). A scenario approach for ecosystem-service changes.

Futures, 96, 23-31.

L Calvet-Mir., E Corbera., A Martin., J Fisher and N Gross-Camp. (2015). Payments for ecosystem services in the tropics: a closer look at effectiveness and equity. *Environmental Sustainability.* 14, 150-162.

Balvanera. P, Uriarte. M., Almeida-Leñero. L., Altesor. A., DeClerck. F., Gardner. T., Hall. J., Lara. A., Laterra. P., Peña-Claros. M., Dalva M. Silva Matos, Adrian L. Vogl, Luz Piedad Romero-Duque, Luis Felipe Arreola, Ángela Piedad Caro-Borrero, Federico Gallego, Meha Jain, Christian Little, Rafael de Oliveira Xavier, José M. Paruelo, Jesús Emilio Peinado, Lourens Poorter, Nataly Ascarrunz, Francisco Correa, Marcela B. Cunha-Santino, Amabel Paula
Hernández-Sánchez, María Vallejos. Ecosystem services research in Latin America: The state of the art. (2012). *Ecosystem Services*. 2, 56-70.

Eastwood. A., Brooker. K., Irvine. R.J., Artz. R.R.E., Norton. L.R., Bullok. J.M., Roos. L., Fielding. L., Ramsay. S.,

Roberts. J., Anderson. W., Dugan. D., Cooksley. S., Pakerman. R.J. (2016). Does nature conservation enhance ecosystem services delivery?. *Ecosystem Services.* 17, 152-162.

Mancini, M. S., Galli, A., Coscieme, L., Niccolucci, V., Lin, D., Pulselli, F., y otros. (2018). The law, ecosystem services and ecosystem functions: An in-depth overview of coverage and interrelation. *Ecosystem Services, 29*, 190-198.

La Rosa. D., Spyra. M., Inostroza. L. (2016). Indicators of Cultural Ecosystem Services for urban planning: A review. *Ecological Indicator.* 61, 74-89.

Nora Fagerholma,b,∗, Mario Torralbaa, Paul J. Burgess c, Tobias Plieninger. (2016). A systematic map of ecosystem services assessments around European agroforestry. *Ecological Indicator.* 62, 47-65.

Beck, K. and Ralph, J., 1994. Patterns Generates Architectures. *Proceedings of European Conference of Object-Oriented Programming.* Bologna, Italy, pp. 139-149.

IPBES (2016): The methodological assessment report on scenarios and models of biodiversity and ecosystem services. S. Ferrier, K. N. Ninan, P. Leadley, R. Alkemade, L. A. Acosta, H. R. Akçakaya,

L. Brotons, W. W. L. Cheung, V. Christensen, K. A. Harhash, J. Kabubo-Mariara, C. Lundquist, M. Obersteiner, H. M. Pereira, G. Peterson, R. Pichs-Madruga, N. Ravindranath, C. Rondinini and B. A. Wintle (eds.). Secretariat of the Intergovernmental Science-Policy Platform on Biodiversity and Ecosystem Services, Bonn, Germany. 348 pages.

COGNITIVE INFORMATION SYSTEMS OVERVIEW AND RESEARCH PROPOSAL

Bálint Molnár and Dóra Mattyasovszky-Philipp
Information Systems Department, Eötvös Loránd University, ELTE, Pázmány Péter Sétány 1/C, Budapest, Hungary

ABSTRACT

The rapid change of world causes new challenges in the business environment and in many other operational areas of enterprises. Those challenges likely increase the chance for client or customer satisfaction meanwhile improve companies' efficiency, improve cost saving, optimize processes in operation and/or manufacturing, enhance security, reduce errors etc. Due to the complexity and to the rapid alterations within the environment, changes in the processes of enterprises are not able to answer these challenges easily in time, e.g. predicting the potential future events as one of the key elements of the long-term success, these events might have a direct impact on the organization future. Those required skills to manage the actual situation are rarely available in one single person or in one team, sometimes it is not affordable or not efficient, therefore one of the possible solution is to leverage the capability of a cognitive information system. There are many unanswered questions, unclear and sometimes misleading information about the cognitive information systems. The aim of the publication is to clarify the meaning of the cognitive system. To expand one of the definitions, meanwhile differentiate the cognitive information system from the traditional information systems, then conceptualize the primary areas of operation. Help to understand and imagine the future of cognitive informatics systems, cognitive operation and analyses in different segments, industries and in the world of enterprises with examples. In the areas presented, point to the potential benefits of the application and highlighting the importance of it.

KEYWORDS

Business Information Systems, Cognitive Information Systems, Information Systems, Modelling, Application

1. INTRODUCTION

The concept of Cognitive Information Systems appeared as an intersection and shared area of Information Systems and Cognitive Science. Modelling, analyzing, and designing information systems in the most recent technological advancement makes it possible and – at the same time – requests for architectural and design principles that combine the development of technology and theories of Cognitive Science. We think of architecture of information systems within enterprises in the sense of Zachman (Zachman, 1987) and TOGAF framework (Josey, 2011). The technology advancement in the field of information systems can be captured in the concept of Data Science and semantics.

Cognitive Science offers the analysis of cognitive tasks, i.e. the investigation of the decision making, reasoning skills of the examined subject whilst the subjects treat the set of complex information (Rogers, 2011). Interdisciplinary research on human expertise and domain specific cognition has yielded theoretical and methodological background that can be employed to create architecture and design principles that can assist in the realization of cognitive information systems (Miller, 2003). Cognitive science studies "the principles, architectures, organization, and operation of natural and artificial intelligence systems" (Grigoriev, 2011), thereby cognitive science is an intersection of scientific domains among artificial intelligence, psychology, linguistics, anthropology, neurosciences, and education. The approaches of informatics that can be exploited on the common field of cognitive science and information systems are as follows: knowledge representation, ontologies, description logic, computational linguistic, machine learning, and computational intelligence. The goal of this paper is to analyze the literature, to collect the provisional definitions and to determine whether what could be the research direction within information technology and business information systems. The objective is to clarify the concept of cognitive information systems in the light of computer science, cognitive science, and modeling of information systems.

The research methodology that were applied during the research analyses and assessment of the available publications pursued the comparative study pattern, i.e. studying and comparing the result published in articles, then a case study paradigm has been used for observing and monitoring the work with a cognitive information system during daily) operation.

2. LITERATURE SURVEY

Cognitive information systems can be regarded as an interdisciplinary research topic that has emerged as an interaction between information systems and cognitive sciences including psychology, neuroscience, cognitive modelling, cognitive ergonomics, linguistics, biology, anthropology, and various branches of artificial intelligence (Miller, 2011). The most essential characteristics of the research area:

Taking into account of the cognitive capability: it is an abstract notion that incorporates the temporal and contextual environment to be considered within the analysis and design of cognitive information systems.

An overarching viewpoint: the consideration in the interaction between humans and silicon agents ("computers") does not constrain the investigation of *cognitive capability* only onto the human party but it involves the automated part of the system. The business services and the supporting functional services of information systems come into being during alteration in business environment, then the analysis of business processes that concludes the design and implementation of the related function. Emerging business services: the simplistic stimulus-reaction model for function-centered viewpoint is expanded with the perspective of the dynamic evolution, i.e. the business services that are developed for fulfilling certain goals are included dynamically in constant changes into functional services of cognitive information systems. The answer to the question what makes a system cognitive is the following according to Hurwitz: *"Three important concepts help make a system cognitive: contextual insight from the model, hypothesis generation (a proposed explanation of a phenomenon), and continuous learning from data across time."* (Hurwitz, 2015.) Wang postulates that a "denotation mathematical" approach is required that own structures, tools, and methods beyond the traditional mathematical logic (Wang, 2007). Ogiela (Ogiela, 2012, pp. 17-18) collected areas of application of informatics and information technology where cognitive information processing techniques are incorporated into various systems. The wide spectrum of the applications covers business information systems, biomedical systems, identity and access management, autonomy and embedded systems etc. The business applications that are listed in Ref (Ogiela, 2012, pp. 17-18) undoubtedly has impacts on business and delivers advantages for the business. Economic ratio interpretation within the decision-making analysis for an enterprise; usually linked to some decision which can be transformed in some way to financial benefit (Park, 2007). The stock exchange games (belonging to decision-making analysis too) can be perceived by the same way, i.e. due to the nature of the analyses is not far from ratio analyses considering cognitive resonance. The cognitive resonance linked to the market expectations as any investment on stock exchange movements (Ogiela, 2014). The concept of cognitive resonance is one of the attempts that try to make sense of the modelling activities in the most recent world of data analytics that uses tools out of data science. However, there are cognitive information systems, which apparently analyze unstructured data without two facets data interpretation, but in fact there are deep semantic analyses behind of data integration. The semantic analysis is the overarching concept for cognitive information systems. The major elements are as follows: data pre-processing, data representation, linguistic perception, pattern classification, data classification, and finally cognitive resonance and data understanding (Ogiela, 2014). The information architecture that can provide an opportunity for creating a framework to describe the information exchange between the human parties along with her/his supporting silicon agent and cognitive information systems can be grounded in Enterprise Architecture (Josey, 2011; Zachman, 1987) and LIDA (Kahneman, 2011; Franklin 2014). The advantage of the LIDA model as an architecture is that it focuses on the cognitive processes and their structure at both conceptual and computational level (Faghihi 2015).

2.1 Understanding Based Cognitive Systems

There is a classification of cognitive information systems as understanding based cognitive systems (UBCCS, Understanding Based Cognitive Categorization Systems) (Ogiela, 2012). Within that categorization, there are enterprises and management related systems as UBDSS (Understanding Based Decision Support Systems),

UBMSS (Understanding Based Management Support Systems). The case studies referenced publication of (Ogiela,2012) in the form of proposal for developing systems investigate single, double and multi-factor analysis approaches that use Net Present Value (NPV), Internal Rate of Return (IRR), and discount rate. The presented approaches are based on formal languages, that describe building blocks for cognitive analysis that can be considered as semantic analysis that is based on logical predicates in the form of rules and concepts. The toolset that is utilized in this approach is grounded in finite state machines, automaton and theories of formal languages to deduce the assessment of the formalized situation. (Ogiela, 2014). Beside the systems with the single factor analysis (IRR, NPV), there is a description of systems with dual and multi-factor analysis. All the proposed systems pursue the same methods, i.e. defining a grammar, capturing the essential concepts in terminal and non-terminal symbols within the grammar, and predicates of decision making are formulated as rewriting rules of the grammar initiating state transitions within the realm of analysis. (Ogiela, 2012). The basic version of the UBMSS have been refined further into several sub-classes in (Ogiela, 2014), namely UBMLRSS (understanding based management liquidity ratios support systems), UBMPRSS (understanding based management profitability ratios support systems), UBMARSS (understanding based management activity ratios support systems), UBMFLRSS (understanding based management financial leverage ratios support systems). All of them use the data from the balance sheet, out of extracts from the general ledger and data from sub-systems. This data set is used in creating Business Case, Strategic Business Plan and in application for credits from banks. These data play important role in the life of a company and its future, these data serve as basis for further decision making.

2.2 Illustrative Example with Criticism

However, Ogiela mentioned IRR analyses by UBMSS system is as a most important method. (Ogiela, 2012, pp. 63). From financial perspective, NPV analyses more preferred by financial decision makers, due to the fact that IRR method is easy to use as long as cash inflows are even from year to year. In the current rapidly changing business environment this hardly can be forecasted or planned in advance that the steady cash flow can be anticipated. The general rule related to IRR is the following: The IRR can be found selecting the rate and discount the cash inflows. If the PV (present value) > I (initial investment) then select the higher rate until one is equal with the PV, because IRR is the rate of interest that equates the initial investment (I) with the present value (PV) of the future cash inflows, which happens at the rate of the IRR when either I=PV or NPV (net present value) = 0. Therefore, the result of decision rule is "accept" if the investment if IRR exceeds the cost of capital, otherwise reject it. Advantage of IRR method that use PV/NPV as time value of money; however, it cannot be used to compare multiple projects. Also, it might generate a problem when there are multiple reversals in the cash flow stream, the project could yield more than one internal rate of return. Due to the above described anomalies, IRR is not acceptable in all cases by decision makers. In case of alternative investments evaluation, the used calculation methodology is the NPV evaluation. Therefore, it would be preferable capability of a cognitive information system that uses NPV method parallel in the same time related to alternative investments. In this way, the NPV value of the alternative investments would bring decision makers in a real decision making position. It is not visible how the UBMSS system can handle the evaluation of IRR with the supposed capability of cognitive analysis. The data from the balance sheet, out of the extracts of general ledger and the reports from controlling are broadly used in business administration. There was a long-term evolution of application of various methods starting with the traditional statistical methods then the modern data mining, computational intelligence and machine learning approaches were employed that are able to create predictive and prescriptive results of the analysis (Brabazon, 2006; Lawrence, 1997; Rabuñal, 2005). The proposed varieties of UBMSS systems cannot identify the patterns that are crucial for recognizing problem areas in the life of a company by senior management. Properties of the cognitive information system defined by Hurwitz, UBMSS systems use well known mathematical models without any new hypotheses and thereby this fact causes that there is no continuous learning from the new models and from the new hypotheses by machine, the silicon agent, because this is an important features of a cognitive information system (Hurwitz, 2015).

3. FUTURE RESEARCH DIRECTION

A cognitive information system in an enterprise environment can be defined as a socio-technological information system that unifies the enterprise architecture and cognitive architecture (e.g. LIDA) in an overarching architecture approach. Considering the Zachman framework as an overarching approach, a cognitive information system belongs to the views of Business Analyst / Strategic Planner, and System Analyst and System Designer. The cognitive information system is involved in the process/function and data perspectives. The cognitive information systems exploit the achievements of data science stepping beyond the traditional stimulus-reaction metaphor for conceptualizing of functional services, it is an adaptive system that can handle the dynamically changing business environment and can incorporate the alteration of business processes by a way that the realization of changes is implemented in a systematic and consistent manner through the three seasons of business processes, i.e. analysis, design and implementation/operation (Bell, 2008). The above presented analysis about the concept of cognitive information systems in enterprises pinpoints the deficiencies of the recent advancements. Firstly, there is a need for integration of enterprise architecture and cognitive architecture approaches in the socio-technological environment of an organization. The architecture integration would lay the groundwork for an overall architecture that main objective would be to provide design principles for cognitive information systems to achieve cognitive resonance among the stakeholders. Secondly, enterprises come across regularly business problems as business process efficiency and effectiveness. The data set raised as the subject of the analysis in the case of UBMSS plays only minor role in the daily operation and strategic planning of companies. The data analytics as applied Data Science is a new source of information for enterprises to chase efficiency and effectiveness in their operations. The data warehouse and data mart technologies provide the opportunity to define objective measures that can describe the quality and quantity of the business process. The poly-structured data (structures, semi-structures and unstructured) can be the subject of various methods of data analytics. Some examples for areas of enterprises where the data science and cognitive approaches can be combined are considered in the following section. The distribution of tasks can be made better that improving employee satisfaction and productivity. The data analytics can help to move the focus from internal performance assessment to customer-oriented assessment of services. Three stages for enabling of processes for data analytics should be defined. The objective of data analytics procedure is to acquire knowledge out of collected data through discovering associations and relationships. The system analysis and design methods that are used are as follows: data modelling, entity-relationship modelling, designing interfaces for ETL (extract, transform, load), methods, techniques, and tools for data-cleansing, and creating semantic description that can partly be interpreted by machines and perceived by humans. Within the realm of predictive analytics, a set of techniques can be used that belong primarily to classification techniques as e.g.: decision tree analysis, statistical analysis, neural networks, case-based reasoning, Bayesian classifiers, genetic algorithms, rough sets. The future research should concentrate much more on the *model creation* for application of data science with the assistance of cognitive architectures. *The results of the analysis* as patterns, relationships, association etc. *should be interpreted for human cognition*. The concept of cognitive resonance is a handy notion for perception and description of the real problem. The major task of the research is to exploit the cognitive architectures in line with enterprise architecture for defining models, determining results and exhibit the outcomes for stakeholders-. Naturally, the available cognitive architectures should be investigated what can be integrated to the requirements of enterprise architecture and architectures of data science (Langley, 2009). To create design principles for supporting model creation, model perception and interpretation will be the task of the research in the sense of Design Science Research paradigm (March, 1995).

4. CONCLUSION

According to the most recent literature, the definition of cognitive information systems refers to the cognitive architectures, data processing, models for insights hypotheses for new phenomenon and opportunity for the silicon agents for the continuous learning. However, UBMSS like, the proposed systems cannot live up to expectations. The cognitive architecture and information system architecture is not integrated. The cognitive resonance provides a framework for describing the information interchange between human and automated systems. Although, the ideas of economic analysis that were raised in case studies of possible applications are superficial from point of operating enterprises where the management and information systems should solve in tandem serious problems.

Hence, the research has plenty to do on developing the idea of cognitive information systems in economics, reconciling the enterprise and cognitive architectures to leverage the tools of data science for business efficiency and effectiveness. The scientific and technological literature contains the description of massive cognitive information systems with the enormous resource requirements that may be accessible by huge international enterprises even taking into account some kind of cloud service as Software-as a-Service and its cost. The subject of the research is two-pronged, on the side of the practice the main aim is to grasp the notion of cognitive information systems that can be used for micro, small and medium enterprises, on the other side of formal approach the goal is to establish a model that define the business and information architecture, the major services exploiting the formal and semi-formal tool set of computer science.

ACKNOWLEDGEMENT

The project has been supported by the European Union, co-financed by the European Social Fund (EFOP-3.6.3-VEKOP-16-2017-00002).

REFERENCES

Beck, K. and Ralph, J., 1994. Patterns Generates Architectures. *Proceedings of European Conference of Object-Oriented Programming.* Bologna, Italy, pp. 139-149.

Bell, M., 2008. *Service-oriented modeling (SOA): Service analysis, design, and architecture.* John Wiley & Sons.

Brabazon, A. and O'Neill, M., 2006. *Biologically inspired algorithms for financial modelling.* Springer Science & Business Media.

Chen, Z., Jia, X. and Xiao, Z., 2015. A computational cognitive model of user applying creativity technique in creativity support systems. *Procedia Computer Science, 55*, pp.818-824.

Faghihi, U., et al., 2015. A cognitive model fleshes out Kahneman's fast and slow systems. *Biologically Inspired Cognitive Architectures, 11*, pp.38-52.

Grigoriev, E.A., 2001. The cognitive role of intuitive hypotheses and visual image of simulated reality. CASC' 2001, pp: 5-16.

Josey, A., 2011. *TOGAF® Version 9.1 A Pocket Guide.* Van Haren.

Kahneman, D., 2011. *Thinking, fast and slow.* Macmillan.

Langley, P., et al., 2009. Cognitive architectures: Research issues and challenges. *Cognitive Systems Research, 10*(2), pp.141-160.

Lawler, E.K., Hedge, A. and Pavlovic-Veselinovic, S., 2011. Cognitive ergonomics, socio-technical systems, and the impact of healthcare information technologies. *International Journal of Industrial Ergonomics, 41*(4), pp.336-344.

Lawrence, R., 1997. Using neural networks to forecast stock market prices. *University of Manitoba.*

March, S.T. and Smith, G.F., 1995. Design and natural science research on information technology. *Decision support systems, 15*(4), pp.251-266.

Miller, G.A., 2003. The cognitive revolution: a historical perspective. *Trends in cognitive sciences, 7*(3), pp.141-144.

Ogiela, L. and Ogiela, M.R., 2012. *Advances in cognitive information systems* (Vol. 17). Springer Science & Business Media.

Ogiela, L. and Ogiela, M.R., 2014. Cognitive systems for intelligent business information management in cognitive economy. *International Journal of Information Management, 34*(6), pp.751-760.

Ogiela, L., 2013. Semantic analysis and biological modelling in selected classes of cognitive information systems. *Mathematical and Computer Modelling, 58*(5), pp.1405-1414.

Park, C.S., et al., 2007. Engineering economics. *Pearson Prentice Hall, New Jersey.*

Rabuñal, J.R. ed., 2005. *Artificial neural networks in real-life applications.* IGI Global.

Rogers, Y., et al., 2011. *Interaction design: beyond human-computer interaction.* John Wiley & Sons.

Wang, Y., 2007. The theoretical framework of cognitive informatics. *International Journal of Cognitive Informatics and Natural Intelligence (IJCINI), 1*(1), pp.1-27.

Zachman, J.A., 1987. A framework for information systems architecture. *IBM systems journal, 26*(3), pp.276-292.

Hurwitz, J., et al., 2015. *Cognitive Computing and Big Data Analytics* Published by John Wiley & Sons, Inc. 10475 Crosspoint Boulevard Indianapolis, IN 46256 .

INTEGRATION OF CONOPS AND TOGAF ADM TO BENEFIT ADAPTIVE ENTERPRISE ARCHITECTURE

Nada Olayan and Shuichiro Yamamoto
Graduate School of Information Sciences,
Nagoya University furo-cho, Chikusa-ku, Nagoya, Aichi, 464-8601 Japan

ABSTRACT

Concept of operation document (ConOps) is an important component for understanding any system clearly and for guiding a better change process from current state to desired state. In our research we work on integrating ConOps to enterprise architecture using ArchiMate Architectural modeling language as a common representation between the both. To able to integrate ConOps as a textual document to EA, we propose a ConOps metamodel as bases for the alignment. In this paper we present our ConOps metamodel and a description of the integration of TOGAF and ConOps elements.

KEYWORDS

Concept of Operation, Enterprise Architecture, TOGAF, ArchiMate, Adaptive Enterprise Architecture

1. INTRODUCTION

In a previous study, we examined the role of the motivation extension of ArchiMate (ArchiMate is a modeling tool for Enterprise Architecture) and its relation to the adaptiveness of the EA. We believe that certain natural language documents could be a factor in the improvement of adaptive EA. Based on the previous examination, we found out that the Concept of Operation document (ConOps IEEE Std 1362™-1998) is the ideal document to serve as the bases for our research for so many reasons. ConOps document is used to guide the transition of systems; based on (Standards.ieee.org, 1998) it provides a clear description of the current and desired system as well as the description of transition and change. A connection between ConOps and ArchiMate has been established in a previous research (Olayan et al., 2018). In this paper we present a metamodel for conops and a suggest integration table for TOGAF ADM iteration cycles and ConOps elements based on ConOps analysis.

2. RELATED WORK

2.1 TOGAF Enterprise Architecture Framework

We refer to TOGAF framework for our Enterprise Architecture framework (EA). TOGAF is considered as the basis for customized Enterprise Architecture (EA). Its most important element is the Architecture Development Methodology (ADM). According to (The Open Group, 2016) The ADM defines the full life cycle processes to create EA, phases of the ADM from TOGAF shown in Figure 1.

2.2 ConOps IEEE 1362-1998 Standard

Concept of operations (CONOP) is a document describing the system and what it does in natural language. There are three major ConOps standards: IEEE 1362-1998 – IEEE guide for ConOps document, ANSI/AIAA guide from American National Standards Institute and DoD data item description for ConOps document. We choose ConOps IEEE 1362-1998 standard as basis because it is the only concept of operation standard that describes current state of system, justifications for change and the concept for the proposed system clearly, which contributes to guiding the transition from current state to future state (Standards.ieee.org, 1998). ConOps could improve the quality of enterprise architecture because the quality of the architecture depends on the ability to capture and analyze the goals and requirements to be realized by the architecture in such way that the "change process" of goals and requirements would be easy. Such quality measure can assure that the gathered data in analytical models and tools are used efficiently to support operational and strategic necessities.

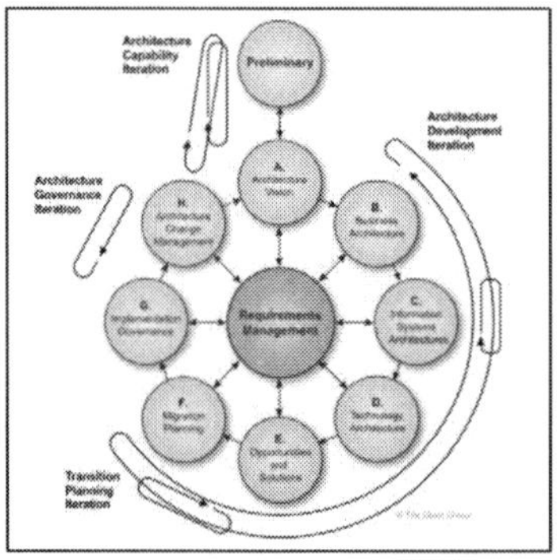

Figure 1. TOGAF ADM Iteration Cycles from the. Graph from (The Open Group, 2012)

2.3 ArchiMate

ArchiMate is an open independent modeling and common language for enterprise architecture with clear concepts and uniform structure; as described by (The Open Group, 2012) it is used for describing, analyzing and visualizing of relationships between architecture domains. ArchiMate 3.0 was introduced in 2016, it consists of core language, which focuses on the description of the four architecture domains defined by TOGAF standard: business architecture, data architecture, application architecture and technology architecture and two extensions: motivation & Strategy and Implementation &migration (The Open Group, 2012), according to (OpenGroup.org, 2016) there were many improvements in the latest addition including the addition of the strategy elements.

2.4 ConOps and ArchiMate

The main challenge in aligning ConOps with EA at first was that ConOps is a textual document with no specific metamodel or graphical representation. For ConOps to be aligned and integrated within EA, we had to find a common reference and representation modeling language that could help integrate and validate the integration. We believe that ArchiMate can serve as common reference and its concepts can represent ConOps graphically because they covered common related elements and concepts. Integrating ConOps into EA adds value either by using already written ConOps documents to aid EA or by updating or creating new ConOps from an EA prospective. In order to properly integrate ConOps into EA we need a metamodel. However no conops metamodel description can be found in literature, for this reason we decided to create general ConOps metamodel first. Different standards lack traceability from document specification to implementation. Giving ConOps a holistic visibility by presenting a metamodel would solve this problem and would also aid the process of creating ConOps at the analysis phase. For this reason our focus was mainly on the problem and solution space represented by traditional system engineering and ArchiMate Motivation Extension.

3. CONOPS ANALYSIS AND METAMODEL

In order to conceptualize and create ConOps metamodel, we employed expert's knowledge as engagement scholarship, literature review and represented the finding in a structure to assist the meta design following the research by (Ostrowski, Helfert and Xie, 2012).Our method include analyzing and identifying core concepts from ConOps standards, industry ConOps documents and related literature taking into consideration ConOps in relation to EA. To cover the domain of problem and solution we also identify related possible requirement engineering elements along with elements from traditional system engineering.In our previous research (Olayan et al., 2018), we extensively examined a number of online accessible ConOps documents (IEEE standard in government and industry) in each document we analyzed each Conops element and extracted all the concepts from ArchiMate and map them to their existence in each element based on ArchiMate standard definition and ArchiMate ontologies based on the work of (Azevedo, C, 2011) the concept had to occur in all the examined documents in the specific ConOps element for the mapping to be acknowledged. Based on a study on different types of conops standards by (Frittman, Edson, 2009), 6 categories of commonly occurring information were identified: background, system descriptions, and analysis of the system, impacts, supportability and operational scenarios. The categories are broken into subcategories, which can be referred to as ConOps elements. Using the previously mentioned categories, analysis of ConOps standards and previous our analysis of ConOps documents based on ArchiMate concepts and traditional systems engineering, we were able to preliminarily identify ConOps main core concepts as shown below in Table 1.

For metamodel representation, we referred to each concept`s definition from ArchiMate layers metamodels and ArchiMate motivation extension Ontology definition (Azevedo, C, 2011). However since ArchiMate doesn't cover all the derived concepts for our metamodel, we defined the rest of the concepts in the context of following literature: definition of ConOps creation methods based on system thinking by (Frittman, Edson, 2009) and their guidelines for creating ConOps (Frittman, Edson, 2008), Cloutier et al. (2009, p.39-p.42) also proposed an Agile ConOps creation process stages where we referred to their conceptual and specification phase to identify and define some concepts. Figure 2 consolidates our meta-model.

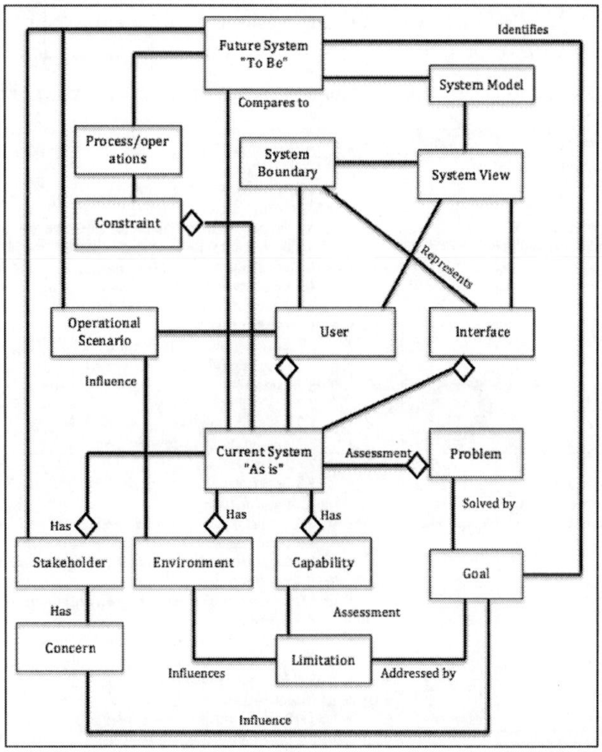

Figure 2. Basic Metamodel for ConOps Concepts and Main Elements

Table 1. Assignment of our derived Conops Core Concepts to Main Common ConOps Categories

Categories of commonly occurring information in ConOps(Frittman,Edson,2009)	Derived preliminary ConOps core concepts
Background	Problem, Goal, Concern, Description of Future system "To be", User
System descriptions	Description of Current system "As is", Constraints, Future system "To be".
Analysis of the system	Capabilities, limitation, Goal, Environment, System View, Interface, System model
Impacts	Process, stakeholders
Supportability	System boundary
Operational scenarios	Operational scenario

4. CONOPS SUPPORTING TOGAF ADM CYCLE

We first proposed that ConOps could support EA because ConOps can play an important role in bridging the current status where we want to move from to the desired status that we wish to reach. According to IEEE The heart of the IEEE standard is described in the following clauses of the ConOps document: "clause3 Description of existing system" (of which user wish to replace), "clause 4 for justification for a new or modified system" and clause 5 which describes the proposed system. This format could serve in tracing and applying changes in a consistent manner according to (The MITRE Corporation guide). Based on our analysis of main elements and clauses of the ConOps document, we observed potential alignment between ConOps and EA. To support TOGAF we decided to aid the ADM, which is the iterative Core of TOGAF.

The whole Architecture Development Methodology (ADM) wheel is iterative; there are several iterations within the ADM iteration cycle as shown in Figure 1. Iteration cycles for ADM includes: "Architecture context iteration", "architecture definition iteration", "transition planning iteration" and "architecture governance iteration". The development of ConOps is iterative and by aligning the related ADM phases and cycles we could achieve better responsive architecture with less ambiguity and better communication. Conops can be used for any type of system (Standards.ieee.org, 1998); our target ConOps for this research is associated with "architectural requirement" and not "system requirements". Suggested integration of ConOps elements from the IEEE 1362-1998 into ADM phases Iteration is shown in Table 2.

Table 2. Table Suggesting Integration of ConOps Elements and ADM Cycle Iterations

TOGAF ADM phases iteration	ConOps elements
Architecture context and Capability Iteration: Preliminary Phase A. Architecture vision H. Architecture change management	**1.Architecture Scope** ▪ 1.3 Architecture Overview **3.Current Architecture** ▪ 3.1 Architecture background, objective and scope ▪ 3.2 Operational policies and constraints **4.Justification for and nature of changes** ▪ 4.1 Justification of change (factors to influence the Architecture change) ▪ 4.2 Description of desired changes **5.Proposed Architecture** ▪ 5.1 Background, objective and scope of the proposed architecture ▪ 5.2 Operational policy and constraints for the proposed architecture **7.Summary of impacts** ▪ 7.1 Operational impacts ▪ 7.2 Organizational impacts ▪ 7.3 Impacts during development
Baseline iteration: B. Business Architecture C. Information system architecture D. Technology architecture	**3.Current Architecture** ▪ 3.3 Description of the current architecture (current component description) ▪ 3.4 Modes of operation for the current architecture ▪ 3.5 User classes and other involved personal in the current architecture ▪ 3.6 Support environment for the current architecture **5.Proposed Architecture** ▪ 5.3 Description of the proposed architecture (proposed component description) ▪ 5.4 Modes of operation for the proposed architecture ▪ 5.5 User classes and other involved personal ▪ 5.6 Support environment. **6.Operational Scenario** ▪ Architectural Operational scenario
Transition planning iteration: E. Opportunity and solution F. Immigration planning	**Justification for and nature of changes** ▪ Priorities among changes (based on factors) ▪ Changes considered but not included

5. CONCLUSION

In this research we presented a metamodel based on the IEEE 1362-1998 ConOps standard and suggested an integration of TOGAF ADM iteration cycles and ConOps elements. Our suggestion came from the open need for a better quality adaptive EA architecture, which promotes better understandability and responsiveness to changes. In future research we will complete the definition of integration between ConOps and EA and present metamodel evaluation using evaluation case study.

REFERENCES

Azevedo, C.,J. P. A. Almeida et al (2011). An Ontology-Based Semantics for the Motivation Extension to ArchiMate. IEEE 15th International Enterprise Distributed Object Computing Conference.

Cloutier, R., Mostashari, A., McComb, S., Deshmukh, A., Wade, J., Kennedy, D. and Korfiatis, P., 2009. Investigation of a graphical CONOPS development environment for agile systems engineering (No. SERC-2009-TR-003). Stevens Inst of Technology Hoboken Nj.

Edson, R. and Frittman, J. (2010). Illustrating the Concept of Operations (CONOPs) Continuum and Its Relationship to the Acquisition Lifecycle. Monterey, CA: Naval Postgraduate School: proceedings of the 7th annual acquisition research symposium, (pp.238-257)

Frittman, J. and Edson, R., 2009. A Systems Thinking Based Approach to Writing Effective Concepts of Operations (CONOPs). In Proc. Conf. Syst. Eng. Res. (pp. 17-19)

Nelson, G. (2007). [The ConOps in a Self-Similar Scale Hierarchy for Systems Engineering. proceedings of Conference on Systems Engineering Research, p.vol. 69.

Olayan, N., Morisaki, S., Kobayashi, N. and Yamamoto, S., (2018). A Proposal on a Method of ArchiMate based Concept of Operation (ConOps). IJCSIS.

Olayan, N. and Yamamoto, S., (2016). System Thinking Approach to Create CONOPS for the Adaptive Enterprise Architecture, proc. on Asia Pacific Conference on Information Management 2016, Vietnam National University Press, Hanoi (pp. 37-39,).

Ostrowski, L., Helfert, M. and Xie, S. (2012). A Conceptual Framework to Construct an Artefact for Meta-Abstract Design Knowledge in Design Science Research. 2012 45th Hawaii International Conference on System Sciences.

Opengroup.org.(2016). What is New in ArchiMate® 3.0? | The Open Group. [online] Available at: http://www.opengroup.org/subjectareas/enterprise/archimate/3.0-whats-new-page2 [Accessed 1 Feb. 2018].

Roberts, N., & Edson, R. (2008, October). System concept of operations: Standards, practices and reality. Presented at the NDIA 11th Annual Systems Engineering Conference, San Diego, CA.

Standards.ieee.org.(1998). IEEE 1362-1998 - IEEE Guide for Information Technology - System Definition - Concept of Operations (ConOps) Document. [online] Available at: http://standards.ieee.org/findstds/standard/1362-1998.html [Accessed 1 Feb. 2018].

The Open Group (2016). TOGAF version 9.1. Zaltbommel: Van Haren Publishing.Group, T. (2012). ArchiMate® 2.0 Specification. Zaltbommel: Van Haren Pub.

The MITRE Corporation.Concept of Operations. [online] Available at: https://www.mitre.org/publications/systems-engineering-guide/se-lifecycle-building-blocks/concept-development/concept-of-operations [Accessed 1 Feb. 2018].

TRENDS AND ISSUES OF ONLINE PHARMACIES IN SAUDI ARABIA

Ramlah Hussein, Afnan Abdulqader Almohammadi, Wed Muhammad Alweldi,
Abrar Mohammad Alshik, Saadia Malik and Arwa Mashat
Faculty of Computing and Information Technology in Rabigh, King Abdulaziz University, Saudi Arabia

ABSTRACT

Online pharmacies are companies that sell medicines over the internet and deliver them by mail. The objective of the study is to look into the current and future trends and issues of online pharmacies in Saudi Arabia. Questionnaires were distributed through Google forms to obtain the perception of online pharmacy in Saudi Arabia. A total of 331 respondents filled up the questionnaire. Questions pertaining to awareness of existence of online pharmacy, type of services and type of medical products were captured.
The results showed interesting findings, 31.4% are aware of the existence of online pharmacy, while 84.9% found online pharmacy is useful, and 71.3% will consider buying the medical and healthcare products online. For the question on preferred services to be offered by online pharmacy, in order of preference, 60.4% would like to have quality assurance of products, 54.7% would like fast and reliable of product delivery, 50.5% would like to have the service of consultant pharmacist in the online pharmacy, 33.8% preferred the pharmacy to show customer review for each product, 21.5% would like tracking of delivery of products and 15.7% preferred online payment.
Looking at the growing interest of online pharmacy in Saudi Arabia, concerns on regulations and policies of online drug and medication use need to be addressed. The limitation of this study only focus percentages of responses. Further study could look into other perspective of data collection and data analysis tools. Further analysis on customers' preference according to age and gender could also be further investigated.

KEYWORDS

Online Pharmacy, E-pharmacy, Saudi Arabia

1. INTRODUCTION

Online pharmacies are companies that sell medicines over the internet and deliver them by mail. E- pharmacy or online pharmacy,

'*refers to the existence of an online pharmacy that offers medical care providers the ability to prescribe medications for patients online. These medications can then be delivered to patients without ever requiring them to leave the confines of their homes. In some, cases prescriptions can be filled without a physician ever having physical contact with the patient.*' (Joseph, J.L. 2008).

In the United States, the growth of online pharmacies started in the year 1990 (Orizio et al., 2011). By the year 2010, the National Association of Boards of Pharmacy found that 5859 outlets are selling prescription medication online (NABP, 2010).

Abanmy (2017) studied the extent of use of online pharmacies in Saudi Arabia. Anbamy (2017) found that very few of the respondents were aware of the existence of online pharmacies and only a small percentage had bought medicines over the internet in Saudi Arabia. In the same study, respondents were also asked if they would consider purchasing the medicines online, interestingly majority of the respondents would consider purchasing medicine online and majority had some experience in buying products online (Anbamy, 2017).

An online pharmacy has both benefits and concerns. The two major benefits are simplicity and convenience (Carlisle, 2003). Other benefits include speed of access search for information of medicines and advice from pharmacists or health care practitioners. (Chetturvedi, et al., 2011). The responsibilities of pharmacist in an online pharmacy includes checking and dispensing of prescription medicines, providing advice on medicine selection and usage to patients, provide information on disease prevention and the proper use of medicines. (Carlisle, 2003, Chetturvedi, et al., 2011). Besides the benefits mentioned above, Carlisle (2003) list other benefits such as privacy, anonymity and availability of alternative treatments.

Among the concerns include self-treatment and self-medication without proper prescription. Other issues include high shipping cost (Chetturvedi, et al., 2011), online prescription without physical examination by medical practitioners (Carlisle, 2003, Henny, 2000), dispensing drug without prescription, availability of unapproved or illegal product and drug resistance (Carlisle, 2003). The unregulated online pharmacies in UK has a risk and growing threat to public health as prescription only analgesics, including controlled opioids, are readily available without a prescription (Raine et al., 2009). In Europe, various direct and indirect barriers to the free circulation of pharmaceuticals are highlighted in (Makinen et al., 2005). The objective of the study is to look into the current and future trends and issues of online pharmacies in Saudi Arabia.

2. METHODOLOGY

This study used a survey questionnaire to capture data on issues and trends of online pharmacies in Saudi Arabia. The questionnaire was adapted from the study of (Abanmy, 2017). Data was collected using Google forms through social media. The questions used two languages, English and Arabic. The questionnaire comprised of eleven questions with regards to online pharmacy in Saudi Arabia as follows:

1. Are you aware of the existence of online pharmacies?
2. Have you ever purchased medical products online?
3. Do you prefer to buy from a regular or electronic pharmacy?
4. If you buy from a regular pharmacy, are you satisfied with your purchase?
5. If you buy from an electronic pharmacy, are you satisfied with your purchase?
6. Which products do you like to have in the digital pharmacy?
7. Do you think the products in the online pharmacy are more quality than the traditional pharmacy?
8. What services would you like to provide in an online pharmacy
9. What are the problems you often encounter when you order online?
10. Do you think having an online pharmacy is useful for the community?
11. Will you consider buying medicines and healthcare products online in the future?

Except for items numbers 6, 8 and 9, 'Yes' and 'No' responses are used to measure the participants' preference. Besides the above data, two demographic factors comprised of age and gender are also captured.

3. RESULT AND DATA ANALYSIS

Data were analysed using Google analysis. The results are shown in the Table 1. A total of 331 participants responded to the survey. The age of respondents are as follows: 15-25 (41.7%), 25-35 (27.8%), 35-45 (25.7%), 45-55 (4.22%) and over 55 (0.6%) respectively. Majority of the respondents are female (95.8%). With respect to the questionnaire item on awareness of online pharmacy, 31.4% are aware of the existence of online pharmacy. Out of the total number respondents, 22.7% have purchased medical products online. Out of those who have purchased medical product online, 55% are satisfied with the products.

On the question of preference of products in online pharmacy, in order of preference, 96.5% preferred beauty & care products, vitamins and supplements (45.6%), Diet & Fitness Products (35.3%) and medical equipment (20.55%) respectively. For the question on preferred services to be offered by online pharmacy, in order of preference, (60.4%) would like to have quality assurance of products, (54.7%) would like fast and reliable of product delivery, (50.5%) would like to have the service of consultant pharmacist in the online pharmacy,

Table 1. Results of Survey

Question	Answer	Result (%)
Age:	15-25 25-35 35-45 45-55 55 and above	41.7 % 27.8% 25.7% 4.2% 0.6%
Gender:	Female Male	95.8% 4.2%
Are you aware of the existence of online pharmacies?	Yes No	31.4% 68.6%
Have you over purchased medical products online?	Yes No	22.7% 77.3%
Do you prefer to buy from a regular or electronic pharmacy?	Regular pharmacy Electronic pharmacy	83.7% 16.3%
If you buy from an electronic pharmacy, are you satisfied with your purchase?	Yes No	55% 45%
If you buy from a regular pharmacy, are you satisfied with your purchase?	Yes No	86% 14%
Which products do you like to have in the digital pharmacy?	Beauty & care products Vitamins and supplements Medical product Diet & Fitness Products	96.5% 45.6% 20.5% 35.3%
Do you think the products in the online pharmacy are more quality than the traditional pharmacy?	Yes No I don't Know	9.4% 24.2% 66.5%
What services would you like to provide in an online pharmacy?	Fast and reliable product delivery. Show customer review for each products Quality assurance of products. Service of consultant Pharmacist. Online payment. Tracking of products.	54.7% 33.8% 60.4% 50.5% 15.7% 21.5%
What are the problems you often encounter when you order online?	Order delay Order is incomplete or damaged Lack of licenses for some products Shipping cost.	42% 24.5% 37.5% 56.5%
Do you think having an online pharmacy is useful for the community?	Yes No	84.9% 15.1%
Will you consider buying medicines and healthcare products online in the future?	Yes No	71.3% 28.7%

(33.8%) preferred the pharmacy to show customer review for each product, (21.5%) would like tracking of delivery of products and (15.7%) preferred online payment.

On the issues of ordering the products online, in the order of highest to lowest of problems encountered, the highest concerned issue is about shipping cost (56.5%), followed by delay of orders (42%), lack of licenses for some products (37.5%) and the product ordered is either damaged or incomplete (24.5%) respectively.

The last two questions were used to capture data on the future of online pharmacy in Saudi Arabia. On the question of the usefulness of having online pharmacy for the community, (84.9%) found it useful. The last question on considering buying medicines and healthcare products online in the future, interestingly (71.3%) will consider buying the medical products online.

4. DISCUSSION

From the results of the survey questionnaire, the findings suggest that the trends of online pharmacy in the future in Saudi Arabia is growing. From the previous study conducted by Abamny, 2017, only 23.1% were aware of the existence of online pharmacy, 31.4% were aware of the existence of online pharmacy, an increase of 8.3%. On purchasing products through online pharmacy, the previous study (Abanmy, 2017) found that only 2.7% have bought medicines online however in the current study 22.7% have purchased medical products online, an increase of 20% from the previous study. The increase of responses in purchasing medical products online is an interesting finding, however, perhaps the medical products understood by the respondents include cosmetics and natural products besides medicines.

The most preferred product that they would like to be available in online pharmacy is the beauty and care products, the findings suggest that considering the majority are female respondents these products would be their first choice, second on the list is vitamins and supplements followed by diet and fitness. Again the response for diet and fitness suggest that female are more concerned on the health and beauty.

From previous study, 42.7% will consider buying medicine online (Abanmy, 2017), an increase of 28.6% compared to the current study (71.3%). This trend shows that the online pharmacy in Saudi Arabia is gaining acceptance among its citizens. The study also found the online pharmacy is useful to the community.

From the findings, the three main issues relating to services offered by the online pharmacy are the assurance of quality products, fast and reliable service and providing consultant service by pharmacist. Whereas, the three major problems encountered by online ordering of pharmacy products include shipping cost, order delayed, and concern on lack of license for some products.

On the issues of services offered by online pharmacy, the findings suggest that the respondents are concerned on the quality assurance of the product and they also would like the online pharmacy to offer consultation service on products use and care by the consultant pharmacist. These two issues are important to be highlighted in discussing services provided by online pharmacies. In this perspective, consultation by pharmacist in guiding the patients on how to use the products and other advice are crucial. Gallagher and Colizzi (2000) stated that pharmacies were providing the consulting service 24/7 through online pharmacies. The patients felt more comfortable to ask question through email rather than seeing the pharmacist face to face (Gallagher and Colizzi, 2000). Quality assurance of products is also an issue that needs further attention. Some product may pass the expiry date or some products of questionable quality may have adverse effect or can be harmful or ineffective (Carlisle, 2003).

The problems of ordering online as mentioned earlier include shipping cost, order delayed and lack of license for some products. Shipping cost may be a disadvantage to online pharmacy especially if the online store is located outside Saudi Arabia such the United States or United Kingdom. Although the two countries may carry quality products but in terms of shipping cost this will incur additional cost to the customers in Saudi Arabia. Chetturvedi et al. (2011) highlighted the issue of high shipping cost as a result of inability to participate in many insurance plan. Another concern is on the license of the product, in this perspective, the respondents are also particularly aware of the need to have licensed product sold in the online pharmacies (Chetturvedi et al. 2011). This awareness is important to ensure that the customers will get quality products that follow certain standards set by the Saudi Arabia, US, UK or other government bodies where the pharmacy is located.

5. CONCLUSION

The objective of study is to investigate the trends and issues of online pharmacy in Saudi Arabia. The findings will help organisations including government bodies and interested parties to get an insight of the trends and future of online pharmacy in this country. Looking at the positive acceptance of the online pharmacy in this country, the current regular pharmacies or new pharmacies will have an idea on the perception of users and prospective customers towards online pharmacy. Hence, this valuable information is useful for them to introduce and develop online pharmacy stores in Saudi Arabia.

However, the concerns on quality and licensed products and shipping costs need to be addressed by the appropriate parties. Other concern include fast and reliable delivery also needs further attention.

Looking at the growing interest of online pharmacy in Saudi Arabia, concerns on regulations and policies of online drug and medication use also need to be addressed.

The limitation of this study only focus percentages of responses. Further study could look into other perspective of data collection and data analysis tools. Further analysis on customers' preference according to age and gender could also be further investigated.

REFERENCES

Abanmy, N (2017). The extent of use of online pharmacies in Saudi Arabia. Saudi Pharmaceutical Journal. www.sciencedirect.com

Carlisle, G. (2003). Internet pharmacies: Global Threat require global regulation. Hertfordshire Law Journal 4(1) 12 -25.

Chetturvedi, A.K., Singh, U.K. and Kumar, A. (2011). An E-Strategy for Communication, International Journal of Pharmaceutical Frontier Research.

Gallagher, J.C. and Colaizzi, J.L. (2000). Issues in Internet Pharmacy Practice. Annals of Pharmacotheraphy.

Joseph J.L. and Cook, D.P. (2011). Medical Ethical and Policy Issues Arising from RIA. Journal of Medical Internet Research.

Makinen M.M.,Rautava P.T., Forsstrom J.J. (2005) Do OPs fit European internal markets? Health Policy. 2005;72: 245–252.

National Association of Boards of Pharmacy Progress report for State and Federal Regulators: April.2010. [2011-02-04]. http://www.nabp.net/news/assets/InternetReport1-11.pdf.

Orizio, G., MD, Merla, A, Schulz, P.J. and Gelatti, U. (2010). Quality of Online Pharmacies and Websites Selling Prescription Drugs: A Systematic Review. Journal of Medical Internet Research.

Raine, C., Webb D., Maxwell S. (2009) The availability of prescription-only analgesics purchased from the internet in the UK. Br. J. Clin. Pharmacol. 2009; 67(2):250–254.

DESIGNING STUDENT'S GUIDE - INFORMATION SYSTEM MODEL BASED ON STUDENTS' NEEDS

Elena Vlahu-Gjorgievska, Yiran He, Siliang Tang and Yapu Wu
School of Computing and Information Technology, University of Wollongong
Northfields Ave, Wollongong NSW 2522, Australia

ABSTRACT

University students always need to deal with many problems in their college life. Although there are several existing applications that can help students solve the problems, it is not easy to find and use them. Therefore, there is demand for a general information system that will save students time and effort from swiping among different applications. The aim of this paper is to deliver a high-level design of a completely integrated Student Guide information system model to assist students in their campus life. The expectation of the presented system model is to be compatible with most of the universities' current systems. The information system features list is based on the needs analysis of the all relevant stakeholders. The features/functionalities are integrated into four main modules, which are study life, campus life, administration and personal accounts. The system model architecture is based on Client-Server model (C/S). Some of the features are local services, while others are provided as Web Services.

KEYWORDS

Student Guide, Information System, Mobile Application, University

1. INTRODUCTION

Online services facilitate daily life and provide a more convenient environment for everyone. However, this may lead to complexity since the functionalities are dispersive in different platform and places.

This paper presents a design of the Student's Guide – information system model based on the students' needs. We have analyzed the needs of possible stakeholders and designed features list showing the functionalities that should be provided. The proposed solution includes four main modules: Daily Life, Administration, Study and My Account. The most important features are campus map, campus life helper, subject management and study discussion group. The system uses Client-Server model (C/S), client-side application and its own server. The client-side will access directly to the third-party server for some functions like maps, university e-mail box or timetable. The modules provide a general solution of integrated campus applications that are expected to stimulate the amount of interaction between students and campus.

In the next section, related work is covered. The design of the Student's Guide system model is presented in the third section. The fourth section concludes the paper.

2. RELATED WORK

There is a considerable number of articles and applications that are related to students' activities and life at the campus. Articles published in this area are mainly focused on special features or integrated solutions of the information systems (or applications) provided for university students.

Augmented Reality (AR) and Virtual Reality (VR) are some of the technologies, elaborated in the literature that can be used to improve the interactivity, enhance the campus tour experience and help students and visitors get familiar with the campus and its characteristics (Özcan et al., 2017; Mines & Tang, 2015). Interactions between users and campus can also be provided by using cyber-physical interaction system, indoor positioning system, and augmented-reality system (Subakti & Jiang, 2016).

Garofalakis et al. (2007) discuss the implementation of a special feature - simulation of a classic map by giving the user opportunity to take notes and marks on the map by clicking on the device's screen. Two other applications (Cardei et al., 2013; Battin & Markande, 2016) apply the Google Maps API to provide the users with an interactive map feature.

Xinyu and Jinyu (2016) present a solution that can help students to enlarge their social network. "iCampus" application (Bromuri et al., 2012) is combining the functionalities of navigation, event informing, and online social interaction. A similar application called "iCollege" (Chen et al., 2016) provides daily advice based on the data collected from users to further facilitate students study and campus life.

For the purpose of the paper, several applications from Google Play and Apple store were reviewed. Appsbuyout Dev (2017) provides features including timetable and scheduling events. Application My Study Life (2017) provides additional share functions, which allow teachers to create and share their schedule. Students-Timetable (2017) allows users to import and export schedule by e-mail, or Bluetooth. In addition, it provides a diary. Although these applications provide only functions that are independent of school/University systems, some applications provide features related to the University systems. MyUOW (2017) accesses the information in university's system and display information on user's device. UA Student App (2017) allows students to get academic dates, academic results and university news. Other applications focus on the travel needs of students which help them to get familiarize with surrounding transportation of the university or helps students to find their lecture theatre, coffee shop, carpark, bus stop, sports field, toilet, even nearest vending machine (UOW Shuttle, 2017 & Lost on campus, 2017).

Some of the reviewed papers and applications provide solutions in which the map features are based on Google API, which reduces the implementation and design of the applications. However, the features provided are with a limited focus that could be extended into further interaction and other functionalities. Comparing to the solutions, reviewed in this section, that mainly focus on few features, the solution presented in this paper integrates the all the features needed by the students.

3. STUDENT'S GUIDE DESIGN

The proposed design follows three main principles: the design should be interactive, focused on the information integration and customization, and platform independent.

3.1 Features

Student's guide has several stakeholders: students, student clubs, IT administration, executive administrators, coordinators, tutors, lecturers, visitors and retailers. The stakeholders are grouped into four groups: Internal-Operational, Internal-Executive, External-Operational, and External-Executive group.

Internal-Operational Group has two stakeholders: IT administrators and IT developers. The administrators should receive IT maintenance notification, user feedback and university mail notification. The developers care more about the expansibility of the system. Internal-Executive Group consists of executive administrators, coordinators, lecturers, tutors and the university itself. They all require university information notification (like e-mail, news and event) and easy-to-use subject modification functions. External-Operation Group stakeholders are students, campus stores and student clubs. Campus stores need to do advertising, get customer feedback and online ordering. Student clubs need requirements of posting and managing club information, such as club description, recruitment information and events. External-Executive Group has two stakeholders. They are visitors and off-campus retailers. All stakeholders have some common requirements. Some of the most frequent requests are campus navigation, retrieve bus information and parking information, online communication and facility information features.

Students are the main users of the system. Apart from the basic (in common) requirements, students also need features related to: integrated timetable, subject management, university administration system instruction, university mail notification, access to e-learning system, student clubs' information, event enrollment, and students' internal communication (like trade with other students, students mutual help, find classmates).

The requirements of stakeholders are divided into 3 parts: Daily Life Assistant, Administrative Assistant and Study Assistant. The complete features list is summarized in a diagram shown on Figure 1(a).

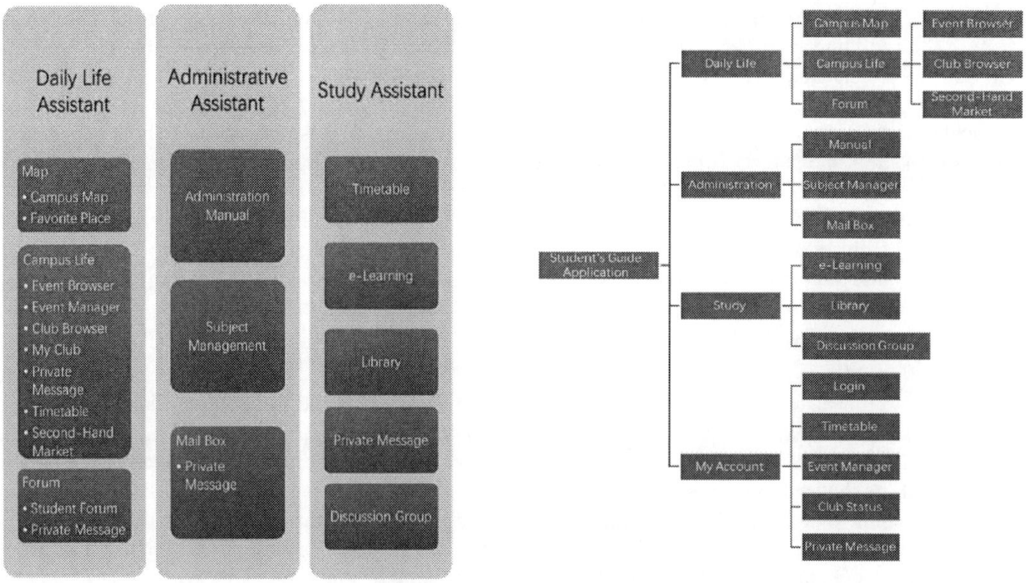

(a) (b)

Figure 1. (a) Features' Diagram; (b) Function Modules

Campus Map feature meets the needs of campus navigation, and retrieve bus, parking and facility information. It is an electronic interactive map with a navigation function. It may be accompanied with rating and reviewing system and Favorite Place feature, which helps users to record the frequently used places and the places they are interested in. Campus Map contains the parking lots information and their current capacity condition, as well as bus station locations, line information and timetables.

Features that meet the needs of event management and student club management are Event Browser, Event Manager, Club Browser, Club Manager and Private Message. Event Browser provides a platform that displays event list. Users with a special account can post and edit events. Students can choose events to attend. The selected event will be stored in Event Manager for reviewing or cancelling. Private Message shall be sent on notification purpose when an event has been chosen, or the events in the Event Manager has been modified. In addition, if a location, such as the building location, has been associated with the event, the user can be linked to Campus Map. Club Browser provides a platform to display club information. It has a club list. Users with club accounts can post club information on its own block. Students can browse the list and choose the club to sign in. Students' club enrollment status shall be recorded in Club Manager for the future management. Event Manager will be automatically renewed when the club (the student joined) has new events posted on the Event Browser, and a Private Message shall be sent for notification purpose. Event date and time information are also stored in the Timetable.

Features Student Forum and Private Message are designed to fulfil the needs of students' mutual help and communication. Student Forum provides a platform for students to ask questions, ask for help or find friends by posting messages. Private Message provides a personal mailbox for private communication. Lecturers, tutors and IT staffs can broadcast notification and information through Private Message. Second-Hand Market feature is a platform for students to sell second-hand goods. This feature allows only the exchange of information, without online transactions. It contains posting, editing, searching, commenting, and filtering functions. To communicate with each other, users can use Private Message function.

To satisfy the needs of university e-mail notification, there are Mail Box and Private Message features. The Mail Box retrieves university's e-mail information from the built-in system. A notification shall be sent as a Private Message when receiving new e-mail.

Features Administration Manual and Subject Management help students and administrative staff to use the university's built-in administration system. The Administration Manual is a help page of university's administration system. It also contains FAQ and the instruction of some administrative processes. Subject Management is a service that uses university system's information.

E-Learning feature presents subject information based on enrollment and listing information posted by lecturers. This feature gathers information from current e-Learning system. Assignment due date, exam date, lecture time and tutorial time are automatically collected from e-Learning system and stores in the Timetable. Library feature can help the user to access University's online library.

One relatively special feature provided is the Discussion Group. It supports the communication between students that are taking the same subject. A discussion group, which is consisted of the students who have enrolled in the same subject, the subject's lecturer and its tutors, is established automatically. This feature facilitates the communication and allows students to find their classmates.

Proposed system model contains built-in features that depend mainly on the University's administration system. The features for off school commercial activities are not provided since retailers and companies have their needs and requirements in carrying out the business on campus.

3.2 Function Modules

According to the stakeholders' division, proposed system model should have three main function modules. But, in order to group some of the overlapping functions in different genres, function module My Account is added. This module is dealing with user identification and repeatedly occurred features. The Function Modules of the Student's guide are shown on Figure 1(b).

My Account module is a special module, different from other three modules. This module has five features: Login, Timetable, Event Manager, Club Status and Private Message. The Login is used to perform user authentication, and the rest of features are based on the user's identity. The workflow of this module is shown on Figure 2(a). The user needs to login or register in the system. After that, the system will perform user authentication in the back-end. Once the user is successfully logged in, the system will display the user information and wait for the user to select a subcategory of My Account module and display the corresponding information.

Daily Life Module has three submodules and five child modules in total. For all three submodules, the system gets information from the database and displays it to the user. For example, when the user selects one event to enroll or a club to join, it will be recorded to the server-side and stored as user's personal data. The system then goes into a listening state and checks (in a certain period of time) the booked event's and club's status. If there are any changes or updates, the system will send a private message to the user as a notification. The Second-Hand Market has a slightly different behaviour. Its operations rely on the Private Message feature.

The Forum submodule is an internet BBS (Bulletin Board System) platform. This platform is mainly used for students to communicate with each other (make friends, chat, share experience, help each other). The Forum's account is using the same user account as other modules.

Administration submodules are Manual, Subject management and Mailbox. The Manual lists quick links to the different help pages of the university. Users also can search for information they want in a spotlight bar. In order to achieve this functionality, local response and external response are used. Storing the links within the local device can provide a quicker response. The search function is a web-based function. In Subject Management, submodule students can add, transfer and withdraw subjects and tutorials. The Mailbox submodule provides the entry to the university mailbox.

Study module has three submodules: E-learning, Library and Discussion Group. E-learning and Library provide the e-learning platform as well as library web page which universities supply to their students. Discussion Group is a functionality for students to communicate study information. The system is grouping the students into the same discussion group according to the subject they have enrolled. Students in the discussion group can discuss the subject and study issue by using this functionality.

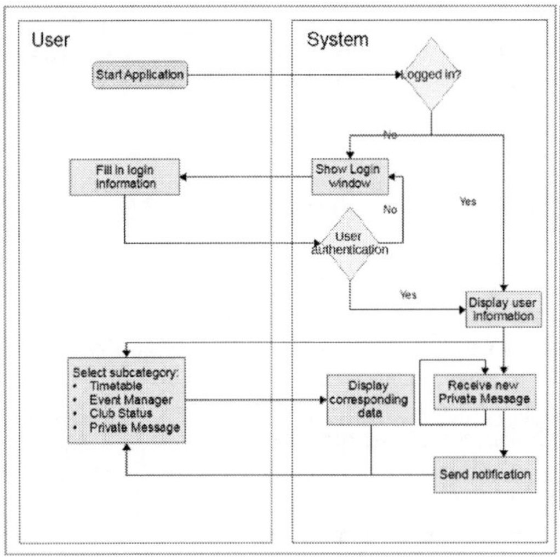

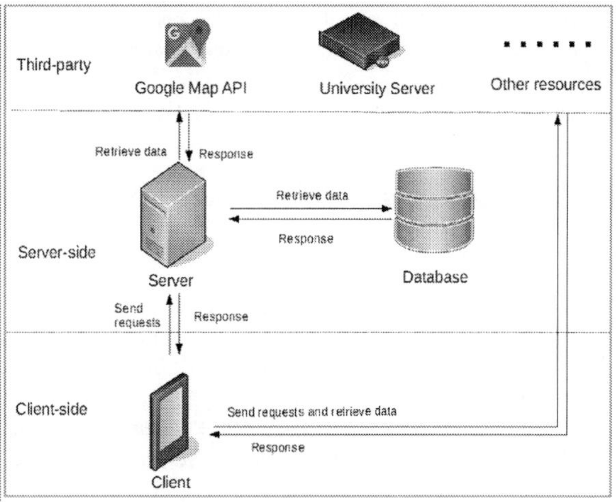

(a) (b)

Figure 2. (a) My account workflow; (b) Architecture Overview

3.3 System Model Architecture

The architecture of the Student's Guide is based on Client-Server model (C/S). Presented architecture (Figure 3) is a hybrid model with three layers: Client-side, Server-side and Third-party resources. Most of the services are presented as web services. The client-side can directly respond to the user's requests or send requests to other internet resources in order to respond to the user's requests. Although other internet resources can be involved, in the diagram on Figure 3 only the university server and the Google Map API are included as they represent essential parts of the proposed architecture.

Some modules can produce a significant amount of data. This information is basically stored on the server-side. Some students may feel unsafe to store their personal information on the server. Based on these security and privacy concerns, any third-party usernames and passwords (e.g. university account and google account) are not stored on the system's server. This information will be cached on the local client-side and will allow faster access, as well as managing (deleting) the information by the users. In addition, the users can choose which data can or can't be shared.

4. CONCLUSION

This paper presents an integrated information system model (Student's Guide) for student campus living. Student's Guide integrates various features in one simple and easy-to-use system. The presented solution helps students in various activities on a daily basis. Student's Guide is a highly functional integrated system model that not only satisfies the needs of the students but also reduces the public costs in the campus.

Presented system model has four modules: Daily Life, Administration, Study and My Account. Daily Life module provides many features that can help students to have an improved campus social life and finding recreational activities. Features like Event Browser and Club Browser, to best of our knowledge, are not provided in any other similar systems or applications. The Administration and Study module incorporate some features that help students to manage their study, like discussion groups for students enrolled in the same subjects. These features will help students to communicate with their classmates, thus improve their performance.

The presented model is a general solution for an integrated system that can assist in the students' life on the campus. Although there is a wide range of features designed to help the students, there is still room for new functionalities that can be developed in future. Additionally, some of the features of the system need to be aligned with the university information system during the implementation phase.

REFERENCES

Appsbuyout Dev, 2017. Student Agenda. [Online] Available at: https://play.google.com/store/apps/details?id=com.clawdyvan.agendadigitalaluno&hl=en [Accessed 20.8.2017].

Battin, P. and Markande, S.D., 2016. Location based reminder Android application using Google Maps API. *In IEEE International Conference on Automatic Control and Dynamic Optimization Techniques*. pp. 649-652.

Bromuri, S., Urovi, V. and Stathis, K., 2012. iCampus: A connected campus in the ambient event calculus. *Innovative Applications of Ambient Intelligence: Advances in Smart Systems*, IGI Global , pp. 58-64.

Cardei, M., Zankina, I., Cardei, I. and Raviv, D., 2013. Campus assistant application on an android platform. *In the Proceedings of IEEE SoutheastCon*. pp. 1-6.

Chen, G., Niu, P. and Yao, H., 2016. An Intelligent Application Platform for Campus Life Based on Mobile Internet. *International Journal of Security and Its Applications*, Vol. 10, No.6, pp. 304-314.

Students – Timetable, 2017. Crazy Students. [Online] Available at: https://play.google.com/store/apps/details?id=crazy.students.student&hl=en [Accessed 20.8.2017].

Garofalakis, J., Papapoulias, P. and Plessas, A., 2007. Representation of Classic MAPS for Mobile Devices. An Interactive Mobile Map Application. *In IEEE 18th International Symposium on Personal, Indoor and Mobile Radio Communications*. pp. 1-5.

Lost On Campus, 2017. Student Services Australia. [Online] Available at: https://play.google.com/store/apps/details?id=com.studentservices.lostoncampus&hl=en [Accessed 20.08.2017].

Maines, C. and Tang, S., 2015. An Application of Game Technology to Virtual University Campus Tour and Interior Navigation. *In 2015 International Conference on Developments of E-Systems Engineering*. pp. 341-346.

My Study Life - School Planner, 2017. My Study Life, Ltd. [Online] Available at: https://play.google.com/store/apps/details?id=com.virblue.mystudylife&hl=en [Accessed 20.08.2017].

MyUOW, 2017. University of Wollongong. [Online] Available at: https://play.google.com/store/apps/details?id=au.edu.uow.myuow&hl=en [Accessed 20.08.2017].

Özcan, U., Arslan, A., İlkyaz, M. and Karaarslan, E., 2017. An augmented reality application for smart campus urbanization: MSKU campus prototype. *In the 5th International Smart Grid and Cities Congress and Fair.* Istanbul, Turkey, pp. 100-104.

Subakti, H. and Jiang, J.R., 2016, December. A marker-based cyber-physical augmented-reality indoor guidance system for smart campuses. *In IEEE 18th International Conference on High Performance Computing and Communications; IEEE 14th International Conference on Smart City; IEEE 2nd International Conference on Data Science and Systems*. pp. 1373-1379.

UA Student App, 2017. University of Adelaide, [Online] Available at: https://play.google.com/store/apps/details?id=com.uofa.student_app&hl=en [Accessed 20.08.2017].

UOW Shuttle, 2017. University of Wollongong. [Online] Available at: https://play.google.com/store/apps/details?id=edu.uow.unishuttle&hl=en [Accessed 20.08.2017].

Xinyu, Z. and Jinyu, S., 2016. Design and development of campus dating social application based on Android. *In 2016 IEEE International Conference on Engineering and Technology*. pp. 1241-1244.

EXPLORING BITCOIN: OPPORTUNITIES AND THREATS OF USE IN OMAN

Tahani Al-Hatmi, Razan Al-Rawas, Marwa Al-Noufali, Hajer Al-Buloshi
and Yousuf Salim AlHinai
Sultan Qaboos University, Oman

ABSTRACT

Bitcoin is a cryptocurrency which operates without any central bank. The main feature is the simplicity of exchange and transfer of money, and all transactions are done automatically. Bitcoin is also open-source, so that no one possesses or controls it and everybody can use it. The main objective of this paper is to understand the opportunity for and threats to Bitcoin in Oman. The research uses two methodologies: primary research interviews with experts and secondary research which consists of existing research papers and research subjects or experiments. The study has found that Bitcoin has an extremely secure database, that there are no international regulations or laws forbidding Bitcoin, that individuals benefit from it more than governments and that the use of Bitcoin in Oman is very low.

KEYWORDS

Cryptocurrency, Investment, E-payment, Security, Regulations, Blockchain, Bitcoin, Oman

1. INTRODUCTION

Bitcoin is a peer-to-peer transaction network which operates without any central bank; it is the simplest way to exchange money at very low cost and where everything is done within and by the system. It is also open-source, meaning that no one possesses or controls it but everybody can use it. In addition, it is not covered by any previous systems. In general, Bitcoin has three main features: fast peer-to-peer transactions, worldwide payment, and low processing fees. Knowledge about Bitcoin gained from this study will benefit individuals in many ways, as Bitcoin has benefits of security and control; in addition, mobile payment is made easy, it works everywhere and makes international payment fast. It will also benefit businesses in that they can choose their own fees, be protected against fraud, and make fast international payments without a payment card industry (PCI). Transactions can also be set up as multi-signature, and accounting is transparent. Developers can also benefit from this study, as it shows that most of the security is on the client's side, that there are new payment possibilities and many third-party payment processing services (API); Bitcoin also offers the simplest of all payment systems. Through exploring these factors, the main objective of this paper, then, is to understand the opportunities and threats that Bitcoin can present in Oman. The specific objectives are threefold

- To explain the opportunities and threats of Bitcoin in areas of investment, security and regulation
- To show who will benefit from using Bitcoin (individuals and/or government)
- To describe the current status of Bitcoin in Oman

The study uses two methodologies: primary research (interviews) and secondary research (literature review).

2. LITERATURE REVIEW

2.1 Electronic Currencies

The term currency traditionally referred to money which is exchanged between all the countries in the world. Nowadays, however, we also have what are known as Virtual Currencies; these have been developed by their own creators and used in their digital worlds (D He, KF Habermeier, RB Leckow, V Haksar, 2016). There are numerous virtual currencies; some of the best-known are Lite coin (LTC) which is used as a network for payment but is not controlled by any outside authorization system (EB Centralny, 2015). Ethereum (ETH) is another such currency, a decentralized source whose functions include running smart contracts and distributed applications, again without any external control. Zcash (ZEC) is yet another virtual currency: its main focus is on improving the security of transactions by providing greater privacy in the recording of transactions. There are several further examples. Dash, for instance, came into the market with the aim of taking decentralized master code networks and making them untraceable. (XRP) stands for Ripple and is a network that emphasizes low-cost and certain international payments. Monero (XMR) is a decentralized currency that uses ring signatures to provide privacy (Sachs, 2014).

2.2 Electronic Payment Systems

The process of any cash system or electronic payment system should include a buyer and a seller who exchange commodities or services; it also contains at least one financial institution that relates these to money. In this payment system, the money moves from a payer to a payee, the two members of the process which depends on the existence of real money moving from an issuer to an acquirer (N. Asokan, 1996).

In the past two decades, the huge development in E-business technologies has made significant changes in the ways that business activities are conducted. Many people around the world currently use online shopping services that require them to pay electronically using Net Banking or Credit cards. This process is now done online routinely and without any complexity (Vishal Vadgama, 2012). In today's environment where everything is online, this use of E-Payment services had prepared the world to accept and use an innovative payment network and a new kind of money, which is known as Bitcoin (Kubát, 2015).

2.3 Bitcoin

In the last decade, a number of crypto currencies have appeared; these include Bitcoin, LiteCoin, PeerCoin, AuroraCoin, DogeCoin, and Ripple. Bitcoin has become the most prominent, due to the huge increase in its price (Pavel Ciaian, 2015).

Most writers define Bitcoin as a decentralized open-source peer-to-peer crypto currency protocol (Simon Barber, 2012). It was first presented in a paper published by Nakamoto (2008) on October 31, 2008, and was announced on January 11, 2009 on the cryptography mailing list. Bitcoin is an electronic cash system that can be used to purchase goods and services on the internet in the same way that printed currencies are used (Sebasti, H., Duarte, A. and Guesrreiro, G., 2017). The currency has many other uses, such as funding companies, investing cash and transferring money without fees. It is also a decentralized currency, meaning that no government, individual or group has any kind of the authority over it; nobody can control it in any way (Yermack, 2014). For this reason, Bitcoin is available anywhere in the world and for anyone who would like to use it; the only restriction is that the other party to the transaction must also accept bitcoins as payment.

Bitcoins can be created mathematically using software programs through creators solve mathematical formula to create their own Bitcoins. The mathematical formula is available and free, so that anyone can check it. It also involves using a computer to solve complex math problems in the network (Bartos, 2015). It keeps its value through its sacristy where there are only 21000000 Bitcoins around the world. Also, you can obtain it if you accept it as a currency and buy it via exchange such as Indacoin or Coinbase.

2.4 Advantages of Bitcoin

There are many advantages to using the Bitcoin technology, such as:

- Bitcoin has low exchange costs: Payments will be sent rapidly through the network, with low exchange costs (Grinber, 2011)
- Bitcoin can be used as an investment: It benefits individuals regardless of government stability (Sheehan, 2015). Businesses will also benefit from its security, its trustworthiness and its potential for long-term investment. In terms of security and trust, the believability of any new technology or currency is profoundly dependent on the general population's conviction that they can exchange it for products and that it will be steady over time. Its trustworthiness, the second attribute, is unlike that of traditional currencies. Yermack (2013), answering queries about the advisability of companies using Bitcoin, explains that the value of Bitcoin shows little or no correlation to the value of traditional currencies, a fact which implies that Bitcoin is still going through a speculative phase of its existence. Because of this, it must depend on the trust of the population and the convenience of its use. Thirdly, long-anyone thinking about long-term investment should be aware that Bitcoin involves both high risks but also the potential for high profits. It is high risk because some people see it as illegal, while others believe that it can generate large gains (Vieira, 2014).
- Ease of use: it is very easy to use and accessible for everyone. (Mariani, 2013/2014).
- No limits: because it is open, source, and there aren't any restrictions on who can use it (Barnes, 2015).
- Low or no fees (Yu, 2015).
- Accepted by many sites: Bitcoin can be used as payment on many key websites, such as Wordpress.com, Reddit and the new file hosting service, Mega.
- Does not need a payment processor: No external bank is involved; the network directly transfers the payment to the user, and Bitcoin can be exchanged and transferred at anytime and anywhere (Badea, 2013). Virtual currency supports many payment systems and savings in terms of making it more available (Segendorf, 2014).

2.5 Disadvantages of Bitcoin

The main risks associated with Bitcoin relate to its situation as a decentralized, open-source software, subject to operational software risks, like its sensitivity to the hacking into the adoption of new releases (Walch, 2016).

- High volatility: Bitcoin is extremely volatile. In some weeks in fall 2013, its value soared by 400 per cent as the exchange rate rose from 200 USD to 800 USD. The uncertainty of the exchange rate may prevent companies from accepting Bitcoin currency. One way to mitigate this is to convert Bitcoin to local currencies on a regular basis, thus keeping only small budgets at risk. (M Möser, R Böhme, D Breuker, 2014).
- Large-scale hacks on Bitcoin companies although the digital signature in a Bitcoin transaction prevents any manipulation, an attacker will be able to double his own use of Bitcoin and create earnings for himself and can also prevent the timestamp of the transaction (J Becker, D Breuker, T Heide, J Holler, 2013).
- No safety mechanisms: Because the existence of unredeemed transaction output is public knowledge, the theft or loss of private keys can take place, as well as the forgery of a digital signature. If this happens, it is equivalent to the loss of 'real' money in the non-virtual world (Simon Barber, Xavier Boyen, Elaine Shi and Ersin Uzun, 2012).
- Untraceable: A recording of the 40 Bitcoin exchanges that was done over three years ago found that there have been 18 since the closure and the client account balance has often disappeared. While some cases may be the result of fraud, this is not the only cause. Using the proportional risk model, the trading volume of the exchange can indicate whether it is likely to close, with the less popular exchanges more likely become popular deals. Also, the present logical regression shows that a popular exchange is more likely to suffer from security vulnerabilities (T Moore, N Christin, 2013).
- Government regulation: The regulation of Bitcoin is still in its infancy and is both a challenge and an added value of the study especially in the early stages of regulation; attention should be given to the rationality of power, not just the assessment of material (Rella, 2015). Government attitudes to cryptocurrencies are not clear, but the risk of regulation is real because at present Bitcoin is not taxed (Zohar, 2015). Some have stressed the need to risk Bitcoin's secrecy in order to regulate against its potential use for money laundering, the drug trade, and terrorism (Bryans, 2014). Others are more concerned about the potential it creates for transnational movement of funds and tax evasion (JA Roman - Rev. Banking & Fin. L., 2014)
- Investment risk: The volatility of Bitcoin means that investors can incur heavy losses. "You try to sell it, and by the time the order goes through, the price may have dropped," says Matthew Elbeck.

3. METHODOLOGY

This paper is based on interviews conducted with Blockchain and Bitcoin experts who were interviewed face-to-face at the Block chain Oman symposium in Oman from 6th of November, 2017 to 9th of November, 2017. The interviewees included: Yobie Benjamin, Chief Technical Officer (CTO) and Board Member at the US Federal Reserve Work Group; Bénédicte Nolens, Senior Director of Risk and Strategy, Security and Futures Commission, Hong Kong; Pierre-Edouard Wahl, Former Vice President of Innovation and Block chain at Credit Suisse; and a number of Omani experts including Mr. Khalid Tahhan CEO of Blockchain Company in Oman; and Muhanna Al-Harthi Experienced Telecom & Technology Program Manager, Solution Architect, and Data Mining Specialist. From discussions with these experts with various expertise and background, the information in this paper was gathered.

4. DISCUSSION

4.1 Bitcoin in Oman

As mentioned earlier, this research will present the opportunities and threats of using Bitcoin in Oman, dividing the topic into several sub-objectives, which will discuss: the opportunities and threats of Bitcoin in the areas of security, regulation and investment; who will benefit from using Bitcoin (individuals and/or government); and the current status of Bitcoin use in Oman.

4.2 Opportunities and Threats

The table below sets out the opportunities and threats of Bitcoin in the areas of security, regulation and investment.

Table 1. Opportunities and Threats of Bitcoin

Opportunities	Threats
Security	
• It is very hard to attack Bitcoin, as it is the most secure public database in existence. Since its inception in 2009, there have been no hacks on the Bitcoin block chain. • Bitcoin transactions are fully traceable and recorded.	• Bitcoin has faced hacking because of the carelessness and lack of awareness of individuals using it.
Regulation	
• Oman has issued an organizational decision to regulate the use of Bitcoin. • Buying and selling Bitcoin is legal in Oman and all secure websites used in this process are allowed.	• There is no law regulating the use of Bitcoin. • Bitcoin can • be used for illegal activities such as tax evasion and money laundering.
Investment	
• It facilitates investment and transfers between individuals by making the process flexible and saving time. • People can own Bitcoin because itis a good store of value. Like gold, its value comes from its scarcity and it maintains its value in the same way. • People can mine and search for Bitcoin and invest in it. • Bitcoin is useful for countries facing global payment problems, for instance, Iran facing international fees and sanctions.	• Bitcoin cannot be an asset for the government because it has the potential for many dangerous activities • Government stands to incur greater losses than individuals when investing in it. • The rise of alternative cryptocurrencies such as Ethereum threatens to decrease the store value of Bitcoin.

Bitcoin is very secure and fully traceable, so there is no doubt that it is the best secured crypto currency till now. The main obstacle in this factor is awareness and carelessness of individuals to maintain their funds. This obstacle can be overcome through spreading the awareness and creating for people a new culture that is familiar with this technology. The other obstacle that that Bitcoin is not organized because it depends on differences from culture to culture therefore there are no laws and regulations that organize Bitcoin usage. Internationally, Bitcoin exchange and investment transactions are legal but it is possible to use in illegal ways such as Tax evasion and Money laundering and these things are done in different currencies even with cash. Yet, these two factors may encourage people to invest in it. In addition, Bitcoin contains many features to facilitate investment between people since there is no central system to control it which lead to make the process easier and flexible and saving time as well and people can carry different types of projects through it. Furthermore, is a good store of value because there are only 21 million Bitcoins in existence and that means it will be treated as any other rare commodity. Bitcoin creates new type of investment which is to explore and mine Bitcoin itself. Since it is a decentralized system identified globally it can play as speculator for countries that face international issues. However, Bitcoin might be affected negatively by other crypto currencies which leads to the decrease of its value.

4.2.1 Who will benefit from using Bitcoin (individuals and /or government)?

This research recognises that individuals will benefit more from Bitcoin more than governments, especially in the field of investment. This is because individuals will invest for their own self-interest while government will invest for the whole country. This means that if losses are incurred, government will suffer far more than individuals, and their losses will be heavier. In addition, government cannot handle Bitcoin as a dependable asset because its decentralization means that they cannot control its inflation and deflation, which makes its use too risky.

4.2.2 The status of Bitcoin in Oman

The Information Technology Authority (ITA) recently issued an organizational decision to regulate the use of Bitcoin, which means that the country is keeping up with new technologies. Majority of people prefer to use friendly apps. That's what bitcoin done, by facilitated money transformation between countries. On the other hand, if banking system integrated with block chain it become efficient as bitcoin. Furthermore, people already familiar with banking services and that's what Oman trying to do through establishment of the Block chain Club during the Blockchain Oman Symposium for spreading awareness and knowledge for the society to push the digital future transformation. However, it will be difficult for Oman to adapt to any crypto currencies in the near future, mainly because the culture is not yet familiar with this type of technology.

This research examined the average exchange transactions of Bitcoin in Oman through the local Bitcoin website. The evidence shows that the use of Bitcoin in Oman is very limited, and that most of (few) exchanges were done in the capital, Muscat. Omani expert don't recommend Omani people to trade or invest in bitcoin because through it they may lose money. Support what Facebook and Google do about blocking crypto currencies trading advertisements.

5. CONCLUSION

The main findings of this exploratory study can be summarized in the following:

- Bitcoin is secure and only its misuse makes it insecure.
- There are no global laws regulating the use of Bitcoin; this makes space for it to be used for illegal and undesirable activities.
- Investing in Bitcoin is an opportunity for individuals more than governments.
- Oman is not ready currently to adopt this technology.
- Not recommended that Omani people to invest in bitcoin currently.
- The adoption of banks in block chain it generate the same features of bitcoin.

This study contributes to both theory and practice. Theoretically, this paper can be considered as the first study of Bitcoin in Oman and therefore provides current understanding of this new phenomenon and establishes good grounds for future research in this area. Practically, it establishes the importance of understand the FinTech sector in general and cryptocurreny in specific and recommends that governments should introduce this subject area into the education system. It also encourages safe investment in Bitcoin by highlighting the various aspects of this electronic currency. This will help governments to make informed plans to decrease the ambiguities of this new technology.

REFERENCES

Barber S., Boyen X., Shi E., Uzun E. (2012) Bitter to Better — How to Make Bitcoin a Better Currency. In: Keromytis A.D. (eds) Financial Cryptography and Data Security. FC 2012. Lecture Notes in Computer Science, vol 7397. Springer, Berlin, Heidelberg

Barber, S., Boyen, X., Shi, E., & Uzun, E. (2012, February). Bitter to better—how to make Bitcoin a better currency. In International Conference on Financial Cryptography and Data Security (pp. 399-414). Springer, Berlin, Heidelberg.

Barnes, D. (2015). Blockchain manoeuvres: applying Bitcoin's technology to banking. The Banker, 14.

Bartos, Jakub (2015). Does Bitcoin follow the hypothesis of efficient market?. International Journal of Economic Sciences, Vol. IV(2), pp. 10-23. , DOI: 10.20472/ES.2015.4.2.002

Becker, J., Breuker, D., Heide, T., Holler, J., Rauer, H. P., & Böhme, R. (2013). Can we afford integrity by proof-of-work? Scenarios inspired by the Bitcoin currency. In The Economics of Information Security and Privacy (pp. 135-156). Springer Berlin Heidelberg.

Centralny, E. B. (2015). Virtual currency schemes–a further analysis.

Ciaian, P., Rajcaniova, M., & Kancs, D. A. (2016). The economics of Bitcoin price formation. Applied Economics, 48(19), 1799-1815

Grinberg, R. (2012). Bitcoin: An innovative alternative digital currency. Hastings Sci. & Tech. LJ, 4, 159.

He, D., Habermeier, K. F., Leckow, R. B., Haksar, V., Almeida, Y., Kashima, M., ... & Yepes, C. V. (2016). Virtual Currencies and Beyond: Initial Considerations (No. 16/3). International Monetary Fund.

Mariani, S. (2014). Bitcoin: an "alternative" currency or an investment opportunity?.

Okamoto, T. (2015). Financial Cryptography and Data Security.

Rogojanu, A., & Badea, L. (2014). The issue of competing currencies

Sachs, G. (2014). All about Bitcoin. Top of Mind, 21, 3-21.

Sebastião, H., Duarte, A. P., & Guerreiro, G. (2017). Where is the information on USD/Bitcoins hourly price movements? (No. 2017-05). Centre for Business and Economics Research (CeBER), University of Coimbra.

Segendorf, B. (2014). What is Bitcoin. Sveriges Riksbank Economic Review, 2, 71-87.

Sheehan, S. (2015). Advantages and Challenges of Incorporating Virtual Currency into Small Businesses.

Vadgama, V., Tanti, B., Modi, C., & Doshi, N. (2012). A novel approach for e-payment using virtual password system. arXiv preprint arXiv:1208.3859.

Vieira, R. (2014). Should my company use Bitcoin? (Doctoral dissertation).

Virtual currency Bitcoin in the scope of money definition and store of value Max Kubát University of Economics, Winston Churchill sq. 4, Prague 130 67, Czech Republic

Walch, A. (2015). The Bitcoin blockchain as financial market infrastructure: a consideration of operational risk.http://www.independent.org/pdf/tir/tir_20_03_12_luther.pdf

Walfish, M., & Blumberg, A. J. (2015). Verifying computations without reexecuting them. Communications of the ACM, 58(2), 74-84.

Yu, K. Y. (2015). Bitcoin: Currency of the Future or Investment Property.

Zohar, A. (2015). Bitcoin: under the hood. Communications of the ACM, 58(9), 104-113.

Reflection Papers

REVIEW OF BIG DATA: POSSIBLE OPPORTUNITIES AND CHALLENGES FOR ORGANISATIONS

Gizem Erboz
Department of Business and Management, Szent Istvan University
Gödöllő, Páter Károly u. 1, 2100, Hungary

ABSTRACT

Big Data has become a significant technology due to emerging needs of staying competitive for organisations; however, the various challenges also must be considered with the improvements of Big Data regarding the characteristics of this concept. Therefore, in this paper, the concepts of Big Data would be analysed; the opportunities and challenges are identified by addressing the Volume, Velocity and Variety (3Vs) of Big Data. Besides, current research expands the dimensions of Big Data (BD) into 5Vs by including Value and Veracity. Therefore, this paper attempts to understand the different perspectives around the concept of Big Data and analyse how the previous studies identify the opportunities and challenges for organisations using Big Data. Although the paper is concluded with some opportunities and challenges, in light of the characteristics of Big Data, the concept is still in infant stage to be discovered in both theory and empirical research.

KEYWORDS

Big Data, Opportunities, Challenges, Business Analytics, Data Analytics

1. INTRODUCTION

In the last few years, enormous datasets have been created through the improving technologies; therefore, now the world is faced with the new challenges of processing large data tools by traditional methods. Now, many of the industries are interested in big data to boost their decision support systems as well as the many government agencies, which announced that they have major plans to achieve Big Data and its applications. The data raise at 50 percent a year or more than doubling every two years (Lohr, 2012). Therefore, this concept takes the highest attention of many Internet companies, managers, and the people who would like increase digitalization on their business.

George et al (2014) defines that Big Data is generated from a multitude of sources including internet clicks, mobile transactions, user generated content and social media and also, generated content through sensor networks or business transactions such as sales queries and purchase transactions. The data generated must be analysed using powerful computational techniques to help decision support systems by using extremely large datasets taken from real time life events (Khan et al, 2014; Demchenko et al, 2013). By doing so, both information and time gaps would be reduced. However, as a consequences of large dataset usage, the more data generated and to be processed in the world. For instance, there are some leading companies which process data on terabytes and petabytes such as Google (hundreds of PB), Facebook (10 PB per month), Baidu and Taobao, a subsidiary of Alibaba. Youtube needs to process average 72 hours of videos in every minute. Such data in both quantity and mutual relations will far surpass the capacities of the IT architectures and infrastructure of existing enterprises. Also, frequency of real-time events will also greatly stress the available computing capacity. The increasingly growing data led to a challenge of how to store and manage such huge heterogeneous datasets with moderate requirements on hardware and software infrastructure (Chen et al, 2014).

This paper provides the short description and the characteristics of Big Data distinguished from traditional sources. Therefore, new opportunities and challenges will be analysed through the effects of this concept.

2. CHARACTERISTICS OF BIG DATA

The current studies (McAfee et al,2012; Ranjan, 2014) in the field of Big Data identify the three dimensions of Big Data; variety, volume, velocity. Besides, some studies (Demchenko et al, 2013; Wamba et al, 2015) discuss the five dimensions of Big Data by adding value and veracity.

Variety of data explains type of data. Data is generated not only from single category, neither only traditional data-sets but also from some sources such as pages, Web Log Files, social networking data, e-mail documents, RFID sensor features, streamed video and audio as semi-structured data. The data could be in different forms like raw, structured, semi-structured and unstructured data. The type of unstructured data is the most difficult to be handled by the organisations through traditional methods.

Volume of data explains the size of data such as terabytes (TB), petabytes (PB), zettabytes (ZB) etc. The growing number of data could be hard to be managed unless the techniques are improved because as of 2012, 2.5 exabytes are created by each day and this number is doubled in 40 months (McAfee et al, 2012). The present data is generated in petabytes; however, in the near future, it might be increased to zettabytes. Only the social networking sites produce in terabytes everyday. Therefore, the volume of data has a significant impact on processing data in using traditional tools.

Velocity of data refers to the speed of data, both the incoming data and data flows from several sources; how the data is produced by millisecond, second, minute hour, day, week, month and year. The frequency of processing data depends on user requirements, the data could be processed in real time, either might be when it is needed. Velocity is based upon occasional, frequent and real time of data. The high frequency generates more volume of data; therefore, traditional methods would not be adequate to process them.

Value of data is the extent of which data is worthy behind the value of organisation, or what kind of benefits could be generated by the extraction of Big Data. For instance, Big Data is used for improving patient outcomes by Premier Healthcare Alliance while decreasing spending by $2.85 billion (Wamba et al, 2015). Value could bring value added into process, activity or predictive analysis.

Veracity of data highlights the quality of data and level of trust from different data sources. Therefore, if data is not of adequate quality by the time, it integrates by the other data and pushes the organisations into wrong decisions on their business.

The literature indicates that the dimensions of data is strategically important to define the opportunities and challenges in Big Data environment, because Big Data is differentiated from traditional databases in terms of its characteristics. Those characteristics of data increase the opportunities as well as challenges for the organisations.

3. OPPORTUNITIES OF BIG DATA

3.1 Improving Management and Forecasting

BD plays a role in predictive analytics; therefore, it gives better management systems and forecasting opportunities on demand. In manufacturing, Big Data could be used in improving demand forecasting, Supply Chain Planning, sales support, developed production operations and web search based applications while in retail, it could be applied to behaviour analysis in store, variety and product optimisation, product placement design, improve performance, labor inputs optimisation, distribution and logistics optimisation, web based markets (Sagıroglu and Sinanc, 2013; Waller and Fawcett, 2013).

3.2 Operations and Supply Chain Efficiency

The impact of competitive advantage through Supply Chains, Information Technology (IT) has become a pioneer tool on the operations. Therefore, the effects of Big Data could not be underestimated as it gives ample opportunities on analysis of the Supply Chain risks, measuring supplier performance or identifyng the credible areas for optimisation. Big Data can be used as the feasible solution for operational challenges to give accurate decisions and as a result, supporting Supply Chains (Tenkorang and Helo, 2016).

Big Data offers more and more samples behind its machine learning techniques; therefore, the risks overfitting is becoming smaller over time. The data analysts deal with the billions of data to be processed; therefore, the risks are minimised while the benefits gained are maximised (Zhou et al,2014).

3.3 Marketing

The new insights also would be generated with increased number of data by users directly or indirectly thanks to advanced technologies on data storage and mining. The purchasing trends could be analysed by companies to set the better marketing strategies and for the target customers; in addition, the customers could make their decisions through their mobile phones about the characteristics of the shops where they would like to purchase their products (Michael and Miller, 2013).

4. CHALLENGES OF BIG DATA

4.1 Ownership

As data is with huge size of amount; therefore, the data can be transferred by different parts of distributors so no one holds the whole data. Therefore, different data owners could restrict the access of their own data by different access rights. Even though the data owners provide some parts or whole data to the third parties; then another challenge of transporting and storing the data arise since the data is huge. In addition, data provided to the other parties could be hard to be managed because of label quality and label noise in different places (Zhou et al, 2014).

4.2 Privacy and Security Issues

The ruining of traditional defensive environments united with attackers' abilities to survive traditional security systems requires organisations to adopt an intelligence driven security model that is more risk aware, contextual and agile. Intelligence driven security relies on big data analytics. Big data involve both the breadth of sources and the information depth needed for programs to specify risks accurately, to defend against illegal activity and advanced cyber threats (Sagıroglu and Sinanc, 2013).

4.3 Communication Costs

The communication cost is one of the leading concerns on computer network; therefore, the leading issue is to minimize the communication cost with satisfied capacity of extra storage and data requirement for processing Big Data. The challenges must be eased by the communication between the clients and the cloud server. The machine learning techniques are the way of overcoming those challenges (Suthaharan, 2014).

4.4 Analytics Challenge

Processing Big Data is another challenge because of various types of decision and optimisation models. The data could be descriptive, estimative, predictive, and prescriptive; therefore, this leads to several models to be developed such as game theory, control theory, or simulation models. Big data is ready for changing data sets on different conditions by staying agile, advanced and predictive analytics. The services and operations could be improved easily by the streams of huge datasets (Kaisler et al, 2013).

Also, as growing data-sets, traditional methods are not capable of storing and processing data; therefore, highly efficient techniques and technologies must be needed. The continuous growth of Big Data could be handled by the techniques such as Hadoop Distributed File Systems (HDFS), Cloud technology and Hive database to become both time sensitive and predictive for the future.

5. CONCLUSION

Big Data is strategically important concept for organisations because of the effects of new technological developments. It represents the huge datasets generated by various sources such as sensors, public webs, and social media; therefore, the characteristics of Big Data could be classified as volume, variety, velocity and in some research also add value and veracity in last years. The opportunities could be taken in business as well as the challenges through 5Vs. In this paper, the review of the articles gives insight to the future improvements of Big Data. The paper suggests that the traditional methods are not capable to overcome the challenges of Big Data; therefore, the new techniques and technologies must be developed in order to maintain the significant effects of this concept. However, Big Data is still in its initial stage, therefore, more research must be identified in its development.

REFERENCES

Chen, C. P., & Zhang, C. Y. (2014). Data-intensive applications, challenges, techniques and technologies: A survey on Big Data. *Information Sciences*, *275*, 314-347.

Demchenko, Y. et al. (2013). Architecture framework and components for the big data ecosystem. *Journal of System and Network Engineering*, 1-31.

George, G. et al. (2014). Big data and management. *Academy of Management Journal*, *57*(2), 321-326.

Kaisler, S. et al. (2013). Big data: Issues and challenges moving forward. In *System Sciences (HICSS), 2013 46th Hawaii International Conference on* (pp. 995-1004). IEEE.

Khan, N. et al. (2014). Big data: survey, technologies, opportunities, and challenges. *The Scientific World Journal*, *2014*.

Lohr, S. (2012). The age of big data. *New York Times*, *11*(2012).

McAfee, A. et al. (2012). Big data: the management revolution. *Harvard business review*, *90*(10), 60-68.

Michael, K., & Miller, K. W. (2013). Big data: New opportunities and new challenges. *Computer*, *46*(6), 22-24.

Ranjan, R. (2014). Streaming big data processing in datacenter clouds. *IEEE Cloud Computing*, *1*(1), 78-83.

Sagiroglu, S., & Sinanc, D. (2013, May). Big data: A review. In *Collaboration Technologies and Systems (CTS), 2013 International Conference on* (pp. 42-47). IEEE.

Suthaharan, S. (2014). Big data classification: Problems and challenges in network intrusion prediction with machine learning. *ACM SIGMETRICS Performance Evaluation Review*, *41*(4), 70-73.

Waller, M. A., & Fawcett, S. E. (2013). Data science, predictive analytics, and big data: a revolution that will transform supply chain design and management. *Journal of Business Logistics*, *34*(2), 77-84.

Wamba, S. F. et al. (2015). How 'big data'can make big impact: Findings from a systematic review and a longitudinal case study. *International Journal of Production Economics*, *165*, 234-246.

Zhou, Z. H et al. (2014). Big data opportunities and challenges: Discussions from data analytics perspectives [discussion forum]. *IEEE Computational Intelligence Magazine*, *9*(4), 62-74.

TOWARDS LONGEVITY OF KNOWLEDGE

Dr.-Ing. Federico Grasso Toro
Physikalisch-Technische Bundesanstalt, Abbestrasse 2-12. 10587. Berlin. Germany

ABSTRACT

In the current big data cloud based machine learning blockchain oversaturated world, the lack of clear patterns from data to become science is the most significant problem that must be faced, not only to help Ph.D. candidates to find procedures to arrive to certainty in scientific fields, but also the general approach as regarding research and the longevity of knowledge. A newly developed Ontology of Knowledge provides a clear structure to subsequently process all available data into scientific certainty, by articulating existing theories into research-specific patterns. The use of this Ontology of Knowledge to develop everlasting scientific and engineering knowledge combines existing technologies with new approaches to develop knowledge, aiming to find static procedures that will allow permanent looped research. Solutions are proposed for problems such as the lack of clarity for longevity of knowledge and the needed approaches to deal with Big Data by re-thinking knowledge as the amalgamation of Data Science and a newly stablished ontology point of view from Epistemology. This reflection paper seeks to find common ground to start the needed discussions towards achieving longevity of knowledge, not just understood as the long existence and perpetration of acquired knowledge, but also as the meaningful and everlasting service of scientific and engineering structured-knowledge as human contribution.

KEYWORDS

Ontology, Knowledge, Data Science, Longevity

1. INTRODUCTION

When Don DeLillo suggested in his novel Zero K the need for adopting a new hand-based semantic towards the longevity of language for potential cryogenic applications that might drift people into the unknown and distant future, I started wondering how could knowledge, but especially scientific and engineering knowledge lasting over time. The latter can be transfer to how-to manual, but even that adaptation of knowledge lacks means to secure its future correct interpretation. Hence, the current big data cloud based machine learning blockchain oversaturated world, lacks clear patterns to find certainty in scientific knowledge and to store it for future usage. Nowadays we are already suffering the lack of planning to transfer knowledge in institutions and academia, where the supposedly achieved scientific knowledge, as well as the supposedly acquired engineering knowledge, rediscovers itself once and again in a cycle lasting decades. The scientific revolution feedback loop that has fed power, resources usage and new research to be developed, presented in Harari, 2014, is modified in Figure 1. The loop seems to be morphing into the repetitiveness of specialization and generalization for understanding and using scientific and engineering knowledge, getting lost in every generation to be eventually re-discovered, causing the permanent problem of knowledge longevity and its applications.

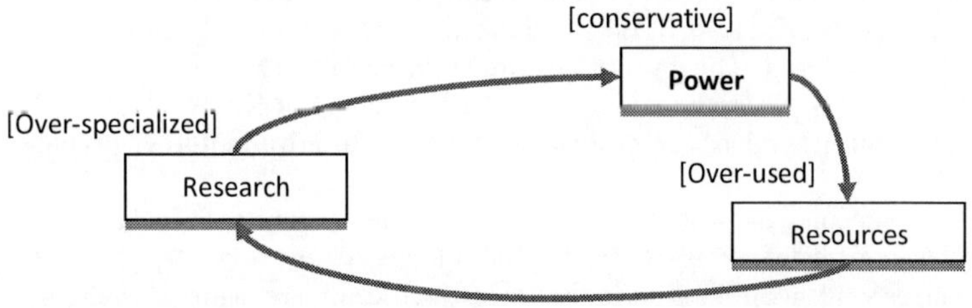

Figure 1. [Modified] Scientific Revolution Feedback Loop (Yuval Noah Harari, 2014)

This proposed loop for scientific development carries out two main problems: How to deal with the newly acquired knowledge? And how to preserve it for further development? Currently, challenges for dealing with Big Data can be solved by approaching data capture, storage, analysis, search, sharing, transfer, visualization, querying and updating from a data scientist point of view and not from the statistician point of view, as proposed in Tukey, 1977. But although the solution has been presented, no clear pattern for its usage has been developed or implemented. Also, while science approaches complex models of mind and the future of conscience, AI technologies focus in potential future collaboration with humanity for more complex contributions. This might be the turning point for future implementations, but the lack of a pure language to continue the exchange of issues and concepts over time might break any solidified advances to coordinate the proper longevity of this combined knowledge.

2. BODY OF PAPER

This newly developed Ontology of Knowledge aims to provide a clear structure to subsequently process all available data into certainty clauses, for both scientific and engineering knowledge, by means of articulating existing theories into reproducible research patterns, consolidating the figure of research into concrete processes from data to results, reducing uncertainty in scientific fields while stating certainty clauses.

In the present reflection paper, I try to present the general idea underneath the ongoing Ontology of Knowledge, used within IT research in a Ph.D. level as the current case study. I provide research patterns to Ph.D. candidates throughout three minimal loops: 1) Bibliography loop: the analysis and description of the current state of the art; 2) Methodology loop: the conjunction process of all previously existing related methods and any newly developed methodologies aimed to solve specific problems; and finally 3) Demonstrator loop: the development of a prototype/model to demonstrate by results the objectively measurable concrete improvement within the situation stated by the specific problems, concluding in the reduction of uncertainty and the production of whether scientific knowledge (for further research) or engineering knowledge (for application purposes). Therefore, by using the Ontology of Knowledge summarized in Figure 2, each produced thesis within the IT research shall be able to describe, process and apply newly developed technics to data for the creation of certainty clauses within the studied field.

The presented Ontology of Knowledge currently applied to IT research is the result of my experience of years as teacher and researcher, producing and applying scientific and engineering knowledge in three continents. It is also the main subject of my current postdoctoral studies in applied epistemology for research of research.

The systematic approach of three loops, applying this Ontology of Knowledge, avoids blockages while stablishing static research patterns for Ph.D. candidates, by the following functionalities:

1) Filter function: it filters the existing data into newly acquired information;
2) Classifier function: it classifies the acquired information into stablished spheres of knowledge;
3) Articulator function: it articulates the newly acquired knowledge into:
    i) Craft: spheres of knowledge related to how to use research;
    ii) Expertise: spheres of knowledge related to how to further research;
4) Applier function: it applies the craft/expertise sphere(s) to produce certainty clauses.

The research patterns described above allows any Ph.D. candidate to develop organized scientific research, based on the three levels of mind analysis presented in Marr, 2010:

I) Computational Level: The level of the mind that answers which tasks are performed.
II) Algorithmic Level: The level of the mind that answers how these tasks are performed.
III) Implementation Level: The level of the mind that answers how these tasks are implemented.

The structure constructed between the newly developed Ontology of Knowledge and the already existing theories of computation, such as Marr 2010, aims to converge "the two cultures" problem stated in Snow, 1959.

In Figure 2 the two schemes used as the bases for the current study case in IT research are presented. While the Ontology of Knowledge expands the structured loops for research patterns, from the data level to the usage level, its correspondent application in the IT research can be recognized in the three levels of mind by Marr as:

I) Construction of structured knowledge: passage between computational and algorithmic levels;

II) Development of scientific knowledge: passage between algorithmic and implementation levels;
II) Application of engineering knowledge: passage between the implementation level and real life.

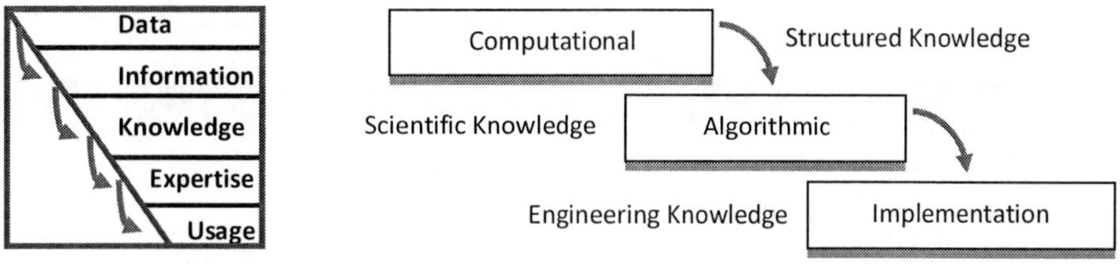

Figure 2. Ontology of Knowledge and Levels of Analysis (David Marr, 2010)

The resulting elastic process determines, explores and creates new structured knowledge to expand into craft/expertise for further usage or transfer, reducing uncertainty for further developments while converging the advantages of structured knowledge to solve the longevity problem with the advantages of scientific research pattern to solve the application problem of advancing engineering knowledge.

Lastly, the always present problem of inaccurate language to transfer knowledge over extended periods of time can be dealt with by means of controlled natural language, e.g. Gellish, as proposed in Van Renssen 2005, allowing future generations to conceive knowledge as stablished certainty clauses and research as the never-ending completion of knowledge by stablished research patterns to reduce uncertainty.

The exemplary case for IT research development is in its ongoing stage, but it has already shown real-life result, proving improvements in IT research in topics such as data management, cloud computing and cryptographic applications. By connecting the abstract-level representation of the presented Ontology of Knowledge into concrete IT scientific research examples, future results will prove if the implementation of the Ontology of Knowledge will provide better research patterns than previously developed research in similar fields by similar institutions, only if it remains stablished for further research in the field beyond the scope of my postdoctoral research.

Further studies for this Ontology of Knowledge will focus on developing the first AI-Researcher demonstrator, an AI-based pattern recognition machine for the developed research patterns; aimed to produce a new scientific revolution of research by means of AI-based assistants. The future publications regarding the ongoing Ontology of Knowledge will abridge the barriers between data science and epistemology, towards increasing dual-field contributions and reducing uncertainty. Figure 3 presents the potential expansion from the already stablished divisions of data science, in Tukey 1977, towards the divisions to be developed in epistemology. By applying the Ontology of Knowledge into epistemology, a list of potential divisions can be stated parallel to Tukey's division for data science. The merge between data science and epistemology in both theoretical and practical levels can be seen in Figure 3.

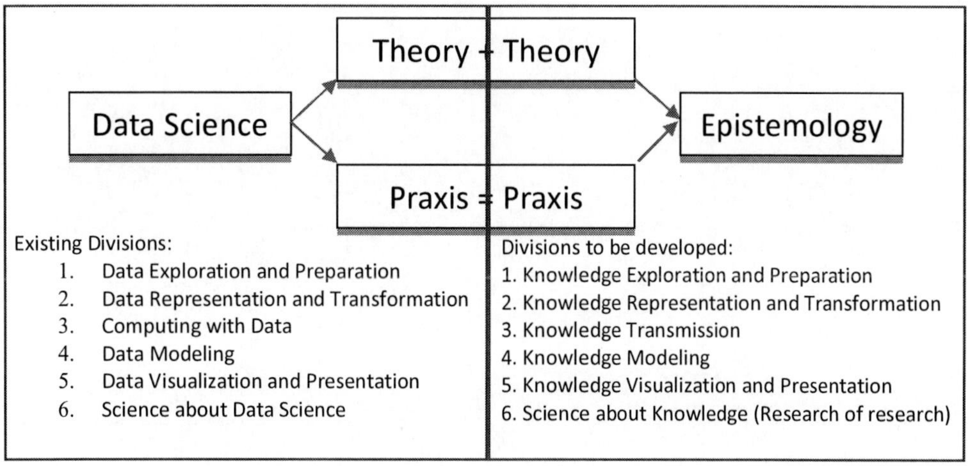

Figure 3. Description of Data Science (Tukey, 1977) [Extended to Epistemology]

3. CONCLUSION

Setting the research patterns to achieve the longevity of knowledge from an anthropological point of view can help humanity to concretely establish scientific certainty. This potential development can result in an everlasting transfer of scientific and engineering knowledge. Aided by the standardization of controlled natural languages, this can produce semantic frameworks for procedures to reduce uncertainty in several research fields achieving the longevity of knowledge by:

1) The craft of applying how-to-use-research;
2) The expertise of developing how-to-research-research.

The resulting patterns by attending longevity of knowledge will be studied and used to develop an AI-based pattern recognition machine, in the frame of AI-based Research Assistants, allowing humanity to begin a new stage of structured-knowledge research.

REFERENCES

DeLillo, D., 2016. *Zero K.* Scribner, New York, USA.

Harari, Y. N., 2014. *Sapiens: A Brief History of Humankind*, Harper, UK.

Marr, D., 2010. *Vision: A Computational Investigation into the Human Representation and Processing of Visual Information.* MIT, Cambridge, USA.

Van Renssen, A., 2005. *Gellish: A Generic Extensible Ontological Language*. Delft University. Delft, The Netherlands.

Snow, C. P., 1959. *The Two Cultures*, OUP, Oxford, UK.

Tukey, J. W., 1977. *Exploratory data analysis.* Addison-Wesley, Boston, USA.

BIG DATA SYSTEMS: A RENEWED DEFINITION OF THE CONCEPT

Everist Limaj[1] and Edona Bilali[2]
[1]*WU Wien, Austria*
[2]*FH Burgenland, Austria*

ABSTRACT

Big data are increasingly being adopted by modern organizations as a competitive way to gain new insights, inform decisions, and unfold business value. Correspondingly, there has been a growing number of studies investigating big data, yet the originating literature is dispersed and the definition of big data varies among studies. In this article, we first explore various current views on the ambiguous term of big data. Then, we propose a renewed definition that synthesizes existing perspectives and adds agency, as the missing link to value creation.

KEYWORDS

Big Data Systems, Literature Review, Definition

1. INTRODUCTION

Many companies nowadays generate up to petabytes of information in the course of the year through social media, clickstreams, transaction records, search indices, online forums, smartphones, digital images, videos, email, documents, consumer demographics, sensor data from active and passive systems, and more (Sakr and Gaber 2014). Different use cases creating value by exploiting these high volumes of data can be found across industries. For instance, Walmart, the largest retailer in the world, uses timely analysis of circa 200 billion rows of sales transactions from most recent weeks to understand their customers' needs and provide them with products they want to buy (Walmart 2015). Netflix, the streaming movie and TV service, has been building a business around predicting exactly what the user enjoy to watch by using cutting-edge analytical techniques (such as recommendation algorithms and content decisions) on data collected from millions of subscribers (Madrigal 2014). Rolls Royce, a manufacturing company of enormous engines, uses sophisticated computer techniques on tens of terabyte of data simulated from jet engines to visualize the quality of products they designed. (Rolls Royce 2009). In line with these increasing applications, there has been an increasing interest among IS researchers to investigate big data. Yet, the big data discourse calls for a comprehensive view on the subject, as the definitions and conceptualizations of big data remain ambiguous and vary among IS studies (Boyd and Crawford 2012, Floridi 2012).

The growth of big data parallels a number of surveys suggesting a variety of conceptualizations and definitions related to the term (Chen et al. 2014, De Mauro et al. 2016, Gandomi and Haider 2015, Ward and Barker 2013). The perspective of these studies, however, are very different and view big data (as we point out in the next section) as either an information asset, a phenomenon (cultural, technological, and scholarly), a dataset, a technology, an analytic technique, a process, or some combination of these views. These contributions generally support organizations to conceive big data platforms. However, in order to create real benefits, the main challenge is not only creating such a system, but also understanding it and the many opportunities it presents. The first step to address this challenge is to bring more clarity on the big data concept. This paper sets to fulfil this gap by providing a renewed conceptualization and a definition that is both comprehensive and precise. To achieve this goal, we first review previous work in this area taking into consideration past and current contribution trying to define big data. Then we offer a clear definition of what we refer to as "big data systems", which synthetizes current perspectives and adds a new element "agency" to increase our understanding on the link between big data and value creation.

2. METHODOLOGY

The literature on big data is interdisciplinary and has found applications in numerous fields. In this paper, we follow recommendations suggested by Webster and Watson (2002) and Boell and Cecez-Kecmanovic (2014) and perform a topic-centric, small-scale literature search among Information Systems and Management disciplines. We used Google Scholar as a large literature reference database to identify articles that engage with defining the term big data or are frequently cited with regard to their big data conceptualization. The identification process developed iteratively through many hermeneutic circles and resulted in 12 selected articles (see Table 1, next page). While this was a systematic, replicable approach (Boell and Cecez-Kecmanovic 2014), we recognize that the criterions upon which the articles were selected are subjective and might not be accounted.

Next, the selected articles were assessed with the main aim to summarize and synthetize what has been done regarding the conceptualization of big data. To achieve this goal, we take into consideration the structure of each definition composed of genus, differentia, and vocation. A genus is an object, a class or a predefined term that can include other sub-classes. The differentia describes the characteristics or properties of a genus. For instance, if we consider online social networks as a genus, related differentia include user-based, relationships, or interactivity. The structure of the genus-differentia definition is an early conception of Aristotle's philosophy and has been applied among various disciplines (Ackrill 1961). For the purposes of this paper, we add to this structure a third element, which we name vocation. Vocation describes what are the main purposes or outcomes, or what can be achieved (in our case with big data). Again, if we consider online social networks, some related vocations would be linking people, building communities, or sharing information.

3. PRESENT VIEWS ON BIG DATA IN IS LITERATURE

The result of our analysis exploring big data definitions in terms of their genus, differentia, and vocation is summarized in Table 1 (see next page). While analyzing the definitions, we discovered two interesting findings.

First, the result suggests that there are many perspectives in use when it comes to defining big data. One common approach is to see big data principally as a dataset that has some particular properties, such as (among others) being too large, expanding too fast and not fitting in traditional databases (Chen and Zhang 2014, Chen et al. 2014, Dumbill 2013). Another approach views big data merely as a technology and extends on the features needed to achieve desired outcomes (Baru et al. 2013, Tambe 2014). An alternative approach portrays big data as an information asset encompassing the "V"- requirements, such as volume, velocity, variety, veracity, and value (Beyer and Laney 2012, De Mauro et al. 2016). Other studies conceptualize big data to some extent as a combination of data, technology, and analytical techniques (Chen et al. 2012, De Mauro et al. 2016, Hashema et al. 2015, Ward and Barker 2013). Somehow similar, Boyd and Crawford (2012) consider big data as a phenomenon (cultural, technological, and scholarly) which lies on the interplay between technology, analysis, and mythology. In another way, Sharma et al. (2014) considers big data as a process that can be performed (by many actors) in order to reach an outcome, such as discovering new insigh

Second, although the many existing perspectives, it appears that there is one important aspect missing regarding big data. The analysis of the selected studies associates different genuses (such as data, technology and complementary assets) with various vocations, however, these genuses alone are not sufficient to generate business value. One essential determinant missing that links big data with value creation is the agency perspective. Agency, as addressed by Giddens (1984), can be understood as human action, or the capability of an actor to intentionally utilize his knowledge to achieve a particular outcome. What is important with regard to big data is that agency stresses the organization's role in terms of the ability to recognize what to do with big data and act intentionally to exploit those opportunities producing consequences that ultimately add business value. In the next section, we propose a new definition of big data systems that synthesizes the aforementioned perspectives and adds agency as the missing link.

Table 1. Exploring Big Data definitions

Author(s)	Definition	Genus	Differentia	Vocation
(Beyer anc Laney 201	...high-volume, high-velocity, high-veracity and/or high-variety information assets that require new forms of processing to enable enhanced decision making, insight discovery and process optimization.	Information assets	Volume, Velocity, Veracity, Variety	Process data, Make decisions, Discover insights, Process optimization
(Dumbill 2013)	...data that exceeds the processing capacity of conventional database systems. The data is too big, moves too fast, or doesn't fit the structures of your database architecture.	Data	Volume, Velocity, Current database is not able to cope with it	Analysis, Generate insights
(Ward and Barker 2013)	...the storage and analysis of large and or complex data sets using a series of techniques including, but not limited to: NoSQL, MapReduce and machine learning.	Datasets Techniques Technologies	Volume, Complexity,	Storage, Analysis
(Boyd and Crawford 2012)	...a cultural, technological, and scholarly phenomenon that rests on the interplay of technology, analysis and mythology.	Phenomenon	Technology, Analysis, Mythology	Compute, Analyze, Make claims
(Baru et al 2013)	...a platform flexible in processing diverse data genres, such as transaction logs, connection graphs, and natural language text, with algorithms characterized by multiple communication patterns.	Technology	Flexibility, Diversity, Various algorithms, Multiple communication patterns	Processing
(Chen et al 2014)	...datasets that could not be perceived, acquired, managed, and processed by traditional IT and software/hardware tools within a tolerable time.	Dataset	Data change over time and differ among applications, Traditional IT cannot cope with it, Maximum tolerable processing time.	Data generation, Acquisition, Storage, Analysis
(Chen and Zhang 201	...a collection of very huge data sets with a great diversity of types so that it becomes difficult to process by using state-of-the-art data processing approaches or traditional data processing platforms.	Dataset	Volume, Heterogeneity, Difficult to process, Traditional approaches cannot cope with it	Business productivity, Science progress
(De Maurc et al. 2016	...the information asset characterized by such a high volume, velocity and variety to require specific technology and analytical methods for its transformation into value.	Information asset	Volume, Velocity, Variety, Specific technology and analytics	Analysis, Value creation
(Hashema al. 2015)	...a set of techniques and technologies that require new forms of integration to uncover large hidden values from large datasets that are diverse, complex, and of a massive scale.	Techniques Technologies Datasets	New forms of integration, Volume, Variety, Velocity, Value	Uncover value from data
(Chen et al 2012)	...data sets and analytical techniques in applications that are so large ... and complex ... that they require advanced and unique data storage, management, analysis, and visualization technologies.	Datasets Techniques Applications	Large and complex applications, Advanced and unique technologies	Storage, Management, Analysis, Visualization
(Tambe 2014)	...allow firms to extract business intelligence from petabyte-scale data in nearly real time...	Technologies	Petabyte-scale data, Real time processing	Extract business intelligence
(Sharma et al. 2014)	...the process of generating insights from data generally involving multiple actors...	Process	Managerial decisions, Multiple actors	Generate insights

4. BIG DATA SYSTEMS DEFINED

We define big data as a system (BDS) composed of interconnected elements, including datasets, technology, analytics and agency that dynamically interact with each other, are characterized by complexity, can change over time and can serve different purposes. To illustrate, in Figure 1 we provide a conceptual framework followed by a more detailed description of each BDS component.

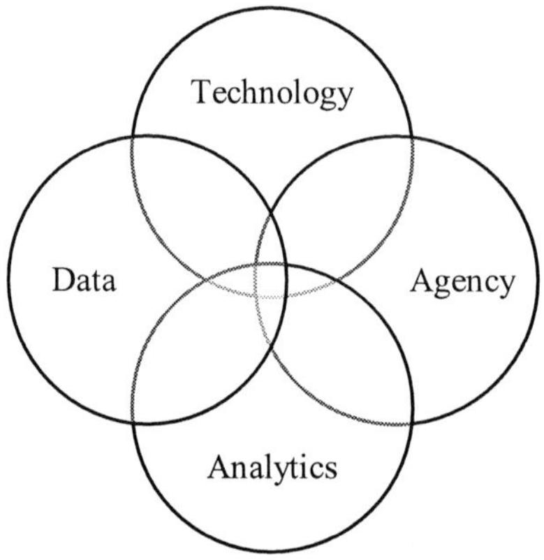

Figure 1. A conceptual framework of Big Data System

A dataset refers to a collection of heterogeneous data that (i) traditional databases are not able to cope with, (ii) come in a high-volume, high-velocity, high-veracity and/or high-variety, (iii) can change over time and (iv) differ among different applications. In combination with other elements that compose the BDS, these data can be stored, collected, processed, visualized and analyzed, yet allowing to discover or generate new insights that can create business value, for instance in terms of making informed decisions, optimizing productivity and/or processes, or creating breakthrough innovations.

Technology refers to modern repositories and flexible applications that can accommodate the aforementioned datasets, for instance in terms of storing or processing. A common example is Apache Hadoop that creates more flexibility in terms of handling different kind of data formats and enables the creation of a so-called "data lake". A data lake combines an enormous scalable storage repository with processing engines that can ingest data without compromising their structure (Miloslavskaya and Tolstoy 2016). It functions like a man-made reservoir where you initially dam the end (build a cluster) and then fill it up with water (data). Once you build the lake, you can use the water (data) for drinking, cleaning, cooling, and food preparation (testing propositions, predictive analysis, visualization, cyber security, etc.)

Analytics refers to the black art applied to tackle data including a collection of skills, methods and techniques that help us to ask and answer questions or, in other words, to discover new business facts. Common examples are predictive or statistical analysis, data mining and visualization, artificial intelligence and natural language processing (Russom 2011), or genetic algorithms, machine learning, social network analysis, sentiment analysis, and signal processing (Chen et al. 2012).

Agency refers to the capacity of an actor to act in a given environment, for instance in terms of recognizing BDS opportunities and efficiently governing the combination of the aforementioned BDS elements (datasets, technology and analytics) to create business value. This includes, but is not limited to, taking timely, appropriate managerial decisions that positively impact discovering new insights, such as composing suitable teams or defining appropriate organizational structures, routines and processes (Sharma et al. 2014).

This renewed conceptualization is important as it synthetizes and extends current views, in particular, by adding agency as an integral component of the big data system. Besides, it stresses the high complexity of the system and the interaction needed between changing elements to generate new insights serving different purposes. Evidently, more research on the current topic is needed to investigate how parts of the system and their relationships initiate collective behavior and how the big data system interrelates with its environment.

REFERENCES

Ackrill, J. L. (1961) *Aristotle's Categories and De Interpretatione, Clarendon Aristotle Series,* Oxford: Clarendon Press.

Baru, C., Bhandarkar, M., Nambiar, R., Poess, M. and Rabl, T. (2013) Benchmarking Big Data Systems and the BigData Top100 List. *Big Data, 1*(1), pp. 60-64.

Beyer, M. A. and Laney, D. (2012) The importance of data: A definition. *Stamford, CT: Gartner.*

Boell, S. and Cecez-Kecmanovic, D. (2014) A hermeneutic approach for conducting literature reviews and literature searches. *Communication of the AIS, 34*(1), pp. 256-286.

Boyd, D. and Crawford, K. (2012) Critical Questions For Big Data - Provocations for a cultural, technological, and scholarly phenomenon. *Information, Communication & Society, 15*(5), pp. 662-679.

Chen, C. L. P. and Zhang, C.-Y. (2014) Data-intensive applications, challenges, techniques and technologies: A survey on Big Data. *Information Sciences, 275*, pp. 314-347.

Chen, H., Chiang, R. H. L. and Storey, V. C. (2012) Business Intelligence and Analytics: From Big Data to Big Impact. *MIS Quarterly, 36*(4), pp. 1165-1188.

Chen, M., Mao, S. and Liu, Y. (2014) Big Data: A Survey. *Mobile Netw Appl, 19*(2), pp. 171-209.

De Mauro, A., Greco, M. and Grimaldi, M. (2016) A formal definition of Big Data based on its essential features. *Library Review, 65*(3), pp. 122-135.

Dumbill, E. (2013) Making Sense of Big Data *Big Data, 1*(1), pp. 1-2.

Floridi, L. (2012) Big Data and Their Epistemological Challenge. *Philosophy & Technology, 25*(4), pp. 435-437

Gandomi, A. and Haider, M. (2015) Beyond the hype: Big data concepts, methods, and analytics. *International Journal of Information Management, 35*(2), pp. 137–144.

Giddens, A. (1984) *The constitution of society,* Berkeley: University of California Press.

Hashema, I. A. T., Yaqoob, I., Anuar, N. B., Mokhtar, S., Gani, A. and Khan, S. U. (2015) The rise of "big data" on cloud computing: Review and open research issues. *Information Systems, 47*, pp. 98-115.

Madrigal, A. C. (2014) *How Netflix Reverse Engineered Hollywood*, Available: http://www.theatlantic.com/technology/archive/2014/01/how-netflix-reverse-engineered-hollywood/282679/ [Accessed 25 January 2017].

Miloslavskaya, N. and Tolstoy, A. (2016) Big Data, Fast Data and Data Lake Concepts. *Procedia Computer Science, 88*, pp. 300-305.

Rolls Royce (2009) *Engine health management* Available: http://www.rolls-royce.com/about/our-technology/enabling-technologies/engine-health-management.aspx#sense [Accessed 25 January 2017].

Russom, P. (2011) *Big Data Analytics*. TDWI best practices report No. fourth quarter, 2011. tableau.com.

Sakr, S. and Gaber, M. M. (2014) *Large Scale and Big Data - Processing and Management,* Boca Raton, Florida: CRC Press.

Sharma, R., Mithas, S. and Kankanhalli, A. (2014) Transforming decision-making processes: a research agenda for understanding the impact of business analytics on organisations. *European Journal of Information Systems, 23*(4), pp. 433-441.

Tambe, P. (2014) Big Data Investment, Skills, and Firm Value. *Management Science, 60*(6), pp. 1452-1469.

Walmart (2015) *When Data Met Retail: A #lovedata story*, Available: https://careersblog.walmart.com/when-data-met-retail-a-lovedata-story/ [Accessed 25 January 2017].

Ward, J. S. and Barker, A. (2013) Undefined By Data: A Survey of Big Data Definitions. *Databases*, pp. available at: arXiv:,1309.5821[cs.DB].

Webster, J. and Watson, R. (2002) Analyzing the past to prepare for the future: Writing a literature review. *MIS Quarterly, 26*(2), pp. 13.

ALZHEIMER EARLY DETECTION BY HADOOP DATA-MINING

Dror Ben-Ami*
Moldova State University, Moldova
**On my last year PhD. Studies, Moldova State University, Informatica, Moldova*

ABSTRACT

Someone in the world develops dementia every 3 seconds! Around 50 million people in 2017 already have dementia. The gloomy forecast: reaching 75 million in 2030 and over 131 million in 2050. The total estimated worldwide cost of dementia is US$ 818 billion in 2015, which represents 1.09% of global GDP. By 2018, the global cost of dementia will rise above a US$ trillion (The global Voice on Dementia). Around 75% of the dementia people have Alzheimer. These figures explain why lot of efforts and means are invested to diagnose AH as early and professionally as possible. The research is focused on two main objectives. The first is "Prediction": Early AH detection by predicted-based algorithms, for those who currently have or probably will have AH. The second is "Efficiency": Improving the current diagnostics process; specifically, regarding the time-consuming parameter. All these, by computers' data mining algorithms: mainly clustering, classification and neural-networks; by using advanced computers' architectures, such HADOOP, and by other computer-based means.

KEYWORDS

Data Mining[DM], Alzheimer[AH] Disease, Hadoop, Clustering, Classification, Neural-Network

1. INTRODUCTION

The paper verifies that Alzheimer's diagnostics can be done by using data mining methods, techniques and specific descriptive and predictive algorithms. These techniques and algorithms are described as general data mining concept (Hand) (Dunham). In addition, and much specifically to Alzheimer disease, this is mentioned, spot and specified in the following articles/links: (Benyoussef) (Gamberger). Regarding the technical environment for implementing and running these AH diagnostics data mining algorithms, attached few bibliographic references. These references reinforce the usage of Hadoop distributed computing as convenient possible technology and architectural environment (Rajendran) (Punekar). So far, the references show that once an algorithm was established, the entire process was performed under Hadoop effectively. Although the novelty and the innovation of the research is based on utilizing Hadoop environment technique differently from current used ways, especially in AH diagnostics. The novelty is based on activating and running few different DM algorithms at once, to make crosstab checks between the models' results. Thus, instead of running in serial order, parallel order was established, and a lot of time was saved. The general algorithms which were part of the research include 5 well-known algorithms: Classification; (2-3-4) Clustering: Fuzzy-C-Means, K-Means, DBSCAN; (5) Neural-Network: Multi-Layer Perceptron.

2. METHOD AND RATIO

The research merge and examines the above data mining algorithms into one overall phase, as interpreted later. The basic concept of *Data Mining Clustering* assumes that we can find similarities between data elements (Hand) (Dunham). The groups which can be found through the process are called *clusters.* If points on a graph describe single data elements, we can assume that the closer points are one to each other, the more similar they are. Thus, we can assume that they belong to the same cluster. If the geometrical distance between the points is greater, we can assume that the data elements do not have "too much" in common, and thus, they cannot belong to the same cluster. So, what is the distance or the magnitude that according to it the belonging of a point to the cluster determines? This is an active check by the automatic computer algorithms, which controls the sensitivities of size and range and other parameters as well. One of the data mining clustering technique distinguishes between two categories: Hard and Soft clustering. The distinguished rule relates to the question whether a point/data-element, belongs to one group/cluster, or to a few groups (clusters). If our demand is for single belonging ONLY, it means that we want to use the *HARD*-clustering method. If our demand enables single data element belonging to few clusters at the same time, it means that we want to use the *SOFT*-clustering method (Punekar) (Soumi). This research examines which algorithm is better for diagnosing the disease centers and focuses in the patient's brain. The reason of using clustering in this research relies on the following accepted-known facts: MRI, *Magnetic Resonance Imaging* is a diagnostic device to scan the brain in Dementia and Alzheimer. The MRI is considered as having less "noise" than other devices. The noise can be identified and reflected by mainly using the colors: *black*, *white*, *grey* and their diversities, rather than images with large spectrum of colors. It is also proved in previous image analysis researches that those algorithms, which belong to Clustering sub-group, are used effectively in the required diagnostics (Vinh). In addition, it is important to mention that clustering is usually used as feasibility and practicability model for the classification model and usually for some other data mining techniques. The DBSCAN algorithm adds the abilities of density measurements, which is crucial and major part in AH MRI-image processing. The Neural network by itself adds another level of data analysis process: the learning stage. This model is conceptually working differently from the others, and empower the ability of the entire research to have some references to the machine-learning stages, based on the data: images on one hand, and textual database text files on the second hand. Regarding to the technological-architectural environments, the industrial and academic organizations, are familiar with different environments, architectures and implementation ways for AH diagnosis, by computer means. Two major concepts and ways to accomplish and manage the research's analysis process were verified: The first is based on one standalone autonomous multi-processor computer, which would perform all the data analysis process. This standalone machine has several processors, which are working simultaneously, but under the same single computer and operation system. This is principally not pure parallel processing; some might think of it much more like serial working process, step by step, in continuous time range. The computer manages its multithreading and other parallelism techniques, but in a very limited source, as a single machine. The second implementation way is based on distributed computing concept, by using the Hadoop platform; which means that all the stages can run in simultaneously in real parallel mode, by automatic distribution of the algorithms' set into few servers/nodes at once. The number of servers/nodes was specified and was limited to three, as equivalence to the 3 multi-processors machine. Also, just as a temporary decision and based on hiring servers' costs. Conceptually, the distributed computing, Hadoop, can save a lot of time, whilst parallelism can be established. This is the case under research objectives. Another significant parameter must be considered: the amounts of data which must be analyzed. The research includes big chunks of data, organized in over than 128MB per one single file: images, databased tables. Hadoop prefers to work with big files, as part of the architectural efficiency.

3. HADOOP SPECS

Hadoop is differently structured from other distributed environments. Thus, it overcomes the entire usual problems of distributed-system, such as: pay for scalability by adding complexity, availability, data consistency, event synchronization, bandwidth limitations, partial failure and more.

Hadoop supports large-scale data storage and data analysis by horizontal scalability techniques, besides other useful solutions, such as: relative isolation for jobs, proportional load capacities, running jobs concurrently, and by clusters structures, which are built from industry-standard hardware. The store and process stages are done on the same machine; which saves a lot of time, specially in the overhead factor. Optimization can be established under Hadoop effectively, which enables significant improvements in the entire jobs performances. All these make Hadoop attractive and suitable for AH detection effectively.

4. SUMMARY OF THE FINDINGS

1. Time consuming: Hadoop environment runs much faster than one standalone 3-multiprocessored machine. This can be shown on Table 1 below.
2. Codes Complexity: all the algorithms were based on Java. The standalone machine had internal KNIME (www.knime.com) package for the data mining exploration. The Hadoop environment includes mainly open-codes which had to be suited to the distributed computing platform. Thus, some more work had to invested in the code adaptation to the Hadoop architecture. However, this stage saved a lot of time during the running stage. The "quality" of the written codes was not compared in this research. The assumption is that all the codes were written by professionals.
3. System Utilization: all the checked parameters, such as: memory consumptions, OS page faults, speed rates – show significantly that Hadoop utilization is higher significantly from the multi-processor standalone computer.

Table 1. Main Results

	SINGLE MACHINE 3 multi-processors	HADOOP 3 Nodes	COMMENT
TIME CONSUMING	~9 hours	~30 minutes	Hadoop faster 18 times
CODE COMPLEXITY	Less complex: most elements are "ready" to use	More complex: part of the codes must be adapted	Very difficult to estimate and to measure

5. CONCLUSIONS

Three main initial conclusions can be derived from this early research: the first is: The proposed approach of the research suggests expanding the Hadoop usage, and utilizing its architecture differently, by activating and running the necessary algorithms at once. Running Hadoop on this way, shows clearly that time can be saved for the main issue of diagnosing AH and the entire process can be speed-up and in much efficient way than before. The second is: Continuous deep learning techniques must be examined and implemented to find out the ultimate data mining algorithms to predict AH early. The third is: What is the optimum nodes for running the Hadoop for AH purposes? This question must be analyzed and researched in much wide and deep research.

REFERENCES

Benyoussef M., A. et al, Nov. 2017, *"Data Mining Approaches for Alzheimer's Disease Diagnosis"*, Lecture Notes in Computer Science book series (LNCS, volume 10542).

Dunham, M.H., 2003, *"Data Mining: Introductory and Advanced Topics"*, Prentice Hall, Pearson Education Inc.

Gamberger D. et al, July 2017, *"Scientists use new data mining strategy to spot those at high Alzheimer's risk"*, Duke University Medical Center. https://medicalxpress.com/news/2017-07-scientists-strategy-high-alzheimer.html

Hand D. et al, 2001, *"Principles of Data Mining"*, MIT press.

Punekar D. et al, 2014, *"Analysis of Image Matching Towards the Hard Clustering"*, International Journal of Scientific and Research Publications, Volume 4, Issue 4, ISSN.

Rajendran K, 2017, *"Journal of Applied Technology and Innovation"*, Asia Pacific University, E-ISSN: 2600-7304, Volume 1, Issue 2, p. 10-27, APU Press.

Soumi G. and K.D. Sanjay, 2013, *"Comparative Analysis of K-Means and Fuzzy C–Means Algorithms"*, (IJACSA) International Journal of Advanced Computer Science and Applications, Vol. 4, No.4.

The global Voice on Dementia: https://www.alz.co.uk/research/statistics

Vinh Q.D., 2009, *"Investigating Data Mining Techniques for Extracting Information from Alzheimer's Disease Data"*, Edith Cowan University.

Posters

GRAPH BASED DISCOVERY IN BIOMEDICAL INFORMATION SYSTEMS CONNECTING SCIENTIFIC TEXTS WITH STRUCTURED EXPERT KNOWLEDGE

Jens Dörpinghaus, Marc Jacobs and Juliane Fluck
Fraunhofer Institute for Scientific Computing and Algorithms SCAI,
Sankt Augustin, Germany

ABSTRACT

In this poster we describe a novel approach for knowledge discovery in biomedical information systems utilizing the Biological Expression Language (BEL). This language is widely used for network-based approaches in text mining for a better understanding of biological mechanisms. Storing all relevant data of decomposed documents, the ontologies and BEL statements in Semantic Digital Assets (SDA) leads to a knowledge graph capable of answering semantic questions and making more biomedical knowledge available for analyses.

KEYWORDS

Knowledge Management, Knowledge Discovery, Graph Theory, Biomedical Information Systems, BEL

1. INTRODUCTION

For a long time network-based approaches have been used to encode and curate biomedical information in a computable form. This is usually done using information systems holding the knowledge of biomedical literature. The Biological Expression Language (BEL, see www.openbel.org) is widely used by domain experts for this purpose. In addition, several information systems have been introduced to support curators generating these networks. SCAIView is a highly efficient information system used for information retrieval, semantic searches and knowledge discovery in biomedical publications.

Currently information from different systems and databases are not connected, but due to the increasing number of datasets this is an important need. The new version of SCAIView will also store Semantic Digital Assets (SDA), which decompose documents and whole literature databases like PubMed or PMC into semantic document elements and annotations. We will introduce two other layers or subsets of the database to utilize SDAs for knowledge discovery using BEL in biomedical documents.

This approach is completely novel, since SDAs have not been used to connect different information layers. We expect new insights and a better integration and less complexity and more speed in terms of computability.

2. METHOD

A Semantic Digital Asset (SDA) is an outer layer surrounding the signal of a message, which can either be a picture, a table or a part of text or speech. It wraps some properties around that digital asset. They were introduced as the four semiotic properties: The identifier (called **sigmatic**), the purpose (Document, Header, Paragraph, Named Entity; called **pragmatic**), the kind of annotation (Named Entity ID, Author, Title; this is called **semantic**), a specification of the content (binary/text called **syntax**). Using this approach, it is very easy to store and access meta-data or annotations for scientific documents. We will use SCAIView for storing and accessing this data model (see scaiview.com). This software has a long history for knowledge discovery (Malhotra et al 2013). Named entities are detected with JProMiner (Fluck et al. 2007).

We will now describe two new information layers stored in this novel format. They provide new links (e.g. nodes in our knowledge graph) that concatenate all three layers.

2.1 Three Layers: Document Elements, Ontologies and BEL Relations

Storing all document elements in SDAs leads to a total decomposition of documents in nested hierarchical structures. Thus we can easily access sections, paragraphs, sentences and their annotated named entities. These are linked to the ontologies and are the basis for BEL relations.

Ontologies are stored in a graph structure containing the ontologies, their class hierarchy and the instances. They have novel links to all BEL and textual elements that map these concepts related to their instances. The BEL relations are semantic triples that consist of named entities and functions (Fluck et al. 2013). They are all stored in SDAs beginning with the named entities and functions that combine them to relations. For example *p(HGNC:CCND1)* contains two SDAs: an entity *HGNC:CCND1* and a function *p*. Combining this with function => to *act(p(HGNC:CDK4))* leads to a tree of statements. The root element would be a BEL document containing different statements.

2.2 Analyzing the Graph

The union of these three layers leads to a graph where all three parts are easily accessible. See figure 1 for an illustration. We now have connections between nodes in the ontologies and documents, as well as documents and ontologies and BEL statements. Thus a total new approach is possible.

We can now utilize this graph to answer semantic questions, proof hypotheses and statements from the literature in this database. "Which papers or authors described first the impact of gene A on process B in the context of disease C"? "What is the probability that for patients suffering A and B drug C leads to side effect D?"

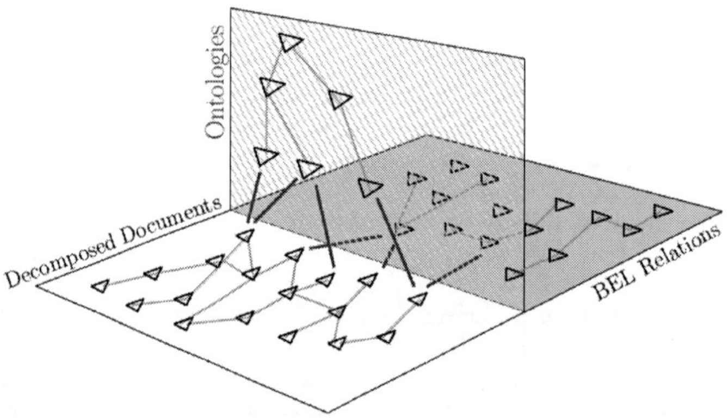

Figure 1. All three layers and their new connections (red): Scientific Documents, Ontologies and BEL relations

This novel approach can first of all be used to compute similarities between documents, sentences and relations. Given a named entity, it is easy to answer the question "Which documents contain this entity?". It is more complex to answer the question "Which documents include or contradict this relation?" – we will use graph isomorphism to solve this issue. In terms of visualization it will also be possible to generate a BEL knowledge graph containing all information stored in a document.

From a technical point of view, storing all relevant data in a Solr/Lucene and Accumulo database will make the information efficiently available. Thus it will be easy to query documents from one layer. All analyses steps will be implemented as microservices using the Apache UIMA framework.

This new result also leads to an easier interaction between experts writing BEL statements and scientific community. Storing these new edges in the graph makes it easy to find documents that contain similar statements, patterns of named entities or even to suggest antithesis. We can also map ontologies to document data and evaluate the focus of publications.

3. FURTHER RESEARCH AND CONCLUSION

Summing up the discussed approach opens the complete graph theoretical toolbox to information systems on biomedical data. This will produce a novel approach for knowledge discovery that is also from a algorithmic point of view far more easy.

Our next step is to connect our BEL curation software to SCAIView to evaluate the results of human generated networks. For this purpose we will implement a BEL2SDA converter and utilize the Ontology Lockup Service (OLS).

REFERENCES

Fluck, J et al. BEL Networks derived from qualitative translations of BioNLP Shared Task annotations. *Proceeding of the 2013 Workshop on Biomedical Natural Language Processing*. 2013

Fluck, J et al. Pro Miner: recognition of human gene and protein names using regular updated dictionaries. *Proceedings of the second BioCreAtivE challenge evaluation workshop*. CNIO, 2007.

Malhotra, A et al. 'HypothesisFinder': a strategy for the detection of speculative statements in scientific text. *PLoS Comput Biol*. 2013.

SDA: TOWARDS A NOVEL KNOWLEDGE DISCOVERY MODEL FOR INFORMATION SYSTEMS

Marc Jacobs, Sven Hodapp and Jens Dörpinghaus
Fraunhofer Institute for Scientific Computing and Algorithms SCAI,
Sankt Augustin, Germany

ABSTRACT

Here, we present a novel model for knowledge discovery in biomedical sciences which has already been used for analyzing millions of journal articles from PMC and PubMed. We decompose each scientific document into semantic digital assets (SDA) that help to build an efficient workflow to retrieve single statements and hypothesis from huge and heterogeneous collections of large documents instead of complete articles. This new approach is so general applicable, that it will also be useful for information systems in other domains.

KEYWORDS

Knowledge Representation, Document Element, Sematic Digital Asset, Key-Value Store, Apache Accumulo, Apache UIMA

1. INTRODUCTION

We have a long standing history in document retrieval in the biomedical sciences. SCAIView is a highly efficient information system used for information retrieval, semantic searches and knowledge discovery (see https://www.scaiview.com). Also several other approaches have been published in the last 10 years serving the wish of the researcher to find interesting articles in a special area to gain insights in biological processes and mechanisms: "Give me all articles that mention a set of genes and proteins in the context of disease B."

Currently we see a trend in requesting the retrieval of single hypotheses and statements instead of retrieving the full article. E.g. "Which paper/author has first stated that gene A is involved in process B in the context of disease C. Show me that evidence sentence or paragraph." Over the last few years new domain specific languages (DSL) and knowledge representations like RDF, BEL (Haupt, 2011) have been proposed to publish and store this kind of statements and findings. Coding free text into a DSL is a time consuming and tedious process for the domain expert. Automatic text mining solutions may help but are far from being perfect.

2. MATERIAL AND METHODS

We have developed a new IS prototype which combines the traditional approach of document retrieval systems based on full text indices like Lucene with the new statement centric knowledge representations.

The novel idea is to split the documents in the atomic parts to gain more flexibility in handling the semantics, keeping track of the provenance and implementing efficient storage or retrieval. Each document (especially a full text document like a scientific article or a patent) is decomposed in small semantic parts (building blocks) which we have named *document elements*. A typical document element is a sentence, a figure, an image, a caption, a heading, a reference, a mathematical formula, a semantic concept like a gene or row in a table etc. We have chosen a 4-tuple as the formal representation of a document element being the key and the contents of the element as value: which we termed *semantic digital asset* (c.f. figure 1). The four fields are:

Sigmatics: Allows to cluster connected SDAs under one identifier. With the sigmatics we are able to talk about it.

Pragmatics: Refers to a certain purpose or a group of persons (or even programs) who can deal with it.

Semantics: Provides the actual meaning. We should use here references to controlled vocabulary.

Syntax: Reference to the specification how the (binary/text) signal is assembled (like a MIME type).

Since we process large document collections like PubMed (NCBI, 2017) with more than 26 million abstracts, PMC (about 4.2 million full text documents, eligible for text mining are only about 2 million documents, https://www.ncbi.nlm.nih.gov/pmc/) or patents (several hundred thousand documents) billions of these document elements have to be handled. For example, a typical full text article with ten pages from PMC contains about 300 document elements. Thus we need a technical backend that can handle those amounts of data. We use Apache Accumulo (Cordova, 2015) as a *Big table* approach (Chang, 2006), which is highly scalable and capable of storing data as sorted distributed key-value pairs (see https://accumulo.apache.org). All other parts were implemented as microservices using the Apache UIMA framework (see Hodapp, 2016):

- An XML importer (an UIMA reader) is used to convert the large zipped files delivered by PubMed into a CAS for each document. During the conversion the document is already annotated with sections, paragraphs, sentences and meta information like authors, title, journal. It generates a JMS message and sends it to the annotation queue.
- Then ProMiner (Hanisch., 2004), the gene and protein UIMA annotator microservice, which is subscribed to this queue, gets the message, annotates gene information into the CAS, and sends the result to the SDA generation queue.
- The UIMA consumer service creates from all the document parts and annotations a corpus of SDAs, and transfers them to the Accumulo storage.

sigmatics	semantics	syntax	pragmatics	signal
PMID:2674115	header	title	en	[Spontaneous antepartal RhD
PMID:2674115	header	authors	text:plain	M Studničková, I Holusková, V
PMID:2674115	header	publicationDate	ISO:8601	31.12.2015
PMID:2674115	header	source	URI	http://www.ncbi.nlm.nih.gov/pubmed/
PMID:2674115	header	journal	text:plain	Ceska gynekologie. 2016 Dec;80(6):401-
PMID:2674115	header	id	text:plain	26741153
PMID:2674115	header	edition	topology:editio	{"edition": "medline18@38abb9bf-528b-
PMID:2674115	header	child	topology:item	{"edition": "medline18@38abb9bf-528b-
outline:39fb2e5	section	title	en	AIM OF THE STUDY
outline:39fb2e5	section	rhetorical	text:plain	OBJECTIVE
outline:39fb2e5	section	level	text:plain	Section
outline:39fb2e5	section	child	topology:item	{"edition": "medline18@38abb9bf-528b-
outline:b90aa8f	section	title	en	DESIGN
outline:b90aa8f	section	rhetorical	text:plain	METHODS
outline:b90aa8f	section	level	text:plain	Section
front-	front-	child	topology:item	{"edition": "medline18@38abb9bf-528b-
document-	document	child	topology:item	{"edition": "medline18@38abb9bf-528b-
front-	front-	child	topology:item	{"edition": "medline18@38abb9bf-528b-
sentence:S153:1	sentence	original	en	[Spontaneous antepartal RhD
sentence:S153:1	Mus_mus	MM137098:Rhd	annotation@v1	{"begin": 24,"end": 27,"attr":
sentence:S153:1	CLO_Efo	CTEF044766:all	annotation@v1	{"begin": 28,"end": 44,"attr":
sentence:A220:1	sentence	original	en	Assess the incidence of spontaneous
sentence:C452:-	sentence	original	en	Clinical study.
sentence:D163:9	sentence	original	en	Department of Obstetrics and
sentence:A000:1	sentence	original	en	A total of 906 RhD negative women with

Figure 1. A semantic digital asset (SDA) can be easily placed in a column store as a row. These are the first of 248 SDAs resulting from the article taken from https://www.ncbi.nlm.nih.gov/pubmed/26741153

3. QUANTITATIVE RESULTS

We have processed the PubMed 2017 database, which contained at that point 26,808,489 abstracts. In here, the median of document elements per document was 14 and the average amount of gene NER tags per sentence with at least one gene mentioned was 1.8. In addition, we processed the PMC 2017 database which contained 1,912,920 full text articles. Here we found 307 document elements per document and again 1.8 gene NER tags per sentence thus having the same information density, but having more details (a factor of about 20). Thus we can conclude that the processing of huge data is possible and our chosen infrastructure is scalable and leads to valuable results.

4. SUMMARY AND OUTLOOK

We created first results for PubMed 2017 and PMC 2017 databases and gave a proof of concept that the corpus deconstruction based on document elements is possible. The most important advantage is that corpus creation and search can be mixed with the semantic annotated figures, plots or any other digital asset contents. No element will be duplicated, since same sentences can be reused in different documents and even those SDAs with similar semiotic properties will concatenate. The result is a highly searchable full text of documents with semantic annotations. This leads to a graph of SDAs which can be used for knowledge retrieval. Since till now we only have a technical proof of concepts the next step is the development of a user interface and the extension of the previous SCAIView. Further research has to be done on the graph theoretical background, heuristics and algorithms to retrieve knowledge and their interpretation.

REFERENCES

Chang, F et al. Bigtable: A distributed storage system for structured data. *7th Symposium on Operating Systems Design and Implementation.* 2016.

Cordova, A et al. *Accumulo: Application Development, Table Design, and Best Practices.* O'Reilly, 2015.

Hanisch, D et al. Prominer : Organism-specific protein name detection using approximate string matching the ProMiner system. *Proceedings of BioCreative: Critical Assessment for Information Extraction in Biology*. 2004.

Haupt, C et al. Representing Text Mining Results for Structured Pharmacological Queries. *ISWC.* 2011

Hodapp, S et al.: Integration of UIMA Text Mining Components into an Event-based Asynchronous Microservice Architecture. *Proceedings of the Workshop on Cross-Platform Text Mining and Natural Language Processing Interoperability*. 2016.

NCBI, Resource Coordinators. Database Resources of the National Center for Biotechnology Information. *Nucleic acids research* 45.D1. 2017.

AUTHOR INDEX